ALIVE IN CHRIST

GRADE 4 CATECHIST EDITION

The Moral Life

aliveinchrist.osv.com

OurSundayVisitor

The Subcommittee on the Catechism, United States Conference of Catholic Bishops, has found the doctrinal content of this manual, copyright 2014, to be in conformity with the *Catechism of the Catholic Church*.

Nihil Obstat
Rev. Fr. Jeremiah L. Payne, S.Th.L.
Censor Librorum, Diocese of Orlando

Imprimatur
✠ Most Rev. John Noonan
Bishop of Orlando
April 30, 2013

Alive in Christ Parish Grade 4 Catechist Edition
ISBN: 978-1-61278-029-0
Item Number: CU5117
3 4 5 6 7 8 9 10 015016 22 21 20 19 18
Webcrafters, Inc., Madison, WI, USA; May 2018; Job # 136715

ALIVE IN CHRIST Table of Contents

Vision and Philosophy

❝ I am the way and the truth* and the life… I am the resurrection and the life. ❞

John 14:6, 11:25

❝ Jesus Christ not only transmits the word of God: he is the Word of God. Catechesis is therefore completely tied to him. Thus what must characterize the message transmitted by catechesis is, above all, its 'christocentricity'. ❞[1]

General Directory for Catechesis, 98

Jesus Christ at the Center

Welcome to *Alive in Christ*. Christ is at the center of our faith, our Church, our catechesis. *Alive in Christ* is intentional in its focus on the life, mission, and saving work of Jesus Christ. This lays a foundation for a relationship with Jesus, who continually leads us to his Father's love and calls us through the Spirit to share in the divine life through his Church (see *Catechism of the Catholic Church*, 426).

Mirroring the Divine Pedagogy

The catechetical process of *Alive in Christ* mirrors the divine pedagogy—the gradual and relational way God teaches us so that we can know him and his truth, be guided by the Holy Spirit to respond with faith and love, and accept the gift of new life in Christ.

In this unique and effective pedagogy, each lesson encourages a personal and ongoing relationship with God, beginning with God's invitation through Sacred Scripture and leading children to reflect on his Word, deepen their understanding of our Sacred Tradition, and respond with a lived faith within the home and among friends, within the Church and in the community.

Building Knowledge of, and Reverence for, Sacred Scripture

Sacred Scripture from the *New American Bible Revised Edition* is foundational to every lesson in *Alive in Christ*. Scripture from both the Old Testament and New Testament is presented in a variety of ways that encourage children to listen to the voice of God in his written Word and learn about the people and stories of the Bible. Each lesson offers several distinct encounters with Sacred Scripture, giving children the opportunity to pray with, reflect on, study, and apply God's Word to their lives.

Comprehensive Presentation of Catholic Teaching

Alive in Christ provides an authentic and comprehensive presentation of the essentials of the Catholic faith and has been found by the United States Conference of Catholic Bishops' Subcommittee on the Catechism to be in conformity with the *Catechism of the Catholic Church*.

Following a systematically organized scope and sequence, key themes of Catholic teaching are repeated each year, through a grade-level focus, building on the child's knowledge of the faith at each developmental stage. This presentation of Catholic teaching—coupled with a purposeful emphasis on Catholic practices, images, and models of faith—promotes a common language of faith and builds a vibrant Catholic identity.

Developmentally Responsive and Appropriate

Created by a team of experts in catechesis, theology, and child psychology, *Alive in Christ* incorporates the most trusted research on how children learn and communicate. Definitions, activities, questions, and reading passages have been reviewed for developmental appropriateness. Targeted on-page interactions help children more effectively learn or reinforce lesson content.

Topics are presented at important developmental "windows"—ages when research in child development tells us that learning about a particular topic would be most effective. Illustrations, Catholic art, and photos emphasize Scripture and visually present the chapter objectives in ways children can understand and relate to.

Complete and Purposeful Approach to Prayer and Worship

Every grade level intentionally incorporates each of the five forms of prayer mentioned in the *Catechism*—blessing and adoration, petition, intercession, thanksgiving, and praise (see CCC, 2626–2643). Children learn about and pray these basic prayer forms and are introduced to traditional prayers and devotions of the Church. They are taught how to talk with God in their own words and listen silently as he speaks to them. Each grade level also presents many opportunities to deepen children's understanding of the feasts and seasons of the Church year and how we celebrate the Paschal Mystery through them.

Putting Faith into Practice

Alive in Christ presents and effectively implements the six fundamental tasks of catechesis (see *General Directory for Catechesis*, 84–85). Exercises, features, and questions throughout the text prompt children to relate knowledge of our Catholic faith with their life experience. Every chapter has on-page activities for immediate application as well as concrete suggestions for children to live out the faith at school, at their parish, and in their homes and communities.

Each lesson's Our Catholic Life section provides practical examples of the ways we worship, live, pray, and serve together as Catholics. It introduces children to Catholic figures who stand as models of heroic virtue in everyday life. Every lesson has connections to the Catholic social tradition, and each grade level provides catechesis on the seven major themes of the Church's Social Teaching.

Practical Ways to Involve Families in Their Children's Faith Formation

The "Family + Faith" page and an extensive website give parents the tools they need to know what their children are learning, talk about the faith, and recognize how they can more consciously live the faith in their daily family life.

On each lesson's take home page, parents will find information about children's developmental understanding, discussion prompts, and resources for family prayer. Taking into consideration the aims of the New Evangelization, each page includes an opportunity for adult reflection on their own relationship with Jesus and the Church.

Online resources offer multimedia tools to foster family interaction and reinforce the lesson at home.

A Commitment to Support Both New and Experienced Catechists

Alive in Christ Catechist Editions empower catechists with easy-to-use and effective tools for lesson planning, teaching and reinforcing faith concepts, and growing in their own relationship with Christ and his Church.

The key concepts and chapter objectives are fully explained and conveniently located at the beginning of each lesson along with background information to strengthen catechist understanding and nurture personal faith. A clear, concise, wraparound lesson plan leads the catechist page-by-page through the effective three-step process with integrated background on Sacred Scripture and doctrine, teaching tips, and connections to music, liturgy, and Catholic Social Teaching.

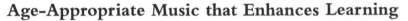

Extensive Online Resources for Catechists and Families

Alive in Christ provides catechists and leaders comprehensive program level resources and unit, chapter, and seasonal specific tools and activities. Online support includes lesson planning tools, catechist formation, custom test building and eAssessments, connections to the Sunday readings, and the option to share lesson plans via social media.

This extensive site provides children and families access to web-based assessments, interactive games and reviews, and articles and resources targeted specifically to adults—all to support faith sharing and continued learning in the home.

Age-Appropriate Music that Enhances Learning

With the knowledge that music is a means for forming children in Sacred Scripture, Church teachings, and Catholic Identity, *Alive in Christ* integrates multiple music options into every lesson. A variety of music from OCP (Oregon Catholic Press), John Burland, Dr. Jo Ann Paradise, and other sources is tied to chapter objectives and themes.

Music is suggested at point-of-use in the Catechist Edition, with multiple song suggestions for each chapter. Many prayer pages feature a song to be used within the prayer service. Music can be sampled and downloaded.

Also, we now have an all-new music component, *Songs of Scripture: Deepening Children's Understanding of the Word of God*, which features songs that teach, reinforce, and unfold the meaning of Scripture stories presented in the Student Book.

Alive in Christ Development Team

Greg Erlandson
President and Publisher

Beth McNamara
General Manager

Sabrina Magnuson
Associate Publisher

Dr. Jo Ann Paradise   **Dr. Joseph White**

Ana Arista   Heidi Busse   David Dziena   Dr. Hosffman Ospino   Denise Utter

Alive in Christ Structural Framework

Alive in Christ follows a systematic Scope and Sequence organized around key themes of Catholic teaching that repeat each year within a grade-level focus, building on the child's knowledge of the faith at each developmental stage.

This organizational structure takes into account research in child development that tells us at which age learning about a particular topic is most effective. These developmental "windows" help us to understand when the spiritual, cognitive, emotional, sociological, moral, and physical abilities of a child are "ripe" for learning. Included in the sequence, then, is a sensitivity to when children are ready to learn. A grade-level focus based within the structural framework of the seven essential themes allows for optimal learning.

The seven essential, foundational themes of the faith—Revelation, Trinity, Jesus Christ, The Church, Morality, Sacraments, and Kingdom of God—provide the structural framework that organizes the content of the grade. Progressing from first to sixth grade, the child deepens understanding as he or she is presented content that is theologically precise and developmentally appropriate.

As you study the Scope and Sequence, you will see how the objectives across grades move the learner to examine and appropriate a greater knowledge of our Catholic faith and how those objectives help to form a vibrant Catholic Identity.

Grade Level Focus	
1: Jesus Christ	"For through faith you are all children of God in Christ Jesus." **Galatians 3:26**
2: Sacraments of Penance and the Eucharist	"This is my body, which will be given for you; do this in memory of me." **Luke 22:19**
3: The Church	"I am the vine, you are the branches. Whoever remains in me and I in him will bear much fruit…" **John 15:5**
4: The Moral Life	"This is my commandment: love one another as I love you." **John 15:12**
5: The Seven Sacraments	"The water I shall give will become in him a spring of water welling up to eternal life." **John 4:14**
6: The Word of God in the Old Testament	"Your word is a lamp for my feet, / a light for my path." **Psalm 119:105**

 Go to **aliveinchrist.osv.com** for an overview of the developmental windows for each grade level focus and full program Scope and Sequence.

Program Scope and Sequence

This graphic gives a visual image of the scope and sequence as a fourth grader in your group will experience it. The circles on the outside name the foundational themes that are the framework (unit structure) for every grade level. The child is holding key developmental factors or "windows" that lead to the grade level focus (for more on this, see page CE29). No matter what unit you are teaching, some component of the grade level focus is being treated.

Unit 1
Revelation

Unit 2
Trinity

Unit 3
Jesus Christ

Unit 4
The Church

Unit 5
Morality

Unit 6
Sacraments

Unit 7
Kingdom of God

**Snapshot of Developmental Factors
Fourth Grade— The Moral Life**

- Children this age are beginning to internalize standards of behavior. Their consciences are growing quickly, and they are gaining a sense of "right" and "wrong" that goes beyond just what might bring them punishments or rewards. This is a great time to work with them on what it means to be disciples of Jesus.

- They are good at using their reasoning skills, but they still don't have a firm grasp on hypothetical reasoning. This means they have difficulty imagining things or situations they haven't experienced. Acting out making good choices in a moral dilemma will be especially effective, since all of us are more likely to do the things we practice.

Alive in Christ Parish Edition Program Components

Student Books Grades 1–6

Student Books follow a seven unit structure with a grade level focus on a foundational topic in our Catholic faith. They are the perfect tool to teach children to know, love, and live their Catholic faith through Sacred Scripture, doctrine, prayer, practices of the faith, and seasonal celebrations.

Catechist Editions Grades 1–6

The Catechist Editions help to build confident, capable, and successful catechists with comprehensive background and lesson preparation pages, timed wrap around lesson plans, optional activities, and point of use information. They are spiral bound and conveniently sized to match the Student Book.

People of Faith Collection Grades 1–6

This beautifully illustrated collection of Saints, Blesseds, and Venerables are connected to specific chapters. Children will learn

about models of our Catholic faith while deepening their relationship with God and the Church.

Music Resources

Catechists are provided options for developmentally appropriate music that enhances learning. *Alive in Christ* integrates music into each step of the lesson. A variety of music from Oregon Catholic Press is tied to chapter objectives and themes.

A unique, all new music component, *Songs of Scripture: Deepening Children's Understanding of God's Word*, features songs by John Burland and Dr. Jo Ann Paradise that teach, reinforce, and unfold the meaning of Scripture stories presented in the Student Book.

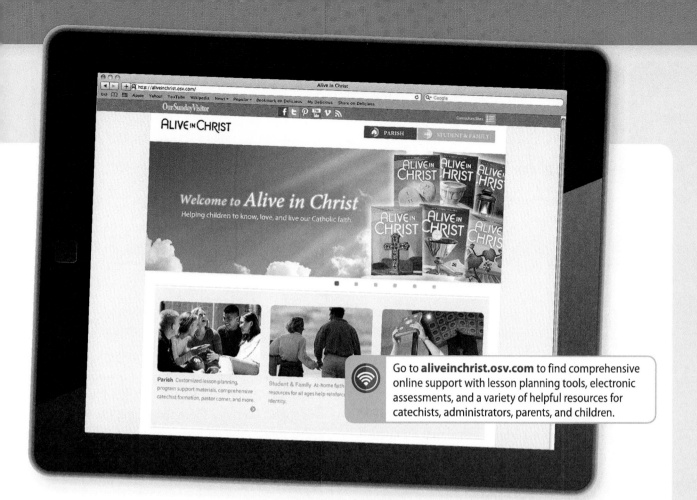

Go to **aliveinchrist.osv.com** to find comprehensive online support with lesson planning tools, electronic assessments, and a variety of helpful resources for catechists, administrators, parents, and children.

Online Resources for the Catechist

- Online lesson planning helps catechists to plan using chapter, seasonal, or Catholic Social Teaching lessons
- Share lesson plans via social media such as Facebook & Twitter
- Unit- and chapter-specific tools, assessments, activities, and multimedia resources
- Build a Custom Test allows catechists to build, print, and distribute tests using a bank of multiple choice, matching, fill in the blank, and long answer questions
- Assign eAssessments to children for completion online
- Catechetical formation and professional development tools are designed to help catechists hone their skills and grow in the knowledge of God's love
- Sample and download chapter-specific music to enhance catechetical learning or for prayer

Online Resources for the Student & Family

- Interactive Reviews offer children an opportunity for web-based assessment, preparation, and practice
- At-home faith formation resources for all ages help reinforce Catholic identity
- Faith-sharing features and resources geared to parents, children, and families encourage continued learning at home via games, multimedia activities, Lectionary-connected resources, social media interaction, and topical articles
- Sample and download chapter-specific music to enhance catechetical learning or for prayer

Online Resources for the Leader

- Program-level tools and resources provide directors, administrators, and leaders with higher-level materials from correlations to in-service models
- Sample and download chapter-specific music to enhance catechetical learning or for prayer

Responding to Your Vocation

66 Give thanks to the Lord for the gift of your vocation, through which Christ has called you from among other men and women to be instruments of his salvation. Respond with generosity to your vocation and your names will be written in heaven. 99

— Pope Saint John Paul II, *Guide for Catechists*, 37

These words, taken from a talk by Pope Saint John Paul II to the catechists of Angola, are both awe inspiring and challenging! You have been called, he said, called by Christ from among other men and women. Have you ever wondered why you responded to the talk of the pastor or DRE that spoke about the need for catechists? Why did the bulletin article that outlined the responsibilities of a catechist stir your heart and prompt you to respond? Who gave your name to the catechetical leader in your parish?

No matter how the invitation came, it was Christ who called you. And by the power of the Holy Spirit, you, like Mary, responded, "Yes!" The vocation to catechesis, like all vocations, first comes from the grace of Baptism, is strengthened in Confirmation, and is sustained by the Eucharist and Penance. "The Church awakens and discerns this divine vocation and confers the mission to catechize….This personal call of Jesus Christ and its relationship to him are the true moving forces of catechetical activity. 'From this loving knowledge of Christ springs the desire to proclaim him, to "evangelize," and to lead others to the "Yes" of faith in Jesus Christ'2" (GDC, 231).

You have been called by Christ and been given the mission by his Church to be instruments of his work. Take a moment and ponder that statement. With so many responsibilities and demands on our time, we might sometimes lose sight of this, and being a catechist becomes just one of the many things we must do each week. This cannot be so. Every time you gather with your children, you take your place in the long line of those who have for 2,000 years held the sacred duty of bringing others into "communion, in intimacy, with Jesus Christ" (*Catechesi Tradendae*, 5).

Your Role as Catechist

To support and nurture children in their baptismal call to a lifetime of growing closer to and more like Jesus, the Church sets out some essential instructions. In order to provide a presentation of the "entire treasure of the Christian message" while adapting it to the "capacity of those being catechized" (GDC, 112), a catechist must do several things.

Teach the comprehensive course of study outlined by the United States Conference of Catholic Bishops' Subcommittee on the Catechism. In *Alive in Christ*, you find these doctrines and practices presented in the objectives of the lesson. (See GDC, 112.)

Respect the developmental level of your children by understanding how they learn. (See GDC, 112.)

Use various methods as they are a "sign of life and richness" that will address multiple learning styles and special needs (GDC, 148).

Model a Catholic life through your own behaviors and practices, for the "charism given to [the catechist] by the Spirit, a solid spirituality and transparent witness of life constitutes the soul of every method" (GDC, 156).

Proclaim with joy and enthusiasm that "God so loved the world he sent his only Son" (John 3:16). In the words of Pope Benedict XVI, "Today too, there is a need… to rediscover the joy of believing and the enthusiasm for communicating the faith" (*Porta Fidei*, 7).

As you accept this sacred and challenging vocation, be assured that the Holy Spirit will lead and guide you in handing on our Catholic faith to the next generation. Let the love of God pour through so that they see in you the image and heart of our loving God.

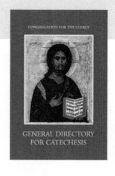

General Directory for Catechesis

As Jesus Formed His Disciples

There are six fundamental tasks in the ministry of catechesis. These six tasks are named and treated in the *General Directory for Catechesis* (see GDC , 85), and later in the *National Directory for Catechesis* (see NDC, 20). Each of these tasks corresponds to an aspect of faith in Jesus. The following are the six tasks of catechesis.

Promoting Knowledge of the Faith

We cannot live a faith we do not know. For this reason, studying the teachings of Jesus and his Church is an essential task of catechesis. The U.S. Bishops' Subcommittee on the Catechism and the conformity review process direct what is to be contained in this comprehensive presentation of the faith. According to the *National Directory for Catechesis*, this task of catechesis is a response to the individual's desire that God plants in the heart of every person to know. This desire comes naturally when individuals have had opportunities to encounter Christ and his message and have experienced an initial conversion. *Alive in Christ* begins each lesson by giving children an opportunity to meet God in his Word and to wonder about his life and love, followed by a process of helping them to know more about him through Sacred Tradition—the teaching of the Church. In this way, we help children frame questions that drive their desire to know more.

Liturgical Education

This task relates to learning about the ways in which the Church worships and celebrates, including the Seven Sacraments, the Order of Mass, and the liturgical year. According to the *General Directory for Catechesis*, liturgical education includes teaching about the form and the meaning of liturgical celebrations, but also means helping individuals prepare their minds and hearts to enter into these mysteries of our faith. As you use *Alive in Christ*, you will teach your students about the liturgy both through the doctrine presented in the core chapters as well as through seasonal activities and prayerful experiences that echo the words and rhythms of our liturgical celebrations.

Moral Formation

This task of catechesis involves forming the consciences of learners through the moral teachings of Jesus and his Church and fostering understanding of what it means to live these teachings in one's daily life. Morality in the Christian life involves standards and guidelines, but it is more than learning a list of rules. Morality is about discipleship. As you use *Alive in Christ*, you will find opportunities to challenge children to apply what they have learned about the Ten Commandments, Jesus' command to love as he has loved, and the Beatitudes to situations at home and school and in the community.

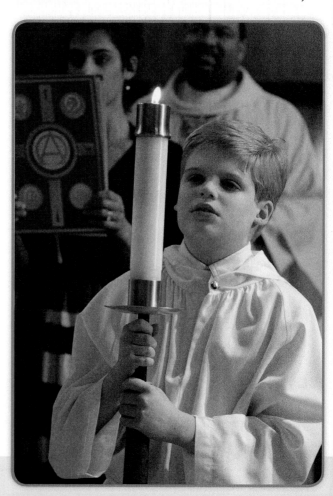

Teaching to Pray

"When catechesis is permeated by a climate of prayer, the assimilation of the entire Christian life reaches its summit" (GDC, 85). The "climate of prayer" in catechesis invites individuals into an ever deeper relationship with God. Teaching to pray is more than merely "teaching prayers"; it involves fostering an understanding of prayer as conversation with God—helping children learn how to talk with God in their own words as well as how to listen to God.

This task of catechesis involves teaching the traditional prayers of the Church and the various forms and expressions of prayer mentioned in the *Catechism of the Catholic Church*. *Alive in Christ* incorporates experiences of all five forms of prayer. You will also have opportunities to help children speak to God in their own words.

Education for Community Life

This task of catechesis relates to developing an understanding of what it means to be a part of the Christian community, including respecting the authority and structure of the Church as well as living out Jesus' New Commandment to love one another as he has loved us. "Catechesis prepares the Christian to live in community and to participate actively in the life and mission of the Church" (GDC, 86). Catechesis should prepare us to live and work with one another, both within the Church and in society as a whole. The

bishops write that catechesis should encourage a spirit of simplicity and humility, a special concern for the poor, particular care for the alienated, a sense of fraternal correction, common prayer, mutual forgiveness, and a fraternal love that embraces all these attitudes. (See GDC, 86.) Various chapter features, as well as the "Live Your Faith" sections on Catholic Social Teaching will assist you in this task of catechesis.

Missionary Initiation

While only some may be called to other lands to minister in Christ's name, by Baptism, all are called to live in such a way that we serve as witnesses of the faith to those who are around us. This task of catechesis prepares the learner to share his or her faith with others. *Alive in Christ* helps to form children in the language of the Catholic faith and the behaviors and practices of the faith. Forming them in a vibrant Catholic identity gives them the skills necessary to be strong witnesses of the faith. This is reinforced in the tools we provide the parents in the Family + Faith page, as it equips the parents to talk about faith with their children.

Our bishops state, "all efforts in evangelization and catechesis should incorporate these tasks" (NDC, 20). In this way, we pay attention to several different dimensions of faith, with the ultimate goal of helping children grow into deeper communion with Christ so that they live as disciples in faith, word, and deed.

The Divine Pedagogy

As catechists, we always hold two realities: the "what" and the "how" of catechesis. What do we want our children to know and love about our faith and how do we best communicate the treasure of our faith?

We use the word *pedagogy* to speak about the art, science, or profession of teaching. In other words, pedagogy is the "how" of faith formation. We are called to hand on the truths of our faith by echoing God's own way of teaching us his truths. The *General Directory for Catechesis* tells us that,

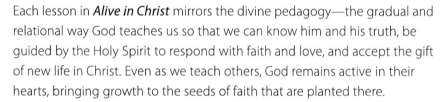

" Catechesis, as communication of divine Revelation, is radically inspired by the pedagogy of God, as displayed in Christ and in the Church. [It is the Church's mission to be] a visible and actual continuation of the pedagogy of the Father and of the Son. "

GDC, 143, 141

Each lesson in *Alive in Christ* mirrors the divine pedagogy—the gradual and relational way God teaches us so that we can know him and his truth, be guided by the Holy Spirit to respond with faith and love, and accept the gift of new life in Christ. Even as we teach others, God remains active in their hearts, bringing growth to the seeds of faith that are planted there.

Here are five important characteristics of the divine pedagogy that are at the heart of each lesson of *Alive in Christ*.

The pedagogy of God is invitational and person-centered.
God initiates a relationship with each person. He does so by first creating us with a desire to know him and the capacity to respond to him. The ultimate invitation to relationship comes in Jesus. Pope Saint John Paul II tells us that the purpose of all catechesis is to bring people into intimacy with Jesus.

As God enters into dialogue with us, we are called to follow this example by providing catechesis that it is rooted in interpersonal relationships and involves a process of dialogue. (See GDC, 143.) God also meets us where we are and accommodates for our particular needs. Therefore, effective catechesis should be developmentally appropriate and should make allowances for adapting to special needs.

God's pedagogy is incarnational.
Dei Verbum points out the "inner unity" of deeds and words in God's plan of revelation: "the deeds wrought by God in the history of salvation manifest and confirm the teaching and realities signified by the words, while the words proclaim the deeds and clarify the mystery contained in them" (2).

From speaking the universe into existence, to his promise to Noah and his covenants with Abraham and Moses, to the Word made flesh in Jesus Christ, it is evident that God's Word becomes action.

An effective pedagogy should make the faith come to life through hands-on activities and applications and multisensory teaching methodologies. It should give learners clear ways to go out and live the Gospel they have received.

The pedagogy of God is familial and communal.
God reveals himself as a communion of persons—Father, Son, and Holy Spirit—and creates human beings to be in communion with one another.

Effective catechesis should build community among the children, involve parents and families as primary catechists, and connect children to the larger parish community. Connecting the families to the life of the parish, particularly through participation in the Sunday Eucharist, is vital in building up the Body of Christ.

God's pedagogy is structured and comprehensive.
In salvation history, God reveals himself to humanity gradually as people are able to understand. One revelation builds upon the next, until Revelation reaches its fullness in the Person of Jesus Christ. Effective catechesis also presents key truths of the faith gradually as the learner is able to receive them.

The pedagogy of God is perpetual.
We read in **Isaiah 55:11**, "So shall my word be / that goes forth from my mouth; / It shall not return to me empty, / but shall do what pleases me, / achieving the end for which I sent it." God's truths are handed on through the generations in the forms of Sacred Scripture and Sacred Tradition, which is the living memory of the Church. God's covenants do not end, but come to greater fulfillment and realization.

A catechesis based on the divine pedagogy prepares the learner to share the Gospel with others, in word and deed, so that the Good News of salvation is handed on to others and to future generations.

Three-Step Catechetical Process

Alive in Christ's catechetical methodology mirrors the divine pedagogy by following a three-step process of **Invite**, **Discover**, and **Live**. This process encourages a personal and ongoing relationship with the Holy Trinity.

1. **The Invite Step** begins the lesson with God's invitation through Sacred Scripture. Children open their minds and hearts to what God is saying to them in Scripture, reflect on it, and transition to the Discover step and chapter objectives.

2. **The Discover Step** helps form Catholic identity through the study of Scripture, knowledge of Church teaching, and an understanding of Catholic practices. It presents the doctrine of the lesson in developmentally appropriate language and images. Charts, on-page questions, and gold star activities prompt children to interact directly with the page, and aid in understanding and retention. With large on page activities, children are given the opportunity to process and reinforce what they have learned and apply it to their own lives and the experience of the Church.

3. **The Live Step** helps children relate knowledge of the faith and the ways we worship, live, pray, and serve together as Catholics. Children are given the tools to connect their faith to everyday life and to deepen their relationship with God and the Church through the prayer experiences at the end of each lesson.

If you follow this three-step process, you will in fact mirror the divine pedagogy by offering children the opportunity to know God and his truth through Sacred Scripture and Sacred Tradition. You will inspire them to be open to the Holy Spirit so that they will respond in faith and love and accept the gift of new life in Christ!

As a catechist, during the **Invite** step you:

- Call the children together to begin in **prayer**.
- Prepare the children to hear the **Word of God**.
- Guide the children through the **Scripture reflection** process, proclaiming God's Word and inviting quiet thought. (See CE22 for a full description of the Scripture reflection process.)
- After proclamation of the Scripture, allow time (governed by what is developmentally appropriate) for sacred **silence**.
- Invite children **to share** what they have experienced, what they felt God was saying to them or what he wanted them to know in a special way today. Assure them sharing is voluntary.
- Prompt continued thought about God's Word and move to chapter objectives by using the "**What Do You Wonder**" questions.

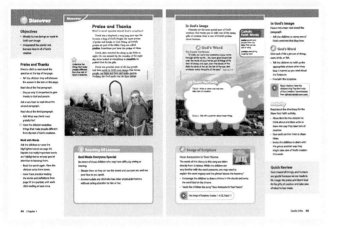

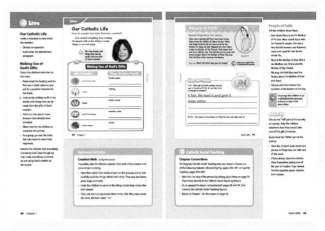

As a catechist, during the **Discover** step you:

- Teach the **objectives** of the lesson, which are identified in the Catechist Edition in two places: the overview Lesson Plan in the catechist background section and in the top left-hand corner of each Discover spread. The Quick Review, highlighted in the bottom right hand corner of the Discover spread, allows you to check that you have fully covered the objectives.

- Follow the **instruction** in the vertical side columns, which walks you through the entire lesson. Note that the activities are an integral part of the lesson. They emphasize the essential elements of Church teaching and help the children apply those truths to worship, prayer, and daily life.

- Present the **Catholic Faith Words**, which are highlighted in the text and called out in the side boxes. These words build a common language of faith and are explained with precise theological language that is developmentally appropriate.

- Use the **boxes** framed in green at the bottom of the page that provide additional Scripture and doctrinal background, optional activities, quick tips, ways to adapt for special needs, suggestions for including music, and more.

As a catechist, during the **Live** step you:

- Guide the children through a graphic organizer, chart, or reflection activity to **synthesize** what they have learned in the chapter.

- Hold up the Communion of Saints, and introduce the children to a **Saint**, **Blessed**, or **Venerable** whose life exemplifies the content of the lesson. What better way to encourage faith-filled living than through Catholic heroines and heroes?

- Give the children the opportunity through a closing **activity** to relate their knowledge of the faith to their lives, and invite them to commit themselves more deeply to what it means to be Catholic with concrete action and future steps.

- Conclude with a **prayer celebration**. Make sure to leave time at the end of the lesson to pray with the children. If the prayer calls for it, you may want to assign parts a week ahead of time.

- Send home the **Family + Faith** page. As the children live their faith primarily in the circle of their families, this page is an excellent resource to connect the children's learning with their home and to form their parents in faith.

Lesson Preparation

Alive in Christ Catechist Editions give you everything you need for lesson planning, teaching and reinforcing faith concepts, and growing in your own relationship with Christ and his Church.

Each chapter has catechist-specific content provided in the planning and background pages. These are the five pages that provide scriptural, doctrinal, and methodological background and formation. You will also find pages that address the different ways children process, understand, and learn lesson content at any given grade level.

Catechist Background easy-to-understand theological background on the chapter content. The Reflect questions help connect faith concepts with the catechist's own life experience.

Key Concept for each lesson is clearly stated at the start of each chapter.

Doctrinal Content correlates to paragraphs from the *Catechism of the Catholic Church.*

Tasks of Catechesis relate lesson components to one of the six Tasks of Catechesis as outlined in the *National Directory for Catechesis.*

Catechist's Prayer offers a moment of reflection for the catechist before planning each lesson.

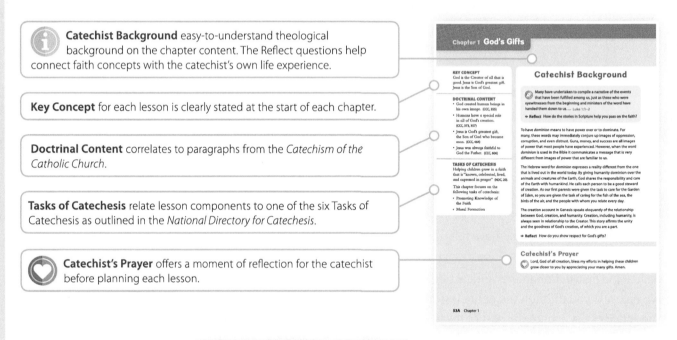

Timed Lesson Plan clearly stated chapter objectives, step-by-step instructions, and a suggested time frame to complete each step of the lesson.

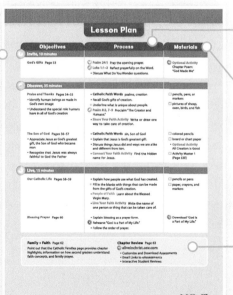

Process Column notes prayer, Scripture, activities, and Catholic Faith Words in each step.

Materials Column materials and online resources needed for the lesson.

Family + Faith / Chapter Review reminders to share chapter content with families and directs catechists to various opportunities for review and assessment.

Sharing the Message offers insight on the relationship between the lesson objectives and the child's developmental level of understanding of those topics.

How Grade Level Children Understand provides background on where children this age typically are in terms of cognitive, social, spiritual, and emotional development.

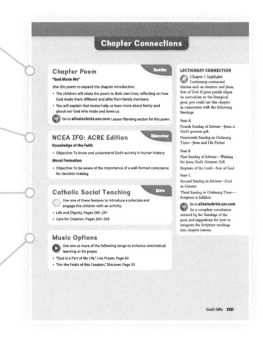

Online Resources are clearly labeled throughout the Catechist Edition and direct you to downloads, lesson planning tools, interactive reviews, eAssessments, and more.

Chapter Story or poem provides an opportunity to extend the Invite step of the process with additional life experience connections.

NCEA IFG: ACRE Edition correlates the lesson objectives to the domains of *NCEA Information for Growth: Assessment of Children/Youth Religious Education* (2013) and helps catechists measure children's understanding and appropriation of lesson content.

Catholic Social Teaching identifies which principles of Catholic Social Teaching/Live Your Faith pieces connect to this chapter and provides direction for how to integrate them into the Live step of the process. These connections are also noted at point of use in the bottom band of the lesson plan.

Music Options are provided to enhance catechetical learning and the prayer celebration. These options are also called out at point of use in the wraparound lesson plan.

Sacred Scripture

66 For in the sacred books, the Father who is in heaven meets His children with great love and speaks with them; and the force and power in the word of God is so great that it stands as the support and energy of the Church…. 99

Dei Verbum, 21

Catholic Bible
✝
NABRE

New American Bible Revised Edition

Sacred Scripture from both the Old Testament and New Testament is at the heart of **Alive in Christ**. The children are invited to understand the importance of Sacred Scripture, as a font of Divine Revelation and the guide for their lives. The Word is always given prominent visual importance to highlight its significance, with a parchment background, an icon, and a logo. Children are led to know, love, and be formed by God's Word.

Scripture in the Catechetical Process

The children always **pray** with Scripture in the opening prayer of the Invite step and often in the prayer experience in the Live step.

The practice of Scripture **reflection** is an essential element in the Invite step of every lesson and the means by which we enter into the divine pedagogy.

Children are formed by this practice of reflecting on Scripture and being open to the Word of God personally speaking to them. Listening with the ear of the heart and reflecting on Scripture prepares children for practices such as *Lectio Divina*.

Sacred Scripture is **studied** in the Discover step as children learn about God's action throughout salvation history and see how Scripture is a source of Church teaching. Key Scripture accounts are presented in multiple grade levels to encourage biblical literacy, familiarity, and understanding.

Throughout the Discover and Live steps, the children **apply** the Word of God to their lived experience and acquire the behaviors and practices of a Catholic life.

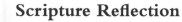

Scripture Reflection

CHAPTER 3 — Invite

God's Commandments

◯ Let Us Pray

Leader: Loving Father, you made us to know you and your desire for us.

"I delight to do your will, my God; your law is in my inner being!" Psalm 40:9

All: O God, help us to learn how to listen for your voice so that we will know how to follow you. Amen.

📖 Scripture

"When [Moses] looked, although the bush was on fire, it was not being consumed.... When the LORD saw that he had turned aside to look, God called out to him from the bush: Moses! Moses! He answered, 'Here I am.' God said: Do not come near! Remove your sandals from your feet, for the place where you stand is holy ground." Exodus 3:2b, 4–5

? What Do You Wonder?
- How does God speak to people today?
- How do the Ten Commandments help you to know God and what ...

⏰ **Invite**

❤️ **Let Us Pray**

Invite children to gather in the prayer space and make the Sign of the Cross. Begin with leader's p... and have a volunteer pray alou... psalm verse from a Bible. Pron... the group's response.

Have the children move out o... prayer space and back to thei...

Say: God wanted Moses to lead ... People, who were slaves, to freedom. The Word of God we will hear ... of Moses' journey of faith.

📖 **Scripture**

Guide the children through ... process of Scripture reflection.

- Invite them to close their eyes and open their minds and hearts to what God is saying to them by being silent and still.
- Proclaim the Scripture.

Step 1: Begin by using the directions provided on the Invite page of the lesson or you may use the recorded preparation, titled "Mantra," included in both the *Songs of Scripture* CDs.

Step 2: Help the children enter into sacred space by prominently displaying the Bible, lighting or turning on a candle, and guiding them to become quiet and still.

Step 3: Read the passage in a slow and steady voice, one complete sentence at a time.

Step 4: Ask the question, "What did you hear God say to you today?" This reflection is critical in providing the children an opportunity to encounter God through his Word. It prepares the child to receive and respond in faith to God's personal invitation.

Sacred Tradition

What is necessary for the children to know so that they will develop a vibrant Catholic identity and be able to express their faith with competence, understanding, and love?

The Church guides us, teaching that the catechetical message has "a 'comprehensive hierarchical character'³ which constitutes a vital synthesis of the faith" (GDC, 114). The truths of the faith are organized in a hierarchy around the mystery of the most Holy Trinity, in a Christ-centered (or *Christocentric*) perspective.

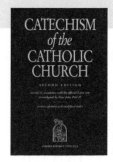

Catechism of the Catholic Church

> ❝ The mutual connections between dogmas, and their coherence, can be found in the whole of the Revelation of the mystery of Christ.⁴ 'In Catholic doctrine there exists an order or "hierarchy" of truths, since they vary in their relation to the foundation of the Christian faith.'⁵ ❞
>
> CCC, 90

In other words, some truths are so basic and foundational to what we believe as Catholics that they must be presented first, and then other related truths can be better understood.

To help us know what is basic and foundational, the USCCB's Subcommittee on the Catechism has identified the truths of the faith deemed essential to the formation of children. *Alive in Christ* has been found to be in conformity with the *Catechism of the Catholic Church*.

In salvation history, God has revealed himself to people in a systematic and gradual way, showing us more of himself as we are capable of understanding. (See GDC, 38 and CCC 54–65.) Our catechesis models this divine pedagogy and includes all of the foundational elements of the faith, presenting them in a gradual and systematic way as the learner is ready to hear them.

Alive in Christ organizes the foundational truths around seven key themes of Catholic teaching that repeat each year within a grade level focus.

Systematic and Comprehensive

The content of Sacred Scripture and Sacred Tradition are systematically presented in precise theological language in the **lesson objectives** of each lesson. The objectives are found on your Lesson Plan and at point of use where they are presented to the children.

Important **Catholic Faith Words** are highlighted in every chapter with definitions that grow as children's understanding does, and their repetition across grades helps to promote the common language of faith.

Each **Unit Opener** summarizes key concepts being presented and identifies *Catechism of the Catholic Church* references for each of these faith statements.

At the back of each Student Book the **Our Catholic Tradition** reference section reinforces the faith basics presented in the lessons. It is referenced in your lesson plan with specific instructions on how to integrate the content into the lesson.

The Theory Behind It

At one point or another in your family life and your ministry as a catechist, you've likely found yourself explaining to a child, "It's not just what you say, it's how you say it." The message is as important as the delivery. You can't separate the *what* from the *how*. Similarly, doctrine and method are not two ends of a spectrum. They are interdependent. In catechesis, you can't have one without the other. And it goes a step further, for it's not just *what* we teach, and how we teach it, but *how* the learner receives it.

"Consequently catechesis starts out with…the integral structure of the Christian message, and proceeds to explain it in a manner adapted to the capacity of those being catechized" (GDC, 112).

When we teach things in a theologically accurate way, and in a manner sensitive to where the children are developmentally, we provide the best chance that they will appropriate the content—process and understand it in a way that has meaning to them and that they can then apply to their own lives.

According to the National Association for the Education of Young Children (NAEYC), *developmental appropriateness* includes multiple components.

1. It is important to know how children develop and learn at particular ages and stages and to create learning environments that are responsive to these general needs.

2. Because every child is unique, knowing the individual children and how they learn best is essential.

3. It is important to know what is culturally appropriate for different ages and stages of development.

The Practice of It

Alive in Christ provides you with carefully selected topics and activities that meet the developmental level of the children you are teaching as well as tips for addressing individual needs. The program includes prayers, Saints, activities, and stories that represent the

Presentation of Text

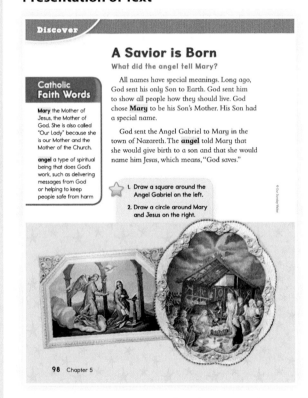

Discover

A Savior is Born
What did the angel tell Mary?

All names have special meanings. Long ago, God sent his only Son to Earth. God sent him to show all people how they should live. God chose **Mary** to be his Son's Mother. His Son had a special name.

God sent the Angel Gabriel to Mary in the town of Nazareth. The **angel** told Mary that she would give birth to a son and that she would name him Jesus, which means, "God saves."

Catholic Faith Words

Mary the Mother of Jesus, the Mother of God. She is also called "Our Lady" because she is our Mother and the Mother of the Church.

angel a type of spiritual being that does God's work, such as delivering messages from God or helping to keep people safe from harm

1. Draw a square around the Angel Gabriel on the left.

2. Draw a circle around Mary and Jesus on the right.

98   Chapter 5

- Information is sequenced and organized in smaller "chunks" to make reading and understanding faster and easier.

- Sentences are shorter in length for younger grades.

- Fonts and type sizes are set with consideration given to the reading level of the child.

- Words are defined consistently at point-of-use and highlighted for easy identification.

- Terms and concepts are introduced, reinforced, and then further defined in advanced ways as they develop across grades.

diversity of cultures found in our Church and introduces these traditions at developmentally-appropriate times.

Alive in Christ takes into account the experience level of today's children with various topics and how they are used to receiving and processing those topics. So, the series is developmentally appropriate not just in what

kids learn at particular ages, but how they learn it.

As a catechist, you can feel confident that you are giving the children the most precise presentation of Church teaching in the most developmentally appropriate way. That's what excellent catechesis is all about.

Use of Visuals

- Fine art, illustrations, and photos advance in detail and sophistication as grades progress.
- Graphic organizers, charts, and callouts are used to present content in easy to track and access formats.
- Captions are used to aid in learning, and the content and purpose of captions advance as the grades do.
- The text-to-art ratio is intentional and customized for each grade level.

Teaching Strategies

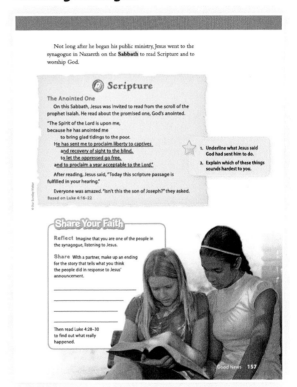

- Questions focus reading, prompt reflection, and reinforce learning.
- On-page activities and teaching strategies incorporate dynamic, interactive learning methods.
- Chapter Reviews use multiple formats to accommodate different learning styles.
- The Catechist Edition includes a Teaching This Grade page that gives details on how children at this age might understand lesson objectives.
- Ideas for customizing content are found in the Reaching All Learners boxes in some chapters.

The Use of Images

❝ In order to communicate the message entrusted to her by Christ, the Church needs art. ❞

—*Letter of Pope Saint John Paul II to Artist* (1999), 12

While educational research assures us that children make meaning through the interplay of text and images (Carney and Levine, 2002), any adult who has spent time with a young child knows that verbal and visual both tell the story. For hundreds of years, the Church has used sacred art and stained glass windows to teach Catholic doctrine and provide a physical presentation of the truths of our faith. Jesus often used images when he preached, giving his disciples a glimpse into his Father's mystery and the Kingdom.

Alive in Christ mirrors the divine pedagogy through its use of photos, illustrations, and images of fine art, stained glass, and statues—each one specifically selected for this program.

Educational research (Carney and Levine, 2002) and our own experience tell us that photos, illustrations, and art closely tied to text

- improve the reader's learning and recall
- direct the child's attention to what's most important on the page
- make the text more understandable and memorable
- help the child connect and apply what's been learned to their lived experience.

In *Alive in Christ* lessons, developmentally appropriate visuals—Scripture illustration, fine art, stained glass, statues, icons, photos, and accompanying captions—meet lesson objectives and build Catholic identity.

You will find historically accurate, child friendly Scripture and Saint illustrations that grow in sophistication and detail as grades advance. This promotes a common visual language of faith and builds a vibrant Catholic identity.

Grade 2   Grade 6
Saints Thérèse of Lisieux and Teresa of Ávila

Grade 1   Grade 3
The Sacred Heart of Jesus in statue and fine art

Grade 2   Grade 5
The Parable of the Good Samaritan

The Role of Music

The use of music in *Alive in Christ* is both intentional and purposeful. The music has been chosen to form children in the lesson content and Catholic identity. It is age appropriate and includes children's voices. It has both a formative and an informative purpose.

Long-term Retention

It has been demonstrated that the repeated rehearsal of information has a positive effect on long-term retention. Activities from the arts, such as music integrated into classroom content, can be used as prompts to recall information. Combining music with movement further enhances a child's learning. We "encode" information through both verbal and motor activity. In other words, when we sing and move, we are learning in both our bodies and our minds.

Sustain Attention

Music and movement also sustain attention. Translating material into actions (role-playing a song) helps learners not only recall a story but can also help them connect that story to a concept they have learned. Besides, moving to music is a universal response, and, with the proper disposition, can enhance prayer.

Emotional and Spiritual Connection

Music can also affect us on an emotional level. Who of us has not been moved by a song to feel something deep within our hearts? Music has helped form us as Catholics throughout the ages and has enabled us to both experience God's presence and respond to him from the depths of our being.

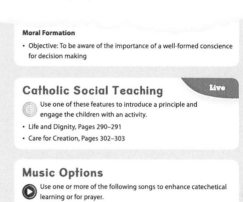

Moral Formation
- Objective: To be aware of the importance of a well-formed conscience for decision making

Catholic Social Teaching   Live

Use one of these features to introduce a principle and engage the children with an activity.
- Life and Dignity, Pages 290–291
- Care for Creation, Pages 302–303

Music Options

Use one or more of the following songs to enhance catechetical learning or for prayer.
- "God Is a Part of My Life," Live Prayer, Page 60
- "For the Fruits of this Creation," Discover, Page 55

First Sunday of Advent—Waiting for Jesus, God's Greatest Gift
Baptism of the Lord—Son of Go

Year C
Second Sunday in Advent—God as Creator
Third Sunday in Ordinary Time—Scripture is fulfilled.

Go to **aliveinchrist.osv.com** for a complete correlation ordered by the Sundays of the year and suggestions for how to integrate the Scripture readings into chapter lessons.

Music options are integrated into every lesson and can be used to celebrate prayer or enhance learning. You will find these options both at point of use in the wraparound and on the Chapter Connections page in the box titled, "Music Options."

 Play chapter-specific music to enhance catechetical learning or for prayer. Go to **aliveinchrist.osv.com** to sample and download.

Songs of Scripture Music CDs

To support the commitment to Sacred Scripture, an all-new, original resource, *Songs of Scripture Deepening Children's Understanding of God's Word*, by John Burland and Jo Ann Paradise, unfolds one of the Scripture passages in each unit. Activities for these songs are found in bottom-band boxes in the Catechist Edition.

 Go to **aliveinchrist.osv.com** to order the *Songs of Scripture* CDs and for more information.

Reaching All Learners

" Growth in faith is related to human development and passes through stages. Individuals develop as human beings and faithful followers of Christ in different ways and according to their own pace…The Church's catechesis—and even more so, the catechist—must take into consideration all the human factors of a particular age level in order to present the Gospel message in a vital and compelling way. "

NDC, 48

Benefitting from the work of educators in the past decades, religious educators now have new tools in providing children the fullness of the faith in developmentally appropriate ways.

Not only must we teach the faith related to children's level of human development, we must also meet the individual needs of our children. When working with any group of children, it does not take long to realize that they learn in different ways. Many have written about how to best provide strategies to address different learning styles. Dr. Howard Gardner's research on Multiple Intelligences provides particular insight. His theory looks at eight different ways people learn. Applying his theory to your planning will help you reach each child with the Good News of salvation.

Throughout *Alive in Christ*, a variety of teaching strategies are employed within the lesson process. Working with words and reading Scripture (Verbal/ Linguistic), using photos and illustrations to prompt discussion (Visual/Spatial), and listening to, singing, and reflecting on songs (Musical) are just a few examples. Additional features, such as Reaching All Learners and Optional Activities, address various methods to help students with different learning styles and abilities connect with the lesson.

Multiple Intelligences	
Verbal/ Linguistic	This learning occurs best through reading, writing, telling stories, and discussing ideas.
Logical/ Mathematical	This learning occurs best through problem solving, analyzing, and applying logic.
Musical	This learning occurs best through singing, listening to music, and remembering melodies.
Bodily/ Kinesthetic	This learning occurs best through physically moving, dancing, acting, and making things.
Visual/Spatial	This learning occurs best through looking at pictures, drawing, and creating.
Interpersonal	This learning occurs best through sharing about one's feelings, talking with others, and collaborating with others on tasks.
Intrapersonal	This learning occurs best through working alone and reflecting.
Naturalist	This learning occurs best through exploring nature and living things.

Go to **aliveinchrist.osv.com** for additional resources on meeting the challenges of providing for special needs in your faith formation sessions.

Teaching Fourth Graders

It's a blessing to be a catechist to fourth graders. This is an exciting time in the life of a child, when children have a clear sense of cause and effect, making them curious about how and why things work the way they do.

Cognitive and Verbal

Fourth graders are growing in their cognitive and verbal skills, and many adults are impressed at how fourth graders can carry on adult-like conversations at times. However, their thinking differs from adults in some important ways.

They are good at using their reasoning skills, but they still don't have a firm grasp on hypothetical reasoning. This means they have difficulty imagining things or situations they haven't experienced.

Fourth graders are very concrete and will learn best by what they experience through their senses. They need us, as catechists, to "make the faith real" through hands-on activities that allow them to put what they are learning into practice.

Social

Fourth graders are growing socially as well. Many children this age have "best friends" of the same gender with whom they choose to spend most of their time. These best friend pairings usually happen around common interests; children this age are most attracted to children they perceive as being most like them.

They might enjoy working in pairs with friends in a catechetical setting. They should also be challenged at times, however, to "branch out" and learn from others who are less similar to themselves.

Another challenge, socially speaking, for fourth graders is taking another person's viewpoint. It's still difficult for children this age to understand how something feels for someone else. For this reason, they can sometimes be hurtful to one another. It's helpful for them to hear when they have hurt someone's feelings and how it felt for that person.

Moral Reasoning

This is an age of particular growth in moral reasoning. Fourth graders are beginning to internalize standards of behavior. Their consciences are growing quickly, and they are gaining a sense of "right" and "wrong" that goes beyond just what might bring them punishments or rewards.

This is a great time to work with them on what it means to be disciples of Jesus and challenge them to set behavioral goals for themselves throughout the week.

Acting out making good choices in a moral dilemma will be especially effective, since all of us are more likely to do the things we practice.

Living and Learning Together

In the *General Directory for Catechesis* we are told that the "childhood religious awakening which takes place in the family is irreplaceable"[6] (226). The role of the catechetical leader and the catechist in the parish is to help form and support families in this sacred journey.

The Family + Faith page gives families the tools they need to talk about faith and more consciously live the faith in their homes and daily lives. The resources on this page are invaluable in providing adults the practical help they need to grow in faith themselves and to nurture the faith of their children.

Your Child Learned
This section summarizes key Catholic teaching covered in the chapter and introduces families to the Scripture and Person of Faith presented.

Children at This Age
This feature helps families understand the relationship between the content presented and the child's developmental level of understanding. It provides a look at the content through the eyes of the child and equips parents with a perspective that is necessary in order to nurture their child's faith.

FAMILY + FAITH
LIVING AND LEARNING TOGETHER

YOUR CHILD LEARNED >>>
This chapter is about God's gift of creation and the special place humans have in it because we are made in the image and likeness of God.

God's Word
Read **Luke 1:1–2** to learn more about those who have worked to tell God's story.

Catholics Believe
- God is the Creator of all that is good.
- Jesus is God's greatest gift. Jesus is the Son of God.
To learn more, go to the *Catechism of the Catholic Church* #256, 319, and 454 at usccb.org.

People of Faith
This week, your child met the Blessed Virgin Mary who we honor as the Mother of God and the Mother of the Church.

CHILDREN AT THIS AGE >>>
How They Understand God's Creation Most second-graders have a strong sense of cause and effect. This makes it natural for them to believe in a Creator when they see the created world. They also have a strong sense that everything has a purpose. For this reason, it is an excellent time for them to learn that everything in the natural world is a gift from God and has a God-given role or meaning.

CONSIDER THIS >>>
When was the last time that God's creation amazed you?

Do you realize creation is one of the many ways God shows himself to you? God… "is living and personal, profoundly close to us in creating and sustaining us. Though he is totally other, hidden, glorious, and wondrous, he communicates himself to us in Jesus Christ, whom we meet in the Church, especially in Scripture and the Sacraments. In these many ways, God speaks to our hearts where we may welcome his loving presence" (*USCCA, p. 51*).

LET'S TALK >>>
- Ask your child to talk about God's gifts. Which is his greatest? (Jesus)
- Talk about ways your family uses God's gifts of creation in your daily routines.

LET'S PRAY >>>
Mary, Mother of God, pray for our family and help us always love your Son, Jesus. Amen.

For a multimedia glossary of Catholic Faith Words, Sunday readings, seasonal and Saint resources, and chapter activities go to aliveinchrist.osv.com.

Alive in Christ, Grade 2 Chapter 1 **61**

Consider This
Through the use of targeted questions that encourage reflection, adults are given the opportunity to reflect on their experience and inform that experience with the teaching of the Church.

Let's Talk
Adult-specific questions or directions help to facilitate discussion with the child about the lesson content.

Let's Pray
This provides families with a short prayer that incorporates the key concept of the lesson.

Go to **aliveinchrist.osv.com**.
The Family + Faith page sends adults to aliveinchrist.osv.com so that families can reinforce and assess their learning, as well as find suggestions for family discussions and ways to apply faith to family life.

 The **aliveinchrist.osv.com** Student/Family pages extend learning, foster family faith sharing, and provide session plans and tools for home-based catechesis.

Catholic Social Teaching

Pope Saint John Paul II reminded us that one of the fundamental tasks of the Christian family is to remember that the family is always at the service of God's Kingdom. While the family is to "guard, reveal, and communicate love," it does so knowing that their love is not only to be shared within itself, but meant to be shared with the world (*Familiaris Consortio*, 17). We are called to reach out past our family to build relationships of love and justice in our neighborhoods, communities, and beyond.

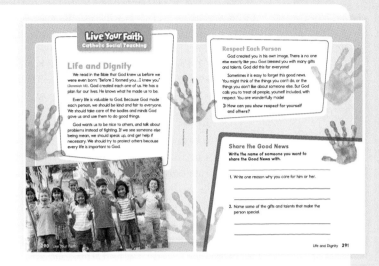

Each grade level of *Alive in Christ*, presents the seven principles of Catholic Social Teaching, articulated by the United States Conference of Catholic Bishops. In this **Live Your Faith** component, the scriptural and doctrinal foundations of the principles help the children connect their faith to a life of peace and justice. While peace and justice are taught in many of the core chapters, the seven principles are intentionally treated in Live Your Faith.

You can use these Catholic Social Teaching features in a variety of ways. Every core chapter and seasonal lesson has a Catholic Social Teaching connection integrated into the lesson plan. A **bottom band box** will provide you with suggestions on how to incorporate the Live Your Faith component with the lesson. Combining these components with the seasonal lessons can help your children connect how Catholics worship with how Catholics live.

Your catechetical leader may choose to schedule these components so that all the children will be focusing on the same principle at the same time. If you schedule your own sessions, you may choose to combine several of the principles and present them at one time.

This presentation of Catholic teaching builds a vibrant Catholic identity and prepares us to evangelize the world through faith and action as we work in service of God's Kingdom.

Using This Feature

Lesson Connection

Use this feature to enhance, or in place of, the Live section of the following chapters:

Chapter 1, page 53	**Chapter 5**, page 97
Chapter 3, page 73	**Chapter 12**, page 175
Chapter 4, page 87	**Chapter 20**, page 267

Use this feature after the Discover section, before the Live prayer begins in the following seasonal lessons:

Ordinary Time: All Saints, page 15

Christmas, page 25   **Easter, We Rejoice**, page 43

Unit	Chapter		Lesson Concepts
1 REVELATION	CHAPTER 1	The Creator's Work	• God created human beings in his image and likeness. • Creation is a gift from God that shows his goodness; it is the work of the Holy Trinity. • Humans have the responsibility to care for all of creation, especially each other.
	CHAPTER 2	The Church Gathered	• The Bible is the Word of God written in human words. It is the holy book of the Church. • The Church is the community of all baptized people who believe in God and follow Jesus. • The Church helps us understand God's Word, teaches us about God's love, and gathers us to honor and worship God.
	CHAPTER 3	Families Teach Love	• Families teach us how to care for, respect, and help one another. • We honor Mary as the Mother of God, the greatest of Saints, and our Mother, too. • The Hail Mary begins with the words Elizabeth used to greet Mary. • The Catholic family is the domestic Church where we experience love and learn about God and how we pray and live as Catholics.
2 TRINITY	CHAPTER 4	The Holy Trinity	• A mystery is a truth that is difficult to perceive or understand with our senses, but is known through faith and through signs. • Jesus teaches us about God his Father and the Holy Spirit. • God the Father, God the Son, and God the Holy Spirit are a perfect communion of love. • The Creed is a statement of the Church's beliefs.
	CHAPTER 5	The Church Celebrates	• At the Last Supper Jesus celebrated the Passover with his Apostles. • Liturgy is the public prayer of the Church. It includes the Seven Sacraments and forms of daily prayer. • Catholics are required to attend Mass on Sundays and Holy Days of Obligation. • The Blessed Sacrament is the Holy Eucharist, especially the Body of Christ, which is kept in the Tabernacle.
	CHAPTER 6	Pray Always	• In the Lord's Prayer, Jesus taught his followers to pray to God the Father. • Daily prayer is important. We can pray using traditional prayers and our own words, out loud or silently, and at any time. • The five basic forms of prayer are blessing and adoration, praise, petition, intercession, and thanksgiving.
3 JESUS CHRIST	CHAPTER 7	The Good News	• The Gospel message is the Good News of God's Kingdom and his saving love. • The four Gospel books in the New Testament are about Christ's life, teaching, Death, and Resurrection. • The Kingdom of God is the world of love, peace, and justice that is in Heaven and is still being built on Earth. • In his miracles and parables, Jesus shows us that God's Kingdom is here and yet to come fully.
	CHAPTER 8	The Paschal Mystery	• Jesus offered the greatest sacrifice: he gave his life to save us from sin so that we could have new life with God in Heaven. • The Resurrection is the event of Jesus being raised from Death to new life by God the Father through the power of the Holy Spirit. • The Paschal Mystery is the mystery of Jesus Christ's suffering, Death, Resurrection, and Ascension. • The Church celebrates the Paschal Mystery in each of the Seven Sacraments.
	CHAPTER 9	The Body of Christ	• With the help of the Holy Spirit, members of the Church continue Jesus' work here on Earth. • The Church is the Body of Christ of which Christ is the head. • All the baptized use their gifts and talents to serve others. • Stewardship is the way we appreciate and use God's gifts, including our time, talent, and treasure and the gift of creation.
4 THE CHURCH	CHAPTER 10	Church Leaders	• The Apostles are the twelve disciples Jesus chose to be his closest followers to share in his work and mission in a special way. • Peter was the leader of the Apostles and first Pope, head of the entire Church. • The bishops are successors of the Apostles. • The Pope, bishops, priests, and deacons lead, guide, and make the Church holy.
	CHAPTER 11	One and Holy	• The Marks of the Church are the four characteristics that identify Christ's Church: one, holy, catholic, and apostolic. • Pentecost is the feast that celebrates the coming of the Holy Spirit fifty days after Easter. • The Holy Spirit continues to unify the Church and make her holy. • The Communion of Saints is everyone who believes in and follows Jesus, people on Earth and in Purgatory and Heaven.

Go to **aliveinchrist.osv.com** for complete program Scope and Sequence.

Sacred Scripture	Catechism of the Catholic Church	Tasks of Catechesis	Catholic Faith Words	People of Faith	Catholic Social Teaching
You Formed Me Psalm 139:13–15; The Creation of the World Genesis 1:1–23	355, 293, 292, 2415	Promoting Knowledge of the Faith, Moral Formation	creation, Holy Trinity, image of God	Bl. Rabanus Maurus	Life and Dignity, Care for Creation
Jesus Prays John 17:20–23; Helping One Another Acts 2:42–47	105–106, 1213, 2030, 942, 1816	Promoting Knowledge of the Faith, Education for Community Life	Bible, Church, Sacred Tradition	St. Francis of Assisi	Call to Community, Human Solidarity
Those Who Hear and Act on the Word of God Luke 8:19–21; Mary Visits Elizabeth Luke 1:39–56	1657, 2207, 963, 435, 2676, 2204	Promoting Knowledge of the Faith, Education for Community Life	Visitation, Mary, domestic Church	Bls. Luigi and Maria	Life and Dignity, Call to Community
This Is How We Know 1 John 4:13–14, 16; The Father and the Spirit John 14:6–7, 16–17	237, 240, 2780, 850, 187	Promoting Knowledge of the Faith, Education for Community Life	mystery, Incarnation, creed, Apostles' Creed	St. John of Matha	Call to Community, Human Solidarity
They Were Hungry Mark 6:34–42; The Last Supper Luke 22:14–20	2097, 1339–1340, 1069–1070, 1389, 1379	Promoting Knowledge of the Faith, Liturgical Education	Seven Sacraments, Last Supper, liturgy, Nicene Creed, Tabernacle, Blessed Sacrament	St. Mary MacKillop	Call to Community, Rights and Responsibilities
Pray Quietly Matthew 6:5–6; The Lord's Prayer Matthew 6:9–13; Praying Well Matthew 6:5–8	2765, 2659, 2644	Teaching to Pray, Liturgical Education	prayer, Lord's Prayer, blessing, adoration, praise, petition, intercession, thanksgiving	St. Gertrude the Great	Life and Dignity, Human Solidarity
The Woman and the Lost Coin Luke 15:8–10; The Rejection at Nazareth Luke 4:16–21; The Mustard Seed Mark 4:30–32	125, 120, 127, 2818–2819, 546	Promoting Knowledge of the Faith, Moral Formation	Gospel, Messiah, Kingdom of God, miracle, parable	St. Isaac Jogues	Life and Dignity, Rights and Responsibilities
No Greater Love John 15:12–13; Mary Meets Jesus John 20:11–18	619, 623, 648, 571, 1113	Promoting Knowledge of the Faith, Liturgical Education	sacrifice, Resurrection, Ascension, Paschal Mystery	St. Mary Magdalene	Life and Dignity, Human Solidarity
Gifts of the Spirit 1 Corinthians 12:4–7; Those Who Helped Matthew 25:31–40	1287–1288, 792, 791, 1937, 2402	Education for Community Life, Liturgical Education	parish, Body of Christ, stewardship	St. Joseph Vaz	Call to Community, Option for the Poor
Jesus Sent Out the Twelve Matthew 10:5–10; Peter and Jesus Matthew 16:15–19, 26:69–75, John 21:15–17	551, 552, 861–862, 939	Education for Community Life, Liturgical Education	Pope, bishop, Magisterium, Apostolic Succession	St. Gregory the Great	The Dignity of Work, Care for Creation
Jesus Preached Peace Ephesians 2:19–21; The Coming of the Spirit Acts 2:1–12	811, 731, 2623–2625, 960–962	Education for Community Life, Liturgical Education	Marks of the Church, one, holy, catholic, apostolic, Pentecost, Saint, Communion of Saints	Sts. Perpetua and Felicity	Call to Community, Human Solidarity

Unit	Chapter	Lesson Concepts
4	**CHAPTER 12** Catholic and Apostolic	• Saint Paul was one of the first to take the message of Jesus across many countries, establishing Church communities and writing them letters that became part of the New Testament. • All Church members participate in her mission to announce the Good News of God's Kingdom to people of all nations. • The Church is catholic because she is everywhere and welcomes everyone. • The Church is apostolic because Jesus gave his Apostles the mission of sharing his Good News with people all over the world.
5 MORALITY	**CHAPTER 13** Choose Love	• The Story of Joseph in the Old Testament shows us to forgive and love. • Jesus teaches us to love our enemies. • The Beatitudes are teachings of Jesus that show the way to true happiness and tell how to live in God's Kingdom. • Jesus' New Commandment is for his disciples to love one another as he has loved us.
	CHAPTER 14 Live in the Light	• Vocation is God's plan for our lives, the purpose for which he made us. • Virtues are good spiritual habits that make you stronger and help you do what is right and good. • The Theological Virtues of faith, hope and charity are gifts from God that help us live in relationship with the Holy Trinity. • Virtues grow over time with our practice and openness to God's grace.
	CHAPTER 15 Help With Choices	• Conscience is an ability given to us by God that helps us make choices about right and wrong. • The Precepts of the Church are some of the minimum requirements given by Church leaders for deepening our relationship with God and the Church. • The Holy Spirit and the teachings of the Church help us to make good choices. • In the Sacrament of Penance and Reconciliation, we receive God's forgiveness and the grace to help us change.
6 SACRAMENTS	**CHAPTER 16** Sacraments of Initiation	• People of all ages can be baptized into the Church. • The Sacraments of Initiation celebrate membership into the Catholic Church: Baptism, Confirmation, and Eucharist. • Baptism removes Original Sin, forgives personal sin, and gives new life in Christ. Confirmation seals and completes Baptism. • In the Eucharist, Jesus Christ shares himself with us, giving us the gift of his Body and Blood.
	CHAPTER 17 Sacraments of Healing	• In the Sacraments of Healing, God's forgiveness and healing are given to those suffering physical and spiritual sickness. • In Penance and Reconciliation, we confess our sins to a priest who forgives in the name of Christ and his Church. • In the Anointing of the Sick, the priest prays that God will send his healing love to the person who is being anointed.
	CHAPTER 18 Sacraments at the Service of Communion	• Sacraments at the Service of Communion celebrate people's commitment to serve God and the community and help build up the People of God. • Holy Orders is the Sacrament in which baptized men are ordained as deacons, priests, or bishops to lead and serve the Church. • Matrimony joins a baptized man and a baptized woman in Christian marriage to serve God by loving and serving each other and any children God gives them.
7 KINGDOM OF GOD	**CHAPTER 19** The Church Through Time	• A covenant is a sacred promise or agreement between God and humans. • God established a covenant with Abraham, and from that came the beginning of God's People. • As the Son of God, Jesus fulfills God's promise and his covenant extends to all people. • The first Christians faced difficult times, but they tried to be faithful to him and to the covenant, and the Church grew.
	CHAPTER 20 The Work of the Church	• The Church continues Jesus' work on Earth through her worship, teaching, care for others, and work for peace and justice. • The Church is a sign of God's Kingdom and helps people share in the love of the Holy Trinity. • By our Baptism, we are called to participate in the Church's mission to share the Good News and serve God and others.
	CHAPTER 21 Everlasting Life	• Jesus' Resurrection is proof of his promise of eternal life. • The Particular Judgment is the individual judgment by God at the time of a person's death when God decides where that person will spend eternity according to his or her faith and works. • The Last Judgment is God's final triumph over evil, when Christ will come again and bring the Kingdom of God to its fullness. • The last book of the Bible, Revelation, ends with John's vision of a new creation, God's everlasting Kingdom.

Go to **aliveinchrist.osv.com** for complete program Scope and Sequence.

Sacred Scripture	Catechism of the Catholic Church	Tasks of Catechesis	Catholic Faith Words	People of Faith	Catholic Social Teaching
Do Everything in the Name of Jesus Colossians 3:16–17; Doing God's Work 1 Corinthians 3:5–9	849, 856, 863, 830–831, 869	Education for Community Life, Missionary Initiation	evangelization, mission, missionaries	St. Elizabeth Ann Seton	Option for the Poor, The Dignity of Work
Pray for Those Who Mistreat You Luke 6:27–28, 31; The Story of Joseph Genesis 37–45; Love of Enemies Matthew 5:43–47	312, 1825, 1716, 1970–1971	Promoting Knowledge of the Faith, Moral Formation	Beatitudes, mercy, New Commandment	St. Peter Canisius	Life and Dignity, Option for the Poor
The Light of the World John 8:12; Your Light Must Shine Matthew 5:14–16	1877, 1803, 1813, 1830	Promoting Knowledge of the Faith, Moral Formation	vocation, virtues, Theological Virtues, faith, hope, charity	St. Genevieve	Rights and Responsibilities, Care for Creation
You Know My Thoughts Psalm 139:23–24; Saul and Jesus Acts 9:1–30	1777, 2041, 1783–1785, 1422–1423	Promoting Knowledge of the Faith, Moral Formation	grace, conscience, Precepts of the Church, sin	St. Pio of Pietrelcina	Rights and Responsibilities, The Dignity of Work
A People Chosen by God 1 Peter 2:9–10; Many Are Baptized Acts 2:38–41	1247, 1250, 1212, 1217, 1323	Promoting Knowledge of the Faith, Liturgical Education	Sacred Chrism, Sacraments of Initiation, Real Presence, Eucharist	St. John the Baptist	Life and Dignity, Call to Community
All Were Healed Matthew 14:34–36; Jesus Gives New Life Luke 8:40–42, 49–56	1421, 1424, 1517	Promoting Knowledge of the Faith, Liturgical Education	Sacraments of Healing	St. Marianne Cope	Rights and Responsibilities, The Dignity of Work
Called to Be Free Galatians 5:13–14; Servants of Christ 1 Corinthians 3:21–4:2	1534, 1536, 1601	Liturgical Education, Moral Formation	vows, priest, deacon, Sacraments at the Service of Communion	St. Jean-Baptiste de La Salle	Call to Community, Human Solidarity
They Lived Together Acts 2:42; I Will Be Your God Genesis 17:1–19	56-58, 72, 73, 706, 2471–2472	Promoting Knowledge of the Faith, Liturgical Education	covenant, proclaim, faithful	St. Clement of Rome	Rights and Responsibilities, Human Solidarity
Be Happy 2 Corinthians 13:11; The Commissioning of the Twelve Matthew 10:5–14	759, 763, 2044–2046	Moral Formation, Missionary Initiation	justice, peace	St. Peter Claver	Rights and Responsibilities, The Dignity of Work
Whoever Knows Jesus Has Life 1 John 5:11–12; The New Heaven and the New Earth Revelation 21:1–4; Alpha and Omega Revelation 22:13	655, 1022, 1038–1040, 1044–1045	Promoting Knowledge of the Faith, Moral Formation	Heaven, Hell, Purgatory, Last Judgment	St. Joseph	Life and Dignity, Rights and Responsibilities

Grade 4 Scope and Sequence

Unit	Chapter	Lesson Concepts
1 REVELATION	**CHAPTER 1** God's Providence	• The first creation account teaches the goodness of all of God's creation. • Providence is God's loving care for all things; his will and plan for creation. • Divine Revelation is the way God tells humans about himself and makes his plan known. • God reveals himself through Sacred Scripture and the Sacred Tradition of the Church.
	CHAPTER 2 God Is Faithful	• Death, suffering, ignorance and the inclination to sin all came into the world as a result of Original Sin. • God always remains faithful and promises salvation, desiring humans to be free and faithful to him. • A covenant is a sacred promise or agreement between God and humans. • God called Abraham, and because of his belief and trust in God, God established a covenant with him.
	CHAPTER 3 God's Commandments	• God created people to be free and live as his People, and he called Moses to lead his People from slavery in Egypt. • The Ten Commandments are the summary of laws that God gave Moses on Mount Sinai that tell us what is necessary in order to love God and others. • God gave the Ten Commandments to help us be faithful to him and his covenant.
2 TRINITY	**CHAPTER 4** In God's Image	• Human dignity comes from being made in God's image and likeness with the ability to love, think, and make choices. • The soul is the spiritual part of a human that lives forever. • Sin is a deliberate thought, word, deed, or omission contrary to the law of God. • Every person is worthy of respect because he or she is created in God's image and made to love.
	CHAPTER 5 Living in Community	• The mission of God the Son and the Holy Spirit is to bring all people into the love of the Holy Trinity. • Morality is living in right relationship with God, yourself, and others. • God created all people for one another and we must all work for the common good. • Our love of our neighbor reflects the love of the Holy Trinity.
	CHAPTER 6 Making Good Choices	• Free will is the God-given freedom and ability to make choices. • God gives us grace, the Ten Commandments, and the Church to help us make good choices and deepen our relationship with him. • We need to know God's laws and form, or strengthen, our conscience so it will help us make good decisions. • Conscience is the God-given ability that helps us judge whether actions are morally good or wrong.
3 JESUS CHRIST	**CHAPTER 7** The Beatitudes	• The Beatitudes guide us to show mercy and be a blessing to others. • The word beatitude means "blessing" or "happiness." God put the desire for happiness inside each of us. • The Beatitudes are Jesus' teachings about the way to true happiness and living in God's Kingdom now and always. • God wants all of us to have eternal life—to live forever with him and all who die in his friendship.
	CHAPTER 8 Love God and Neighbor	• The Great Commandment is the two-fold command to love God above all and your neighbor as yourself. • The Theological Virtues of faith, hope, and charity are gifts from God that help us to believe in him, trust his plan for us, and love him with all our heart, soul, and mind. • Loving God leads to sharing his love with others, and the Corporal and Spiritual Works of Mercy guide us in the ways to do so.
	CHAPTER 9 Honoring God	• The First Commandment teaches us to worship and honor only God, and not to place things or other people before him. • The Second Commandment calls us to always use the name of God with reverence and respect. • Blasphemy is the sin of showing disrespect for the name of God, Jesus Christ, Mary, or the Saints in words or actions. • We observe the Third Commandment through participation in the Sunday Eucharist, rest, time with family, and works of service.
4 THE CHURCH	**CHAPTER 10** Called to Serve	• Vocation is God's plan for our lives; the purpose for which he made us. • Priesthood, consecrated religious, committed single life, and married life are four distinct ways people respond to God's call. • All baptized members of the Church are called to serve God and the Church using their gifts.
	CHAPTER 11 Models of Virtue	• A Saint is a person who the Church declares has led a holy life and is enjoying eternal life with God in Heaven. • Mary is the perfect model of holiness, accepting God's will throughout her life and remaining faithful to him. • The Immaculate Conception is the truth that God kept Mary free from sin from the first moment of her life. • Mary is called the Mother of the Church because she holds her Son's followers close to her heart.

Go to **aliveinchrist.osv.com** for complete program Scope and Sequence.

Sacred Scripture	Catechism of the Catholic Church	Tasks of Catechesis	Catholic Faith Words	People of Faith	Catholic Social Teaching
God's Plan Psalm 33:9, 11–12; The Story of Creation Genesis 1:1-31, 2:1–3; The Call of Jeremiah Jeremiah 1:4–8	299, 302–303, 50, 81–82	Promoting Knowledge of the Faith	providence, Sacred Scripture, Divine Revelation, Sacred Tradition	St. Kateri Tekakwitha	Life and Dignity, Care for Creation
The Promise Hebrews 10:16–17, 23; In the Garden Genesis 3; Abram's Call and Journey Genesis 12:1–8; God's Promise 15:1–5, 18; 17:5–9, 15; 21:1–3	402–405, 55, 56–58, 59–60	Promoting Knowledge of the Faith, Moral Formation	Original Sin, salvation, covenant, faithful	St. Bridget of Sweden	Rights and Responsibilities, Human Solidarity
Holy Ground Exodus 3:2b, 4–5; Joseph and His Brothers Genesis 37:1–4, 42:6–8, 44:1–12, 45:4–5; The Exodus from Egypt Exodus 2:1–10, 14:10–31, 15:19–21	2057, 2061, 2062–2063	Promoting Knowledge of the Faith, Moral Formation	Ten Commandments, ark of the covenant	St. Raymond of Peñafort	Call to Community, Rights and Responsibilities
Worthy of the Lord Colossians 1:10, 12–15; In His Image Genesis 1:27	355–357, 366, 1849, 1440, 1700	Promoting Knowledge of the Faith, Moral Formation	human dignity, soul, sin, mortal sin, venial sin	St. Germaine Cousin	Life and Dignity, Care for Creation
Love One Another 1 John 4:9, 11–13, 16b; The Communal Life Acts 2:42–45	258–260, 1950–1951, 1905–1906, 1878	Promoting Knowledge of the Faith, Education for Community Life	Holy Trinity, morality, common good	St. Dominic	Call to Community, Option for the Poor
The Lord's Judgment Isaiah 11:1–4a; The Parable of the Good Samaritan Luke 10:30–35	1704, 1785, 1783–1784, 1777	Promoting Knowledge of the Faith, Moral Formation	free will, grace, conscience	St. Charles Lwanga	Rights and Responsibilities, Option for the Poor
Hear and Observe the Word of God Luke 11:27–28; The Sermon on the Mount Matthew 5:3–10	2444, 1718, 1716, 1720–1721	Moral Formation, Missionary Initiation	mercy, Beatitudes, eternal life, peace	St. Yi Sung-hun	Option for the Poor, Human Solidarity
Live as Jesus Commanded Ephesians 5:1–5; The Greatest Commandment Matthew 22:37–40; The Rich Young Man Matthew 19:16–22	2055, 1814, 1817, 1822, 2447–2448	Moral Formation, Missionary Initiation	Great Commandment, Theological Virtues, faith, hope, charity, Corporal and Spiritual Works of Mercy	St. Katharine Drexel	Life and Dignity, Human Solidarity
Worthy Are You, Lord Revelation 4:11; 7:12; The Golden Calf Exodus 32:1–20	2110, 2142–2143, 2148, 2176–2177	Liturgical Education, Moral Formation	worship, idolatry, blasphemy, Resurrection	St. Mary Ann of Quito	Life and Dignity, Care for Creation
Saul Is Chosen 1 Samuel 10:20–22; The Call of the First Disciples Matthew 4:18–22	1877, 871–873, 912–913	Education for Community Life, Missionary Initiation	vocation, Kingdom of God, vows, laity	Bl. Frédéric Ozanam	Call to Community, The Dignity of Work
Light of the World Matthew 5:14–16; The Canticle of Mary Luke 1:46–50	828, 829, 491, 963	Promoting Knowledge of the Faith, Teaching to Pray	canonization, Saint, beatification, Mary, Immaculate Conception, patron Saint	St. Bernadette Soubirous	Call to Community, Option for the Poor

Unit	Chapter	Lesson Concepts
4	**CHAPTER 12** The Church Teaches	• Jesus chose Peter to be the shepherd of his flock, leader of the Apostles, and head of his Church. • Jesus gave Peter and the Apostles, and their successors the Pope and bishops, the authority to teach and lead in his name. • The Magisterium is the teaching office of the Church, which is all of the bishops in union with the Pope. • The Holy Spirit directs the Magisterium in teaching and guiding the People of God. • The Precepts of the Church are some of the minimum requirements for deepening our relationship with God and Church.
5 **MORALITY**	**CHAPTER 13** Family Love	• God created humans to live in families and wants family members to respect, love, and protect one another. • The Fourth Commandment teaches children to honor and obey parents, who are to provide for, love, and share faith with them. • The Sixth and Ninth Commandments are about faithful love and commitment between husband and wife, but require all of us to keep promises, be faithful, and act appropriately. • The Cardinal Virtues help us to act wisely, use self-control, give God and others their due, and be disciplined.
	CHAPTER 14 Respect Life	• Life comes from God. Every human life is sacred from the moment of conception until the time of natural death. • All actions that respect and protect life uphold the Fifth Commandment. • Actions that deliberately harm human life, including that of the unborn, the sick, and elderly, are grave sins. • The Fifth Commandment calls us to respect and take care of our bodies.
	CHAPTER 15 Live in the Truth	• A martyr is a person who gives up his or her life to witness to the truth of Christ and the faith. • God is the source of all truth. His Word and his law call people to live in the truth. • The Eighth Commandment calls us to be honest in words and actions and forbids lying, gossip, and any acts against the truth.
6 **SACRAMENTS**	**CHAPTER 16** The Liturgical Year	• The Paschal Mystery is the mystery of Jesus' suffering, Death, Resurrection, and Ascension through which he saved all humans from the power of sin and everlasting death. • The liturgical year is made up of the feasts and seasons of the Church calendar that celebrate the Paschal Mystery of Christ. • The seasons of the Church year are Advent, Christmas, Ordinary Time, Lent, Triduum, and Easter.
	CHAPTER 17 The Seven Sacraments	• God the Father sent his only Son, Jesus, as a sign of his love for all people. • The Seven Sacraments are effective signs of God's life, instituted by Christ and given to the Church, so that Jesus can continue his saving work in the world. • The visible signs and Divine actions in each celebration give grace and allow us to share in God's work. • The Sacrament of the Eucharist, in which we receive the gift of Jesus Christ's Body and Blood, is at the heart of Catholic life.
	CHAPTER 18 Healing and Reconciliation	• Conversion involves turning away from sin and responding to God's love and forgiveness. • In the Sacrament of Penance and Reconciliation, we receive God's forgiveness of sins through the Church and are strengthened by grace to make peace and avoid temptation. • The Sacrament of the Anointing of the Sick brings Jesus' healing touch to strengthen, comfort, and forgive the sins of those who are seriously ill or close to death.
7 **KINGDOM OF GOD**	**CHAPTER 19** A Generous Spirit	• Being detached from our possessions enables us to work for peace and justice in God's Kingdom. • The Seventh and Tenth Commandments teach about the right attitude toward material possessions and require generosity. • Theft, greed, and envy are sins against these Commandments. • God created the world for all creatures and called humans to stewardship.
	CHAPTER 20 The Church in the World	• The mission of the Church is to proclaim the Gospel and work for the good of all people. • Evangelization is sharing the Good News of Jesus through words and actions in a way that invites people to accept the Gospel. • The Church is made up of people of many cultures and they are all united by their belief in Christ. • Missionaries spread the Gospel message and Jesus' care for all people to countries all around the world.
	CHAPTER 21 Eternal Life with God	• Heaven is a state of eternal happiness with God. • To spend eternity with God, we must grow in friendship with God. Through the Holy Spirit, God helps us respond to his grace and grow in friendship with him. • At the time of our death, we will be judged by God. This is called the Particular Judgment. • The Last Judgment refers to Jesus' coming in glory at the end of time to judge all the living and the dead and the coming of God's Kingdom in its fullness.

Sacred Scripture	Catechism of the Catholic Church	Tasks of Catechesis	Catholic Faith Words	People of Faith	Catholic Social Teaching
Building the Body of Christ Ephesians 4:11–13; You Are the Messiah! Mark 8:27–30	881, 85, 890–891, 892, 2041–2043	Moral Formation, Education for Community Life	Magisterium, Precepts of the Church	St. Mary Magdalen Postel	Call to Community, Rights and Responsibilities
Obey Your Parents Colossians 3:20–21; The Boy Jesus and His Family Luke 2:41–52	2203, 2199, 2348–2350, 1804–1805	Moral Formation, Education for Community Life	Cardinal Virtues, temperance, fortitude, modesty, chastity	Sts. Louis Martin and Marie-Azélie Martin	Life and Dignity, Call to Community
You Will Answer for Your Actions Matthew 5:21–22; The Choice Deuteronomy 30:19–20; Love of Enemies Matthew 5:43–45	2258, 2302, 2268–2269, 2288	Moral Formation, Education for the Community Life	sacred, murder	St. Gianna Molla	Life and Dignity, Option for the Poor
Keep Your Promises Matthew 5:33, 37; The Truth Will Set You Free John 8:31–32, 14:6	2473, 2465, 2464, 2487	Moral Formation, Education for the Community Life	martyr, reparation, prudence	St. Joan of Arc	Rights and Responsibilities, Human Solidarity
Trust God Psalm 62:8–9; The Right Time Ecclesiastes 3:1–8	571, 1171, 1168–1169	Promoting Knowledge of the Faith, Liturgical Education	Ascension, Paschal Mystery, liturgical year	St. Juan Diego	Call to Community, Human Solidarity
His Grace Ephesians 1:3, 7–8; The Last Supper Luke 22:17–20	458, 1127, 1128, 1131, 1322, 1324	Promoting Knowledge of the Faith, Liturgical Education	Incarnation, Seven Sacraments, Eucharist	St. Margaret Mary Alacoque	Option for the Poor, Human Solidarity
I Confess Psalm 32:1–3, 5; The Story of Zacchaeus Luke 19:1–10; The Man Born Blind John 9:1–38	1427–1428, 1468–1469, 1532	Liturgical Education, Moral Formation	repent, Penance and Reconciliation, Confession, temptation, sacramental seal, penance, absolution, Anointing of the Sick	V. Matt Talbot	Rights and Responsibilities, Option for the Poor
Give Luke 6:38; The Parable of the Rich Fool Luke 12:16–21; The Poor Widow's Contribution Mark 12:41–44	2545–2546, 2401, 2534, 2408, 2536, 2538, 2402	Promoting Knowledge of the Faith, Moral Formation	envy, greed, humility, justice, stewardship	St. Margaret of Scotland	Call to Community, The Dignity of Work
Be My Witnesses Acts of the Apostles 1:8; The Commissioning of the Disciples Matthew 28:18–20	849, 853–854, 849–851, 781	Education for Community Life, Missionary Initiation	Gospel, mission, evangelization	St. Junipero Serra	Option for the Poor, Human Solidarity
Whoever Has the Son Has Life 1 John 5:1–3, 11–12; The Judgment of the Nations Matthew 25:34–40	1024, 1039–1041, 1021–1022, 682, 1038	Promoting Knowledge of the Faith, Education for Community Life	Heaven, Gifts of the Holy Spirit, Particular Judgment, Purgatory, Hell, Last Judgment	St. Martin de Porres	Life and Dignity, Rights and Responsibilities

Scope and Sequence

Unit	Chapter		Lesson Concepts
1 REVELATION	CHAPTER 1	God's Plan for All Creation	• Being made in his image and likeness, humans can praise God for his goodness and care for one another and creation. • God revealed himself in a unique way through Sacred Scripture and Sacred Tradition. • Providence is God's loving care for all things, his will and plan for all creation. • The gifts of the Earth used in the Seven Sacraments are signs of God's presence and power.
	CHAPTER 2	Made to Be With God	• Our longings are part of the desire God put in our hearts to be truly happy with him. • Grace is a free, loving gift of a participation in the life of the Holy Trinity. • Faith is a belief and trust in God and the things that he has revealed to us, both a gift from God and a human choice. • The Sacrament of Baptism is the beginning of the journey of faith.
	CHAPTER 3	Signs of God's Presence	• God uses signs, such as the Burning Bush speaking to Moses, to communicate that he is with us and acting in our lives. • The Passover meal was a sign of the covenant between God and the People he saved. • The Seven Sacraments are signs of the new covenant made through the life and sacrifice of Jesus. In each Sacrament, visible signs and divine actions give grace and allow us to share in God's work.
2 TRINITY	CHAPTER 4	The Mystery of the Trinity	• Jesus invites us into a deeper understanding of the mystery of God whom we cannot see except through him. • Those who are baptized enter into the very life of the Holy Trinity, who is love. • The Theological Virtues of faith, hope, and charity help us obey the First Commandment and live in relationship with the Trinity.
	CHAPTER 5	Prayer and Worship	• King David and Jesus teach us that prayer and worship are ways to show reverence for God and to respond to his love. • When we worship God, we adore and praise him, especially in prayer and in the liturgy of the Church. • In the liturgy, we participate along with the whole Body of Christ in the saving work accomplished through Jesus' life, Death, Resurrection, and Ascension. • The Holy Trinity is at work in the celebration of the liturgy.
	CHAPTER 6	A Life of Virtue	• In his discussion on the Great Commandment, Jesus teaches that showing love for God and neighbor is an act of worship. • The Cardinal Virtues are habits acquired by human effort in cooperation with grace that help us live as God's children. • The virtues strengthen our ability to know right from wrong, helping us act for good and grow as God's children.
3 JESUS CHRIST	CHAPTER 7	Living Image of Christ	• The word Incarnation means "coming into flesh." It is the mystery that the Son of God became man in order to save all people. • Jesus is the Savior who came into the world to save all people lost through sin and lead them back to God his Father. • God created all people in his image and likeness, with free will, a soul, and the ability to love. • We are given God's very life and the help to be a living image of Christ every day.
	CHAPTER 8	Proclaim the Kingdom	• The Kingdom of God is God's Reign of peace, justice, and love that exists in Heaven, but has not yet come in its fullness on Earth. • Jesus' parables and miracles helped his followers experience and understand the meaning of the Kingdom, which Christ made present but is not yet complete until he comes again. • Christ's words and actions, and his presence in the Seven Sacraments, teach about the need for conversion in our own lives.
	CHAPTER 9	Celebrating the Paschal Mystery	• By his sacrifice and Resurrection, Jesus is the Redeemer—bringing us back from the slavery of sin and everlasting death. • The Paschal Mystery is Christ's work of Redemption through his suffering, Death, Resurrection, and Ascension. • Each of the Sacraments is a celebration of and participation in the Paschal Mystery.
4 THE CHURCH	CHAPTER 10	The Church's Message	• The four Marks of the Church distinguish Christ's Church and her mission to bring Christ to the world. • The Church is an assembly, a gathering of the People of God, the Body of Christ. • The Church is one because the power of the Holy Spirit unites all the members in one faith, in the celebration of the Sacraments, and under the authority of the Pope.
	CHAPTER 11	The Teaching Church	• Jesus gave the Apostles a mission and the authority to spread the Good News of his Father's Kingdom. • The bishops, in union with the Pope, are the successors of the Apostles and share in their authority to faithfully pass on what God has revealed through his Son, Jesus. • The Magisterium is the teaching office of the Church, including all of the bishops in union with the Pope. • The Pope and the bishops, guided by the Holy Spirit, protect and explain the Word of God.

Go to **aliveinchrist.osv.com** for complete program Scope and Sequence.

Sacred Scripture	Catechism of the Catholic Church	Tasks of Catechesis	Catholic Faith Words	People of Faith	Catholic Social Teaching
Let Us Sing Joyfully Psalm 95:1–2, 6–7; The Coming of God Psalm 98:4–9	299, 81–82, 302, 1145	Promoting Knowledge of the Faith, Liturgical Education	Divine Revelation, Sacred Scripture, Sacred Tradition, providence, stewardship	St. Hildegard	Life and Dignity, Care for Creation
You Are My God Psalm 63:2, 4–5; Martha and Mary Luke 10:38–42; The Samaritan Woman John 4:7–29	27, 2652, 1997, 26, 153–154, 189	Promoting Knowledge of the Faith, Liturgical Education	religion, grace, faith, Messiah	St. Augustine	Life and Dignity, Call to Community
Temple of the Living God 2 Corinthians 6:16; The Burning Bush Exodus 3:1–15	1146–1147, 204, 1334, 1122–1123	Promoting Knowledge of the Faith, Liturgical Education	covenant, Seven Sacraments	St. Benedict	Call to Community, Human Solidarity
The Baptism of Jesus Mark 1:9-11; John the Baptist's Testimony to Jesus John 1:32–34	250, 426, 265, 1813	Promoting Knowledge of the Faith, Moral Formation	mystery, Holy Trinity, virtues	St. Athanasius	Rights and Responsibilities, Human Solidarity
Rejoice in the Lord Philippians 4:4–7; The Ark Brought to Jerusalem 2 Samuel 6:1–15; The Early Church Gatherers Acts 2:46–47a	2579, 2098–2100, 1082–1083, 2655	Liturgical Education, Teaching to Pray	reverence, worship, liturgy	St. Cecilia	The Dignity of Work, Human Solidarity
Walk Humbly Micah 6:8; The Greatest Commandment Mark 12:28–34	2055, 2083, 1805, 1834, 1803	Promoting Knowledge of the Faith, Moral Formation	Cardinal Virtues	St. Thomas More	Rights and Responsibilities, Option for the Poor
God Created Mankind Genesis 1:26–27; The Visit of the Magi Matthew 2:1–12	461, 430, 41, 355, 1877	Promoting Knowledge of the Faith	Incarnation, Savior, free will, soul	Bl. Maria Vicenta Rosal Vasquez	Life and Dignity, Option for the Poor
Around Galilee Matthew 4:23; The Parable of the Sower Luke 8:5–8	2816, 2819, 546, 547, 1127, 1129	Promoting Knowledge of the Faith, Missionary Initiation	Kingdom of God, parable, miracles, conversion	St. Catherine of Siena	Rights and Responsibilities, Option for the Poor
They Will Be His People Revelation 21:3–6; The Resurrection of Jesus Luke 24:5b–9	1173, 606–607, 1085, 1115	Promoting Knowledge of the Faith, Liturgical Education	Original Sin, sacrifice, Paschal Mystery	St. Paul Miki	Life and Dignity, Option for the Poor
Live in a Manner Worthy Ephesians 4:1–6; God's House and People 1 Peter 2:4–5	775, 811, 804–805, 813	Education for Community Life, Missionary Initiation	Marks of the Church, Body of Christ	St. Robert Bellarmine	Call to Community, Human Solidarity
I Am with You Always Matthew 28:18–20; Peter's Confession about Jesus Matthew 16:15–19	858, 857, 86, 85	Promoting Knowledge of the Faith, Education for Community Life	Magisterium, infallibility	Pope Saint John Paul II	Call to Community, Rights and Responsibilities

Unit	Chapter	Lesson Concepts
4	CHAPTER 12 — Lives of Holiness	• To be holy is to be unique and pure, set apart for God and his purposes. • Saints are models of heroic virtue who responded to the Holy Spirit's call, accepting God's grace and living in his friendship. • The Church honors Mary, the Mother of God, as the Queen of Saints. The Annunciation and Assumption teach us about her obedience and faith. • Canonization is a declaration by the Pope naming a person as a Saint whose life can be a model for all Christians.
5 MORALITY	CHAPTER 13 — Evil in the World	• The disobedience of our first parents and its effect for all humans is called Original Sin. • Jesus' Death and Resurrection were God's plan for the Redemption he had promised his Chosen People. • Mortal and venial sin are personal sins that break or weaken a person's relationship with God.
	CHAPTER 14 — New Life in Christ	• Through the Sacraments of Initiation, we enter into a relationship with Christ and membership into the Catholic Church. • Through the Sacrament of Baptism, we participate in the role of Jesus as priest, prophet, and king. • Confirmation seals us with a special outpouring of the Gifts of the Holy Spirit, deepens baptismal grace, and strengthens us. • The Rite of Christian Initiation of Adults (RCIA) is the process by which adults, and some children, become members of the Catholic Church through the Sacraments of Initiation.
	CHAPTER 15 — Forgiveness and Healing	• Christ continues to share God's forgiving and healing love in the Sacraments of Healing. • The Sacrament of Penance, called by different names, always has four parts: contrition, confession, penance, and absolution. • In the Anointing of the Sick Christ strengthens, comforts, and forgives the sins of those who are seriously ill or close to death.
6 SACRAMENTS	CHAPTER 16 — Gathered as One	• The Mass is central to Catholic life because it unites Christ's followers more closely to him and to one another. • Real Presence is the teaching that Jesus Christ is really and truly with us in the Eucharist—Body, Blood, Soul and Divinity. • In the Mass we are joined more closely to the Communion of Saints and remember in a special way those who have died. • Participation in the Mass is a duty and privilege. We are led by the ordained ministers and others serve to help us worship.
	CHAPTER 17 — Liturgy of the Word	• The Old Testament is the first part of the Bible about God's relationship with the Chosen People before Jesus was born. • The New Testament is the second part of the Bible about the life and teaching of Jesus, his followers, and the early Church. • Sacred Scripture is interpreted through the teaching of the Church. • The Liturgy of the Word, the first main parts of the Mass, begins with the first reading from the Old Testament and ends with the Prayer of the Faithful.
	CHAPTER 18 — Liturgy of the Eucharist	• Jesus Christ, the Bread of Life, received in the Eucharist, offers lasting spiritual nourishment and the promise of eternal life. • Instituted at the Last Supper, the Eucharist is both a holy meal and a sacrifice during which we give thanks, remember Jesus' sacrifice, and receive the Body and Blood of Christ. • The consecration is the part of the Eucharistic Prayer in which the priest prays the words of Jesus Christ over the bread and wine, and these elements become the Body and Blood of Christ.
7 KINGDOM OF GOD	CHAPTER 19 — The Call to Serve	• A vocation is a particular way to answer God's call to serve him and others, whether as a member of the ordained ministry, a consecrated religious, or a lay person (married or single). • Each of us needs to learn to listen for God's call in our own lives. • The Sacraments at the Service of Communion celebrate people's commitment to serve God and the Church.
	CHAPTER 20 — The Last Things	• The Last Judgment is God's final triumph over evil at the end of time when Christ returns and judges all the living and the dead. • At the time of death, each person will be judged and God will decide where he or she will spend eternity. • We prepare for eternal life by accepting God's grace, growing in his friendship, and serving him and one another right now. • The symbols used at a Mass of Christian Burial connect to our Baptism and Jesus' Resurrection.
	CHAPTER 21 — Bring the Good News	• By his words and actions, Jesus showed how the prophecy of Isaiah was fulfilled in him. • Evangelization is giving witness to the faith by proclaiming the Good News of Jesus through words and deeds in a way that invites people to accept the Gospel. • In the Sacraments, especially the Eucharist, we are given grace to become more like Christ, to love God and others better. • The Corporal and Spiritual Works of Mercy are actions that address the physical and spiritual needs of others.

Go to **aliveinchrist.osv.com** for complete program Scope and Sequence.

Sacred Scripture	Catechism of the Catholic Church	Tasks of Catechesis	Catholic Faith Words	People of Faith	Catholic Social Teaching
Every Spiritual Blessing Ephesians 1:3–5; The Handmaid of the Lord Luke 1:30–31, 38	2013–2015, 2030, 971, 828	Promoting Knowledge of the Faith, Moral Formation	salvation, Fruits of the Holy Spirit, Mother of God, Annunciation, Assumption, canonization, beatification	Queenship of Mary	Dignity of Work, Care for Creation
God Proves His Love Romans 5:8, 19; Dependence on God Matthew 6:25–30a	375, 417, 571, 601, 1855–1856, 1862–1863	Promoting Knowledge of the Faith, Moral Formation	Original Holiness, sin, mortal sin, venial sin	St. Gemma Galgani	Life and Dignity, Rights and Responsibilities
We Too Might Live Romans 6:3–5; Freedom from Sin; Life in God Romans 6:10–11	1212, 1241, 1294–1296, 1232	Liturgical Education, Education for Community Life	Confirmation, Sacred Chrism, Rite of Christian Initiation of Adults (RCIA), catechumen	St. Cyril of Jerusalem	Call to Community, Human Solidarity
Repentance for Sinners Luke 5:30–32; The Parable of the Lost Son Luke 15:11–32	1421, 1423, 1503, 1532	Promoting Knowledge of the Faith, Liturgical Education	confession, reparation, contrition, absolution	St. John Vianney	Life and Dignity, Option for the Poor
Gather the People Joel 2:15b–16; Communal Life Acts 2:46–47; Church Order 1 Thessalonians 5:14–18	2181–2182, 1378, 1090, 1411, 2180–2181	Liturgical Education, Education for Community Life	Real Presence, Communion of Saints	St. Louis Montfort	Call to Community, Human Solidarity
True Blessedness Luke 11:27–28; Gratitude in Your Hearts Colossians 3:16	103, 120–121, 124–125, 132–133, 136	Promoting Knowledge of the Faith, Liturgical Education	Book of Gospels, psalms, creed	St. Jerome	Call to Community, Rights and Responsibilities
Participation in the Body of Christ 1 Corinthians 10:16; Feeding of the Five Thousand Luke 9:12–17; The Lord's Supper Matthew 26:26–28	1419, 1382, 1377	Promoting Knowledge of the Faith, Liturgical Education	consecration, transubstantiation, Blessed Sacrament	St. Clare of Assisi	Call to Community, Human Solidarity
Whoever Serves Me John 12:26; 13:4–5, 12–15; The Compassion of Jesus Matthew 9:35–38	825, 897–899, 160, 1534	Liturgical Education, Missionary Initiation	vocation, laity, consecrated religious life, vows	St. Francis Xavier	The Dignity of Work, Care for Creation
God of the Living Luke 20:37–38; The Judgment of the Nations Matthew 25:31–40	759, 1022, 2794–2795, 1681–1683	Promoting Knowledge of the Faith, Education for Community Life	Heaven, Hell, eternal life, Purgatory, Particular Judgment, viaticum	St. Stephen	Rights and Responsibilities, Option for the Poor
Hope Is in the Lord Psalm 146:5–10; Fulfilled in Your Hearing Luke 4:16–21	2472, 436, 712–714, 905, 1392, 1394, 2447	Education for Community Life, Missionary Initiation	missionaries, Gifts of the Holy Spirit, evangelization, Corporal and Spiritual Works of Mercy	St. Vincent de Paul	Rights and Responsibilities, Option for the Poor

Endnotes:

1. Cf. CCC 426-429; CT 5-6; DCG (1971) 40.

2. CCC 429.

3. Cf. CT, 31; CT 31 which expounds the integrity and organization of the message; cf. DCG (1971) 39 and 43.

4. Cf. Vatican Council I: DS 3016: *nexus mysteriorum*; LG 25.

5. UR 11.

6. CT 68.

Opening Lesson
&
Church Year Feasts and Seasons

Opening Lesson

The Church Year Feasts and Seasons

KEY CONCEPT
The key concept for each lesson is clearly stated at the start of each chapter.

DOCTRINAL CONTENT
- The doctrinal content for each chapter will be found in this section. It will show how the chapter correlates to paragraphs from the *Catechism of the Catholic Church*.

TASKS OF CATECHESIS
The six tasks of catechesis are outlined in the *National Directory for Catechesis*. The relevant tasks of catechesis for a chapter will be found in this section.

Catechist Background

But God, who is rich in mercy, because of the great love he had for us, even when we were dead in our transgressions, brought us to life with Christ (by grace you have been saved).
Ephesians 2:4–5

→ **Reflect** In what ways do you need God's mercy?

The Catechist Background includes a short essay that provides easy-to-understand theological background on the chapter content for both novice and experienced catechists.

The catechetical process of **Alive in Christ** mirrors the divine pedagogy—the gradual and relational way God teaches us so that we can know him in his truth, be guided by the Holy Spirit to respond with faith and love, and accept the gift of new life in Christ. Each lesson encourages this personal and ongoing relationship, beginning with God's invitation through Sacred Scripture. This leads children to reflect on his Word, deepen their understanding of our Sacred Tradition, and respond with a lived faith within the home and in the community.

Alive in Christ incorporates the most trusted research on how children learn and communicate. Topics are presented at important developmental "windows"—ages when research in child development tells us that learning about a particular topic would be most effective. For example, in Grade Four, the children will discover how Jesus teaches us to love God and others by following his Commandments and living the Beatitudes. While fourth graders are practical, concrete thinkers, they are also beginning to better understand morality. For example, the Commandments will begin to make sense as children this age internalize what they are learning about living a Christian life.

→ **Reflect** Throughout your life, in what ways has God invited you to be in relationship with him?

Catechist's Prayer

Lord, thank you for calling me to the ministry of catechesis. It is a great privilege and an awesome responsibility to echo your Word to others. Draw me closer to you, so that I may teach by word and example.

A New Year

Let Us Pray

Leader: Our Father, out of love you gave us commands to help us honor you and live with others. Help us follow your ways and the teachings of your Son.

"All the paths of the LORD are mercy and truth toward those who honor his covenant and decrees." **Psalm 25:10**

All: Thank you, God, for leading us and forgiving us when we stray from your paths.

Scripture

But because of his great love for us, God, who is rich in mercy, made us alive with Christ even when we were dead in transgressions—it is by grace you have been saved.

Based on Ephesians 2:4–5

© Our Sunday Visitor

? What Do You Wonder?

- Why do we need God's mercy?
- How does God invite us to be in relationship with him?

A New Year 1

(i) Catechist Background

Reflecting on Scripture

Each chapter in **Alive in Christ** begins with a focus on Sacred Scripture. On the *Invite* page, the children are called to open their minds and hearts to God's message.

- The Psalm verse and New Testament excerpt set the theme for the chapter. The passage from Ephesians is especially appropriate for this opening lesson, as it is repeated on the back cover of the book and was the source of/inspiration for the series name.

- For more information on the use of Sacred Scripture throughout the chapters, refer to page CE22.

Invite

✦ Ask children how they feel when they are invited somewhere. Point out the *Invite* heading on the page, and explain that every lesson will begin with an invitation.

Let Us Pray

Introduce the children to the prayer space and invite them into it. Lead them in the Sign of the Cross. Read aloud the leader's prayer and the Psalm verse. Prompt the children's response.

Have the children move from the prayer space back to their seats.

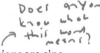
Does anyone know what this word means?

Scripture

Explain that *transgressions* are sins or wrong choices. Guide the children in reflecting on the Scripture.

- Invite them to close their eyes and concentrate on the message in this passage.
- Proclaim the Scripture.
- Pause for several moments.
- *Ask:* What message did you hear in this passage?
- Invite volunteers to share.

What Do You Wonder?

Point out the picture and ask what would happen if the bikers went off the path. Discuss how God's mercy saves us when we stray from his paths.

Invite the children to respond to the questions. Ask what else they might wonder about in their relationship with God.

Objectives

- Chapter objectives relating to this Discover section are clearly stated here
- Begin to understand what is going to be learned this year, especially about God's covenant with his People

Fourth Grade

Ask the children to define the word *discover*.

Point out that the Discover pages in this book will help them find out important things about their faith.

Explain that the children will use this book to deepen their relationship with God.

- Have the children investigate the book by looking at titles in the table of contents.
- Let them preview the illustrations and headings.
- Ask the children to report on what they will learn.

Point out the icons on the page and invite the children to speculate on what they signal. Use the text to expand on their responses.

- As you define the icons, reinforce the importance of Scripture, prayer, and songs in learning about God.
- Call attention to the photograph.
- Ask the children to explain how it relates to your group.
- Invite the children to interpret the meaning of the many faces on the cross.

Fourth Grade

What are we going to learn this year?

You are about to begin the next mile of your faith journey, but you do not travel alone. Your family, friends, and the whole parish community travel with you. And so does God's Word.

This symbol lets you know that the story or reading that follows is from the Bible. In every lesson you will spend time with God's Word in Scripture. Through these stories you will learn more about God's plan for all people, whom he created in his image and likeness. You will grow closer to Jesus as you learn more about his life and the teachings of his Church.

You will begin and end each lesson with a prayer. Each time you are together, you have the chance to thank God, ask his help, pray for the needs of others, and praise God for being God. God the Holy Spirit helps you pray.

You will sing songs to praise God and celebrate our faith. During the year, you'll explore the feasts and seasons of the Church year, and you will meet many Saints, heroes of the Church.

Every chapter has exercises to help you better understand what's being taught. You may be underlining, circling, writing, matching, or more.

© Our Sunday Visitor

2 Opening Lesson

✓ Quick Tip

Lesson Structure

The chapters in this book will all follow the same three-step process:

- *Invite* begins with prayer that includes Sacred Scripture and calls the children to be open to God's Word.
- *Discover* presents Scripture, Church teachings, and Catholic practices with developmentally appropriate language and art and contains activities to reinforce and apply learning.
- *Live* connects the children's faith knowledge with the ways that Catholics worship, live, pray, and serve in community. It also contains the concluding prayer for the chapter.
- For more information on the lesson process, see pages CE18–CE19.

Living as Jesus' Disciples

During this year, you'll be learning a lot about God's **covenant** with his People, and the laws he gave them to live by the covenant. Important Catholic Faith Words are **highlighted** in yellow to focus your attention and defined again on the sides of the pages.

You'll see how Jesus teaches us to love God and others by following the Ten Commandments and living the Beatitudes. Scripture stories will remind you that no matter what we do, God will always forgive us if we are truly sorry and ask his forgiveness.

All you do in class will help you follow Jesus' example and be part of the Church.

Three times a chapter you'll see green words like the ones below. You'll take a break to think about your faith and special people in your life; make connections to what you do at home, with friends, at Church; and see how living your faith can make a difference.

> ### Catholic Faith Words
>
> **covenant** a sacred promise or agreement between God and humans

 Circle one thing you want to learn more about this year.

Share Your Faith

Reflect Name some teachings of Jesus that you've heard often.

_____

_____

_____

Share Talk with a partner about why these teachings are important and who taught them to you.

Blessed are the peacemakers

(i) Catechist Background

Focus on Fourth Graders

Alive in Christ presents key themes of Catholic teaching in a developmentally appropriate sequence. For more information on how the series framework supports faith development, see pages CE8–CE9.

- The Grade 4 Focus is The Moral Life.
- This year's lessons have been designed to address the children's growing awareness of standards of behavior and their developing consciences.
- For more information on the abilities and perspectives of the children you are teaching, see pages CE9 and CE29.

Living as Jesus' Disciples

Elicit from the children that the word *disciple* means "follower."

- *Ask:* How do you follow Jesus?
- Point out that to be good followers, they will need to know what Jesus taught.

Read aloud the first four paragraphs to explain what they will learn about Jesus' teachings.

Work with Words

Call attention to the word *covenant* in the first paragraph and the Catholic Faith Words definition on the side of the page. Tell the children that they will learn many new words this year.

Activity

Point out the *Share Your Faith* feature.

- Point out that this feature and others like it will help them think about their faith and share it.
- Read aloud the directions.
- Allow time for the children to work independently. Then have them share their ideas with a partner.
- ⭐ Invite the children to circle one item on the page that they want to learn more about this year.
- Invite volunteers to share their ideas.

Quick Review

This book will teach about Jesus and how to follow him. It contains Scripture, prayers, songs, and exercises to help us learn.

Discover

Objectives

- Learn that Sacred Scripture is the inspired Word of God written by humans
- Be able to find the different parts of the Bible

God's Word

Explain that we use words to teach important ideas. God also uses words to teach us.

Read aloud the first two paragraphs to show the importance of God's Word.

- Call attention to the Catholic Faith Word *Sacred Scripture*.
- Tell the children that the Bible is a collection of books that were written at many different times and by many different people. The books tell the story of God's relationship with his People.

The Old Testament

Read aloud the text to acquaint the children with the Old Testament.

- Emphasize that this part of the Bible tells about before Jesus was born.
- Point out the table that shows the different types of books in the Old Testament. Tell the children that this book will have many tables that will help them learn.

Use the caption to explain the illuminated manuscript's purpose.

Catholic Faith Words

Sacred Scripture another name for the Bible; Sacred Scripture is the inspired Word of God written by humans

God's Word

Another name for the Bible is **Sacred Scripture**. It is the inspired Word of God written by humans. We read and pray with Scripture with our families, during parish gatherings, and in religion classes. We hear readings from Scripture during Mass and the other Sacraments.

The Catholic Bible has seventy-three books—forty-six in the Old Testament and twenty-seven in the New Testament.

The Old Testament

The first part of the Bible is about God's relationship with the Hebrew people before Jesus was born. It includes laws, history, messages of the prophets, and stories of God's faithfulness and actions in the lives of his People.

Before the invention of the printing press, the Bible had to be copied by hand. Many times when copying the text, monks would also illuminate, or illustrate, Scripture passages.

The Old Testament	
The Pentateuch	Genesis, Exodus, Leviticus, Numbers, Deuteronomy
The Historical Books	Joshua, Judges, Ruth, 1 Samuel, 2 Samuel, 1 Kings, 2 Kings, 1 Chronicles, 2 Chronicles, Ezra, Nehemiah, Tobit, Judith, Esther, 1 Maccabees, 2 Maccabees
The Wisdom Books	Job, Psalms, Proverbs, Ecclesiastes, Song of Songs (Ecclesiasticus), Wisdom, Sirach
The Prophetic Books	Isaiah, Jeremiah, Lamentations, Baruch, Ezekiel, Daniel, Hosea, Joel, Amos, Obadiah, Jonah, Micah, Nahum, Habakkuk, Zephaniah, Haggai, Zechariah, Malachi

© Our Sunday Visitor

❤ Liturgy Link

Bible Readings

The Old Testament and New Testament are the core of the Liturgy of the Word. However, the priests, deacons, and readers do not read directly from the Bible; they read from the Lectionary and Book of Gospels, which contain passages from the Bible.

- Typically, the first reading on a Sunday is from the Old Testament, followed by a responsorial Psalm. The next reading is usually from a New Testament Epistle, and the last is always from the Gospels.

 Visit **aliveinchrist.osv.com** for weekly Scripture readings and seasonal resources.

The New Testament

The second part of the Bible tells of God's love for people after the coming of Jesus. It is about the life and teaching of Jesus, his followers, and the early Church.

The New Testament	
The Gospels	Matthew, Mark, Luke, John
The Acts of the Apostles	
The New Testament Letters	Romans, 1 Corinthians, 2 Corinthians, Galatians, Ephesians, Philippians, Colossians, 1 Thessalonians,
	2 Thessalonians, 1 Timothy, 2 Timothy, Titus, Philemon, Hebrews, James, 1 Peter, 2 Peter, 1 John, 2 John, 3 John, Jude
Revelation	

Connect Your Faith

Locate Bible Passages To practice finding a particular Bible passage, use the example of Luke 10:25–28. Luke is the name of a book in the Bible. The chapter number always comes directly after the name of the book, so 10 is the chapter number. The numbers 25–28 refer to the verses. With a partner, find this passage in your Bible and discuss what this passage means to you. Write some of your thoughts here.

_____

_____

_____

A New Year   **5**

✓ Quick Tip

Sacred Traditions

Part of the richness of the Catholic faith resides in Sacred Tradition, accrued through two millennia of Church history.

- Every lesson in this book presents truths of the faith.
- At the back of the Student Book, the Our Catholic Tradition reference section expands on the lesson contents. Your lesson plans will contain specific references to this reference section when appropriate.
- You may want to have the children explore this section. For more on Sacred Tradition, see page CE23.

The New Testament

Invite a volunteer to read aloud the first paragraph.

Allow time for the children to explore the information about the New Testament.

- Explain that the New Testament begins with Jesus' birth.
- Reinforce that this part of the Bible is about Jesus and the early Church.
- Point out that the readings that we hear during Mass are from both the Old Testament and New Testament. The Gospel that we hear at Mass is always from one of the four Gospels.
- Explain that in Biblical times, one of the main ways to communicate was with letters. The books of Letters were written by Jesus' disciples to members of the early Church. They explain the lessons that Jesus taught.

Activity

Explain that activities like this one will be seen throughout the book. They will help the children learn more about particular aspects of their faith.

- Distribute Bibles and assist the children with finding the passage.
- Allow time for the children to find the passage and discuss it with a partner.

Quick Review

The Bible has two parts. The Old Testament tells about God's People before Jesus was born. The New Testament tells about Jesus and the early Church.

Our Catholic Life

Point out the *Live* heading on the page.

- Explain that each chapter in this book has a section that will help the children live as good Catholics. Read the text to further explain this.
- ☆ Read the directions and have the children complete the matching activity.
- As a group, discuss the relationship between each phrase in the first column and its partner in the second column.
- Reinforce that the children will learn about these ways of being a disciple throughout the year.

People of Faith

Read aloud this paragraph.

- Help the children understand that Venerables and Blesseds are holy people who have not yet been declared Saints.

Activity

As a group, complete the activity.

- Have a volunteer write the list on the board or on chart paper.

Our Catholic Life

Each chapter in your book has an Our Catholic Life section. It builds on what's in the chapter and focuses in a special way on what it means to be Catholic. Words, images, and activities help us better understand how to grow closer to Jesus and the Church.

☆ Match the ways to grow as disciples on the left with the descriptions on the right.

Growing as Disciples of Jesus

Know more about our faith	Understand and live the Beatitudes and the Great Commandment
Understand and take part in the Sacraments	Participate in the mission and community life of your parish
Live as Jesus calls us to	Understand and pray in adoration, praise, thanksgiving, petition, and intercession
Talk and listen to God in prayer	Show the Gospel by the choices we make and way we treat others
Be an active member of the Church	Celebrate the Eucharist and participate in Reconciliation
Help others know Jesus through our words and actions	Learn about God's plan for us all through Sacred Scripture and Sacred Tradition

© Our Sunday Visitor

People of Faith

You will also be introduced to People of Faith, holy women and men who loved God very much and did his work on Earth. They are officially recognized by the Church as Venerables, Blesseds, or Saints.

 Live Your Faith

Describe what's happening in the picture. How are these people being active members of the Church?

Name some ways you can take part in your parish activities and worship.

6 Opening Lesson

ⓘ Catechist Background

Six Tasks of Catechesis

As a catechist, you are charged with six fundamental tasks as contained in the *National Directory for Catechesis*.

- Each of these tasks corresponds to an aspect of faith in Jesus. They are: Promoting Knowledge of the Faith, Liturgical Education, Moral Formation, Teaching to Pray, Education for Community Life, and Missionary Initiation.
- For more information on these tasks, refer to pages CE14–CE15.

Let Us Pray

Pray Together

Every chapter has a prayer page. Over the course of the year, you'll talk and listen to God using different prayer types. You may listen to God's Word, read from the Bible, pray for the needs of others, call on the Saints to pray for us, and praise God the Father, Son, and Holy Spirit in words and songs.

Gather and begin with the Sign of the Cross.

Leader: Blessed be God.

All: Blessed be God forever.

Leader: Let us pray.

Bow your heads as the leader prays.

All: Amen.

Leader: A reading from the holy Gospel according to Luke.

Read Luke 10:25–28.

The Gospel of the Lord.

All: Praise to you, Lord Jesus Christ.

 Sing "Alive in Christ"

We are Alive in Christ
We are Alive in Christ
He came to set us free
We are Alive in Christ
We are Alive in Christ
He gave his life for me
We are Alive in Christ
We are Alive in Christ

A New Year **7**

Let Us Pray

Pray Together

Read the first paragraph aloud to the children.

- Explain that every chapter will end with prayer.

Prepare

Assume the role of leader.

Show the children where their responses are on the page.

 Rehearse "Alive in Christ," downloaded from **aliveinchrist.osv.com**.

Gather

Lead the children into the prayer space.

- Begin with the Sign of the Cross.
- Invite the children to be still and listen to the reading.

Pray

Follow the order of prayer on the student page.

Conclude by processing around the room with the children singing "Alive in Christ."

Songs of Scripture

Songs for Deepening Children's Understanding of God's Word

In addition to all of the chapter-specific songs available for download, a program component, *Songs of Scripture: Songs for Deepening Children's Understanding of God's Word* by John Burland and Dr. Jo Ann Paradise helps celebrate faith and support catechesis.

- Two CDs, Grades 1–3 and Grades 4–6, offer songs that teach, reinforce, or unfold the meaning of Scripture stories.
- These and other songs are available through **aliveinchrist.osv.com** and searchable by grade and chapter level.

Family + Faith

Distribute the page to the children or parents/adult family members.

Point out the chapter highlights: insights on how fourth graders understand concepts, the opportunity for the adults to reflect on their own experience and faith journey, and the family prayer.

Your Child Learned is a summary of the Catholic teaching that was covered in the chapter and introduces families to the Scripture and the Person of Faith that was presented.

Children At This Age helps parents become aware of how their child comprehends what was taught and suggests ways to help the child gain a deeper understanding of the material.

Consider This invites parents to ponder some of their own experiences and listen as the Church speaks to their personal journey of faith.

Let's Talk offers parents developmentally appropriate questions that lead to discussion of the week's lesson.

Let's Pray provides a short family prayer based on the Person of Faith featured in the lesson.

Online Resources offers multimedia tools to encourage family interaction and reinforce the lesson at home.

FAMILY+FAITH
LIVING AND LEARNING TOGETHER

YOUR CHILD LEARNED >>>

This page encourages you to share your faith and identify the many ways you already live the faith in daily family life. In this section, you will find a summary of what your child has learned in the chapter.

Scripture

 This introduces you to the opening Scripture, and provides direction for more reading.

Catholics Believe

- Bulleted information highlights the main points of doctrine of the Chapter.

People of Faith

Here you meet the holy person featured in People of Faith.

CHILDREN AT THIS AGE >>>

This section gives you a sense of how your child will likely be able to understand the topics taught. It suggests ways you can help your child better understand and live their faith.

How They Understand Children this age typically want to be independent, and doing things together with their peers is important to them. However, they are just beginning to "come out of themselves." Some days they will appear older than their years and other days they will seem younger. Remember to be patient with your child as he or she experiments with new ways of talking or behaving.

At this age children will have begun to internalize and express a moral code that is shaped in your family as well as in school and by the Church. They may seem very concerned about fairness and rights. Rules and regulations are the measure of right and wrong for them. At times they may appear legalistic and judgmental of themselves and others.

You can nurture your child's sense of Catholic morality. Give him or her opportunities to consider better or best choices, not just right or wrong choices. Help him or her see how their words and actions can affect others.

CONSIDER THIS >>>

These questions invite you to reflect on your own experience and consider how the Church speaks to you on your faith journey.

LET'S TALK >>>

Here you will find some practical questions that prompt discussion about the lesson's content, faith sharing, and making connections with your family life.

- What are you and your child looking forward to learning about your faith this year?

LET'S PRAY >>>

 Encourages family prayer connected to the example of our People of Faith.

Holy men and women, you model faith, hope, and love. Pray for us as we journey through this year. Amen.

For a multimedia glossary of Catholic Faith Words, Sunday readings, seasonal and Saint resources, and chapter activities go to **aliveinchrist.osv.com**.

Optional Activity

Explore the Student Book

In addition to what is presented in this opening lesson, there are many other features that help you present the Catholic faith to your students. Ask them to find the following features in their books.

- The Church Year: Children learn about Church feasts and seasons.
- Unit Openers: Preview the doctrinal theme with photos and art that convey the richness of our Catholic Tradition.
- Catholic Social Teaching/Live Your Faith: Introduce the children to important teachings of Jesus and the Church that help us live Jesus' New Commandment to love as he loved.

The Church Year Overview

The children will:

- discuss the sorrows in Mary's life
- identify the Sorrowful Mysteries of the Rosary

Catholic Social Teaching
Live Your Faith
- Option for the Poor and Vulnerable
- Solidarity of the Human Family

The children will:

- understand the doctrine of the Incarnation
- discuss the changes during Advent that bring us closer to Jesus

Catholic Social Teaching
Live Your Faith
- Life and Dignity of the Human Person
- Option for the Poor and Vulnerable

The children will:

- recognize the Epiphany to mean that Jesus came to show God to all people

Catholic Social Teaching
Live Your Faith
- Call to Family, Community, and Participation
- Solidarity of the Human Family

The children will:

- explain the disciplines and practices of Lent
- discuss ways children can apply the Lenten practices

Catholic Social Teaching
Live Your Faith
- Call to Family, Community, and Participation
- Rights and Responsibilities of the Human Person

The children will:

- recognize Holy Week, especially Triduum, as a special time
- explore the meaning of the Cross

Catholic Social Teaching
Live Your Faith
- Life and Dignity of the Human Person
- Rights and Responsibilities of the Human Person

The children will:

- explain that Easter celebrates the Resurrection of Jesus
- discuss ways Jesus is present today

Catholic Social Teaching
Live Your Faith
- Solidarity of the Human Family
- Care for God's Creation

The children will:

- explore the story of the Ascension
- discuss our belief in eternal life

Catholic Social Teaching
Live Your Faith
- Life and Dignity of the Human Person
- Rights and Responsibilities of the Human Person

The children will:

- explain that the coming of the Holy Spirit at Pentecost marked when the work of the Church began
- discuss the work of the Holy Spirit today

Catholic Social Teaching
Live Your Faith
- Rights and Responsibilities of the Human Person
- Dignity of Work and Rights of Workers

Check out the activities and resources available for the seasons of the Church Year at the following websites.
Go to **aliveinchrist.osv.com** and click on the Resource Library tab and select a season.
Go to **teachingcatholickids.com** and click on the current month's newsletter.

LESSON OBJECTIVES
- Discuss the sorrows in Mary's life
- Identify the Sorrowful Mysteries of the Rosary

ENVIRONMENT
Bible or Lectionary
White tablecloth
Crucifix
Icon of Our Lady of Sorrows (optional)

- Cover the prayer table with the white cloth, and place the crucifix, Bible, and icon of Our Lady of Sorrows on the table.

 MUSIC OPTIONS
Go to **aliveinchrist.osv.com** to sample and download,
"Salve Regina"
"Holy Mary"
"Immaculate Mary"
"Kyrie"
"Mary, a Woman of Faith"
"Mary, Our Mother"

 CATHOLIC SOCIAL TEACHING
- **Option for the Poor and Vulnerable**, Pages 296–297
- **Solidarity of the Human Family**, Pages 300–301

Catechist Background

"Behold, this child is destined for the falling and the rising of many in Israel, and to be a sign that will be contradicted (and you yourself a sword will pierce) so that the thoughts of many hearts may be revealed." Luke 2:34–35

➜ **Reflect** How do you think Mary felt after hearing Simeon's words?

The period of Ordinary Time is devoted to the mystery of Christ in all of its aspects. This liturgical season is called Ordinary Time because the weeks are numbered in order, not because the season is "ordinary" in the usual sense of that word.

Through the celebration of the Saints, the Church comes in contact with important aspects of the mystery of Christ. Most prominent among these celebrations are the many feasts in honor of the Virgin Mary. The Feast of Our Lady of Sorrows, celebrated on September 15, is one such remembrance.

Although Mary rarely speaks in the Gospels, her presence and sorrowful acceptance of Jesus' mission give strong testimony to the way in which new life can emerge from suffering and death. When the disciples could not understand why Jesus had to suffer and die, Mary remained as a model of acceptance and faith. She came to share fully in the fruits of that suffering: Christ's Resurrection and his promise of new life for all.

➜ **Reflect** How does faith help you in times of suffering, distress, or crisis?

Catechist's Prayer

 Loving God, may Mother Mary inspire me to faithfully trust in your providence, especially in difficult times. Amen.

Sorrowful Mother

♥ Let Us Pray

Leader: Lord God,
In times of doubt, sadness and difficulty.
We trust in you, as our Mother Mary did.
We know you are with us.

"But I trust in you, LORD;
I say, 'You are my God.'" Psalm 31:15

All: Amen.

📖 Scripture

The child's father and mother were amazed at what was being said about him. Then Simeon blessed them and said to his mother Mary, "This child is destined for the falling and the rising of many in Israel, and to be a sign that will be opposed so that the inner thoughts of many will be revealed—and a sword will pierce your own soul too." Based on Luke 2:33–35

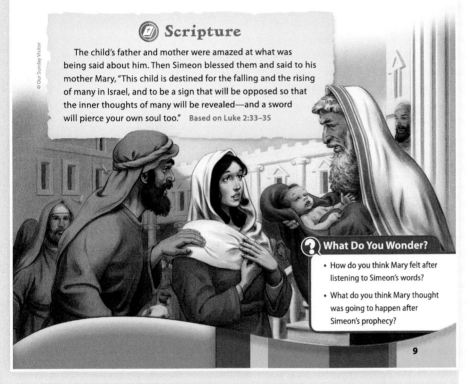

© Our Sunday Visitor

❓ What Do You Wonder?

- How do you think Mary felt after listening to Simeon's words?
- What do you think Mary thought was going to happen after Simeon's prophecy?

9

📖 Lectionary Connection

Luke 2:33–35

This Gospel passage is part of the Gospel for the Feast of the Holy Family, Year B. It is also the Gospel for the Feast of the Presentation of the Lord on February 2.

- In this Gospel, Simeon's hopes are fulfilled when he sees the child Jesus. Simeon predicted Mary's sorrow, which would result from her Son's role in the world.
- Even Mary, so loved by God, was to endure suffering.

Invite

♥ Let Us Pray

Invite the children to gather in the prayer space and make the Sign of the Cross. Choose a child to be the leader. Read aloud the Psalm verse from a Bible. Prompt the children's response.

Have the children move out of the prayer space and back to their seats.

Say: It is easy to trust God when good things are happening but we also need to trust God when things are not so good. No matter how good we are, hard things will happen to us.

📖 Scripture

Guide the children through the process of Scripture reflection.

- Invite them to close their eyes, be still and open their minds and hearts to what God is saying to them in this passage.
- Proclaim the Scripture.
- Maintain several moments of silence.
- *Ask:* What did you hear God say to you today?
- Invite volunteers to share.

What Do You Wonder?

Say: All of the Christmas stories talk about joy and happiness. In this one Mary heard she would also face sorrow.

Invite the children to respond to the questions. Ask what else they might wonder about Mary and what Jesus' suffering and Death was like for her.

Ordinary Time

Invite volunteers to read aloud the Ordinary Time box.

- Ask the children to name the liturgical color for Ordinary Time.
  green
- Point out that the priest wears white on Mary's feast days.

Help the children focus by asking them to close their eyes and think of a sad time in their lives or in the lives of their families.

- Exercise discretion and tact. Offer an example of a sad time from your own life, or ask a volunteer to do so.
- Ask the children whether they think the Holy Family had sad times, too.

Read aloud the first paragraph.

Call attention to the photo and caption.

- Read aloud the caption.
- Explain that this statue depicts one of the sad times in Mary's life.
- Tell the children that they are going to learn about other sad times in Mary's life.

Mary, Our Model of Faith

Invite volunteers to read aloud the paragraphs.

- Have the children retell the three sorrows that took place during Jesus childhood.

 Music Option: Have the children sing "Holy Mary" or "Mary, a Woman of Faith," downloaded from **aliveinchrist.osv.com**.

Michelangelo's sculpture *Pietà*, on display in St. Peter's Basilica in Vatican City, depicts Mary holding Jesus after his body had been taken down from the Cross.

© Our Sunday Visitor

Ordinary Time

The Church honors Mary in every season. The feast days of Mary often remember happy events in her life, such as the day we celebrate her birth or her Assumption into Heaven. But on September 15 during Ordinary Time, the Church honors Mary as Our Lady of Sorrows. This feast is a time to recall some of the sorrows in Mary's life.

Ordinary Time

- The life and ministry of Jesus are the focus of Ordinary Time. Mary and the Saints are also remembered throughout the year.

- In Ordinary Time, the priest wears green, a sign of growth and life.

- The priest wears white on Mary's feast days.

Mary, Our Model of Faith

There were seven especially sad times in Mary's life. They are called the seven sorrows of Mary.

Three of the sorrows happened during Jesus' childhood. The first was Simeon's prophecy that Jesus' life would make Mary sad. Next was the difficult trip into Egypt to escape Herod's plan to kill Jesus. Later, Mary worried when Jesus was missing and teaching in the Temple.

10 The Church Year

(i) Catechist Background

Liturgical Colors

Although the Feast of Our Lady of Sorrows occurs in Ordinary Time, the liturgical color for its celebration is white—the color for all Marian feasts.

Because this feast follows the Feast of the Triumph of the Holy Cross, the color red is sometimes worn to represent the great sorrow Mary endured at the foot of the Cross.

The last four sorrows came at the end of Jesus' life. Mary must have been sad to see Jesus carrying his Cross and being crucified. As any mother would, she must have felt sorrow when he was taken down from the Cross and buried in the tomb. But in difficult and sad times, Mary always believed in her Son. She acted with courage and cared for others. Mary can be a model for you, too, in the sad times of your life.

→ What can we do when we have difficult times?

Number the Seven Sorrows of Mary above.

Compassion

Mary watched as her Son suffered and died at the hands of those who did not understand him. Sorrow is still felt today whenever someone sees a loved one hurting. But from your sorrow can grow greater caring and compassion for the suffering of others. Compassion for others is more powerful than pain. We hear this message in the Gospels.

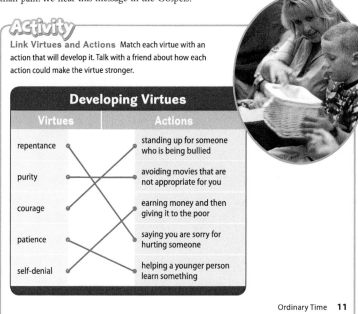

Activity

Link Virtues and Actions Match each virtue with an action that will develop it. Talk with a friend about how each action could make the virtue stronger.

Developing Virtues

Virtues	Actions
repentance	standing up for someone who is being bullied
purity	avoiding movies that are not appropriate for you
courage	earning money and then giving it to the poor
patience	saying you are sorry for hurting someone
self-denial	helping a younger person learn something

Ordinary Time **11**

Optional Activity

The Rosary *Intrapersonal*

Refer to page 326 in the Our Catholic Tradition reference section in the back of the Student Book for how to pray the Rosary.

- Point out all the mysteries of the Rosary, calling attention to the Sorrowful Mysteries.
- Pray the Sorrowful Mysteries of the Rosary with the children.

Mary, Our Model of Faith, *continued*

Read aloud the paragraph.

- Discuss the last four sorrows Mary had to face. Liken them to some of the sorrows that the children face. For example, Mary watched as Jesus faced rejection. She did not become hateful, but instead continued to trust in God.
- *Ask:* How can Mary be a model during personal times of sadness?
- *Ask:* Who are some other role models of faith in your life?
- ☆ Have the children number the Seven Sorrows of Mary in the text.
- *Ask:* What can we do when we have difficult times?

Compassion

Read aloud the paragraph.

- Introduce and explain the word *compassion*, which comes from a Latin word meaning "to suffer with."
- Explain that compassion is more than sympathy. When we feel compassion for someone we feel their suffering in a special way. We also have the desire to provide relief from the suffering.
- *Ask:* When have you felt sorrow when someone you loved was hurting?

 Music Option: Have the children sing "Mary, Our Mother," downloaded from **aliveinchrist.osv.com**.

Activity

Read aloud the directions.

- Have the children work with a partner to complete and discuss the activity.

People of Faith

Point out the chart.

- Explain to the children that each chapter of their book teaches about a Saint or person of faith.
- The left column shows the chapter number of the book.
- The middle column shows who is taught in each chapter.
- The right column shows the feast day for the person.

Read through the names of the People of Faith one at a time.

- As you read, pause after each person and invite the children to raise their hands if they have heard of the person.
- Encourage those who raise their hands to share what they remember about the person.
- Summarize by telling the children that throughout the year, they will be learning about each of these holy people.

 Encourage the children to go to **aliveinchrist.osv.com** at home to find out more about Mary and the Saints.

People of Faith

Chapter	Person	Feast Day
1	Saint Kateri Tekakwitha	July 14
2	Saint Bridget of Sweden	July 23
3	Saint Raymond of Peñafort	January 7
4	Saint Germaine Cousin	June 15
5	Saint Dominic	August 8
6	Saint Charles Lwanga	June 3
7	Saint Yi Sung-hun	September 20
8	Saint Katharine Drexel	March 3
9	Saint Mary Ann of Quito	May 26
10	Blessed Frédéric Ozanam	September 9
11	Saint Bernadette Soubirous	April 16
12	Saint Mary Magdalen Postel	July 16
13	Saint Louis Martin and Saint Marie-Azélie Martin	July 12
14	Saint Gianna Beretta Molla	April 28
15	Saint Joan of Arc	May 30
16	Saint Juan Diego	December 9
17	Saint Margaret Mary Alacoque	October 16
18	Venerable Matt Talbot	
19	Queen Saint Margaret of Scotland	November 16
20	Saint Junípero Serra	July 1
21	Saint Martin de Porres	November 3

© Our Sunday Visitor

12 The Church Year

 Catholic Social Teaching

Chapter Connections

To integrate Catholic Social Teaching into your lesson, choose one of the following features: Option for the Poor and Vulnerable, pages 296–297; or Solidarity of the Human Family, pages 300–301.

- To expand the lesson, move to the Catholic Social Teaching feature after completing page 12.
- Return to the prayer on page 13.

Let Us Pray

Prayer for Mercy

Gather and pray the Sign of the Cross together.

Leader: Blessed be God.

All: Blessed be God forever.

Sing together.

Leader: Christ Jesus, you have given us Mary as a model of courage and patience. As we remember Mary's sorrows, we express sorrow for our failure to love. Lord, have mercy.

All: Lord, have mercy.

Guided Reflection

Sit in silence before the cross as the leader leads you in a reflection on Our Lady of Sorrows.

Leader: Let us pray . . .

All: Amen.

Go Forth!

Leader: Let us go forth in Mary's spirit of faith, hope, and love for her Son.

All: Thanks be to God.

 Sing "Holy Mary"

13

 **Liturgy Link**

Lord, Have Mercy

One purpose of the *Kyrie*, or *Lord, Have Mercy*, is to help unify the worshipping community.

- This prayer is about asking for personal forgiveness and about reflecting on who we are and who we are called to be.

- The *Kyrie* emphasizes praising God's mercy for those times when we have not acted as the Body of Christ in the world.

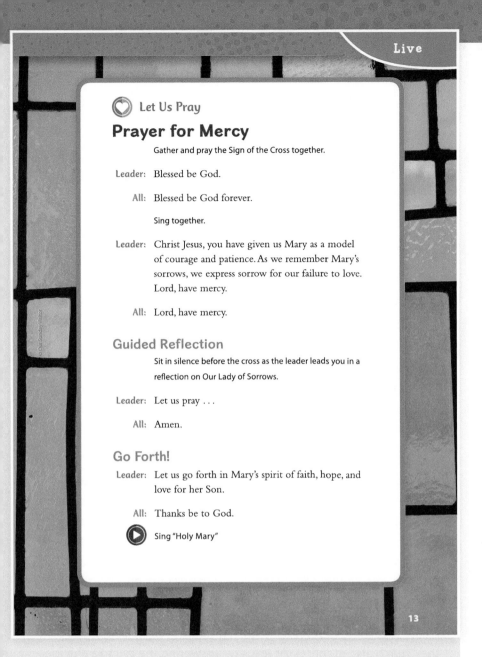

Let Us Pray
Prayer for Mercy

Rehearse "Holy Mary," downloaded from **aliveinchrist.osv.com**.

Follow the order of prayer on the student page.

Guided Reflection

Have the children close their eyes.

- *Say the following, pausing between each sentence*: When you are hurt or suffering, imagine a kind person with an arm around you, saying, "I know how you feel." Your hurt may not go away completely, but that touch and soft voice may make your suffering easier. Mary is Jesus' Mother and she is your Mother, too.

- *Leader's prayer:* Jesus, help us remember that we can always turn to you and your Mother.

Conclude by singing together "Holy Mary."

Distribute this page to the children or parents/adult family members.

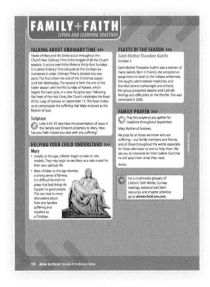

LESSON OBJECTIVES

- Understand the doctrine of the Incarnation
- Discuss the changes during Advent that bring us closer to Jesus

ENVIRONMENT

Table
Purple cloth
Advent wreath
Candles for wreath or battery operated candles

- If possible, place the children's desks or chairs in a circle.
- Put the prayer table in the center of the circle.
- Prepare the prayer table with the cloth and Advent wreath.

 MUSIC OPTIONS
Go to **aliveinchrist.osv.com** to sample and download,
"Through My Fault"
"Candles of Advent"
"God Keeps His Promises"
"Jesus Is Our Friend"

 CATHOLIC SOCIAL TEACHING

- **Life and Dignity of the Human Person**, Pages 290–291
- **Option for the Poor and Vulnerable**, Pages 292–293

Catechist Background

> "Do not be afraid, Mary, for you have found favor with God. Behold, you will conceive in your womb and bear a son, and you shall name him Jesus." Luke 1:30–31

→ **Reflect** In what ways do you prepare for the coming of Christ into your life?

The four-week season of Advent marks the beginning of the liturgical year of the Church. Until December 16, the focus of the season is an anticipation of the Second Coming of Christ. Then, from December 17 through December 24, liturgies prepare the faithful to celebrate Christ's birth on Christmas.

John the Baptist is a prominent figure during Advent. He invited people to be baptized in water as they acknowledged their sins. John emphasized that accepting this baptism meant a change of heart as well as a change of behavior. At the same time, he made it clear that his mission was to prepare the way for someone greater than himself. The one who would follow John would baptize not only with water but also with the Holy Spirit and with fire (see Matthew 3:11).

As the preaching of John the Baptist prepared for the coming of Christ, the Church also prepares for Jesus by answering the call to a change of heart.

→ **Reflect** What great things has God done for you or your family?

Catechist's Prayer

Loving God, may the Holy Spirit help me to prepare my heart for the Second Coming of Christ and help me to hear the call to a change of heart. Amen.

Prepare for Jesus

Let Us Pray

Leader: Lord God, as we prepare for the feast of Christmas.
We thank you for the gift of your Son, Emmanuel,
God with us.

"The LORD has done great things for us;
     Oh, how happy we were!"   Psalm 126:3

All: Amen.

Scripture

"In the sixth month, the angel Gabriel was sent from God to a town of Galilee called Nazareth, to a virgin betrothed to a man named Joseph, of the house of David, and the virgin's name was Mary. And coming to her, he said, 'Hail, favored one! The Lord is with you.' Then the angel said to her, 'Do not be afraid, Mary, for you have found favor with God. Behold, you will conceive in your womb and bear a son, and you shall name him Jesus. He will be great and will be called Son of the Most High . . .'"   Luke 1:26–32a

© Our Sunday Visitor

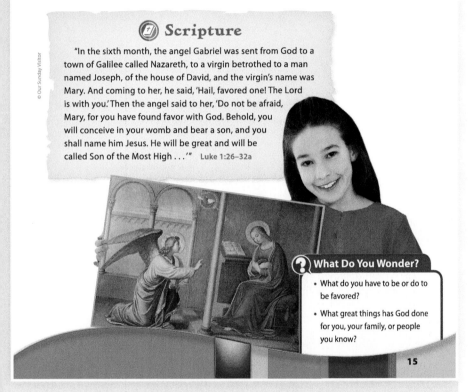

? What Do You Wonder?

- What do you have to be or do to be favored?
- What great things has God done for you, your family, or people you know?

15

Lectionary Connection

Luke 1:26–32a

This Gospel passage is part of a larger reading (Luke 1:26–38) that is read on the Fourth Sunday of Advent, Year B.

- This Gospel tells the story of the Annunciation. An angel tells Mary that she is going to give birth to a son and name him Jesus. He will be the Son of God.
- Mary said "yes" to God. Mary had faith in and trusted God.
- The Church reminds us during the Advent season that we, too, need to be prepared.

Let Us Pray

Invite the children to gather in the prayer space and make the Sign of the Cross. Choose a child to be the leader. Read aloud the Psalm verse from a Bible. Prompt the children's response.

Have the children move out of the prayer space and back to their seats.

Explain that God does great things for all of us.

Say: Mary was prepared for God's great invitation to be the Mother of his Son. Listen to the angel's words to Mary.

Scripture

Guide the children through the process of Scripture reflection.

- Invite them to close their eyes, be still and open their minds and hearts to what God is saying to them in this passage.
- Proclaim the Scripture.
- Maintain several moments of silence.
- *Ask:* What did you hear God say to you today?
- Invite volunteers to share.

What Do You Wonder?

Say: You are also a favored child of God. Just as God invited Mary to be part of his plan, he will invite you to do his work too.

Invite the children to respond to the questions. Ask what else they might wonder about Mary and the great things God does.

Change Our Hearts

Quiet the children with a moment of silence.

- Call attention to the purple cloth draped over the table in the prayer area.

- Explain to the children that purple is the color for Advent. Tell them that purple means both *penance* and *preparation*.

- *Ask:* What do Catholics prepare for during Advent? to celebrate Jesus' Second Coming into the world at the end of time

Have a volunteer read aloud the opening paragraph.

- Invite the children to share any Advent family traditions.

- Explain that all our family and parish traditions have a purpose. Then read aloud the chart.

- Ask volunteers to read the last two paragraphs.

- *Ask:* What is one way you will prepare for Jesus' coming during Advent this year?

 Music Option: Have the children sing "Candles of Advent" or "God Keeps His Promises," downloaded from **aliveinchrist.osv.com**.

Discover

Change Our Hearts

Advent is the first season of the Church year. During the four weeks of Advent, the whole Church prepares to celebrate Jesus' Second Coming into the world at the end of time.

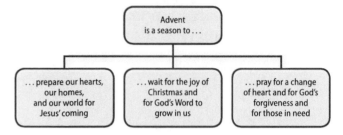

Advent is a season to . . .

. . . prepare our hearts, our homes, and our world for Jesus' coming

. . . wait for the joy of Christmas and for God's Word to grow in us

. . . pray for a change of heart and for God's forgiveness and for those in need

Purple is the Advent color. The priest wears purple vestments. The church is decorated with purple decorations.

During this season, Catholics prepare for Christmas by reflecting on the gift of the Incarnation, when God sent his only Son to become one of us and to be the Savior of all people.

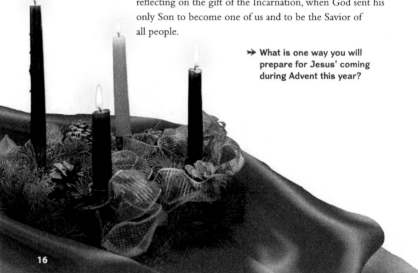

➜ What is one way you will prepare for Jesus' coming during Advent this year?

16

© Our Sunday Visitor

Catechist Background

Liturgical Colors

Violet (or purple) is the seasonal color of Advent. Reserved for royalty in ancient times, today it is a symbol of preparation for Christ the King.

- The Advent wreath, from Germanic tradition, was lit during winter as a symbol of hope for the coming spring.

- Christians use this symbol for hope in Christ, the everlasting light.

The Path of Love

Taking time for daily prayer before the Advent wreath with your family gives you time to reflect on Jesus' love. Small acts of sacrifice and penance can help you turn your heart toward Jesus and show greater love for others.

John told the people who were waiting for the Messiah that they would have to change. He said, "Prepare the way of the Lord, make straight his paths" (Mark 1:3).

➜ What changes can you make to straighten your path and bring you closer to Jesus?

Show Your Love In the space below, create a list of loving actions you can do for members of your family. You might include things like reading a book to a younger sibling, washing the dog, cleaning up your room without complaining, or taking someone else's turn doing the dishes. Create a coupon book to give to each member of your family this Christmas.

Advent **17**

Optional Activity

Prepare the Way *Visual/Spatial*

Have each child use a separate sheet of paper to draw a pathway with a symbol of Jesus at the end of the path.

- Have the children create road signs along the path that indicate ways in which they will prepare for the coming of Christ.
- For example, a "Stop" sign could say: Help Mom clean a mess my little brother made.

The Path of Love

Invite volunteers to read aloud the paragraphs.

- Help the children understand what is meant by "small acts of sacrifice and penance." Brainstorm a list of specific acts.
- *Ask:* What changes can you make to straighten your path and bring you closer to Jesus?
- Have the children discuss this question with a partner.
- After the discussion, invite volunteers to share their ideas with the rest of the group.

 Music Option: Have the children sing "Jesus Is Our Friend," downloaded from **aliveinchrist.osv.com**.

Activity

Read aloud the activity directions.

- Provide the children with paper and scissors.
- If time permits, give the children an opportunity to make at least one coupon for each family member.
- If no time remains, assign the activity as homework.
- At the next session, be sure to ask the children how their family reacted to this activity.

Prepare for Jesus **17**

Celebrate Forgiveness

 ### Let Us Pray

Explain to the children that they will be praying a penitential prayer. They will be asking for God's loving mercy and forgiveness.

Prepare

Choose a reader.

Show the children their responses.

 Rehearse "Through My Fault," downloaded from **aliveinchrist.osv.com**.

Pray

Follow the order of prayer on the student pages.

- Lead the children in praying the Sign of the Cross.
- *Leader's prayer:* God, our Father, open our hearts to change. Show us how to become more like your Son, Jesus.
- Pray the Penitential Act.

 Sing together "Through My Fault."

Celebrate Forgiveness

This prayer is a penitential prayer. In a penitential prayer, we ask for God's loving mercy and forgiveness.

 ### Let Us Pray

Gather and pray the Sign of the Cross together.

Leader: Our help is in the name of the Lord.

All: Who made Heaven and Earth.

Leader: Let us pray.

Bow your heads as the leader prays.

All: Amen.
I confess to almighty God
and to you, my brothers and sisters,
that I have greatly sinned,
in my thoughts and in my words,
in what I have done and in what I have failed to do,

Gently strike your chest with a closed fist.

through my fault, through my fault,
through my most grievous fault;
therefore I ask blessed Mary ever-Virgin,
all the Angels and Saints,
and you, my brothers and sisters,
to pray for me to the Lord our God.

Amen.

 Sing "Through My Fault"

© Our Sunday Visitor

18

Catholic Social Teaching

Chapter Connections

To integrate Catholic Social Teaching into your lesson, choose one of the following features: Life and Dignity of the Human Person, pages 290–291; or Option for the Poor and Vulnerable, pages 296–297.

- To expand the lesson, move to the Catholic Social Teaching feature after completing page 17.
- Return to the prayer on page 18.

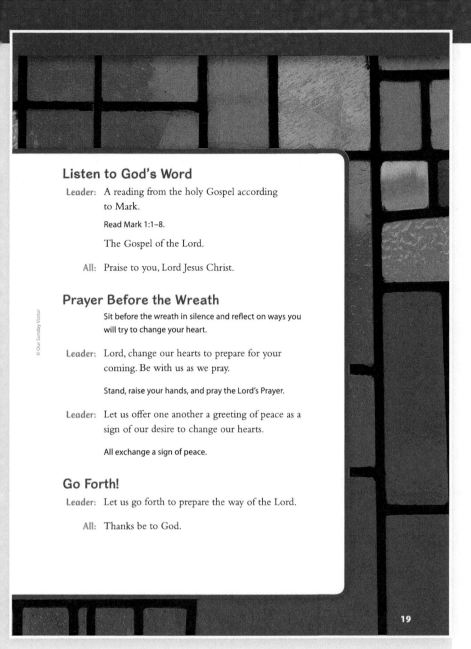

Listen to God's Word

Leader: A reading from the holy Gospel according to Mark.

Read Mark 1:1–8.

The Gospel of the Lord.

All: Praise to you, Lord Jesus Christ.

Prayer Before the Wreath

Sit before the wreath in silence and reflect on ways you will try to change your heart.

Leader: Lord, change our hearts to prepare for your coming. Be with us as we pray.

Stand, raise your hands, and pray the Lord's Prayer.

Leader: Let us offer one another a greeting of peace as a sign of our desire to change our hearts.

All exchange a sign of peace.

Go Forth!

Leader: Let us go forth to prepare the way of the Lord.

All: Thanks be to God.

© Our Sunday Visitor

19

Listen to God's Word

Invite the children to stand for the proclamation of the Gospel.

Prayer Before the Wreath

Invite the children to sit.

- After lighting one of the Advent candles, ask the children to reflect silently on ways they can "prepare the way of the Lord" in their hearts.

- After a few minutes, signal the children to stand. Ask the children to raise their hands and join you in praying the Lord's Prayer.

- Invite the children to exchange a sign of peace.

Go Forth!

Conclude the session by having the children slowly and reverently process back to their seats.

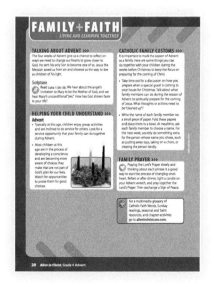

Distribute this page to the children or parents/adult family members.

♥ Liturgy Link

Penitential Act

The Penitential Act includes a moment of silent reflection.

- It is not a moment to ask God to forgive personal sins sacramentally.
- It is a time to ask God to forgive our collective failure to live as a sign of Christ's presence in the world.

Christmas: God's Greatest Gift

LESSON OBJECTIVE

- Recognize the Epiphany to mean that Jesus came to show God to all people

ENVIRONMENT

Nativity scene, including statuettes of the three Magi

Candle or battery-opperated candle

White cloth

- Cover the prayer table with the white cloth.
- Place the crèche or Nativity scene on the table, and set the Magi to one side.
- Clear enough room to allow the children to process around the prayer space.

 MUSIC OPTION
Go to **aliveinchrist.osv.com** to sample and download, "We Three Kings"

 CATHOLIC SOCIAL TEACHING

- **Call to Family, Community, and Participation**, Pages 292–293
- **Solidarity of the Human Family**, Pages 300–301

Catechist Background

> But when the kindness and generous love of God our savior appeared, not because of any righteous deeds we had done but because of his mercy, he saved us through the bath of rebirth and renewal by the holy Spirit. Titus 3:4–5
>
> → **Reflect** How do you feel when someone does something special for you for no apparent reason?

The Christmas season extends from the vigil of Christmas to the Sunday after the Feast of Epiphany. The Birth of Christ is called the Incarnation (meaning "in the flesh").

The Feast of Epiphany commemorates the three Magi who traveled from afar to bring homage to the child whose star they had seen. The gifts that they offered testify to the greatness they recognized in the child Jesus. Because these visitors were not Jewish, the story also reveals that the gift of God's only Son is given to all humankind.

God's gift of Christ to the world is an event that continues every day. Each time the Church gathers for Mass, a procession with gifts of bread and wine ends at the altar. Through the power of the Holy Spirit, God gives himself to humans by transforming these gifts into the Body and Blood of Christ.

→ **Reflect** In what ways do you bring the gift of God's only Son to other people?

Catechist's Prayer

 Loving God, send me your Holy Spirit, so that I may share the gifts of love, joy, and peace with all I meet. Amen.

God's Greatest Gift

 Let Us Pray

Leader: Faithful God, you loved us so much you sent us
          your only Son. Strengthen us to return your love
          by living as his faithful followers.

          "I will sing of your mercy forever, LORD
             proclaim your faithfulness through all ages."
             Psalm 89:2

All: Amen.

> **Scripture**
>
> But when the goodness and loving-kindness of Jesus our Savior came to Earth, he saved us. Humans did not do anything to deserve being saved. God sent Jesus to save us just because he wanted to. He saved us because he was merciful and forgiving. We were saved by his grace so we might inherit the hope of eternal life.   **Based on Titus 3:4–7**

© Our Sunday Visitor

? What Do You Wonder?

- What makes it possible that a person forgives over and over again?
- What does it mean to inherit good things?

21

Lectionary Connection

Titus

This passage is the Second Reading on the Feast of the Nativity of the Lord—Mass at Dawn (Christmas morning).

- The important message of this reading is that God sent his Son, Jesus, to save us, not because we did anything to deserve it, but because God loved us. We have been saved by God's grace.

- When Jesus came to Earth, he came with the message that God's love is for everyone, not just a certain few.

Let Us Pray

Invite the children to gather in the prayer space and make the Sign of the Cross. Choose a child to be the leader. Read aloud the Psalm verse from a Bible. Prompt the children's response.

Have the children move out of the prayer space and back to their seats.

Explain that God is faithful to us always and forever. His love is a gift to all people.

Say: God's love is meant for you and me and for everyone God created. That's the Good News of Christmas.

Scripture

Guide the children through the process of Scripture reflection.

- Invite them to close their eyes, be still and open their minds and hearts to what God is saying to them in this passage.
- Proclaim the Scripture.
- Maintain several moments of silence.
- *Ask:* What did you hear God say to you today?
- Invite volunteers to share.

What Do You Wonder?

Say: In the reading, Saint Paul tells Titus that Jesus was born to save us because God loved us that much. So much, that if we respond to God's love, we will live with him forever.

Invite the children to respond to the questions. Ask what else they might wonder about God's faithfulness and his gift of eternal life.

The Season of Christmas

Ask the children to name the Magi who came to visit the baby Jesus.

- List the children's responses on the board or on chart paper.
- Tell the children that the Bible never names the Magi, but Tradition calls them Caspar, Balthazar, and Melchior. Their story is important because they represent all the people of the world that Jesus came to save.

Invite volunteers to read aloud the first two paragraphs.

- Emphasize that the Christmas season begins on December 24 and continues through the Feast of the Baptism of the Lord.

Precious Gifts

Invite volunteers to read aloud the three paragraphs.

- Discuss the meaning of *Epiphany*.
- Invite three volunteers to read the captions under each gift.
- Talk about the gifts of gold, frankincense, and myrrh. Make sure that the children understand the symbolism of each gift.
- *Ask:* What gifts of reverence and worship can you offer Jesus?
- Encourage the children to keep a list of the group's responses and try to act on them during the coming week.

The Season of Christmas

The Church's season of Christmas begins with the Christmas Eve Vigil on December 24. Christmas is a joyful and festive season. The priest wears white or gold vestments. During the Christmas season, Jesus' birth and childhood are proclaimed and celebrated.

The Feast of Epiphany comes in the middle of the Christmas season. The season ends in January with the Feast of the Baptism of the Lord, after Epiphany.

Precious Gifts

The word Epiphany means "showing forth." On Epiphany the Church remembers the visit of the three Magi, often called wise men, to the Infant Jesus.

The Magi came from distant lands, followed a bright star to find the Infant Jesus, honored him, and gave glory to God. Epiphany celebrates the belief that Jesus came to Earth to save everyone.

To honor the Savior and show him reverence, the Magi brought him gifts of gold, frankincense, and myrrh.

➔ **What gifts of reverence and worship can you offer Jesus?**

The gift of gold, a precious metal, showed that the Magi thought of Jesus as worthy of the highest honor.

Frankincense, an incense with a pleasing smell, represented the holiness of Jesus.

Myrrh is a symbol of preserving and saving. This gift was a sign that Jesus would die for the salvation of all people.

22 The Church Year

Optional Activity

Give Gifts *Interpersonal*

Brainstorm with the children some ways they can bring the gifts of frankincense (holiness), myrrh (salvation), and gold (honor) to others.

- Encourage the children to share these gifts with others during the coming weeks.
- Ask the children the record the things they have done. Discuss their results.

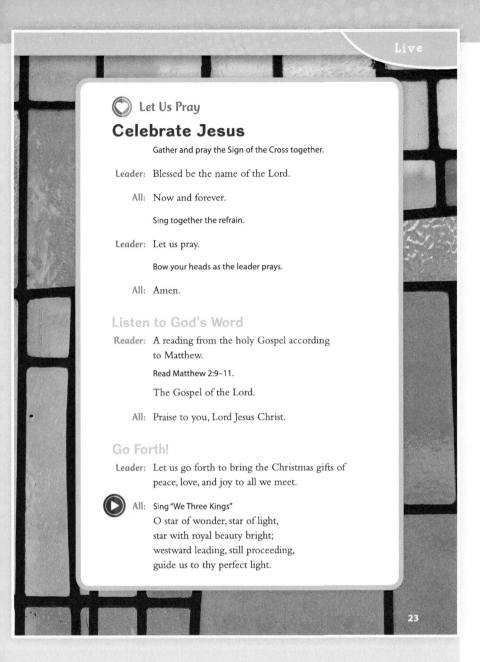

Let Us Pray

Celebrate Jesus

Gather and pray the Sign of the Cross together.

Leader: Blessed be the name of the Lord.

All: Now and forever.

Sing together the refrain.

Leader: Let us pray.

Bow your heads as the leader prays.

All: Amen.

Listen to God's Word

Reader: A reading from the holy Gospel according to Matthew.

Read Matthew 2:9–11.

The Gospel of the Lord.

All: Praise to you, Lord Jesus Christ.

Go Forth!

Leader: Let us go forth to bring the Christmas gifts of peace, love, and joy to all we meet.

 All: Sing "We Three Kings"
O star of wonder, star of light,
star with royal beauty bright;
westward leading, still proceeding,
guide us to thy perfect light.

23

Let Us Pray

Celebrate Jesus

Show the children their responses in the Student Book.

- Invite a child to read the Gospel.

 Rehearse "We Three Kings," downloaded from **aliveinchrist.osv.com**.

- Invite the children to process to the prayer space. Have each child bring their book.

Follow the order of prayer on the student page.

- Lead the children in the Sign of the Cross.

Listen to God's Word

Have the children remain standing for the proclamation of the Gospel.

Go Forth!

Conclude by singing together "We Three Kings."

Catholic Social Teaching

Chapter Connections

To integrate Catholic Social Teaching into your lesson, choose one of the following features: Call to Family, Community, and Participation, pages 292–293; or Solidarity of the Human Family, pages 292–293.

- To expand the lesson, move to the Catholic Social Teaching feature after completing page 22.
- Return to the prayer on page 23.

Distribute this page to the children or parents/adult family members.

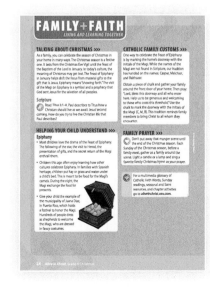

God's Greatest Gift **23–24**

Lent: A Time to Pray

LESSON OBJECTIVES

- Explain the disciplines and practices of Lent
- Discuss ways children can apply the Lenten practices

ENVIRONMENT

Purple cloth
Willow branches
Cross (not a crucifix)
Container of water
Small plant

- Drape the purple cloth on the table, and decorate it with a few of the branches and the cross.

....

 MUSIC OPTIONS
Go to **aliveinchrist.osv.com** to sample and download,
"Ashes"
"Lord, Teach Me Your Ways"
"Show Us Your Mercy"
"With These Ashes"

 CATHOLIC SOCIAL TEACHING

- **Call to Family, Community, and Participation**, Pages 292–293
- **Rights and Responsibilities of the Human Person**, Pages 294–295

Catechist Background

 "It is Christ [Jesus] who died, rather, was raised, who also is at the right hand of God, who indeed intercedes for us."
Romans 8:34

→ **Reflect** What does it mean to you that God is on your side?

The season of Lent begins with Ash Wednesday and lasts for forty days until the Easter Triduum. Lent is a period of purification and enlightenment, and a time of penance. Through prayers and penitential practices, members of the Church acknowledge their complete dependence on the mercy and compassion of God.

Dying to one's self is an important requirement of discipleship, and Lent provides Christians an opportunity to make it a deeper part of their lives. Ashes symbolize the call to die to sin and selfishness; prayer, fasting, and almsgiving aid in the process.

Christians recognize that Jesus' suffering and Death brought about reconciliation between God and humans. The faithful witness to this reconciliation by their willingness to participate in a life of sacrifice.

→ **Reflect** What are the ways that dying to self brings life to you or to others?

Catechist's Prayer

 Loving God, during this season of Lent, help me to turn toward you and to live as a follower of Christ. Amen.

A Time To Pray

♥ Let Us Pray

Leader: Lord God, send your Holy Spirit to open our hearts to see what we need to change. We pray the Holy Spirit will show us where we can be less selfish and more like your Son. Through Christ, our Lord.

"I shall walk before the LORD in the land of the living." Psalm 116:9

All: Amen.

✝ Scripture

"What then shall we say to this? If God is for us, who can be against us? He who did not spare his own Son but handed him over for us all . . .

It is Christ [Jesus] who died, rather, was raised, who also is at the right hand of God, who indeed intercedes for us." Romans 8:31–32, 34

? What Do You Wonder?

- In what ways is God on your side?
- Why doesn't God always give you what you ask for?

© Our Sunday Visitor

25

✝ Lectionary Connection

Romans 8:31b–34

This passage is the Second Reading we hear on the Second Sunday of Lent, Year B.

- This reading tells of God's complete faithfulness. God loved all people so much that he did not spare his own Son.
- Jesus is a model of unselfishness for us. Lent gives us time to look at ways we can be more like him.

Invite

♥ Let Us Pray

Invite the children to gather in the prayer space and make the Sign of the Cross. Choose a child to read aloud the Psalm verse from a Bible. Prompt the children's response.

Have the children move out of the prayer space and back to their seats.

Explain that God gave his very own Son because of his faithfulness to all people.

Say: God did not spare his very own Son. Jesus suffered and died for us.

✝ Scripture

Guide the children through the process of Scripture reflection.

- Invite them to close their eyes, be still and open their minds and hearts to what God is saying to them in this passage.
- Proclaim the Scripture.
- Maintain several moments of silence.
- *Ask:* What did you hear God say to you today?
- Invite volunteers to share.

What Do You Wonder?

Say: God never lets us down. Even when we may not feel his presence, we can trust that he is always with us.

Invite the children to respond to the questions. Ask what else they might wonder about how God is for us.

An Unselfish Spirit

Bring in a plant that needs pruning; a miniature rosebush, for example.

- Ask the children which branches need pruning and why.
- Discuss how pruning will help the plant grow.
- Invite a volunteer to read aloud the paragraph.

Spiritual Discipline

Invite two volunteers to read aloud the two paragraphs.

- Explain to the children the meanings of *fasting* and *almsgiving*.
- Ask the children what "spiritual growth" means. Possible response: a better relationship with God
- Point out that fasting and almsgiving are forms of sacrifice. Discuss how sacrifice helps a person grow and change.
- *Ask:* What good can you produce if you cut away bad habits?

Invite three volunteers to read aloud the Lent box.

- Emphasize that prayer, fasting and almsgiving are the three principal practices of Lent.

Music Option: Have the children sing "Lord, Throughout These Holy Days," downloaded from **aliveinchrist.osv.com**.

An Unselfish Spirit

Trees and vines can grow wild when no one takes care of them. They produce fruit too small or too sour to enjoy. That is why it is important to prune trees and vines. Pruning means cutting off dead and unhealthy branches so that the best fruit can grow. Trees and vines also require plenty of soil, water, and sunlight.

Spiritual Discipline

During the Season of Lent, the Church reminds us that good pruning is needed to produce good fruit. You can produce good fruit by cutting away bad habits and selfishness. Then the good fruit of love, sharing, and forgiveness can grow in you.

Prayer, fasting, and almsgiving are the three principal practices of Lent. These are the practices of disciples of Jesus. Prayer is the foundation for all spiritual discipline. It is like the soil a tree needs to grow. It gives you spiritual nourishment and deepens your relationship with God.

Lent
- Lent is a forty-day season set aside for the People of God to reflect on our relationship with God and others.
- Purple, the liturgical color for Lent, reminds us we are called to change. It is a sign of penance.
- During Lent, the Church fasts, prays, and gives alms.

→ What good can you produce if you cut away bad habits?

26

© Our Sunday Visitor

Optional Activity

Growth in Christ *Naturalist*

Provide each child with a pot (paper cup), a seed, and soil. Have the children plant their seeds and place them near a light source.

- Encourage the children to care for their seedlings during Lent.
- Remind the children that as their plants are growing, so is their relationship with Christ.

Growing Spiritually

Your body is growing every day. Growing in spirit is equally important. Just as you feed your body, so must your soul be fed. The spiritual discipline of prayer strengthens you so that you can avoid sin and prepare for the joy of Easter.

On Good Soil Around the tree, list two or three ways you could try to deepen your life of prayer during Lent. Try a different way during each of the six weeks of Lent.

Lent **27**

Growing Spiritually

Water the rosebush or other plant that you displayed to the group.

- Explain that just as we need to feed and care for a plant in order for it to grow, we need to feed and care for our soul in order to grow spiritually.
- Read aloud the paragraph.
- *Ask:* What habits of prayer do you already have?
- *Ask:* What is your plan for strengthening your life of prayer during Lent?

Refer to page 312 in the Our Catholic Tradition reference section in the back of the Student Book for more about Lent.

Read aloud the activity directions.

- Give the children time to complete the activity.
- Encourage the children to display their lists at home as reminders. After Easter, invite volunteers to share how well their suggestions worked.

🌐 Catholic Social Teaching

Chapter Connections

To integrate Catholic Social Teaching into your lesson, choose one of the following features: Call to Family, Community, and Participation, pages 292–293; or Rights and Responsibilities of the Human Person, pages 294–295.

- To expand the lesson, move to the Catholic Social Teaching feature after completing page 27.
- Return to the prayer on page 28.

Celebrate Lent

 Let Us Pray

Explain to the children that during this celebration of the Word, they will listen to and reflect on God's Word.

Prepare

Show the children their responses in the Student Book.

Select a reader.

 Rehearse "Ashes," downloaded from **aliveinchrist.osv.com**.

Invite the children to process to the prayer space. Have each child bring his or her book.

Pray

Follow the order of prayer on the student pages.

- Lead the children in the Sign of the Cross.
- *Leader's prayer:* God, our Father, during the Season of Lent, grant us the grace to repent and believe in the Gospel.

Listen to God's Word

Have the children stand for the proclamation of the Gospel.

Dialogue

Have the children sit in a circle for discussion.

- If the children have trouble with the second question, tell them to think of "good fruit" as "good deeds."

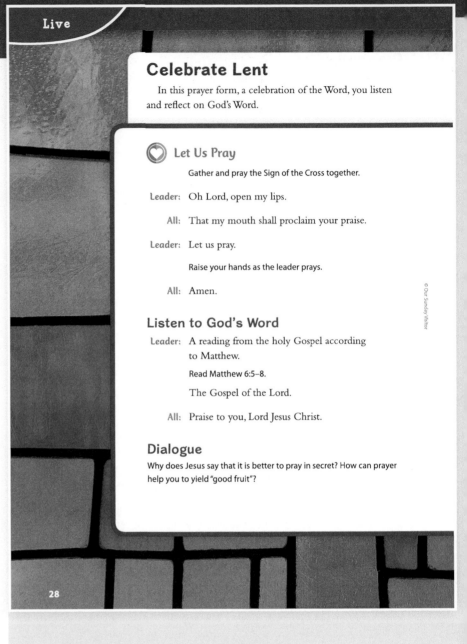

Live

Celebrate Lent

In this prayer form, a celebration of the Word, you listen and reflect on God's Word.

 Let Us Pray

Gather and pray the Sign of the Cross together.

Leader: Oh Lord, open my lips.

All: That my mouth shall proclaim your praise.

Leader: Let us pray.

Raise your hands as the leader prays.

All: Amen.

Listen to God's Word

Leader: A reading from the holy Gospel according to Matthew.

Read Matthew 6:5–8.

The Gospel of the Lord.

All: Praise to you, Lord Jesus Christ.

Dialogue

Why does Jesus say that it is better to pray in secret? How can prayer help you to yield "good fruit"?

© Our Sunday Visitor

28

Liturgy Link

The Body and Prayer

The *orans* position is suggested for the opening prayer of the celebration. Simply stand with hands open and palms facing upwards.

- This posture suggests praise, pleading, and vulnerability.
- It is often used by the priest during the Liturgy of the Eucharist.

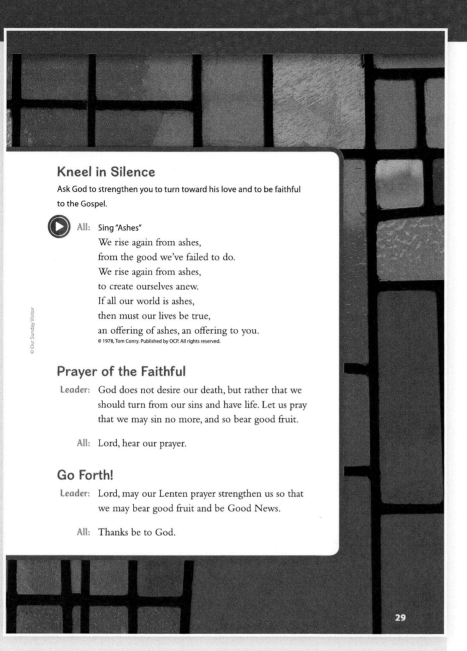

Kneel in Silence

Ask God to strengthen you to turn toward his love and to be faithful to the Gospel.

 All: Sing "Ashes"

We rise again from ashes,
from the good we've failed to do.
We rise again from ashes,
to create ourselves anew.
If all our world is ashes,
then must our lives be true,
an offering of ashes, an offering to you.

Prayer of the Faithful

Leader: God does not desire our death, but rather that we should turn from our sins and have life. Let us pray that we may sin no more, and so bear good fruit.

All: Lord, hear our prayer.

Go Forth!

Leader: Lord, may our Lenten prayer strengthen us so that we may bear good fruit and be Good News.

All: Thanks be to God.

29

Kneel in Silence

Invite the children to kneel and pray silently for God's help in bearing good fruit during Lent.

 Sing together "Ashes."

Prayer of the Faithful

Leader's intercessions:

Lord God, may our celebration of Lent turn our lives to God and the life that comes from believing in his Son, Jesus. (Response)

Lord God, be with us as we pray together, and when we pray alone. (Response)

Lord God, may our lives be lived in fruitful service to you and our neighbors. (Response)

Go Forth!

Conclude the session by having the children slowly and reverently process back to their seats.

 Lectionary Connection

Matthew 6:5–8

The reading for the celebration is found in the Lectionary for the Fifth and Sixth Sundays of Easter, respectively in Year B.

- Vines and branches are multi-layered symbols. In the Scriptures, Israel, divine Wisdom, and the Son of Man are depicted as vines. Jesus' followers are the branches.

Distribute this page to the children or parents/adult family members.

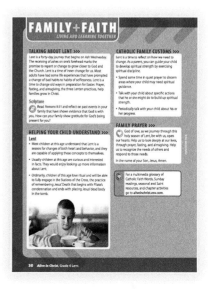

LESSON OBJECTIVES

- Recognize Holy Week, especially Triduum, as a special time
- Explore the meaning of the Cross

ENVIRONMENT

Red cloth
Pictures of a heart, a stop sign, and a cross
Cross or crucifix

- Place the prayer table in the center of the worship space.
- Cover the table with a red tablecloth, and place the cross in the center.
- Use as little light as possible for this celebration. Dim the room lights and do not light a candle.

 MUSIC OPTIONS
Go to **aliveinchrist.osv.com** to sample and download, "Were You There" "Pange Lingua"

 CATHOLIC SOCIAL TEACHING

- **Life and Dignity of the Human Person**, Pages 290–291
- **Rights and Responsibilities of the Human Person**, Pages 294–295

Catechist Background

He humbled himself, becoming obedient to death, even on a cross. Because of this, God greatly exalted him and bestowed on him the name that is above every name…
Philippians 2:8–9

➜ **Reflect** What helps you to do the right thing, even when it may be difficult or painful to do so?

The Easter Triduum begins with the Mass of the Lord's Supper on the evening of Holy Thursday and ends with evening prayer on Easter Sunday. The high point of the Triduum is the Easter Vigil. In this celebration, which always occurs during the night before Easter Sunday, the Church awaits the Resurrection and celebrates the Sacraments of Initiation with those who have been preparing as catechumens.

The Good Friday liturgy recalls the Passion and Death of Christ. The Liturgy of the Word proclaims the story of Jesus' suffering and Death. Then, those gathered intercede for the Church and for the world. The second part of the liturgy offers Christians an opportunity to venerate the cross. Finally, the Church shares the Eucharist that was consecrated on Holy Thursday.

Without the eyes of faith, the Cross could signify only death and destruction. Christians venerate the cross because they have come to see that Christ's willing sacrifice has transformed an instrument of death into a vehicle of unending life.

➜ **Reflect** What are the images and thoughts that come to mind when you reflect on the Cross of Christ?

Catechist's Prayer

 God, our Father, thank you for the gift of your Son, Jesus. May my life give honor to his great sacrifice. Amen.

Triduum

 Let Us Pray

Leader: Lord, God, sometimes we do things we
should not do.
We are sorry. Send your Holy Spirit
to guide us to right and loving actions.
Through Christ, our Lord.

"The Lord GOD is my help,
therefore I am not disgraced." Isaiah 50:7a

All: Amen.

 Scripture

"He humbled himself,
becoming obedient to death,
even death on a cross.
Because of this, God greatly exalted him
and bestowed on him the name
that is above every name." Philippians 2:8–9

What Do You Wonder?

• Why did Jesus choose to be obedient?
• What helps people do the right thing?

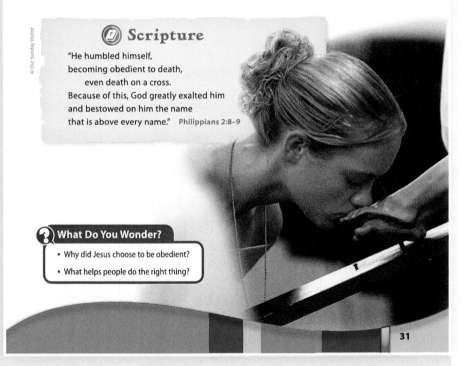

© Our Sunday Visitor

31

(🗓) **Lectionary Connection**

Philippians 2:8–9

This Scripture passage is part of the Second Reading on Palm Sunday
of the Lord's Passion.

• Jesus trusted his Father and always did his will. Jesus was obedient
even to death on a Cross.

• Christ humbled himself. Because of this, God greatly exalted him.

(♡) **Let Us Pray**

Invite the children to gather in the
prayer space and make the Sign of
the Cross. Choose a child to be the
leader. Prompt the children's
response.

Have the children move out of the
prayer space and back to their seats.

Explain that sometimes it is not easy
to do the right thing. In fact, we
often need help to do the right thing.

Say: We do need help to do the
right thing. That is why we often
pray asking for God's help. We can
also think about Jesus as Saint Paul
describes him to the Philippians.

(🗓) **Scripture**

Guide the children through the
process of Scripture reflection.

• Invite them to close their eyes, be
still and open their minds and
hearts to what God is saying to
them in this passage.

• Proclaim the Scripture.

• Maintain several moments of
silence.

• *Ask:* What did you hear God say
to you today?

• Invite volunteers to share.

What Do You Wonder?

Say: Sometimes it is hard to
imagine that a person could be
obedient even if it meant death, but
Jesus was.

Invite the children to respond to the
questions. Ask what else they might
wonder about Jesus' obedience or
doing the right thing.

The Cross

Show the children a picture of a heart, a stop sign, and a cross.

- Ask the children what each shape means, and write their responses on the board or on chart paper.

Invite two volunteers to read aloud the paragraphs.

- Recall with the children that Palm, or Passion, Sunday begins the holiest week of the liturgical year.
- Review with the children that the Triduum begins with Holy Thursday, moves into Good Friday, continues through the Easter Vigil and ends with evening prayer on Easter Sunday.

Suffering Servant

Invite two volunteers to read aloud the paragraphs.

- Discuss the Way of the Cross. Focus on the sacrifices that Jesus made along the journey to Calvary while knowing he was going to die.

Point out the photo.

- Invite the children to describe what they see.
- Explain that some communities reenact the Stations of the Cross on Good Friday, walking through the city streets.

The Cross

On Palm (Passion) Sunday, with the procession of palms and the reading of the Passion of Jesus, the Church begins the holiest week of the year. We call to mind all the events that led to Jesus' dying and rising to new life.

The last three days of Holy Week are called the Triduum. Triduum starts with the Holy Thursday Mass, moves into Good Friday, continues through the Easter Vigil, and ends with evening prayer on Easter Sunday.

Suffering Servant

On Good Friday the Church remembers the suffering Jesus endured for the sake of every person.

A Good Friday procession reenacts Jesus carrying the Cross to Golgotha, the place of his Crucifixion.

Jesus' journey carrying his Cross from the place he was condemned to the place where he was crucified is called the Way of the Cross. It was a painful journey. The Romans used the crucifixion as an instrument of punishment and death. Yet through Jesus the cross became a sign of new life.

© Our Sunday Visitor

32   The Church Year

Optional Activity

Sacrificial Love *Visual/Spatial*

Jesus showed us the joy that comes when we sacrifice for others. The children can share this joy.

- Have the children create Easter cards and distribute them at a convalescent home or retirement community during Holy Week.
- Encourage the children to sacrifice their time to make extra cards.

Because of Jesus' Death on the Cross and his Resurrection to new life, you receive forgiveness and share in God's life.

Today, the cross is a symbol of Jesus' love for all. The cross can inspire you to love in both word and action.

➜ **Where do you see crosses?**

New Life

The passage from the Book of Isaiah was written long before Jesus was born. Isaiah told the people that someday one of God's servants would suffer for the sins of many. Jesus suffered and died to free all people from sin and to bring them back to God's friendship. That is why the Church calls Jesus the Suffering Servant.

Activity

In Word and Action Think about an act of kindness or sacrifice that you will make during Holy Week. Then write some more ways you can imitate the love of Jesus in word and action.

_____
_____
_____
_____
_____
_____
_____
_____
_____
_____

Triduum   **33**

🌐 Catholic Social Teaching

Chapter Connections

To integrate Catholic Social Teaching into your lesson, choose one of the following features: Life and Dignity of the Human Person, pages 290–291; or Rights and Responsibilities of the Human Person, pages 294–295.

- To expand the lesson, move to the Catholic Social Teaching feature after completing page 33.
- Return to the prayer on page 34.

Suffering Servant,
continued

Invite a volunteer to read aloud the paragraphs.

- Reflect again on the symbol of the cross. Discuss how a symbol of death became a symbol of new life.
- *Ask:* Where do you see crosses?
- Tell the children to pay special attention during the coming week and notice any crosses they see around them.

New Life

Invite a volunteer to read aloud the paragraph.

- *Ask:* What are some ways you can imitate the love of Jesus in word and action?

Refer to page 313 in the Our Catholic Tradition reference section in the back of the Student Book for more about the Triduum.

 Music Option: Have the children sing "Pange Lingua," downloaded from **aliveinchrist.osv.com**.

Activity

Read aloud the activity directions.

- Invite the children to brainstorm together acts of kindness or sacrifice they can make during Holy week. Then have them choose one and write it down.
- Together brainstorm more ways that fourth graders can imitate the love of Jesus in word and action. Have the children write down the ones they are most likely to do.

Live

Celebrate Triduum

Let Us Pray

Explain to the children that they will have an opportunity to reverence the cross during the prayer. Tell them that they may choose to bow before the cross, kiss the cross, or offer some other sign of reverence.

Prepare

Show the children their responses in the Student Book.

Select a reader.

 Rehearse "Were You There," downloaded from **aliveinchrist.osv.com**.

- Invite the children to process to the prayer space. Have each child bring their book.

Pray

Follow the order of prayer on the student pages.

- Lead the children in the Sign of the Cross.

Listen to God's Word

Have the reader proclaim the Scripture.

 Sing together "Were You There?"

Dialogue

Make sure the children understand the connection between Isaiah's words and Christ's sacrifice.

Celebrate Triduum

This prayer form reverences the cross in a celebration of the Word. In the celebration you reflect on God's Word. In reverencing the cross, you use movement to pray.

Let Us Pray

Gather and pray the Sign of the Cross together.

Leader: O Lord, open my lips.

All: That my mouth may proclaim your praise.

Leader: Let us pray.

Bow your heads as the leader prays.

All: Amen.

Listen to God's Word

Leader: A reading from the Book of the prophet Isaiah.

Read Isaiah 53:10b–12.

The word of the Lord.

All: Thanks be to God.

Sing together.

Sing "Were You There?"

Dialogue

The Book of Isaiah was written long before the birth of Jesus. Why do you think the Church reads this passage on Good Friday?

34

(i) Catechist Background

Liturgical Colors

Black was once used as the liturgical color for Good Friday. Black symbolized the absence of light and the attitude of mourning.

- Today, red vestments are usually worn on Good Friday. Red symbolizes suffering and the blood of Jesus.

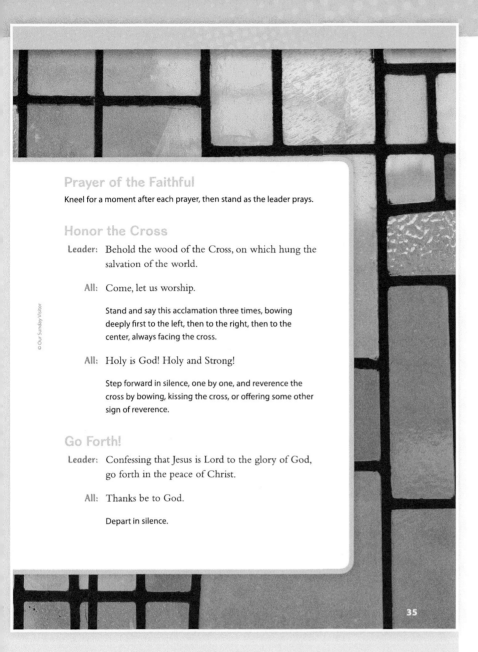

Prayer of the Faithful

Kneel for a moment after each prayer, then stand as the leader prays.

Honor the Cross

Leader: Behold the wood of the Cross, on which hung the salvation of the world.

All: Come, let us worship.

Stand and say this acclamation three times, bowing deeply first to the left, then to the right, then to the center, always facing the cross.

All: Holy is God! Holy and Strong!

Step forward in silence, one by one, and reverence the cross by bowing, kissing the cross, or offering some other sign of reverence.

Go Forth!

Leader: Confessing that Jesus is Lord to the glory of God, go forth in the peace of Christ.

All: Thanks be to God.

Depart in silence.

© Our Sunday Visitor

35

Prayer of the Faithful

Invite the children to kneel after each prayer for a moment of silence, and then stand as the leader prays.

Leader prayers:

Jesus, thank you for loving us, even to the point of the Cross. Help us to love others, even when it becomes difficult to do. (Response)

Lord Jesus, give us true vision to see those who are suffering around us and to comfort them. (Response)

Father, help us to celebrate the Triduum this year with grateful hearts for what Jesus did for us on the Cross. (Response)

Honor the Cross

Demonstrate how the children are to reverence the cross and then invite them to come forward individually.

- When all have reverenced the cross, pause for silent reflection.

Go Forth!

Instruct the children to return in silence to their places.

Distribute this page to the children or parents/adult family members.

Liturgy Link

Venerate the Cross

The practice of unveiling and venerating the cross on Good Friday began in the Church of Jerusalem.

- Three times during the liturgy, while the cross is unveiled, the choir sings, "Behold the wood of the Cross, on which hung the salvation of the world," and the assembly responds with "Come, let us adore" (*Roman Missal*).

LESSON OBJECTIVES

- Explain that Easter celebrates the Resurrection of Jesus
- Discuss ways Jesus is present today

ENVIRONMENT

White cloth
Large candle to represent the Paschal (Easter) Candle
Alleluia banner
Bowl filled with holy water

- Cover a table with the cloth.
- Place the bowl of water on the table, and place the banner next to it.
- Place the candle next to the table, or if a small candle is used, place it on the table.

 MUSIC OPTIONS
Go to **aliveinchrist.osv.com** to sample and download,
"He Is Risen, Alleluia"
"Alleluia"
"Easter Alleluia"
"I Want to Walk as a Child of the Light"
"Walk in the Light"

 CATHOLIC SOCIAL TEACHING

- **Solidarity of the Human Family**, Pages 300–301
- **Care for God's Creation**, Pages 302–303

Catechist Background

"The community of believers was of one heart and mind, and no one claimed that any of his possessions was his own, but they had everything in common." **Acts 4:32**

➜ **Reflect** How would you feel about living this way?

During each Mass of the Easter season, the Paschal Candle burns brightly in a central place in the sanctuary. The words of the Easter Proclamation, or *Exsultet*, which was sung during the Easter Vigil, convey the significance of this candle. This is the light that pierces through the darkness of sin and evil. This is the light that shines forth like the dawn of Christ's Resurrection. This light is Christ himself.

Whenever Catholics are baptized, the Paschal Candle is also lit. The newly baptized receive baptismal candles that are lit from the Paschal Candle. This signifies that those who are baptized receive the light of Christ. The Church prays that this light of Christ will be preserved by faith and burn brightly all the days of these new Catholics' lives.

➜ **Reflect** How does the light of Christ help you see your life in a new or different way?

Catechist's Prayer

 God, our Father, help me to live in the light of Easter every day. Amen.

He Lives

♡ Let Us Pray

Leader: Lord, God, bless all your people with the joy of
Easter and the continued presence of your Son
forever. Through Christ our Lord.

"Give thanks to the LORD, for he is good,
his mercy endures forever." Psalm 118:1

All: Amen.

ⓘ Scripture

"The community of believers was of one heart and mind, and
no one claimed that any of his possessions was his own, but
they had everything in common. With great power the apostles
bore witness to the resurrection of the Lord Jesus, and great
favor was accorded them all. There was no needy person among
them, for those who owned property or houses would sell
them, bring the proceeds of the sale, and put them at the feet
of the apostles, and they were distributed to each according to
need." Acts 4:32–35

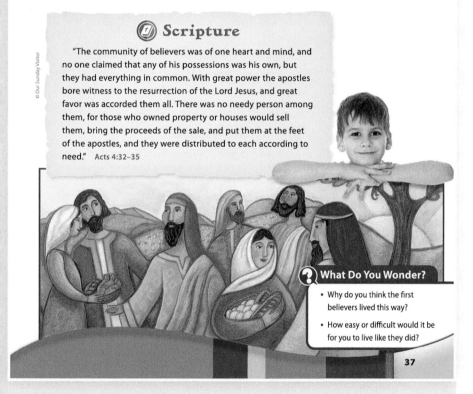

? What Do You Wonder?

- Why do you think the first
believers lived this way?

- How easy or difficult would it be
for you to live like they did?

37

ⓘ Lectionary Connection

Acts of the Apostles 4:32–35

This Scripture passage is the First Reading on the Second Sunday of
Easter, Year B.

- This passage describes the early followers of Jesus. The first
Christians were of "one heart and mind" (Acts 4:32).

- The distribution and sharing of possessions continues the
teachings of Jesus in the Gospel of Luke (Luke 12:33, 16:9, 11, 13).

♡ Let Us Pray

Invite the children to gather in the
prayer space and make the Sign of
the Cross. Choose a child to be the
leader. Prompt the children's
response.

Have the children move out of the
prayer space and back to their seats.

Explain that the first followers of
Jesus lived in community.

Say: The joy of Easter and God's
presence are still with us today, two
thousand years later. The early
followers of Jesus formed a loving
community. Listen to how they lived.

ⓘ Scripture

Guide the children through the
process of Scripture reflection.

- Invite them to close their eyes, be
still and open their minds and
hearts to what God is saying to
them in this passage.

- Proclaim the Scripture.

- Maintain several moments of
silence.

- *Ask:* What did you hear God say
to you today?

- Invite volunteers to share.

What Do You Wonder?

Say: The early Christian community
cared about each other and shared
what they owned. They were a good
example to others. When people
saw how they lived, they came to
believe in Jesus, too.

Invite the children to respond to the
questions. Ask what else they might
wonder about the first Christians.

Light of the World

Turn off the lights, and then light a candle or a single lamp.

- After a moment of silence, ask the children to describe the light. What effect does it have on the room?

- Write the children's responses on the board or on chart paper.

- Ask the children to name some of the things that light can do. Possible responses: brighten, warm, show the way, help plants grow

Have volunteers read aloud the text.

- *Ask:* What are some of the signs of joy that can be seen and heard during the Easter season? the Alleluia, flowers and plants, white cloth

- Call attention to the photo.

- Invite the children to name the signs of joy they see in the photo.

 Music Option: Have the children sing "Alleluia," downloaded from **aliveinchrist.osv.com**.

At Easter, we often see Resurrection crosses inside and outside churches. White cloths and flowers to help proclaim Jesus' being raised to new life.

Light of the World

On Easter the Church celebrates Jesus' Resurrection. When Jesus was raised from the dead on the third day, he conquered sin and death. The Church celebrates Easter for fifty days, from Easter Sunday to Pentecost.

The Easter season is one of joy and gladness. Alleluias are sung once again. Flowers and plants fill the churches, as signs of the new life Christ brings. Choirs sing Glory to God! and the altar is draped in white cloth. All are signs of the light that Jesus brings into the world.

In the northern hemisphere, Easter comes as the darkness of winter gives way to spring. Leaves appear on trees, and flowers blossom. Spring is a season of new life.

38 The Church Year

 ## Songs of Scripture

He Lives!

This song is filled with joy. Both the tempo and the words speak to the urgency to announce the Good News that Jesus is Risen. He Lives!

- Give each child a length of tin foil the circumference of their head. Have them twist the foil and then connect the ends, making a halo.

- Teach the children the song. During the chorus, have them imagine they are the angel speaking to the women at the tomb.

 Use *Songs of Scripture*, Grades 4–6 CD, Track 13

Let Your Light Shine

Jesus' Resurrection is a sign of the new life that bursts forth in the bright light of the sun. Jesus triumphed over the selfishness that leads people away from God. He turned the darkness of sin into the light of love. That is why Jesus is called the Light of the World.

Did you ever notice that outside on a dark night, away from the lights of the city, the stars seem brighter? In a similar way, the light of Christ brightens the darkness of the world. In the midst of sadness and violence, Christ's light shines even more brightly. In the midst of loneliness or rejection, the light of Christ's love is there to warm the heart that is hurting.

➜ What are some ways Jesus is light for you?

➜ How can you help others to know the light of Christ's love?

The Light of the World Decorate the candle with symbols of Jesus as the Light of the World.

In the seven rays of light radiating from the candle flame, write things you and your family can do each week during the Easter season to bring Christ's light into your neighborhood and community. Share your ideas with your family.

Easter **39**

Catholic Social Teaching

Chapter Connections

To integrate Catholic Social Teaching into your lesson, choose one of the following features: Solidarity of the Human Family, pages 300–301; or Care for God's Creation, page 302–303.

- To expand the lesson, move to the Catholic Social Teaching feature after completing page 39.

- Return to the prayer on page 40.

Let Your Light Shine

Invite volunteers to read aloud the paragraphs.

- Recall with the children the discussion they had about light.

- Remind them that Jesus is light in the darkness of sin, confusion, and death.

- *Ask:* What are some ways Jesus is light for you?

- *Ask:* What are some things you can do to help others to know the light of Christ's love?

Refer to page 313 in the Our Catholic Tradition reference section in the back of the Student Book for more about the Easter season.

> Music Option: Have the children sing "I Want to Walk as a Child of the Light" or "Walk in the Light," downloaded from **aliveinchrist.osv.com**.

Activity

Read aloud the activity directions.

- Discuss possible responses with the group.

- Provide time for the children to complete the activity on their own.

- When everyone has finished, invite volunteers to share what they have written with a partner.

Celebrate Easter

 Let Us Pray

Explain to the children that this prayer is a celebration of the Word and an act of praise and thanksgiving. A celebration of the Word is a moment of prayer with the Church using the Scriptures.

Prepare

Select a reader.

Show the children their responses in the Student Book.

 Rehearse "He Is Risen, Alleluia!" downloaded from **aliveinchrist.osv.com**.

- Lead the children in procession to the prayer area. Have the children bring their books.

Pray

Follow the order of prayer on the student pages.

- Lead the children in praying the Sign of the Cross.
- *Leader's prayer:* God, our Father, Jesus rose victorious over the darkness of sin. May we live in the light of Easter each day of our lives.

Listen to God's Word

Have the children stand for the proclamation of the Gospel.

Celebrate Easter

This prayer is a celebration of the Word and an act of praise and thanksgiving. A celebration of the Word is a moment of prayer with the Church using the Scriptures.

 Let Us Pray

Gather and pray the Sign of the Cross together.

Leader: Light and peace in Jesus Christ our Lord. Alleluia.

All: Thanks be to God, Alleluia.

Reader: Christ is our light in the darkness!

All: Alleluia, Alleluia, Alleluia.

Reader: Christ is the Way, the Truth, and the Life!

All: Alleluia, Alleluia, Alleluia.

Leader: Let us pray.

Bow your heads as the leader prays.

All: Amen, Alleluia.

Listen to God's Word

Reader: A reading from the holy Gospel according to Matthew.

Read Matthew 28:1–10.

The Gospel of the Lord.

All: Praise to you, Lord Jesus Christ.

40

🔖 Lectionary Connection

Matthew 28:1–10

The Gospel used for the celebration is taken from the Gospel for the Easter Vigil, Year A.

- The women found an empty tomb. They did not yet understand what Jesus had taught about his Death.
- The Good News that greeted the women was frightening and confusing, yet they went forth to share the news.

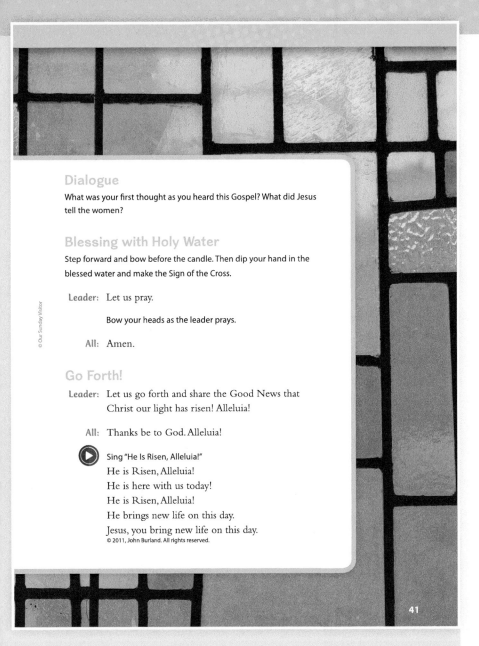

Dialogue

What was your first thought as you heard this Gospel? What did Jesus tell the women?

Blessing with Holy Water

Step forward and bow before the candle. Then dip your hand in the blessed water and make the Sign of the Cross.

Leader: Let us pray.

> Bow your heads as the leader prays.

All: Amen.

Go Forth!

Leader: Let us go forth and share the Good News that Christ our light has risen! Alleluia!

All: Thanks be to God. Alleluia!

 Sing "He Is Risen, Alleluia!"
He is Risen, Alleluia!
He is here with us today!
He is Risen, Alleluia!
He brings new life on this day.
Jesus, you bring new life on this day.
© 2011, John Burland. All rights reserved.

41

Dialogue

Ask the children to imagine how they would feel if they walked down the street and saw a friend whom they knew had just died. Help the children understand the feelings that the women in the Gospel must have experienced.

- Invite the children to discuss and reflect on the dialogue questions.
- Point out that Jesus calls all of his followers to spread the Good News.

Blessing with Holy Water

Model making the Sign of the Cross with holy water.

- Guide the children one by one through the ritual action.
- *Leader's prayer:* Jesus, Light of the World, continue to help and guide us throughout our lives. May we always give you praise and honor for the gifts of light and new life.

 Sing together "He Is Risen, Alleluia!"

Distribute this page to the children or parents/adult family members.

♥ Liturgy Link

Praise God!

The word *alleluia* comes from the Hebrew words for "Praise God!"

- The *Alleluia* is a prayer of community rejoicing in the greatness of God.
- The body can aid in creating a spirit of prayer and praise. Invite the children to sing *Alleluia* with arms raised.

LESSON OBJECTIVES

- Explore the story of the Ascension
- Discuss our belief in eternal life

ENVIRONMENT

White cloth
Large bowl or container
Poster board cut into leaf shapes, large enough to write 2-3 names on each one

- Cover the prayer table with the white cloth.
- Place the bowl on the table.
- Clear enough room for the children to move in the prayer space.

 MUSIC OPTIONS
Go to **aliveinchrist.osv.com** to sample and download, "Rise Up with Him" "Save Us, Lord" "We Proclaim Your Death, O Lord"

 CATHOLIC SOCIAL TEACHING

- **Life and Dignity of the Human Person**, Pages 290–291
- **Rights and Responsibilities of the Human Person**, Pages 294–295

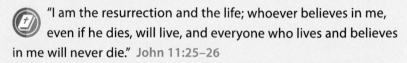

Catechist Background

 "I am the resurrection and the life; whoever believes in me, even if he dies, will live, and everyone who lives and believes in me will never die." John 11:25–26

➔ **Reflect** How does your belief in eternal life affect how you live today?

The Feast of the Ascension celebrates the fact that Jesus who is both God and human is returning to the Father and will return again in the Second Coming. The Ascension is the final piece of the Paschal Mystery, which consists also of Jesus' Passion, Crucifixion, Death, Burial, Descent among the Dead, and Resurrection. Along with the Resurrection, the Ascension was put forth as proof of Jesus' claim that he was the Messiah. The Ascension is also the event in which humanity is taken into Heaven. It symbolizes the victory of Jesus Christ over the power of sin and death.

This feast is an appropriate time to remember and pray for those who have died in the hope of rising again and living in communion with God in Heaven for all eternity.

➔ **Reflect** What are your hopes for life after death?

Catechist's Prayer

God, our Father, help me to live each day with gratitude for the gift of eternal life. Amen.

Ascension

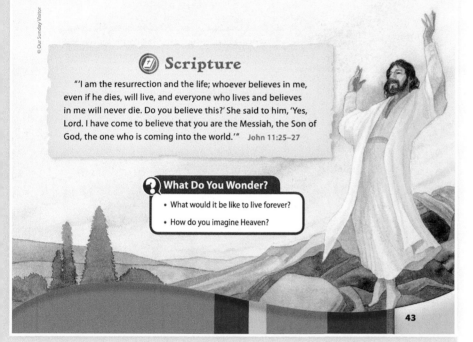

💙 Let Us Pray

Leader: Dear Lord,

Help us to understand that your will is for us to enjoy eternal happiness with you in Heaven. Give us the help of the Holy Spirit to live as faithful followers here, so that one day we will enjoy that happiness. In your name we pray.

"The LORD has set his throne in heaven; his dominion extends over all." Psalm 103:19

All: Amen.

© Our Sunday Visitor

✡ Scripture

"'I am the resurrection and the life; whoever believes in me, even if he dies, will live, and everyone who lives and believes in me will never die. Do you believe this?' She said to him, 'Yes, Lord. I have come to believe that you are the Messiah, the Son of God, the one who is coming into the world.'" John 11:25–27

? What Do You Wonder?

• What would it be like to live forever?

• How do you imagine Heaven?

43

✡ Lectionary Connection

John 11:25–27

This reading is proclaimed the Third Sunday of Lent, Year A. It is also often chosen as the Gospel for funerals and Masses for the Dead.

• The most important fact of this story is that Jesus is the resurrection and life for the believer. The passage emphasizes the importance of faith.

• This whole story is one of the most evocative of Jesus' humanity since it shows his grief at Lazarus' death and his obvious personal ties to the family.

Invite

💙 Let Us Pray

Invite the children to gather in the prayer space and make the Sign of the Cross. Invite a child to read aloud the Psalm verse from a Bible. Prompt the children's response.

Have the children move out of the prayer space and back to their seats.

Explain that God is faithful to us always and forever. His love is a gift to all people.

Say: Jesus' Death, Resurrection and Ascension show us that he conquered death. It reminds us of his words to Mary when her brother Lazarus died.

✡ Scripture

Guide the children through the process of Scripture reflection.

• Invite them to close their eyes, be still and open their minds and hearts to what God is saying to them in this passage.

• Proclaim the Scripture.

• Maintain several moments of silence.

• *Ask:* What did you hear God say to you today?

• Invite volunteers to share.

What Do You Wonder?

Say: In the reading, Jesus tells Mary that people who believe in him will never die even though their bodies do.

Invite the children to respond to the questions. Ask what else they might wonder about Heaven or the gift of eternal life.

Death and Dying

Read aloud the text.

- Have volunteers share stories about those close to them who have died.

- Reassure the children that God wants all of us to be happy with him in Heaven.

The Offer

Read aloud the introduction in the first box of the chart.

- Explain that God wants every person to go to Heaven. We are invited to accept this offer.

Ask four individuals to each read aloud one of the remaining boxes of the chart.

- After each item, discuss ways children do or can do each of those things.

- Point out that each of the items is a way of living out Jesus' Great Commandment of love.

- Have the children check off the things that they already do. Have them circle something they will do in the future. Then have them add one idea to the list.

Refer to page 308–309 in the Our Catholic Tradition reference section in the back of the Student Book for more about how the Ascension fits into the Paschal Mystery of Jesus Christ.

> ▶ Music Option: Have the children sing "Save Us, Lord" or "We Proclaim Your Death, O Lord," downloaded from **aliveinchrist.osv.com**.

Discover

Death and Dying

Jesus died and rose and then ascended into Heaven to be with his Father forever. All of us will die some day, too. But we have the chance to be with Jesus and his Father in Heaven. We are always sad when someone close to us dies because we miss that person. Jesus' Resurrection and his Ascension give us faith and hope that when a person dies, his or her life continues, but it is different.

Death is a passing from this life to new life. Our body dies but our soul lives on. However, our bodies will also rise at the end of time On the Feast of the Ascension, the Church celebrates Jesus' return to his Father in Heaven. Ascension Thursday is celebrated forty days after Easter.

 Check off the things that you already do. Circle something you will do in the future. Then add one idea to the list.

The Offer

God calls everyone at all times and offers us the gift of salvation. We accept God's gift of salvation through our faith in Jesus Christ. Real faith will show itself in the things we do.

☐ We take time to listen and talk to God.

☐ We are kind and respectful to others.

☐ We take care of all God's gifts.

☐ We reach out to the poor, to those who are sick, and to those who are outcasts.

_____

_____

44 The Church Year

 ## Songs of Scripture

Least of My Brothers

Show the children a drawing of a wagon wheel with Jesus' name written on the hub.

- Discuss that we relate to everyone through Jesus just as the spokes relate to each other through the hub.

- Teach the song.

> ▶ Use *Songs of Scripture*, Grades 4–6 CD, Track 16

Let Us Pray

Remember the Ascension

Gather to sing and pray the Sign of the Cross together.

Leader: We proclaim your Death, O Lord,
and profess your Resurrection
until you come again.
Let us pray.

Bow your heads as the leader prays.

All: Amen.

Listen to God's Word

Leader: A reading from the holy Gospel according to John.

Read John 14:1–3
Silent Reflection

Presentation of Names

Leader: One way to give witness to the Resurrection is to
commend those who have died to God. Write the
names of people who have died whom you wish
to remember in prayer. Then place your list in the
bowl in the front of the room.

After the last child has come forward, the intercessions
begin. Respond to each intercession with these words.

All: I place my trust and hope in God.

Go Forth!

Leader: Let us offer a prayer of praise to God—Father,
Son, and Holy Spirit.

 Sing "Rise Up with Him"

45

Let Us Pray

Remember the Ascension

Select a reader.

 Rehearse "Rise Up with Him"
downloaded from
aliveinchrist.osv.com.

Leader's Prayer: God, our Father, you revealed your Son, Jesus, to the world as the source of our life and the destroyer of death. Through him, may we live so as to be with you for eternity.

Presentation of Names

On the leaves, have the children write the names of loved ones who have died.

Leader prayers of intercession: Lord for all those whose names we have placed here that they are enjoying happiness with you in Heaven.

Lord, for all who will die today that you will bless them with eternal rest.

Lord, for ourselves and our loved ones that we will have peaceful, happy deaths.

Distribute this page to the children or parents/adult family members.

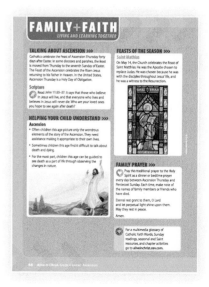

Catholic Social Teaching

Chapter Connections

To integrate Catholic Social Teaching into your lesson, choose one of the following features: Life and Dignity of the Human Person, pages 290–291; or Rights and Responsibilities of the Human Person, pages 294–295.

- To expand the lesson, move to the Catholic Social Teaching feature after completing page 44.
- Return to the prayer on page 45.

LESSON OBJECTIVES

- Explain that the coming of the Holy Spirit at Pentecost marked when the work of the Church began
- Discuss the work of the Holy Spirit today

ENVIRONMENT

Red cloth
Symbol of the Holy Spirit
Bible
Cross
Candle or battery-opperated candle
Bowl of water

- Cover the table with the red cloth.
- Open the Bible and place it on the table.
- On the table, place a symbol of the Holy Spirit, candle, and bowl of water.

MUSIC OPTIONS

Go to **aliveinchrist.osv.com** to sample and download,
"Come, Holy Ghost"
"Come to Us, Holy Spirit"
"Gifts"
"Come to Us, Spirit of Jesus"
"The Holy Spirit"

CATHOLIC SOCIAL TEACHING

- **Rights and Responsibilities of the Human Person**, Pages 294–295
- **The Dignity of Work and Rights of Workers**, Pages 298–299

Catechist Background

"There are different kinds of spiritual gifts but the same Spirit; there are different forms of service but the same Lord; there are different workings but the same God who produces all of them in everyone." **1 Corinthians 12:4–6**

➜ **Reflect** How do the Gifts of the Holy Spirit help you to live a holy life?

Although Pentecost marks the end of the Easter Season, for the Church it signals a new beginning in carrying out the mission of Christ in the world. At Pentecost we celebrate the outpouring of the Holy Spirit that takes root in the hearts of believers. The readings for Pentecost recall how the first disciples were transformed from fearful self-doubters to courageous missionaries.

The Lectionary includes a sequence, or poem, for the Feast of Pentecost. Entitled *Veni, Sancte Spiritus* (Come, Holy Spirit), this ancient hymn recalls ways in which the Church has experienced the gift of the Holy Spirit. Among these are the Holy Spirit as "father of the poor," "the soul's most welcome guest," and "most blessed light divine."

➜ **Reflect** In what unique ways has God blessed you with the power of the Holy Spirit?

Catechist's Prayer

Come, Holy Spirit, fill the heart of your faithful servant. Strengthen me with your gifts, so that I may work with God as he builds his Kingdom. Amen.

Pentecost

 Let Us Pray

Leader: Come Holy Spirit
send us your power and your gifts,
that we may be instruments
of the coming of God's Kingdom.
Through Christ, our Lord.

"Bless the LORD, my soul!
LORD, my God, you are great indeed!"

Psalm 104:1

All: Amen.

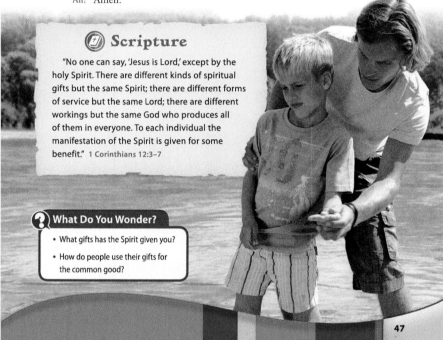

Scripture

"No one can say, 'Jesus is Lord,' except by the holy Spirit. There are different kinds of spiritual gifts but the same Spirit; there are different forms of service but the same Lord; there are different workings but the same God who produces all of them in everyone. To each individual the manifestation of the Spirit is given for some benefit." 1 Corinthians 12:3–7

? What Do You Wonder?

- What gifts has the Spirit given you?
- How do people use their gifts for the common good?

47

Lectionary Connection

1 Corinthians 12:3b–7, 12–13

Part of this passage comes from the Second Reading on the Second Sunday in Ordinary Time, Year C.

- Saint Paul explains that there are many spiritual gifts that all come from the same Spirit.
- In the Sacrament of Confirmation, we are sealed with the Gift of the Holy Spirit. The Holy Spirit helps us to live lives of holiness.

 Let Us Pray

Invite the children to gather in the prayer space and make the Sign of the Cross. Choose a child to be the leader. Read aloud the Psalm verse from a Bible. Prompt the children's response.

 Music Option: Have the children sing "Come to Us, Holy Spirit" or "Gifts," downloaded from **aliveinchrist.osv.com**.

Have the children move out of the prayer space and back to their seats.

Say: The Holy Spirit gives us power and gifts to help us spread the Good News.

Scripture

Guide the children through the process of Scripture reflection.

- Invite them to close their eyes, be still and open their minds and hearts to what God is saying to them in this passage.
- Proclaim the Scripture.
- Maintain several moments of silence.
- *Ask:* What did you hear God say to you today?
- Invite volunteers to share.

What Do You Wonder?

Say: The Gifts of the Holy Spirit are given to help each other and to build the Church. Each of us has a responsibility to use our gifts.

Invite the children to respond to the questions. Ask what else they might wonder about the Gifts of the Holy Spirit and the Kingdom of God.

Pentecost Today

Point out the liturgical color for the Feast of Pentecost in the prayer center.

- Ask the children to explain what red symbolizes, and write their responses on the board or on chart paper.

- Explain that red symbolizes the fire of the Holy Spirit. A dove, fire and wind are all symbols of the Holy Spirit.

Invite a volunteer to read aloud the text.

- Emphasize that Pentecost celebrates the gift of the Holy Spirit to the Church.

⭐ Have the children underline the Holy Spirit's action in and for the Church from Pentecost through today.

- *Ask:* How is the Holy Spirit active in the world today?

Refer to page 309 in the Our Catholic Tradition reference section in the back of the Student Book for more about the Holy Spirit and the Gifts of the Holy Spirit.

 Music Option: Have the children sing "Come to Us, Spirit of Jesus" or "The Holy Spirit," downloaded from **aliveinchrist.osv.com**.

Discover

Pentecost Today

Today the Church rejoices in the Resurrection of the Lord for fifty days after Easter. Then on Pentecost, the Church celebrates the gift of the Holy Spirit to the Church. The Holy Spirit gave the first disciples the wisdom and courage they needed to preach the Gospel.

⭐ Underline the Holy Spirit's action in and for the Church from Pentecost through to today.

- The Feast of Pentecost celebrates the coming of the Holy Spirit on Mary and the Apostles.

- Pentecost occurs fifty days after Easter and marks the end of the Easter season.

- On Pentecost the priest wears red vestments. Red reminds us of the fire of the Holy Spirit.

The coming of the Holy Spirit marked the beginning of the Apostles' active ministry of spreading the Gospel after Jesus' Ascension. From this time onward, the Church has been empowered by the Holy Spirit to spread the Good News by word and action. He builds up the Church, empowers her for service, and is the source of her holiness.

➜ **How is the Holy Spirit active in the world today?**

48   The Church Year

🌐 Catholic Social Teaching

Chapter Connections

To integrate Catholic Social Teaching into your lesson, choose one of the following features: Rights and Responsibilities of the Human Person, pages 294–295; or the Dignity of Work and Rights of Workers, pages 298–299.

- To expand the lesson move to the Catholic Social Teaching feature after completing page 48.

- Return to the prayer on page 49.

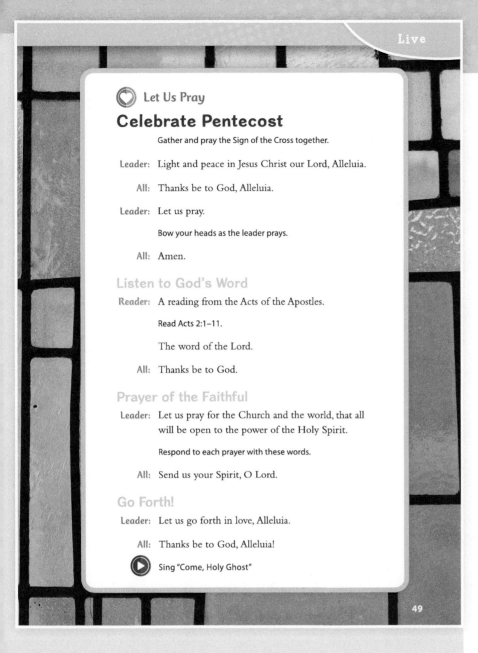

 Let Us Pray

Celebrate Pentecost

Gather and pray the Sign of the Cross together.

Leader: Light and peace in Jesus Christ our Lord, Alleluia.

All: Thanks be to God, Alleluia.

Leader: Let us pray.

Bow your heads as the leader prays.

All: Amen.

Listen to God's Word

Reader: A reading from the Acts of the Apostles.

Read Acts 2:1–11.

The word of the Lord.

All: Thanks be to God.

Prayer of the Faithful

Leader: Let us pray for the Church and the world, that all will be open to the power of the Holy Spirit.

Respond to each prayer with these words.

All: Send us your Spirit, O Lord.

Go Forth!

Leader: Let us go forth in love, Alleluia.

All: Thanks be to God, Alleluia!

▶ Sing "Come, Holy Ghost"

49

 Let Us Pray

Celebrate Pentecost

Select a reader.

> ▶ Rehearse "Come, Holy Ghost," downloaded from **aliveinchrist.osv.com**.

Follow the order of prayer on the student page.

- *Leader's prayer:* God our Father, you have given us new birth in Baptism. Strengthen us with your Holy Spirit, and fill us with your light.

Listen to God's Word

Have the children stand for the proclamation of God's Word.

Prayer of the Faithful

Invite the children to offer their own intentions.

Go Forth!

▶ Sing together "Come, Holy Ghost."

Distribute this page to the children or parents/adult family members.

❤ Liturgy Link

Music and Song

The voice is the primary instrument in liturgical worship. Music, too, expresses emotions and communicates a message.

- Music allows worshippers a window into the sacred.
- Though not indispensible to liturgy, music enhances one's participation in worship.
- Invite the children to share the name of their favorite hymn about the Holy Spirit.

Core
Chapters

Units at a Glance

Revelation

Our Catholic Tradition

- God communicates a loving plan for all of creation. We learn of this in Sacred Scripture and Sacred Tradition. (CCC, 50, 81)

- God stays true and faithful to his promises. Through his covenants, God keeps telling and showing people that he will be faithful, even though we sin. (CCC, 211)

- God helps us understand how to be faithful to him. Through the Ten Commandments, God revealed how he wants all of his children to live. (CCC, 2060)

How does God show he is faithful to his covenant through the lives of Abraham, Joseph, and Moses?

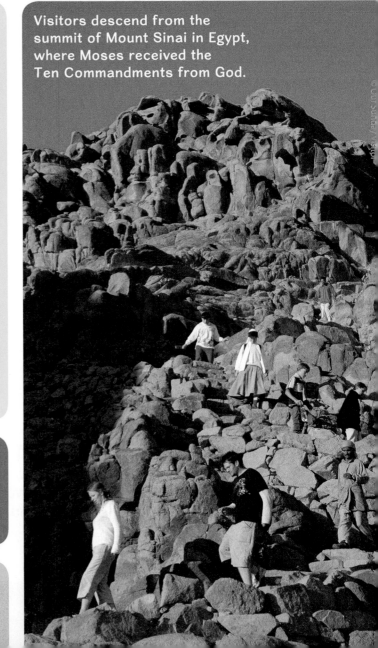

Visitors descend from the summit of Mount Sinai in Egypt, where Moses received the Ten Commandments from God.

Unit 1 Overview

Chapter 1

The children will:

- recognize that the first creation account teaches the goodness of all God's creation
- define providence as God's loving care for all things; his will and plan for creation
- describe Divine Revelation as the way God tells humans about himself and makes his plan known
- recall that God reveals himself through Sacred Scripture and the Sacred Tradition of the Church

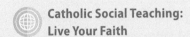

Catholic Social Teaching: Live Your Faith

- Life and Dignity of the Human Person, Pages 290–291
- Care for God's Creation, Pages 302–303

Chapter 2

The children will:

- discuss how death, suffering, ignorance, and the inclination to sin all came into the world as a result of Original Sin
- understand that God always remains faithful and promises salvation, desiring humans to be free and faithful to him
- describe a covenant as a sacred promise or agreement between God and humans
- appreciate that God called Abraham, and because of his belief and trust in God, God established a covenant with him

 Songs of Scripture
"Abraham"

 Catholic Social Teaching: Live Your Faith

- Rights and Responsibilities of the Human Person, Pages 294–295
- Solidarity of the Human Family, Pages 300–301

Chapter 3

The children will:

- understand that God created people to be free and live as his People, and he called Moses to lead his People from slavery in Egypt
- identify the Ten Commandments as the summary of laws that God gave Moses on Mount Sinai
- explain that God gave the Ten Commandments to help us be faithful to him and his covenant

 Catholic Social Teaching: Live Your Faith

- Call to Family, Community, and Participation, Pages 292–293
- Rights and Responsibilities of the Human Person, Pages 294–295

Preview Unit Theme

Ask: What is the unit theme?

Summarize that the unit focuses on God's Revelation.

Invite volunteers to read aloud each of the bullets in Our Catholic Tradition.

Explain to the children that they will learn about these things in the next three chapters.

Have the children study the photos and images. Invite volunteers to describe what they see. What do these images say about the unit theme?

Ask: How does God show he is faithful to his covenant through the lives of Abraham, Joseph, and Moses?

After some discussion, explain to the children that they will be exploring this question in the next three chapters.

KEY CONCEPT

God loves and cares for all creation and has a plan for the world. Everything God wants you to know about him is contained in Sacred Scripture and in the Tradition of the Church.

DOCTRINAL CONTENT

- The first creation account teaches the goodness of all of God's creation. (CCC, 299)
- Providence is God's loving care for all things; his will and plan for creation. (CCC, 302–303)
- Divine Revelation is the way God tells humans about himself and makes his plan known. (CCC, 50)
- God reveals himself through Sacred Scripture and the Sacred Tradition of the Church. (CCC, 81–82)

TASKS OF CATECHESIS

Helping children grow in a faith that is "known, celebrated, lived, and expressed in prayer" (NDC, 20).

This chapter focuses on the following task of catechesis:

- Promoting Knowledge of the Faith

Catechist Background

 But the plan of the LORD stands forever, the designs of his heart through all generations. Psalm 33:11

➔ **Reflect** What do you find most amazing in everything God created? How do you know God's plan for you?

Around you are many signs of the presence of God. From the simplicity of a single cell to the vastness of the cosmos, you have much to marvel at and much that shows you the graciousness of our Creator. Who else but a loving God would begin and sustain such intricate patterns of life?

Creation is the means by which your reason and experience help you understand God's plan for you. But God helps you even more. He reveals himself through Sacred Scripture and Sacred Tradition as well. In Sacred Scripture you see that humanity's history has been filled with times of salvation and grace. In Sacred Tradition you see how people are chosen to celebrate, teach, and serve as God's own family. Just as God named all creation "good," you are continually called in your time to be a co-worker in that same plan for goodness, justice, and peace.

As you experience the gift of creation, you learn that God brought everything into being and that he continues to care deeply for all created things. He provides what is needed for all of creation to grow toward perfection. This is an essential teaching. It affirms that God is neither detached nor distant, but with you always. His loving care for all creation is called *providence*. One response is to care for others as he cares for you.

➔ **Reflect** When have you been most aware of the providence of God in your life?

Catechist's Prayer

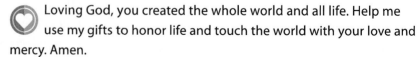 Loving God, you created the whole world and all life. Help me use my gifts to honor life and touch the world with your love and mercy. Amen.

Lesson Plan

Objectives	Process	Materials
Invite, 10 minutes		
God's Providence Page 53	Psalm 32:28 Pray the opening prayer.	Optional Activity Chapter Poem: "God Said, 'It Is Good!'"
	Psalm 33:9, 11–12 Reflect prayerfully on the Word.	
	• Discuss What Do You Wonder questions.	
Discover, 35 minutes		
God's Creation Pages 54–55	• Recall God's amazing plan for creation.	☐ pencils
• Recognize that the first creation account teaches the goodness of all God's creation	Genesis 1:1–31, 2:1–3 Proclaim "The Story of Creation."	☐ kaleidoscopes
	☆ Circle the word *good* in the Scripture story and name what was learned about God from this Scripture story.	
	• Share Your Faith Activity Name ways the world shows God's love and care for creation.	
A Plan of Loving Goodness Pages 56–57	• **Catholic Faith Words** providence, Sacred Scripture, Divine Revelation, Sacred Tradition	☐ pencils
• Define providence as God's loving care for all things; his will and plan for creation	• Recall God's loving care and plan for all creation.	☐ index cards
• Describe Divine Revelation as the way God tells humans about himself and makes his plan known	Jeremiah 1:4–8 Proclaim "The Call of Jeremiah."	
	• Explain that God makes himself known through Divine Revelation—Sacred Scripture and Sacred Tradition.	
• Recall that God reveals himself through Sacred Scripture and the Sacred Tradition of the Church	• Connect Your Faith Activity Define the word *providence*.	
Live, 15 minutes		
Our Catholic Life Pages 58–59	• Identify how to create a prayer space.	☐ pencils
	☆ Add ideas in the spaces provided.	• Optional Activity Caring for Creation
	• People of Faith Learn about Saint Kateri Tekakwitha.	☐ Activity Master 1 (Page 53E)
	• Live Your Faith Activity Design a prayer space.	
Psalm Prayer of Praise Page 60	• Teach gestures for the Psalm refrain.	Download "I Sing the Mighty Power of God."
	▶ Rehearse "I Sing the Mighty Power of God."	
	• Follow the order of prayer.	

Family + Faith Page 61

Point out that the Catholic Families page provides chapter highlights, information on how fourth graders understand faith concepts, and family prayer.

Chapter Review Page 62

 aliveinchrist.osv.com

- Customize and Download Assessments
- Email Links to eAssessments
- Interactive Student Reviews

ONLINE RESOURCES

 Go to **aliveinchrist.osv.com**

You will find:

- Interactive lesson planning with web specific content and additional activities
- Step by step lesson instruction from printed Catechist Edition for integrated lesson planning
- Custom-built assessments to download and eAssessment links
- Interactive reviews that provide scores and the option to review answers
- Sunday readings with background and questions of the week

 Go to **osvparish.com**

You will find:

- Ask the Experts Q and A
- General Catechist Helps
- Community Connections and Blogs

Sharing the Message with Fourth Graders

God's Plan The logical nature of children's thinking at this age leads them to a sensible conclusion about God's creation: If God made everything, then he made everything for a reason. It's helpful to talk with them about the purpose behind created things and especially the idea that they are made for a unique purpose as well.

Teaching Tip: Throughout the year, talk about the wonder of God's plan. As you discuss various created things, talk about the purpose they serve in God's design. Remind the children that they have a God-given purpose as well.

How Fourth Graders Understand

- Provide fourth graders the opportunity to act out or retell Bible stories. This will help them understand what the stories really mean.
- Fourth graders are capable of working in groups or with a partner. Be sure to give them clear directions.
- Fourth graders are creative. Drawing, painting, writing, sculpture, and acting can improve learning.

"I like to create things. Give me activities that let me draw and write."

Chapter Connections

Chapter Poem

Invite

"God Said, 'It Is Good!'"

Use this poem to expand the chapter introduction.

- Children will relate the poem to their own lives, reflecting on God's amazing creation.
- Connect learning about God to creation.

 Go to **aliveinchrist.osv.com** Lesson Planning section for this poem.

NCEA IFG: ACRE Edition

Discover

Knowledge of the Faith

- Objective: To know and understand basic Catholic teaching about the Incarnate Word Jesus Christ as the way, truth, and life

Catholic Social Teaching

Live

 Use one of these features to introduce a principle and engage the children with an activity.

- Life and Dignity of the Human Person, Pages 290–291
- Care for God's Creation, Pages 302–303

Music Options

 Use one or more of the following songs to enhance catechetical learning or for prayer.

- "I Sing the Mighty Power of God," Live Prayer, Page 60
- "For the Fruits of This Creation," Discover, Page 55
- "To You, O God, I Lift My Soul," Live, Page 58

LECTIONARY CONNECTION

 Chapter 1 highlights Lectionary-connected themes such as Sacred Scripture, grace and creation. If your parish aligns its curriculum to the liturgical year, you could use this chapter in connection with the following Sundays.

Year A

The Baptism of the Lord—Baptism, mission

Second Sunday in Ordinary Time—Baptism, Jesus

Year B

First Sunday of Advent—Second Coming, Kingdom of God

First Sunday of Lent—Baptism, covenant, Holy Trinity

Fourth Sunday of Lent—Jesus as Savior, grace

Year C

Fourth Sunday of Advent—Kingdom of God, covenant

Thirty-third Sunday in Ordinary Time—God the Father, Jesus Christ, Good News

Our Lord Jesus Christ, King of the Universe—Kingdom of God, Holy Trinity

Go to **aliveinchrist.osv.com** for a complete correlation ordered by the Sundays of the year and suggestions for how to integrate the Scripture readings into chapter lessons.

Name _____ Date _____

Caring for Creation

Read the statements below. Put a plus sign (+) in front of ways that respect creation.
Put a minus sign (–) in front of ways that destroy or harm creation.

1. _____ You throw garbage from a car window.

2. _____ You write graffiti on your school desk.

3. _____ You recycle aluminum cans.

4. _____ You use household products that will not harm the environment.

5. _____ You save food that is not eaten for another meal.

6. _____ You destroy a bird's nest.

7. _____ You leave lights on as you leave a room.

8. _____ You let the water run when you are not using it.

9. _____ You care for the needs of your pet.

10. _____ You care for the feelings of others.

In each container, write one way
to respect creation.

12.

11.

13.

14.

God's Providence

 Let Us Pray

Leader: Gracious God, we thank you for caring for and
guiding us.

"I will instruct you and show you the way
you should walk,
give you counsel with my eye upon you."
Psalm 32:8

All: God our Father, your great love for us never ends.
We trust that following your plan for us will bring
us happiness and peace. Amen.

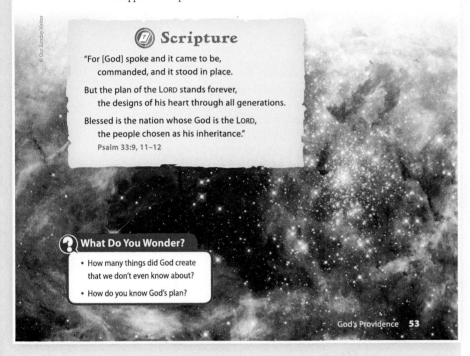

Scripture

"For [God] spoke and it came to be,
commanded, and it stood in place.

But the plan of the LORD stands forever,
the designs of his heart through all generations.

Blessed is the nation whose God is the LORD,
the people chosen as his inheritance."
Psalm 33:9, 11–12

? What Do You Wonder?

- How many things did God create
  that we don't even know about?
- How do you know God's plan?

God's Providence   **53**

Optional Activity

Chapter Poem: "God Said, 'It Is Good!'"   *Verbal/Linguistic*

Use this poem after the opening prayer, before explaining that God
had a plan as he created the world and everything in it.

- Have a volunteer read aloud the poem.
- *Ask:* What do you find most amazing about God's creation?
- Have the children write their own two line stanza for the poem.
- After connecting how we learn about God through creation,
  transition back to the lesson instruction.

  Go to **aliveinchrist.osv.com** for Chapter Poem.

 Let Us Pray

Invite the children to gather in the
prayer space and make the Sign of
the Cross. Invite a child to read
aloud the leader's prayer and Psalm
verse. Prompt the children's
response.

Have the children move out of the
prayer space and back to their seats.

Say: When someone creates
something new they start with a
plan or a design. God had a plan as
he created the world and
everything in it. Let's listen to what
the Bible tells us about God's plan.

Scripture

Guide children through the process
of Scripture reflection.

- Invite them to close their eyes
  and open their minds and hearts
  to what God is saying to them by
  being silent and still.
- Proclaim the Scripture.
- Maintain several moments of
  silence.
- *Ask:* What did you hear God say
  to you today?
- Invite volunteers to share.

What Do You Wonder?

Say: It is hard to imagine how God
could have designed everything in
creation from an acorn to our
human bodies. How powerful and
awesome God is!

Invite the children to respond to the
questions. Ask what else they might
wonder about God's creation and
his plan for them.

Objective

• Recognize that the first creation account teaches the goodness of all God's creation

God's Creation

Ask: What did God say about all that he had made?

• Write the children's responses on the board or on chart paper.

Read aloud the first paragraph.

• Discuss kaleidoscopes. Invite volunteers to explain what a kaleidoscope is. If you brought one in, pass it around for the children to look through.

• *Ask:* How is the world like a kaleidoscope?

• Have the children tell what they know about creation from the Bible.

 Scripture

Explain to the children that there are two accounts of creation in the Bible. You will be reading the first account.

• Invite the children to follow along as you proclaim "The Story of Creation."

☆ Tell the children to circle the word *good* every time it appears in the Scripture story.

God's Creation

What did God say about all that he had made?

The world is something like a kaleidoscope. Its complex patterns and movements give clues to God's amazing plan for creation. This Scripture account teaches us about God and his creation.

Scripture

The Story of Creation

In the beginning, when God created the heavens and the earth, the earth was a formless wasteland. It was completely dark. A mighty wind swept over the waters.

Then God said, "Let there be light," and there was light. He separated the light from the darkness. God called the light "day" and the darkness "night." God saw that it was good. This was the first day.

Then God said, "Let there be a dome in the middle of the waters." God made the dome. It separated the water above from the water below. God called the dome "the sky." God saw that it was good. This was the second day.

Then God said, "Let the water under the sky be gathered into a single basin." The water was gathered into a single basin and dry land appeared. God called the dry land "earth." He called the water "the sea." God saw that it was good.

Then God said, "Let there be plants, and trees of every kind." The earth brought forth every kind of plant and every kind of fruit tree. God saw that it was good. This was the third day.

54   Chapter 1

© Our Sunday Visitor

 Scripture Background

Genesis 1:1–31, 2:1–3

This is the first account of Creation from the Book of Genesis. From it we learn important truths about God, his creation, and humans' role in it.

• We learn of the magnitude of God's love and his desire to create out of nothing so we might share in his glory.

• Humans were created in God's image and likeness, unique from all other creation, to live together in joy and peace with God and one another.

• Humans were given special care and responsibility for all of creation.

Then God said, "Let there be lights in the dome of the sky, to separate day from night." God made two great lights. He made the sun for the day and the moon for the night. Then God made the stars. God saw that it was (good) This was the fourth day.

Then God said, "Let the seas be filled with living creatures and the sky with flying birds." God created all kinds of swimming creatures and all kinds of birds. God saw that it was (good) This was the fifth day.

Then God said, "Let the earth be filled with all kinds of living creatures." God made wild animals, cattle, and all kinds of creeping things. God saw that it was (good) Then God said, "Let there be people, made in my own image and likeness." God created people, a man and a woman. He blessed them and told them to take care of the earth, the seas, and all the plants and living creatures. God looked at everything he made and saw that it was very (good) This was the sixth day.

After God had finished creating the world, he rested. He blessed the seventh day and made it holy.

Based on Genesis 1:1–31, 2:1–3

1. Circle the word *good* every time it appears in the Scripture passage.

2. Tell what you learned about God from this Scripture passage.

© Our Sunday Visitor

Share Your Faith

Reflect On the globe, fill in some of the ways the world shows God's love and care for his creation.

Share Talk about some of these ways with a partner.

PEOPLE
ANIMALS
PLANTS
SEAS

God's Providence **55**

The Story of Creation,
continued

- *Say:* Raise your hand if you have heard this Scripture account before.
- *Ask:* What is one thing you heard in this account today that was new to you?

Invite volunteers to name what God created on each day.

☆ Have the children tell what they learned about God from the Scripture account.

- Emphasize that we learn about God's loving care and generosity from what we see in creation. Remind them that everything that God created is good, especially themselves.

 Music Option: Have children sing "For the Fruits of this Creation," downloaded from **aliveinchrist.osv.com**.

Activity

Read aloud the directions for the Share Your Faith activity.

- Have the children work independently to write their ideas.
- After a short time, have them discuss their responses with a partner.

Quick Review

God's creation is good. His love, care, and generosity can be seen in all that he made.

Objectives

- Define providence as God's loving care for all things; his will and plan for creation
- Describe Divine Revelation as the way God tells humans about himself and makes his plan known
- Recall that God reveals himself through Sacred Scripture and the Sacred Tradition of the Church

A Plan of Loving Goodness

Ask: How does God reveal his plan to us?

- Write the children's responses on the board or on chart paper.

Read aloud the opening paragraph.

Work with Words

Have each child create their own packet of vocabulary index cards.

- Distribute index cards.
- Have the children write the word *providence* on the front of the card and its definition on the back of the card.

Read aloud the second paragraph.

 Scripture

Proclaim "The Call of Jeremiah."

- Ask a volunteer to retell the story.
- Direct children's attention to the picture of Jeremiah. Ask volunteers to share what is happening in the picture.
- Discuss the questions.

A Plan of Loving Goodness

How does God reveal his plan to us?

From the beginning, God has had a loving plan for all creation. As God's plan unfolds, he keeps everyone and everything in his loving care. This is called **providence**. God has a plan for you and for everyone.

Once, long before Jesus was born, there was a young man who lived in the tiny kingdom of Judah, where the nation of Israel is today. His name was Jeremiah, which means "the Lord raises up." Jeremiah was called by God to speak the truth to his people in a time of great danger. They had lost their way and were being invaded by powerful nations. This is how Jeremiah remembered God calling him.

> **Catholic Faith Words**
>
> **providence** God's loving care for all things; God's will and plan for creation

 Scripture

The Call of Jeremiah

The word of the LORD came to me:
Before I formed you in the womb I knew you,
 before you were born I dedicated you,
 a prophet to the nations I appointed you.

"Ah, Lord GOD!" I said,
 "I do not know how to speak. I am too young!"

But the LORD answered me,
 Do not say, "I am too young."

To whomever I send you, you shall go;
 whatever I command you, you shall speak.

Do not be afraid of them,
 for I am with you to deliver you.
 Jeremiah 1:4–8

→ When have you felt that God wanted you to do something or to make a certain choice?
→ How did you know?

© Our Sunday Visitor

56 Chapter 1

 Scripture Background

Jeremiah 1:4–8

The prophets called people back to live by the covenant with God. Their message was ultimately one of hope, reminding people of God's faithfulness.

- Jeremiah prophesied during the destruction of Jerusalem.
- His prophecies included a covenant, written on the hearts of the people, and the rebuilding of Jerusalem.

Jeremiah answered God's call, or command, and followed his plan. The story of Jeremiah is in the Old Testament of the Bible. The Bible, also called **Sacred Scripture**, is God's Word written in human words. There are many more stories in the Old Testament that can show you how others have followed God's plan.

Then, in the New Testament, you can see God's Son, Jesus, answering his Father's call perfectly. Through Jesus, you can learn how you are to respond to God's plan for you. The Holy Spirit, whom Jesus sent to the Church, will help you.

God's Revelation

God has made himself known gradually throughout history by words and deeds and in the experience of people. The way God shares the truth about himself and his plan is called **Divine Revelation**. Revelation is found in Sacred Scripture and in the **Sacred Tradition** of the Church.

Catholic Faith Words

Sacred Scripture another name for the Bible; Sacred Scripture is the inspired Word of God written by humans

Divine Revelation the way God makes himself, and his plan for humans, known to us

Sacred Tradition God's Word to the Church, safeguarded by the Apostles and their successors, the bishops, and handed down verbally—in her creeds, Sacraments, and other teachings—to future generations

Connect Your Faith

Define Providence Explain *providence* in your own words.

God's Providence   **57**

✓ Quick Tip

Vocabulary Cards

Have the children continue building their set of vocabulary cards to use in matching games throughout the year.

- End each lesson with a quick review.
- Frequent practice will help the children articulate their faith.

A Plan of Loving Goodness, *continued*

Ask a volunteer to read aloud the first paragraph on page 57.

- Distribute index cards, and have the children write the term *Sacred Scripture* on the front of the card and its definition on the back of the card.

Ask a volunteer to read the second paragraph aloud.

God's Revelation

Have the children read the paragraph silently.

- Distribute index cards, and have the children make vocabulary cards for the terms *Divine Revelation* and *Sacred Tradition*.
- Discuss the term *Divine Revelation*. Invite the children to tell some of the things they know about God and list these on chart paper.

Activity

- Read the directions for the Connect Your Faith activity to the children.
- Have the children work with a partner.
- When everyone has finished, invite each pair to share their ideas with the rest of the group.

Quick Review

God's loving plan for everyone is called providence. God reveals himself through Sacred Scripture and the Sacred Tradition of the Church.

Our Catholic Life

Ask: Where do you pray?

- Write the children's responses on the board or on chart paper.

Invite a volunteer to read aloud the paragraph.

Make Your Own Prayer Space

Discuss the importance of having a quiet place to pray.

Read the text aloud. Pause occasionally to permit the children to envision their own prayer space.

- You might like to brainstorm places for prayer and Bible stories with the group before asking them to complete the activity on their own.

☆ Invite the children to fill in their ideas in the spaces provided.

- Remind the children that we pray using our own words, traditional prayers of the Church, and sometimes no words at all.

- Refer the children to page 325 in the Our Catholic Tradition reference section in the back of the Student Book for some traditional prayers they may not yet be familiar with.

- *Ask:* Why is it important to have quiet spaces and quiet times?

- Encourage the children to try this exercise at home. Emphasize the importance of praying every day.

 Music Option: Have the children sing "To You, O God, I lift My Soul," downloaded from **aliveinchrist.osv.com**.

Our Catholic Life

Where do you pray?

Prayer is talking and listening to God. It is raising your mind and heart to God. Prayer helps you learn about God's plan for you. Quiet time and a special place make it easier to think and pray. A prayer space is a place you can go to feel close to God.

☆ Add your ideas in the spaces provided.

Make Your Own Prayer Space

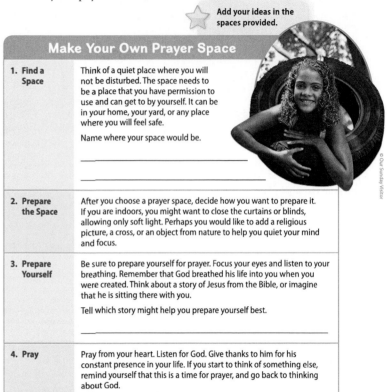

1. Find a Space	Think of a quiet place where you will not be disturbed. The space needs to be a place that you have permission to use and can get to by yourself. It can be in your home, your yard, or any place where you will feel safe. Name where your space would be. _____ _____
2. Prepare the Space	After you choose a prayer space, decide how you want to prepare it. If you are indoors, you might want to close the curtains or blinds, allowing only soft light. Perhaps you would like to add a religious picture, a cross, or an object from nature to help you quiet your mind and focus.
3. Prepare Yourself	Be sure to prepare yourself for prayer. Focus your eyes and listen to your breathing. Remember that God breathed his life into you when you were created. Think about a story of Jesus from the Bible, or imagine that he is sitting there with you. Tell which story might help you prepare yourself best. _____
4. Pray	Pray from your heart. Listen for God. Give thanks to him for his constant presence in your life. If you start to think of something else, remind yourself that this is a time for prayer, and go back to thinking about God.

58 Chapter 1

Optional Activity

Activity Master 1: Caring for Creation

Distribute copies of the activity found on catechist page 53E.

- Tell the children to use what they have learned in this chapter to complete the activity.

- As an alternative, you may wish to send this activity home with the children.

People of Faith

Saint Kateri Tekakwitha, 1656–1680

July 14

Saint Kateri Tekakwitha's father was a Mohawk warrior. Her mother was an Algonquian woman who was Christian. Kateri is the first Native American to be canonized. She learned about Jesus from Jesuit missionaries. Because she lived so close to nature and found God in the natural world, she is the patron of ecology, nature, and the environment. Kateri often spent time praying in the woods, where she would talk to God. She would hear him in her heart and through the wonders of creation. One of her titles is the "Lily of the Mohawks."

Discuss: What in nature reminds you of God?

 Learn more about Saint Kateri at aliveinchrist.osv.com

Live Your Faith

Design a prayer space for your room. What would be important to have in this space?

Identify three things on your sketch.

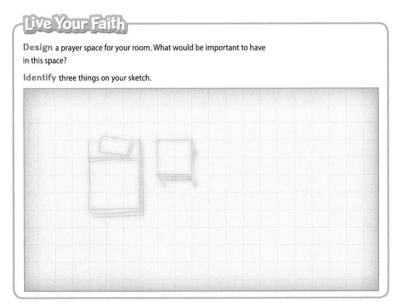

God's Providence **59**

Catholic Social Teaching

Chapter Connections

To integrate Catholic Social Teaching into your lesson, choose one of the following features: Life and Dignity of the Human Person, pages 290–291; or Care for God's Creation, pages 302–303.

- Start the Live step of the process by talking about Saint Kateri Tekakwitha on page 59. Then move directly to the Catholic Social Teaching feature.
- Or, to expand the lesson, complete both pages 58 and 59, then move to the Catholic Social Teachings feature.
- Return to Chapter 1 for the prayer on page 60.

People of Faith

Tell the children about Saint Kateri Tekakwitha.

- Invite a volunteer to read aloud the People of Faith story.
- In October 2012, Saint Kateri Tekakwitha was the first Native American to be canonized. Her favorite devotion was to make crosses out of sticks. She placed the crosses throughout the forest where they served as a reminder for her to pray.
- Invite volunteers to share which things in nature remind them of God.

Encourage the children to go to **aliveinchrist.osv.com** at home to find out more about Saint Kateri Tekakwitha.

Activity

Read aloud and discuss the directions for the Live Your Faith activity as a group.

- Brainstorm what the children might like to include in their prayer space.
- Allow time for the children to complete the activity.
- Invite volunteers to share their drawings.

Live

 Let Us Pray

Psalm Prayer of Praise

Explain to the children that this Psalm prayer, a prayer of praise from the Book of Psalms, praises our loving, compassionate God, who is more than we can ever imagine.

Prepare

Select five readers.

Teach the gestures for the Psalm refrain so that all may pray this portion of the Psalm with words and gestures.

- *The Lord*: Sign language for *Lord* which is the letter *L* with the right thumb and forefinger. Move right hand from the left shoulder and go towards the right hip; it models a sash.
- *is compassionate*: Cross arms over your chest
- *toward all his works*: Uncross arms in an outward gesture

 Rehearse "I Sing the Mighty Power of God," downloaded from **aliveinchrist.osv.com**.

Gather

Lead the children into the prayer space.

Pray

- Follow the order of prayer on the student page.
- *Leader's prayer:* Compassionate God, your care and love for us is overwhelming. Thank you! Help us, too, to be caring, compassionate, and loving in our world.

 Conclude by playing "I Sing the Mighty Power of God."

Live

 Let Us Pray

Psalm Prayer of Praise

This prayer, taken from the Book of Psalms in the Bible, is a prayer of praise. We give praise to our loving and compassionate God, who is more than we can ever imagine.

Gather and begin with the Sign of the Cross.

Leader: Compassionate God, we praise you for your wondrous works, your kindness and love, your marvelous plan for your creation.

Reader 1: The Lord is gracious and compassionate, filled with great kindness and rich in love.

Reader 2: The Lord is good to all and compassionate toward all his works.

All: The Lord is compassionate toward all his works.

Reader 3: Let all your works give you thanks, O Lord, and let your holy People bless you.

Reader 4: The eyes of all look to you and you give them all they need.

All: The Lord is compassionate toward all his works.

Reader 5: The Lord is just in all his ways and loving toward all that he has created.

All: The Lord is compassionate toward all his works. **Based on Psalm 145**

Leader: Let us pray.

 All: Sing "I Sing the Mighty Power of God"

 Liturgy Link

Prayer of Praise

Praise is one of the five forms of Christian prayer. The other four forms of Christian prayer are adoration, petition, intercession and thanksgiving.

- We praise God and give him glory not for what he has done, but simply because he is God.
- Many of the Psalms in the Old Testament are Psalms of praise.

 Go to **aliveinchrist.osv.com** for Sunday readings, Scripture background, questions of the week, and seasonal resources.

FAMILY+FAITH
LIVING AND LEARNING TOGETHER

YOUR CHILD LEARNED >>>
This chapter explains that God reveals himself through Sacred Scripture and the Sacred Tradition of the Church.

Scripture
 Read **Psalm 25:1–2a, 4–5** to find out about God's plan for us.

Catholics Believe
- God loves and cares for all creation and has a plan for the world.
- Everything God wants you to know about him is contained in Scripture and in the Tradition of the Church.

To learn more, go to the *Catechism of the Catholic Church #80–83, 302–308* at **usccb.org.**

People of Faith
This week, your child learned about Saint Kateri Tekakwitha, a patron of ecology and the first Native American to be canonized.

CHILDREN AT THIS AGE >>>
How They Understand God's Plan The logical nature of children's thinking at this age leads them to a sensible conclusion about God's creation: If God made everything, then he made everything for a reason. It's helpful to talk with your child about the purpose behind created things and especially the idea that he or she is made for a unique purpose as well.

CONSIDER THIS >>>
Do you ever wonder about God's plan for you?

You are God's greatest creation because he has created you in his image. He created you with a plan and purpose for your life. As Catholics, we know that "God guides his creation toward its completion or perfection through what we call his *Divine Providence.* This means that God has absolute sovereignty over all that he has made and guides his creation according to the divine plan of his will" (*USCCA, p. 56*).

LET'S TALK >>>
- Ask your child to tell you the Bible account of creation in his or her own words.
- Share a way that God has made himself known to you recently.

LET'S PRAY >>>
O God, help us to learn to know and love you through your creation as Saint Kateri did. Amen.

> For a multimedia glossary of Catholic Faith Words, Sunday readings, seasonal and Saint resources, and chapter activities go to **aliveinchrist.osv.com.**

Chapter 1 Review

(A) Work with Words
Fill in the circle next to the answer that best completes each statement.

1. God's plan for _____ is revealed gradually.
   - ○ the Bible
   - ● creation
   - ○ animals

2. People experience God _____.
   - ● throughout their lives
   - ○ only after death
   - ○ never

3. God's plan for everything that exists _____.
   - ● continues today
   - ○ is finished
   - ○ has not started

4. God's loving care and plan for all creation is called _____.
   - ○ Scripture
   - ○ Tradition
   - ● providence

5. Jesus always _____ God the Father's plan for him.
   - ○ ignored
   - ● followed
   - ○ changed

(B) Check Understanding
Complete the following statements.

6. God's Divine Revelation is found in Sacred Scripture and _____ **Sacred Tradition** _____.

7. _____ **Sacred Scripture** _____ is the inspired Word of God written in human words.

8. _____ **Divine Revelation** _____ is the way God makes himself, and his plan for humans, known to us.

9. Prayer is _____ **talking** _____ and listening to God.

10. _____ **Prayer** _____ involves raising your heart and mind to God.

> Go to **aliveinchrist.osv.com** for an interactive review.

Family + Faith

Distribute the page to the children or parents/adult family members. Point out the chapter highlights, insights on how fourth graders understand concepts, the opportunity for the adults to reflect on their own experience and faith journey, and the family prayer.

Chapter Review

Use Catechist Quick Reviews to highlight lesson concepts.

(A) Work with Words
Direct the children to fill in the circle beside the correct answer.

(B) Check Understanding
Have the children fill in the blanks to complete each statement.

> Go to **aliveinchrist.osv.com** to prepare customized and downloadable assessments, send eAssessments, and assign interactive reviews.

God's Providence   **61–62**

KEY CONCEPT

God's covenant with Abraham reveals that God is always faithful to his People. Sin is present in the world because of human choice.

DOCTRINAL CONTENT

- Death, suffering, ignorance, and the inclination to sin all came into the world as a result of Original Sin. (CCC, 402–405)

- God always remains faithful and promises salvation, desiring humans to be free and faithful to him. (CCC, 55)

- A covenant is a sacred promise or agreement between God and humans. (CCC, 56–58)

- God called Abraham, and because of his belief and trust in God, God established a covenant with him. (CCC, 59–60)

TASKS OF CATECHESIS

Helping children grow in a faith that is "known, celebrated, lived, and expressed in prayer" (NDC, 20).

This chapter focuses on the following tasks of catechesis:

- Promoting Knowledge of the Faith
- Moral Formation

Catechist Background

"This is the covenant I will establish with them after those days, says the Lord: 'I will put my laws in their hearts, and I will write them upon their minds…. Their sins and their evildoing I will remember no more.'" **Hebrews 10:16–17**

→ **Reflect** How does God show that he is faithful to you? Who or what helps you strengthen your faith in God?

The disobedience of Adam and Eve in the Genesis story shows that from the beginning of creation, humans have sometimes chosen to turn away from God. The choice of the first humans resulted in Original Sin, a condition in which all people share; but it also resulted in God's promise to send a redeemer. Today, even though you know the ways in which you have turned away from God, you also know that he is always faithful and always calls you back to himself.

The covenant that God made with Noah and with Abraham and Sarah established a permanent and durable connection between God and his people. This covenant continues through each succeeding generation of the Jewish people, and reached its ultimate fulfillment with the institution of the new covenant in Jesus Christ. His Death, Resurrection, and Ascension forged the sacred relationship between God and his people into one that promises eternal life and happiness. As a result of your Baptism, you too participate in this covenant relationship with God. He, who will never abandon you, continually calls you deeper into relationship with him.

→ **Reflect** When have you experienced the patient faithfulness of God in your life?

Catechist's Prayer

Dear God, thank you for calling me to be a part of a community of faith. With your grace, I can work with you as you build your Kingdom. Amen.

Lesson Plan

Objectives	Process	Materials

⏱ Invite, 10 minutes

God Is Faithful Page 63

- ♡ Psalm 89:2–3 Pray the opening prayer.
- 📖 Hebrews 10:16–17, 23 Reflect prayerfully on the Word.
- Discuss What Do You Wonder questions.

⊛ **Optional Activity**
Chapter Poem:
"A Very Bad Day"

⏱ Discover, 35 minutes

The First Sin Pages 64–65

- Discuss how death, suffering, ignorance, and the inclination to sin all came into the world as a result of Original Sin
- Understand that God always remains faithful and promises salvation, desiring humans to be free and faithful to him

- **Catholic Faith Words** Original Sin, salvation
- 📖 Genesis 3 Proclaim "In the Garden."
- Discuss God's faithfulness to Noah.
- ☆ Underline what happened because of Original Sin.
- **Share Your Faith Activity** Identify examples of the effects of Original Sin in the world and how God wants us to act in those situations.

☐ pencils
- **Optional Activity**
Review the story of Noah

A Sacred Promise Pages 66–67

- Describe a covenant as a sacred promise or agreement between God and humans
- Appreciate that God called Abraham, and because of his belief and trust in God, God established a covenant with him

- **Catholic Faith Words** covenant, faithful
- Introduce God's covenant with Abram.
- 📖 Genesis 12:5–8; 15:1–5, 18; 17:5–9, 15; 21:1–3 Proclaim "Abram's Call and Journey," and "God's Promise."
- Explain God's covenant with Abraham.
- **Connect Your Faith Activity** Name how to show faithfulness to God.

☐ pencils
☐ highlighter markers, 2 for each child
☐ index cards

⏱ Live, 15 minutes

Our Catholic Life Pages 68–69

- Discuss patience when we ask God for help and guidance.
- ☆ Write about a time when you asked God for help.
- **People of Faith** Learn about Saint Bridget of Sweden.
- **Live Your Faith Activity** Circle actions that describe how to follow God's example.

☐ pencils
- **Optional Activity**
Being Faithful
☐ Activity Master 2 (Page 63E)

Covenant Prayer Page 70

- Reflect on how you have been faithful to God.
- ▶ Rehearse "God Keeps His Promises."
- Follow the order of prayer.

⊛ Download "God Keeps His Promises."

Family + Faith Page 71

Point out that the Catholic Families page provides chapter highlights, information on how fourth graders understand faith concepts, and family prayer.

Chapter Review Page 72

⊛ aliveinchrist.osv.com

- Customize and Download Assessments
- Email Links to eAssessments
- Interactive Student Reviews

God Is Faithful **63B**

ONLINE RESOURCES

 Go to **aliveinchrist.osv.com**

You will find:

- Interactive lesson planning with web specific content and additional activities
- Step by step lesson instruction from printed Catechist Edition for integrated lesson planning
- Custom-built assessments to download and eAssessment links
- Interactive reviews that provide scores and the option to review answers
- Sunday readings with background and questions of the week

 Go to **osvparish.com**

You will find:

- Ask the Experts Q and A
- General Catechist Helps
- Community Connections and Blogs

Sharing the Message with Fourth Graders

God's Faithfulness As they grow in social skills and awareness, fourth graders have deeper friendships than younger children. They understand that trust and loyalty are essential to being in relationship with someone else. This provides a natural context in which to learn about God's covenants and his faithfulness in keeping his promises—even when we as human beings do not live up to our commitments to God.

Teaching Tip: As much as possible throughout this year, relate stories from the Old Testament to the fulfillment of God's promises in Jesus Christ.

How Fourth Graders Understand

- Most fourth graders understand that it is important to be a loyal friend and enjoy hearing stories about kids who are loyal to one another.
- Teamwork helps fourth graders learn to work with others. Try some team activities with your group.
- Fourth graders value faithfulness in friends and family. To help them understand the value of being true to others, use examples from their experience, such as supporting a friend who is being teased.

"I am learning how important it is to keep promises. Keep yours to me."

Chapter Connections

Chapter Poem

Invite

"A Very Bad Day"

Use this poem to expand the chapter introduction.

- The children will relate the poem to their own lives, reflecting on how God is always with them even when they are having a very bad day.

 Go to **aliveinchrist.osv.com** Lesson Planning section for this poem.

NCEA IFG: ACRE Edition

Discover

Knowledge of the Faith

- Objective: To know and understand basic Catholic teaching about the Incarnate Word Jesus Christ as the way, truth, and life

Moral Formation

- Objective: To be knowledgeable about the teachings of Jesus and the Church as the basis of Christian morality and to understand Catholic Social Teaching

Catholic Social Teaching

Live

 Use one of these features to introduce a principle and engage the children with an activity.

- Rights and Responsibilities of the Human Person, Pages 294–295
- Solidarity of the Human Family, Pages 300–301

Music Options

 Use one or more of the following songs to enhance catechetical learning or for prayer.

- "God Keeps His Promises," Live Prayer, Page 70
- "Holy God, We Praise Thy Name," Invite, Page 63
- "God of Abraham," Discover, Page 67

LECTIONARY CONNECTION

 Chapter 2 highlights Lectionary-connected themes such as covenant, trust in God, and Baptism. If your parish aligns its curriculum to the liturgical year, you could use this chapter in connection with the following Sundays.

Year A

The Holy Family of Jesus, Mary, and Joseph—God's faithfulness, Original Sin, covenant

The Baptism of the Lord—Baptism, covenant

Second Sunday of Lent—God's faithfulness, grace

Year B

Fourth Sunday of Advent—covenant, trusting God

First Sunday of Lent—Baptism, covenant

Second Sunday of Lent—trusting God, covenant

Year C

First Sunday of Advent—God's plan, Jesus' Second Coming

Second Sunday of Lent—covenant, Abraham

Go to **aliveinchrist.osv.com** for a complete correlation ordered by the Sundays of the year and suggestions for how to integrate the Scripture readings into chapter lessons.

God Is Faithful **63D**

Name _____ Date _____

Being Faithful

Read each statement. If the sentence tells of faithfulness, color the letter that has the sentence number beneath it. The colored letters will reveal a secret message.

1. Eve chose to disobey God.

2. God continues to love our first parents, called Adam and Eve.

3. Abram offers thanksgiving to the Lord.

4. God promises Abram the land of Canaan.

5. God promises Abraham and Sarah many descendants.

6. You make fun of someone.

7. God continues to love humans.

8. You remember to pray.

9. You spread a rumor about another person.

10. God creates a beautiful world.

11. You go out of your way to help others.

12. You disobey your parents.

God Is Faithful

 Let Us Pray

Leader: Lord of all faithfulness, gather us as your people and keep us close to your heart.

"I will sing of your mercy forever, LORD
proclaim your faithfulness through all ages.
For I said, 'My mercy is established forever;
my faithfulness will stand as long as the
heavens.'" Psalm 89:2–3

All: Faithful God, thank you for making us your own. Thank you for believing in us. Thank you for giving us faith. Amen.

 Scripture

"This is the covenant I will establish with
them after those days, says the Lord:

'I will put my laws in their hearts,
and I will write them upon their minds. . . .
Their sins and their evildoing I will remember no more.'

Let us hold unwaveringly to our confession that gives us hope, for he who made the promise is trustworthy."
Hebrews 10:16–17, 23

 What Do You Wonder?

- How did God show his faithfulness to the first humans?
- Who or what helps you strengthen your faith in God?

© Our Sunday Visitor

God Is Faithful **63**

Optional Activity

Chapter Poem: "A Very Bad Day" *Interpersonal*

Use this poem after the opening prayer, before explaining that God always loves us.

- Ask volunteers to share experiences of having a bad day.
- Read aloud "A Very Bad Day."
- Remind the group that God is always faithful even when we are having a bad day.
- Transition back to the lesson instruction.

 Go to **aliveinchrist.osv.com** for Chapter Poem.

 Let Us Pray

Invite the children to gather in the prayer space and make the Sign of the Cross. Have a volunteer pray aloud the leader prayer and Psalm verse. Prompt the group's response.

▶ Music Option: Have the children sing "Holy God, We Praise Thy Name," downloaded from **aliveinchrist.osv.com**.

Explain that God always loves us.

Say: God is forever faithful. Even if our belief in God wavers, he continues to believe in us.

Have the children move out of the prayer space and back to their seats.

Scripture

Guide the children through the process of Scripture reflection.

- Invite them to close their eyes and open their minds and hearts to what God is saying to them by being silent and still.
- Proclaim the Scripture.
- Maintain several moments of silence.
- *Ask:* What did you hear God say to you today?
- Invite volunteers to share.

What Do You Wonder?

Say: Faith is a gift, a heartfelt gift from a faithful God. It is a gift not only to appreciate but to practice. It is a treasure to be cherished and shared.

Invite the children to respond to the questions. Ask what else they might wonder about God's faithfulness.

Objectives

- Discuss how death, suffering, ignorance, and the inclination to sin all came into the world as a result of Original Sin

- Understand that God always remains faithful and promises salvation, desiring humans to be free and faithful to him

The First Sin

Ask: How did Adam and Eve's choice affect all of us?

- Write the children's responses on the board or chart paper.

Direct the children's attention to the stained glass window.

- Invite a volunteer to read the caption aloud.

Tell the children that the Bible begins with the Book of Genesis. This book introduces Adam and Eve.

Invite a volunteer to read aloud the paragraph.

Refer the children to page 304 in the Our Catholic Tradition reference section in the back of the Student Book for more on the Pentateuch.

Scripture

Proclaim "In the Garden."

- Stress that Adam and Eve are responsible for their actions.
- *Ask:* How did life change for Adam and Eve after they sinned? They felt ashamed; everything got harder; they had to leave the garden; they had to work; jealousy, sadness, and fighting entered the world.

64 Chapter 2

In the biblical Creation accounts, we learn about our first parents, known as Adam and Eve.

The First Sin

How did Adam and Eve's choice affect all of us?

For Adam and Eve, there was a time when every day was a good day. But one day, Satan, a fallen angel who was God's enemy, came to Eve in the form of a snake and tempted her. We learn from the Book of Genesis what Adam and Eve did. Genesis is the first book of the Bible. Together, the first five books of the Bible are called the Pentateuch. The five books are: Genesis, Exodus, Leviticus, Numbers, and Deuteronomy.

 Catholic Faith Words

Original Sin the sin of our first parents, Adam and Eve, which led to the sinful condition of the human race from its beginning

salvation the loving action of God's forgiveness of sins and the restoration of friendship with him brought by Jesus

Scripture

In the Garden

In the Garden of Eden was one special tree that God told Adam and Eve not to touch. But Satan convinced Eve that if she and Adam ate the fruit of that tree, they could be more like God. Adam and Eve did as Satan said; but after they sinned, they felt ashamed. They learned how it felt to do something wrong.

Everything got harder for Adam and Eve. God sent them away from the garden. They had to work to find food and shelter. From then on, jealousy, sadness, and fighting were in the world. **Based on Genesis 3**

64 Chapter 2

Scripture Background

Genesis 3

The creation story conveys important religious truths rather than historical events.

- The story of our first parents, Adam and Eve, shows how sin affects relationships with God.
- Biblical accounts emphasize that it was humans' choice, not God's, that changed humanity's initial relationship with God.
- God has always demonstrated an intimate and loving care for creation.

Consequences

Humans were created to share God's life and to be happy with God forever. By disobeying God, Adam and Eve broke their friendship with God. This sin of our first parents is called **Original Sin** because ever since that choice was made, sin has been present throughout the world. Original Sin affects every human. The inclination to sin, suffering, and death all came into the world as a result of Original Sin.

Even though God sent Adam and Eve away from the garden, he did not abandon them. He remained faithful and promised **salvation**. He wanted all humans to be free and faithful to him, so they could be happy forever.

The Book of Genesis then tells another important story, the story of Noah. The point of Noah's story is that even when people continued to sin and to disobey God, God was faithful.

 Underline what happened because of Original Sin.

Share Your Faith

Reflect Find some stories in the news that are examples of the effects of Original Sin in the world today.

Share In a small group, talk about ways that people can act as God wants them to in these situations.

Optional Activity

Noah *Musical*

Spend time reviewing the story of Noah with the children.

- Emphasize that the flood was a consequence of human sin and that the rainbow was a symbol of God's faithful promise.
- Ask the children to write a song about Noah to the tune of a popular song or simple children's song.

Consequences

Read aloud the first and second paragraphs.

 Point out the gold star direction. Have a volunteer read aloud the direction. Give the children a minute to complete the activity, and then encourage the children to share their responses.

Invite a volunteer to read aloud the last paragraph.

- Ask a volunteer to tell the story of Noah. Fill in any missing details.
- Discuss how God was faithful to Noah.

Work with Words

- Have each child make vocabulary cards for the terms *Original Sin* and *salvation*.

Activity

Read aloud the direction for the Share Your Faith activity.

- Distribute newspaper clippings on various topics.
- Have the children work in small groups to choose articles that provide examples of the effects of Original Sin in the world. Then have the groups complete the activity.
- Display the articles on poster board.

Quick Review

God is always faithful, even when humans disobey. God made humans to be free to make choices and to experience faith and true happiness.

Objectives

- Describe a covenant as a sacred promise or agreement between God and humans
- Appreciate that God called Abraham, and because of his belief and trust in God, God established a covenant with him

A Sacred Promise

Ask: What did God ask of and promise to Abram?

- Write the children's responses on the board or on chart paper.

Tell the children that they are now going to explore the story of Abram.

- Read the definition for the Catholic Faith Word *covenant*.
- Explain that God made a covenant with Abram.

 Scripture

Distribute highlighters of different colors.

- Ask the group to read silently.
- Have the children highlight the words of Abram with one color and the words of God in another.

Tell the children that Abram built altars of thanksgiving to maintain his relationship with God through trying times.

Have the children work in groups of three.

- Give each group a sheet of paper and ask them to draw three or four large stars.
- Inside each star have them write one thing that they believe God wants for them.

66 Chapter 2

Discover

A Sacred Promise

What did God ask of and promise to Abram?

After a long time, God called a man named Abram to help humans remain faithful.

 Scripture

Abram's Call and Journey

The LORD called Abram, promising to bless him and make of him a great nation. Abram took his wife, Sarai, his brother's son Lot, and their possessions on the long journey to the new land as God directed.

Abram and his family were never alone on their difficult journey. They knew that God was always with them. Every time Abram reached a stop on the journey, he built an altar of thanksgiving to the LORD. **Based on Genesis 12:1–8**

© Our Sunday Visitor

God's Promise

Many years later, after Abram had settled in the land of Canaan, the LORD spoke again to him, saying, "Don't be afraid! I will protect and reward you."

Abram replied, "LORD, you have given me everything I could ask for, except children."

The LORD told Abram, "Look at the sky and count the stars. That is how many descendants you will have."

God spoke to Abram again. God made a covenant with Abram and his descendants for all time. God told Abram, "To your descendants I give this land . . . I am making you the father of a multitude of nations." The land of Canaan would belong to Abram and his descendants forever, and these people would be God's people.

Based on Genesis 15:1–5, 18; 17:5–9, 15; 21:1–3

66 Chapter 2

 Songs of Scripture

Abraham

God's call to Abraham includes the command to move to a new land.

- Discuss the last verse of the song and ask the children how they can listen for God's voice in their lives today.
- The rhythm of this song invites movement. Let the children make up some simple gestures.
- Invite the children to stand and do the gestures with the song.

 Use *Songs of Scripture*, Grades 4–6 CD, Track 5

God's Covenant with Abraham

God revealed his plan to Abram in a new way by making a **covenant**, or sacred promise or agreement, with him. As a sign of the covenant, God changed the names of Abram and Sarai to Abraham and Sarah. Soon after that, even though Sarah was old, she had a son, whom the couple named Isaac.

Abraham and Sarah never turned away from God. Like Abraham and Sarah, you are **faithful** to God every time you obey his laws and make loving choices.

Abraham is considered an ancestor in faith of Christianity, Judaism, and Islam. These religions see their origins in Abraham's free response to God's revelation that he was the one God Abraham should believe in and follow.

> **Catholic Faith Words**
>
> **covenant** a sacred promise or agreement between God and humans
>
> **faithful** to be constant and loyal in your commitments to God and others, just as he is faithful to you

In prayer before the Blessed Sacrament, we are in the presence of Christ, who remained faithful to God the Father and fulfilled the covenant.

Connect Your Faith

Show Faith Write your first name in colorful letters below. Around your name, write words that tell how you show that you are faithful to God.

✓ Quick Tip

Keep Promises

By seeing that God keeps promises, humans learn how to keep promises. God's covenant with Abraham is a model.

- Point out that promises are special pledges people make to one another.
- Discuss how people feel about broken promises.
- Remind the children to make only those promises that they will be able to keep.

God's Covenant with Abraham

Read the first two paragraphs.

- Emphasize that God made and kept promises.
- *Ask:* How were Abraham and Sarah faithful to God? Possible responses: They trusted God and his promises; they obeyed his laws; they made loving choices; they followed his call.

Tell the children that Abraham and Sarah's story is important to people of many faiths. Have them read the last paragraph to learn why.

Work with Words

Introduce the Catholic Faith Words *covenant* and *faithful* and have the children make a vocabulary cards.

- Refer the children to page 305 in the Our Catholic Tradition reference section to read about covenant.

Direct the children's attention to the photo. Invite a volunteer to read the caption aloud. Then emphasize Christ's faithfulness.

 Music Option: Have the children sing "God of Abraham," downloaded from **aliveinchrist.osv.com**.

Activity

Read aloud the directions for the Connect Your Faith activity.

Quick Review

God made a covenant with Abraham. He promised Abraham that his descendants would be God's people forever.

Our Catholic Life

Ask: How do you remain faithful?

- Write the children's responses on the board or chart paper.

Read the opening paragraph aloud.

- *Ask:* What helps you trust that God will answer your prayers?

Have volunteers read aloud the next two paragraphs.

- Emphasize the importance of being faithful in prayer. God does answer our prayers. However, the answer might not come as quickly as we would like or the answer may not be what we had expected.

Jessica's Story

Read the story aloud.

- *Ask:* How did God help Jessica?
- *Say:* There is a saying, "God helps those who help themselves."
- *Ask:* What do you think this saying means?
- *Ask:* Do you agree?

Your Story

- ⭐ Point out the activity directions to the children.
- Encourage the children to write about their own experience.
- Remind the children that God gives us everything we need to live and be happy.

Our Catholic Life

How do you remain faithful?

Often we ask God for help and guidance. Sometimes his help does not come as quickly as we would like. Or it may not be the help we expect. It may be difficult to be faithful. But, we continue to pray and trust that God will give us the help we need to get through whatever we face.

Abraham and Sarah prayed and waited for many years before they had their first child. They were shocked to learn they would have a child so late in life. But, their son, Isaac, arrived according to the timing of God's plan.

At times, God's answer is not easy to see. Many times when you ask for his help, God gives you the ability to help yourself. Jessica learns this in the following situation.

⭐ Write about a time when you asked God for help and later realized that he had given you what you needed to help yourself.

Jessica's story

Jessica wanted the video game she saw at the store. She prayed, asking God for the game. She continued to pray for several weeks, but still she did not get the game. One day her neighbor offered Jessica $5 to water his plants while he was out of town. Another neighbor asked Jessica to walk her dog. At the end of the week, Jessica had $10. She realized that she could save her money for the game. With her parents' permission, Jessica started asking neighbors whether they had odd jobs for her to do. After two months, Jessica had enough money to buy the video game.

Your story

_____
_____
_____
_____
_____
_____
_____
_____
_____
_____
_____

68

© Our Sunday Visitor

Optional Activity

Activity Master 2: Being Faithful

Distribute copies of the activity found on catechist page 63E.

- The children should use what they have learned in this chapter to complete the activity.
- As an alternative, you may wish to send this activity home with the children.

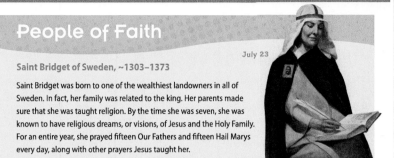

People of Faith

Saint Bridget of Sweden, ~1303–1373

July 23

Saint Bridget was born to one of the wealthiest landowners in all of Sweden. In fact, her family was related to the king. Her parents made sure that she was taught religion. By the time she was seven, she was known to have religious dreams, or visions, of Jesus and the Holy Family. For an entire year, she prayed fifteen Our Fathers and fifteen Hail Marys every day, along with other prayers Jesus taught her.

Discuss: Tell about a time when you waited for God to answer a prayer.

 Learn more about Saint Bridget at **aliveinchrist.osv.com**

Live Your Faith

Circle the actions below that describe how you can follow God's example, being loyal and trustworthy to friends, family, and most especially God.

being friendly

helping in class

lying

telling the truth

sharing possessions

stealing

God Is Faithful **69**

 ## Catholic Social Teaching

Chapter Connections

To integrate Catholic Social Teaching into your lesson, choose one of the following features: Rights and Responsibilities of the Human Person, pages 294–295; or Solidarity of the Human Family, pages 300–301.

- Start the Live step of the process by talking about Saint Bridget of Sweden on page 69. Then move directly to the Catholic Social Teaching feature.
- Or, to expand the lesson, complete both pages 68 and 69, then move to the Catholic Social Teaching feature.
- Return to Chapter 2 for the prayer on page 70.

People of Faith

Tell the children about Saint Bridget of Sweden.

- Invite a volunteer to read aloud the People of Faith story.
- Explain that Saint Bridget lived about 700 years ago. Unlike many Saints, she was married and had eight children. One of her daughters also became a Saint, Saint Catherine of Sweden.
- Saint Bridget of Sweden is the patron Saint of Sweden. Some call her the patron Saint of failures because practically nothing she ever set out to do was ever realized. Yet she was the only woman to found a religious order.
- Invite volunteers to tell about a time when they waited for God to answer a prayer.

 Encourage the children to go to **aliveinchrist.osv.com** at home to find out more about Saint Bridget of Sweden.

Activity

Read aloud the directions for the Live Your Faith activity.

- Allow time for the children to complete the activity.
- Invite volunteers to share their answers.

Let Us Pray

Covenant Prayer

Explain to the children that this prayer recalls and promises some of the ways we are faithful to our loving God.

Prepare

Have the children think of one way they have been faithful to God this week. Explain that they will share this during the prayer.

 While the children are reflecting, play "God Keeps His Promises," downloaded from **aliveinchrist.osv.com**.

Gather

Lead the children into the prayer space. Have each child bring their book.

- Invite the children to be seated and prepare their minds and hearts for prayer.

Pray

Follow the order of prayer on the student page.

- Begin by leading the children in the Sign of the Cross.
- Invite the children to name one way that they have been faithful to God this week. After each person speaks, invite the group to respond, "God Ever Faithful, we are your covenant People."

 Conclude by singing with the children "God Keeps His Promises."

Live

 Let Us Pray

Covenant Prayer

This covenant prayer recalls and promises some of the ways we are faithful to our loving God.

Gather and begin with the Sign of the Cross.

Leader: God Ever Faithful, we gather, aware of your constant faithfulness to us.

All: Thank you for your gift of faithfulness, O God. Help us to trust in you. We are your covenant People.

Name ways you have made loving choices and been faithful. Then respond:

God Ever Faithful, we are your covenant People.

Leader: Let us pray.

 All: Sing "God Keeps His Promises"
God keeps his promises.
God keeps his promises
God keeps his promises to us
God keeps his promises
God keeps his promises
Every word he says you can trust!
© 2010, Chet A. Chambers. Published by Our Sunday Visitor, Inc.

 Liturgy Link

Thanksgiving

Thanksgiving is one of the five types of prayer, which are adoration, petition, intercession, praise, and thanksgiving. The letters of Saint Paul often begin and end with thanksgiving.

- "Give thanks in all circumstances" (1 Thess 5:18).
- "Persevere in payer, being watchful in it with thanksgiving (Col 4:2).

 Go to **aliveinchrist.osv.com** for Sunday readings, Scripture background, questions of the week, and seasonal resources.

FAMILY+FAITH
LIVING AND LEARNING TOGETHER

YOUR CHILD LEARNED >>>
This chapter explains Original Sin, its consequences, and how God loves us despite our choices to act against his plan for our happiness and salvation.

Scripture
 Read Hebrews 10:16–17, 23 to find out about God's promises of love.

Catholics Believe
• God's covenant with Abraham reveals that God is always faithful to his People.
• Sin is present in the world because of human choice.
To learn more, go to the *Catechism of the Catholic Church #59–61, 385–389* at **usccb.org.**

People of Faith
This week, your child learned about Saint Bridget of Sweden. She is known for her faithfulness in prayer.

CHILDREN AT THIS AGE >>>
How They Understand God's Faithfulness As he or she grows in social skills and awareness, your child has deeper friendships than before. Your child understands that trust and loyalty are essential to being in relationship with someone else. This provides a natural context in which to learn about God's covenants and his faithfulness in keeping his promises—even when we as human beings do not always live up to our commitments to God.

CONSIDER THIS >>>
How can making good choices make you happy?

God created us to live in happiness with him forever. When we sin, we turn away from God and our relationship with him. As Catholics, we realize that "though venial sin does not completely destroy the love we need for eternal happiness, it weakens that love and impedes our progress in the practice of virtue and the moral good. Thus, over time, it can have serious consequences" (*USCCA, p. 313*).

LET'S TALK >>>
• Ask your child to tell you about God's covenant with his People and why it was needed.
• Talk with each other about what it means to be trustworthy and loyal to God and one another.

LET'S PRAY >>>
Dear God, help us to pray faithfully to you like Saint Bridget did. Amen.

For a multimedia glossary of Catholic Faith Words, Sunday readings, seasonal and Saint resources, and chapter activities go to **aliveinchrist.osv.com.**

Family + Faith

Distribute the page to the children or parents/adult family members. Point out the chapter highlights, insights on how fourth graders understand concepts, the opportunity for the adults to reflect on their own experience and faith journey, and the family prayer.

Chapter 2 Review

A Work with Words Complete each sentence with the correct word from the Word Bank.

Word Bank
- faithful
- sin
- covenant
- names
- friendship

1. By disobeying God, Adam and Eve broke their __friendship__ with him.

2. One consequence of the disobedience of Adam and Eve is the inclination to ____sin____.

3. God always remains ___faithful___ to his People.

4. God made a ___covenant___ with Abraham and his descendants.

5. As a sign of the covenant, God changed the ___names___ of Abram and Sarai.

B Check Understanding Fill in the circle of the choice that best completes each sentence.

6. God created humans to be _____ with him forever.
   - ● happy
   - ○ confused
   - ○ out of relationship

7. _____ is the child of Abraham and Sarah.
   - ○ Adam
   - ● Isaac
   - ○ Eve

8. The choice of our first parents, Adam and Eve, to disobey God is called _____ .
   - ● Original Sin
   - ○ Original Temptation
   - ○ Original Suffering

9. _____ is the loving action of God's forgiveness of sins and the restoration of friendship with God through Jesus.
   - ○ Happiness
   - ○ Honesty
   - ● Salvation

10. Abraham is an _____ in faith.
   - ○ author
   - ● ancestor
   - ○ official

 Go to **aliveinchrist.osv.com** for an interactive review.

© Our Sunday Visitor

Chapter Review

Use Catechist Quick Reviews to highlight lesson concepts.

A Work with Words
Review the Word Bank with the children. Direct the children to use the words from the Word Bank to complete each statement.

B Check Understanding
Direct the children to fill in the circle beside the correct answer.

Go to **aliveinchrist.osv.com** to prepare customized and downloadable assessments, send eAssessments, and assign interactive reviews.

KEY CONCEPT

God gave you the Ten Commandments to help you be faithful to him and his covenant. The Commandments tell you ways to love God and others.

DOCTRINAL CONTENT

- God created people to be free and live as his People, and he called Moses to lead his People from slavery in Egypt. (CCC, 2057)

- The Ten Commandments are a summary of laws that God gave Moses on Mount Sinai that tell us what is necessary in order to love God and others. (CCC, 2061)

- God gave the Ten Commandments to help us be faithful to him and his covenant. (CCC, 2062–2063)

TASKS OF CATECHESIS

Helping children grow in a faith that is "known, celebrated, lived, and expressed in prayer" (NDC, 20).

This chapter focuses on the following tasks of catechesis

- Promoting Knowledge of the Faith

- Moral Formation

Catechist Background

God called out from the bush: Moses! Moses! He answered, "Here I am." God said: Do not come near! Remove the sandals from your feet, for the place where you stand is holy ground. Exodus 3:4–5

→ **Reflect** How does God speak to you? How do the Ten Commandments help you to know what God wants for you?

In the Ten Commandments, the struggling Israelites were presented with the simple wisdom of God's will for them. For the Israelites, the keeping of the Commandments made the difference between life in a new land and death in the desert.

Today the simplicity of the Ten Commandments speaks to you clearly. If you respect the lives and property of others, you live in peace. If you honor your body and promote human dignity, you open yourself to love and respect. If you honor and thank your God, your mission and priorities fall into place. Sin can enslave you and restrict your access to these good things. Faithfulness to the Ten Commandments—through incorporation into the Paschal Mystery through the Seven Sacraments—releases you from the bondage of sin.

Throughout their history the Israelites were sustained by the covenant they made with the one true God. They tried to be faithful to his Commandments. Jesus, however, perfectly fulfilled and built upon the Law of Moses. The Mosaic Law led directly to the new law of Jesus— the Great Commandment of love.

→ **Reflect** When and how have you experienced the freedom of living one of the Commandments?

Catechist's Prayer

 Lord of love, free my heart from prejudice and lack of concern. Help me teach love for you and others through my actions. Amen.

Lesson Plan

Objectives	Process	Materials

🕐 Invite, 10 minutes

God's Commandments Page 73

🔵 Psalm 40:9 Pray the opening prayer.

📖 Exodus 3:2b, 4–5 Reflect prayerfully on the Word.

• Discuss What Do You Wonder questions.

🎧 **Optional Activity**
Chapter Story: "Monkey Bars"

🕐 Discover, 35 minutes

From Slavery to Freedom
Pages 74–75

• Understand that God created people to be free and live as his People, and he called Moses to lead his People from slavery in Egypt

• Recall that God created humans to be free.

📖 Genesis 37:1–4, 42:6–8, 44:1–12, 45:4–5 Proclaim "Joseph and His Brothers."

• Explain how the choices of Joseph's brothers affected Joseph and his family.

📖 Exodus 2:1–10, 14:10–31, 15:19–21 Proclaim "The Exodus from Egypt."

• **Share Your Faith Activity** Reflect on and discuss the effects of forgiveness.

☐ pencils

Laws to Guide Us Pages 76–77

• Identify the Ten Commandments as the summary of laws that God gave Moses on Mount Sinai

• Explain that God gave the Ten Commandments to help us be faithful to him and his covenant

• **Catholic Faith Words** Ten Commandments, ark of the covenant

• Identify how to apply the Ten Commandments to everyday life.

☆ Underline why God gave people the Ten Commandments.

• **Connect Your Faith Activity** Identify how you have followed the Ten Commandments.

☐ pencils
☐ index cards
• **Optional Activity**
The Ten Commandments
☐ Activity Master 3 (Page 73E)

🕐 Live, 15 minutes

Our Catholic Life Pages 78–79

• Review the Ten Commandments

☆ Identify which Commandment each action relates to.

• **People of Faith** Learn about Saint Raymond of Peñafort.

• **Live Your Faith Activity** Apply the Ten Commandments to scenarios.

☐ pencils

Psalm Prayer of Praise Page 80

• Select four readers.

▶ Rehearse "My Ten Commandments."

• Follow the order of the prayer.

🎧 Download "My Ten Commandments."

Family + Faith Page 81

Point out that the Catholic Families page provides chapter highlights, information on how fourth graders understand faith concepts, and family prayer.

Chapter Review Page 82

🎧 aliveinchrist.osv.com

• Customize and Download Assessments
• Email Links to eAssessments
• Interactive Student Reviews

ONLINE RESOURCES

 Go to **aliveinchrist.osv.com**

You will find:

- Interactive lesson planning with web specific content and additional activities
- Step by step lesson instruction from printed Catechist Edition for integrated lesson planning
- Custom-built assessments to download and eAssessment links
- Interactive reviews that provide scores and the option to review answers
- Sunday readings with background and questions of the week

 Go to **osvparish.com**

You will find:

- Ask the Experts Q and A
- General Catechist Helps
- Community Connections and Blogs

Sharing the Message with Fourth Graders

The Ten Commandments Fourth graders are practical, concrete thinkers, but they are beginning to understand that morality involves more than what people see on the outside. Commandments of the heart such as "You shall not covet" are beginning to make sense as children this age internalize what they are learning about living the Christian life. In this process, conscience formation and character-building is reaching a new level.

Teaching Tip: When possible, talk about how the things in our heart express themselves in our actions. Discuss ways to cultivate God's love in our hearts so we desire to do his will.

How Fourth Graders Understand

- Most fourth graders like to hear stories about the heroes of the Bible, such as Joseph or Moses. Share these stories in a variety of ways.
- Many fourth graders are good at and like memorizing. Encourage them to memorize the Ten Commandments. Use games to help them.
- Most fourth graders have developed respect for authority and rules, and they understand that rules protect people for the betterment of everyone.

"Help me understand why rules are important. Let me help you make the rules for our group."

Chapter Connections

Chapter Story

"Monkey Bars"

Use this story to expand the chapter introduction.

- The children will relate the story to their own lives, reflecting on the importance of school rules.

 Go to **aliveinchrist.osv.com** Lesson Planning section for this story.

NCEA IFG: ACRE Edition *Discover*

Knowledge of the Faith

- Objective: To know and understand basic Catholic teaching about the Incarnate Word Jesus Christ as the way, truth, and life

Moral Formation

- Objective: To be knowledgeable about the teachings of Jesus and the Church as the basis of Christian morality and to understand Catholic Social Teaching

Catholic Social Teaching *Live*

 Use one of these features to introduce a principle and engage the children with an activity.

- Call to Family, Community, and Participation, Pages 292–293
- Rights and Responsibilities of the Human Person, Pages 294–295

Music Options

 Use one or more of the following songs to enhance catechetical learning or for prayer.

- "My Ten Commandments," Live Prayer, Page 80
- "Go Down, Moses," Discover, Page 75
- "Moses, Set Them Free," Discover, Page 75
- "God's Good Rules," Discover, Page 77

LECTIONARY CONNECTION

Chapter 3 highlights Lectionary-connected themes such as the Ten Commandments, sin and freedom. If your parish aligns its curriculum to the liturgical year, you could use this chapter in connection with the following Sundays.

Year A

Fourth Sunday of Lent—social sin, freedom

Third Sunday of Easter—faith, trust in God

Twenty-ninth Sunday in Ordinary Time—First Commandment, stewardship

Year B

Second Sunday of Advent—sin, freedom

Third Sunday of Lent—Ten Commandments, God's will

Thirty-first Sunday in Ordinary Time—Ten Commandments, Great Commandment

Year C

Fourth Sunday of Easter— covenant, the Great Commandment

Twenty-fifth Sunday in Ordinary Time—Ten Commandments, love of others

 Go to **aliveinchrist.osv.com** for a complete correlation ordered by the Sundays of the year and suggestions for how to integrate the Scripture readings into chapter lessons.

Name _____ Date _____

The Ten Commandments

On the lines to the right, unscramble the words to complete the Ten Commandments.

1. I am the Lord your God. You shall not have **egasrtn dsog** before me.

   _____   _____

2. You shall not **etka** the name of the Lord your God in **aniv**.

   _____   _____

3. **memReerb** to keep **ylho** the Lord's day.

   _____   _____

4. Honor your **fteahr** and your **tomhre**.

   _____   _____

5. You **llhsa** not **ikll**.

   _____   _____

6. You shall not **mocmit adtrulye**.

   _____   _____

7. You **halls** not **lstae**.

   _____   _____

8. You shall not bear **flsae tiwnses** against your neighbor.

   _____   _____

9. You shall not **vocet** your neighbor's **weif**.

   _____   _____

10. You shall not **cotve** your neighbor's **gdoos**.

    _____   _____

God's Commandments

 Let Us Pray

Leader: Loving Father, you made us to know you and your desire for us.

"I delight to do your will, my God;
your law is in my inner being!"   Psalm 40:9

All: O God, help us to learn how to listen for your voice so that we will know how to follow you. Amen.

 Scripture

"When [Moses] looked, although the bush was on fire, it was not being consumed.... When the LORD saw that he had turned aside to look, God called out to him from the bush: Moses! Moses! He answered, 'Here I am.' God said: Do not come near! Remove your sandals from your feet, for the place where you stand is holy ground."   Exodus 3:4–5

What Do You Wonder?

• How does God speak to people today?

• How do the Ten Commandments help you to know God and what he wants for you?

God's Commandments   **73**

Optional Activity

Chapter Story: "Monkey Bars"   *Interpersonal*

Use this story after the opening prayer, before explaining that Moses was a great person of faith.

• Invite volunteers to share the rules they need to follow at school.

• *Ask:* What do you think Michelle did at recess that day?

• *Ask:* Why are rules important?

• After explaining that God gives us rules to help us live together and follow him, transition back to the lesson instruction.

 Go to **aliveinchrist.osv.com** for Chapter Story.

 Invite

 Let Us Pray

Invite the children to gather in the prayer space and make the Sign of the Cross. Begin with the leader's prayer and have a volunteer pray aloud the Psalm verse from a Bible. Prompt the group's response.

Have the children move out of the prayer space and back to their seats.

Say: God wanted Moses to lead his People, who were slaves, to freedom. The Word of God we will hear is part of Moses' journey of faith.

 Scripture

Guide the children through the process of Scripture reflection.

• Invite them to close their eyes and open their minds and hearts to what God is saying to them by being silent and still.

• Proclaim the Scripture.

• Maintain several moments of silence.

• *Ask:* What did you hear God say to you today?

• Invite volunteers to share.

What Do You Wonder?

Say: Moses was like a shepherd taking care of his sheep when he noticed the burning bush. He paid attention to hear God and know what God wanted him to do. God gave Moses the Ten Commandments so that his People would know how to live.

Invite the children to respond to the questions. Ask what else they might wonder about how God speaks to us today and them directly.

Objective

- Understand that God created people to be free and live as his People, and he called Moses to lead his People from slavery in Egypt

From Slavery to Freedom

Ask: How does God give his People freedom?

- Write the children's responses on the board or on chart paper.

Read aloud the introduction to the Scripture story.

- Review with the children that God created us with free will so that we can choose whether or not to follow God. God created us with free will because he wants us to choose good.

Point out the stained glass window and invite a volunteer to read the caption aloud.

- Invite volunteers to share what they see in the window.

 Scripture

Proclaim "Joseph and His Brothers."

- Tell the children to listen carefully as you read and to think about a time when they acted as Joseph did.
- Have the children list the major events in the story.
- Have the children discuss the question in their books: When have you forgiven someone as Joseph did?

From Slavery to Freedom

How does God give his people freedom?

God created human beings to be free. He asks us to use the gift of free will to answer his call to live as his People. Because of sin, we know that there are times when others try to take away our freedom. Here are two Bible stories about how God led his People from slavery to freedom.

God gave Joseph the ability to interpret dreams. After he explained the Pharaoh's dreams, Pharaoh called Joseph "a man so endowed with the spirit of God" (Genesis 41:38).

© Our Sunday Visitor

 Scripture

Joseph and His Brothers

Jacob, one of Abraham's descendants, had twelve sons. Jacob's older sons hated their younger brother Joseph because he was their father's favorite.

One day Joseph's brothers threw him into a dry well. Then, they sold him as a slave in Egypt. They told their father that wild animals had killed Joseph. Now, more of their father's goods would belong to them.

Over the years, Joseph's power to tell the meaning of dreams won him a place of honor with Pharaoh, the leader of Egypt. During a famine, Joseph's brothers came to the court to beg for grain. The brothers did not recognize Joseph, but Joseph knew them.

To test them, Joseph had servants fill the brothers' sacks with grain and put a silver cup into the sack of his brother Benjamin. Later, he had his servants follow them and discover the silver cup in the sack. Joseph then told the brothers that Benjamin was to be his slave.

Benjamin's brother Judah pleaded for him, saying that their father would be brokenhearted if Benjamin did not return. At this news, Joseph wept and told the men that he was their brother. He forgave them.

Based on Genesis 37:1–4, 42:6–8, 44:1–12, 45:4–5

➜ When have you forgiven someone as Joseph did?

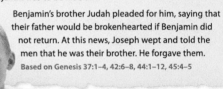 **Reaching All Learners**

Role-Play

Some children with language difficulties may prefer to role-play the story of Joseph.

- Organize the children into small groups, and have them practice performing the scene in which Joseph tests his brothers and then forgives them.
- Invite the small groups to perform the scene.

God Calls Moses

When Joseph's brothers sold him as a slave, they caused problems for themselves as well. It was only when Joseph forgave his brothers that his family knew real freedom and happiness again.

 Scripture

The Exodus from Egypt

Many years later, God's People, the Israelites, were slaves in Egypt. Their male children were being killed, so one Israelite mother hid her baby boy in a basket near the Nile River. When Pharaoh's daughter found the baby, she kept him and named him Moses. She raised him at court as her son.

When Moses grew older, God called him to be a leader of his people. God asked Moses to tell Pharaoh to stop hurting the Israelites, but Pharaoh did not listen.

Finally, Moses was able to lead the Israelites out of Egypt. At the Red Sea, Moses raised his staff and the waters parted for the Israelites to pass through.

Based on Exodus 2:1–10, 14:10–31, 15:19–21

➔ Who was Moses and what did he do?

Share Your Faith

Reflect How did forgiveness help Joseph's family experience happiness again?

Share Tell how you felt after you were forgiven for something you'd done or said.

God's Commandments **75**

 © Our Sunday Visitor

 Scripture Background

Exodus 2:1–10, 14:10–31

Review with the group that when Moses and the Israelites were crossing the desert, God helped Moses part the Red Sea so that the Israelites could escape from the Egyptians.

- Tell them that this incident reveals that when people put their faith in God, he will provide for them.
- He may not provide for you in the way you expect, but you need to trust in his love and care.

God Calls Moses

Emphasize how the choices of Joseph's brothers affected Joseph and his family.

- Ask the children how forgiveness helped both Joseph and his brothers.

 Scripture

Have the children read the Scripture passage silently.

- *Ask:* Who was Moses and what did he do?
- Discuss why Moses led the Israelites out of Egypt.
- *Ask:* Do you think it was hard for Moses to leave Pharaoh's court? Why or why not?

> **▶** Music Option: Have the children sing "Go Down, Moses" or "Moses, Set Them Free," downloaded from **aliveinchrist.osv.com**.

Activity

Point out the Share Your Faith activity and read aloud the directions.

- Discuss the question together as a large group.
- Have the children share with a partner.

Quick Review

Joseph and Moses helped show the way to freedom. God wants his People to live in freedom.

Discover

Objectives

- Identify the Ten Commandments as the summary of laws that God gave Moses on Mount Sinai
- Explain that God gave the Ten Commandments to help us be faithful to him and his covenant

Laws to Guide Us

Ask: How do the Ten Commandments help us to be faithful?

- Write the children's responses on the board or on chart paper.

Tell the children that they will learn that the Ten Commandments showed the Israelites how to live.

- Talk with the group about what things guide them through life.
- Invite volunteers to read the text aloud.

Work with Words

Have the children make vocabulary cards for the terms *ark of the covenant* and *Ten Commandments*.

Living God's Covenant

Recall aloud the definition of *covenant.* a sacred promise or agreement between God and his People

Read the paragraph aloud.

⭐ Have a volunteer read the directions aloud. Invite the children to share what they underlined.

Refer to student page 305 in the Our Catholic Tradition reference section to read how the Ten Commandments are part of God's covenant with the Israelites.

76 Chapter 3

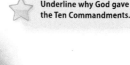

Discover

Laws to Guide Us

How do the Ten Commandments help us to be faithful?

The Israelites were free from slavery, but they still needed God's help. After they crossed the Red Sea, they wandered in the desert for years. They forgot that God had saved them from slavery in Egypt. Moses struggled to keep order among God's People and to find food and water for them. He complained to God about his hard job, and God helped him.

In the desert, God called Moses up to Mount Sinai. After God showed his power with thunder and lightning, he gave Moses the **Ten Commandments** as laws to show the people how they were to live.

Moses and the Israelites built a special container, called the **ark of the covenant**, to house the tablets of the Ten Commandments. They carried the ark with them wherever they went as a reminder that God was with them.

Living God's Covenant

Just as the Ten Commandments helped the Israelites live their covenant relationship with God, the Commandments are also a guide for you. They tell you the minimum that is required to love God and others. The first three Commandments show you how to be faithful to God. The last seven show you how to treat other people with love. The chart on the next page names the Ten Commandments and explains what each one means for you.

 Underline why God gave his People the Ten Commandments.

Catholic Faith Words

Ten Commandments the summary of laws that God gave Moses on Mount Sinai. They tell what is necessary in order to love God and others.

ark of the covenant a wooden chest that housed the tablets of the Ten Commandments. The Israelites carried it wherever they went as a reminder that God was with them.

© Our Sunday Visitor

ⓘ Catechist Background

The Ten Commandments

Explain to the children that the Ten Commandments were given to the Israelites as reminders of the way God wanted them to live. They were rules that helped God's People put him first and also protect the community. The agreements between God and the community gave people guidance in their relationships with God and one another.

- Point out that love for God, ourselves, and others is at the heart of the Ten Commandments.
- Encourage the children to memorize the Ten Commandments.

The Ten Commandments	
The Commandment	**What the Commandment Means**
1. I am the Lord your God. You shall not have strange gods before me.	• Place your faith in God alone. • Worship, praise, and thank the Creator. • Believe in, trust, and love God.
2. You shall not take the name of the Lord your God in vain.	• Speak God's name with reverence. • Don't curse. • Never call on God to witness to a lie.
3. Remember to keep holy the Lord's Day.	• Gather to worship at the Eucharist. • Rest and avoid unnecessary work on Sunday.
4. Honor your father and your mother.	• Respect and obey your parents, guardians, and others who have proper authority.
5. You shall not kill.	• Respect and protect the lives of others and your own life.
6. You shall not commit adultery.	• Be faithful and loyal to friends and family. • Be pure and act appropriately to respect God's gift of sexuality.
7. You shall not steal.	• Respect the things that belong to others. • Share what you have with those in need.
8. You shall not bear false witness against your neighbor.	• Be honest and truthful. • Do not brag about yourself. • Do not say untruthful or negative things about others.
9. You shall not covet your neighbor's wife.	• Practice modesty in thoughts, words, and dress.
10. You shall not covet your neighbor's goods.	• Rejoice in others' good fortune. • Do not be jealous of others' possessions. • Do not be greedy.

© Our Sunday Visitor

Connect Your Faith

Commandments and You Talk with a partner about a decision you made this week, and tell which Commandment you followed when you made that decision.

God's Commandments **77**

The Ten Commandments

Organize the children into small groups, and assign one or two of the Ten Commandments to each group.

- Allow five minutes for each group to discuss examples of ways that they could apply the Commandments to their everyday lives.
- Ask one person from each group to share the group's examples with the rest of the children.
- Write the words *God* and *Others* on a piece of chart paper. Ask volunteers to tell which of the Commandments honor God and which tell how to treat others. Record the responses under the appropriate headings.

Activity

Read aloud the directions for the Connect Your Faith activity.

- Tell the children that thinking carefully about each of the Commandments will help them respond.
- Invite volunteers to share their decisions.

Quick Review

The Ten Commandments are the summary of laws that God gave Moses on Mount Sinai. They helped the Israelites be faithful to God and his covenant, loving God and neighbor.

Optional Activity

Activity Master 3: The Ten Commandments

Distribute copies of the activity found on catechist page 73E.

- Ask the children to unscramble the words to complete the Ten Commandments.
- Review their answers.

God's Commandments **77**

Live

Our Catholic Life

Ask: How can you live as the Ten Commandments require?

- Write the children's responses on the board or on chart paper.

Summarize the first paragraph.

- *Ask:* How do the Ten Commandments help us to live in a way that is pleasing to God? The Ten Commandments teach us how to love God and others.

- Read aloud the second paragraph.

The Ten Commandments

- Call attention to the table. Have the children review the Ten Commandments on page 77.

- Discuss how the Commandments relate to the list on this page. Point out that the list on this page gives examples of how we can live each of the Ten Commandments.

 Invite the children to write the correct Commandment number next to each example. Then have them fill in the last line with one way to live out the Fourth Commandment.

- You might like to have the children work in pairs or trios to complete the activity.

- Invite volunteers to share their responses.

Live

Our Catholic Life
How can you live as the Ten Commandments require?

God gave Moses the Ten Commandments to share with his People. These Commandments help us live in a way that is pleasing to God.

Page 77 lists explanations of each Commandment. Here are some other ways to live out the Commandments.

 Write the correct Commandment number next to each example. Then fill in the last section with one way to live out the Fourth Commandment.

© Our Sunday Visitor

The Ten Commandments
☐ Remember that religious holidays, such as Christmas and Easter, are about Jesus, not about gifts and candy.
☐ When someone lends you something, treat it with great care. Always return it in good condition.
☐ On Sunday, go to Mass and spend time in quiet reflection about your week.
☐ Listen when your parents ask you to do something. Don't make them ask you repeatedly.
☐ Use the names of God and Jesus with reverence and respect.
☐ Treat people and animals with care.
☐ Behave with decency.
☐ Follow Jesus' example of respecting himself and his friends.
☐ Be thankful for what you have, and share with others.
☐ Speak honestly about others.
☐ _____

(i) Catechist Background

Discern What Is Right

The Ten Commandments are one of God's gifts that help people make moral decisions. We are also guided by:

- Scripture, in both the Old Testament and New Testament.
- Church teachings.
- examples from good people in the community.
- examples from the lives of the Saints.

People of Faith

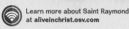

January 7

Saint Raymond of Peñafort, c. 1175–1275

Many of our Church laws are based on the Ten Commandments. Laws that are written for the Church are called "canon laws." Saint Raymond of Peñafort was a priest who studied canon law. There were many canon laws, but they were not organized into one place. The Pope asked Raymond to put all the canon laws in one book. He had to make sure no law was repeated. It was a big job! When all the laws were in one book, Saint Raymond became the head of the Dominican Order. He lived about 800 years ago.

Discuss: How do you follow the Ten Commandments?

 Learn more about Saint Raymond at **aliveinchrist.osv.com**

Live Your Faith

Write the number of the Commandment that is not being followed in each of the two pictures below.

Talk with a partner about what you would do in each situation. Then draw a picture of yourself keeping one Commandment.

People of Faith

Tell the children about Saint Raymond of Peñafort.

- Invite a volunteer to read aloud the People of Faith story.
- Saint Raymond of Peñafort was a bright young man who finished his studies in law and canon law at an early age. Then he became a famous teacher. Eventually he left teaching to join a religious order. He lived into his hundredth year.
- Saint Raymond is known as the patron Saint of lawyers.
- Invite volunteers to share how they follow the Ten Commandments.

 Encourage the children to go to **aliveinchrist.osv.com** at home to find out more about Saint Raymond of Peñafort.

Activity

As a group, read aloud and discuss the directions for the Live Your Faith activity.

- Brainstorm what the children might like to include in their picture.
- Allow time for the children to complete the activity.
- Invite volunteers to share their drawings.

Catholic Social Teaching

Chapter Connections

To integrate Catholic Social Teaching into your lesson, choose one of the following features: Call to Family, Community, and Participation, pages 292–293; or Rights and Responsibilities of the Human Person, pages 294–295.

- Start the Live step of the process by talking about Saint Raymond on page 79. Then move directly to the Catholic Social Teaching feature.
- Or, to expand the lesson, complete both pages 78 and 79, then move to the Catholic Social Teachings feature.
- Return to Chapter 3 for the prayer on page 80.

Live

 Let Us Pray

Psalm Prayer of Praise

Tell the children that they will sing and pray the way the Israelites did when they escaped from Egypt.

Prepare

- Choose four readers. You will be the leader.
- Teach the children their responses.

 Rehearse "My Ten Commandments," downloaded from **aliveinchrist.osv.com**.

Gather

Invite the children to gather in the prayer space.

- Direct the children to be seated and prepare their minds and hearts for prayer.
- Have the readers stand in front of the group.

Pray

- Follow the order of prayer on the student page.
- *Leader's Prayer:* Thank you, God, for giving us your holy words. Help us follow your Commandments faithfully.

 Conclude by singing together "My Ten Commandments."

 Let Us Pray

Psalm Prayer of Praise

Gather and begin with the Sign of the Cross.

Leader: The Lord gives us the Commandments as a way of living. Let us praise God for the gift of salvation.

Reader 1: Then was our mouth filled with laughter, on our lips there were songs.

All: God has done great things for us.

Reader 2: What marvels the Lord worked for us! Indeed, we were glad.

All: God has done great things for us.

Reader 3: Those who are sowing in tears will sing when they reap.

All: God has done great things for us.

Reader 4: They go out, they go out, full of tears; they come back, they come back, full of song.

All: God has done great things for us.

Leader: Let us pray.

Bow your head as the leader prays.

All: Amen. Based on Psalm 126

 Sing "My Ten Commandments"

80 Chapter 3

Liturgy Link

Songs

Songs are an integral part of the liturgy, and an engaging tool for children to learn and express faith.

- Include familiar liturgical songs as well as catechetical songs using children's voices and lyrics that children understand.
- Encourage the children to sing in loud, clear voices to show their love for God.

Go to **aliveinchrist.osv.com** for Sunday readings, Scripture background, questions of the week, and seasonal resources.

FAMILY+FAITH
LIVING AND LEARNING TOGETHER

YOUR CHILD LEARNED >>>
This chapter explains that the Ten Commandments teach us how to respond to God, who first loved us, and how to love others.

Scripture
 Read **Exodus 3:2b, 4–5** to find out how God communicated to Moses through the burning bush.

Catholics Believe
- God gave you the Ten Commandments to help you be faithful to him and his covenant.
- The Commandments tell you ways to love God and others.

To learn more, go to the *Catechism of the Catholic Church #2055, 2060–2061* at **usccb.org**.

People of Faith
This week, your child learned about Saint Raymond of Peñafort. Saint Raymond was known for compiling all the Church's canon laws into one book.

CHILDREN AT THIS AGE >>>
How They Understand the Ten Commandments Your child is probably a practical, concrete thinker, but children this age are also beginning to understand that morality involves more than what people see on the outside. Commandments of the heart such as "You shall not covet" are beginning to make sense as your child internalizes an understanding of living a Christian life. In this process, conscience formation and character building are moving toward the next stage of development.

CONSIDER THIS >>>
What does setting limits for your child teach him or her about love?

Out of love, we set limits for our children to keep them safe and healthy as well as teach them how to treat others with respect. As Catholics, we understand that "before God gave the Commandments at Sinai, he entered into a covenant of love with the community of Israel (cf. Exodus 19:3–6). Once the covenant was established, God gave the people the Ten Commandments in order to teach them the way to live the covenant of love" (*USCCA, p. 325*).

LET'S TALK >>>
- Ask your child to tell you about Joseph and his brothers.
- Talk together about what positive things we can do when we are feeling jealous.

LET'S PRAY >>>
 Dear God, help us to always keep your Commandments. Amen.

For a multimedia glossary of Catholic Faith Words, Sunday readings, seasonal and Saint resources, and chapter activities go to **aliveinchrist.osv.com**.

Alive in Christ, Grade 4 Chapter 3　**81**

Distribute the page to the children or parents/adult family members. Point out the chapter highlights, insights on how fourth graders understand concepts, the opportunity for the adults to reflect on their own experience and faith journey, and the family prayer.

Chapter 3 Review

A **Work with Words** Match each description in Column 1 with the correct term in Column 2.

Column 1	Column 2
1. forgave his brothers	Moses
2. place of law-giving	Pharaoh
3. Israelites' place of slavery	Mount Sinai
4. leader of Egypt	Joseph
5. led Israelites to freedom	Egypt

B **Check Understanding** Circle True if a statement is true, and circle False if a statement is false. Correct any false statements.

6. God gave Moses the Ten Commandments on Mount Sinai.

(**True**)　　False

7. The Third Commandment requires you to avoid gossip.

True　　(**False**)

The Third Commandment requires you to keep holy the Lord's Day.

8. The Ten Commandments were only for Moses to keep for himself.

True　　(**False**)

The Ten Commandments were for all of the Israelites.

9. Moses led his followers out of Egypt.

(**True**)　　False

10. Joseph was the leader of Egypt.

True　　(**False**)

Pharaoh was the leader of Egypt.

 Go to **aliveinchrist.osv.com** for an interactive review.

82　Chapter 3 Review

Use Catechist Quick Reviews to highlight lesson concepts.

A **Work with Words**
Have the children match the description in Column 1 to the correct term in Column 2.

B **Check Understanding**
Have the children circle *True* if the statement is true and *False* if it is false. Correct any false statements.

Go to **aliveinchrist.osv.com** to prepare customized and downloadable assessments, send eAssessments, and assign interactive reviews.

God's Commandments　**81–82**

Use Catechist Quick Reviews in each chapter to highlight lesson concepts for this unit and prepare for the Unit Review.

Have the children complete the Review pages. Then discuss the answers as a group. Review any concepts with which the children are having difficulty.

(A) Work with Words

Have the children use the clues to solve the puzzle. Have them write the answer to each clue in the boxes. When they finish, have them read down the column with the cicles to find the hidden word you can use to answer number 10.

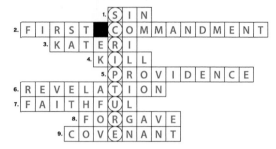

(A) Work with Words Use the clues to solve the puzzle. Write the answer to each clue in the boxes. When you have finished, read down the column with the circles to find the hidden word you can use to answer number 10.

1. S I N
2. F I R S T C O M M A N D M E N T
3. K A T E R I
4. K I L L
5. P R O V I D E N C E
6. R E V E L A T I O N
7. F A I T H F U L
8. F O R G A V E
9. C O V E N A N T

© Our Sunday Visitor

1. Original _____ is what we call Adam and Eve's choice to disobey God.
2. "You shall not have strange gods before me" is part of the _____.
3. _____ Tekakwitha is the first Native American to be canonized.
4. The Fifth Commandment forbids us to do this.
5. God's loving care for all things; his will and plan for creation
6. Divine _____ is the way God makes himself and his plan for humans known.
7. Steadfast and loyal in your commitment to God
8. What Joseph did after his brothers pleaded for Benjamin to be spared
9. A sacred promise or agreement between God and humans
10. Sacred _____ is another name for the Bible, or the inspired Word of God written in human words.

B Check Understanding Complete each sentence with the correct word from the Word Bank.

Word Bank
- plan
- Pharaoh's
- journey
- Moses
- jealous

11. God asked Abram and Sarai to go on a long ___journey___ and live in a new land called Canaan.

12. God has a ___plan___ for all of his People.

13. Joseph's brothers sold him into slavery because they were ___jealous___.

14. God gave the Ten Commandments to ___Moses___ to share with his People.

15. As a baby, Moses was left in a basket by the Nile River, where he was found by ___Pharaoh's___ daughter.

C Make Connections Write a response to each question.

16. Why is it important for you to find a quiet place to pray?
___Possible responses: to be able to hear God's will for___
___my life; to be free of distractions___

17. What is the lesson of the story of Abraham and Sarah's waiting many years to have a child?
___Possible response: It is important to trust in God's___
___plan for our lives; all things are possible for God.___

Use the terms in the Word Bank in a paragraph to explain how you keep the Third Commandment.

18–20. ___Responses will vary.___

Word Bank
- Sunday
- worship
- rest
- Lord's Day

B Check Understanding
Have the children complete each sentence with the correct word from the Word Bank.

C Make Connections
16–17. Have the children write a response to each question or statement.

18–20. Have the children use the terms in the Word Bank to explain how they keep the Third Commandment.

Go to **aliveinchrist.osv.com** to prepare customized and downloadable assessments, send eAssessments, and assign interactive reviews.

Trinity

Our Catholic Tradition

- You are made in God's image and likeness and are to live and love in community. (CCC, 1604)

- Showing love to others is a way we reflect the love of the Holy Trinity. The failure to do so is sin. (CCC, 735)

- The Divine Persons of the Holy Trinity help you to do good and avoid evil. You do this by using your free will and following your conscience. (CCC, 1704)

How does a conscience, informed by Sacred Scripture and Sacred Tradition, interpreted by the Church, help us to love as God loves?

Unit 2 Overview

Chapter 4

In God's Image 87
The children will:

- recognize that dignity of the human person comes from being made in God's image and likeness
- distinguish the soul as the spiritual part of a human that lives forever
- define sin as a deliberate thought, word, deed, or omission contrary to the law of God
- recognize that sin is a failure to love that affects individuals and the whole Church community
- recall that every person is worthy of respect because he or she is created in God's image and made to love

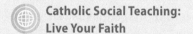 **Catholic Social Teaching: Live Your Faith**

- Life and Dignity of the Human Person, Pages 290–291
- Care for God's Creation, Pages 302–303

Chapter 5

Living in Community 97
The children will:

- recognize that the mission of God the Son and the Holy Spirit is to bring all people into the love of the Holy Trinity
- define morality as living in right relationship with God, yourself, and others
- appreciate that God created all people for one another and we must all work for the common good
- connect that our love of our neighbor reflects the love of the Holy Trinity

 **Catholic Social Teaching: Live Your Faith**

- Call to Family, Community, and Participation, Pages 292–293
- Dignity of Work and Rights of Workers, Pages 298–299

Chapter 6

Making Good Choices 107
The children will:

- define free will as the God-given ability to choose between good and evil
- recall that God gives us grace, the Ten Commandments, and the Church to help us make good choices and to deepen our relationship with him
- understand that knowing God's laws and forming, or strengthening, our conscience will help us make good decisions
- identify conscience as the God-given ability that helps us judge whether actions are morally good or wrong

 Songs of Scripture
"The Good Samaritan"

 Catholic Social Teaching: Live Your Faith

- Rights and Responsibilities of the Human Person, Pages 294–295
- Option for the Poor and Vulnerable, Pages 296–297

Preview Unit Theme

Ask: What is the unit theme?

Summarize that the unit focuses on the Holy Trinity.

Invite volunteers to read aloud each of the bullets in Our Catholic Tradition.

Explain to the children that they will learn about these things in the next three chapters.

Have the children study the photos and images. Invite volunteers to describe what they see. What do these images say about the unit theme?

Ask: How does a conscience, informed by Sacred Scripture and Scared Tradition, interpreted by the Church, help us to love as God loves?

After some discussion, explain to the children that they will be exploring this question in the next chapters.

KEY CONCEPT

Every person is worthy of respect because he or she is created in God's image. Each person has a soul that will live forever.

DOCTRINAL CONTENT

- Human dignity comes from being made in God's image and likeness with the ability to love, think, and make choices. (CCC, 355–357)

- The soul is the spiritual part of a human that lives forever. (CCC, 366)

- Sin is a deliberate thought, word, deed or omission contrary to the law of God. (CCC, 1849)

- Sin is a failure to love that affects individuals and the whole Church community. (CCC, 1440)

- Every person is worthy of respect because he or she is created in God's image and made to love. (CCC, 1700)

TASKS OF CATECHESIS

Helping children grow in a faith that is "known, celebrated, lived, and expressed in prayer" (NDC, 20).

This chapter focuses on the following tasks of catechesis.

- Promoting Knowledge of the Faith
- Moral Formation

Catechist Background

Live in a manner worthy of the Lord, so as to be fully pleasing, in every good work bearing fruit and growing in the knowledge of God. **Colossians 1:10**

➜ **Reflect** How can sin hurt your relationship with God and others?

Humans have a spiritual dimension that is no less real than the physical one. This spiritual dimension of humans is called the *soul*. Humans, however, are not divided creatures, one part body and another part soul. We are simultaneously physical and spiritual.

Humans are made in God's image. All humans are bound as brothers and sisters, regardless of individual differences. Being created in God's image is humanity's most profound common trait. Body and soul share in the dignity of the image of God. The soul is the gift of life breathed into humans by the Creator. The soul is immortal and will transcend even the death of the physical body.

Human dignity comes first from the fact that all people are creations of God. Therefore, humans are products of love, wisdom, and goodness beyond understanding. Respect for life at all stages is the only appropriate response to such divine generosity. Human life is sacred because all humans are offspring of God. There can be no greater dignity than this.

➜ **Reflect** In what ways does your life show honor to God and respect for others?

Catechist's Prayer

God and Father of all, help us always to remember that we are created in your image. Guide us to see your Son, Jesus, in every person we meet. Amen.

Lesson Plan

Objectives	Process	Materials

🕐 Invite, 10 minutes

In God's Image Page 87

- 💬 Psalm 139:13–14 Pray the opening prayer.
- 📖 Colossians 1:10, 12–15 Reflect prayerfully on the Word.
- Discuss What Do You Wonder questions.

🌐 **Optional Activity**
Chapter Story: "Rosa Parks"

🕐 Discover, 35 minutes

Reflect God's Love Pages 88–89
- Recognize that dignity of the human person comes from being made in God's image and likeness
- Distinguish the soul as the spiritual part of a human that lives forever

- **Catholic Faith Words** human dignity, soul
- Explain that all people have human dignity because they are created in God's image.
- 📖 Genesis 1:27 Proclaim the Scripture.
- Explain that Saint Marianne Cope honored the human dignity of people.
- **Share Your Faith Activity** Describe human dignity.

☐ pencils
☐ index cards
- **Optional Activity** Human Dignity in Scripture
☐ Activity Master 4 (Page 87E)

Created to Be with God Pages 90–91
- Define sin as a deliberate thought, word, deed, or omission contrary to the law of God
- Recognize that sin is a failure to love that affects individuals and the whole Church community
- Recall that every person is worthy of respect because he or she is created in God's image and made to love

- **Catholic Faith Words** sin, mortal sin, venial sin
- Explain that sin is failure to love.
- Compare and contrast mortal sin and venial sin.
- Recall that all people are equal, have human dignity, and are worthy of respect.
- **Connect Your Faith Activity** Identify mortal sins and venial sins.

☐ pencils
☐ index cards
- **Optional Activity** Write a group prayer

🕐 Live, 15 minutes

Our Catholic Life Pages 92–93

- Explain that both nature and people show God's glory.
- ☆ Name how nature and people are signs of God's glory.
- **People of Faith** Learn about Saint Germaine Cousin.
- **Live Your Faith Activity** Create a poster.

☐ pencils
☐ crayons or markers

Prayer for Dignity and Respect Page 94

- Select four readers.
- ▶ Rehearse "O God, You Search Me."
- Follow the order of prayer.

🌐 Download "O God, You Search Me."

Family + Faith Page 95

Point out that the Catholic Families page provides chapter highlights, information on how fourth graders understand faith concepts, and family prayer.

Chapter Review Page 96

🌐 aliveinchrist.osv.com

- Customize and Download Assessments
- Email Links to eAssessments
- Interactive Student Reviews

ONLINE RESOURCES

 Go to **aliveinchrist.osv.com**

You will find:

- Interactive lesson planning with web specific content and additional activities
- Step by step lesson instruction from printed Catechist Edition for integrated lesson planning
- Custom-built assessments to download and eAssessment links
- Interactive reviews that provide scores and the option to review answers
- Sunday readings with background and questions of the week

 Go to **osvparish.com**

You will find:

- Ask the Experts Q and A
- General Catechist Helps
- Community Connections and Blogs

Sharing the Message with Fourth Graders

Being Created in God's Image Fourth graders are now past those early childhood years in which they thought anything was possible. They are becoming painfully aware of their limitations and need to remember that they are valuable human beings by virtue of their creation in God's image. Knowing this, they can also begin to explore the idea that they were created for a purpose—God has a design for their lives.

Teaching Tip: Periodically ask various children in your group what they think might be God's plan for their lives. Encourage them to watch for signs of God's plan through their talents and interests, opportunities that arise for them, and the things they hear from others.

How Fourth Graders Understand

- Fourth graders are concerned about fairness. Encourage them to speak up when they see others treated unfairly.
- Sometimes fourth graders want to be like everyone else. Help them appreciate their own unique gifts.
- Show respect for differences by encouraging the children to share their unique gifts. Some are talkers. Others are listeners, writers, artists, or dancers.

"I am curious about other lands and cultures. Give me opportunities to learn about all kinds of people."

Chapter Connections

Chapter Story
Invite

"Rosa Parks"

Use this story to expand the chapter introduction.

- The children will relate the story to their own lives, reflecting on God creating every person in his image.
- Connect all people being created in God's image to all people deserving respect.

 Go to **aliveinchrist.osv.com** Lesson Planning section for this story.

NCEA IFG: ACRE Edition
Discover

Knowledge of the Faith

- Objective: To know and understand basic Catholic teaching about the Incarnate Word Jesus Christ as the way, truth, and life

Moral Formation

- Objectives: To be knowledgeable about the teachings of Jesus and the Church as the basis of Christian morality and to understand Catholic Social Teaching; to be aware of the importance of a well-formed conscience for decision making

Catholic Social Teaching
Live

 Use one of these features to introduce a principle and engage the children with an activity.

- Life and Dignity of the Human Person, Pages 290–291
- Care for God's Creation, Pages 302–303

Music Options

 Use one or more of the following songs to enhance catechetical learning or for prayer.

- "O God, You Search Me," Live Prayer, Page 94
- "God Is Our Father," Discover, Page 88
- "You Are Near," Live, Page 92

LECTIONARY CONNECTION

 Chapter 4 highlights Lectionary-connected themes such as dignity, respect for life and created in God's image. If your parish aligns its curriculum to the liturgical year, you could use this chapter in connection with the following Sundays.

Year A

Twenty-fifth Sunday in Ordinary Time—dignity

Twenty-eighth Sunday in Ordinary Time—respect for life

Thirty-first Sunday in Ordinary Time—sin

Year B

Baptism of the Lord—created in God's image

Second Sunday of Lent—children of God

Second Sunday of Easter—respect for life

Year C

Second Sunday of Advent—salvation

Fourth Sunday of Lent—created in God's image

Fourth Sunday of Easter—Good Shepherd

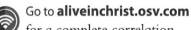 Go to **aliveinchrist.osv.com** for a complete correlation ordered by the Sundays of the year and suggestions for how to integrate the Scripture readings into chapter lessons.

Name _____   Date _____

Human Dignity and Scripture

Every person is created in God's image and is worthy of respect. Jesus respected the dignity of everyone he met, especially the outcasts of society.

Look up and read the Bible verses listed below, and complete the chart.

Scripture	Whom did Jesus treat with dignity?	How did Jesus show that he respected the person?
1. Matthew 8:1–4		
2. Mark 2:13–17		
3. Luke 7:36–50		
4. Luke 19:1–10		
5. John 4:4–42		

In God's Image

 Let Us Pray

Leader: Creator Father, we give you thanks for making us as we are and who we are.

"You formed my inmost being;
   you knit me in my mother's womb.
I praise you, because I am wonderfully made;
   wonderful are your works!"   Psalm 139:13–14

All: O God, you are more than our maker. You are our loving Father. Help us grow to be like you more and more each day. Amen.

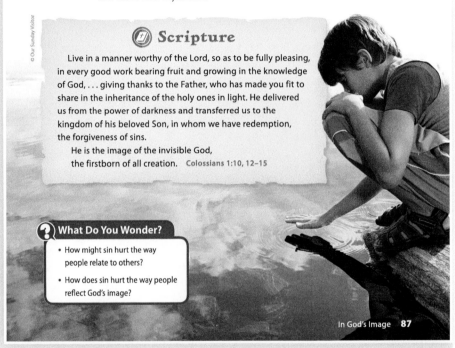

Scripture

Live in a manner worthy of the Lord, so as to be fully pleasing, in every good work bearing fruit and growing in the knowledge of God, . . . giving thanks to the Father, who has made you fit to share in the inheritance of the holy ones in light. He delivered us from the power of darkness and transferred us to the kingdom of his beloved Son, in whom we have redemption, the forgiveness of sins.

He is the image of the invisible God,
   the firstborn of all creation.   Colossians 1:10, 12–15

What Do You Wonder?

- How might sin hurt the way people relate to others?
- How does sin hurt the way people reflect God's image?

In God's Image   **87**

© Our Sunday Visitor

Optional Activity

Chapter Story: "Rosa Parks"   *Verbal/Linguistic*

Use this story after the opening prayer, before explaining how we are made in God's image.

- Read the story aloud. Ask the children to think about how they might feel if they were treated as Rosa was.
- Emphasize that because all humans are created in God's image, everyone has human dignity and is worthy of respect. When finished, transition back to the lesson instruction.

 Go to **aliveinchrist.osv.com** for Chapter Story.

 **Invite**

 Let Us Pray

Invite the children to stand and make the Sign of the Cross. Choose a child to read the Psalm verse from a Bible. Prompt the children's response.

Have the children move out of the prayer space and back to their seats.

Explain that God created all people in his image.

Say: What does the term "made in God's image" mean? Let's listen and learn.

Scripture

Guide the children through the process of Scripture reflection.

- Invite them to close their eyes, be still and open their minds and hearts to what God is saying to them in this passage.
- Proclaim the Scripture.
- Maintain several moments of silence.
- *Ask:* What did you hear God say to you today?
- Invite volunteers to share.

What Do You Wonder?

Say: What does it mean to be made in God's image? The best answer is found in the Person of Jesus. He is our model to follow. In him, we see the best example of someone who shows us God's image. Our challenge is to be the kind of person he was, to relate to God and to others as he did, and to serve as he served.

Invite the children to respond to the questions. Ask what else they might wonder about sin or about being made in God's image.

Objectives

- Recognize that dignity of the human person comes from being made in God's image and likeness
- Distinguish the soul as the spiritual part of a human that lives forever

Reflect God's Love

Ask: What does it mean to be created in God's image?

- Write the children's responses on the board or on chart paper.

Read aloud the paragraph.

 Scripture

Proclaim the Scripture Story.

- Tell the children that this passage comes from the first account of creation. Explain that people have dignity because they are created in the image of God.

Ask the children to silently read the last paragraph.

⭐ Have the children draw one way they are an image of love. Invite sharing.

Work with Words

Have the children create vocabulary cards for *human dignity* and *soul*.

 Music Option: Have the children sing "God Is Our Father," downloaded from **aliveinchrist.osv.com**.

Discover

Reflect God's Love

What does it mean to be created in God's image?

God has given you life. He has created you and all people to reflect his own image of love. God's image is meant to shine in each of us. As Catholics, we believe that all people have **human dignity** because they are created in God's image.

Catholic Faith Words

human dignity the worth each person has because he or she is made in the image of God

soul the spiritual part of a human that lives forever

 Scripture

God created mankind in his image;
in the image of God he created them;
male and female he created them.   Genesis 1:27

God made you with a human body, and you have a **soul** that will live forever. God gave you the ability to think, to love, and to make choices. You can choose to do good every day and let God's image of love shine through.

⭐ In the mirror, draw one way you are an image of love.

88   Chapter 4

 Scripture Background

Genesis 1:27

Humans are the only creatures created in God's image and likeness because they are the only ones who have immortal souls. The human body shares in the dignity of this image of God.

- Because humans have both a body and a soul, their creation unites the world of matter and spirit.
- God created people with the capacity to share in his divine nature. This is the source of human dignity and worth.

Saint Marianne Cope

The story of Saint Marianne Cope shows how one person reflected God's love. She treated others, especially the poor and sick, with dignity and respect.

When she was a child, Barbara Cope knew that she wanted to become a religious sister. Because her family was poor, she worked in a factory to help support them. When her brothers and sisters were finally grown, she entered the religious community of the Sisters of Saint Francis.

In the convent, she was known as Sister Marianne. She taught and helped her Sisters establish hospitals which were special at that time because they treated people of any nationality, religion, or color. In the hospitals, she worked for patients' rights and promoted cleanliness.

The King and Queen of Hawaii invited the Sisters to work in hospitals there. Mother Marianne, as she was then called, took a group of Sisters to answer the call. Within a few years, they transformed a dirty hospital for lepers (people with a contagious skin disease) into a beautiful facility and made other improvements to help lepers and their families.

Over the years, Mother Marianne also helped found hospitals in New York.

→ **How did Mother Marianne's work honor the dignity of people?**

Share Your Faith

Reflect In your own words, describe what the term *human dignity* means.

Share Explain your description to a partner.

In God's Image **89**

Optional Activity

Activity Master 4: Human Dignity and Scripture

Distribute copies of the activity found on catechist page 87E.

- Help the children locate the Scripture passages.
- As an alternative, you may wish to send this activity home with the children.

Saint Marianne Cope

Introduce the biography of Saint Marianne Cope by summarizing the first paragraph. Ask the children if they think it is possible for a person to give dignity to other people.

- Read aloud the biography of Saint Marianne Cope.
- Emphasize that because all humans are created in God's image, everyone has human dignity and is worthy of respect.
- Saint Marianne demonstrated this in her work with persons with leprosy. Explain that people incorrectly thought that leprosy was a highly contagious disease, so it was difficult to find people to take care of lepers.
- *Ask:* How did Mother Marianne's work honor the dignity of people?

Activity

Read aloud the directions for the Share Your Faith activity.

- Have the children work independently to write their ideas.
- After a short time, have them discuss with a partner.

Quick Review

All people are created in God's image and are equal in human dignity. It is important to treat all people with respect.

Discover

Objectives

- Define sin as a deliberate thought, word, deed or omission contrary to the law of God
- Recognize that sin is a failure to love that affects individuals and the whole Church community
- Recall that every person is worthy of respect because he or she is created in God's image and made to love

Created to Be with God

Ask: What is a failure to love?

- Write the children's responses on the board or on chart paper.

Read aloud the first paragraph to introduce the topic of sin.

- Ask the children what happens when they act in a loving way.
- Explain that "failure to love" is one definition of sin.

Have the children silently read the second paragraph.

Personal Sin

Read aloud the last sentence about mortal sin and venial sin that is above the chart. Then, introduce the chart.

- Invite volunteers to read aloud each column.

Work with Words

Point out the Catholic Faith Words.

- Distribute index cards and provide time for the children to create a vocabulary card for each term: *sin*, *mortal sin*, and *venial sin*.
- Invite volunteers to define each term in their own words.

Created to Be with God

What is a failure to love?

God created you to be united to him and to all people. Every time you act in a loving way, you deepen your connection to God and to the members of the Church, the Body of Christ. When you choose to treat someone badly, you hurt this person and the whole community of faith. You choose not to show love and respect.

Sin is always a failure to love. A sinful thought, word, or act also hurts your friendship with God and other people. Sin affects you, too, and keeps you from becoming the person God wants you to be. There are two kinds of personal sin—**mortal sin** and **venial sin**.

© Our Sunday Visitor

Personal Sin

Venial Sins	Mortal Sins
• sins that weaken your friendship with God and others, but do not destroy it	• sins that cause a person's relationship with God to be broken
• things that you do, such as disobeying, cheating, and lying. These are sins of commission.	• serious sins, such as murder
• bad habits that you develop, such as being lazy or dishonest	• In order for a sin to be mortal, (1) the act must be seriously wrong, (2) you must know that it is seriously wrong, and (3) you must freely choose to do it anyway.
• A failure to act sometimes is a sin of omission; for example, to remain silent when someone tells a joke that makes fun of another person or group is a sin.	

 Quick Tip

Sin

Help the children distinguish sins from accidents.

- Remind them that bad things can happen despite people's good intentions. These are accidents, not sins. Knocking over a vase and breaking it is not a sin.
- A sin is a wrong action that is done on purpose. Purposely breaking a vase because you are angry with a parent is a sin.

Love and Respect

All people are equal. Every person has human dignity and is worthy of respect because he or she is made in God's image. Because he is the Son of God, Jesus is the perfect image of God. You are called to become more like Jesus and to reflect the love and care that he shows all people.

Connect Your Faith

Identify Sins For each statement below, write an M in the blank if it describes a mortal sin. Write a V in the blank if it describes a venial sin.

- M a serious sin
- V lying or cheating
- M destroys a person's relationship with God and others
- M murder
- V hurts a person's relationship with God and others
- V being lazy or disobeying

Catholic Faith Words

sin a deliberate thought, word, deed, or omission contrary to the law of God. Sins hurt our relationship with God and other people.

mortal sin serious sin that causes a person's relationship with God to be broken

venial sin a sin that weakens a person's relationship with God but does not destroy it

In God's Image 91

Love and Respect

Invite a volunteer to read aloud the paragraph.

- Remind the children that every person has dignity and is worthy of respect because he or she is made in God's image.
- Refer to page 318 in the Our Catholic Tradition reference section in the back of the Student Book for more information on human dignity.
- Emphasize that Jesus is the perfect image of God and that we are all called to become more like Jesus.

Activity

Point out the Connect Your Faith activity.

- Have a volunteer read aloud the directions.
- Have the children work independently to complete the activity.
- Review the answers with the children and answer any questions they may have.

Quick Review

Sin is a failure to love. It hurts you, others, and your relationship with God.

Optional Activity

Write a Group Prayer *Interpersonal*

Have the children write a group prayer.

- Print the words to the prayer on the board or chart paper.
- Have the children create gestures that correspond to the words of the prayer.
- Pray the prayer before the end of the session and at other appropriate times throughout the year.

Our Catholic Life

Ask: Where do you see God's glory?

- Write the children's responses on the board or on chart paper.

Invite a volunteer to read aloud the first paragraph.

Ask a volunteer to read aloud "Nature Gives Glory to God."

- Ask the children to name ways in which nature gives glory to God.

 Inside the sunflower, have the children write one way nature is a sign of God's glory.

Ask a volunteer to read aloud "People Show the Glory of God."

- Ask the children to name people who have shown them God's love, power, wonder, or wisdom.

☆ Inside the soccer ball, have the children write about a time when they have seen the reflection of God in another person.

> ▶ Music Option: Have the children sing, "You Are Near," downloaded from **aliveinchrist.osv.com**.

Our Catholic Life

Where do you see God's glory?

God shows you something of what he is like through his image in people and through the world he created. If you pay attention you will learn many things about him.

1. Inside the flower, write one way nature is a sign of God's glory.
2. Inside the soccer ball, write about a time when you have seen a reflection of God in another person.

Nature Gives Glory to God

The loveliness of a flower or the brilliance of a sunset tells you something about God's power and goodness. Reflecting on his glory may bring about feelings of gratitude or peace. Take time to look closely at and appreciate nature.

People Show the Glory of God

Think about people who have shown you love: your parents or guardians, a good friend, an understanding teacher, or a devoted grandparent. A baby may make you think of God's power and wonder. An older person may remind you of God's wisdom.

92   Chapter 4

✓ Quick Tip

Recognize God's Presence

Encourage the children to look for the presence of God in their lives and in the world.

- Begin with the question: "Where have you seen God today?"
- Ask each child to write a brief paragraph answering the question, "Where do you see God's glory?"

People of Faith

Saint Germaine Cousin, 1579–1601

June 15

Saint Germaine Cousin reminds us that each of us is made in God's image and worthy of respect. She had a crippled hand and a deformed neck. After her mother died, her father remarried. Her stepmother made her sleep in a cupboard under the stairs. Germaine never complained. Instead, she prayed for her stepmother. Finally, her stepmother realized that Germaine was very holy and wanted her to live in the house. But Germaine stayed in her cupboard and was a model of prayer and holiness.

Discuss: What can you do to help someone who has a disability?

 Learn more about Saint Germaine at **aliveinchrist.osv.com**

Live Your Faith

Create a poster that explains how you can treat others with dignity and see the glory of God in everyone.

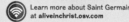
DIGNITY

In God's Image **93**

Catholic Social Teaching

Chapter Connections

To integrate Catholic Social Teaching into your lesson, choose one of the following features: Life and Dignity of the Human Person, pages 290–291; or Care for God's Creation, pages 302–303.

- Start the Live step of the process by talking about Saint Germaine Cousin on page 93. Then move directly to the Catholic Social Teaching feature.
- Or, to expand the lesson, complete both pages 92 and 93, then move to the Catholic Social Teaching feature.
- Return to Chapter 4 for the prayer on page 94.

People of Faith

Tell the children about Saint Germaine Cousin.

- Invite a volunteer to read aloud the People of Faith story.
- Explain that Saint Germaine Cousin was treated so poorly by her stepmother that she was not allowed to go to school. Instead she spent her days in the field tending the sheep.
- Instead of feeling lonely, Saint Germaine found a friend in God. She had a rosary made of knots and string.
- Every day she would leave her sheep in God's care and go to Mass.
- One day when rain had caused the river to rise to flood stage, a villager saw the river part so that Saint Germaine could cross to get to church in time for Mass.
- *Ask:* What can you do to help someone who has a disability?

Encourage the children to go to **aliveinchrist.osv.com** at home to find out more about Saint Germaine Cousin.

Activity

Read aloud the directions and discuss the Live Your Faith activity together as a group.

- Allow time for the children to create their posters.
- Invite volunteers to share their drawings.

Let Us Pray
Prayer for Dignity and Respect

Explain that this celebration will be a prayer that honors names for God.

Prepare

Choose a reader for the prayer.

- Ask the children to identify the names for God used in the prayer service.

 Rehearse "O God, You Search Me," downloaded from **aliveinchrist.osv.com**.

Gather

Invite the children to gather in the prayer space with their books.

- Have the children remain standing and prepare their minds and hearts for prayer.

Pray

Lead the children in praying the Sign of the Cross.

- Follow the order of prayer on the student page.

 Conclude by singing together "O God, You Search Me."

 Let Us Pray
Prayer for Dignity and Respect

Gather and begin with the Sign of the Cross.

Reader 1:	God of life,
All:	We pray for the dignity of life.
Reader 2:	God of creation,
All:	We pray for the dignity of life.
Reader 3:	God, the source of all life,
All:	We pray for the dignity of life.
Reader 4:	God, the protector of humanity,
All:	We pray for the dignity of life.
Leader:	God, we give you praise and thanks for all creation. Based on Psalm 139
All:	Amen.

 Sing "O God, You Search Me"
O God, you search me and you know me.
All my thoughts lie open to your gaze.
When I walk or lie down you are before me:
Ever the maker and keeper of my days.

 Liturgy Link

Choose a Reader

Make sure that each child acts as prayer leader or reader sometime during the year.

- Be aware of what the leader or reader is required to do in each prayer service.
- In this celebration, the reader reads short phrases rather than a long passage. This is a good time to select a child who is not a strong reader.

Go to **aliveinchrist.osv.com** for Sunday readings, Scripture background, questions of the week, and seasonal resources.

FAMILY+FAITH
LIVING AND LEARNING TOGETHER

YOUR CHILD LEARNED >>>
This chapter explains that God created all people in his image and therefore each of us has human dignity and deserves respect.

Scripture
 Read **Colossians 1:10, 12–15** to find out how God created us to live.

Catholics Believe
• Every person is worthy of respect because he or she is created in God's image.
• Each person has a soul that will live forever.

To learn more, go to the *Catechism of the Catholic Church #355–357, 362–366* at **usccb.org**.

People of Faith
This week, your child learned about Saint Germaine Cousin, who was born with some severe disabilities.

CHILDREN AT THIS AGE >>>

How They Understand Being Created in God's Image
Your child is probably now past those early childhood years in which he or she thought anything was possible. Some children this age are becoming painfully aware of their limitations and need to remember that they are valuable human beings by virtue of their creation in God's image. Knowing this, they can also begin to explore the idea that they were created for a purpose, and that God has a design for their lives.

CONSIDER THIS >>>
Is it easier to show respect to a stranger or to someone in your own family?

It may be more difficult to show respect to people with whom we live because we see their flaws up close. All people deserve our respect because they are made in the image of God. As Catholics, we know that "to be made in the image of God includes specific qualities. Each of us is capable of self-knowledge and of entering into communion with other persons through self-giving. These qualities—and the shared heritage of our first parents—also form a basis for a bond of unity among all human beings" (*USCCA, p. 67*).

LET'S TALK >>>
• Ask your child to explain why all people have dignity.
• Share a personal story about a time when you were not treated with dignity and how you felt.

LET'S PRAY >>>
O God, may we always be respectful of all people, knowing we are all your children. Amen.

For a multimedia glossary of Catholic Faith Words, Sunday readings, seasonal and Saint resources, and chapter activities go to **aliveinchrist.osv.com**.

Chapter 4 Review

(A) Work with Words Circle True if the statement is true, and circle False if the statement is false. Correct any false statements.

1. A bully can never reflect God's image.

    True   **(False)**

Everyone reflects God's image. _____

2. God is with everyone at all times in all places.

    (True)   False

_____

3. You commit a mortal sin when you cheat on a spelling test.

    True   **(False)**

You commit a venial sin. _____

4. Mortal sin causes a person's relationship with God to be broken.

    (True)   False

_____

5. Each person is unique and created by God.

    (True)   False

_____

(B) Check Understanding Complete the following statements.

6. The _____soul_____ is the spiritual part of you that lives forever.

7. Human ____dignity____ is the worth each person has because he or she is made in God's image.

8. A ____venial____ sin hurts your friendship with God.

9. ____People____ and ____nature____ show the glory of God.

10. You are ____called____ to show God's love and care to others, as Jesus did.

Go to **aliveinchrist.osv.com** for an interactive review.

Family + Faith

Distribute the page to the children or parents/adult family members. Point out the chapter highlights, insights on how fourth graders understand concepts, the opportunity for the adults to reflect on their own experience and faith journey, and the family prayer.

Chapter Review

Use Catechist Quick Reviews to highlight lesson concepts.

(A) Work with Words
Have the children identify each statement as *True* or *False*. Ask volunteers to share how they changed the false statements to make them true.

(B) Check Understanding
Have the children complete each statement.

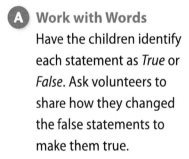 Go to **aliveinchrist.osv.com** to prepare customized and downloadable assessments, send eAssessments, and assign interactive reviews.

In God's Image   **95–96**

KEY CONCEPT

God created people for one another, and all must work for the common good. Such love of neighbor reflects the love of the Holy Trinity. No one can believe alone, just as no one can live alone.

DOCTRINAL CONTENT

- The mission of God the Son and the Holy Spirit is to bring all people into the love of the Holy Trinity. (CCC, 258–260)
- Morality is living in right relationship with God, yourself and others. (CCC, 1950–1951)
- God created all people for one another and we must all work for the common good. (CCC, 1905–1906)
- Our love of our neighbor reflects the love of the Holy Trinity. (CCC, 1878)

TASKS OF CATECHESIS

Helping children grow in a faith that is "known, celebrated, lived, and expressed in prayer" (NDC, 20).

This chapter focuses on the following tasks of catechesis:

- Promoting Knowledge of the Faith
- Education for Communal Life

Catechist Background

> Beloved, if God so loved us, we also must love one another. No one has ever seen God. Yet, if we love one another, God remains in us, and his love is brought to perfection in us.
> 1 John 4:11–12

→ **Reflect** Where do you look for help in living a moral life?

Morality begins with relationships—your conscious choice to share in God's own life and to live with others in peace and with compassion. The more you choose the good, alone or with others, the better your relationships will be with others and with God. Choosing what is morally good involves following the pattern of living given to us by Jesus Christ and accepting the grace God offers us to do so. Christ's teachings are our practical guides to morality.

Your loving God always supports you in living by his laws. Your relationships with those in your community—in your parish, for example—help you by surrounding you with other believers. Your relationships with God and others help you form a correct conscience and develop life-affirming habits.

All communities, from your immediate family to entire nations, survive and thrive only when there is recognition of the common good, the needs of the group and all its members. Working for the common good is not simply enlightened self-interest; it is an authentic Christian practice. As a Catholic, you are called by the grace of your Baptism to respect all persons and to promote the well-being of everyone. Promoting the common good is central to the mission of Christ.

→ **Reflect** How have you promoted the common good?

Catechist's Prayer

Loving God, thank you for the community of faith that supports me as I teach these children. May it support them as they work for the common good. Amen.

Lesson Plan

Objectives	Process	Materials
Invite, 10 minutes		
Living in Community Page 97	◎ **Psalm 133:1** Pray the opening prayer. 📖 **1 John 4:9, 11–13, 16b** Reflect prayerfully on the Word. • Discuss What Do You Wonder questions.	🌐 **Optional Activity** Chapter Poem: "The Chain of Life"
Discover, 35 minutes		
Created to Love Pages 98–99 • Recognize that the mission of God the Son and the Holy Spirit is to bring all people into the love of the Holy Trinity	• **Catholic Faith Words** Holy Trinity • Explain that God's plan is for people to live together in love. ☆ Underline the mission of God the Son and God the Holy Spirit. 📖 **Acts 2:42–45** Proclaim "The Communal Life." • **Share Your Faith Activity** Name ways to show love for others in a community or parish.	☐ pencils ☐ index cards • **Optional Activity** Illustrate Laws
Living as Catholics Pages 100–101 • Define morality as living in right relationship with God, yourself and others • Appreciate that God created all people for one another and we must all work for the common good • Connect that our love of our neighbor reflects the love of the Holy Trinity	• **Catholic Faith Words** morality, common good • Explain that our families and our parish help us live a moral life. • Explain that people who live in community work for the common good. • **Connect Your Faith Activity** Explain how to work for the common good.	☐ pencils ☐ index cards • **Optional Activity** Board Game ☐ Activity Master 5 (Page 97E)
Live, 15 minutes		
Our Catholic Life Pages 102–103	• Explain that our actions affect the lives of others. ☆ Identify guidelines for living in community. • **People of Faith** Learn about Saint Dominic. • **Live Your Faith Activity** Identify one way to create a more loving community.	☐ pencils ☐ crayons or markers
Lectio Divina Page 104	• Designate Side 1 and Side 2. ▶ Rehearse "Raise Your Voice for Justice." • Follow the order of prayer.	🌐 Download "Raise Your Voice for Justice."

Family + Faith Page 105

Point out that the Catholic Families page provides chapter highlights, information on how fourth graders understand faith concepts, and family prayer.

Chapter Review Page 106

🌐 **aliveinchrist.osv.com**
- Customize and Download Assessments
- Email Links to eAssessments
- Interactive Student Reviews

ONLINE RESOURCES

 Go to **aliveinchrist.osv.com**

You will find:

- Interactive lesson planning with web specific content and additional activities
- Step by step lesson instruction from printed Catechist Edition for integrated lesson planning
- Custom-built assessments to download and eAssessment links
- Interactive reviews that provide scores and the option to review answers
- Sunday readings with background and questions of the week

 Go to **osvparish.com**

You will find:

- Ask the Experts Q and A
- General Catechist Helps
- Community Connections and Blogs

Sharing the Message with Fourth Graders

Being Created for One Another Most fourth graders are very social. But the social skills of fourth graders have moved beyond the early childhood years of simply wanting to play with other children to forming real bonds of friendship. This is the time of "best friends," when children form close relationships with one or a few children they prefer to spend their time with. It is the beginning of the deeper relationships they will hopefully enjoy for the rest of their lives.

Teaching Tip: Be sure to make time for children to cultivate friendships within the group. Providing group and partner learning activities can be one way to encourage this.

How Fourth Graders Understand

- Fourth graders like to solve problems. Have them brainstorm solutions that benefit the group.
- Fourth graders can help build community. Show them how to be supportive of others.
- Fourth graders want to know more about other people. Help them understand how people of all cultures make our community special and unique.

"I understand that in order for my group or team to succeed, everyone must work together; everyone must develop his or her skills."

Chapter Connections

Chapter Poem

Invite

"The Chain of Life"

Use this poem to expand the chapter introduction.

- The children will relate the poem to their own lives, reflecting on the people who help and support them, such as parents and teachers.
- Connect those who care and support the children to how all humans are connected.

   Go to **aliveinchrist.osv.com** Lesson Planning section for this poem.

NCEA IFG: ACRE Edition

Discover

Knowledge of the Faith

- Objective: To know and understand basic Catholic teaching about the Incarnate Word Jesus Christ as the way, truth, and life

Communal Life

- Objectives: To know the origin, mission, structure, and communal nature of the Church; to know the rights and responsibilities of the Christian faithful

Catholic Social Teaching

Live

 Use one of these features to introduce a principle and engage the children with an activity.

- Call to Family, Community, and Participation, Pages 292–293
- Dignity of Work and Rights of Workers, Pages 298–299

Music Options

 Use one or more of the following songs to enhance catechetical learning or for prayer.

- "Raise Your Voice for Justice," Live Prayer, Page 104
- "Loving Others," Discover, Page 98
- "The Trinity," Discover, Page 98
- "Right and Just," Discover, Page 101
- "Peacemaker," Live, Page 102

LECTIONARY CONNECTION

 Chapter 5 highlights Lectionary-connected themes such as communal life, love for others, and the Holy Trinity. If your parish aligns its curriculum to the liturgical year, you could use this chapter in connection with the following Sundays.

Year A

Third Sunday in Ordinary Time—communal life

Second Sunday of Easter—communal life

Sixth Sunday of Easter—Holy Spirit

Year B

Fifth Sunday of Easter—love one another

Sixth Sunday of Easter—Holy Trinity

Year C

Third Sunday of Advent—children of God

Fourth Sunday of Lent—love of neighbor

 Go to **aliveinchrist.osv.com** for a complete correlation ordered by the Sundays of the year and suggestions for how to integrate the Scripture readings into chapter lessons.

Name _____   Date _____

Board Game

Instructions

Cut apart the game markers below. Give one to each player. Then, cut apart the numbers as well. Put all of the game marker pieces at the start line. Turn the numbers face down, and mix them up.

One at a time, each player chooses a number, moves the appropriate number of spaces, and then gives an example of how, when, or if they followed what is described in the space. The first player to reach the finish wins.

You asked a new student to eat lunch with you. **Move ahead 1 space.**

You let someone go before you in line. **Move ahead 1 space.**

FINISH

You hit someone on the playground. **Move back 2 spaces.**

You didn't tell the whole truth. **Move back 1 space.**

You cleaned your room without being asked. **Move ahead 2 spaces.**

You didn't laugh when a classmate fell. **Move ahead 1 space.**

You talked back to your mom or dad. **Move back 2 spaces.**

You gave $1.00 of your own money to charity. **Move ahead 2 spaces.**

You made fun of someone's clothes. **Move back 1 space.**

You prayed for a friend who is sick. **Move ahead 1 space.**

START

You shared your snack with a friend. **Move ahead 1 space.**

Living in Community

 Let Us Pray

Leader: God of unity and communion, God who is one and three-in-one, unite us in love.

"How good and how pleasant it is,
    when brothers dwell together as one!"
    Psalm 133:1

All: God of unity and communion, God who is one and three-in-one, unite us in love. Amen.

Scripture

In this way the love of God was revealed to us: God sent his only Son into the world so that we might have life through him. . . . Beloved, if God so loved us, we also must love one another. No one has ever seen God. Yet, if we love one another, God remains in us, and his love is brought to perfection in us. This is how we know that we remain in him and he in us, that he has given us of his Spirit. . . . God is love, and whoever remains in love remains in God and God in him.

1 John 4:9, 11–13, 16b

? What Do You Wonder?

- What are some things you do to keep a friendship going strong?
- Where can you look for help in living a moral life, or a life of love?

© Our Sunday Visitor

97

Optional Activity

Chapter Poem: "The Chain of Life" *Verbal/Linguistic*

Use this poem after the opening prayer, before explaining that God is one in three Divine Persons.

- Invite volunteers to each read one line of the poem.
- *Ask:* Who are three links in your chain of life?
- Invite the children to share some ways that all humans are connected. Remind them to refer to the poem to help them. When finished, transition back to the lesson instruction.

 Go to **aliveinchrist.osv.com** for Chapter Poem.

 **Let Us Pray**

Invite the children to gather in the prayer space and make the Sign of the Cross. Invite a child to take the role of leader. Prompt the children's response to the Psalm verse.

Have the children move out of the prayer space and back to their seats.

Explain how God is one in three Divine Persons.

Say: God lives not only in Heaven, but also in community, in true and deepening relationship. The Father gives us Jesus, who, in turn, reveals the Father and sends the Spirit.

Scripture

Guide the children through the process of Scripture reflection.

- Invite them to close their eyes, be still and open their minds and hearts to what God is saying to them in this passage.
- Proclaim the Scripture.
- Maintain several moments of silence.
- *Ask:* What did you hear God say to you today?
- Invite volunteers to share.

What Do You Wonder?

Say: God the Holy Trinity has created us to be like himself—to give ourselves in love to one another. Self-giving love is not always easy, but we reflect God when we give of ourselves.

Invite the children to respond to the questions. Ask what else they might wonder about relationships and living a moral life.

Objective

- Recognize that the mission of God the Son and the Holy Spirit is to bring all people into the love of the Holy Trinity

Created to Love

Ask: What does love of neighbor have to do with love of God?

- Write the children's responses on the board or on chart paper.

Work with Words

Point out the definition of *Holy Trinity*.

- Provide index cards and have the children make a vocabulary card.

Read aloud the first paragraph. Confirm the children's understanding of the Holy Trinity as God the Father, God the Son (Jesus Christ), and God the Holy Spirit.

- Refer to the Our Catholic Tradition reference section on page 308 of the Student Book for more about the Holy Trinity.

Invite volunteers to read aloud the last two paragraphs.

- ⭐ Direct the children to underline the mission of the Holy Trinity.
- Emphasize that God's plan is for people to live together in love, in community.

 Music Option: Have the children sing, "Loving Others" or "The Trinity," downloaded from **aliveinchrist.osv.com**.

Discover

Created to Love

What does love of neighbor have to do with love of God?

You learned in the last chapter that God made all people in his image. You are more clearly an image of God when you reflect the love of the **Holy Trinity** to others. The Holy Trinity is the mystery of one God in three Divine Persons: God the Father, God the Son, and God the Holy Spirit. God reveals himself as three unique Divine Persons, but the Father, Son, and Holy Spirit are one God.

Jesus is both divine and human, God and man. Jesus tells us that the mission of God the Son and God the Holy Spirit is to bring people into the love of the Holy Trinity—the perfect love that exists in the Father, Son, and Holy Spirit. God's plan is for people to live together in love.

From the time of the first humans, people have formed groups. When a group of people live together in love, it is a community. In a community like this, the people have common beliefs, hopes, and goals.

Jesus teaches his disciples.

> **Catholic Faith Words**
>
> **Holy Trinity** the mystery of one God in three Divine Persons: Father, Son, and Holy Spirit

> ⭐ Underline the mission of God the Son and God the Holy Spirit.

98   Chapter 5

Optional Activity

Illustrate Laws   *Mathematical/Logical*

God has laws that help people live together. So do communities.

- Discuss laws that help people live together in community. For example, speed limits help keep the streets safe.
- Ask the children to name a community law and illustrate how that law helps people.

Right and Responsibility

Each person has individual rights that are balanced with a responsibility to respect and protect the rights of others. No one has unlimited freedom or an unlimited right to the Earth's goods. When everyone's rights are in balance, the Kingdom of God is close at hand.

You can see a good example of this in the story of the early Christians. In this passage, we learn how they lived in the years just after Jesus' Resurrection and Ascension—praying, teaching, and caring for others.

 Scripture

The Communal Life

They devoted themselves to the teaching of the apostles and to the communal life, to the breaking of the bread and to the prayers. Awe came upon everyone, and many wonders and signs were done through the apostles. All who believed were together and had all things in common; they would sell their property and possessions and divide them among all according to each one's need. *Acts 2:42–45*

© Our Sunday Visitor

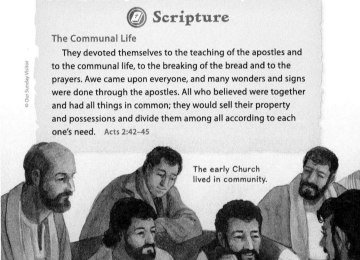

The early Church lived in community.

Share Your Faith

Reflect What are some practical ways people in a community show their love for one another?

Share Tell a partner about one way this happens in your parish today.

Living in Community **99**

 Scripture Background

Acts 2:42–45

The Acts of the Apostles are sometimes referred to as "the acts of the Holy Spirit" because this Book recognizes the guidance of the Holy Spirit in the development of community life.

- The Book of Acts provides important information about life in the earliest Christian communities, such as sharing of goods, the celebration of the Eucharist, and their early attempts at organization.

Right and Responsibility

Invite a volunteer to read aloud the first paragraph.

- Tell the children that a community tries to achieve a balance between rights and responsibilities.

Scripture

Invite a volunteer to read aloud the second paragraph to introduce the Scripture story.

Proclaim "The Communal Life."

- Invite the children to imagine what it might have been like to live among the first Christians.
- *Ask:* How is your parish like the early Christians?

Activity

Read aloud the directions for the Share Your Faith activity.

- Have the children work independently to write their ideas. After a short time, have them share their ideas with a partner.
- In pairs, have the children tell one way their parish community shows love for one another.

Quick Review

Christians form communities that reflect the love of the Holy Trinity. People in communities have both rights and responsibilities.

Objectives

- Define morality as living in right relationship with God, yourself, and others

- Appreciate that God created all people for one another and we must all work for the common good

- Connect that our love of our neighbor reflects the love of the Holy Trinity

Living as Catholics

Ask: What does it mean to live a moral life?

- Write the children's responses on the board or on chart paper.

Love One Another

Read this section aloud.

- Point out that the early Christians took Jesus' example as their model and that Christians today do the same.

Moral Living

Ask the children to read this section to identify what helps a Christian lead a moral life.

- *Ask:* How are you called to live as part of the larger community of faith?

Work with Words

Have the children make vocabulary cards for the Catholic Faith Words: *morality* and *common good*.

Living as Catholics

What does it mean to live a moral life?

Love One Another

The early Christians formed a community based on a common faith in Jesus Christ and his message. Their faith and love are an example for you today. Faith is your "yes" to all that God has revealed. God created all men and women equal in dignity and in his image. So respect for the rights and needs of others is part of faith.

Just as you cannot live in isolation from others, so you cannot believe alone. You believe as part of a larger community of faith. As a Catholic, you are called to live a good moral life.

Catholic Faith Words

morality living in right relationship with God, yourself, and others. It is putting your beliefs into action.

common good the good of everyone, with particular concern for those who might be most vulnerable to harm

Moral Living

The moral life is a way of living in right relationship with God, yourself, and others. Catholic **morality** includes following the Ten Commandments, the teachings of Jesus, and the teachings of the Church. It also includes following the good and just laws that work for the **common good**.

Catholic families and your parish community are places where you can learn to live the Catholic moral life.

➡ How are you called to live as part of a larger community of faith?

An altar server places the Procession Cross during the Introductory Rites of the Mass.

100

Optional Activity

Activity Master 5: Board Game

Distribute copies of the activity found on catechist page 97E.

- Playing the game will reinforce what types of actions are involved in living a moral life.

- As an alternative, you may wish to send this activity home with the children.

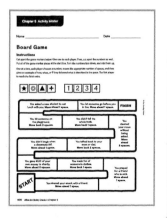

The Common Good

People who live in true communities work for the common good by

- respecting the human dignity of each person and acknowledging each person's right to freedom and self-expression, as long as others are not hurt.
- making sure that every person has a way to get the things that are necessary for life, such as food, shelter, clothing, and access to doctors.
- providing peace, security, and order in the community.

Connect Your Faith

For the Common Good Beside each picture, explain how these people in your neighborhood or parish work for the common good.

respecting the human dignity of each person

_____
_____
_____

making sure that people can get the things that are necessary for life

_____
_____
_____

providing peace, security, and order

_____
_____
_____

Living in Community **101**

The Common Good

Read the introductory statement.

Invite volunteers to each read aloud one of the bullets.

- Remind the children of the definition of the *common good*. Tell them that the common good is important for everyone, and especially for those who might be most vulnerable in the world.

 Music Option: Have the children sing, "Right and Just," downloaded from **aliveinchrist.osv.com**.

Activity

Point out the Connect Your Faith activity.

- Read aloud the directions and talk through the activity with the group.
- Have the children work independently to write their responses.
- Invite volunteers to share their answers with the group.

Quick Review

Christian morality helps people live as a community of faith. People in communities work for the common good.

✓ Quick Tip

Think Globally

In his encyclical, *The Hundredth Year*, Pope Saint John Paul II emphasized the world's interconnectedness.

- Point out to the children that despite our differences, we are one human family.
- Discuss how a person's actions affects everyone. Provide sinful examples such as killing or stealing as well as positive examples like feeding the poor or recycling.

Our Catholic Life

Ask: How should you live as part of a community?

- Write the children's responses on the board or on chart paper.

Read the text aloud.

Living in Community

 Read aloud the directions to the activity.

- Encourage the children to work on their own to complete the activity.
- When everyone has finished, invite volunteeers to share their answers.

Organize the children into five groups.

- Assign each group one of the guidelines.
- Have each group list concrete suggestions for following the assigned guideline.
- Invite each group to share their list with the rest of the children.

> Music Option: Have the children sing, "Peacemaker," downloaded from **aliveinchrist.osv.com**.

Live

Our Catholic Life

How should you live as part of a community?

Your actions affect the lives of others. As part of the community of God's family, you have a responsibility to those around you. When you act responsibly, you help create a more loving community.

Here are some guidelines for becoming a good member of the community.

1. Choose words from the Word List to complete the sentences.
2. Circle what you are already doing to live as a good community member.
3. Write one way you can be a better community member.

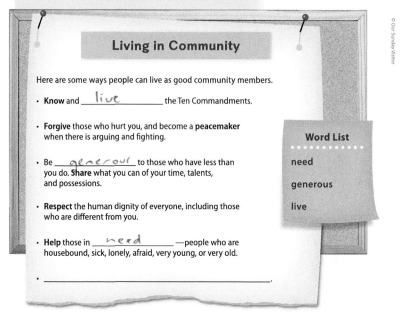

Living in Community

Here are some ways people can live as good community members.

- **Know** and ___live___ the Ten Commandments.

- **Forgive** those who hurt you, and become a **peacemaker** when there is arguing and fighting.

- Be ___generous___ to those who have less than you do. **Share** what you can of your time, talents, and possessions.

- **Respect** the human dignity of everyone, including those who are different from you.

- **Help** those in ___need___ —people who are housebound, sick, lonely, afraid, very young, or very old.

- _____.

Word List

need

generous

live

© Our Sunday Visitor

 Quick Tip

Offer Solidarity

Part of living in a community is showing solidarity. Watch for situations in your community in which the children can show that they care.

- Be alert to situations in which people have suffered a tragedy, such as a fire, a natural disaster, or a death.
- Help the children find ways to show care and concern, such as by writing notes, making cards, or raising money.

People of Faith

Saint Dominic, 1170–1221

August 8

Saint Dominic knew that it was important for people who work for God to be together. He founded a religious order called the Order of Preachers. Sometimes they are called *Dominicans*, after him. His motto was: "to praise, to bless, to preach." He wanted his followers to always praise God, bless everyone they met, and preach the Gospel. He also wanted them to live together in community. They shared all they had, like the earliest followers of Jesus did. Even today, Dominicans dedicate their lives to telling people the Good News, and they still live in community.

Discuss: How does your family work together for the good of each person?

 Learn more about Saint Dominic at **aliveinchrist.osv.com**

Live Your Faith

Look at what the people in the pictures are doing to help one another.

Decide on one thing you can do next week to help create a more loving community.

List the steps you will take to make this happen.

To do list
☐
☐
☐
☐
☐

Living in Community **103**

🌐 Catholic Social Teaching

Chapter Connections

To integrate Catholic Social Teaching into your lesson, choose one of the following features: Call to Family, Community, and Participation, pages 292–293; or Dignity of Work and Rights of Workers, pages 298–299.

- Start the Live step of the process by talking about Saint Dominic on page 103. Then move directly to the Catholic Social Teaching feature.
- Or, to expand the lesson, complete both pages 102 and 103, then move to the Catholic Social Teaching feature.
- Return to Chapter 5 for the prayer on page 104.

People of Faith

Tell the children about Saint Dominic.

- Invite a volunteer to read aloud the People of Faith story.
- Explain that Saint Dominic founded a religious order called the Order of Preachers, also known as the Dominicans.
- The worldwide popularity of the Rosary is attributed to Saint Dominic. For centuries, Dominicans have helped to spread the Rosary and emphasized the Catholic belief in the power of the Rosary.
- When Saint Dominic was a young student, he gave away his money, and sold his clothes and furniture to feed the poor.
- *Ask:* How does your family work together for the good of each person?

 Encourage the children to go to **aliveinchrist.osv.com** at home to find out more about Saint Dominic.

Activity

Read aloud the directions for the Live Your Faith activity.

- As a group discuss the first part of the activity.
- Allow time for the children to complete the activity on their own.
- Invite the children to share their ideas with a partner.

Let Us Pray
Lectio Divina
Explain to the children that this ancient prayer of the Church, probably dating back to the third century, is a slow praying of the Scriptures in which we listen for what the Holy Spirit wants us to hear.

Prepare
Designate Side 1 and Side 2.

> ▶ Rehearse "Raise Your Voice for Justice," downloaded from **aliveinchrist.osv.com**.

Gather
Invite the children to process to the prayer space. Have each child bring their book.

- Have the Side 1 children stand together in one place and the Side 2 stand together in another.
- Invite the children to prepare their minds and hearts for prayer.

Pray
- *Before the first reading:* Invite the children to listen to the Scripture reading, listening for the one word or one phrase that is meaningful to them.
- *First Reflection:* Invite the children to choose their word or phrase and have them think about what it means to them.
- *Prior to second reading:* Invite the children to listen to the Scripture reading a second time.
- *Second Reflection:* Ask the children to think about what their word or phrase calls them to do.

> Conclude by singing together "Raise Your Voice for Justice."

 Let Us Pray
Lectio Divina
This ancient prayer of the Church is a slow praying of the Scriptures in which we listen for what the Holy Spirit wants us to hear.

Gather and begin with the Sign of the Cross.

Leader: Come Holy Spirit. Open our ears;

All: open our minds; open our hearts.

Leader: Read John 14:27
First Reflection

Leader: Read John 14:27
Second Reflection

Leader: United as one community, committed to grow as one in God, we pray:

Side 1: Glory be to the Father

Side 2: and to the Son

Side 1: and to the Holy Spirit,

Side 2: as it was in the beginning

Side 1: is now, and ever shall be

Side 2: world without end.

All: Amen.

 Sing "Raise Your Voice for Justice"

 Liturgy Link

Lectio Divina
This method of prayer has its roots in the monastic tradition of Christianity.

- It is translated as "holy reading," "meditative reading," or "spiritual reading."
- The method is divided into five steps: *reading, meditation, prayer, contemplation,* and *action.*

> Go to **aliveinchrist.osv.com** for Sunday readings, Scripture background, questions of the week, and seasonal resources.

FAMILY + FAITH
LIVING AND LEARNING TOGETHER

YOUR CHILD LEARNED >>>
This chapter explains that the Holy Trinity—God the Father, God the Son, and God the Holy Spirit—shows us how to live in right relationship with God, ourselves, and one another.

Scripture
Read **1 John 4:9, 11–13, 16b** to find out why God sent his Son, Jesus, to live among us.

Catholics Believe
- God created people for one another, and all must work for the common good. Such love of neighbor reflects the love of the Holy Trinity.
- No one can believe alone, just as no one can live alone.

To learn more, go to the *Catechism of the Catholic Church #1905–1912* at **usccb.org.**

People of Faith
This week, your child learned about Saint Dominic, the founder of the Dominican Order. His life motto was "to praise, to bless, to preach."

CHILDREN AT THIS AGE >>>
How They Understand Being Created for One Another Most children this age are very social. But the social skills of your child have probably moved beyond the early childhood years of simply wanting to play with other children to forming real bonds of friendship. This is a time of "best friends," when children form close relationships with one or a few children they prefer to spend their time with. It is the beginning of the deeper relationships they will hopefully enjoy for the rest of their lives.

CONSIDER THIS >>>
When a Catholic says, "God is love," what do we mean?

As Catholics, we believe God's nature is a relationship of perfect love—a communion of love between Father, Son, and Holy Spirit. God, "ever-faithful and forgiving, is ultimately experienced by human beings through his Son, Jesus Christ, and the Holy Spirit. His love is stronger than a mother's love for her child or a bridegroom for his beloved. [. . .] Jesus has revealed that God's very being is love" (*USCCA, p. 51*).

LET'S TALK >>>
- Ask your child to explain the connection between love of neighbor and love of God.
- Talk about how people in your community work for the common good.

LET'S PRAY >>>
Dear God, help us always live in peace and work for the good of each person in our family. Amen.

 For a multimedia glossary of Catholic Faith Words, Sunday readings, seasonal and Saint resources, and chapter activities go to **aliveinchrist.osv.com.**

Chapter 5 Review

A Work with Words **Solve the crossword puzzle.**

Down
1. A group of people with similar beliefs, working together toward a common goal
2. Living in right relationship with God, self, and others
4. Members of a community _____ on one another.

Across
3. The result of respecting and working for everyone's rights in a community
5. When we show this to others, we follow God's way and live a moral life.

Crossword answers:
- 1 Down: COMMUNITY
- 2 Down: MORALITY
- 3 Across: COMMON GOOD
- 4 Down: DEPEND
- 5 Across: LOVE

B Check Understanding **Circle the word that best completes each statement.**

6. Your (beliefs/**actions**) affect the lives of others.
7. Your individual rights are (**balanced**/unconnected) with your responsibility to respect and protect the rights of others.
8. God created (some/**all**) men and women equal in human dignity and in his image.
9. A Catholic community where you can worship and learn is called a (**parish**/city).
10. As a Catholic, you are called to live a (**good**/partly) moral life.

 Go to **aliveinchrist.osv.com** for an interactive review.

Family + Faith

Distribute the page to the children or parents/adult family members. Point out the chapter highlights, insights on how fourth graders understand concepts, the opportunity for the adults to reflect on their own experience and faith journey, and the family prayer.

Chapter Review

Use Catechist Quick Reviews to highlight lesson concepts.

A **Work with Words**
Have the children solve the crossword puzzle.

B **Check Understanding**
Have the children circle the word that best completes the sentence.

Go to **aliveinchrist.osv.com** to prepare customized and downloadable assessments, send eAssessments, and assign interactive reviews.

Living in Community **105–106**

KEY CONCEPT

God's grace helps us use reason and free will to make good choices. Conscience is our God-given ability that helps us judge right from wrong.

DOCTRINAL CONTENT

- Free will is the God-given freedom and ability to make choices. (CCC, 1704)
- God gives us grace, the Ten Commandments, and the Church to help us make good choices and deepen our relationship with him. (CCC, 1785)
- We need to know God's laws and form, or strengthen, our conscience so it will help us make good decisions. (CCC, 1783–1784)
- Conscience is the God-given ability that helps us judge whether actions are morally good or wrong. (CCC, 1777)

TASKS OF CATECHESIS

Helping children grow in a faith that is "known, celebrated, lived, and expressed in prayer" (NDC, 20).

This chapter focuses on the following tasks of catechesis:

- Promoting Knowledge of the Faith
- Moral Formation

Catechist Background

Not by appearance shall he judge, nor by hearsay shall he decide, But he shall judge the poor with justice, and decide fairly for the land's afflicted. Isaiah 11:3b–4a

→ **Reflect** What helps you to know what is right and just?

God wants humans to come freely to his love. Free will gives you the ability to make choices and to act on them. This is both the right and the responsibility of Catholics trying to be disciples of Jesus. Humans don't always choose to do good. Sometimes they choose to sin. But we are given free will so we might freely choose good. If you cannot freely decide how to act, you cannot truly choose what is good.

You mature spiritually and morally as you exercise your free will. You learn from your good choices as well as from your mistakes. Free will makes you accountable. God asks you to be part of his plan and then lets you choose your response.

Within every person is a conscience that moves him or her to make good choices and avoid bad choices. Sacred Scripture and Sacred Tradition feed and inform your growing conscience as you navigate through the various choices in your life. The Holy Spirit is always ready to assist you. Your informed conscience brings you closer to God and the Christian community.

→ **Reflect** What people or events have been most important in forming your conscience?

Catechist's Prayer

God of Wisdom, open the minds and hearts of the children in my group to use the gifts of free will and conscience to make good choices. Guide them to recognize your voice. Amen.

Lesson Plan

Objectives	Process	Materials

🕐 Invite, 10 minutes

Making Good Choices Page 107

- ♥ Psalm 119:66 Pray the opening prayer.
- 📖 Isaiah 11:1-4a Reflect prayerfully on the Word.
- Discuss What Do You Wonder questions.

◉ **Optional Activity**
Chapter Poem:
"Too Many Choices"

🕐 Discover, 35 minutes

Choices and Consequences
Pages 108–109

- Define free will as the God-given ability to choose between good and evil
- Recall that God gives us grace, the Ten Commandments, and the Church to help us make good choices and to deepen our relationship with him

- **Catholic Faith Words** free will, grace
- Explain that all choices have consequences.
- Explain that we grow closer to God when we use free will to make a good choice.
- ☆ Underline ways God helps us make good decisions.
- **Share Your Faith Activity** Describe how Julia felt after she made her choice.

☐ pencils
☐ index cards

God's Gift of Conscience
Pages 110–111

- Understand that knowing God's laws and forming, or strengthening, our conscience will help us make good decisions
- Identify conscience as the God-given ability that helps us judge whether actions are morally good or wrong

- **Catholic Faith Words** conscience
- Explain that good choices help us grow as a moral person.
- 📖 Luke 10:30-35 Proclaim "The Good Samaritan."
- Explain that our conscience is a gift from God.
- ☆ Identify ways to form a conscience.
- **Connect Your Faith Activity** Offer advice for scenarios.

☐ pencils
☐ index cards
- **Optional Activity**
Word Puzzle
☐ Activity Master 6 (Page 107E)

🕐 Live, 15 minutes

Our Catholic Life Pages 112–113

- Explore four steps for making good decisions.
- **People of Faith** Learn about Saint Charles Lwanga.
- **Live Your Faith Activity** Draw steps used to make a good decision.

☐ pencils
☐ crayons or markers

Prayer of Reflection Page 114

- Introduce contemplation as a form of prayer.
- ▶ Prepare the instrumental music.
- Follow the order of prayer.

◉ Download instrumental music.

Family + Faith Page 115

Point out that the Catholic Families page provides chapter highlights, information on how fourth graders understand faith concepts, and family prayer.

Chapter Review Page 116

◉ aliveinchrist.osv.com
- Customize and Download Assessments
- Email Links to eAssessments
- Interactive Student Reviews

Teaching This Grade

ONLINE RESOURCES

 Go to **aliveinchrist.osv.com**

You will find:

- Interactive lesson planning with web specific content and additional activities
- Step by step lesson instruction from printed Catechist Edition for integrated lesson planning
- Custom-built assessments to download and eAssessment links
- Interactive reviews that provide scores and the option to review answers
- Sunday readings with background and questions of the week

 Go to **osvparish.com**

You will find:

- Ask the Experts Q and A
- General Catechist Helps
- Community Connections and Blogs

Sharing the Message with Fourth Graders

Free Will and Conscience Fourth grade children understand well that adults do not always see what they say and do. They also know that there are limits to the ability of authority figures in their life to enforce their will. Being a moral person, then, becomes a series of choices. They need to understand that these choices are given to us so that we can have the freedom to choose the good. This is also the beginning of the understanding of conscience. As children become more aware of their inner thought lives, they can form and listen to the voice inside that will help them make good choices.

Teaching Tip: Emphasize that conscience is not necessarily the same as what we feel like doing. We each need to form our consciences with Scripture and Church teaching to ensure that our conscience is a faithful guide.

How Fourth Graders Understand

- Fourth graders can do simple chores. Chores help them become more responsible.
- Fourth graders need practice making choices. Allow them to help decide on room rules and procedures.
- Give fourth graders opportunities to consider better or best choices, not simply right or wrong choices.

"I like to role-play. Give me chances to enact modern day scenes and Bible stories."

Chapter Connections

Chapter Poem

Invite

"Too Many Choices"

Use this poem to expand the chapter introduction.

- The children will relate the poem to their own lives, reflecting on the choices they make.
- Connect that some choices are more important than others.

 Go to **aliveinchrist.osv.com** Lesson Planning section for this poem.

NCEA IFG: ACRE Edition

Discover

Knowledge of the Faith

- Objective: To know and understand basic Catholic teaching about the Incarnate Word Jesus Christ as the way, truth, and life

Moral Formation

- Objectives: To be knowledgeable about the teachings of Jesus and the Church as the basis of Christian morality and to understand Catholic Social Teaching; to be aware of the importance of a well-formed conscience for decision making

Catholic Social Teaching

Live

 Use one of these features to introduce a principle and engage the children with an activity.

- Rights and Responsibilities of the Human Person, Pages 294–295
- Option for the Poor and Vulnerable, Pages 296–297

Music Options

 Use one or more of the following songs to enhance catechetical learning or for prayer.

- Instrumental background music, Live Prayer, Page 114
- "Choices," Discover, Page 109
- "Open My Eyes," Page 111

LECTIONARY CONNECTION

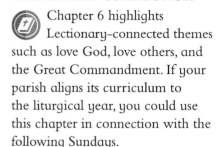 Chapter 6 highlights Lectionary-connected themes such as love God, love others, and the Great Commandment. If your parish aligns its curriculum to the liturgical year, you could use this chapter in connection with the following Sundays.

Year A

Twenty-third Sunday in Ordinary Time—love, law

Thirtieth Sunday in Ordinary Time—Great Commandment

Year B

Thirty-first Sunday in Ordinary Time—love God and neighbor

Fifth Sunday of Easter—love God and others

Year C

Fifth Sunday of Easter—love one another

Fifteenth Sunday in Ordinary Time—Great Commandment

Go to **aliveinchrist.osv.com** for a complete correlation ordered by the Sundays of the year and suggestions for how to integrate the Scripture readings into chapter lessons.

Name _____   Date _____

Word Puzzle

Complete each sentence, and write the answer on the lines provided. Then transfer the letter to the numbered spaces at the bottom of the page. You will discover a sentence that gives some good advice.

1. You can use the gift of free will to make _____ choices

   ☐ ☐ ☐ ☐
   13 5 5 14

2. _____ weakens your relationship with God.

   ☐ ☐ ☐
   15 10 9

3. Prayer and _____ help you think things through.

   ☐ ☐ ☐ ☐ ☐
   15 3 6 14 4

4. Disobeying a _____ can have unfortunate consequences.

   ☐ ☐ ☐ ☐
   7 6 1 11

5. God will give you a second chance to make a _____ choice.

   ☐ ☐ ☐ ☐ ☐ ☐
   12 2 3 3 2 7

6. You can _____ on the Holy Spirit to help you.

   ☐ ☐ ☐ ☐
   7 2 1 4

7. Good choices help you grow _____ to God.

   ☐ ☐ ☐ ☐ ☐ ☐
   8 1 5 15 2 7

☐ ☐ ☐ ☐ ☐ ☐ ☐
1 2 3 4 5 6 7

☐ ☐ ☐ ☐ ☐ ☐ ☐ ☐ ☐ ☐
8 5 9 15 8 10 11 9 8 11

☐ ☐ ☐ ☐ ☐ ☐ ☐ ☐ ☐ ☐ ☐
12 2 4 5 6 7 13 6 10 14 11

Making Good Choices

 Let Us Pray

Leader: O God, give us a faith strong enough to see what is right and just.

"Teach me wisdom and knowledge, for in your commandments I trust." **Psalm 119:66**

All: O God, give us the wisdom and knowledge to make choices that are true to that faith. Amen.

 Scripture

A shoot shall sprout from the stump of Jesse, and from his roots a bud shall blossom. The spirit of the LORD shall rest upon him: a spirit of wisdom and of understanding, A spirit of counsel and of strength, a spirit of knowledge and of fear of the LORD, and his delight shall be the fear of the LORD. Not by appearance shall he judge, nor by hearsay shall he decide, But he shall judge the poor with justice, and decide fairly for the land's afflicted.

Isaiah 11:1–4a

What Do You Wonder?

- Who or what helps you choose what is right and just?
- What are some ways you can form your conscience in order to choose what is right and just?

© Our Sunday Visitor

107

Optional Activity

Chapter Poem: "Too Many Choices" *Verbal/Linguistic*

Use this poem after the opening prayer, before explaining that God created us with the ability to make choices.

- Read aloud the poem as the children follow along.
- *Ask:* What is an important choice you have made?
- *Ask:* What helps you make a choice? What makes it harder?
- After the discussion, transition back to the lesson instruction.

 Go to **aliveinchrist.osv.com** for Chapter Poem.

 **Invite**

 Let Us Pray

Invite the children to gather in the prayer space and make the Sign of the Cross. Choose a volunteer to read the Psalm. Prompt the children's response.

Have the children move out of the prayer space and back to their seats.

Say: We have the ability to choose right or wrong. Making the right choice is not always easy. That is why God promised to send a Savior who would show us the way to choose.

Scripture

Guide the children through the process of Scripture reflection.

- Invite them to close their eyes, be still and open their minds and hearts to what God is saying to them in this passage.
- Proclaim the Scripture.
- Maintain several moments of silence.
- *Ask:* What did you hear God say to you today?
- Invite volunteers to share.

What Do You Wonder?

Say: God gives us the freedom to choose as well as a Savior who shows us how to choose. God also gives us a conscience. When it is properly formed, our conscience can tell us whether a choice is a wise choice.

Invite the children to respond to the questions. Ask what else they might wonder about making choices and knowing right from wrong.

Discover

Objectives

- Define free will as the God-given ability to choose between good and evil
- Recall that God gives us grace, the Ten Commandments, and the Church to help us make good choices and to deepen our relationship with him

Choices and Consequences

Ask: What is the proper use of free will?

- Write the children's responses on the board or on chart paper.

Julia Decides

Read aloud the story. Ask two volunteers to pantomime the story as you read.

- *Ask:* What is something that happened because of Julia's choice? She improved and won the award.

- Ask the children to think about the consequences that might have occurred if another choice had been made in the story.

- Offer other examples of choices and consequences, such as whether a child should go along when a friend is making a bad decision, or help that friend make a better choice, or whether they should ignore it when they see someone being bullied, or speak to an adult.

Discover

© Our Sunday Visitor

Choices and Consequences

What is the proper use of free will?

You have the freedom to make choices, but all choices have consequences. In this story, Julia learns a lesson from a choice she makes.

Julia Decides

"Come on, Julia!" said Monica. "I really want to see the new movie at the Crosstown Cinema. I thought you wanted to see it, too."

"I do want to see it," Julia replied. "Maybe we can see it next week.

108 Chapter 6

My coach just called an extra soccer practice for this afternoon. I have to go."

"Well, you can go to soccer practice if you want to," said Monica. "I am going to the movie."

After Monica left, Julia got ready for practice. "I can see that movie later with my sister Lila," she thought as she tied her shoes. "Right now I have to work on my goal tending. The team is counting on me."

When Julia finally saw the movie, she enjoyed it. However, not as much as she enjoyed winning the award for most improved player at the end of the season!

 Catechist Background

Freedom

Fourth graders' ideas about freedom usually revolve around freedom from rules or restrictions. You can deepen their understanding.

- Instead of freedom from something, emphasize freedom to do something—in this case freedom to make good choices.
- The children should come to realize that freedom to make choices does not grant them freedom from responsibility for those choices.

Freedom and Responsibility

Julia's story shows that all choices have consequences. You are responsible for your choices, too.

When God created you in his image, he gave you **free will**. With your free will, you make choices. Sometimes your choices are between right and wrong. Sometimes, as in Julia's case, they are between better and best. Whenever you make a good choice, you use God's gift of free will properly and you grow closer to God.

God Helps You

God gives you many gifts to help you make good choices. God's most important gift is **grace**, which is God's free and loving gift to you of his own life and help. You received grace in a special way in the Sacrament of Baptism. You grow in God's grace through the Sacraments, prayer, and good moral choices.

In addition to his <u>grace</u>, God gives you <u>the Ten Commandments</u> and the <u>Church</u> to help you. God is always helping you develop a more loving relationship with him.

Catholic Faith Words

free will the God-given freedom and ability to make choices. God created us with free will so we can have the freedom to choose good.

grace God's free and loving gift to humans of his own life and help

Underline three ways God helps you make good choices.

Share Your Faith

Reflect What was most difficult about Julia's choice? What two words would you use to describe how she felt after she made her choice?

_____

_____

Share Design a ribbon for Julia's Most Improved Player award.

Making Good Choices **109**

✓ Quick Tip

Be Positive

Emphasize to the children the positive message of the Catholic faith. Tell them that God's power is greater than the power of sin.

- Focus your presentation on the gift of God's grace.
- Emphasize that the Ten Commandments show us how to live in right relationships.
- Do not deny the reality of sin or the harm that sin does but also show the children how making good choices draws us closer to God.

Freedom and Responsibility

Tell the children to read silently these two paragraphs.

- Read aloud the last sentence of the section.
- Emphasize that growing closer to God is a consequence of making a good choice.

Work with Words

Point out the terms *free will* and *grace*.

- Distribute index cards and have the children use them to make vocabulary cards.

God Helps You

As a group, read aloud the text.

- Recall those gifts of God that help humans do good and avoid wrong.
- For a list of the Ten Commandments, refer the children to page 316 in the Our Catholic Tradition reference section of the Student Book.

> ▶ Music Option: Have the children sing, "Choices," downloaded from **aliveinchrist.osv.com**.

Activity

Read aloud the directions for the Share Your Faith activity.

- Have the children work independently to write their ideas.
- After a short time, have them discuss their ideas with a partner.

Quick Review

People are given the ability to make choices, and they have help in making good decisions.

Discover

Objectives

- Understand that knowing God's laws and forming, or strengthening, our conscience will help us make good decisions
- Identify conscience as the God-given ability that helps us judge whether actions are morally good or wrong

God's Gift of Conscience

Ask: What is a well-formed conscience?

- Write the children's responses on the board or on chart paper.

Summarize the paragraph to introduce the Scripture story.

Scripture

Draw attention to the picture. Ask the children to tell what they see happening in the picture.

Invite a volunteer to proclaim "The Parable of the Good Samaritan."

- Point out that Jewish listeners would have expected the priest and the Jewish leader to help others.
- *Ask:* What was difficult about the choice the Samaritan made?
- *Ask:* When is it difficult for you to make good choices?

God's Gift of Conscience

What is a well-formed conscience?

Good choices help you grow as a moral person. They build good habits and strengthen your relationship with God and others. One day Jesus told this story about showing love, even toward people whom we do not know.

Catholic Faith Words

conscience the God-given ability that helps us judge whether actions are right or wrong. It is important for us to know God's laws so our conscience can help us make good decisions.

Scripture

The Parable of the Good Samaritan

Jesus told the story of a Jewish traveler going from Jerusalem to Jericho who was attacked by robbers that beat, robbed, and left him on the side of the road.

A priest saw the injured traveler and moved to the other side of the road. Later, a Jewish leader came to the same place, and when he saw the traveler, he too moved to the other side of the road. Finally, a Samaritan came to the place where the traveler lay dying. Unlike the others, the Samaritan stopped. He treated and bandaged the traveler's wounds. He carried him on his own animal to an inn, where he cared for him. The next day, when the Samaritan was leaving, he gave the innkeeper money and told him, "Take care of this man. If you spend more than what I have given you, I will repay you when I return." **Based on Luke 10:30–35**

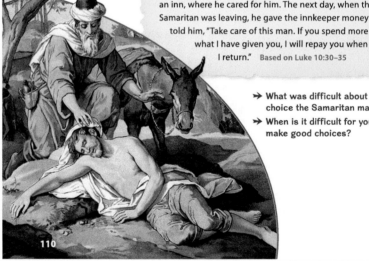

→ What was difficult about the choice the Samaritan made?
→ When is it difficult for you to make good choices?

110

Songs of Scripture

The Good Samaritan

This song retells the Scripture story in the verses while the chorus continually reminds us that a neighbor is the one who helps and stays.

- Invite the children to listen to the song and to volunteer to be the main characters. These children can act out the story as it is sung.
- The remainder of the children can participate in the chorus. Invite this group to create gestures for the words of the chorus.

  ▶ Use *Songs of Scripture*, Grades 4–6 CD, Track 6

Know the Difference

Good choices strengthen your relationship with God and others. Sin weakens or destroys that relationship. Sin is always a failure to love God and others. When you use your free will to sin, you always become less free.

You probably know when you have done something wrong, even if no one has seen you. You know that you have acted against God's plan. Your **conscience** is a gift from God that helps you to know the difference between right and wrong. Conscience is your free will and your reason working together. They direct you to choose what is good and avoid what is wrong. It is your job to strengthen, or form, your own conscience. You cannot do this alone.

1. Place a check mark next to one thing you want to know more about.

2. Draw a star next to one way you will form your conscience this week.

Forming Your Conscience

The Holy Spirit	strengthens you to make good choices	☐
Prayer and study	help you think things through	☐
Scripture and Church teaching	guide your decisions	☐
Parents, teachers, and wise people	give you good advice	☐

© Our Sunday Visitor

Connect Your Faith

The Right Choice
For each scenario, what advice would you give to help a friend use God's gift of conscience to make the right choice? Take turns sharing with a partner.

Making Good Choices **111**

Optional Activity

Activity Master 6: Word Puzzle

Distribute copies of the activity found on catechist page 107E.

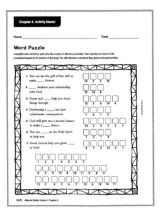

- Tell the children that when they solve the puzzle, they will find some good advice.

- As an alternative, you may wish to send this activity home with the children.

Have the children read silently the first two paragraphs.

Work with Words
Point out the term *conscience* and explain that it is the God-given ability to make choices.

- Distribute index cards and have the children each make a vocabulary card.

- Invite volunteers to talk about times when they have listened to their conscience.

☆ Read the directions aloud and have the children complete the activity on their own.

> ▶ Music Option: Have the children sing "Open My Eyes," downloaded from **aliveinchrist.osv.com**.

Activity

Point out the Connect Your Faith activity and read aloud the directions.

- As a group, talk through each scenario.

Quick Review

A well-developed conscience helps you avoid sin and reminds you that everyone is a neighbor to be loved and respected.

Our Catholic Life

Ask: How do you make decisions?

- Write the children's responses on the board or chart paper.

Read aloud the first two paragraphs.

Making Good Decisions

- Invite four volunteers to each read a box in the chart.
- After each child has read aloud his or her box, invite volunteers to share experiences in which using that step has been helpful in making a choice.

Discuss some common situations that children face, such as teasing, bullying, or making decisions about the use of time or money.

- Help the children look at the situations from various points of view.
- Choose an example, and have the children use the four steps to make good decisions.

Our Catholic Life

How do you make decisions?

Making good moral decisions takes practice. Remember the words *stop, think, pray,* and *choose.* They are steps to help you make decisions. These words will remind you what to do when you are faced with a moral choice.

These four steps may not help you make the easiest choice or the most popular choice, but they will help you make the best choice. This choice will strengthen your relationship with God and others.

Making Good Decisions

STOP	THINK
Take your time Do not make a snap decision or act on your first idea. • Important choices can affect you, others, and your relationship with God. • Give yourself time, and you are more likely to make a good decision.	**Consider your choices** Think about what might happen if you make each choice. • Say a prayer to the Holy Spirit for guidance. • Listen to your conscience. • Consider what the Bible and the Church teach you. • Consult with your family and teachers.
PRAY	**CHOOSE**
Ask for help in choosing Reflect on what God is calling you to do. • Pray again for help and guidance from the Holy Spirit. • Ask for wisdom and courage to make the best choice.	**Make up your mind** Decide what you will do. • Be confident that if you think and pray about your decision, you will make the right choice. • Act on your choice.

© Our Sunday Visitor

112

Quick Tip

Accountability

Fourth graders may not know the word *accountability*. However, they will understand its meaning when you teach them that choices have consequences not only for themselves and for their spiritual life, but also for the rest of society. Their choices can

- lead to habits of good or bad behavior.
- help or harm others, both loved ones and strangers.
- strengthen or damage their relationship with God.

People of Faith

Saint Charles Lwanga, d. 1886

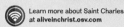
June 3

Saint Charles Lwanga was a young servant in the king's court in Uganda. The king hated Christians. He commanded his servants to join in immoral activities. Charles refused, choosing to follow his conscience and obey God, not the king. Charles and twenty-one other Christians were tortured before they were executed in an effort to get them to do what the king wanted. As Charles was dying, he prayed aloud and said that he knew he was going to Heaven. Charles and his companions are known as the African Martyrs.

Discuss: Tell about a time when you followed your conscience.

 Learn more about Saint Charles at **aliveinchrist.osv.com**

Live Your Faith

Think about a time when your conscience helped you to make a good moral decision. Then draw the steps you took to make that decision.

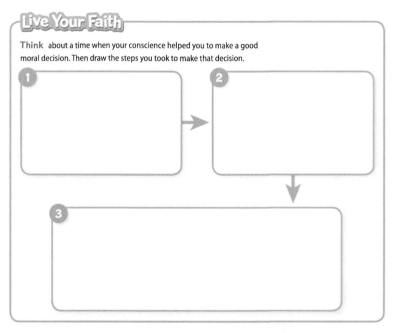

1

2

3

© Our Sunday Visitor

Catholic Social Teaching

Chapter Connections

To integrate Catholic Social Teaching into your lesson, choose one of the following features: Rights and Responsibilities of the Human Person, pages 294–295; or Option for the Poor and Vulnerable, pages 296–297.

- Start the Live step of the process by talking about Saint Charles Lwanga on page 113. Then move directly to the Catholic Social Teaching feature.
- Or, to expand the lesson, complete both pages 112 and 113, then move to the Catholic Social Teaching feature.
- Return to Chapter 6 for the prayer on page 114.

People of Faith

Tell the children about Saint Charles Lwanga.

- Invite a volunteer to read aloud the People of Faith story.
- Explain that Saint Charles Lwanga was only twenty-five years old when he died for his faith. He died not only because he would not submit to immoral acts, but also because he was protecting young boys who were studying the faith.
- Unfortunately King Mwanga's hatred could not be subdued and many Christians in Uganda died for their faith over the course of two years.
- Invite the children to tell about a time when they followed their conscience.

 Encourage the children to go to **aliveinchrist.osv.com** at home to find out more about Saint Charles Lwanga.

Activity

Read aloud the directions and discuss the Live Your Faith activity together as a group.

- Allow time for the children to complete the activity.
- Invite volunteers to share their drawings.

Live

 Let Us Pray

Prayer of Reflection

Tell the children that reflection is a form of prayer that will help them focus on and think about God.

Prepare

Explain to the children that today, you will be both the leader and reader.

 Select an instrumental song or download one from **aliveinchrist.osv.com**.

Gather

Invite the children to process to the prayer area.

- Make sure that the children are seated comfortably in the prayer space.
- Have the children prepare their minds and hearts for prayer.

Pray

Follow the order of prayer on the student page.

- Set the tone of the prayer by reading with a quiet voice and slower pace.

 Play instrumental music during the reflection.

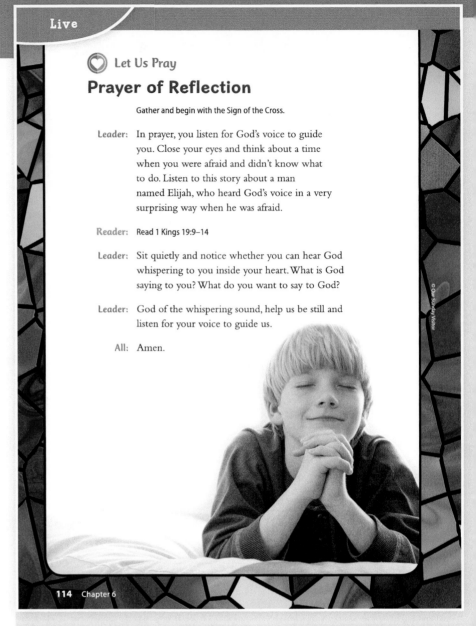

Live

 Let Us Pray

Prayer of Reflection

Gather and begin with the Sign of the Cross.

Leader: In prayer, you listen for God's voice to guide you. Close your eyes and think about a time when you were afraid and didn't know what to do. Listen to this story about a man named Elijah, who heard God's voice in a very surprising way when he was afraid.

Reader: Read 1 Kings 19:9–14

Leader: Sit quietly and notice whether you can hear God whispering to you inside your heart. What is God saying to you? What do you want to say to God?

Leader: God of the whispering sound, help us be still and listen for your voice to guide us.

All: Amen.

114 Chapter 6

 Liturgy Link

Silence

Silence is important in prayer. The Church community experiences silence in prayer after the Scripture is proclaimed at Mass.

- Include short periods of quiet within your prayer experiences.
- Respect for silence helps teach reverence.

Go to **aliveinchrist.osv.com** for Sunday readings, Scripture background, questions of the week, and seasonal resources.

FAMILY+FAITH
LIVING AND LEARNING TOGETHER

YOUR CHILD LEARNED >>>
This chapter explains that it is necessary to develop a well-formed conscience in order to choose good over evil.

Scripture
 Read **Isaiah 11:1–4a** to find out about the Savior God promised to send.

Catholics Believe
- God's grace helps us use our reason and free will to make good choices.
- Conscience is our God-given ability that helps us judge right from wrong.

To learn more, go to the *Catechism of the Catholic Church #1776–1782* at **usccb.org.**

People of Faith
This week, your child learned about Saint Charles Lwanga, an African martyr who was known for following his conscience.

CHILDREN AT THIS AGE >>>
How They Understand Free Will and Conscience Fourth grade children understand well that adults do not always see what they say and do. They also know that there are limits to the ability of authority figures in their life to enforce their will. Being a moral person, then, becomes a series of choices. They need to understand that these choices are given to us so that we can have the freedom to choose the good. This is also the beginning of the understanding of conscience. As children become more aware of their inner thoughts, they can form and listen to their conscience to help them make good choices.

CONSIDER THIS >>>
Have you ever considered the difference between a well-formed conscience and your opinion?

It can be all too easy to seemingly speak with authority even when we may not be well informed. There is a distinction between opinion and our conscience. As Catholics, we know that "a good conscience makes judgments that conform to reason and the good that is willed by the Wisdom of God. A good conscience requires lifelong formation. Each baptized follower of Christ is obliged to form his or her conscience according to objective moral standards" (*USCCA, p. 314*).

LET'S TALK >>>
- Ask your child to explain how all choices have consequences.
- Talk about a time when someone in the family had to make an important decision. How did the family help him or her?

LET'S PRAY >>>
 Saint Charles, pray for us that we may follow our consciences, even when it hard to do so. Amen.

For a multimedia glossary of Catholic Faith Words, Sunday readings, seasonal and Saint resources, and chapter activities go to **aliveinchrist.osv.com.**

Family + Faith

Distribute the page to the children or parents/adult family members. Point out the chapter highlights, insights on how fourth graders understand concepts, the opportunity for the adults to reflect on their own experience and faith journey, and the family prayer.

Chapter 6 Review

(A) Work with Words Complete each sentence with the correct term from the Word Bank.

Word Bank
moral
free will
conscience
God
grace

1. _____Free will_____ is the God-given freedom and ability to make choices.

2. Your _____conscience_____ is the God-given ability that helps us judge actions as right or wrong.

3. Good choices help you grow as a _____moral_____ person.

4. Sin weakens or destroys your relationship with _____God_____ and with others.

5. God's gift of his own life and help is _____grace_____.

(B) Make Connections Write responses on the lines below.

6. What is the lesson of the Parable of the Good Samaritan?
   Possible response: We should help our neighbors.

7. How do prayer and study help you?
   Possible response: Prayer and study help form my conscience.

8. What can help you make good decisions?
   Possible response: Grace, Scripture, and Church teachings help guide my decisions.

9. What happens when you choose to sin?
   Possible response: Sin hurts my relationship with God.

10. To whom can you go when you need advice?
    Possible response: parents, guardians, teachers, or other wise people

 Go to **aliveinchrist.osv.com** for an interactive review.

Chapter Review

Use Catechist Quick Reviews to highlight lesson concepts.

(A) Work with Words Complete each sentence with the correct term from the Word Bank.

(B) Check Understanding Write responses to the questions.

 Go to **aliveinchrist.osv.com** to prepare customized and downloadable assessments, send eAssessments, and assign interactive reviews.

Making Good Choices   **115–116**

Use Catechist Quick Reviews in each chapter to highlight lesson concepts for this unit and prepare for the Unit Review.

Have the children complete the Review pages. Then discuss the answers as a group. Review any concepts with which the children are having difficulty.

A **Work with Words**
Have the children write the correct word after each definition, then find the word in the word search. Explain that some words may be written backwards.

Unit Review

UNIT
2

A Work with Words Write the correct word after each definition. Then find the word in the word search. Some words may be written backwards.

F	C	D	E	V	Q	T	Y	Y	L
O	L	N	C	P	I	U	H	T	T
C	M	J	A	K	E	P	S	I	R
I	L	M	R	I	X	U	X	N	L
W	D	I	G	N	I	T	Y	U	C
J	D	Y	P	P	V	S	K	M	B
C	R	E	A	T	E	I	N	M	Y
E	C	N	E	I	C	S	N	O	C
X	V	Z	O	O	R	E	S	C	C

© Our Sunday Visitor

1. God's free and loving gift to us of his own life and help _____ grace
2. To make something from nothing _____ create
3. The God-given ability that helps you judge right from wrong _____ conscience
4. A group of people with common beliefs and goals _____ community
5. The worth each person has from being made in God's image _____ dignity

UNIT 2 — Unit Review

B Check Understanding Match each description in Column 1 with the correct term in Column 2. Terms may be used more than once.

Column 1	Column 2
6. cheating on homework	sin of omission
7. staying silent while someone is being teased	
	venial sin
8. lying to a friend	
9. a deliberate thought, word, deed, or omission contrary to the law of God	sin
10. murder	mortal sin

Match each description in Column 1 with the correct term in Column 2.

Column 1	Column 2
11. the spiritual part of a human that lives forever	conscience
12. ability from God to judge right from wrong	free will
13. a Catholic community with shared spiritual beliefs and worship	morality
14. living in right relationship with God, yourself, and others	parish
15. the freedom God has given you to make choices	soul

C Make Connections Write responses on the lines below.

16. What is the difference between mortal sin and venial sin?

<u>Possible response: Mortal sin causes a person's</u>
<u>relationship with God to be broken; venial sin</u>
<u>weakens a person's relationship with God.</u>

17. How does God help you make good choices?

<u>Possible responses: He gives us grace,</u>
<u>the Ten Commandments, and the Church.</u>

18. How can you work for the common good?

<u>Possible responses: respect the freedom and rights</u>
<u>of others, obey the rules in your community</u>

19. How would you describe morality?

<u>Possible responses: to honor and love God, to avoid</u>
<u>sin, to participate in the Church, to work for the</u>
<u>common good</u>

20. How can you develop your conscience?

<u>Possible responses: read Scripture, learn Church</u>
<u>teachings, seek advice of wise people, pray to the</u>
<u>Holy Spirit</u>

B Check Understanding

6–10. Have the children match the correct description in Column 1 with the correct term in Column 2. Explain that terms may be used more than once.

11–15. Match each description in Column 1 with the correct term in Column 2.

C Make Connections
Have the children write responses on the lines provided.

Go to **aliveinchrist.osv.com** to prepare customized and downloadable assessments, send eAssessments, and assign interactive reviews.

Jesus Christ

Our Catholic Tradition

- Jesus wants people to be happy and to carry his message of the goodness of God's Kingdom into the world. He shared that message in his teachings, most especially the Beatitudes. (CCC, 851, 1724)

- Jesus calls us to trust in the Father and to be a blessing to others by living the Great Commandment of love. (CCC, 2055)

- Jesus teaches us to praise God with worship, by honoring his name, and by keeping Sunday holy. (CCC, 2083)

How does Jesus' teaching in the Beatitudes help us to live the Ten Commandments?

Hagia Maria Sion Abbey stands just outside the Old City of Jerusalem, on Mt. Zion.

Unit 3 Overview

Chapter 7

The children will:

- describe how the Beatitudes guide us to show mercy and be a blessing for others
- understand that *beatitude* means "blessing" or "happiness." God put the desire for happiness inside each of us
- define the Beatitudes as teachings of Jesus that show the way to happiness and tell how to live in God's Kingdom now and always
- connect that because God first blessed us, everyone can be a blessing to others

 Songs of Scripture
"The Beatitudes"

 Catholic Social Teaching: Live Your Faith

- Option for the Poor and Vulnerable, Pages 296–297
- Solidarity of the Human Family, Pages 300–301

Chapter 8

The children will:

- describe the Great Commandment as the twofold command to love God above all else and your neighbor as yourself
- deepen understanding of the Theological Virtues as gifts from God that help us to believe in him, trust his plan for us, and love him with all our heart, soul, and mind
- connect that loving God leads to sharing his love with others, and the Corporal and Spiritual Works of Mercy guide us in the ways to do so

 Catholic Social Teaching: Live Your Faith

- Life and Dignity of the Human Person, Pages 290–291
- Solidarity of the Human Family, Pages 300–301

Chapter 9

The children will:

- recognize that the First Commandment teaches us to worship and honor only God, and not to place things or other people before him
- recognize that the Second Commandment calls us to always use the name of God with reverence
- define *blasphemy* as the sin of showing disrespect for the name of God, Jesus Christ, Mary, or the Saints
- appreciate that we observe the Third Commandment through participation in the Sunday Eucharist and rest

 Catholic Social Teaching: Live Your Faith

- Life and Dignity of the Human Person, Pages 290–291
- Care for God's Creation, Pages 302–303

Preview Unit Theme

Ask: What is the unit theme?

Summarize that the unit focuses on Jesus Christ.

Invite volunteers to read aloud each of the bullets in Our Catholic Tradition.

Explain to the children that they will learn about these things in the next three chapters.

Have the children study the photos and images. Invite volunteers to describe what they see. What do these images say about the unit theme?

Ask: How does Jesus' teaching in the Beatitudes help us to live the Ten Commandments?

After some discussion, explain to the children that they will be exploring this question in the next three chapters.

KEY CONCEPT

The Beatitudes are eight teachings that describe the Reign of God that Jesus announced when he lived on Earth. The Beatitudes show you how to live and act as a follower of Jesus.

DOCTRINAL CONTENT

- The Beatitudes guide us to show mercy and be a blessing to others. (CCC, 2444)

- The word *beatitude* means "blessing" or "happiness." God put the desire for happiness inside each of us. (CCC, 1718)

- The Beatitudes are teachings of Jesus that show the way to true happiness and tell how to live in God's Kingdom now and always. (CCC, 1716)

- God wants all of us to have eternal life—life forever with him for all who die in his friendship. (CCC, 1720–1721)

TASKS OF CATECHESIS

Helping children grow in a faith that is "known, celebrated, lived, and expressed in prayer" (NDC, 20).

This chapter focuses on the following tasks of catechesis:

- Moral Formation
- Missionary Initiation

Catechist Background

 Jesus replied, "Rather, blessed are those who hear the word of God and observe it." Luke 11:28

➜ **Reflect** What does it mean to be blessed?

God has been blessing the world from the beginning. After the Fall, God took a world that was headed toward death and turned it back toward life. He brought the Chosen People out of slavery, bestowed on them the gift of the Law, spoke through the prophets, and gave them his only Son, Jesus.

Because you are a baptized Catholic, blessing is your work, too. Your actions, like those of Christ, can be a source of blessing for others. When you ask God's blessing on a meal or on another person, you acknowledge that it is God who gives all gifts and makes them holy. When you bring God's peace to another person, you are doing the work of blessing that will bring you true happiness.

Jesus taught the Beatitudes in the Sermon on the Mount. In the light of the Christian message, the Beatitudes reframe the blessings promised to the Israelites. The Beatitudes reflect the way that Jesus lived his life. Jesus' actions brought to the world the peace, love, and justice that God desires. This Reign of God will reach its fullness at the end of time.

➜ **Reflect** What can you do today to be a blessing for others?

Catechist's Prayer

 God of peace, I thank you for the ways that your Spirit sustains me. Help me live the Beatitudes and teach by my example. Amen.

Lesson Plan

Objectives	Process	Materials

Invite, 10 minutes

The Beatitudes Page 121

- Psalm 33:12 Pray the opening prayer.
- Luke 11:27–28 Reflect prayerfully on the Word.
- Discuss What Do You Wonder questions.

Optional Activity
Chapter Story:
"Game Night"

Discover, 35 minutes

Jesus Brings God's Blessing
Pages 122–123

- Describe how the Beatitudes guide them to show mercy and be a blessing for others
- Understand that *beatitude* means "blessing" or "happiness." God put the desire for happiness inside each of us
- Define the Beatitudes as teachings of Jesus that show the way to happiness and tell how to live in God's Kingdom now and always

- **Catholic Faith Words** mercy, Beatitudes, eternal life
- Explain that in the Gospel of Matthew is a summary of what Jesus taught about how to live by God's Word.
- Matthew 5:3–10 Proclaim the Scripture.
- Explain that God wants us to work with him as he builds his Kingdom.
- ☆ Match each Beatitude to its meaning.
- **Share Your Faith Activity** Think of a question to ask Jesus.

☐ pencils
☐ index cards

Be a Blessing Pages 124–125

- Connect that because God first blessed us, everyone can be a blessing to others

- **Catholic Faith Words** peace
- Explain that God first blessed us and we can bless others.
- Read about Pope Saint John XXIII.
- **Connect Your Faith Activity** Describe how to be a blessing to others.

☐ pencils
☐ index cards or paper
- **Optional Activity**
Being a Blessing
☐ Activity Master 7
(Page 121E)

Live, 15 minutes

Our Catholic Life Pages 126–127

- Explain that an intercession is a prayer asking God for something for another person or community.
- ☆ Write examples of when to pray an intercession.
- **People of Faith** Learn about Saint Yi Sung-hun.
- **Live Your Faith Activity** Write a prayer asking for help in living the Beatitudes.

☐ pencils
☐ crayons or markers

Prayer of Blessing Page 128

- Choose a leader and four readers.
- Rehearse "Lead Me, Lord."
- Follow the order of prayer.

Download "Lead Me, Lord."

Family + Faith Page 129

Point out that the Catholic Families page provides chapter highlights, information on how fourth graders understand faith concepts, and family prayer.

Chapter Review Page 130

aliveinchrist.osv.com
- Customize and Download Assessments
- Email Links to eAssessments
- Interactive Student Reviews

ONLINE RESOURCES

 Go to **aliveinchrist.osv.com**

You will find:

- Interactive lesson planning with web specific content and additional activities
- Step by step lesson instruction from printed Catechist Edition for integrated lesson planning
- Custom-built assessments to download and eAssessment links
- Interactive reviews that provide scores and the option to review answers
- Sunday readings with background and questions of the week

 Go to **osvparish.com**

You will find:

- Ask the Experts Q and A
- General Catechist Helps
- Community Connections and Blogs

Sharing the Message with Fourth Graders

The Beatitudes Fourth graders are beginning to understand that morality, in the Catholic life, is not just about what is not allowed. It is about being something, and specifically following someone—the Person of Jesus Christ. Jesus offers us a pattern in the Beatitudes, which involve both outward actions and inner dispositions of the heart. Children this age are growing in their ability to perceive what is inside their hearts, so this is a good time to use the Beatitudes to talk about who God would call us to be.

Teaching Tip: Throughout the year, discuss how various lessons connect to who Jesus calls us to be in the Beatitudes. For example, how does honoring God (Chapter 9) relate to being pure in heart? How does choosing life (Chapter 14) relate to being a peacemaker?

How Fourth Graders Understand

- Fourth graders like working with others and hearing their ideas. Give them time to do activities in pairs or in a large group.
- Fourth graders like to know what to expect when they come to a session. Tell them what the plan is and they will be better members of the group.
- The language of the Beatitudes may be challenging for fourth graders. Help them understand by giving them examples of ways to live each one.

"I like stories! Give me opportunities to use my imagination."

Chapter Connections

Chapter Story

Invite

"Game Night"

Use this story to enhance the chapter introduction.

- The children will relate the story to their own lives, reflecting on the blessings they experience in life.
- Connect the blessings in their life with sharing those blessings.

 Go to **aliveinchrist.osv.com** Lesson Planning section for this story.

NCEA IFG: ACRE Edition

Discover

Moral Formation

- Objective: To be knowledgeable about the teachings of Jesus and the Church as the basis of Christian morality and to understand Catholic Social Teaching

Missionary Spirit

- Objectives: To recognize the centrality of evangelization as the Church's mission and identity embodied in vocation and service; to be aware of how cultures are transformed by the Gospel

Catholic Social Teaching

Live

 Use one of these features to introduce a principle and engage the children with an activity.

- Option for the Poor and Vulnerable, Pages 296–297
- Solidarity of the Human Family, Pages 300–301

Music Options

 Use one or more of the following songs to enhance catechetical learning or for prayer.

- "Lead Me, Lord," Live Prayer, Page 128
- "Love, Jesus, Love," Discover, Page 123

LECTIONARY CONNECTION

 Chapter 7 highlights Lectionary-connected themes such as the Beatitudes, faith, works, and the dignity of the human person. If your parish aligns its curriculum to the liturgical year, you could use this chapter in connection with the following readings.

Year A

Second Sunday of Easter—faith

Fourth Sunday in Ordinary Time—Beatitudes

Twenty-eighth Sunday in Ordinary Time—dignity of all people

Year B

The Ascension of the Lord—followers of Jesus

Twenty-second Sunday in Ordinary Time—morality

Twenty-fourth Sunday in Ordinary Time—faith and works

Year C

Third Sunday of Advent—Beatitudes

Twenty-third Sunday in Ordinary Time—discipleship

Twenty-fifth Sunday in Ordinary Time—dignity of the human person

 Go to **aliveinchrist.osv.com** for a complete correlation ordered by the Sundays of the year and suggestions for how to integrate the Scripture readings into chapter lessons.

Name _____ Date _____

Being a Blessing

For each of the following situations, think of at least two ways that you could be a blessing for others.

Your mother has had a hard day at work and is tired. She is making dinner now, but the phone keeps ringing and your younger brother wants attention.

   1. _____.

   2. _____.

Mr. Hatsumi, who lives next door, has a broken leg. He has a hard time walking his dog and taking his trash to the curb. No one ever visits him.

   3. _____.

   4. _____.

Your best friend is sad and upset because his hamster died. He doesn't want to play or talk on the phone.

   5. _____.

   6. _____.

Your teacher introduces a new student, Bryn, to your class. Bryn doesn't know anyone to sit with at lunch and doesn't know where to catch the bus to go home.

   7. _____.

   8. _____.

The Beatitudes

♡ Let Us Pray

Leader: Thank you, O Lord, for you have
          blessed us in so many ways.

          "Blessed is the nation whose God is the LORD,
              the people chosen as his inheritance."
          Psalm 33:12

All: You have chosen us, O Lord, and made us to be
          happy with you forever. We are truly blessed by
          your gifts. Amen.

📖 Scripture

While [Jesus] was speaking, a woman from the crowd called out and said to him, "Blessed is the womb that carried you and the breasts at which you nursed." He replied, "Rather, blessed are those who hear the word of God and observe it." *Luke 11:27–28*

❓ What Do You Wonder?

- What does it mean to be blessed?
- What directions did Jesus give his followers on how to live?

The Beatitudes   **121**

Optional Activity

Chapter Story: "Game Night"   *Verbal/Linguistic*

Use this story after the opening prayer, before explaining that not only are we blessed, but we can be a blessing for others.

- Read aloud the story.
- Ask for examples from their life experience.
- *Ask:* What do you think it means to be blessed?
- *Ask:* How do you share your blessings with others?
- When finished, transition back to the lesson instruction.

 Go to **aliveinchrist.osv.com** for Chapter Story.

♡ Let Us Pray

Invite the children to gather in the prayer space and make the Sign of the Cross. Choose a leader and someone to read the Psalm. Prompt the children's response.

Have the children move out of the prayer space and back to their seats.

Explain that not only are we blessed, but we can be a blessing.

Say: The Church teaches us that "every baptized person is called to be a 'blessing'" (CCC, 1669). Jesus reminds us that blessing comes from hearing and following God's Word.

📖 Scripture

Guide the children through the process of Scripture reflection.

- Invite them to close their eyes, be still and open their minds and hearts to what God is saying to them in this passage.
- Proclaim the Scripture.
- Maintain several moments of silence.
- *Ask:* What did you hear God say to you today?
- Invite volunteers to share.

What Do You Wonder?

Say: The woman in the crowd was saying that Mary was blessed, because she was the Mother of God. Jesus teaches us that we are all blessed, when we listen to God's Word and follow it.

Invite the children to respond to the questions. Ask what else they might wonder about what it means to be blessed.

Objectives

- Describe how the Beatitudes guide us to show mercy and be a blessing for others
- Understand that *beatitude* means "blessing" or "happiness." God put the desire for happiness inside each of us
- Define the Beatitudes as teachings of Jesus that show the way to happiness and tell how to live in God's Kingdom now and always

Jesus Brings God's Blessing

Ask: What did Jesus teach his disciples about blessings?

- Write the children's responses on the board or on chart paper.

Invite a volunteer to read aloud the paragraph.

- Tell the children that God blesses those who care for others.

Work with Words

Point out the definition of *mercy*.

- Distribute index cards. Have each child make a vocabulary card.

 Scripture

Choose eight children to each read aloud one of the Beatitudes.

- Together, proclaim the Scripture. You will read the introductory lines.
- Ask volunteers to explain what they think each Beatitude means. Record their responses. You may need to clarify words such as *meek*, *persecuted*, and *righteousness*.

Jesus Brings God's Blessing

What did Jesus teach his disciples about blessings?

In the Gospel according to Matthew, we find a summary of what Jesus taught about how to live by God's Word. We learn who is blessed and how to be a blessing for others, and about the kindness and concern know as **mercy**.

Catholic Faith Words

mercy kindness and concern for those who are suffering. God has mercy on us even though we are sinners.

Beatitudes teachings of Jesus that show the way to true happiness and tell the way to live in God's Kingdom now and always

eternal life life forever with God for all who die in his friendship

 Scripture

One day Jesus stood in the midst of his Apostles and a great crowd of followers. He taught them with these words:

"Blessed are the poor in spirit,
for theirs is the kingdom of heaven.

Blessed are they who mourn,
for they will be comforted.

Blessed are the meek,
for they will inherit the land.

Blessed are they who hunger and thirst
for righteousness,
for they will be satisfied.

Blessed are the merciful,
for they will be shown mercy.

Blessed are the clean of heart,
for they will see God.

Blessed are the peacemakers,
for they will be called children of God.

Blessed are they who are persecuted for
the sake of righteousness,
for theirs is the kingdom of heaven."

Matthew 5:3–10

This statue of Christ the Redeemer overlooks Rio de Janeiro, Brazil. A chapel beneath the statue was consecrated in 2006.

 Songs of Scripture

The Beatitudes

Provide each child a "stone" cut from a brown paper bag.

- Direct the children to Matthew 5:3-10 and have the children print one Beatitude on their stone.
- Play the song. When the children hear their Beatitude, have them place their stones on the floor to create a path.

▶ Use *Songs of Scripture*, Grades 4–6 CD, Track 7

The Beatitudes

The Church calls this teaching of Jesus the **Beatitudes**. The word *beatitude* means "blessing" or "happiness." God put the desire for happiness inside each of us. Sometimes we think certain people or things will make us happy. But true happiness comes when we follow the Beatitudes.

The Beatitudes are about how we act, feel, and think. They are about the lasting happiness God wants for you. God wants us to work with him as he builds his Kingdom. He wants us all to have **eternal life**.

⭐ Match the Beatitude on the left with its meaning on the right.

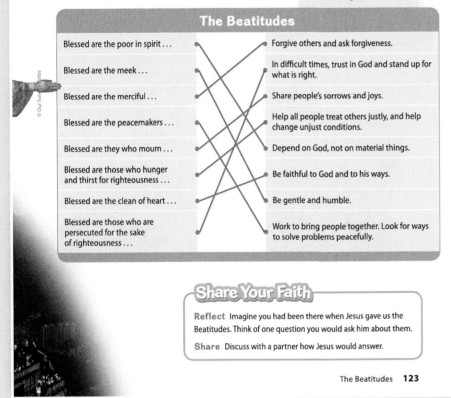

The Beatitudes

Blessed are the poor in spirit . . .	Forgive others and ask forgiveness.
Blessed are the meek . . .	In difficult times, trust in God and stand up for what is right.
Blessed are the merciful . . .	Share people's sorrows and joys.
Blessed are the peacemakers . . .	Help all people treat others justly, and help change unjust conditions.
Blessed are they who mourn . . .	Depend on God, not on material things.
Blessed are those who hunger and thirst for righteousness . . .	Be faithful to God and to his ways.
Blessed are the clean of heart . . .	Be gentle and humble.
Blessed are those who are persecuted for the sake of righteousness . . .	Work to bring people together. Look for ways to solve problems peacefully.

© Our Sunday Visitor

Share Your Faith

Reflect Imagine you had been there when Jesus gave us the Beatitudes. Think of one question you would ask him about them.

Share Discuss with a partner how Jesus would answer.

The Beatitudes **123**

✓ Quick Tip

Graphic Organizer

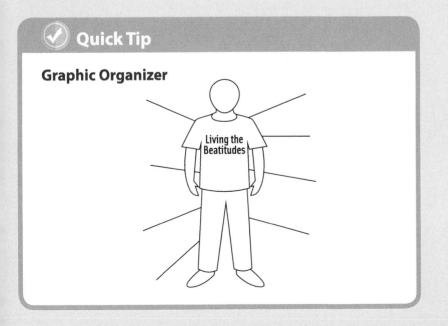

Living the Beatitudes

The Beatitudes

Have the children silently read the first two paragraphs.

- Explain that when we follow the Beatitudes we are a blessing to others. We work with God as he builds his Kingdom.

Work with Words

Point out the definitions of *Beatitudes*, and *eternal life*.

- Have the children make a vocabulary card for each term.

⭐ Have the children complete the activity.

- On the board or chart paper, draw the graphic organizer from the box below.

- Ask volunteers to describe everyday ways that they could live each Beatitude. Write their ideas in the graphic organizer.

- Refer to The Beatitudes on page 317 in the Our Catholic Tradition section of the Student Book.

 Music Option: Have the children sing, "You Are Near," downloaded from **aliveinchrist.osv.com**.

Activity

Read aloud the directions for the Share Your Faith activity.

- Have the children write their questions and discuss with a partner.

Quick Review

The Beatitudes teach how to find lasting happiness with God and to work with him as he builds his Kingdom.

Objective

- Connect that because God first blessed us, everyone can be a blessing to others

Be a Blessing

Ask: What does it mean to be a blessing to others?

- List children's responses on the board or on chart paper.

Introduce the biography by summarizing the introductory paragraph.

Pope John XXIII

Ask the children to think about people who are blessings to them.

- Tell them that this biography will show them how one person was a blessing.
- Read the first part of the biography.

Provide some background on Pope John XXIII (1881–1963).

- Pope John XXIII was known for his simple ways and good nature.
- He wrote encyclicals that promoted social justice and world peace.
- He convened the Second Vatican Council, although he did not live to see its completion.
- He was beatified by Pope Saint John Paul II in 2000, and canonized as a Saint by Pope Francis in 2014.

Be a Blessing

What does it mean to be a blessing to others?

Because God first blessed us, everyone has a chance to be a blessing to others. This story tells how one humble man was a blessing to many people.

Pope Saint John XXIII

Angelo Roncalli grew up in an Italian farming family. He became a priest in 1904 and he helped a bishop run a diocese. He also taught in a seminary and gave inspirational homilies.

A stamp printed in Italy in 1981 commemorates the 100th anniversary of Pope Saint John XXIII's birth.

When Italy became involved in World War I, Angelo was drafted. He became a sergeant and chaplain in the medical corps. He prayed with wounded soldiers, gave them Holy Communion, and heard their confessions. When needed, he performed the Sacrament of the Anointing of the Sick.

After the war, he went back to work at the seminary. Soon, Father Angelo was put in charge of an office in the Vatican that helps those who work in the missions.

While in Bulgaria, he visited and worked with Catholic and other Christian groups. When an earthquake struck, he worked to provide relief to the victims. No matter where Father Angelo was, he served those around him by loving them in God's name.

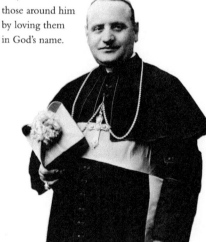

© Our Sunday Visitor

✓ Quick Tip

Map It

Distribute maps of Europe to the children.

- Using the text on student page 124 as a guide, invite them to trace Pope John XXIII's career on the map.
- Point out that the Church is universal. This means that it is for people everywhere. Discuss how Pope John XXIII's career helps show this.
- Discuss how his different work assignments may have helped the future Pope understand different points of view.

Sisters from the Missionaries of Charity amid the rubble of their church after the 2010 earthquake in Port-au-Prince, Haiti.

Sharing Blessings

In the 1930s, Father Angelo worked for the Church in Greece. Then, World War II broke out. He helped prisoners of war communicate with their families. He also helped Jewish families escape by giving them papers that ensured their safe travel.

Angelo was respected in these countries because of his sincere ways and deep holiness. He tried to settle problems by using the teachings about love from the Bible.

In 1958, Father Angelo was elected Pope. He took the name John XXIII. In this position, he was a good servant to his people. He visited people in hospitals and in prisons. He welcomed and met with people from other countries and of other religions. He urged everyone to live in **peace** and settle their problems with kindness and justice. In 1961, Pope Saint John XXIII called a special meeting of all the bishops of the Church. They discussed how the Church could help bring the message of Jesus to the world.

→ How did Pope Saint John XXIII show that God blesses all people?
→ What lesson can you learn from Pope Saint John XXIII?

Catholic Faith Words

peace a state of calm when things are in their proper order and people settle problems with kindness and justice

Connect Your Faith

Be a Blessing Write words beginning with the letters of the word PEACE to describe how you can be a blessing to others.

P _____
E _____
A _____
C _____
E _____

The Beatitudes **125**

Sharing Blessings

Continue reading until the end of the biography.

- Have the children scan the story for actions that were blessings. List these actions on the board.
- Have the children look for evidence that Pope John XXIII was meek and clean of heart. Discuss these terms if the children are unfamiliar with them.
- Discuss the questions.
- Discuss how the children can emulate Pope John XXIII's actions in a small way.

Work with Words

Ask the children to raise their hands if they know what *peace* means.

- Read aloud the definition of peace.
- Distribute index cards and have the children each make a vocabulary card for *peace*.

Activity

Point out the Connect Your Faith activity and read aloud the directions.

- Organize the children in pairs and give them time to complete the activity.
- Invite the pairs to share their ways of being a blessing for others.

Quick Review

God calls each person to be a blessing for others.

Optional Activity

Activity Master 7: Being a Blessing

Distribute copies of the activity found on catechist page 121E.

- Because each situation calls for two solutions, you may wish to have the children work in pairs.
- As an alternative, you may wish to send this activity home with the children.

Live

Our Catholic Life

Ask: How can you share blessings through prayer?

- Write the children's responses on the board or on chart paper.

Read aloud the two paragraphs.

- Emphasize that we offer prayers of intercession at Mass.

- Ask the children to tell what we pray for during the intercessions at Mass.

- Discuss why intercessory prayer is **generous.** You are asking for help for another person.

- Have volunteers read aloud the text in each petal.

⭐ Have the children fill in examples of when they would pray a prayer of intercession.

- Invite the children to silently offer a prayer of intercession.

Live

Our Catholic Life

How can you share blessings through prayer?

Intercession, or petition, is a kind of prayer in which you ask God for something for another person or for the community. It is a generous, thoughtful kind of prayer, and it is one of the types of prayers that Jesus prayed.

Just before the preparation of the gifts at Mass, the whole assembly offers prayers of intercession to God in the Prayer of the Faithful. These prayers are often said for members of the Church, religious and government leaders, and people in the news. Here are some examples of when you might want to say a prayer of intercession.

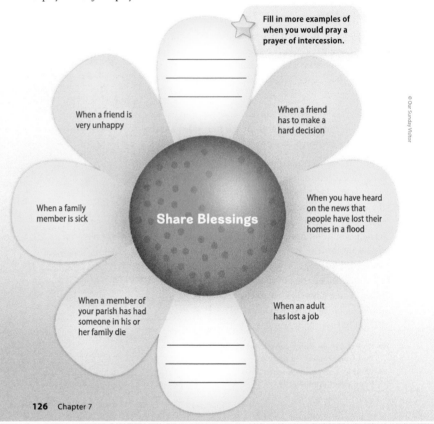

Fill in more examples of when you would pray a prayer of intercession.

When a friend is very unhappy

When a friend has to make a hard decision

When a family member is sick

Share Blessings

When you have heard on the news that people have lost their homes in a flood

When a member of your parish has had someone in his or her family die

When an adult has lost a job

© Our Sunday Visitor

 Quick Tip

Deal with Anxiety

Anxiety is bred by uncertainty, which is often created by events beyond one's control. Ways of dealing with anxiety include:

- exercising—a great stress reliever;
- talking with others—to provide perspective;
- praying—sharing problems or worries with God to impart a sense of peace.

Talk to the children about ways they can overcome anxiety in their lives. Conclude by praying a prayer to the Holy Spirit.

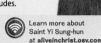

Saint Yi Sung-hun, 1756–1801

September 20

Saint Yi Sung-hun lived in Korea. His family was part of the ruling class. When he was traveling with his father to China, he was baptized. He was one of the first people in Korea to become Catholic. The government did not want people to be Christian. When Yi Sung-hun refused to worship a false god, he was arrested. Many other Korean Christians were arrested too. One hundred and three people were killed for being Christian. When Yi Sung-hun died, he told people not to be sad because he would see them again in Heaven. He placed God first, and was a man of the Beatitudes.

Discuss: How does God bless you? How can you share those blessings with others?

 Learn more about Saint Yi Sung-hun at **aliveinchrist.osv.com**

Live Your Faith

Name one Beatitude that you live by regularly and another that is more difficult for you.

_____

_____

_____

_____

Write a short prayer asking God to help you live these Beatitudes.

_____

_____

_____

_____

_____

_____

_____

The Beatitudes **127**

People of Faith

Tell the children about Saint Yi Sung-hun.

- Invite a volunteer to read aloud the People of Faith story.

- Explain that although Saint Yi Sung-hun had a Catholic aunt, his father fiercely opposed the spread of Catholicism. However, when Yi Sung-hun accompanied his father on a diplomatic trip to China, Yi Sung-hun sought out Catholic priests there and was baptized. He returned to the Catholic community in Seoul with books, crucifixes, and other Catholic artifacts.

- *Ask:* How does God bless you? How can you share those blessings with others?

> Encourage the children to go to **aliveinchrist.osv.com** at home to find out more about Saint Yi Sung-hun.

Activity

Read aloud the directions for the Live Your Faith activity.

- As a group, discuss the first part of the activity.

- Allow time for the children to work independently to write their responses.

- Have the children write a prayer, and invite them to share it with the rest of the group.

🌐 Catholic Social Teaching

Chapter Connections

To integrate Catholic Social Teaching into your lesson, choose one of the following features: Option for the Poor and Vulnerable, pages 296–297; or Solidarity of the Human Family, pages 300–301.

- Start the Live step of the process by talking about Saint Yi Sung-hun on page 127. Then move directly to the Catholic Social Teaching feature.

- Or, to expand the lesson, complete both pages 126 and 127, then move to the Catholic Social Teaching feature.

- Return to Chapter 7 for the prayer on page 128.

Let Us Pray

Prayer of Blessing

Tell the children that they will pray a prayer of petition, asking God to help each of them be a blessing for others.

Prepare

Choose a leader and four readers for the prayer service.

 Rehearse "Lead Me, Lord," downloaded from **aliveinchrist.osv.com**.

Gather

Invite the children to process to the prayer space. Have each child bring their book.

- Direct the children to be seated and prepare their minds and hearts for prayer.

Pray

Follow the order of prayer on the student page.

 Conclude by singing together "Lead Me, Lord."

Live

 ## Let Us Pray

Prayer of Blessing

Gather and begin with the Sign of the Cross.

Leader: Brothers and sisters, praise God, who is rich in mercy.

All: Blessed be God forever.

Reader 1: Read Philippians 4:4–7.

All: Blessed be God forever.

Reader 2: Loving God, you created all the people of the world, and you know each of us by name.

All: Blessed be God forever.

Reader 3: We thank you for our lives. Bless us with your love and friendship.

All: Blessed be God forever.

Reader 4: May we grow in wisdom, knowledge, and grace.

All: Blessed be God forever.

Leader: May we be blessed in the name of the Father, the Son, and the Holy Spirit.

Based on Matthew 5, 7; John 14

All: Amen.

 Sing "Lead Me, Lord"

128 Chapter 7

 ## Liturgy Link

Set the Mood

Before you begin the celebration, ask the children to sit quietly and remind themselves of God's presence.

- Ring a chime or bell to set the mood as you have the children move to the prayer space.
- This sound will reinforce the fact that prayer time is different from other group activity times.

Go to **aliveinchrist.osv.com** for Sunday readings, Scripture background, questions of the week, and seasonal resources.

FAMILY+FAITH
LIVING AND LEARNING TOGETHER

YOUR CHILD LEARNED >>>
This chapter explains that Jesus gave us the Beatitudes to show the way to true happiness and to tell us how to live in God's Kingdom now and always.

Scripture
Read Luke 11:27–28 to find out who Jesus says is blessed and why.

Catholics Believe
• The Beatitudes are eight teachings that describe the Reign of God that Jesus announced when he lived on Earth.
• The Beatitudes show you how to live and act as a follower of Jesus.

To learn more, go to the *Catechism of the Catholic Church #1716–1724* at usccb.org.

People of Faith
This week, your child learned about Saint Yi Sung-hun, a Korean martyr who placed God first and is remembered for sacrificing his life for his belief in Jesus.

CHILDREN AT THIS AGE >>>
How They Understand the Beatitudes Your child is probably beginning to understand that morality, in the Catholic life, is not just about what is not allowed. It is about being something, and specifically *following someone*, Jesus Christ. Jesus offers us a pattern in the Beatitudes, which involve both outward actions and inner dispositions of the heart. Children your child's age are growing in their ability to perceive what is inside their hearts, so this is a good time to use the Beatitudes to talk about who God would call us to be.

CONSIDER THIS >>>
Have you ever felt a blessing in the midst of suffering?

Even in times of suffering, we can count the blessings of those who care for us, listen to us, and share God's love with us. As Catholics, we know that "the Church carries forward Christ's healing ministry in a variety of approaches. Catholic families in countless ways care for family members who are ill. There are numerous inspiring stories of an aging spouse who personally ministers to an ailing spouse in cases of Alzheimer's and other illnesses. Caregivers find that faith and prayer mean a great deal to them in these situations" (*USCCA*, p. 252).

LET'S TALK >>>
• Ask your child to tell you about the Beatitudes.
• Share how God has blessed your family and how your family members are a blessing to one another.

LET'S PRAY >>>
Saint Yi Sung-hun, pray for us that we may put God first in our lives, and always be a blessing for others. Amen.

For a multimedia glossary of Catholic Faith Words, Sunday readings, seasonal and Saint resources, and chapter activities go to aliveinchrist.osv.com.

Chapter 7 Review

A Work with Words **Complete the following paragraph with the correct words from the Word Bank.**

1–5. Jesus gave us the ___**Beatitudes**___ to show us

the way to ___**true**___ happiness.

Through the ___**eight**___ Beatitudes,

Jesus tell us about being blessed by God and living

for God's ___**Kingdom**___ now and always.

He said that people who are ___**meek**___

are blessed because they will inherit the land.

Word Bank
- true
- eight
- Kingdom
- Beatitudes
- meek

B Check Understanding **Fill in the circle next to the answer that best completes each statement.**

6. People who are poor in spirit are those who depend on _____ .
- ○ material things
- ● God
- ○ themselves

7. God wants all people to share _____ with him.
- ● eternal life
- ○ Beatitudes
- ○ material things

8. Working to bring people together is a way to be _____ .
- ○ meek
- ○ poor in spirit
- ● a peacemaker

9. Kindness and concern for those who are suffering is _____ .
- ● mercy
- ○ blessedness
- ○ meekness

10. Prayers of _____ ask God for something for another person or for a community.
- ○ righteousness
- ● intercession
- ○ friendship

Go to aliveinchrist.osv.com for an interactive review.

Family + Faith

Distribute the page to the children or parents/adult family members. Point out the chapter highlights, insights on how fourth graders understand concepts, the opportunity for the adults to reflect on their own experience and faith journey, and the family prayer.

Chapter Review

Use Catechist Quick Reviews to highlight lesson concepts.

A **Work with Words**
Have the children complete the paragraph using words from the Word Bank.

B **Check Understanding**
Have the children fill in the circle next to the answer that best completes each statement.

Go to **aliveinchrist.osv.com** to prepare customized and downloadable assessments, send eAssessments, and assign interactive reviews.

KEY CONCEPT

The Great Commandment is to love God with all your heart, strength, and mind and to love your neighbor as yourself. The Theological Virtues of faith, hope, and charity help us to love God and grow closer to him.

DOCTRINAL CONTENT

- The Great Commandment is the two-fold command to love God above all and your neighbor as yourself. (CCC, 2055)

- The Theological Virtues of faith, hope, and charity are gifts from God that help us to believe in him, trust his plan for us, and love him with all our heart, soul, and mind. (CCC, 1814, 1817, 1822)

- Loving God leads to sharing his love with others, and the Corporal and Spiritual Works of Mercy guide us in the ways to do so. (CCC, 2447–2448)

TASKS OF CATECHESIS

Helping children grow in a faith that is "known, celebrated, lived, and expressed in prayer" (NDC, 20).

This chapter focuses on the following tasks of catechesis:

- Moral Formation
- Missionary Initiation

Catechist Background

 So be imitators of God, as beloved children, and live in love, as Christ loved us. Ephesians 5:1a

➜ **Reflect** What helps you to imitate Christ?

Jesus says that the two greatest Commandments are love for God and love for neighbor. How do you love your neighbor? Wishing someone well or showing common courtesy is a good start, but it is not enough. You are called to show Christian charity to others by caring for their basic needs.

Compassionate service to others is shown through the Corporal, or physical, Works of Mercy. Christians have a responsibility to provide food, drink, shelter, and clothing to those in need; to be truly present and involved with those who are sick and imprisoned; and at the end of life, to bury the dead with dignity and prayer. These works are your ongoing mission. Doing them alone might sometimes be overwhelming. Fortunately, you are not alone! As part of a faith community, whether the parish or an outreach ministry, you can accomplish great works.

Wherever poverty exists, human misery exists, too. Poverty certainly means material deprivation, but it can also mean oppression, physical illness, or emotional and mental turmoil. Jesus always acted with compassion toward those who were suffering. The Church follows this example by working for justice, protection, and liberation, and by calling for preferential love for those who are poor.

➜ **Reflect** What kinds of poverty can you work to alleviate in your parish or community?

Catechist's Prayer

Loving God, open my eyes to the ways in which I can return your love by helping my neighbors. May my hands be ready to do the work of spreading your love. Amen.

Lesson Plan

Objectives	Process	Materials
Invite, 10 minutes		
Love God and Neighbor Page 131	⬭ **Psalm 119:33** Pray the opening prayer. 📖 **Ephesians 5:1–5** Reflect prayerfully on the Word. • Discuss What Do You Wonder questions.	📶 **Optional Activity** Chapter Story: "Signs of Love"
Discover, 35 minutes		
The Great Commandment Pages 132–133 • Describe the Great Commandment as the twofold command to love God above all else and your neighbor as yourself	• **Catholic Faith Words** Great Commandment • Explain that Jesus teaches to love God with our whole heart and soul. 📖 **Matthew 22:37–40** Proclaim "The Greatest Commandment." • Explain why the young man could not give away his possessions. • **Share Your Faith Activity** Design a billboard.	☐ pencils ☐ index cards • **Optional Activity** Share with Others
Love God Pages 134–135 • Deepen understanding of the Theological Virtues as gifts from God that help us to believe in him, trust his plan for us, and love him with all our heart, soul, and mind • Connect that loving God leads to sharing his love with others, and the Corporal and Spiritual Works of Mercy guide us in the ways to do so	• **Catholic Faith Words** Theological Virtues, faith, hope, charity, Corporal Works of Mercy, Spiritual Works of Mercy • Explain that the Corporal Works of Mercy meet the physical needs of others. • **Connect Your Faith Activity** Match the Work of Mercy to the action.	☐ pencils ☐ index cards • **Optional Activity** Corporal Works of Mercy Mobile ☐ Activity Master 8 (Page 131E)
Live, 15 minutes		
Our Catholic Life Pages 136–137	• Recall that people do God's work on Earth when they perform the Works of Mercy. ✩ Write how to help in each scenario. • **People of Faith** Learn about Saint Katharine Drexel. • **Live Your Faith Activity** Draw how to show love for God and others each day.	☐ pencils ☐ crayons or markers
Celebration of the Word Page 138	• Select a leader and four readers. ▶ Rehearse "Whatsoever You Do." • Follow the order of prayer.	📶 Download "Whatsoever You Do."

Family + Faith Page 139

Point out that the Catholic Families page provides chapter highlights, information on how fourth graders understand faith concepts, and family prayer.

Chapter Review Page 140

📶 **aliveinchrist.osv.com**

• Customize and Download Assessments
• Email Links to eAssessments
• Interactive Student Reviews

Teaching This Grade

ONLINE RESOURCES

 Go to **aliveinchrist.osv.com**

You will find:

- Interactive lesson planning with web specific content and additional activities
- Step by step lesson instruction from printed Catechist Edition for integrated lesson planning
- Custom-built assessments to download and eAssessment links
- Interactive reviews that provide scores and the option to review answers
- Sunday readings with background and questions of the week

 Go to **osvparish.com**

You will find:

- Ask the Experts Q and A
- General Catechist Helps
- Community Connections and Blogs

Sharing the Message with Fourth Graders

The Great Commandment The continued concrete thinking of fourth graders means that they will probably continue to see love for God and for neighbor as a series of outward actions. This is not far from the truth, for it is certainly the things that we do that tell whether we really have love for God and neighbor. Children this age are growing in their ability to see relationships between these larger Commandments and smaller choices in everyday life. They can better determine whether or not an individual action is loving towards God or to their neighbor. This new ability will help them to begin to make decisions in new situations.

Teaching Tip: Throughout the year, when talking about moral decision making, ask the group to relate the issue being discussed to how actions could show love for God and neighbor.

How Fourth Graders Understand

- Fourth graders need concrete examples. Model for them how people practice the Works of Mercy. Or, invite guest speakers to share their stories.
- Fourth graders like stories about how Jesus helped people. Provide opportunities for them to read them, hear them, act them out, and apply them to their lives.
- Fourth graders want to be active and involved. Have them make cards for sick parishioners or have them take up a collection of food for the local food pantry.

"I have a real interest in helping people. Let's plan some service projects."

Chapter Connections

Chapter Story

Invite

"Signs of Love"

Use this story to expand the chapter introduction.

- The children will relate the story to their own lives, reflecting on how they experience God's love.
- Connect experiencing God's love to how they show God's love to others.

 Go to **aliveinchrist.osv.com** Lesson Planning section for this story.

NCEA IFG: ACRE Edition

Discover

Moral Formation

- Objective: To be knowledgeable about the teachings of Jesus and the Church as the basis of Christian morality and to understand Catholic Social Teaching

Missionary Spirit

- Objectives: To recognize the centrality of evangelization as the Church's mission and identity embodied in vocation and service; to be aware of how cultures are transformed by the Gospel

Catholic Social Teaching

Live

Use one of these features to introduce a principle and engage the children with an activity.

- Life and Dignity of the Human Person, Pages 290–291
- Solidarity of the Human Family, Pages 300–301

Music Options

 Use one or more of the following songs to enhance catechetical learning or for prayer.

- "Whatsoever You Do," Live Prayer, Page 138
- "This Is My Commandment," Discover, Page 133
- "Loving God," Discover, Page 135
- "Loving Others," Discover, Page 135

LECTIONARY CONNECTION

 Chapter 8 highlights Lectionary-connected themes such as the Great Commandment and the Corporal Works of Mercy. If your parish aligns its curriculum to the liturgical year, you could use this chapter in connection with the following Sundays.

Year A

Fourth Sunday of Easter—Good Shepherd

Thirtieth Sunday in Ordinary Time—Great Commandment

Year B

Second Sunday in Ordinary Time—live as followers of Jesus

Twenty-third Sunday in Ordinary Time—love of neighbor

Thirty-first Sunday in Ordinary Time—love of neighbor

Year C

Second Sunday of Lent—Corporal Works of Mercy

Twenty-fifth Sunday in Ordinary Time—love God and neighbor

 Go to **aliveinchrist.osv.com** for a complete correlation ordered by the Sundays of the year and suggestions for how to integrate the Scripture readings into chapter lessons.

Name _____ Date _____

Corporal Works of Mercy Mobile

Think of a symbol to represent each of the Corporal Works of Mercy. Draw and color your symbols in the shapes below. Then cut out the shapes and glue them to pieces of cardboard. Use different lengths of string or yarn to hang the symbols from a clothes hanger.

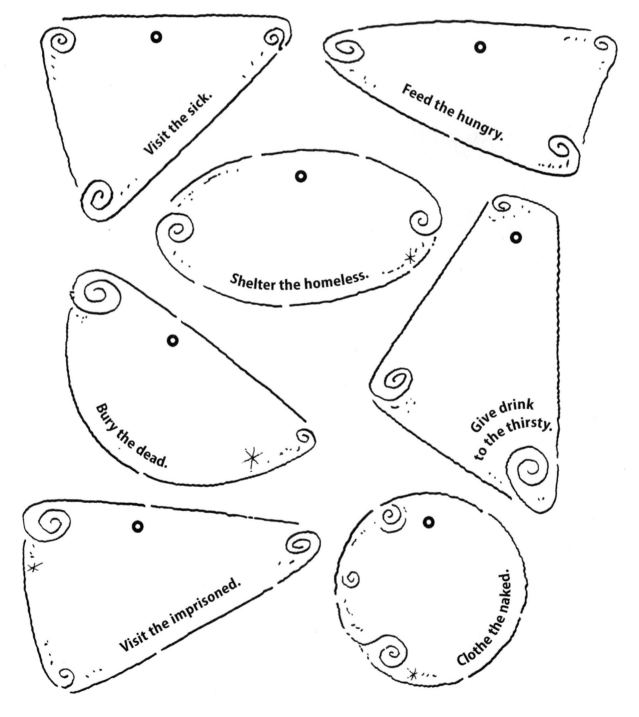

CHAPTER 8

Love God and Neighbor

Let Us Pray

Leader: Merciful God, help us to know and do your will.

"LORD, teach me the way of your statutes;
I shall keep them with care." **Psalm 119:33**

All: You ask us, Lord, to love you with our whole heart and love our neighbor as we love ourselves. Give us the grace to do what you ask. Amen.

Scripture

"So be imitators of God, as beloved children, and live in love, as Christ loved us." Jesus gave himself as a sacrifice of love to his Father for us. So, you holy ones must live as Jesus commanded. Do not ever be greedy, or swear, or be disrespectful. **Based on Ephesians 5:1–5**

What Do You Wonder?

- What helps you imitate Christ, to have faith, hope, and love?
- How can you be generous and help people in need?

131

Optional Activity

Chapter Story: "Signs of Love" *Verbal/Linguistic*

Use this story after the opening prayer, before explaining that being a follower of Jesus means loving God and our neighbor.

- Read aloud the story.
- Ask the children what the pictures in Elena's album might show.
- *Ask:* If this were your album, what picture would you include?
- Ask the children to name three ways they have shown God's love to others. Then, transition back to the lesson instruction.

 Go to **aliveinchrist.osv.com** for Chapter Story.

Invite

Let Us Pray

Invite the children to gather in the prayer space and make the Sign of the Cross. Choose a volunteer to read aloud the Psalm verse from a Bible. Prompt the children's response.

Have the children move out of the prayer space and back to their seats.

Explain that being a follower of Jesus means loving God and our neighbor.

Say: Saint Paul often describes what it means to be a follower of Jesus. He helps us understand what it means to have faith in Jesus and then live what you believe.

Scripture

Guide the children through the process of Scripture reflection.

- Invite them to close their eyes, be still and open their minds and hearts to what God is saying to them in this passage.
- Proclaim the Scripture.
- Maintain several moments of silence.
- *Ask:* What did you hear God say to you today?
- Invite volunteers to share.

What Do You Wonder?

Say: Sometimes generosity involves giving away money. People are also generous with their time and talents. People with generous hearts see what people need and try to help.

Invite the children to respond to the questions. Ask what else they might wonder about imitating Christ.

Objective

- Describe the Great Commandment as the twofold command to love God above all else and your neighbor as yourself

The Great Commandment

Ask: How is the Great Commandment like the Ten Commandments?

- Write the children's responses on the board or on chart paper.

Read aloud the introductory paragraph.

 Scripture

Invite a volunteer to proclaim "The Greatest Commandment."

- Have the children repeat aloud the two parts of the Great Commandment. Encourage them to memorize these verses.

- Read aloud the last paragraph.

- Display a list or poster of the Ten Commandments.

- Point out that the first half of the Great Commandment sums us the first three Commandments, which are ways of loving God. The second half sums up the next seven Commandments, which name ways to treat neighbors.

Work with Words

Point out the definition of *Great Commandment.*

- Have the children make a vocabulary card for the term.

The Great Commandment

How is the Great Commandment like the Ten Commandments?

We all know that rules are important. We understand that obeying rules, even when we don't like them, helps keep order. But Jesus taught that keeping the Ten Commandments includes more than checking off items on a list. Each Commandment shows you a way to love God and love others with your whole heart and soul.

Catholic Faith Words

Great Commandment the twofold command to love God above all and your neighbor as yourself. It sums up all God's laws.

 Scripture

The Greatest Commandment

"You shall love the Lord, your God, with all your heart, with all your soul, and with all your mind. This is the greatest and the first commandment. The second is like it: You shall love your neighbor as yourself. The whole law and the prophets depend on these two commandments." Matthew 22:37–40

Therefore, the **Great Commandment** to love God above all and your neighbor as yourself sums up the Ten Commandments, the whole law, and what the prophets taught.

132

 Scripture Background

Matthew 22:37–40

The Pharisees were known for their zealous observance of the Law. In addition to the Ten Commandments, there were hundreds of rules about worship, morality, and daily life.

- Some of the Pharisees tested Jesus to try to make him look foolish or irreligious.
- Instead, Jesus talked about observing the Law through living the Great Commandment.

Following Jesus

There are many ways that you can follow Jesus by sharing your love with others. Once, Jesus asked a young man to show his love for others in a very generous way.

Scripture

The Rich Young Man

One day when Jesus was teaching, a young man asked, "What must I do to live forever with God?"

Jesus answered, "Keep the commandments."

"Which commandments?" the young man asked. Jesus listed some of the Ten Commandments for him.

"I keep all those commandments!" the young man said happily. "What else do I need to do?"

"If you wish to be perfect," Jesus said, "go, sell what you have and give to [the] poor, and you will have treasure in heaven. Then come, follow me."

The young man's smile faded, for he was very rich. He could not imagine giving everything away, so he went away sad. **Based on Matthew 19:16–22**

Jesus knew that the man's love for his possessions could keep him from loving God completely. When Jesus tested him to see how important his possessions were, the man could not part with them.

➔ **Why could the rich young man not give away his possessions?**

Share Your Faith

Reflect Think about what Jesus tells us about the Great Commandment.

Share With a partner, design a billboard that supports this teaching.

Love God and Neighbor **133**

Optional Activity

Share with Others *Interpersonal*

Jesus loved those who were poor, but he did not love poverty. The Church document *Economic Justice for All* states that dealing with poverty is a moral imperative of the highest priority.

- Work with the children to conduct a toy or book drive to benefit a local homeless shelter, battered women's shelter, or hospital.
- With permission from the director of faith formation, invite other groups to participate.

Following Jesus

Read this paragraph aloud.

Scripture

Proclaim "The Rich Young Man."

- Have the children listen for Jesus' advice.
- Tell the children to imagine how they would respond to Jesus' words.

Read aloud the paragraph following the Scripture story to summarize the message.

- Have the children explain why the young man could not give away his possessions.
- *Ask:* What possession would be the hardest for you to give away? Why?

> Music Option: Have the children sing, "This Is My Commandment," downloaded from **aliveinchrist.osv.com**.

###

Read aloud the directions for the Share Your Faith activity.

- Have the children work with a partner to design a billboard that supports Jesus' teaching.
- Invite volunteers to share their work.

Quick Review

Jesus said to love God with all you are and to love your neighbor as yourself. The Commandments tell you how to do this.

Discover

Objectives

- Deepen understanding of the Theological Virtues as gifts from God that help us to believe in him, trust his plan for us, and love him with all our heart, soul, and mind
- Connect that loving God leads to sharing his love with others, and the Corporal and Spiritual Works of Mercy guide us in the ways to do so

Love God

Ask: How can you live the Great Commandment?

- Write the children's responses on the board or on chart paper.

Invite volunteers to read aloud the first two paragraphs.

Work with Words

Point out the Catholic Faith Words.

- Distribute index cards and have the children make a vocabulary card for each term.

Love Others

Invite a volunteer to read aloud the paragraph.

- Emphasize that Jesus cared most for those who were poor, helpless, and suffering, and he calls his followers to do the same.

Theological Virtues

Invite volunteers to read aloud the text on the chart.

Love God

How can you live the Great Commandment?

The first step in living the Great Commandment is to understand that God wants you to love him. The **Theological Virtues** help you to live in a loving relationship with God. Virtues are good spiritual habits that strengthen you and help you to do what is right and good. They develop over time with our practice and openness to God's grace.

The Theological Virtues of **faith**, **hope** and **charity** are gifts from God. When we use these gifts, we are drawn into a deeper relationship with God. We also come to a deeper understanding that loving God leads to sharing God's love with others.

Catholic Faith Words

Theological Virtues the virtues of faith, hope, and charity, which are gifts from God that guide our relationship with him

faith the theological virtue that makes it possible for us to believe in God and all that he helps us understand about himself. Faith leads us to obey God.

hope the theological virtue that helps us trust in the true happiness God wants us to have and in Jesus' promises of eternal life, and to rely on the help of the Holy Spirit

charity the theological virtue of love. It directs us to love God above all things and our neighbor as ourselves, for the love of God.

Love Others

God the Father sent his Son to show all people how to live in love. Jesus showed that the power of love can make a difference. Jesus cared most for those who were poor, helpless, and suffering. He calls his followers to do the same.

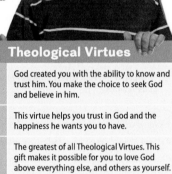
© Our Sunday Visitor

Theological Virtues

Faith	God created you with the ability to know and trust him. You make the choice to seek God and believe in him.
Hope	This virtue helps you trust in God and the happiness he wants you to have.
Charity	The greatest of all Theological Virtues. This gift makes it possible for you to love God above everything else, and others as yourself.

 Reaching All Learners

Be Sensitive

Use language that treats all families respectfully.

- Avoid the overuse of phrases such as, "the less fortunate," "the needy," or "the poor."
- Remind the children that all families and all people need help at times, and that each person has human dignity and worth.

Acts of Charity

The strength of the Holy Spirit, whom Jesus sent, gives you the power to reach out to others in love, as Jesus did. The Holy Spirit breathed charity into you at your Baptism.

Jesus' Great Commandment tells you to love others as you love yourself. Christians see the needs of others and help meet those needs. The Church has named seven acts of kindness you can do to meet the physical needs of others. They are called the **Corporal Works of Mercy**. The **Spiritual Works of Mercy** name what you can do for others to care for the needs of their heart, mind, and soul. See page 317 in the Our Catholic Tradition section of your book for the full list of Works of Mercy.

> **Catholic Faith Words**
>
> **Corporal Works of Mercy** actions that show care for the physical needs of others
>
> **Spiritual Works of Mercy** actions that address the needs of the heart, mind, and soul

Connect Your Faith

Recognize Works of Mercy Draw lines to match the Work of Mercy with an action. Then circle the actions that you have done.

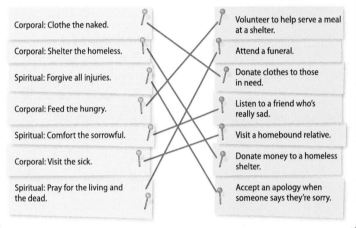

Corporal: Clothe the naked.	Volunteer to help serve a meal at a shelter.
Corporal: Shelter the homeless.	Attend a funeral.
Spiritual: Forgive all injuries.	Donate clothes to those in need.
Corporal: Feed the hungry.	Listen to a friend who's really sad.
Spiritual: Comfort the sorrowful.	Visit a homebound relative.
Corporal: Visit the sick.	Donate money to a homeless shelter.
Spiritual: Pray for the living and the dead.	Accept an apology when someone says they're sorry.

Love God and Neighbor **135**

Acts of Charity

Have two children read aloud the text.

Work with Words

Ask the children to repeat the words *Corporal Works of Mercy*. Explain that *corporal* means "bodily" or "physical."

- Give examples of how practicing the Corporal Works of Mercy will help meet others' physical needs.
- Distribute index cards and have the children make vocabulary cards for *Corporal Works of Mercy* and *Spiritual Works of Mercy*.

> **Music Option:** Have the children sing, "Love God" or "Love Others," downloaded from **aliveinchrist.osv.com**.

Activity

Read aloud the directions for the Connect Your Faith activity.

- Have the children work in pairs to match the Work of Mercy to an action.
- Review the correct answers with the children.

Quick Review

The Corporal Works of Mercy are ways to show God's love to others, as the Great Commandment requires.

Optional Activity

Activity Master 8: Corporal Works of Mercy Mobile

Distribute copies of the activity found on catechist page 131E.

- Suggest that the children look through magazines to find ideas for their symbols.
- As an alternative, you may wish to send this activity home with the children.

Live

Our Catholic Life

Ask: How can you help people as Jesus did?

- Write the children's responses on the board or on chart paper.

Invite two volunteers to read aloud the two paragraphs.

- Remind the children that people do God's work on Earth when they perform the Works of Mercy.
- Emphasize that there are many kinds of needs and it is not always easy to see what those needs are.

Many Ways to Help

Before assigning the activity, read aloud each Corporal Work of Mercy and scenario. Invite the children to share their ideas for how they could help.

 Have the children work independently to write how they could help in each situation.

- Invite volunteers to share their ideas.
- Refer to page 317 in the Our Catholic Tradition reference section of the Student Book, for more on the Corporal and Spiritual Works of Mercy.

Live

Our Catholic Life

How can you help people as Jesus did?

People all over the world are in need. Some of them are in your parish or neighborhood. If you pay attention, you may find that you know people who need your loving help.

When you think of people in need, do you imagine people who are homeless, hungry, and sick? The Corporal Works of Mercy teach us that there are many kinds of need. It is not always easy to see what those needs are. Here are some people you might see who need your help.

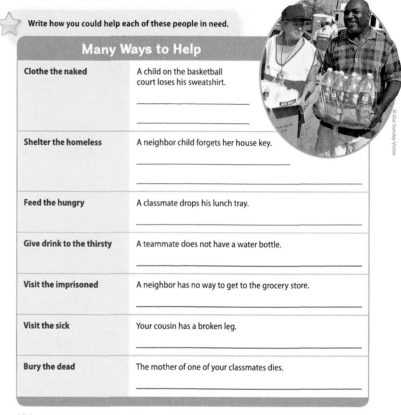

Write how you could help each of these people in need.

Many Ways to Help

Clothe the naked	A child on the basketball court loses his sweatshirt. _____ _____
Shelter the homeless	A neighbor child forgets her house key. _____ _____
Feed the hungry	A classmate drops his lunch tray. _____
Give drink to the thirsty	A teammate does not have a water bottle. _____
Visit the imprisoned	A neighbor has no way to get to the grocery store. _____
Visit the sick	Your cousin has a broken leg. _____
Bury the dead	The mother of one of your classmates dies. _____

© Our Sunday Visitor

136 Chapter 8

✓ Quick Tip

Practice Empathy

Empathy is distinct from *sympathy*. Empathy requires you to identify with a person rather than only to feel sorry for him or her. When we empathize, we understand how something feels for someone else. Cultivate empathy in the children.

- Use sensory language to help the children identify with people who need assistance.
- Encourage the children to role-play as a way to help them understand other points of view.

People of Faith

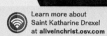

Saint Katharine Drexel, 1858–1955

Saint Katharine Drexel came from a wealthy family, but she devoted her money and her life to those who were poor. She did missionary work among African Americans and Native Americans. She insisted that all people be treated fairly, no matter what their race. She founded the Sisters of the Blessed Sacrament and also established schools on Native American reservations and the first and only Catholic university for African Americans. She believed it was her life's work to live out the Corporal Works of Mercy.

Discuss: What Works of Mercy have you done?

 Learn more about Saint Katharine Drexel at aliveinchrist.osv.com

Live Your Faith

Write or draw one way in which you will try to show your love for God and others on each day next week.

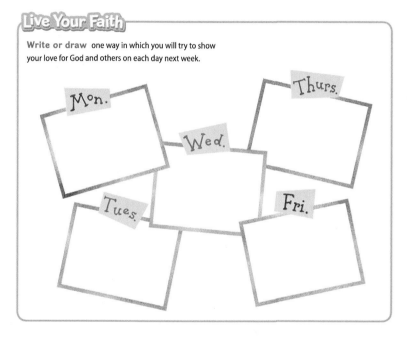

Mon.

Tues.

Wed.

Thurs.

Fri.

© Our Sunday Visitor

⊕ Catholic Social Teaching

Chapter Connections

To integrate Catholic Social Teaching into your lesson, choose one of the following features: Life and Dignity of the Human Person, pages 290–291; or Solidarity of the Human Family, pages 300–301.

- Start the Live step of the process by talking about Saint Katharine Drexel on page 137. Then move directly to the Catholic Social Teaching feature.
- Or, to expand the lesson, complete both pages 136 and 137, then move to the Catholic Social Teaching feature.
- Return to Chapter 8 for the prayer on page 138.

People of Faith

Tell the children about Saint Katharine Drexel.

- Invite a volunteer to read aloud the People of Faith story.
- Explain that Saint Katharine Drexel took a special interest in helping African Americans and Native Americans. She began by donating money, but soon realized that more importantly, people were needed. She dedicated her life and 20 million dollars to her work.
- Because of her life-long dedication to her faith and her selfless service, Pope Saint John Paul II named her a Saint on October 1, 2000. She was the second American-born Saint.
- *Ask:* What Works of Mercy have you done?

 Encourage the children to go to **aliveinchrist.osv.com** at home to find out more about Saint Katharine Drexel.

Activity

As a group, read aloud the directions and discuss the Live Your Faith activity.

- Allow time for the children to complete the activity on their own.
- Invite volunteers to share their ideas.

Live

 Let Us Pray

Celebration of the Word

Prepare

Choose a leader and four readers.

- Teach the children their responses.

 Rehearse "Whatsoever You Do," downloaded from **aliveinchrist.osv.com**.

Gather

Invite the children to process to the prayer space.

- Have the leader stand in the front of the group.
- Direct the children to be seated and prepare their minds and hearts for prayer.

Pray

Follow the order of prayer on the student page.

- Optional reading: *Matthew 25:31–46.*
- *Leader's concluding prayer:* God of love, we ask your help in living the Great Commandment. Teach us to show your love to others.

 Conclude by singing together "Whatsoever You Do."

Live

 Let Us Pray

Celebration of the Word

Gather and begin with the Sign of the Cross.

Leader: God of Mercy, we gather to remind ourselves of your love and mercy.

Reader 1: A reading from the First Letter to the Corinthians.
Read 1 Corinthians 13:2–7.
The word of the Lord.

All: Thanks be to God.

Reader 2: Lord, give us the gift of patience.

All: We want to live in your love.

Reader 3: Lord, give us the gift of kindness.

All: We want to live in your love.

Reader 4: Lord, help us think of others.

All: We want to live in your love.

Leader: Let us pray.

Bow your heads as the leader prays.

All: Amen.

 Sing "Whatsoever You Do"

Whatsoever you do to the least of my people, that you do unto me.

138 Chapter 8

 Liturgy Link

The Bible at Mass

Talk about the readings at Mass.

- Explain to the children that the first of three readings at Mass is usually taken from the Old Testament, the second from the New Testament Letters or Epistles, and the third from one of the Gospels in the New Testament.
- Everyone stands when the Gospel is read, to honor the Lord Jesus.

Go to **aliveinchrist.osv.com** for Sunday readings, Scripture background, questions of the week, and seasonal resources.

FAMILY+FAITH
LIVING AND LEARNING TOGETHER

YOUR CHILD LEARNED >>>

This chapter helps students deepen their understanding of the Theological Virtues and how these virtues help us live the Great Commandment and practice Works of Mercy.

Scripture

 Read **Ephesians 5:1–5** to find out what those who say they love God must have.

Catholics Believe

- The Great Commandment is to love God with all your heart, strength, and mind and to love your neighbor as yourself.
- The Theological Virtues of faith, hope, and charity help us to love God and grow closer to him.

To learn more, go to the *Catechism of the Catholic Church #2055, 2083, 2196* at **usccb.org**.

People of Faith

This week, your child learned about Saint Katharine Drexel, who dedicated her life and her fortune to educating African Americans and Native Americans.

CHILDREN AT THIS AGE >>>

How They Understand the Great Commandment The continued concrete thinking of fourth-graders means that they will probably continue to see love for God and for neighbor as a series of outward actions. This is not far from the truth, for it is certainly the things that we do that tell whether we really have love for God and neighbor. Children your child's age are growing in their ability to see relationships between these larger Commandments and smaller choices in everyday life. They can better determine whether or not an individual action is loving toward God or toward their neighbor. This new ability will help them to begin to make decisions in new situations.

CONSIDER THIS >>>

How does your relationship with God affect how you love others?

The more aware we are of God's love for us, the more that love moves through us. As Catholics, we know that "Scripturally and theologically, the Christian moral life begins with a loving relationship with God, a covenant love made possible by the sacrifice of Christ. The Commandments and other moral rules are given to us as ways of protecting the values that foster love of God and others. They provide us with ways to express love, sometimes by forbidding whatever contradicts love" (*USCCA, p. 318*).

LET'S TALK >>>

- Ask your child to name some of the Works of Mercy.
- Talk about a time of need when someone helped you by performing one of the Works of Mercy.

LET'S PRAY >>>

Saint Katharine, pray for us that we may follow the way of Jesus. Help us live out the Corporal Works of Mercy in our daily lives. Amen.

For a multimedia glossary of Catholic Faith Words, Sunday readings, seasonal and Saint resources, and chapter activities go to **aliveinchrist.osv.com**.

Chapter 8 Review

A Work with Words Use all of the words in the Word Bank to write five of the Corporal Works of Mercy. Use the lines below.

1. Feed the hungry.
2. Bury the dead.
3. Give drink to the thirsty.
4. Shelter the homeless.
5. Clothe the naked.

Word Bank

the
drink
dead
feed
shelter
bury
hungry
clothe
give
thirsty
homeless
naked

B Check Understanding Circle True if a statement is true, and circle False if a statement is false. Correct any false statements.

6. The Spiritual Works of Mercy show care for the physical needs of others.

   True   **(False)**

   They are about the needs of mind, heart, and soul.

7. Only adults have the ability to care for and help others.

   True   **(False)**

   Everyone has the ability to care for and help others.

8. Hope makes it possible for us to believe in God and all he has revealed.

   True   **(False)**

   Faith is the theological virtue that makes belief possible.

9. The Great Commandment can be restated in this way: "First love God, and then love others as you love yourself."

   (True)   False

10. The virtue of charity directs us to love God above all things.

   (True)   False

Go to **aliveinchrist.osv.com** for an interactive review.

Family + Faith

Distribute the page to the children or parents/adult family members. Point out the chapter highlights, insights on how fourth graders understand concepts, the opportunity for the adults to reflect on their own experience and faith journey, and the family prayer.

Chapter Review

Use Catechist Quick Reviews to highlight lesson concepts.

A **Work with Words**
Have the children use words from the Word Bank to write five of the Corporal Works of Mercy.

B **Check Understanding**
Have the children circle *True* or *False*, and correct any false statements.

 Go to **aliveinchrist.osv.com** to prepare customized and downloadable assessments, send eAssessments, and assign interactive reviews.

KEY CONCEPT

The first three Commandments teach you to honor God above all else, respect his name, and worship him on Sunday. These Commandments tell you to believe in, trust, and love God.

DOCTRINAL CONTENT

- The First Commandment teaches us to worship and honor only God, and not to place things or other people before him. (CCC, 2110)

- The Second Commandment calls us to always use the name of God with reverence and respect. (CCC, 2142–2143)

- Blasphemy is the sin of showing disrespect for the name of God, Jesus Christ, Mary, or the Saints in words or actions. (CCC, 2148)

- We observe the Third Commandment through participation in the Sunday Eucharist, rest, time with family, and works of service. (CCC, 2176–2177)

TASKS OF CATECHESIS

Helping children grow in a faith that is "known, celebrated, lived, and expressed in prayer" (NDC, 20).

This chapter focuses on the following tasks of catechesis:

- Liturgical Education
- Moral Formation

Catechist Background

"Worthy are you, Lord our God, to receive glory and honor and power, for you created all things; because of your will they came to be and were created." **Revelation 4:11**

➜ **Reflect** What does it mean to put God first?

An entertainment phenomenon of the early twenty-first century has been the TV talent contest known as "American Idol." The show's format features young singers vying against one another to be voted the most popular. Millions of viewers cast phone ballots to choose their "idol."

Talent is a gift from God, and no one is saying that shows like "American Idol" violate the First Commandment. But fame, beauty, and wealth have certainly become idols to many Americans of all ages. The first three Commandments, with their injunction to put God first, speak as powerfully now as they did long ago, when the Israelites danced before the golden calf.

The first three Commandments lay out a surprisingly simple (though not always easy!) plan for avoiding the false gods that threaten to lead you astray. Get your priorities in order: God comes first. Be careful whom and what you honor (or dishonor) with your words. And put your time where your heart is, honoring God, family, and your own peace of mind with the Sabbath rest.

In a time when there is a "golden calf" on every corner, you can find real joy and certainty in living the first three Commandments. When you put God first, everything else falls into place.

➜ **Reflect** What will you do to keep the Sabbath holy this week?

Catechist's Prayer

Holy God, may my words show reverence for your name. May my actions show my love for you. May the children learn to honor you through their words and deeds. Amen.

Lesson Plan

Objectives	Process	Materials

⏱ Invite, 10 minutes

Honoring God Page 141

- ◉ **Psalm 22:23–24a** Pray the opening prayer.
- ▨ **Revelation 4:11; 7:12** Reflect prayerfully on the Word.
- Discuss What Do You Wonder questions.

◉ **Optional Activity**
Chapter Story:
"A Place of Honor"

⏱ Discover, 35 minutes

Putting God First Pages 142–143

- Recognize that the First Commandment teaches us to worship and honor only God, and not to place things or other people before him

- **Catholic Faith Words** worship, idolatry
- Recall that God created people in his own image.
- ▨ **Exodus 32:1–20** Proclaim "The Golden Calf."
- Explain that the First Commandment requires honor and worship of God alone.
- **Share Your Faith Activity** Write why God is deserving of praise.

☐ pencils
☐ index cards

Respecting God Pages 144–145

- Recognize that the Second Commandment calls us to always use the name of God with reverence
- Define *blasphemy* as the sin of showing disrespect for the name of God, Jesus Christ, Mary, or the Saints
- Appreciate that we observe the Third Commandment through participation in the Sunday Eucharist and rest

- **Catholic Faith Words** blasphemy, Resurrection
- Explain that the Second Commandment teaches treating God's name with reverence and respect.
- ☆ Fill in the missing letters.
- Explain that the Third Commandment teaches honoring God by celebrating Sunday.
- **Connect Your Faith Activity** Identify how to remember the Lord's Day.

☐ pencils
☐ index cards
- **Optional Activity** Names of God
☐ Activity Master 9 (Page 141E)

⏱ Live, 15 minutes

Our Catholic Life Pages 146–147

- Discuss the first three Commandments.
- ☆ Unscramble the words to discover ways to show respect for God.
- **People of Faith** Learn about Saint Mary Ann of Quito.
- **Live Your Faith Activity** Identify how to love God by following the Commandments.

☐ pencils
☐ crayons or markers

Prayer of Praise Page 148

- Select five readers.
- ▶ Rehearse "Holy God, We Praise Thy Name."
- Follow the order of prayer.

◉ Download "Holy God, We Praise Thy Name."

Family + Faith Page 139

Point out that the Catholic Families page provides chapter highlights, information on how fourth graders understand faith concepts, and family prayer.

Chapter Review Page 140

◉ aliveinchrist.osv.com
- Customize and Download Assessments
- Email Links to eAssessments
- Interactive Student Reviews

ONLINE RESOURCES

 Go to **aliveinchrist.osv.com**

You will find:

- Interactive lesson planning with web specific content and additional activities
- Step by step lesson instruction from printed Catechist Edition for integrated lesson planning
- Custom-built assessments to download and eAssessment links
- Interactive reviews that provide scores and the option to review answers
- Sunday readings with background and questions of the week

 Go to **osvparish.com**

You will find:

- Ask the Experts Q and A
- General Catechist Helps
- Community Connections and Blogs

Sharing the Message with Fourth Graders

Honoring God It can be a challenge for many fourth graders to honor God above everything. Fourth graders are practical and concrete, so they are usually very focused on material things. Understanding that they should seek God more than they want the newest video game system or other high tech device can pose a conflict for them. They need to know that if they ask him, God will help them form the desires of their heart so that they are in line with his will.

Teaching Tip: Encourage the children to be honest with themselves and with God about the things that sometimes distract them from the spiritual. They need to know that everyone struggles with this and that God can help them detach themselves from things that won't bring them ultimate happiness.

How Fourth Graders Understand

- Fourth graders are interested in learning all about God. Encourage them to use their own words to talk about God too.
- Fourth graders like to talk about things that happen in their lives. Get to know them and their families.
- Many children feel awe and gratitude for the gifts of creation. Remind them that when they show respect for God's creatures, they show respect to God.

"I can show respect for God. Help me learn the words for holy things and how to use the words properly."

Chapter Connections

Chapter Story Invite

"A Place of Honor"

Use this story to enhance the chapter introduction.

- The children will relate the story to their own lives, reflecting on how they honor their family.
- Connect showing honor for others with showing honor for God.

 Go to **aliveinchrist.osv.com** Lesson Planning section for this story.

NCEA IFG: ACRE Edition Discover

Liturgical Life

- Objective: To know the Paschal Mystery of Jesus: in the Church's liturgical life – feasts, seasons, symbols, and practices; and in the Sacraments as signs and instruments of grace

Moral Formation

- Objectives: To be knowledgeable about the teachings of Jesus and the Church as the basis of Christian morality and to understand Catholic Social Teaching; to be aware of the importance of a well-formed conscience for decision making

Catholic Social Teaching Live

 Use one of these features to introduce a principle and engage the children with an activity.

- Life and Dignity of the Human Person, Pages 290–291
- Care for God's Creation, Pages 302–303

Music Options

 Use one or more of the following songs to enhance catechetical learning or for prayer.

- "Holy God, We Praise Thy Name," Live Prayer, Page 148
- "Father, We Adore You," Discover, Page 143
- "God Is Our Father," Discover, Page 144
- "Praise the Lord," Discover, Page 146

LECTIONARY CONNECTION

 Chapter 9 highlights Lectionary-connected themes such as honoring God, Jesus the Savior, and faith and trust in God. If your parish aligns its curriculum to the liturgical year, you could use this chapter in connection with the following Sundays.

Year A

Second Sunday of Advent—believe and trust in God

The Most Holy Trinity—honoring God

Thirty-second Sunday in Ordinary Time—perseverance in prayer

Year B

Third Sunday of Advent—Jesus the Savior

The Baptism of the Lord—Jesus the Son of God

Fourth Sunday of Easter—Good Shepherd

Year C

Twenty-fourth Sunday in Ordinary Time—honoring God

Twenty-seventh Sunday in Ordinary Time—faith and trust in God

Thirtieth Sunday in Ordinary Time—humility before God

 Go to **aliveinchrist.osv.com** for a complete correlation ordered by the Sundays of the year and suggestions for how to integrate the Scripture readings into chapter lessons.

Name _____ Date _____

Names of God

Read the names of God listed in the box. Then find and circle each name in the word search. The names run from left to right and from top to bottom.

CREATOR	FATHER	JESUS CHRIST	SON
LORD	SAVIOR	HOLY SPIRIT	

A	J	Y	O	Z	U	E	P	T	M	E
J	E	S	U	S	C	H	R	I	S	T
Q	F	A	D	K	M	O	N	Q	D	S
B	W	V	N	L	I	L	G	H	C	Y
C	P	I	R	O	L	Y	D	S	Z	D
M	G	O	Q	R	H	S	O	N	B	L
T	S	R	N	D	R	P	E	D	K	J
K	R	X	G	U	V	I	Z	U	T	N
P	F	A	T	H	E	R	L	W	O	Q
W	B	N	E	D	O	I	B	X	A	B
G	Z	C	R	E	A	T	O	R	J	I

Write one way in which you will use God's name with respect this week.

_____

_____

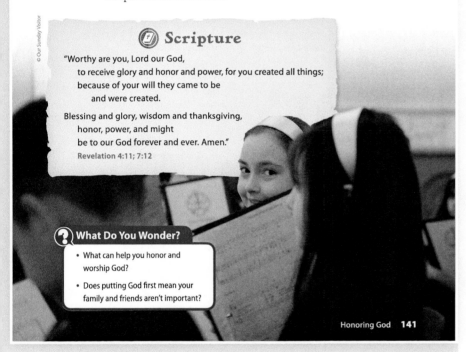

CHAPTER 9

Invite

Honoring God

♥ Let Us Pray

Leader: All glory, praise, and honor to you, great God of grace.

"I will proclaim your name to all I know;
    in the assembly I will praise you:
You who fear the LORD, give praise!
    All descendants of Jacob, give honor."

Based on Psalm 22:23–24a

All: We honor and respect you, Lord, and give to you first place in our lives. Amen.

© Our Sunday Visitor

📖 Scripture

"Worthy are you, Lord our God,
    to receive glory and honor and power, for you created all things;
    because of your will they came to be
      and were created.

Blessing and glory, wisdom and thanksgiving,
    honor, power, and might
    be to our God forever and ever. Amen."

Revelation 4:11; 7:12

❓ What Do You Wonder?

- What can help you honor and worship God?
- Does putting God first mean your family and friends aren't important?

Honoring God **141**

Optional Activity

Chapter Story: "A Place of Honor" *Verbal/Linguistic*

Use this story after the opening prayer, before explaining that we give honor and praise to God.

- Ask two children to read aloud the parts of Vernique and Jeremy.
- Ask the children why the trophy, certificate, the picture and the bowl are going to be displayed in a place of honor.
- *Ask:* What would you put in a place of honor for your family?
- When finished, transition back to the lesson instruction.

📶 Go to **aliveinchrist.osv.com** for Chapter Story.

🕐 **Invite**

♥ Let Us Pray

Invite the children to gather in the prayer space and make the Sign of the Cross. Choose a leader and a reader to read aloud the Psalm verse from a Bible. Prompt the children's response.

Have the children move out of the prayer space and back to their seats.

Explain that that we give honor and praise to God.

Ask: How do we honor God? Put first things first. Put God first. Do your best to know, love, respect, and serve him first of all.

📖 Scripture

Guide the children through the process of Scripture reflection.

- Invite them to close their eyes, be still and open their minds and hearts to what God is saying to them in this passage.
- Proclaim the Scripture.
- Maintain several moments of silence.
- *Ask:* What did you hear God say to you today?
- Invite volunteers to share.

What Do You Wonder?

Say: We respect and give glory to God with both our words and our actions. When we respect and honor him in our lives, everything else will be in good order.

Invite the children to respond to the questions. Ask what else they might wonder about honoring God and putting him first in their lives.

Objective

- Recognize that the First Commandment teaches us to worship and honor only God, and not to place things or other people before him

Putting God First

Ask: What does it mean to praise and honor God?

- Write the children's responses on the board or on chart paper.

Have a volunteer read aloud the paragraph.

- Remind the children that people must honor and respect God because he created everyone and everything.

Scripture

Proclaim "The Golden Calf."

- Ask volunteers to pantomime the parts of Aaron, Moses, and the people as you read.
- *Ask:* Why did it not show respect to God to worship the golden calf?
- Have the children discuss in small groups what the people should have done instead of making the calf.

Putting God First

What does it mean to praise and honor God?

God created each person to be unique, but also alike in a most important way. He created everyone in his own image. Once, the Hebrew people forgot to show God the honor and respect due to the giver of such a gift.

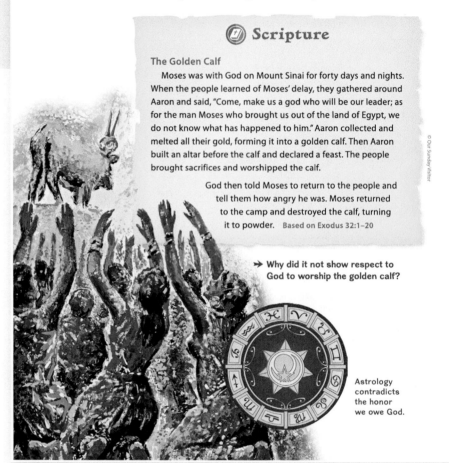

Scripture

The Golden Calf

Moses was with God on Mount Sinai for forty days and nights. When the people learned of Moses' delay, they gathered around Aaron and said, "Come, make us a god who will be our leader; as for the man Moses who brought us out of the land of Egypt, we do not know what has happened to him." Aaron collected and melted all their gold, forming it into a golden calf. Then Aaron built an altar before the calf and declared a feast. The people brought sacrifices and worshipped the calf.

God then told Moses to return to the people and tell them how angry he was. Moses returned to the camp and destroyed the calf, turning it to powder. Based on Exodus 32:1–20

© Our Sunday Visitor

➤ Why did it not show respect to God to worship the golden calf?

Astrology contradicts the honor we owe God.

Scripture Background

Exodus 32:1–20

The golden calf in this Scripture story has both a literal and a symbolic meaning.

- The calf is a graven image or idol, forbidden by the First Commandment.
- The Hebrew people made this idol, emphasizing their doubt about God's faithfulness.
- The idol is gold, symbolizing the people's greed.

The First Commandment

The sin of worshipping the golden calf occurred while Moses was receiving the stone tablets of the Ten Commandments from God. The First Commandment says, "I am the Lord your God. You shall not have strange gods before me."

The First Commandment requires you to honor and worship only God. **Worship** is the adoration and praise that is due to God. You worship God when you celebrate Mass, when you pray, and when you live a life that puts God first. Worshipping an object or a person instead of God, as the people worshipped the golden calf, is called **idolatry**.

When you worship God, you show your belief in him as the source of creation and salvation. You show that you, and all creatures, rely on him for life. You show your trust and hope in him. This is why fortune-telling, or thinking that we can control nature and know the things that God knows, is against the First Commandment.

➔ What are some things that people sometimes place ahead of God?

Catholic Faith Words

worship to adore and praise God, especially in the liturgy and in prayer

idolatry the sin of worshipping an object or a person instead of God. It is letting anything or anyone become more important than God.

Share Your Faith

Reflect Think about the ways you worship God. Write a sentence that explains why God is deserving of praise.

_____

_____

Share Share your responses with a partner.

© Our Sunday Visitor

The First Commandment

Ask the children to silently read this section.

- Have them underline the First Commandment.
- Ask the children what this Commandment reminds people to do. keep God first in our lives, and put our trust and hope in him
- *Ask:* What are some things that people sometimes place ahead of God?
- Explain that these things are not necessarily bad, unless they take attention away from God.

Work with Words

Have the children create vocabulary cards for the words *worship* and *idolatry*.

Music Option: Have the children sing, "Father, We Adore You," downloaded from **aliveinchrist.osv.com**.

Activity

Read aloud the directions for the Share Your Faith activity.

- Allow time for the children to complete the activity and share their responses.
- Point out that doing the things they have listed is a good way for children to honor God.

Quick Review

People worship God and owe him respect and honor because he created all life and offers all people salvation.

ⓘ Catechist Background

Idolatry

The golden calf was thought to be a god. Worshipping the golden calf was sinful, unlike praying before images of Saints.

- Explain that the Church honors Saints for their holiness, but worships only God.
- Prayers are directed to God through the Saints.
- Statues remind people of Jesus, Mary, and the Saints.

Discover

Objectives

- Recognize that the Second Commandment calls us to always use the name of God with reverence
- Define *blasphemy* as the sin of showing disrespect for the name of God, Jesus Christ, Mary, or the Saints
- Appreciate that we observe the Third Commandment through participation in the Sunday Eucharist and rest

Respecting God

Ask: What do the Second and Third Commandments tell you to do?

- Write the children's responses on the board or on chart paper.

Ask a volunteer to read aloud the first paragraph.

Tell the children that to take a name "in vain" means to use it with disrespect.

- Have the children read silently the next paragraph to learn how they are to use God's name.

Work with Words

Review the meaning of *blasphemy*.

- Have the children make vocabulary cards for the term *blasphemy*.

Read aloud the last paragraph.

 Have the children fill in the missing letters.

> ▶ Music Option: Have the children sing, "God Is Our Father," downloaded from **aliveinchrist.osv.com**.

Respecting God

What do the Second and Third Commandments tell you to do?

Catholic Faith Words

blasphemy the sin of showing disrespect for the name of God, Jesus Christ, Mary, or the Saints in words or action

Resurrection the event of Jesus being raised from Death to new life by God the Father through the power of the Holy Spirit

The Second Commandment is connected to the First Commandment: "You shall not take the name of the Lord in vain." God's name is sacred, or holy, because God is sacred. When God called Moses to be the leader of his People, God revealed his name to Moses. God shared his name with his People because he loved and trusted them. In return, God's People are to bless and praise God's holy name.

This Commandment calls you to always use the name of God with reverence and respect. Respecting God's name is a sign of the respect God deserves. It is a sin against God's name to curse or to use God's name to swear to a lie. To seriously dishonor the name of God, Jesus Christ, Mary, or the Saints in words or actions is called **blasphemy**.

You probably use God's name most often in prayer. Calling on God's name strengthens you to live as a child of God and a follower of Christ. The Second Commandment also reminds us that God calls each person by name. A name is a sign of a person's human dignity. You are to use the names of others with respect.

© Our Sunday Visitor

 Fill in the missing letters in the words below.

The Name of God

Every time you make the Sign of the Cross, you call on the name of

the F a t h e r,

of the Son, and of the

H o l y Sp i r i t.

This is a reminder of your

B a p t i s m.

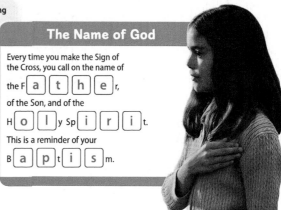

144 Chapter 9

Optional Activity

Activity Master 9: Names of God

Distribute copies of the activity found on catechist page 141E.

- Tell the children to circle the names of God and answer the question.
- As an alternative, consider sending this activity home with the children.

Keeping the Lord's Day

Following the First, Second, and Third Commandments helps you love God and grow closer to him. The Third Commandment teaches you to honor God by celebrating Sunday, the greatest and most special day of the week for Christians. The Third Commandment is this: Remember to keep holy the Lord's Day.

Sunday is the first day of the week. Jesus rose to new life on the first day of the week. This is why Sunday is known as the Lord's Day. Gathering on Sunday for the Eucharist has been the center of the Church's life since the time of the Apostles. This is because Sunday is the day of the Lord's **Resurrection**.

The Lord's Day

Participate in the Sunday celebration of the Eucharist. This is the most important way to observe the Third Commandment.

Rest and enjoy time with your family. Share a meal, read the Bible together, or visit a relative you do not often see.

Take part in parish activities, visit a retirement center, visit people in the community who are sick, or perform a work of service as a family.

Respect the rights of others to rest and observe Sunday.

Connect Your Faith

Sunday Suggestions Circle the actions you could take to remember the Lord's Day.

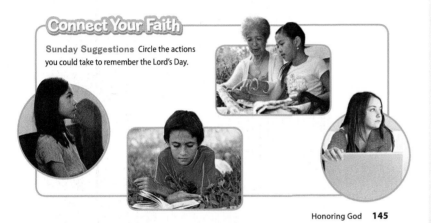

Honoring God   **145**

(i) Catechist Background

The Right to Rest

In his 1981 encyclical *On Human Work*, Pope Saint John Paul II noted that workers have certain rights:

- the right to balance labor with rest;
- the right to have a weekly day to rest, fulfill religious obligations, and spend time with family;
- the right to a vacation.

Review with the children ways they can keep holy the Lord's Day.

Keeping the Lord's Day

Ask the children to share how their families honor the Lord's Day.

Read aloud the first paragraph.

- Remind the children that after God created the world, he rested.

Have the children read silently the next paragraph to learn why Sunday is a special day.

The Lord's Day

Invite four children to each read aloud one of the ways to keep Sunday holy.

Work with Words

Point out the definition of *Resurrection* and have the children make vocabulary cards.

Activity

Point out the Connect Your Faith activity and read aloud the directions.

- Have the children work independently to complete the activity.
- Discuss their responses.

Quick Review

The Second Commandment says to use God's name with respect. The Third Commandment says to honor God by keeping Sundays holy. Keeping these Commandments is a way to grow closer to God.

Our Catholic Life

Ask: Why are the First, Second, and Third Commandments important?

- Write the children's responses on the board or on chart paper.

Read aloud the first paragraph.

Commandments of Respect

Point out the variety of ways in which children can show respect for God.

 Have the children unscramble the words in bold to reveal some ways to show respect for God.

Ask six volunteers to read aloud the text.

- *Ask:* What things in the church should you especially treat with respect? Possible responses: hymnals, people, statues, Bibles

- Emphasize that their responses should include "other people."

- Refer to page 316 in the Our Catholic Tradition reference section of the Student Book for the Ten Commandments.

> ▶ Music Option: Have the children sing, "Praise the Lord," downloaded from **aliveinchrist.osv.com**.

Our Catholic Life

Why are the First, Second, and Third Commandments important?

The first three Commandments are about how you act toward, think about, and worship God. They give you a guide for how you can praise God and show him respect.

Commandments of Respect

God has given you many blessings. In return, he asks that you follow the first three Commandments in worship of him.

Attend Mass Participate in Mass every Sunday or Saturday evening.

Say grace Give thanks to God and ask for his **lbisgssen** before you eat.

<u>blessings</u>

Remember the meaning of religious holidays During the holidays, stop and think about why you are celebrating.

Love others Show kindness and love to people around you. They are made in God's **emgia**.

<u>image</u>

Say a prayer of thanks Thank God for the many blessings in your life.

Do not curse Pay attention to what you are **ysinga**.

<u>saying</u>

> ⭐ Unscramble the letters in the boldfaced words to find some ways to show your respect for God.

© Our Sunday Visitor

146

✔️ Quick Tip

Keep the Lord's Day

Catholic Tradition calls people to honor God by taking a break from work.

- Encourage the children to talk with their families about doing activities they enjoy as a family.

- At your next session, allow volunteers to report on their Sunday activities.

People of Faith

Saint Mary Ann of Quito, 1618–1645

May 26

Saint Mary Ann of Quito was born in Quito, a city in Ecuador, South America. She was from a noble family. At an early age, she promised to live a holy life in poverty. She spent much time in prayer and doing penance. At first her name was Mariana de Paredes. Because she wanted to be sure she always showed her respect for the Name of Jesus, she added his name to hers. When earthquakes and disease came to her city, she prayed. The city was saved. She is considered a national hero of Ecuador.

Discuss: How do you show respect for the name of God?

 Learn more about Saint Mary Ann at **aliveinchrist.osv.com**

Live Your Faith

Describe how the student in the picture is following one of the Commandments.

Illustrate one way you could love God by following one the first three Commandments.

 © Our Sunday Visitor

Honoring God **147**

 Catholic Social Teaching

Chapter Connections

To integrate Catholic Social Teaching into your lesson, choose one of the following features: Life and Dignity of the Human Person, pages 290–291; or Care for God's Creation, pages 302–303.

- Start the Live step of the process by talking about Saint Mary Ann on page 147. Then move directly to the Catholic Social Teaching feature.
- Or, to expand the lesson, complete both pages 146 and 147, then move to the Catholic Social Teaching feature.
- Return to Chapter 9 for the prayer on page 148.

People of Faith

Tell the children about Saint Mary Ann of Quito.

- Invite a volunteer to read aloud the People of Faith story.
- Explain that Saint Mary Ann was a hermit or recluse.
- She had great love for Jesus Christ and his Blessed Mother.
- God gave Saint Mary Ann many wonderful mystical gifts. She could read hearts, heal people, cure diseases, and predict the future. On at least one occasion, she restored a dead person to life.
- She is the first person from Ecuador to be named a Saint.
- Out of her respect for the name of Jesús, she added his name to hers. She is also known as Saint Mariana of Jesus de Paredes.
- *Ask:* How do you show respect for the name of God?

Encourage the children to go to **aliveinchrist.osv.com** at home to find out more about Saint Marianna of Jesus.

Activity

Read aloud the directions and discuss the first part of the Live Your Faith activity.

- Allow time for the children to complete an illustration.
- Invite volunteers to share their drawings.

Let Us Pray

Prayer of Praise

Tell the children that today they will be using different names for God.

Prepare

- Select five readers. You can be the leader.
- Practice the response with the children.

 Rehearse "Holy God, We Praise Thy Name," downloaded from **aliveinchrist.osv.com**.

Gather

Invite the children to process to the prayer space.

- Since you are the leader for this prayer, stand in the front of the group.
- Make sure the children are seated comfortably. Invite them to prepare their minds and hearts for prayer.

Pray

Follow the order of prayer on the student page.

- For an optional Scripture reading, use *Psalm 33:1–5* or *Psalm 34:1–4*.
- *Leader's concluding prayer:* Holy God, may we remember to be thankful for all your blessings and give honor to your holy name.

 Conclude by singing together "Holy God, We Praise Thy Name."

Live

 Let Us Pray

Prayer of Praise

Gather and begin with the Sign of the Cross.

Leader: Respond to each name of God by praying: We praise your name, O God.

Reader: God, our Father,

All: We praise your name, O God.

Reader: All merciful and gracious God,

All: We praise your name, O God.

Reader: God, our Creator,

All: We praise your name, O God.

Reader: Compassionate God,

All: We praise your name, O God.

Reader: God, source of all life,

All: We praise your name, O God.

Leader: Let us pray.

Bow your heads as the leader prays.

All: Amen.

 Sing "Holy God, We Praise Thy Name"

148 Chapter 9

 Liturgy Link

Glory to God

At Mass on most Sundays, the assembly sings or prays an ancient hymn in praise of God—Father, Son, and Holy Spirit.

- Read through the text of this prayer with the children. Have them point out the names of God mentioned in the prayer.
- Teach or review with the children a melody that your parish uses for the Glory to God (*Gloria*).
- Show them how to fold their hands when they pray.

 Go to **aliveinchrist.osv.com** for Sunday readings, Scripture background, questions of the week, and seasonal resources.

FAMILY+FAITH
LIVING AND LEARNING TOGETHER

YOUR CHILD LEARNED >>>
This chapter explains how the First, Second, and Third Commandments help us keep God first in our lives and teach us to worship God and honor his name.

Scripture
 Read **Revelation 4:11; 7:12** to find out why and how to honor God.

Catholics Believe
- The first three Commandments teach you to honor God above all else, respect his name, and worship him on Sunday.
- These Commandments tell you to believe in, trust, and love God.

To learn more, go to the *Catechism of the Catholic Church #2063–2065* at **usccb.org**.

People of Faith
This week, your child learned about Saint Mary Ann of Quito, one of the national heroes of Ecuador.

CHILDREN AT THIS AGE >>>
How They Understand Honoring God It can be a challenge for many fourth-graders to honor God above everything. Children this age are practical and concrete, so they are usually very focused on material things. Understanding that they should seek God more than they want the newest video game system or other high-tech device can pose a conflict for them. They need to know that if they ask him, God will help them form the desires of their heart so that they are in line with his will.

CONSIDER THIS >>>
What would your calendar indicate are the top priorities in your family's life?

Most of our calendars are filled with work, children's activities, and chores to keep the household running. Yet, the Commandments call us to prioritize with God in mind. As Catholics, we understand that "the first three Commandments treat our relationship to God. . . . The First Commandment calls us to have faith in the true God, to hope in him, and to love him fully with mind, heart, and will. . . . The First Commandment fosters the virtue of religion that moves us to adore God alone because he alone is holy and worthy of our praise" (*USCCA, p. 341*).

LET'S TALK >>>
- Ask your child to tell you one way we honor God in our lives.
- Talk about how your family keeps the Lord's Day.

LET'S PRAY >>>
Dear God, may we always respect and honor your name and never use it as a swear word. Amen.

For a multimedia glossary of Catholic Faith Words, Sunday readings, seasonal and Saint resources, and chapter activities go to **aliveinchrist.osv.com**.

Alive in Christ, Grade 4 Chapter 9   **149**

Family + Faith

Distribute the page to the children or parents/adult family members. Point out the chapter highlights, insights on how fourth graders understand concepts, the opportunity for the adults to reflect on their own experience and faith journey, and the family prayer.

Chapter 9 Review

(A) Work with Words **Fill in the circle next to the word that best completes each statement.**

1. Calling on God's name in _____ helps you live as a child of God and follower of Christ.
   - ○ anger
   - ● prayer
   - ○ an oath

2. _____ the name of God, Jesus Christ, Mary, or the Saints in words or actions is called blasphemy.
   - ● Dishonoring
   - ○ Explaining
   - ○ Honoring

3. When you adore and praise God, _____ in the liturgy and in prayer, you are worshipping him.
   - ○ except
   - ○ only
   - ● especially

4. Fortune-telling is against the _____ Commandment.
   - ● First
   - ○ Second
   - ○ Third

5. When you worship God, you show your _____ in him as the source of creation and salvation.
   - ○ disbelief
   - ● belief
   - ○ indifference

(B) Check Understanding **Respond briefly to the following questions.**

6. Who or what should you worship?
   __only God__

7. What did God create in his own image?
   __humans__

8. How can you show respect for God's name?
   __not use it in an angry way__

9. Who is called to worship at Sunday Mass?
   __all Catholics__

10. What do the first three Commandments tell you to do?
    __show respect for God__

Go to **aliveinchrist.osv.com** for an interactive review.

150   Chapter 9 Review

Chapter Review

Use Catechist Quick Reviews to highlight lesson concepts.

(A) Work with Words
Have the children choose the word that best completes each statement.

(B) Check Understanding
Have the children respond briefly to each question.

 Go to **aliveinchrist.osv.com** to prepare customized and downloadable assessments, send eAssessments, and assign interactive reviews.

Honoring God   **149–150**

Use Catechist Quick Reviews in each chapter to highlight lesson concepts for this unit and prepare for the Unit Review.

Have the children complete the Review pages. Then discuss the answers as a group. Review any concepts with which the children are having difficulty.

A) Work with Words

Have the children match each description in Column 1 with the correct term in Column 2.

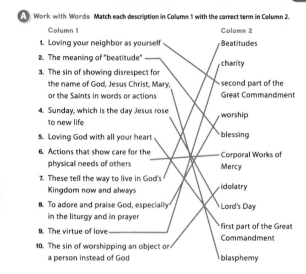

Unit Review

UNIT
3

A) **Work with Words** Match each description in Column 1 with the correct term in Column 2.

Column 1
1. Loving your neighbor as yourself
2. The meaning of "beatitude"
3. The sin of showing disrespect for the name of God, Jesus Christ, Mary, or the Saints in words or actions
4. Sunday, which is the day Jesus rose to new life
5. Loving God with all your heart
6. Actions that show care for the physical needs of others
7. These tell the way to live in God's Kingdom now and always
8. To adore and praise God, especially in the liturgy and in prayer
9. The virtue of love
10. The sin of worshipping an object or a person instead of God

Column 2
Beatitudes
charity
second part of the Great Commandment
worship
blessing
Corporal Works of Mercy
idolatry
Lord's Day
first part of the Great Commandment
blasphemy

© Our Sunday Visitor

Jesus Christ   **151**

B Check Understanding **Complete each sentence with the correct word.**

11. _____Moses_____ received the Ten Commandments from God on Mount Sinai.

12. The _____First_____ Commandment says, "I am the Lord your God. You shall not have strange gods before me."

13. The _____Second_____ Commandment says, "You shall not take the name of the Lord in vain."

14. The _____Third_____ Commandment says, "Remember to keep holy the Lord's Day."

15. The rich young man in the Scripture story could not think of selling his things and giving the _____money_____ to the poor.

Make Connections **Write a response to each question or statement.**

16. Write about one of the Theological Virtues.
_____Responses will vary._____
_____
_____
_____

17. Write about someone who lives out the Theological Virtue you described.
_____Responses will vary._____
_____
_____
_____

18. Explain what the first three Commandments teach about respect.
Possible response: They tell me how to show respect toward God by giving him love, trusting in him, and believing in him; they tell me how to use his name; going to Mass and worshipping on Sunday show respect for God.

19. Explain what the Great Commandment has in common with the Corporal Works of Mercy.
Possible response: We love our neighbor as ourselves when we perform the Corporal Works of Mercy.

20. What do respect and honor mean to you?
Possible response: Respect means treating God and others the way the Ten Commandments require and showing care and obeying authority; honor means putting God above all things.

B Check Understanding
Have the children complete each sentence with the correct word.

C Make Connections
Have the children write a response to each question or statement.

Go to **aliveinchrist.osv.com** to prepare customized and downloadable assessments, send eAssessments, and assign interactive reviews.

The Church

Our Catholic Tradition

- Every person has a vocation to love and honor God, share in his happiness, and become more like Christ as we serve others and work for his Kingdom. (CCC, 1877)

- Mary and the Saints are models and teachers of holiness for all of us. (CCC, 828)

- Jesus gave Church leaders the authority to explain Sacred Scripture and Sacred Tradition to the faithful. The Holy Spirit directs Church leaders in teaching and guiding the faithful. (CCC, 95, 100)

How does your vocation help you to become a Saint?

Unit 4 Overview

Chapter 10

The children will:

- define vocation as God's plan for our lives, the purpose for which he made us
- describe priesthood, consecrated religious life, committed single life, and married life as four distinct ways people respond to God's call
- appreciate that all baptized members of the Church are called to serve God and the Church using their gifts and in ways appropriate to their state of life

 Catholic Social Teaching: Live Your Faith

- Call to Family, Community, and Participation, Pages 292–293
- Dignity of Work and Rights of Workers, Pages 298–299

The children will:

- describe a Saint as a person whom the Church declares has led a holy life and is enjoying eternal life with God in Heaven
- identify Mary as the perfect model of holiness, accepting God's will throughout her life and remaining faithful to him
- recognize the Immaculate Conception as the truth that God kept Mary free from sin from the first moment of her life
- recognize that Mary is called the Mother of the Church because she holds her Son's followers close to her heart

 Songs of Scripture
"Mary's Song of Praise"

 Catholic Social Teaching: Live Your Faith

- Call to Family, Community, and Participation, Pages 292–293
- Option for the Poor and Vulnerable, Pages 296–297

The children will:

- identify Peter as the Apostle Jesus chose to lead the Apostles and the Church
- recognize that Jesus gave Peter and the Apostles, and their successors the Pope and bishops, the authority to teach and lead in his name
- identify the Magisterium as the teaching office of the Church
- explain how the Holy Spirit directs the Magisterium in teaching and guiding the People of God
- retell the Precepts of the Church

 Catholic Social Teaching: Live Your Faith

- Call to Family, Community, and Participation, Pages 292–293
- Rights and Responsibilities of the Human Person, Pages 294–295

Preview Unit Theme

Ask: What is the unit theme?

Summarize that the unit focuses on the Church.

Invite volunteers to read aloud each of the bullets in Our Catholic Tradition.

Explain to the children that they will learn about these things in the next three chapters.

Have the children study the photos and images. Invite volunteers to describe what they see. What do these images say about the unit theme?

Ask: How does your vocation help you to become a Saint?

After some discussion, explain to the children that they will be exploring this question in the next three chapters.

KEY CONCEPT

God calls every person to a vocation. Through your vocation, you can help God increase his Reign.

DOCTRINAL CONTENT

- Vocation is God's plan for our lives; the purpose for which he made us. (CCC, 1877)
- Priesthood, consecrated religious, committed single life, and married life are four distinct ways people respond to God's call. (CCC, 871–873)
- All baptized members of the Church are called to serve God and the Church using their gifts and in ways appropriate to their state of life. (CCC, 912–913)

TASKS OF CATECHESIS

Helping children grow in a faith that is "known, celebrated, lived, and expressed in prayer" (NDC, 20).

This chapter focuses on the following tasks of catechesis:

- Education for Communal Life
- Missionary Initiation

Catechist Background

 Again they consulted the Lord, "Is there still someone else to come forward?" The Lord answered: He is hiding among the baggage. **1 Samuel 10:22**

➔ **Reflect** What will help you respond to God's call?

There has never been a time when God was not in charge! From the first light of creation to this morning's sunrise, all humans have been under the loving dominion of God. His plan for humans also has existed from the beginning. Humanity was created to live in peace, in justice, and in love.

By committing sin, humans strayed from God's plan. Jesus came to bring them back to a right relationship with God and to fulfill God's Reign. Jesus' Death and Resurrection saved humans and gave them a share in the Kingdom. Humans still struggle and long for the completion that will come when Jesus returns. But humans wait in hope, cooperating with God in bringing about his Reign. Christians' patience, faithfulness, and love show others that the Reign of God is both *possible* and *present*—though incompletely—here and now.

God invites you to live a life of meaning and service. Single or married, ordained or lay person, you participate in making the world whole and holy. The wonder of this is that you are asked to live your vocation exactly where you are at the moment. Vocation is God's plan for your life, the purpose for which he made you. Using your gifts to benefit others is answering God's invitation with an open heart and willing hands.

➔ **Reflect** When have you felt that God was calling you?

Catechist's Prayer

 Eternal God, may your loving plan reign in my heart. May my words bring peace to others and my actions show concern for their needs. Amen.

Lesson Plan

Objectives	Process	Materials

🕐 Invite, 10 minutes

Called to Serve Page 155	○ **Psalm 113:1** Pray the opening prayer. 📖 **1 Samuel 10:20–22** Reflect prayerfully on the Word. • Discuss What Do You Wonder questions.	🌐 **Optional Activity** Chapter Story: "A Good Neighbor"

🕐 Discover, 35 minutes

God's Call Pages 156–157 • Define vocation as God's plan for our lives, the purpose for which he made us • Describe priesthood, consecrated religious life, committed single life, and married life as four distinct ways people respond to God's call	• **Catholic Faith Words** vocation, Kingdom of God, vows • Explain that everyone has a vocation. 📖 **Matthew 4:18–22** Proclaim "The Call of the First Disciples." • Explain that vocations can make the Kingdom of God visible. • Explain the four ways in which people respond to God's call to serve. • **Share Your Faith Activity** Share an example of a person who serves God.	☐ pencils ☐ index cards
Serving the Church Pages 158–159 • Appreciate that all baptized members of the Church are called to serve God and the Church using their gifts and in ways appropriate to their state of life	• **Catholic Faith Words** laity • Explain that all the baptized are invited to serve the Church. ☆ Identify roles of the laity that raise interest or questions. • Explore the story of Venerable Anne de Guigné. • **Connect Your Faith Activity** Identify how to help others by using one of God's gifts.	☐ pencils ☐ index cards • **Optional Activity** People of God ☐ Activity Master 10 (Page 155E)

🕐 Live, 15 minutes

Our Catholic Life Pages 160–161	• Recall the Sacrament of Baptism. ☆ Identify ways to live God's call. • **People of Faith** Learn about Blessed Frédéric Ozanam. • **Live Your Faith Activity** Name how to use talents.	☐ pencils ☐ crayons or markers
Prayer of Petition for Vocations Page 162	• Have paper prepared for each child. ▶ Rehearse "Gifts."	🌐 Download "Gifts." ☐ pencils

---

Family + Faith Page 163

Point out that the Catholic Families page provides chapter highlights, information on how fourth graders understand faith concepts, and family prayer.

Chapter Review Page 164

🌐 **aliveinchrist.osv.com**
• Customize and Download Assessments
• Email Links to eAssessments
• Interactive Student Reviews

ONLINE RESOURCES

 Go to **aliveinchrist.osv.com**

You will find:

- Interactive lesson planning with web specific content and additional activities
- Step by step lesson instruction from printed Catechist Edition for integrated lesson planning
- Custom-built assessments to download and eAssessment links
- Interactive reviews that provide scores and the option to review answers
- Sunday readings with background and questions of the week

 Go to **osvparish.com**

You will find:

- Ask the Experts Q and A
- General Catechist Helps
- Community Connections and Blogs

Sharing the Message with Fourth Graders

Their Call from God As fourth graders hear that God has a plan for their lives, they are capable of realizing that this plan is different from the one he has for anyone else, and that they have the free will to choose to follow—or not to follow—God's plan. With help and support from adults, children this age can begin to better identify the talents and interests that can point to God's plan and also to see the opportunities to explore further God's path for their futures.

Teaching Tip: Point out talents, gifts, and interests when you see them represented in the group. Encourage the children to think of ways they can use their talents for God.

How Fourth Graders Understand

- Fourth graders are fascinated by different points of view. Invite speakers or guests to some of the sessions.
- Fourth graders enjoy group activities. Show them how to work peacefully with others.
- Fourth graders are interested in more information. Encourage them to research vocations that interest them.

"I like to make a difference. Give me an opportunity to work on parish projects."

Chapter Connections

Chapter Story

Invite

"A Good Neighbor"

Use this story to expand the chapter introduction.

- The children will relate the story to their own lives, reflecting on what makes the world around them a better place.
- Connect making the world a better place to following God's plan.

 Go to **aliveinchrist.osv.com** Lesson Planning section for this story.

NCEA IFG: ACRE Edition

Discover

Communal Life

- Objectives: To know the origin, mission, structure, and communal nature of the Church; to know the rights and responsibilities of the Christian faithful

Missionary Spirit

- Objectives: To recognize the centrality of evangelization as the Church's mission and identity embodied in vocation and service; to be aware of how cultures are transformed by the Gospel

Catholic Social Teaching

Live

 Use one of these features to introduce a principle and engage the children with an activity.

- Call to Family, Community, and Participation, Pages 292–293
- Dignity of Work and Rights of Workers, Pages 298–299

Music Options

 Use one or more of the following songs to enhance catechetical learning or for prayer.

- "Gifts," Live Prayer, Page 162
- "God Has Chosen Me," Discover, Page 156
- "Build God's Kingdom" or "Seek Ye First," Discover, Page 157
- "All That God Wants You to Be," Live, Page 160
- "Act Justly," Live, Page 161

LECTIONARY CONNECTION

 Chapter 10 highlights Lectionary-connected themes such as vocation, Baptism and the Kingdom of God. If your parish aligns its curriculum to the liturgical year, you could use this chapter in connection with the following Sundays.

Year A

Third Sunday in Ordinary Time—vocation

Most Holy Body and Blood of Christ—God's care

Twenty-seventh Sunday in Ordinary Time—Kingdom of God

Year B

Second Sunday in Ordinary Time—vocation

Twenty-fourth Sunday in Ordinary Time—faith and works

Twenty-ninth Sunday in Ordinary Time—serve others

Year C

Third Sunday of Advent—conversion

The Baptism of the Lord—Baptism

Twenty-third Sunday in Ordinary Time—discipleship

 Go to **aliveinchrist.osv.com** for a complete correlation ordered by the Sundays of the year and suggestions for how to integrate the Scripture readings into chapter lessons.

Name _____   Date _____

People of God

Fill in the missing letters to discover some of the roles that the People of God serve in the Church. Inside the church shape, fill in the name of someone who serves this role in your parish. Use a parish bulletin to help you.

1. C A T ☐ ☐ H I ☐ ☐

2. M ☐ ☐ I C ☐ ☐ N

3. S E ☐ ☐ E ☐

4. D ☐ A ☐ ☐ N

5. L ☐ C T ☐ R

6. Y ☐ ☐ T H

M I ☐ I S T ☐ ☐

7. P ☐ ☐ E S ☐

8. R E ☐ ☐ G I ☐ ☐ ☐

L I F E

1. _____.   2. _____.

3. _____.   4. _____.

5. _____.   6. _____.

7. _____.   8. _____.

Called to Serve

 Let Us Pray

Leader: God of love, we gladly honor and obey you.

"Praise, you servants of the LORD,
praise the name of the LORD." Psalm 113:1

All: In our Baptism, we are called to holiness. You call
us by name to know you and serve your people.
Open our hearts that we may hear your call. Amen.

Scripture

So Samuel had all the tribes of Israel come forward, and
the tribe of Benjamin was chosen. And the family of Matri was
chosen. Finally, Saul, son of Kish, was chosen. But they could not
find him. Samuel asked, "Has he come here?" The Lord answered,
"He is hiding among the baggage." Based on 1 Samuel 10:20–22

© Our Sunday Visitor

? What Do You Wonder?

• How does God call people today?

• What will help you respond to
God's call?

155

Optional Activity

Chapter Story: "A Good Neighbor" *Verbal/Linguistic*

Use this story after the opening prayer, before explaining that God
called Saul to do his work.

• Invite a child to read aloud the story.

• Ask the children to share if any of them have a neighbor who
makes their neighborhood a special place.

• After asking the children to name ways they can make the world
better, transition back to the lesson instruction.

 Go to **aliveinchrist.osv.com** for Chapter Story.

 Invite

Let Us Pray

Invite the children to gather in the
prayer space and make the Sign of
the Cross. Choose a leader. Read
aloud the Psalm verse from a Bible.
Prompt the children's response.

Have the children move out of the
prayer space and back to their seats.

Explain that God called Saul to do
his work.

Say: Saul was the first King of Israel.
When Samuel told Saul that God
had called him to this great work,
Saul was overwhelmed.

Scripture

Guide the children through the
process of Scripture reflection.

• Invite them to close their eyes, be
still and open their minds and
hearts to what God is saying to
them in this passage.

• Proclaim the Scripture.

• Maintain several moments of
silence.

• *Ask:* What did you hear God say
to you today?

• Invite volunteers to share.

What Do You Wonder?

Say: As the people waited to see
who God had chosen to lead them,
they were not expecting to find their
leader hiding in the baggage. Saul
was afraid. Answering God's call
requires courage and a willing heart.

Invite the children to respond to the
questions. Ask what else they might
wonder about hearing and
responding to God's call.

Objectives

- Define vocation as God's plan for our lives; the purpose for which he made us
- Describe priesthood, consecrated religious life, committed single life, and married life as four distinct ways people respond to God's call

God's Call

Ask: What does it mean to have a vocation?

- Write the children's responses on the board or on chart paper.

Read aloud the first paragraph.

- Discuss the meaning of the term *vocation*.

 ## Scripture

Proclaim "The Call of the First Disciples."

- Choose six volunteers to act out the story as you read it a second time.
- Discuss what Jesus meant when he said, "fishers of men."
- *Ask:* Have you ever felt that God wanted you to do something or to make a certain choice?
- Tell the children that like the first disciples, each of them has a vocation or a calling from God.

 Music Option: Have the children sing, "God Has Chosen Me," downloaded from **aliveinchrist.osv.com**.

God's Call

What does it mean to have a vocation?

Everyone has a **vocation**. A vocation is God's plan for our lives: the purpose for which he made us. Sometimes God calls a person to a special role. When Jesus was ready to begin his work, he gathered some friends to help him.

 ### Scripture

The Call of the First Disciples

One day, Jesus was walking by the Sea of Galilee. He saw two brothers, Peter and Andrew. Andrew cast a net into the sea. The brothers were fishermen.

Jesus said to them, "Come follow me. I will make you fishers of men." At once, they left their nets and followed Jesus.

Jesus continued walking. He came upon two more brothers, James and John. They were in a boat with their father, fixing their nets. Jesus called them. Immediately they left their nets and their father and followed Jesus.

Based on Matthew 4:18–22

© Our Sunday Visitor

Scripture Background

Matthew 4:18–22

In this Scripture passage, Jesus begins recruiting his first disciples.

- In contrast to the practice of a rabbi of that time, Jesus chose his disciples rather than his disciples choosing him.
- Jesus' disciples choose to follow not simply to listen and learn. Jesus' disciples will take on an active role as fishers of people.

Vocation and God's Kingdom

Not everyone hears God's call as clearly as the first disciples did. Sometimes it takes many years of praying and listening to know your vocation.

All vocations can make the **Kingdom of God** more visible. God's Reign is the world of love, peace, and justice that God intends. Jesus announced the Kingdom and revealed it in his life and ministry. But God's Kingdom will not be here fully until the end of time when Christ returns in glory. Until then, we are called to help God increase his rule in our lives and in the world.

→ What signs can you see of God's Kingdom?

Ways to Respond to God's Call

The Catholic Church recognizes four ways in which people respond to God's call to serve: through the priesthood, consecrated religious life, committed single life, or the married life. Consecrated religious life is a state of life in which a person usually makes **vows**, or promises, that help them to grow in holiness. Baptism sets us all on the journey of holiness. Priests and married couples take vows as well.

| Priesthood | Consecrated religious life | Committed single life | Married life |

Catholic Faith Words

vocation God's plan for our lives; the purpose for which he made us

Kingdom of God God's rule of peace, justice, and love that exists in Heaven, but has not yet come in its fullness on Earth

vows solemn promises that are made to or before God

Share Your Faith

Reflect Think about two people you know who serve God.

Share Tell a partner how these people are an example of service for you.

Vocation and God's Kingdom

Have the children read these two paragraphs.

Work with Words

Point out and read aloud the definition of *Kingdom of God*.

- Have the children make vocabulary cards.

Spend time on the discussion question. Encourage responses that relate to the Beatitudes.

- Refer the children to page 317 in the Our Catholic Tradition reference section for more about the Beatitudes.

Ways to Respond to God's Call

Ask a volunteer to read aloud the paragraph.

- Invite the children to name people they know who serve God.
- Have the children make vocabulary cards for the term *vows*.

 Music Option: Have the children sing, "Build God's Kingdom" or "Seek Ye First," downloaded from **aliveinchrist.osv.com**.

Activity

Read aloud the directions for the Share Your Faith activity.

- Provide time for the children to share with a partner.

Quick Review

Everyone has a vocation—a call to be a sign of the Kingdom of God.

✓ Quick Tip

States of Life

Invite the children to compare and contrast the states of life.

- On the board or chart paper, create four sections labeled *priesthood, consecrated religious life, married life,* and *single life.*
- Divide each section into two columns. Ask the children to list what they think are the challenges and the rewards of each way of life. List their responses in the appropriate columns.

Discover

Objective

- Appreciate that all baptized members of the Church are called to serve God and the Church using their gifts and in ways appropriate to their state of life

Serving the Church

Ask: How can we use our gifts to serve?

- List the children's responses on the board or on chart paper.

Ask a volunteer to read aloud the paragraph.

Work with Words

Invite a volunteer to read aloud the definition of *laity*.

- Have the children make vocabulary cards for the term *laity*.

Many Gifts

Point out that there are many ways to serve the Church. Explain that in the chart, they will see some ways we can serve in the liturgy. Ask each of seven volunteers to read aloud one item from the list of roles.

- Ask the children to share the names of people they know who serve in these roles.
- ⭐ Invite the children to circle the roles that interest them or that they have a question about.
- Point out the photos. Ask the children to match the people in the photos to the roles they serve.

Discover

Serving the Church

How can we use our gifts to serve?

The Church recognizes that some people may be called to serve God by remaining single. The dedicated single life is also a vocation. Both single and married people are part of the **laity**. All who are baptized are invited to serve the universal Church and the parish community. Here are some ways we do this.

> **Catholic Faith Words**
>
> **laity** all of the baptized people in the Church who share in God's mission but are not priests or consecrated sisters or brothers; sometimes called lay people

 Circle the roles that interest you or that you have questions about.

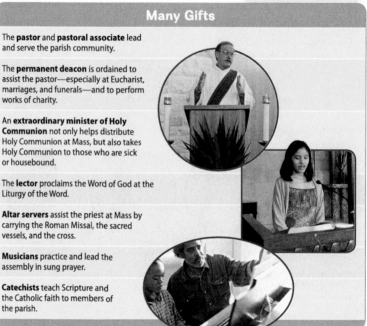

Many Gifts

The **pastor** and **pastoral associate** lead and serve the parish community.

The **permanent deacon** is ordained to assist the pastor—especially at Eucharist, marriages, and funerals—and to perform works of charity.

An **extraordinary minister of Holy Communion** not only helps distribute Holy Communion at Mass, but also takes Holy Communion to those who are sick or housebound.

The **lector** proclaims the Word of God at the Liturgy of the Word.

Altar servers assist the priest at Mass by carrying the Roman Missal, the sacred vessels, and the cross.

Musicians practice and lead the assembly in sung prayer.

Catechists teach Scripture and the Catholic faith to members of the parish.

Optional Activity

Activity Master 10: People of God

Distribute copies of the activity on catechist page 155E.

- Tell the children to think of the people in their parish who perform each role. Provide parish bulletins to help them find the appropriate names.
- As an alternative, you may wish to send this activity home with the children.

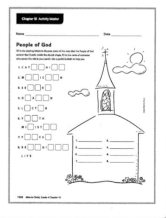

Venerable Anne de Guigné

Venerable Anne de Guigné's beloved "Papa" died when she was four years old. She decided to become as good and as kind as she could. As she grew older, one of her teachers noticed how happy Anne was. The teacher asked Anne for the secret to happiness in life. Anne replied, "Jesus loves me very much, and I love him very much." Anne knew Jesus' love because she had a special gift for prayer. She received her First Holy Communion when she was six. From then on, she offered up her prayers for all those who did not know and love Jesus.

Using Your Gifts

You can already use your gifts from God to make a difference. Discerning your vocation means learning, through prayer, about what God wants you to do. You don't have to do something big and public to make the world a better place. Like Venerable Anne, you can do it quietly and privately.

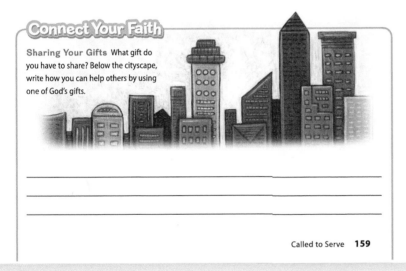

Connect Your Faith

Sharing Your Gifts What gift do you have to share? Below the cityscape, write how you can help others by using one of God's gifts.

_____

_____

_____

Called to Serve **159**

✓ Quick Tip

Guest Speakers

With permission of your director of faith formation, arrange for some parish ministers to speak to your group.

• With your help, the children should prepare questions to ask each visitor about his or her vocation and participation in the ministry of the Church.

• Help the children plan a song, skit, or other activity to welcome the guests.

Venerable Anne de Guigné

Share with the children the story of Venerable Anne de Guigné.

• *Ask:* What was Venerable Anne de Guigné's secret to happiness in life? Anne knew that Jesus loved her very much, and she loved him very much.

Using Your Gifts

Tell the children that Venerable Anne de Guigné had a special gift for prayer, but everyone has their own unique gift to share.

• Discuss with the children different ways that they could begin to discover their gifts.

• Explain that even children their age can serve as tutors to younger children or in the parish nursery, and that adults can serve on parish councils. Catholics of all ages can participate in outreach projects.

Activity

Read aloud the directions for the Connect Your Faith activity.

• Have the children work independently to complete the activity.

• Have the children share their response with a partner.

Quick Review

All Christians can serve God by working for love, peace, and justice.

Live

Our Catholic Life

Ask: What does your Baptism call you to do?

- Write the children's responses on the board or on chart paper.

Invite the children to share any experiences they may have of attending a Baptism.

Invite volunteers to take turns reading aloud a paragraph.

Live Your Call

Invite volunteers to read aloud the text.

- Point out that all baptized people share Jesus' ministry. As Catholics learn and grow, their duties change.
- Point out the photos. Ask the children to tell how each photo is an example of sharing in Jesus' ministry of Priest, Prophet, or King.
- *Ask:* When have you been a priest, prophet, or king for God? Refer the children to the bulleted text if they need help.
- Have the children use the lines to add some other ways to live their call. Have them write their name on the last line.

 Music Option: Have the children sing, "All That God Wants You to Be," downloaded from **aliveinchrist.osv.com**.

Our Catholic Life
What does your Baptism call you to do?

Like the disciples and Venerable Anne de Guigné, you too have a calling. Your call, like that of all Catholics, came to you at your Baptism.

You probably do not remember your Baptism. You might have heard stories about how you cried or smiled. You know the names of your godparents. Now that you are older, you have learned more about the importance of the Sacrament of Baptism.

Through Baptism, you share in Jesus' ministry as priest, prophet, and king. Here are some ways to live your baptismal commitment.

 Add some other ways to these and fill in your name on the last line.

Live Your Call

As Priest
- Learn about God's plan for all creation.
- Pray with and for others.
- _____

As Prophet
- Learn what the Church teaches about morals and justice.
- Help other people make good choices.
- _____

As King
- Take responsibility for your actions and choices.
- Follow Jesus' example by serving and forgiving others, especially those who are most in need of justice, mercy, and loving care.
- _____

_____ , may you live as priest, prophet, and king.

160 Chapter 10

✓ Quick Tip

Use Religious Imagination
When Catholics use religious imagination, they further their relationship with God. Share the following with the children.

- As a priestly people, they use language, symbols, and gestures to pray.
- As prophetic followers of Christ, they use religious imagination to teach others.
- As kings, they lead others to God through their imaginations and through the help of the Holy Spirit.

People of Faith

Blessed Frédéric Ozanam, 1813–1853

September 9

Blessed Frédéric Ozanam was born in Milan, Italy. For a time, he studied law. When he lived in Paris, he discovered a love for literature. His friends challenged him to find a way to live out his strong Christian beliefs in his everyday life. Frédéric realized that he had a call to help those in need. He helped found the Society of Saint Vincent de Paul, which still helps those in need, especially those who are poor. Frédéric was also a university professor and wrote many books. He tried to live out his vocation in all he did.

Discuss: How do you live your call to holiness?

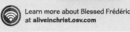 Learn more about Blessed Frédéric at **aliveinchrist.osv.com**

Live Your Faith

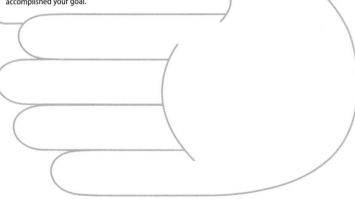

Write On each finger of the hand, write one way you can use your talents in your parish. In the center of the hand, write one way that you can use one of your talents to bring more peace and justice into the world this week. Discuss your idea with a partner and talk next week about how you accomplished your goal.

© Our Sunday Visitor

Called to Serve **161**

 Catholic Social Teaching

Chapter Connections

To integrate Catholic Social Teaching into your lesson, choose one of the following features: Call to Family, Community, and Participation, pages 292–293; or Dignity of Work and Rights of Workers, pages 298–299.

- Start the Live step of the process by talking about Blessed Frédéric Ozanam on page 161. Then move directly to the Catholic Social Teaching feature.
- Or, to expand the lesson, complete both pages 160 and 161, then move to the Catholic Social Teaching feature.
- Return to Chapter 10 for the prayer on page 162.

People of Faith

Tell the children about Blessed Frédéric Ozanam.

- Invite a volunteer to read aloud the People of Faith story.
- Explain that Blessed Frédéric defended his faith with words and modeled how to live the faith with his actions.
- Blessed Frédéric started a newspaper, *The New Era*, that was dedicated to securing justice for the poor and working class.
- He never demeaned the poor; he only offered whatever service he could. Serving the poor taught Blessed Frédéric something about God that he could only learn there.
- *Ask:* How do you live your call to holiness?

 Encourage the children to go to **aliveinchrist.osv.com** at home to learn more about Blessed Frédéric Ozanam.

Activity

Read aloud the directions and discuss the first part of the Live Your Faith activity together.

- Allow time for the children to write in each finger.
- Discuss the second part of the activity as a group.
- Allow time for the children to write their responses and discuss their idea with a partner.
- Do not forget to check with the children next session to see if they accomplished their goals.

 Music Option: Have the children sing, "Act Justly," downloaded from **aliveinchrist.osv.com**.

Called to Serve **161**

Let Us Pray
Prayer of Petition for Vocations

Prepare

Have paper ready for each child. You might have them prepared with the title, "MY VOCATION," at the top.

> Rehearse "Gifts," downloaded from **aliveinchrist.osv.com**.

Gather

Invite the children to gather in the place where it will be most convenient for them to write.

- Have each child bring their book and a pencil.

Pray

Follow the order of prayer on the student page.

God's Call: Invite the children to write their first name down their paper. Ask them—in prayerful reflection—to think of something God is calling them to do for each letter of their first name. It doesn't have to begin with the first letter. For example, using the name *Josh:*

- Bring **J**oy to sad people
- Pray for **O**thers
- **S**ay kind and honest words
- **H**elp people who are lonely

Litany: When they have finished, invite each child to name one of the things God is calling them to do. After each one, all the children will respond: "_____, God calls you."

 Conclude by singing together "Gifts."

Let Us Pray
Prayer of Petition for Vocations

This prayer of petition for vocations is a chance to reflect on how God calls each of us to use our gifts, as Jesus did, to build the Kingdom of God.

Gather and begin with the Sign of the Cross.

Leader: You have called each of us, Loving God, to be all that you created us to be. Send your Spirit to give us the desire to use our gifts to make your world a better place.

God's Call—My Vocation
Litany

All: _____, God calls you.

Leader: God, we give you thanks for the gift of our Baptism. In Baptism, you called us to participate in Jesus' ministry as priest, prophet, and king. Give us the courage, through the power of your Spirit, to be faithful to your call.

All: Amen.

 Sing "Gifts"
We thank you, God,
for giving talents to us.
Now we use those gifts
to serve others and you.
Singing and teaching,
helping each other.
Caring for needs
of our sisters and brothers.
We thank you, God,
as we give our talents back to you!
© 2010, Chet A. Chambers. Our Sunday Visitor, Inc.

Liturgy Link

Renew Baptismal Promises

As part of the baptismal ceremony, promises are made by the candidate or the candidate's parents and godparents.

- These promises are often renewed at First Communion and Confirmation.
- Get the text for the promises from the *Roman Missal*, and renew these promises in a prayer service.

> Go to **aliveinchrist.osv.com** for Sunday readings, Scripture background, questions of the week, and seasonal resources.

YOUR CHILD LEARNED >>>

This chapter explains vocation as God's plan for our lives and the purpose for which he made us; answering God's call and following his plan for us helps us grow in holiness.

Scripture

 Read **1 Samuel 10:20–22** to find out how one person responded to God's call.

Catholics Believe

• God calls every person to a vocation.

• Through your vocation, you can help God increase his Reign.

To learn more, go to the *Catechism of the Catholic Church #941, 2046* at **usccb.org.**

People of Faith

This week, your child learned about Blessed Frédéric Ozanam, who was a cofounder of the Society of Saint Vincent de Paul. Blessed Frédéric is an example for us of someone who answered and lived God's call for his life.

CHILDREN AT THIS AGE >>>

How They Understand Their Call from God As fourth-graders hear that God has a plan for their lives, they are capable of realizing that this plan is different from the one he has for anyone else. They have the free will to choose to follow—or not to follow—God's plan. With help and support from adults like you, your child can begin to better identify the talents and interests that can point to God's plan and also to see the opportunities to further explore God's path for his or her future.

CONSIDER THIS >>>

Do you think of your marriage as part of God's plan for you to grow in holiness?

God invites us to grow in holiness through our vocations. The vocation of marriage helps us become one with God by loving our spouse. As Catholics, we know that "God created man and woman out of love and commanded them to imitate his love in their relations with each other. . . . [Both] are equal in human dignity, and in marriage both are united in an unbreakable bond" (*USCCA, p. 279*).

LET'S TALK >>>

• Ask your child to explain vocation.

• Affirm your child's gifts and talents, naming some ways he or she could use them to bring happiness to others and serve God.

LET'S PRAY >>>

 God, help us answer your call as Blessed Frédéric did, so that we may do your will for our lives. Amen.

For a multimedia glossary of Catholic Faith Words, Sunday readings, seasonal and Saint resources, and chapter activities go to **aliveinchrist.osv.com.**

Family + Faith

Distribute the page to the children or parents/adult family members. Point out the chapter highlights, insights on how fourth graders understand concepts, the opportunity for the adults to reflect on their own experience and faith journey, and the family prayer.

Chapter 10 Review

A **Work with Words** Complete the following paragraph.

1–5. Jesus announced that God's _____Kingdom_____ was at, hand. By this he meant that God's Reign of _____peace_____, _____love_____, and _____justice_____ had begun with him, but was still to come in its fullness. All of us are _____called_____ by God to cooperate with him in bringing his Kingdom to fullness.

B **Check Understanding** Fill in the circle next to the answer that best completes each statement.

6. The purpose for which God made us is known as a _____.
- ● vocation
- ○ vacation
- ○ Commandment

7. _____ people who are baptized can serve a parish.
- ○ Some
- ● All
- ○ No

8. _____ lead the people in prayer when they celebrate Mass.
- ○ Deacons
- ○ Parishioners
- ● Priests

9. Deacons do all of the following EXCEPT _____.
- ○ assist at the Sacraments
- ○ perform works of charity
- ● lead a diocese

10. Both single and married people are part of the _____.
- ○ ordained
- ● laity
- ○ consecrated

Go to **aliveinchrist.osv.com** for an interactive review.

Chapter Review

Use Catechist Quick Reviews to highlight lesson concepts.

A **Work with Words**
Have the children complete the paragraph.

B **Check Understanding**
Have the children fill in the circle next to the answer that best completes each statement.

Go to **aliveinchrist.osv.com** to prepare customized and downloadable assessments, send eAssessments, and assign interactive reviews.

Called to Serve   **163–164**

KEY CONCEPT

The Church's holiness shines in the Saints. All who live their love of God are Saints. Mary is the perfect model of holiness, and she is called the Mother of the Church.

DOCTRINAL CONTENT

- A Saint is a person who the Church declares has led a holy life and is enjoying eternal life with God in Heaven. (CCC, 828)

- Mary is the perfect model of holiness, accepting God's will throughout her life and remaining faithful to him. (CCC, 829)

- The Immaculate Conception is the truth that God kept Mary free from sin from the first moment of her life. (CCC, 491)

- Mary is called the Mother of the Church because she holds her Son's followers close to her heart. (CCC, 963)

TASKS OF CATECHESIS

Helping children grow in a faith that is "known, celebrated, lived, and expressed in prayer" (NDC, 20).

This chapter focuses on the following tasks of catechesis:

- Promoting Knowledge of the Faith

- Teaching to Pray

Catechist Background

 "Just so, your light must shine before others, that they may see your good deeds and glorify your heavenly Father."
Matthew 5:16

➔ **Reflect** How do you let your light shine before others?

Some people are extraordinary. They rise above the norm, they try harder, and they succeed in the face of adversity. Often you try to be like them because they inspire you. But they are human like you—or else they would be too remote to be inspiring!

These achievers in the community of faith are those the Church honors as Saints. They were not perfect. If you read the stories of their lives, you see that they too had moments of doubt and fear. They failed from time to time and even grew despondent. But they continued to say "yes" to God, even in the face of disappointments or great challenges.

Canonized Saints are people whom the Church officially recognizes as public examples of virtue and holiness. They are your models, but you must remember that all Christians are called to be Saints. They are sanctified by Christ and led by the Holy Spirit. Sainthood is your destiny, too.

The teaching that Mary was immaculately conceived (without sin from the moment of her conception) is directly related to her role as the Mother of God. This dogma was proclaimed by Pope Pius IX in 1854. Mary's freedom from sin made her the perfect mother for Jesus. Her willingness to obey God makes her the perfect model for your Christian discipleship.

➔ **Reflect** How is Mary a model for you? When do you feel favored by the Lord?

Catechist's Prayer

Jesus Christ, Son of God, be with me this day. I ask all the Saints, especially your Mother Mary, to surround me with love and guide me with the light of faith. Amen.

Lesson Plan

Objectives	Process	Materials

🕐 **Invite, 10 minutes**

Models of Virtue Page 165

- Leviticus 11:44 Pray the opening prayer.
- Matthew 5:14–16 Reflect prayerfully on the Word.
- Discuss What Do You Wonder questions.

🌐 **Optional Activity**
Chapter Story: "On Call"

🕐 **Discover, 35 minutes**

Holy Ones of God Pages 166–167

- Describe a Saint as a person whom the Church declares has led a holy life and is enjoying eternal life with God in Heaven

- **Catholic Faith Words** canonization, Saint, beatification
- Explain that the Church honors people whose lives showed others how to do God's will.
- Learn about Saint Catherine of Siena.
- **Share Your Faith Activity** Name why Saint Catherine is a model of faith.

☐ pencils
☐ index cards
☐ map or globe
- **Optional Activity** Saint Catherine of Siena

Models of Holiness Pages 168–169

- Identify Mary as the perfect model of holiness, accepting God's will throughout her life and remaining faithful to him
- Recognize the Immaculate Conception as the truth that God kept Mary free from sin from the first moment of her life
- Recognize that Mary is called the Mother of the Church because she holds her Son's followers close to her heart

- **Catholic Faith Words** Mary, Immaculate Conception, patron Saints
- Explain that Mary is the perfect model of holiness.
- Luke 1:46–50 Proclaim "The Canticle of Mary."
- Explain what it means to be a model of holiness.
- ☆ Circle ways Mary is the perfect model of holiness.
- **Connect Your Faith Activity** Discuss qualities of Mary to model.

☐ pencils
☐ index cards
- **Optional Activity** Saints and Symbols
☐ Activity Master 11 (Page 165E)

🕐 **Live, 15 minutes**

Our Catholic Life Pages 170–171

- Explain how to follow the example of the Saints.
- ☆ Complete an inventory about how to follow the Saints.
- **People of Faith** Learn about Saint Bernadette.
- **Live Your Faith Activity** Name ways of growing in holiness.

☐ pencils
☐ crayons or markers

Litany of the Saints Page 172

- Select two readers.
- ▶ Rehearse "Immaculate Mary."

🌐 Download "Immaculate Mary."

Family + Faith Page 173

Point out that the Catholic Families page provides chapter highlights, information on how fourth graders understand faith concepts, and family prayer.

Chapter Review Page 174

🌐 aliveinchrist.osv.com

- Customize and Download Assessments
- Email Links to eAssessments
- Interactive Student Reviews

ONLINE RESOURCES

 Go to **aliveinchrist.osv.com**

You will find:

- Interactive lesson planning with web specific content and additional activities
- Step by step lesson instruction from printed Catechist Edition for integrated lesson planning
- Custom-built assessments to download and eAssessment links
- Interactive reviews that provide scores and the option to review answers
- Sunday readings with background and questions of the week

 Go to **osvparish.com**

You will find:

- Ask the Experts Q and A
- General Catechist Helps
- Community Connections and Blogs

Sharing the Message with Fourth Graders

The Saints Fourth graders are often very interested in stories about the Saints. It is especially intriguing for them to hear about Saints who were young or who acted heroically in challenging circumstances. Children this age can also understand that the Saints were not perfect, but they allowed God to use them and to form them into what he called them to be.

Teaching Tip: Use pictures of Saints and holy cards as much as possible with your group so kids can identify "heroes" they can connect with as examples.

How Fourth Graders Understand

- Fourth graders admire heroes. Use books, videos, and sacramentals to teach them about the Saints.
- Sometimes it is hard for fourth graders to sit still. Use methods that will allow them to move around and be active.
- Friendship is important to fourth graders. Let them know that the Saints can provide them with help and support.

"I admire heroes. Show me creative ways to learn about the Saints."

Chapter Connections

Chapter Story

Invite

"On Call"

Use this story to expand the chapter introduction.

- The children will relate the story to their own lives, reflecting on how firefighters make a difference.
- Connect the work of volunteer firefighters to our call to holiness.

 Go to **aliveinchrist.osv.com** Lesson Planning section for this story.

NCEA IFG: ACRE Edition

Discover

Knowledge of the Faith

- Objective: To know and understand basic Catholic teaching about the Incarnate Word Jesus Christ as the way, truth, and life

Prayer

- Objective: To recognize and learn how to engage in Catholic forms of personal and communal prayer and ways of deepening one's spiritual life

Catholic Social Teaching

Live

 Use one of these features to introduce a principle and engage the children with an activity.

- Call to Family, Community, and Participation, Pages 292–293
- Option for the Poor and Vulnerable, Pages 296–297

Music Options

 Use one or more of the following songs to enhance catechetical learning or for prayer.

- "Immaculate Mary," Live Prayer, Page 172
- "Litany of Saints," Discover, Page 167
- "We Gather Around Your Throne," Discover, Page 167

LECTIONARY CONNECTION

 Chapter 11 highlights Lectionary-connected themes such as faith, mission, and witness. If your parish aligns its curriculum to the liturgical year, you could use this chapter in connection with the following Sundays.

Year A

Second Sunday of Advent—mission

Third Sunday of Advent—witness

Pentecost Sunday—mission, gifts

Year B

Third Sunday of Advent—witness

Fourth Sunday of Advent—Mary

The Epiphany of the Lord—Mary

Year C

Third Sunday of Easter—mission

Twenty-seventh Sunday in Ordinary Time—faith

Twenty-ninth Sunday in Ordinary Time—faithfulness

 Go to **aliveinchrist.osv.com** for a complete correlation ordered by the Sundays of the year and suggestions for how to integrate the Scripture readings into chapter lessons.

Name _____   Date _____

Saints and Symbols

Saints come from many cultures, and their lives of holiness are sometimes identified with particular images. See how many of these symbols you can recognize. Cut out the symbol boxes at the bottom of the page. Glue each symbol onto the empty box beneath the name of the Saint whose actions suggest the image.

Saint Nicholas
December 6

Saint Blaise
February 3

Saint Peter
June 29

Saint Patrick
March 17

Saint Kateri Tekakwitha
July 14

Saint Catherine of Siena
April 29

Saint Joseph
March 19

Saint Francis of Assisi
October 4

Saint Martha
July 29

Models of Virtue

 Let Us Pray

Leader: We know your name, O Lord. It is
Holy, Holy, Holy.

"I, the LORD, am your God. You shall make
and keep yourselves holy, because I am holy."
Leviticus 11:44

All: We are your namesakes, O Lord. Help us live up
to our name. Amen.

 Scripture

You are the light of the world. A city set on a mountain cannot be hidden. Nor do they light a lamp and then put it under a bushel basket; it is set on a lampstand, where it gives light to all in the house. Just so, your light must shine before others, that they may see your good deeds and glorify your heavenly Father.   Matthew 5:14–16

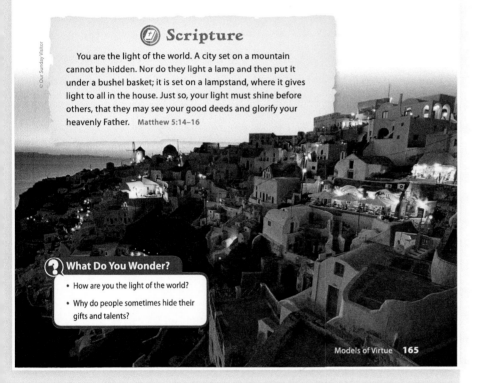

What Do You Wonder?

- How are you the light of the world?
- Why do people sometimes hide their gifts and talents?

Models of Virtue **165**

Optional Activity

Chapter Story: "On Call"   *Verbal/Linguistic*

Use this story after the opening prayer, before explaining about the holiness of God's people.

- Ask the children why it might be difficult to be a volunteer firefighter.
  you never know when you have to go, it can be dangerous
- *Ask:* Why do you think Joseph chooses to be a volunteer firefighter?   Emphasize that Joseph values helping people in need.
- *Ask:* What can children do to help people in need?

 Go to **aliveinchrist.osv.com** for Chapter Story.

 **Invite**

 Let Us Pray

Invite the children to gather in the prayer space and make the Sign of the Cross. Invite a volunteer to read aloud the Psalm verse from a Bible. Prompt the children's response.

Have the children move out of the prayer space and back to their seats.

Explain that God calls all of us to holiness, like the Saints.

Say: We do not become holy because we do so much for God. We are holy because God has done so much for us. Those we call Saints know this. Their faith lights up the way of holiness for us.

 Scripture

Guide the children through the process of Scripture reflection.

- Invite them to close their eyes, be still and open their minds and hearts to what God is saying to them in this passage.
- Proclaim the Scripture.
- Maintain several moments of silence.
- *Ask:* What did you hear God say to you today?
- Invite volunteers to share.

What Do You Wonder?

Say: The holiness of all God's people shines in the Saints. As we grow in faith, we can add our light to theirs.

Invite the children to respond to the questions. Ask what else they might wonder about how to be the light of the world.

Objective

• Describe a Saint as a person whom the Church declares has led a holy life and is enjoying eternal life with God in Heaven

Holy Ones of God

Ask: Who models faith for us?

• Write the children's responses on the board or on chart paper.

Invite the children to silently read the paragraph.

Work with Words

Point out the Catholic Faith Words.

• Invite volunteers to read aloud the definitions of each term.

• Have the children make vocabulary cards for all three terms.

Saint Catherine of Siena

Gather the children in a story circle.

• Show them the location of Italy on a map. Tell them that you are going to read a story about a woman who lived in Italy many years ago.

• Read aloud the biography of Catherine of Siena.

Catholic Faith Words

canonization a declaration by the Pope naming a person a Saint. Canonized Saints have special feast days or memorials in the Church's calendar.

Saint a person whom the Church declares has led a holy life and is enjoying eternal life with God in Heaven

beatification the second step in the process of becoming a Saint, in which a venerable person is recognized by the Church as having brought about a miracle through his or her prayers of intercession

Holy Ones of God

Who models faith for us?

The Church honors certain people whose lives showed others how to do God's will. These models of faith and virtue lived holy lives. To be holy is to be unique and pure, set apart for God and his purposes. These people helped God bring his Reign into the world more fully. Through the process of **canonization**, the Church names each of these people a **Saint**. The second step in the process of canonization is **beatification**. Here is the story of one Saint.

Saint Catherine of Siena

Catherine wanted to serve God through quiet prayer. But Catherine's world was full of problems. God called her to make a difference.

Catherine lived long ago in Siena, Italy. She was very wise and used words well. Although unusual for a woman of her time, Catherine made public speeches and taught priests. She also cared for the sick and those in prison.

166

(i) Catechist Background

Canonization

After a candidate's death, bishops send information to the Vatican.

• If a panel recommends it, the Pope proclaims the person *servant of God* and then *venerable*.

• If the candidate is responsible for a miracle, the Pope can declare the person *beatified*, or *blessed*.

• If another miracle is confirmed, the Pope can declare the candidate a Saint.

Catherine spoke out against injustice. She helped leaders in the Church make peace with one another. For a time, she lived in Rome and served as an adviser to the Pope. Christians learn from Catherine that every member of the Church can make a difference.

Catherine's students called her "Mother" and "Teacher." She has been named a Doctor of the Church, which is an honor that means she is one of the great teachers in our Church. Even though she had no formal education, her writings and teachings have been very influential in the Church.

Catherine of Siena is also a canonized Saint of the Catholic Church. This means that the Church has officially declared that she led a holy life and is enjoying eternal life with God in Heaven.

➜ What are some reasons people admire Catherine?

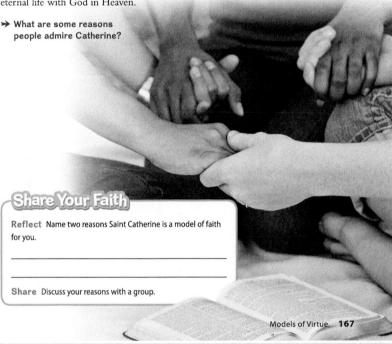

Share Your Faith

Reflect Name two reasons Saint Catherine is a model of faith for you.

_____

_____

Share Discuss your reasons with a group.

Models of Virtue **167**

Optional Activity

Saint Catherine of Siena *Verbal/Linguistic*

Ask volunteers to research more about Saint Catherine.

• Provide books about the Saints or Website addresses that will get the research started.

• Ask the children to report their findings at the next session.

• If possible, display the reports in the room or parish hall.

Saint Catherine of Siena, *continued*

Point out the illustration of Saint Catherine on page 166.

• Invite the children to describe what they see.

Explain that Saint Catherine had a great deal of influence for a woman of her time (1347–1380).

• *Ask:* What do you admire about Saint Catherine of Siena?

• For more information on the Saints, refer the children to page 311 of the Our Catholic Tradition reference section in the back of the Student Book.

 Music Option: Have the children sing, "Litany of Saints" or "We Gather Around Your Throne," downloaded from **aliveinchrist.osv.com**.

Activity

Read aloud the directions for the Share Your Faith activity.

• Have the children work independently to write their ideas.

• After a short time, have them discuss with a partner.

Quick Review

Saints are holy people who are models of faith for Catholic Christians.

Objectives

- Identify Mary as the perfect model of holiness, accepting God's will throughout her life and remaining faithful to him
- Recognize the Immaculate Conception as the truth that God kept Mary free from sin from the first moment of her life
- Recognize that Mary is called the Mother of the Church because she holds her Son's followers close to her heart

Model of Holiness

Ask: How is Mary a model of holiness?

- Write the children's responses on the board or on chart paper.

Read aloud the introductory paragraph.

- Tell the children to listen to learn about Mary, the greatest Saint of the Catholic Church.
- Have the children make a vocabulary card for *Mary*.

 Scripture

Invite a volunteer to proclaim "The Canticle of Mary."

- Explain that many people still call Mary's canticle by its Latin name, the *Magnificat*.

Discover

Model of Holiness

How is Mary a model of holiness?

There are many Saints, but **Mary** is the perfect model of holiness. God chose Mary to be the mother of Jesus. After Mary said "yes" to being the Mother of God's Son, she visited her cousin Elizabeth. Here is how Mary described her joy at the great blessing God had given her.

 Scripture

The Canticle of Mary

"My soul proclaims the greatness of the Lord;
   my spirit rejoices in God my savior.
For he has looked upon his handmaid's lowliness;
   behold, from now on will all ages call me blessed.
The Mighty One has done great things for me,
   and holy is his name.
         His mercy is from age to age
            to those who fear him."

Luke 1:46–50

> **Catholic Faith Words**
>
> **Mary** the Mother of Jesus, the Mother of God. She is also called "Our Lady" because she is our mother and the Mother of the Church.

168 Chapter 11

 Songs of Scripture

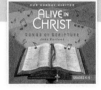

Mary's Song of Praise

This song helps the children learn the "heart" of the words of the *Magnificat*.

- Teach the children the song.
- Hannah, the mother of Samuel, also praises God when she is told she will have a child. Ask the children to open their Bible and read silently along with you 1 Samuel 2:1–10.
- Have the children compare the Scripture to the song.

Use *Songs of Scripture*, Grades 4–6 CD, Track 8

Your Will Be Done

(God created Mary full of grace.) He preserved her from sin from the very first moment of her conception. The Catholic Church calls this gift from God Mary's **Immaculate Conception**.

The word *immaculate* means spotless and clean—without sin. The word *conception* means the very moment when a person's life begins. The Church celebrates the Immaculate Conception of Mary on December 8.

Part of holiness is being able to accept and do the things that God asks. (Mary accepted God's will throughout her life.) Mary cared for and protected Jesus when he was a child. She stood by him all through his life. She was strong enough to be with him when he was crucified.

After Jesus ascended into Heaven, Mary remained on Earth with Jesus' followers. She was there at Pentecost when the Holy Spirit came. Mary is called the Mother of the Church because she holds her Son's followers close to her heart. (She remains an example of love and faith for all.)

A Guide for You

When you were baptized, you may have received the name of one of the Saints. This person is your **patron Saint**—your model of faith who prays for you from Heaven. You walk in the footsteps of your Saint and continue his or her good works in the way you live.

Connect Your Faith

Model of Holiness With a partner, discuss three qualities of Saints that you want to model.

> **Catholic Faith Words**
>
> **Immaculate Conception** the truth that God kept Mary free from sin from the first moment of her life
>
> **patron Saint** a Saint who has a particular connection to a cause, place, type of work, or person. For example, if a person or city shares the name of a Saint, that Saint is a patron.

 Circle the ways in which Mary is the perfect model of holiness.

ST MARTIN DE PORRES

169

© Our Sunday Visitor

Your Will Be Done

Read aloud the first two paragraphs.

- Point out that Mary's Immaculate Conception makes her unique among all the Saints.
- ⭐ Have the children circle the ways in which Mary is the perfect model of holiness.

Work with Words

Read aloud the definition of *Immaculate Conception*.

- Have the children create a vocabulary card for the term.

Invite volunteers to finish reading "Your Will Be Done."

- *Ask:* Have you ever been given a very big responsibility? What did you say or do?

A Guide for You

Have a volunteer read aloud the paragraph.

- Have the children create a vocabulary card for *patron Saint*.
- Encourage the children to find information about their patron Saint and share it with the group during the next session.

Activity

Point out the Connect Your Faith activity and read aloud the directions.

- Have the children work with a partner to complete the activity.

Quick Review

No one can see God, but we know a lot about him through his creation.

Optional Activity

Activity Master 11: Saints and Symbols

Distribute copies of the activity found on catechist page 165E.

- Suggest that the children use the Student Book and reference sources to complete the activity.
- As an alternative, you may want to send this activity home with the children.

Chapter 11 Activity Master

Name _____ Date _____

Saints and Symbols

Saints come from many cultures, and their lives of holiness are sometimes identified with particular images. See how many of these symbols you can recognize. Cut out the symbol boxes at the bottom of the page. Glue each symbol onto the empty box beneath the name of the Saint whose actions suggest the image.

Saint Nicholas December 6	Saint Blaise February 3	Saint Peter June 29
Saint Patrick March 17	Saint Kateri Tekakwitha July 14	Saint Catherine of Siena April 29
Saint Joseph March 19	Saint Francis of Assisi October 4	Saint Martha July 29

165E *Alive in Christ, Grade 4 Chapter 11*

Our Catholic Life

Ask: How can you follow the example of the Saints?

- Write the children's responses on the board or on chart paper.

Ask a volunteer to read aloud the first paragraph.

- Emphasize that the Saints were regular people, just like the children. The Saints chose to live holy lives.

Remind the children that we are all called to be Saints, no matter how old we are and what we think we can do. Then summarize the second paragraph.

Following the Saints

Call attention to the chart.

- Read aloud the three bold face statements and the text that goes with them.
- ☆ In the boxes, have the children write a *D* for the things they are doing, a *G* for the things they are growing in, and a *Q* for the things they have questions about.

Encourage the children to name other ways of growing in holiness.

- *Ask:* When have you felt God's love growing within you?
- Give an example from your own life to start the discussion.

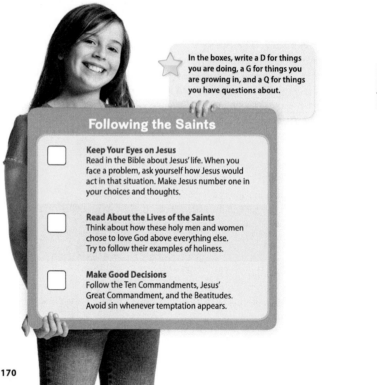

Live

Our Catholic Life

How can you follow the example of the Saints?

The Church honors Saints from around the world. They have lived holy lives, and many of them have done brave things to spread God's Word. You may think that you cannot be like them until you are older, but all of the Saints were your age once. Some Saints acted heroically at a young age.

You can do things now. To spread God's loving message to others, you must first allow God's love to grow within you. To do so, keep in mind the following steps.

In the boxes, write a D for things you are doing, a G for things you are growing in, and a Q for things you have questions about.

Following the Saints

Keep Your Eyes on Jesus
Read in the Bible about Jesus' life. When you face a problem, ask yourself how Jesus would act in that situation. Make Jesus number one in your choices and thoughts.

Read About the Lives of the Saints
Think about how these holy men and women chose to love God above everything else. Try to follow their examples of holiness.

Make Good Decisions
Follow the Ten Commandments, Jesus' Great Commandment, and the Beatitudes. Avoid sin whenever temptation appears.

170

© Our Sunday Visitor

✓ Quick Tip

Social Analysis

You acquire and develop the skill of social analysis when you examine how society's actions further or hinder Christian principles.

- Encourage the children to learn about the Saints and how they fit into their historical era. Many Saints took unpopular stands on social issues while remaining faithful to Church teaching.
- Discuss how current decisions should be resolved by applying Christian principles.

People of Faith

Saint Bernadette, 1844–1879

April 16

Saint Bernadette Soubirous came from a very poor French family. She helped her family by herding sheep. One day, she saw a vision of a beautiful young woman. Over the next five months, she saw the woman seventeen more times. The woman led her to a spring of healing water. When Bernadette asked her who she was, the lady said she was "The Immaculate Conception." People then knew that Bernadette was seeing Mary, the Mother of Jesus. Today, people still go to the spring at Lourdes and pray for healing.

Discuss: What do you know about the Immaculate Conception?

 Learn more about Saint Bernadette at **aliveinchrist.osv.com**

 © Our Sunday Visitor

Live Your Faith

Name one way you can show how you are growing in holiness.

_____

Create two snapshots of yourself that show ways in which you are still growing.

Catholic Social Teaching

Chapter Connections

To integrate Catholic Social Teaching into your lesson, choose one of the following features: Call to Family, Community, and Participation, pages 292–293; or Option for the Poor and Vulnerable, pages 296–297.

- Start the Live step of the process by talking about Saint Bernadette on page 171. Then move directly to the Catholic Social Teaching feature.
- Or, to expand the lesson, complete both pages 170 and 171, then move to the Catholic Social Teaching feature.
- Return to Chapter 11 for the prayer on page 172.

People of Faith

Tell the children about Saint Bernadette.

- Invite a volunteer to read aloud the People of Faith story.
- Explain that some people believed Saint Bernadette when she told about her visions and others did not. The division of opinion caused uproar in the town. Those who believed she was mentally ill demanded that she be put in an asylum.
- People began to follow her everywhere, some out of curiosity and some who thought they might witness a miracle.
- *Ask:* What do you know about the Immaculate Conception?
- Refer to page 169 if the children need assistance.

 Encourage the children to go to **aliveinchrist.osv.com** at home to learn more about about Saint Bernadette.

Activity

Explain the directions for the Live Your Faith activity to the children.

- Brainstorm suitable subjects for the snapshots. Possibilities include receiving a Sacrament, helping others, or studying the Bible.
- Allow time for the children to complete the activity.
- Have the children meet in small groups to share their snapshots.
- Ask each group to choose three snapshots to share with the rest of the children.

Live

 Let Us Pray

Litany of the Saints

Tell the children that they can always call on the Saints to pray for them.

Prepare

Choose two readers, and review the pronunciation of the names.

- Teach the children their response.

 Rehearse "Immaculate Mary," downloaded from **aliveinchrist.osv.com**.

Gather

Invite the children to process to the prayer space.

- Direct the children to be seated the prepare their minds and hearts for prayer.

Pray

Follow the order of prayer on the student page.

- Optional readings are 1 Peter 3: 8–9 and Matthew 5:13–16.
- *Leader's concluding prayer:* God, we thank you for the example of the Saints. Help us grow to be more like them in our love of you.

 Conclude by singing together "Immaculate Mary."

 Let Us Pray

Litany of the Saints

A litany is a prayer with one line that is meant to be repeated over and over again so that those praying are caught up in the prayer itself.

Gather and begin with the Sign of the Cross.

Leader: Respond with *Pray for us* after each Saint's name.

Reader 1: Holy Mary, Mother of God

All: Pray for us.

Reader 2: Saint Michael,
Saint John the Baptist,
Saint Joseph,
Saints Peter and Paul,
Saint Mary Magdalene,
Saint Stephen,
Saint Agnes,
Saint Gregory,
Saint Francis,
Saint Dominic,
Saint Catherine,
Saint Teresa,
Saints Perpetua and Felicity,
Saint Martin,

Leader: Let us pray.

Bow your heads as the leader prays.

All: Amen.

 Sing "Immaculate Mary"

 Liturgy Link

Visual Focus

If possible, include a statue (or other artwork) of Mary in your prayer space.

- Encourage the children to bring in flowers or draw pictures to show their devotion.
- Display the items around the statue as a reminder of Mary's special role in faith.

 Go to **aliveinchrist.osv.com** for Sunday readings, Scripture background, questions of the week, and seasonal resources.

FAMILY + FAITH
LIVING AND LEARNING TOGETHER

YOUR CHILD LEARNED >>>
This chapter teaches that Saints are people whom the Church declares have lived holy lives and are now with God in Heaven.

Scripture
 Read **Matthew 5:14–16** to find out how living a life of holiness can light the way for others.

Catholics Believe
- The Church's holiness shines in the Saints. All who live their love of God are Saints.
- Mary is the perfect model of holiness, and she is called the Mother of the Church.

To learn more, go to the *Catechism of the Catholic Church* #828–829, 963, 967–970 at **usccb.org**.

People of Faith
This week, your child learned about Saint Bernadette of Lourdes, to whom the Virgin Mary appeared.

CHILDREN AT THIS AGE >>>
How They Understand the Saints Your child is probably very interested in stories about the Saints. It is especially intriguing for children this age to hear about Saints who were young or who acted heroically in challenging circumstances. Your child can also understand that the Saints were not perfect, but they allowed God to use them and to form them into what he called them to be.

CONSIDER THIS >>>
Who in your life is open to God's will like Mary?

Saints are ordinary people who live extraordinarily faith-filled lives. Mary's willingness to obey God makes her the perfect model. As Catholics, we know that Mary "occupies a place in the Church which is the highest after Christ and yet very close to us" (*Lumen Gentium*, 54). When God calls Mary to be the Mother of his Son, she consents with deep faith and trust. She is the first and greatest of the disciples (*Based on USCCA p. 143*).

LET'S TALK >>>
- Ask your child to explain why Mary is the perfect model of holiness.
- Share a story about a Saint who means a lot to you or talk about ways your family can honor the Saints.

LET'S PRAY >>>
 Immaculate Mary, keep us safe under your protection. Amen.

 For a multimedia glossary of Catholic Faith Words, Sunday readings, seasonal and Saint resources, and chapter activities go to **aliveinchrist.osv.com**.

Chapter 11 Review

A Work with Words **Complete each sentence with the correct word from the Word Bank.**

Word Bank
- Beatification
- holy
- Mother
- preserved
- wisdom

1. Catherine of Siena was named a Doctor of the Church because of her _____ **wisdom** _____.

2. Immaculate Conception is the teaching that recognizes that God _____ **preserved** _____ Mary from sin from the first moment of her life.

3. _____ **Beatification** _____ is the second step in the process of a person being canonized a Saint.

4. Mary felt great joy at being chosen by God to be the _____ **Mother** _____ of his Son.

5. A Saint is recognized by the Church for living a _____ **holy** _____ life and is in Heaven with God.

B Check Understanding **Respond briefly to the following questions.**

6. What does it mean to be a canonized Saint of the Catholic Church?
   It means that the Church recognizes the person led a holy life and is now enjoying eternal life with God in Heaven.

7. What makes Mary the perfect model of holiness?
   She said "yes" to God and accepted his will throughout her life no matter how difficult.

8. What did Catherine of Siena speak out against?
   She spoke out against injustice.

9. What is a patron Saint?
   Possible responses: a model of faith, a protector, someone people or parishes are named after

10. What can you learn from reading about the lives of Saints?
    Possible responses: how they put God first, how to follow their example

 Go to **aliveinchrist.osv.com** for an interactive review.

Family + Faith

Distribute the page to the children or parents/adult family members. Point out the chapter highlights, insights on how fourth graders understand concepts, the opportunity for the adults to reflect on their own experience and faith journey, and the family prayer.

Chapter Review

Use Catechist Quick Reviews to highlight lesson concepts.

A **Work with Words**
Have the children complete each sentence with a word from the Word Bank.

B **Check Understanding**
Have the children write a brief response to each question.

Go to **aliveinchrist.osv.com** to prepare customized and downloadable assessments, send eAssessments, and assign interactive reviews.

Models of Virtue **173–174**

Chapter 12 The Church Teaches

KEY CONCEPT

Jesus gave leaders of the Church the authority to interpret Scripture and Tradition for the faithful. The Holy Spirit directs the Church in teaching and guiding the People of God.

DOCTRINAL CONTENT

- Jesus chose Peter to be the shepherd of his flock, leader of the Apostles, and head of his Church. (CCC, 881)
- Jesus gave Peter and the Apostles, and their successors the Pope and bishops, the authority to teach and lead in his name. (CCC, 85)
- The Magisterium is the teaching office of the Church, which is all of the bishops in union with Rome. (CCC, 890–891)
- The Holy Spirit directs the Magisterium in teaching and guiding the People of God. (CCC, 892)
- The Precepts of the Church are some of the minimum requirements given by Church leaders for deepening our relationship with God and the Church. (CCC, 2041–2043)

TASKS OF CATECHESIS

Helping children grow in a faith that is "known, celebrated, lived, and expressed in prayer" (NDC, 20).

This chapter focuses on the following tasks of catechesis:

- Moral Formation
- Education for Communal Life

Catechist Background

> [Jesus] gave some as apostles, others as prophets, others as evangelists, others as pastors and teachers, to equip the holy ones for the work of ministry, for the building up the body of Christ.... **Ephesians 4:11–12**

➔ **Reflect** Who is your spiritual guide or mentor?

Jesus was a teacher; his words, his actions, and his life revealed God. His gift of the Holy Spirit empowered his Apostles and disciples to continue teaching. From these first followers, the vital teaching mission comes to the Magisterium of the Church today. The Pope and the bishops are entrusted with interpreting the Word of God, guarding it from error and misuse, and spreading it throughout the world.

All followers of Jesus make moral choices and take actions that can witness to the power of God. As a catechist, though, your responsibility is not only to teach but also to educate yourself. The more you learn about Scripture and Tradition, the better you can share the Good News of salvation with the children you teach.

The Precepts of the Catholic Church describe the minimum necessary for Catholics to consider themselves active members of the faith community. Rather than restricting your behavior, the Precepts actually encourage you to do more. Following these Precepts (loving, praying, worshipping, and living the liturgical year fully) will enrich you with an improved spiritual life and enable you to help build a stronger Church community.

➔ **Reflect** How can Jesus' teaching style shape your teaching style?

Catechist's Prayer

Loving God, I thank you for the opportunity to serve by handing on the faith to others and for the Church community that supports me in this task. Amen.

Lesson Plan

Objectives	Process	Materials
Invite, 10 minutes		
The Church Teaches Page 175	• Psalm 143:10 Pray the opening prayer. • Ephesians 4:11–13 Reflect prayerfully on the Word. • Discuss What Do You Wonder questions.	**Optional Activity** Chapter Story: "A Good Teacher Is…"
Discover, 35 minutes		
Jesus Chooses a Leader Pages 176–177 • Identify Peter as the Apostle Jesus chose to lead the Apostles and the Church	• Explain that the authority to teach was given by Jesus and guided by the Holy Spirit. • Mark 8:27–30 Proclaim "You Are the Messiah!" ✩ Underline what Peter did the night before Jesus died. • **Share Your Faith Activity** Write a prayer including the name of someone who has forgiven them.	☐ pencils
The Church and You Pages 178–179 • Recognize that Jesus gave Peter and the Apostles, and their successors the Pope and bishops, the authority to teach and lead in his name • Identify the Magisterium as the teaching office of the Church • Explain how the Holy Spirit directs the Magisterium in teaching and guiding the People of God • Retell the Precepts of the Church	• **Catholic Faith Words** Magisterium, Precepts of the Church • Explain that it is the Church's mission to share the true message of Jesus. • Explain that Catholics have a duty to live according to the Precepts of the Church. • **Connect Your Faith Activity** Complete the word search.	☐ pencils ☐ index cards • **Optional Activity** Precepts Poem ☐ Activity Master 12 (Page 175E)
Live, 15 minutes		
Our Catholic Life Pages 180–181	• Explain there are many ways to support the Church with time, talent, and money. • Name ways to support the Church. • **People of Faith** Learn about Saint Mary Magdalen Postel. • **Live Your Faith Activity** Draw or write how to share time, talents, or money with the Church.	☐ pencils ☐ crayons or markers
Prayer of Intercession Page 182	• Select three readers. • Rehearse "The Church."	Download "The Church."

Family + Faith Page 183

Point out that the Catholic Families page provides chapter highlights, information on how fourth graders understand faith concepts, and family prayer.

Chapter Review Page 184

aliveinchrist.osv.com
• Customize and Download Assessments
• Email Links to eAssessments
• Interactive Student Reviews

ONLINE RESOURCES

 Go to **aliveinchrist.osv.com**

You will find:

- Interactive lesson planning with web specific content and additional activities
- Step by step lesson instruction from printed Catechist Edition for integrated lesson planning
- Custom-built assessments to download and eAssessment links
- Interactive reviews that provide scores and the option to review answers
- Sunday readings with background and questions of the week

 Go to **osvparish.com**

You will find:

- Ask the Experts Q and A
- General Catechist Helps
- Community Connections and Blogs

Sharing the Message with Fourth Graders

Church Teaching For most fourth graders, the experience of the teaching Church is limited to their own parish or school—the things they learn in faith formation and hear in the Mass, for example. However, children this age are growing in their ability to perceive the larger worldwide Church and to understand the role of the bishops and Pope. Their respect for these leaders will be influenced by the respect shown by adults around them.

Teaching Tip: As a group, write a letter to the bishop of your diocese. Encourage the children to talk about what they are learning and to thank the bishop for his life of service to the Church.

How Fourth Graders Understand

- Fourth graders are interested in the history of their faith. Tell them stories about their faith heritage.
- Fourth graders enjoy belonging to a group. Teach them ways of being a good member of the Catholic community.
- Use games, repetition, or incentives to help the children memorize the Precepts of the Church.

"Role models help me be a better person. Point out people I can follow."

Chapter Story

Invite

"A Good Teacher Is..."

Use this story to expand the chapter introduction.

- The children will relate the story to their own lives, reflecting on the qualities of a good teacher.
- Connect the qualities of a good teacher with the teachers and leaders in the Church.

 Go to **aliveinchrist.osv.com** Lesson Planning section for this story.

NCEA IFG: ACRE Edition

Discover

Moral Formation

- Objective: To be knowledgeable about the teachings of Jesus and the Church as the basis of Christian morality and to understand Catholic Social Teaching

Communal Life

- Objectives: To know the origin, mission, structure, and communal nature of the Church

Catholic Social Teaching

Live

 Use one of these features to introduce a principle and engage the children with an activity.

- Call to Family, Community, and Participation, Pages 292–293
- Rights and Responsibilities of the Human Person, Pages 294–295

Music Options

 Use one or more of the following songs to enhance catechetical learning or for prayer.

- "The Church," Live Prayer, Page 182
- "Go Light Your World," Invite, Page 175
- "Jesus Is with Us Today," Discover, Page 177
- "The Family of God," Discover, Page 179
- "Gifts," Live, Page 180

LECTIONARY CONNECTION

Chapter 12 highlights Lectionary-connected themes such as fidelity, holiness, and the Holy Spirit. If your parish aligns its curriculum to the liturgical year, you could use this chapter in connection with the following Sundays.

Year A

Sixth Sunday of Easter—promise of the Holy Spirit

Ninth Sunday in Ordinary Time—fidelity

Year B

Fourth Sunday of Advent—Mary

Fourth Sunday in Ordinary Time—Moses

Year C

Second Sunday of Advent—holiness

Twenty-ninth Sunday in Ordinary Time—remain faithful

Go to **aliveinchrist.osv.com** for a complete correlation ordered by the Sundays of the year and suggestions for how to integrate the Scripture readings into chapter lessons.

Name _____ Date _____

Precepts Poem

Color and decorate this mini-poster, and display it where you will see it often. The first letter of each line spells an important word for Catholics to remember.

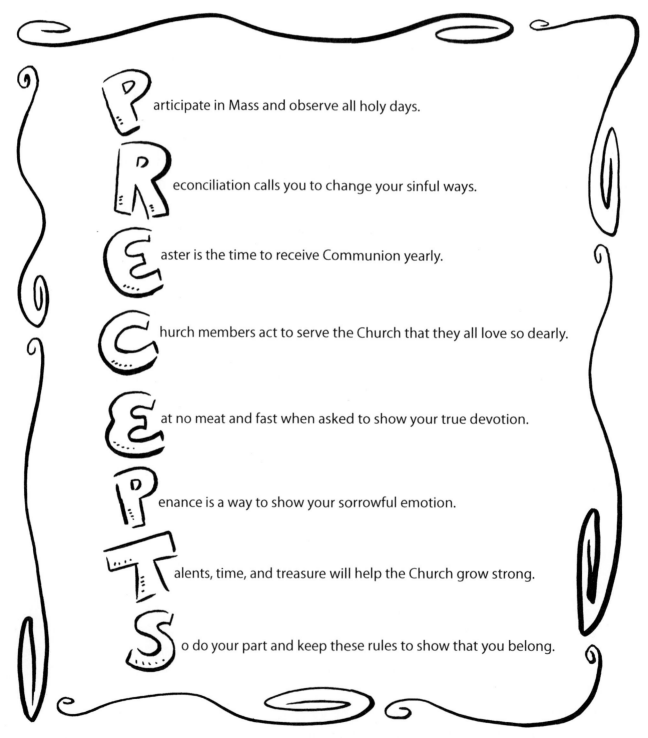

Participate in Mass and observe all holy days.

Reconciliation calls you to change your sinful ways.

Easter is the time to receive Communion yearly.

Church members act to serve the Church that they all love so dearly.

Eat no meat and fast when asked to show your true devotion.

Penance is a way to show your sorrowful emotion.

Talents, time, and treasure will help the Church grow strong.

So do your part and keep these rules to show that you belong.

The Church Teaches

 Let Us Pray

Leader: Jesus, Teacher and Lord, send us good teachers and leaders to guide us to you.

"Teach me to do your will,
for you are my God.
May your kind spirit guide me." Psalm 143:10

All: Help us to follow our leaders, Lord, so that we, too, might show others the way to you.

 Scripture

[Jesus] gave some as apostles, others as prophets, others as evangelists, others as pastors and teachers, to equip the holy ones for the work of ministry, for building up the body of Christ, until we all attain to the unity of faith and knowledge of the Son of God. Ephesians 4:11–13

❓ What Do You Wonder?

- Who are the Church leaders and teachers you know or know about?
- Who guides you in your faith?

175

Optional Activity

Chapter Story: "A Good Teacher Is..." *Verbal/Linguistic*

Use this story after the opening prayer, before explaining that Jesus sent us the Holy Spirit when he returned to his Father in Heaven.

- Encourage the children to share stories about their favorite teachers.
- Have volunteers read aloud the bullet points.
- *Ask:* What are some other qualities of a good teacher?
- *Ask:* Outside of school, who are your teachers?
- Transition back to the lesson instruction.

 Go to **aliveinchrist.osv.com** for Chapter Story.

 Let Us Pray

Invite the children to gather in the prayer space and make the Sign of the Cross. Choose a leader and someone to read aloud the Psalm verse from a Bible. Prompt the children's response.

Have the children move out of the prayer space and back to their seats.

Explain that Jesus sent us the Holy Spirit when he returned to his Father in Heaven.

Say: When Jesus, the Teacher, returned to his Father, he did not leave us on our own.

Scripture

Guide the children through the process of Scripture reflection.

- Invite them to close their eyes, be still and open their minds and hearts to what God is saying to them in this passage.
- Proclaim the Scripture.
- Maintain several moments of silence.
- *Ask:* What did you hear God say to you today?
- Invite volunteers to share.

What Do You Wonder?

Say: Today, the Holy Spirit, our God-given Teacher and Guide, continues to give us teachers and leaders to follow.

Invite the children to respond to the questions. Ask what else they might wonder about Church leaders and teachers.

Objective

- Identify Peter as the Apostle Jesus chose to lead the Apostles and the Church

Jesus Chooses a Leader

Ask: Whom did Jesus choose as the leader of the Apostles?

- List the children's responses on board or on chart paper.

Invite a volunteer to read aloud the paragraph.

- *Ask:* Who has taught you about God, Jesus, or the Church?

 Scripture

Proclaim "You Are the Messiah!"

- Ask a volunteer to read aloud the next paragraph.
- Tell the children that Jesus trusted Peter to teach and govern his Church.
- *Ask:* If Jesus asked you the same question he asked Peter, what would you say?

Point out the picture.

- Ask the children to tell what they see in the picture.

Jesus Chooses a Leader

Whom did Jesus choose as the leader of the Apostles?

We have many teachers who help us learn important lessons. Our parents are our first teachers, and the Church is our most important teacher. The Church's authority, or power to teach, was given by Jesus and is guided by the Holy Spirit. Here is a Gospel passage about the beginnings of the Church's authority to teach.

 Scripture

You Are the Messiah!

Now Jesus and his disciples set out for the villages of Caesarea Philippi. Along the way he asked his disciples, "Who do people say that I am?" They said in reply, "John the Baptist, others Elijah, still others one of the prophets." And he asked them, "But who do you say that I am?" Peter said to him in reply, "You are the Messiah." Then [Jesus] warned them not to tell anyone about him. Mark 8:27–30

© Our Sunday Visitor

Peter believed in Jesus and said so. Jesus gave Peter and the other Apostles a share in the authority he had from his Father. Then Jesus sent them out to preach, teach, forgive, and heal in his name.

→ If Jesus asked you the same question he asked Peter, what would you say?

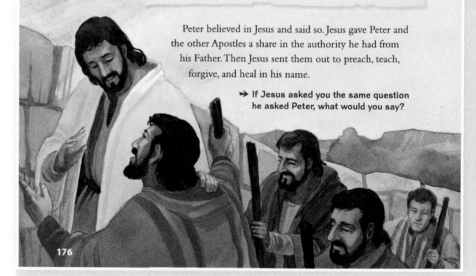

176

 Scripture Background

Mark 8:27–30

The Scripture passage in this lesson marks an important moment in Jesus' life.

- Jesus is ready to reveal himself to his disciples as the Messiah.
- However, the time is not yet right to share this truth with the general public.
- At this point in Jesus' life, most people regarded him as a prophet but not as the promised Savior.

Peter and Jesus

Peter made some mistakes along the way. Much later, at the time of Jesus' crucifixion, Peter and the other disciples were very much afraid. In fact, the night before Jesus died, Peter denied three times that he had ever known Jesus. Afterward, he was ashamed of himself and cried bitterly.

But Jesus never lost faith in Peter. After Jesus' Death and Resurrection, Jesus was talking to Peter and the other disciples on the shore of a lake. Jesus asked three times whether Peter loved him. Of course, Peter said that he did. Jesus said to him, "Feed my lambs. Feed my sheep." (See John 21:15–17.)

In spite of Peter's earlier denials, Jesus made Peter the chief shepherd of all his flock. When he became the leader, Peter made good decisions for the members of the Church.

➜ Why do you think Jesus asked Peter the same question three times?

1. Underline what Peter did before Jesus' death.
2. Circle what the risen Jesus asked Peter.

Reflect Think of some times when you have been forgiven for mistakes you have made.

Share Write a short prayer of thanks for someone who has forgiven you.

✓ Quick Tip

The Magisterium

Catholics depend on the teaching authority of the Church.

- The Church's teachings are rooted in Sacred Scripture and in Jesus' life.
- Pope Saint John Paul II said that the Magisterium's duty is to "discern and promote philosophical thinking which is not at odds with faith" (*Fides et Ratio*).
- Help the children understand that both Sacred Scripture and Sacred Tradition guide the Church and all Catholics, including us.

Peter and Jesus

Explain that although Peter understood that Jesus was the Messiah, he still had more to learn about Jesus.

Read aloud this paragraph.

⭐ Have the children underline what Peter did the night before Jesus died.

- Emphasize that even though he denied Jesus, Peter later repented and learned from his mistake.

Ask two children to play the parts of Jesus and Peter in a skit for the group.

- Ask the children what Jesus meant when he said, "Feed my lambs. Feed my sheep." Take care of my people.
- *Ask:* Why do you think Jesus asked Peter the same questions three times?

 Music Option: Have the children sing, "Jesus Is with Us Today," downloaded from **aliveinchrist.osv.com**.

Activity

Read aloud the directions for the Share Your Faith activity.

- Allow time for the children to write their prayers.

Quick Review

Jesus chose Peter to be the teacher and leader of his Church and also gave other Apostles a share in the authority to teach and lead.

Objectives

- Recognize that Jesus gave Peter and the Apostles, and their successors the Pope and bishops, the authority to teach and lead in his name
- Identify the Magisterium as the teaching office of the Church
- Explain how the Holy Spirit directs the Magisterium in teaching and guiding the People of God
- Retell the Precepts of the Church

The Church and You

Ask: What is your role as a member of the Church?

- Write the children's responses on the board or on chart paper.

Read aloud the first two paragraphs.

- For more on Church authority, refer to page 310 in the Our Catholic Tradition reference section in the back of the Student Book.

Work with Words

Introduce the word *Magisterium* and have the children make vocabulary cards.

Have a child read aloud the last paragraph.

- *Ask:* Who has taught you what the Church teaches?

Draw the graphic organizer on the board or chart paper.

- Ask the children who works through the people listed. Write *Holy Spirit* in the outermost circle.

Catholic Faith Words

Magisterium the teaching office of the Church, which is all of the bishops in union with the Pope

Precepts of the Church some of the minimum requirements given by Church leaders for deepening your relationship with God and the Church

The Church and You

What is your role as a member of the Church?

After Jesus ascended into Heaven, Peter and the Apostles were afraid. Then at Pentecost, the Holy Spirit came and gave them courage to preach the Good News.

The Apostles, with Peter as their head, were the first leaders of the Church. Jesus founded the Church on the Apostles. He gave them the authority to teach and lead his followers. Today, the chief teachers in the Church are the Pope and the bishops, the successors of the Apostles. Their teaching office is called the **Magisterium**. They have the teaching authority to interpret the Word of God found in Sacred Scripture and Sacred Tradition. This is called magisterial authority, and goes back to the authority Christ first gave to the Apostles. The Holy Spirit works through the Church's teachers to keep the whole Church faithful to the teachings of Jesus.

The Church's mission to share the true message of Jesus is not left to the Pope and bishops alone. All members of the Body of Christ have a duty to learn Jesus' message as the Church interprets it and to share it with others. As you do this, you will grow in your love of God and neighbor.

➔ Who has taught you about the teachings of the Church?

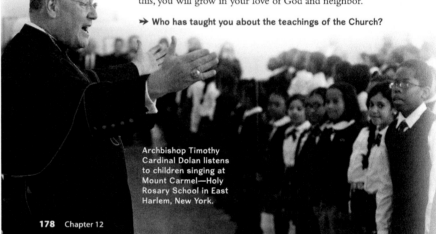

Archbishop Timothy Cardinal Dolan listens to children singing at Mount Carmel—Holy Rosary School in East Harlem, New York.

178 Chapter 12

© Our Sunday Visitor

✓ Quick Tip

Graphic Organizer

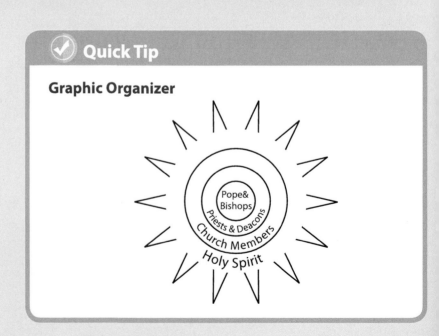

Pope & Bishops

Priests & Deacons

Church Members

Holy Spirit

Rules for Living

Some of the responsibilities of members of the Catholic Church are summed up in the **Precepts of the Church**. The Church's leaders developed these rules and requirements to show you the minimum you should do to live morally and faithfully. As a Catholic, you have a duty to live according to the teachings and Precepts of the Church.

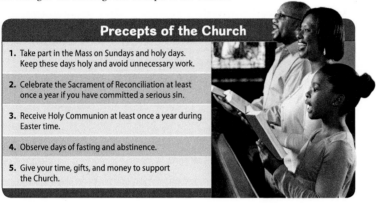

Precepts of the Church

1. Take part in the Mass on Sundays and holy days. Keep these days holy and avoid unnecessary work.

2. Celebrate the Sacrament of Reconciliation at least once a year if you have committed a serious sin.

3. Receive Holy Communion at least once a year during Easter time.

4. Observe days of fasting and abstinence.

5. Give your time, gifts, and money to support the Church.

© Our Sunday Visitor

Connect Your Faith

Word Search

Find at least six words in this word search that relate to the teaching authority of the Church.

Use two of these words in a sentence about your role in the Church.

F	A	I	T	H	O	P	E	A	P
B	P	R	E	C	E	P	T	S	E
H	O	L	Y	S	P	I	R	I	T
A	P	O	S	T	L	E	S	C	E
D	E	B	I	S	H	O	P	S	R

Rules for Living

Tell the children that those who lead and teach the Church have written rules to help people live as faithful followers of Jesus.

- Ask a volunteer to read aloud the paragraph.
- Read the definition of the *Precepts of the Church* and have the children make vocabulary cards for this term.

Precepts of the Church

Have each of five volunteers read aloud one Precept.

- Organize the children into five groups, and assign one Precept to each group.
- Have each group tell how fourth graders can obey the assigned Precept.

 Music Option: Have the children sing, "The Family of God," downloaded from **aliveinchrist.osv.com**.

Activity

Point out the Connect Your Faith activity and read aloud the directions.

- Have the children complete the word search activity.

Quick Review

The Pope and the bishops have the authority to lead and teach the Church in spreading Jesus' message.

Optional Activity

Activity Master 12: Precepts Poem

Distribute copies of the activity found on catechist page 175E.

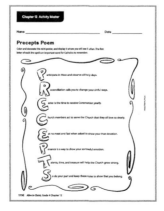

- This Activity Master will reinforce the Precepts of the Church.
- As an alternative, you may wish to send this activity home with the children.

Our Catholic Life

Ask: How can you help support the Church?

- Write the children's responses on the board or on chart paper.

Read aloud or summarize the introductory paragraph.

- Ask a child to read aloud Precept number 5 from Student Book page 179.

Ways to Support Your Parish

Point out the chart.

- Have each of three volunteers read aloud one of the boxes.
- Discuss possible responses to how the children can give of their time, talents, and money to the Church.
- Write the possible responses on the board or on chart paper.
- Provide time for the children to write down their ideas.

 Music Option: Have the children sing, "Gifts," downloaded from **aliveinchrist.osv.com**.

Our Catholic Life

How can you help support the Church?

When each person gives time, gifts, or money, the Church can provide for the needs of her members and can grow in helping meet the needs of others as well.

Ways to Support Your Parish

Giving your time could include participating in any activity in which you volunteer your efforts to help with a parish event. You could help decorate the church for a special liturgy, or donate time to the nursery during Sunday Mass.

Write one way you can give your time to the Church.

_____

Sharing your gifts or talents with the Church community is also important. You could use your computer skills to get others involved, or sing in the children's choir or greet people before Sunday Mass.

Write one way you can share your talents with the Church.

_____

Offering some of your money supports the work of the parish, such as ministering to those who are in need. Money is needed to purchase food and other supplies for shelters. It is also needed to run the parish. For example, the parish has to pay for electricity.

Even if your allowance is small, you should give what you can to your parish.

Write one way you can give of your treasure to support the Church's work.

_____

© Our Sunday Visitor

✓ Quick Tip

Make Changes

Share with the children that sometimes people must make changes in their lives in order to become better followers of Christ.

- Start small—make one commitment and stick to it.
- Do what you enjoy—it will be easiest to keep doing an activity if you enjoy it.
- Work with friends!

People of Faith

Saint Mary Magdalen Postel, 1756–1846

July 16

Saint Mary Magdalen Postel was educated in a Benedictine convent. At eighteen she opened a school for girls in France. It was just before the French Revolution. During the revolution, her school was closed. At that time, Mary Magdalen helped protect fugitive priests. She knew the importance of teaching people about the faith. She wanted everyone to know what the Church teaches. So after the revolution ended, she continued to work in the field of religious education.

Discuss: How does your parish help you to grow in faith?

Learn more about Saint Mary Magdalen Postel at **aliveinchrist.osv.com**

Live Your Faith

Think What chances do you have to use your time, talent, or money to help the Church?

Write or draw one thing you will do next week to share these things with the Church.

The Church Teaches **181**

Catholic Social Teaching

Chapter Connections

To integrate Catholic Social Teaching into your lesson, choose one of the following features: Call to Family, Community, and Participation, pages 292–293; or Rights and Responsibilities of the Human Person, pages 294–295.

- Start the Live step of the process by talking about Saint Mary Magdalen Postel on page 181. Then move directly to the Catholic Social Teaching feature.
- Or, to expand the lesson, complete both pages 180 and 181, then move to the Catholic Social Teaching feature.
- Return to Chapter 12 for the prayer on page 182.

People of Faith

Tell the children about Saint Mary Magdalen Postel.

- Invite a volunteer to read aloud the People of Faith story.
- Explain that in 1807, Saint Mary Magdalen Postel and three other teachers took vows, beginning the Sisters of the Christian Schools of Mercy.
- She was named superior and took the name Mary Magdalen.
- It was several years before the community was able to flourish. In difficult years, they had to move several times.
- Saint Mary Magdalen Postel was honored for her holiness and miracles and was canonized in 1925.
- *Ask:* How does your parish help you grow in faith?

Encourage the children to go to **aliveinchrist.osv.com** at home to learn more about Saint Mary Magdalen Postel.

Activity

Read aloud the directions and discuss the first part of the Live Your Faith activity as a group.

- Allow time for the children write or draw what they will do.
- Invite volunteers to share their work.

Let Us Pray

Prayer of Intercession

Explain to the children that this prayer of intercession is in the form of the Prayer of the Faithful, the prayer we pray during Mass. We place our needs in the hands of God trusting that he will give us what we need.

Prepare

Select three readers for the prayer service.

- Teach the children their response.

> ▶ Rehearse "The Church," downloaded from **aliveinchrist.osv.com**.

Gather

Invite the children to process to the prayer space.

- Have the children sit down and ask them to prepare their minds and hearts for prayer.

Pray

Follow the order of prayer on the student page.

- Encourage the children to add their own intercessions.

 Conclude by singing together "The Church."

 Let Us Pray

Prayer of Intercession

In an intercession, we ask God to act in some way in the lives of others. This prayer follows the order of the Prayer of the Faithful, which we pray at Mass.

Gather and begin with the Sign of the Cross.

Leader: We gather, knowing that God hears us when we pray.

Reader 1: For our Church, that the Holy Spirit will continue to guide her as she teaches the truth revealed by Jesus, let us pray to the Lord.

All: Lord, hear our prayer.

Reader 2: For those in need, that they will experience our care as we live the Beatitudes, let us pray to the Lord.

All: Lord, hear our prayer.

Reader 3: For each person in our community, that the Great Commandment guides us, let us pray to the Lord.

All: Lord, hear our prayer.

Leader: For what else shall we pray?

Name specific prayers.

All: Amen.

 Sing "The Church"

182 Chapter 12

 Liturgy Link

Intercessions

Review with the children that the format of the Prayer of the Faithful includes at least one intention from each of the following:

- Church leaders and the needs of the Church.
- Public authorities and the salvation of the world.
- Those oppressed by any need.
- The local community.

> 🌐 Go to **aliveinchrist.osv.com** for Sunday readings, Scripture background, questions of the week, and seasonal resources.

FAMILY+FAITH
LIVING AND LEARNING TOGETHER

YOUR CHILD LEARNED >>>

This chapter explains the role of Peter and the Apostles continued by the Magisterium and how it interprets Jesus' message through the direction of the Holy Spirit, and describes the Precepts of the Church.

Scripture

Read **Ephesians 4:11–13** to learn about the the diversity of gifts used to build up the Church.

Catholics Believe

- Jesus gave the leaders of the Church the authority to interpret Scripture and Tradition for the faithful.
- The Holy Spirit directs the Church in teaching and guiding the People of God.

To learn more, go to the *Catechism of the Catholic Church #85–87* at usccb.org.

People of Faith

This week, your child learned about Saint Mary Magdalen Postel, who is known for her dedication to religious education.

CHILDREN AT THIS AGE >>>

How They Understand Church Teaching For most fourth-graders, the experience of the teaching Church is limited to their own parish or school; for example, the things they learn in faith formation and hear in the Mass. However, your child is likely growing in his or her ability to perceive the larger worldwide Church and to understand the role of the bishops and Pope. Your child's respect for these leaders will be influenced by the respect shown by adults around them.

CONSIDER THIS >>>

Do you recall when you first realized that you didn't have all the answers?

As we grow wiser, we realize we are limited in our understanding. The Church, guided by the Holy Spirit, brings us the fullness of truth. As Catholics, we know the "entire community of Christians received the Apostles' proclamation of the Gospel, and so the church in her entirety is called 'apostolic.' Under the guidance of the Holy Spirit, the church as a whole remains and will always remain faithful to the teaching of the Apostles" (USCCA, p. 132).

LET'S TALK >>>

- Ask your child to explain some ways the Church teaches us.
- Share a story about someone who helped you understand a Church teaching.

LET'S PRAY >>>

Saint Mary Magdalen, pray for us that we may open our hearts and minds to learn more as we grow in faith and in our love for God. Amen.

For a multimedia glossary of Catholic Faith Words, Sunday readings, seasonal and Saint resources, and chapter activities go to aliveinchrist.osv.com.

Family + Faith

Distribute the page to the children or parents/adult family members. Point out the chapter highlights, insights on how fourth graders understand concepts, the opportunity for the adults to reflect on their own experience and faith journey, and the family prayer.

Chapter 12 Review

(A) Work with Words   Complete each sentence with the correct word or words from the Word Bank.

1. Minimum requirements given by the Church to help you grow closer to God and the Church are called ____**Precepts**____ of the Church.

2. Jesus gave the Church the ____**authority**____ to teach and lead the Body of Christ.

3. You have the duty to __**live according to**__ the rules and laws of the Church.

4. The ____**Magisterium**____ is the teaching office of the Church, all the bishops in union with the Pope.

5. The ____**Holy Spirit**____ guides the Church and the Magisterium.

> **Word Bank**
>
> Holy Spirit
>
> Precepts
>
> authority
>
> live according to
>
> Magisterium

(B) Check Understanding   Circle True if a statement is true, and circle False if a statement is false. Correct any false statements.

6. Only wealthy people can help support the Church. (**True** / **False**)
   <u>Everyone can help support the Church.</u>

7. On Christmas, the Holy Spirit came and gave the disciples courage to go out and preach the Good News. (**True** / **False**)
   <u>On Pentecost, the Holy Spirit came.</u>

8. The Pope and bishops are the chief teachers in the Church. (**True** / **False**)

9. When John became the leader of the Church, he made good decisions for the members. (**True** / **False**)
   <u>When Peter became the leader of the Church, he made good decisions for the members.</u>

10. Jesus sent the Apostles out to preach, teach, forgive, and heal in his name. (**True** / **False**)

Go to **aliveinchrist.osv.com** for an interactive review.

Chapter Review

Use Catechist Quick Reviews to highlight lesson concepts.

(A) **Work with Words**
Have the children complete each sentence with the correct word or words from the Word Bank.

(B) **Check Understanding**
Have the children circle *True* if a statement is true, circle *False* if it is false, and correct any false statements.

Go to **aliveinchrist.osv.com** to prepare customized and downloadable assessments, send eAssessments, and assign interactive reviews.

The Church Teaches   **183–184**

Use Catechist Quick Reviews in each chapter to highlight lesson concepts for this unit and prepare for the Unit Review.

Have the children complete the Review pages. Then discuss the answers as a group. Review any concepts with which the children are having difficulty.

A **Work with Words**
Have the children solve the puzzle with terms from the Word Bank.

Unit Review

UNIT
4

A Work with Words **Solve the puzzle with terms from the Word Bank.**

Down

1. _____ is God's plan for our lives. The purpose for which he made us.

2. God's _____ is here now, but has not yet come in its fullness.

3. Observing days of fasting and abstinence is a _____ of the Church.

4. The teaching office of the Church

6. The Immaculate _____ is the teaching that Mary was preserved from sin from the first moment of her life.

7. A person whom the Church declares has led a holy life and is enjoying life with God in Heaven

10. All the baptized who are not priests or religious brothers or sisters

Across

5. An _____ server assists the priest at Mass.

8. The process by which the Church officially declares someone a Saint

9. A Saint who has a particular connection to a cause, place, type of work, or person.

Word Bank

vocation   canonization   Kingdom   altar
Conception   Saint   patron Saint laity
Magisterium   Precept

© Our Sunday Visitor

B Check Understanding   Complete each sentence with the correct word from the Word Bank.

Word Bank

holiness

Magisterium

call

members

canonization

11. In the story of Catherine of Siena, you learned that Catherine answered God's _____ call _____ .

12. A declaration by the Pope that names a person a Saint is called _____ canonization _____ .

13. Mary is the perfect model of _____ holiness _____ .

14. All _____ members _____ of the Church have a duty to learn Jesus' message and share it with others.

15. The _____ Magisterium _____ is the teaching office of the Church, which is all of the bishops in union with the Pope.

C Make Connections   Write a response to each question or statement.

16. Through Baptism, you share in Jesus' role as priest, prophet, and king. Think about the accounts of Jesus in the Bible. Describe one account that shows Jesus acting as a priest, a prophet, or a king.
Possible responses: priest—Jesus prays for others, the Last Supper; prophet—Jesus preaches the Sermon on the Mount; king—Jesus washes the disciples' feet and forgives a sinner

17. Name two ways in which you can grow in holiness today.
Responses will vary.

18. Explain how supporting the Church by offering your time, gifts, and money strengthens the Church community.
Possible responses: I share in helping the Church help others; I help our parish run

19. Why is Mary so important to our Catholic faith?
Possible responses: Mary is the perfect model of holiness; Mary is the Mother of Jesus; Mary said "yes" to God's will and showed us how to be a follower; she loves us and prays for us

20. Explain the Church's role as a teacher.
The Church teaches with authority to help us understand God's Word in Scripture and Tradition, and to be faithful to the message of Jesus.

B Check Understanding
Have the children complete each sentence with the correct word from the Word Bank.

C Make Connections
Have the children write a response to each question or statement.

Go to **aliveinchrist.osv.com** to prepare customized and downloadable assessments, send eAssessments, and assign interactive reviews.

Morality

Our Catholic Tradition

- The virtues help us do what is good, follow God's Commandments, and give the best of ourselves. (CCC, 1803)

- God created humans to live in strong, loving families and communities. These communities are called to respect life and live in the truth. (CCC, 2207)

- All human life is sacred. (CCC, 2319)

- We learn ways of loving our neighbor and respecting others by practicing the Fourth through Tenth Commandments. (CCC, 2196)

Why is it important for families to respect the dignity of each person in their family and in the world?

© Our Sunday Visitor

Preview Unit Theme

Ask: What is the unit theme?

Summarize that the unit focuses on morality.

Invite volunteers to read aloud each of the bullets in Our Catholic Tradition.

Explain to the children that they will learn about these things in the next three chapters.

Have the children study the photos and images. Invite volunteers to describe what they see. What do these images say about the unit theme?

Ask: Why is it important for families to respect the dignity of each person in their family and in the world?

After some discussion, explain to the children that they will be exploring this question in the next three chapters.

KEY CONCEPT

God created humans to live in strong, loving families. The Fourth, Sixth, and Ninth Commandments provide basic laws of family love and respect.

DOCTRINAL CONTENT

- God created humans to live in families and wants family members to respect, love, and protect one another. (CCC, 2203)

- The Fourth Commandment teaches children to honor and obey parents and parents to provide for, love, and share their faith with children. (CCC, 2199)

- The Sixth and Ninth Commandments are about faithful love and commitment between husband and wife, but require all of us to keep promises, be faithful, and act appropriately. (CCC, 2348–2350)

- The Cardinal Virtues help us to act wisely, use self-control, give God and others their due, and be disciplined in our thoughts and actions. (CCC, 1804–1805)

TASKS OF CATECHESIS

Helping children grow in a faith that is "known, celebrated, lived, and expressed in prayer" (NDC, 20).

This chapter focuses on the following tasks of catechesis:

- Moral Formation
- Education for Communal Life

Catechist Background

Children obey your parents in everything, for this is pleasing to the Lord. Fathers, do not provoke your children, so they may not be discouraged. Colossians 3:20–21

→ **Reflect** How does your family express love for one another?

The Catholic Church gives much importance to the covenant of marriage, basing her teachings on both Sacred Scripture and Sacred Tradition. The wedding feast appears in the Old Testament as a symbol of the union of God and his People. In the New Testament, the feast symbolizes the union of Christ and his Church. Matrimony is more than a human institution.

The love of a husband and wife echoes the love of Christ for his Church. Marriage is a relationship of love and commitment for a lifetime! In marriage, human love and commitment between a man and a woman are bonded with the eternal love and covenant of God.

Marriage is the foundation of family and community life. Parents are to act as co-workers with God in creating new life. The family is a blessing to both parents and children. Parents nurture and guide their children, passing on the faith. Children remind their parents of the calling to share God's love. Together, family members support one another in mutual love. Families are the basic unit of society and of Christian community. Strength and stability in family life promote strength and stability among the People of God.

→ **Reflect** How has your family helped you grow in faith?

Catechist's Prayer

Loving God, be with the families of the children I teach. Heal what needs to be healed. Strengthen what needs to be strengthened. Help me appreciate these children as your children. Amen.

Lesson Plan

Objectives	Process	Materials

⏱ Invite, 10 minutes

Family Love Page 189

- ♡ **Proverbs 1:8** Pray the opening prayer.
- 📖 **Colossians 3:20–21** Reflect prayerfully on the Word.
- Discuss What Do You Wonder questions.

🔊 **Optional Activity**
Chapter Story:
"All Shapes and Sizes"

⏱ Discover, 35 minutes

Honor and Respect Pages 190–191
- Appreciate that God created humans to live in families and wants family members to love one another
- Understand that the Fourth Commandment teaches children to honor parents and parents to love and share their faith with children

- **Catholic Faith Words** Cardinal Virtues
- Explain that the Fourth Commandment is to honor your father and mother.
- 📖 **Luke 2: 41–52** Proclaim "The Boy Jesus and His Family."
- Explain how to honor parents and guardians.
- **Share Your Faith Activity** Draw something your family enjoys doing together.

☐ pencils
☐ index cards
☐ crayons or markers

Faithful Love Pages 192–193
- Understand that the Sixth and Ninth Commandments are about faithful love between husband and wife, but require all of us to be faithful, and act appropriately
- Recognize that the Cardinal Virtues help us to act wisely, use self-control, give God and others their due, and be disciplined in our lives

- **Catholic Faith Words** temperance, fortitude, modesty, chastity
- Explain that we live the Sixth and Ninth Commandments when we keep promises to family, friends, and God.
- ☆ Underline how the Cardinal Virtues help us. Circle ways to practice modesty and chastity.
- Explain that God loves all families.
- **Connect Your Faith Activity** Complete the crossword puzzle.

☐ pencils
☐ index cards
- **Optional Activity**
Blessing Prayer
☐ Activity Master 13 (Page 189E)

⏱ Live, 15 minutes

Our Catholic Life Pages 194–195

- Talk about concrete examples of following Commandments.
- ☆ Identify ways that show how they keep the Commandments.
- **People of Faith** Learn about Saint Louis Martin and Saint Marie-Azélie Martin.
- **Live Your Faith Activity** Name four qualities of good friendships and family love.

☐ pencils
☐ crayons or markers

Prayer of Petition Page 196

- Select three readers.
- ▶ Rehearse "Right and Just."

🔊 Download "Right and Just."

Family + Faith Page 197
Point out that the Catholic Families page provides chapter highlights, information on how fourth graders understand faith concepts, and family prayer.

Chapter Review Page 198
🌐 aliveinchrist.osv.com
- Customize and Download Assessments
- Email Links to eAssessments
- Interactive Student Reviews

ONLINE RESOURCES

 Go to **aliveinchrist.osv.com**

You will find:

- Interactive lesson planning with web specific content and additional activities
- Step by step lesson instruction from printed Catechist Edition for integrated lesson planning
- Custom-built assessments to download and eAssessment links
- Interactive reviews that provide scores and the option to review answers
- Sunday readings with background and questions of the week

 Go to **osvparish.com**

You will find:

- Ask the Experts Q and A
- General Catechist Helps
- Community Connections and Blogs

Sharing the Message with Fourth Graders

Family Love Fourth graders usually have a very strong love for their parents. If they live with both parents, they can often pick up on the quality of their mom and dad's relationship with one another. One area in which they often struggle is in their relationship with siblings. Developmental differences, as well as limited space and attention, can cause rivalries between brothers and sisters. When children understand that the family is like a school where we learn to love each other, they can rise to meet these challenges with God's help.

Teaching Tip: Encourage the children to think about ways they can cultivate an environment of love at home through loving actions towards family members—even siblings who are not always charitable towards them.

How Fourth Graders Understand

- Fourth graders know that there are many types of families. They like to read about families and how they are special.
- Fourth graders are aware that all families sometimes have problems. Be sensitive about asking them to share personal information.
- Explain that the Fourth, Sixth, and Ninth Commandments are positive actions that help keep families strong and united.

"My family is very important to me. Help me appreciate my family's strengths."

Chapter Connections

Chapter Story

Invite

"All Shapes and Sizes"

Use this story to expand the chapter introduction.

- The children will relate the story to their own lives, reflecting on the diversity of families.
- Connect families to sharing God's love.

 Go to **aliveinchrist.osv.com** Lesson Planning section for this story.

NCEA IFG: ACRE Edition

Discover

Moral Formation

- Objective: To be knowledgeable about the teachings of Jesus and the Church as the basis of Christian morality and to understand Catholic Social Teaching

Communal Life

- Objectives: To know the origin, mission, structure, and communal nature of the Church; to know the rights and responsibilities of the Christian faithful

Catholic Social Teaching

Live

 Use one of these features to introduce a principle and engage the children with an activity.

- Life and Dignity of the Human Person, Pages 290–291
- Call to Family, Community, and Participation, Pages 292–293

Music Options

 Use one or more of the following songs to enhance catechetical learning or for prayer.

- "Right and Just," Live Prayer, Page 196
- "God's Good Rules," Discover, Page 190
- "My Ten Commandments," Discover, Page 190
- "Obey Your Parents," Discover, Page 191

LECTIONARY CONNECTION

 Chapter 13 highlights Lectionary-connected themes such as Mary, mission, and faithfulness. If your parish aligns its curriculum to the liturgical year, you could use this chapter in connection with the following Sundays.

Year A

Second Sunday of Advent—mission

Third Sunday of Advent—witness

Pentecost Sunday—mission, gifts

Year B

Third Sunday of Advent—witness

Fourth Sunday of Advent—Mary

The Epiphany of the Lord—Mary

Year C

Third Sunday of Easter—mission

Twenty-seventh Sunday in Ordinary Time—faith

Twenty-ninth Sunday in Ordinary Time—faithfulness

 Go to **aliveinchrist.osv.com** for a complete correlation ordered by the Sundays of the year and suggestions for how to integrate the Scripture readings into chapter lessons.

Name _____ Date _____

Blessing Prayer

This prayer is the closing blessing from the *Rite of Marriage*. Decorate the prayer with a colorful border. Cut it out, roll it into a scroll, and tie it with a brightly colored ribbon. Present it to a married couple whom you know.

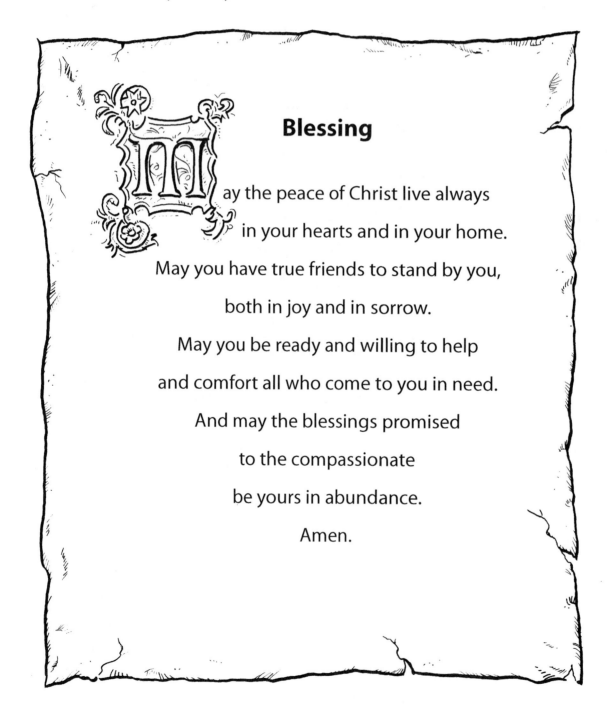

Blessing

May the peace of Christ live always

in your hearts and in your home.

May you have true friends to stand by you,

both in joy and in sorrow.

May you be ready and willing to help

and comfort all who come to you in need.

And may the blessings promised

to the compassionate

be yours in abundance.

Amen.

Family Love

Let Us Pray

Leader: Loving Father, thank you for our parents and families who love us and teach us.

"Hear, my son, your father's instruction,
and reject not your mother's teaching."
Proverbs 1:8

All: Loving God, help us grow with respect and blossom with love. Amen.

Scripture

Children, obey your parents in everything, for this is pleasing to the Lord. Fathers, support your children, so they may not be discouraged. **Based on Colossians 3:20–21**

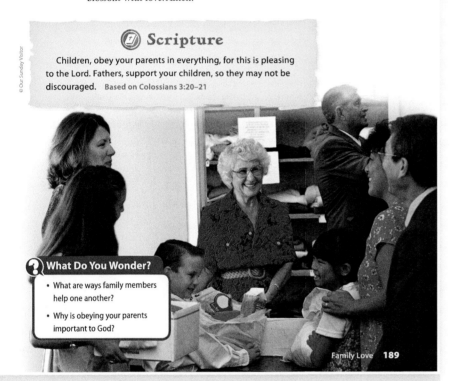

What Do You Wonder?

- What are ways family members help one another?
- Why is obeying your parents important to God?

Family Love **189**

Optional Activity

Chapter Story: "All Shapes and Sizes" *Verbal/Linguistic*

Use this story after the opening prayer, before explaining that our families are God's gift to us.

- Read the story aloud as the children follow along.
- *Ask:* What do you do to share God's love with your family?
- Have the children draw pictures of their family members.
- After having them write captions telling how each person shares God's love, transition back to the lesson instruction.

 Go to **aliveinchrist.osv.com** for Chapter Story.

Invite

♥ Let Us Pray

Invite the children to gather in the prayer space and make the Sign of the Cross. Choose one child to be the leader and one to read aloud the Psalm verse from a Bible. Prompt the children's response.

Have the children move out of the prayer space and back to their seats.

Say: Sometimes it is a challenge to remember that your family is one of God's gifts to you. Listen to God's Word and hear what he says about honoring our parents.

📖 Scripture

Guide the children through the process of Scripture reflection.

- Invite them to close their eyes, be still and open their minds and hearts to what God is saying to them in this passage.
- Proclaim the Scripture.
- Maintain several moments of silence.
- *Ask:* What did you hear God say to you today?
- Invite volunteers to share.

What Do You Wonder?

Say: Your family is God's gift to you. You are also a gift to your family. There are many ways you can help love grow in your family. The love that grows in your family should be so great that it spills out into the rest of the world.

Invite the children to respond to the questions. Ask what else they might wonder about God's gift of a family and obeying parents.

Objectives

- Appreciate that God created humans to live in families and wants family members to love one another
- Understand that the Fourth Commandment teaches children to honor parents and parents to love and share their faith with children

Honor and Respect

Ask: What does the Fourth Commandment require?

- Write the children's responses on the board or on chart paper.

Ask a volunteer to read aloud the two paragraphs and recite the Fourth Commandment.

 Scripture

Invite a child to proclaim "The Boy Jesus and His Family."

- Tell the children to listen carefully and think of how Mary and Joseph felt when Jesus was missing and when they found him.
- *Ask:* How did Jesus live out the Fourth Commandment?

Point out the picture on the page. Ask the children to describe how Mary and Joseph must have felt when they walked into the Temple and saw Jesus.

- *Ask:* Why is it important for you to obey your parents?

 Music Option: Have the children sing "God's Good Rules" or "My Ten Commandments," downloaded from **aliveinchrist.osv.com**.

Honor and Respect

What does the Fourth Commandment require?

It would be hard to imagine our lives without our families. The love of our parents, grandparents, aunts, and uncles helps us to feel cared for and valued. God created humans to live in families. God wants families to be strong, to protect one another, and to live in peace and love.

The Fourth, Sixth, and Ninth Commandments provide basic laws about family love and respect. The Fourth Commandment is this: Honor your father and mother. Jesus is the perfect example for living out this Commandment.

 Scripture

The Boy Jesus and His Family

When Jesus was twelve, he went to Jerusalem with his family to celebrate Passover. As Mary and Joseph were returning home, they realized that Jesus was not with them. They finally found him talking with the teachers in the Temple. Mary told Jesus how worried they had been, and Jesus returned to Nazareth with his parents.

Jesus was obedient as he grew in wisdom and age. His actions were pleasing to God and to all who knew him.
Based on Luke 2:41–52

→ How did Jesus live out the Fourth Commandment?

190

 **Scripture Background**

The Holy Family

This passage points out that Jesus' family was faithful to the religious practices of the time—in this case, traveling to the Temple for Passover.

- The children may be concerned that Mary and Joseph could lose Jesus.
- Families in biblical times traveled in caravans, the men in one group and the women in another. Children traveled in either group. Both Mary and Joseph probably thought that Jesus was with the other group.

Living the Fourth Commandment

The Fourth Commandment teaches you to honor your parents and guardians. You honor them when you

- listen to and obey them in all that is good.
- show gratitude for all that they do for you.
- respect and care for them as they grow older.
- respect people in authority.

Parents and guardians are to provide for your needs, serve as good role models, love you, and share their faith with you. This sharing makes the family a domestic Church, where we first learn about loving others and following Christ. Parents and guardians also encourage you to grow in faith by sharing their own faith and teaching the **Cardinal Virtues**, good habits that help us live as children of God. They help you make good choices and figure out your vocation.

Catholic Faith Words

Cardinal Virtues the four principal moral virtues—prudence, temperance, justice, and fortitude—that help us live as children of God and from which the other moral virtues flow. We strengthen these good habits through God's grace and our own efforts.

Share Your Faith

Reflect Draw something your family enjoys doing together.

Share Talk with a partner about how this activity keeps your family strong and close.

191

Optional Activity

Joyful Events *Intrapersonal*

The finding of Jesus in the Temple is one of the Joyful Mysteries of the Rosary.

- Tell the children about the joyful events in Mary's life (the Annunciation, the Visitation, the Nativity, the Presentation, the Finding of Jesus in the Temple).
- Pray a decade of the Rosary with the children.
- See page 326 in the Our Catholic Tradition reference section of the Student Book for how to pray the Rosary.

Living the Fourth Commandment

Read aloud the first paragraph.

- Explain that these instructions tell what children are to do for their parents.

Invite a volunteer to read the second paragraph.

- Explain that this paragraph tells what responsibilities parents have.
- *Ask:* What does it mean to be a good role model? Who has been a good role model for you?

Work With Words

Invite a volunteer to read aloud the definition for *Cardinal Virtues*.

- Have the children make a vocabulary card.
- Refer to page 319 in the Our Catholic Tradition reference section in the back of the Student Book to find out more about the Cardinal Virtues.

 Music Option: Have the children sing "Obey Your Parents" or "People Who Love Me," downloaded from **aliveinchrist.osv.com**.

Activity

Read aloud the directions for the Share Your Faith activity.

- Have the children work independently to complete their drawings.

Quick Review

God meant humans to live as families. Jesus is the perfect example for living the Fourth Commandment.

Family Love   **191**

Objectives

- Understand that the Sixth and Ninth Commandments are about faithful love between husband and wife, but require all of us to be faithful, and act appropriately

- Recognize that the Cardinal Virtues help us to act wisely, use self-control, give God and others their due, and be disciplined in our lives

Faithful Love

Ask: What do the Commandments teach about love?

- Write the children's responses on the board or on chart paper.

Point out the wedding photo.

- Ask the children to raise their hand if they have been to a wedding.

- Invite the children to share what they saw or heard at the wedding.

Invite volunteers read aloud the text.

- Explain that *covet* means to want something that belongs to someone else.

- Ask the children how they have been faithful in their friendships.

- Then ask why faithfulness is important in relationships.

- *Ask:* Why is the Sacrament of Matrimony important?

Discover

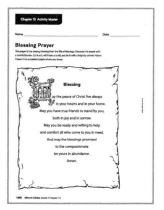

© Our Sunday Visitor

Faithful Love

What do the Commandments teach about love?

The Sixth Commandment is: You shall not commit adultery. The Ninth Commandment is: You shall not covet your neighbor's wife. These Commandments are about the faithful love and commitment between husband and wife.

When a man and woman marry, they make solemn promises to or before God, called vows. They promise to love and honor each other always and to welcome the gift of children.

Part of being faithful is respecting your vows and those of other married couples. Married couples should not act in ways that would weaken their marriage. Adultery means being unfaithful to these vows. The grace of the Sacrament of Matrimony strengthens the couple to be faithful and true.

→ **Why is the Sacrament of Matrimony important?**

Virtues and You

The Sixth and Ninth Commandments apply to everyone. You can live out these Commandments by keeping promises to family, friends, and God.

Catholic Faith Words

temperance the Cardinal Virtue that helps us use moderation, be disciplined, and have self-control

fortitude the Cardinal Virtue that helps you show courage, have strength to get through difficult times, and not give up on doing good

modesty a moral virtue and one of the Fruits of the Holy Spirit that helps us dress, talk, and move in appropriate ways

chastity a moral virtue and one of the Fruits of the Holy Spirit that helps us to act and think in ways that are appropriate and pure

---

Optional Activity

Activity Master 13: Blessing Prayer

Distribute copies of the activity found on catechist page 189E.

- As a group, brainstorm some marital symbols that the children may want to include.

- As an alternative, you may wish to send this activity home.

The four Cardinal Virtues—prudence, **temperance**, justice, and **fortitude**—help us to act wisely, use self-control, give others their due, stand strong, and be disciplined in our thoughts and actions.

Temperance helps us to practice **modesty** and **chastity**. You can dress, talk, and move in ways that honor your own dignity and that of others. You can respect that the differences between males and females are gifts from God.

1. Underline how the Cardinal Virtues help us.
2. Circle ways you practice modesty and chastity.

God's Love Strengthens

Sometimes it is hard for families to live as God intends. Arguments, hurts, and disappointments can keep families from being signs of God's love. Parents and children sometimes hurt one another. Some families are hurt through separation, divorce, or even death.

But God continues to love all families and to help them grow stronger. Every time families are signs of love, they reflect the love that exists within the Holy Trinity.

Connect Your Faith

Crossword Fill in the crossword using the clues.

Across

3. helps us to act and think in ways that are pure
5. helps us use moderation and self-control

Down

1. helps us dress, talk, and move appropriately
2. Cardinal _____ help you live as children of God
4. showing courage and strength

```
1.              2.
M               V
O          3. C H A S T I T Y
D              R
E          4.  R
S          F   T
        5. T E M P E R A N C E
Y          O   E
           R   S
           T
           I
           T
           U
           D
           E
```

✓ Quick Tip

Family Disappointments

Children in your group may live in nontraditional families.

- Avoid the phrase "broken home" or other language that implies that some families are not as good as others.
- Do not single out children. Let the text speak to those who need to hear it.
- Make yourself available to any child who may be interested in talking privately about their personal situation. If a situation does arise, be sure to bring it to the attention of appropriate members of your parish staff.

Virtues and You

Read aloud the last paragraph on page 192.

- Emphasize that we can live the Sixth and Ninth Commandments by keeping promises to family, friends, and God.

Invite volunteers to read aloud the first two paragraphs on page 193.

⭐ Have the children underline how the Cardinal Virtues help us. Then have them circle ways to practice modesty and chastity.

Work with Words

Invite volunteers to read aloud the Catholic Faith Words and their definitions.

- Have the children make a vocabulary card for each term.

God's Love Strengthens

Read aloud or summarize this section.

- *Ask:* What can families do to be signs of God's love?
- Be sensitive to family privacy issues.

Activity

Read aloud the Connect Your Faith activity directions.

- Have the children work in pairs to complete the puzzle.

Quick Review

The Sixth and Ninth Commandments help families to grow in love. God loves families and helps them to grow stronger.

Our Catholic Life

Ask: How can you follow God's Commandments in your family life?

- Write the children's responses on the board or on chart paper.

Recall with the children that the Fourth, Sixth, and Ninth Commandments center on family life.

Read aloud the introductory paragraph.

- Invite each of six volunteers to read aloud one of the hearts.
- After each heart, ask the children for concrete examples of how to follow each suggestion.
- ⭐ Have the children identify the hearts that show the way they are already keeping the Commandments. Then discuss how following the Ten Commandments makes family life better.
- Encourage the children to practice one of the suggestions this week and notice the difference.

Live

Our Catholic Life

How can you follow God's Commandments in your family life?

God asks you to show his love to your family at all times. This is not always easy, but keeping the Fourth, Sixth, and Ninth Commandments will help you.

1. Draw a star next to the hearts that show ways you keep the Commandments now.
2. Discuss how following the Ten Commandments makes family life better.

Remember that being part of a family means forgiving one another as God forgives us when we sin.

Keep the promises you make to your family, friends, and God. Do what you have said you will do.

Practice modesty by dressing decently and by avoiding television programs, movies, books, and music that show disrespect for God's gift of sexuality.

Don't be jealous of other family members. Include others in your friendships.

Share your possessions, your time, and your gifts with family members.

Respect, honor, and obey your parents and other family members. Listen to them, and pay attention to their needs.

© Our Sunday Visitor

 Quick Tip

Conscience Formation

The focus on the Ten Commandments in this chapter can lead to a discussion of conscience formation.

- Tell the children that a person's conscience will be only as good as the information that it receives.
- Ask the children to consider the Ten Commandments and Beatitudes and how these guides call them to act.

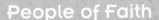

People of Faith

July 12

Saint Louis Martin, 1823–1894
Saint Marie-Azélie Martin, 1831–1877

God loves all families and wants them to be happy. Saints Louis Martin and Marie-Azélie Martin fell in love and got married. Louis was a jeweler and watchmaker. Marie-Azélie made a special kind of lace. They promised to live as holy a life as possible and teach their children about Jesus. The Martins did many things with their family, like take walks and tell stories. All of their five daughters became nuns. One, Thérèse de Lisieux, became a Saint.

Discuss: What does your family like to do together?

 Learn more about Saints Louis and Marie-Azélie at aliveinchrist.osv.com

Live Your Faith

Build with Solid Blocks The family is the building block of the Christian community and of society. In the blocks, write four qualities of good friendships and family love. Tell how your family shows one of these qualities to others.

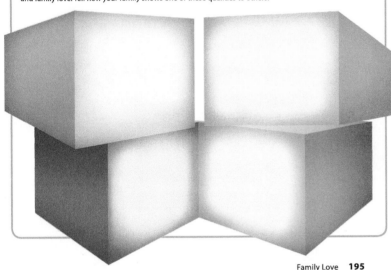

Family Love **195**

© Our Sunday Visitor

🌐 Catholic Social Teaching

Chapter Connections

To integrate Catholic Social Teaching into your lesson, choose one of the following features: Life and Dignity of the Human Person, pages 290–291; or Call to Family, Community, and Participation, pages 292–293.

- Start by talking about the People of Faith on page 195. Then move directly to the Catholic Social Teaching feature.
- Or, to expand the lesson, complete both pages 194 and 195, then move to the Catholic Social Teaching feature.
- Return to Chapter 13 for the prayer on page 196.

People of Faith

Tell the children about the two Saints.

- Invite a volunteer to read aloud the People of Faith story.
- Explain that Saint Marie-Azélie wanted to become a religious sister. To her disappointment, she was turned away by the Sisters of Charity of Saint Vincent de Paul because she had respiratory difficulties and recurrent headaches. So Blessed Marie-Azélie prayed for God to give her children. In the meantime, she became a lace maker.
- Saint Louis wanted to become a monk. However, due to his lack of knowledge of Latin, he was rejected. So, Saint Louis decided to become a watchmaker.
- He later fell in love with Saint Marie-Azélie. They married just three months later. Her lace making business was so successful that Louis sold his watch making business to go into partnership with her.
- *Ask:* What does your family like to do together?

Encourage the children to go to **aliveinchrist.osv.com** at home to learn more about Saint Louis Martin and Saint Marie-Azélie Martin.

Activity

Read aloud the directions and discuss the first part of the Live Your Faith activity as a group.

- Allow time for the children to write four qualities of good friendships and family love.
- Have the children tell a partner how their family shows one of the qualities to others.

Let Us Pray

Prayer of Petition

Tell the children that they will pray for families everywhere.

- Ask the children to draw their families or write names of family members.

Prepare

Choose readers for the prayer.

- Teach the children their responses.

 Rehearse "Right and Just," downloaded from **aliveinchrist.osv.com**.

Gather

Invite the children to process to the prayer space with their pictures or lists. Ask them to think about their families as they pray.

- Direct the children to ready their minds and hearts for prayer.

Pray

Follow the order of prayer on the student page.

- Alternative readings are Sirach 3:2–6, 12–14, or Colossians 3:12–21.
- *Leader's concluding prayer:* God—Father, Son, and Holy Spirit—we ask that you strengthen and bless family life.

 Conclude by singing together "Right and Just."

Live

 Let Us Pray

Prayer of Petition

A prayer of petition is a prayer in which we ask God for something for another person or for the community.

Gather and begin with the Sign of the Cross.

Leader: God, from you every family learns to love. We ask you to strengthen our families.

All: Hear us, O Lord.

Reader 1: May our parents and those who care for us be blessed in their commitment to love us and each other.

All: Hear us, O Lord.

Reader 2: May we and all children find support and security in their families.

All: Hear us, O Lord.

Reader 3: May all families discover your gift of faithful love.

All: Hear us, O Lord.

Leader: Let us pray.

Bow your heads as the leader prays.

All: Amen.

 Sing: "Right and Just"
It is right—the proper thing to do.
It is just—giving God what's due.
When we come to praise our God,
It is right and just.

 Liturgy Link

Prayer Leaders

Preparing leaders is important in setting the tone for a prayer.

- Make sure that each child can read and pronounce the words correctly.
- Review when to sit, stand, or use proper gestures.
- Children's active participation now may inspire them to serve in liturgical ministries in the future.

Go to **aliveinchrist.osv.com** for Sunday readings, Scripture background, questions of the week, and seasonal resources.

FAMILY+FAITH
LIVING AND LEARNING TOGETHER

YOUR CHILD LEARNED >>>

This chapter examines the importance of the Sacrament of Matrimony, the role of family in God's plan, and how the Cardinal Virtues help us to act appropriately and be disciplined.

Scripture

Read **Colossians 3:20** to find out what God's Word says about our parents.

Catholics Believe

- God created humans to live in strong, loving families.
- The Fourth, Sixth, and Ninth Commandments provide basic laws of family love and respect.

To learn more, go to the *Catechism of the Catholic Church* #2197–2200, 2204–2206, 2380–2381, 2521–2524 at **usccb.org**.

People of Faith

This week, your child learned about Saints Louis Martin and Marie-Azélie Martin, the parents of Saint Thérèse of Lisieux.

CHILDREN AT THIS AGE >>>

How They Understand Family Love Fourth-graders usually have a very strong love for their parents. If they live with both parents, they can often pick up on the quality of their mom and dad's relationship with one another. One area in which they often struggle is in their relationship with siblings. Developmental differences, as well as limited space and attention, can cause rivalries between brothers and sisters. When children understand that the family is like a school where we learn to love each other, they can rise to meet these challenges with God's help.

CONSIDER THIS >>>

How has your understanding of what it means to honor your parents changed?

As our parents age, we have an opportunity to show what they taught us about love. As Catholics, we know that "while adult children may sometimes experience a strain between raising their own children and caring for their parents, they must do what they can to help their parents. . . . While it is right for society to help care for the elderly, the family remains the rightful source of support" (*USCCA, pp. 377–378*).

LET'S TALK >>>

- Ask your child to name one thing about the Fourth, Sixth, or Ninth Commandments.
- Talk about ways your family honors one another.

LET'S PRAY >>>

Dear God, please help our family to be happy together, to love each other, and to pray for each other. Amen.

For a multimedia glossary of Catholic Faith Words, Sunday readings, seasonal and Saint resources, and chapter activities go to **aliveinchrist.osv.com**.

Alive in Christ, Grade 4 Chapter 13 **197**

Family + Faith

Distribute the page to the children or parents/adult family members. Point out the chapter highlights, insights on how fourth graders understand concepts, the opportunity for the adults to reflect on their own experience and faith journey, and the family prayer.

Chapter 13 Review

A Work with Words **Complete each sentence with the correct word from the Word Bank.**

1–5. God made humans to live as ____**families**____ who love and respect one another. By following the ____**Fourth**____ Commandment, children ____**honor**____ and obey their parents and guardians. The ____**Sixth**____ and Ninth Commandments are about being ____**faithful**____ in marriage, keeping promises, and acting appropriately.

Word Bank

faithful
Fourth
families
Sixth
honor

B Check Understanding **Write a definition for each of the following terms.**

6. Obey:
to do things or act in ways that are requested by those in authority or to follow rules and laws

7. Vows:
solemn promises that are made to or before God

8. Modesty:
the Cardinal Virtue that helps people dress, talk, and move in appropriate ways

9. Adultery:
being unfaithful to vows of marriage

10. Faithful:
keeping the promises you make

Go to **aliveinchrist.osv.com** for an interactive review.

198 Chapter 13 Review

Chapter Review

Use Catechist Quick Reviews to highlight lesson concepts.

A **Work with Words**
Have the children complete each sentence with the correct word from the Word Bank.

B **Check Understanding**
Have the children write a definition for each of the words.

Go to **aliveinchrist.osv.com** to prepare customized and downloadable assessments, send eAssessments, and assign interactive reviews.

Family Love **197–198**

KEY CONCEPT

All human life is sacred because it comes from God. The Fifth Commandment forbids anything that takes a human life.

DOCTRINAL CONTENT

- Life comes from God. Every human life is sacred from the moment of conception until the time of natural death. (CCC, 2258)

- All actions that respect and protect life uphold the Fifth Commandment. (CCC, 2302)

- Actions that deliberately harm human life, including that of the unborn, the sick, and elderly, are grave sins. (CCC, 2268–2269)

- The Fifth Commandment calls us to respect and take care of our bodies. (CCC, 2288)

TASKS OF CATECHESIS

Helping children grow in a faith that is "known, celebrated, lived, and expressed in prayer" (NDC, 20).

This chapter focuses on the following tasks of catechesis:

- Moral Formation
- Education for Communal Life

Catechist Background

 "But I say to you, whoever is angry with his brother will be liable to judgment...." Matthew 5:22a

➤ **Reflect** What helps you when someone makes you really mad?

You have a choice to make regarding life. You can cooperate with God in creating, sustaining, and protecting life, or you can choose to harm life. Your mandate to protect life stems from the fact that all life is a gift from God. Humans are the stewards, not the owners, of life.

Respect for human life is a broad category that includes society's approach to those who are unborn, elderly, ill, poor, or marginalized. Abortion, homicide, euthanasia, suicide, war, and other life-and-death concerns are grave matters that must be seen in the light of faith and the Ten Commandments.

The Church has many profound teachings that challenge the faithful on issues related to life. Catholics are called to form their consciences and take actions that promote respect for human life and dignity. The use of force is to be the last resort in any situation. And certainly violence against those who are innocent and defenseless (as in abortion) is never acceptable.

➤ **Reflect** How do you show respect for life?

Catechist's Prayer

 O Creator, with tenderness, you loved me into being. With strong arms, you protect me. Thank you for the gift of my life. Amen.

Lesson Plan

Objectives	Process	Materials
Invite, 10 minutes		
Respect Life Page 199	◎ **Psalm 36:10** Pray the opening prayer. ◉ **Matthew 5:21–22** Reflect prayerfully on the Word. • Discuss What Do You Wonder questions.	◉ **Optional Activity** Chapter Story: "A Change of Heart"
Discover, 35 minutes		
All Human Life Is Sacred Pages 200–201 • Deepen their awareness of human life as sacred and a gift from God from the moment of conception until the time of natural death • Recognize that all actions that respect and protect life uphold the Fifth Commandment	• **Catholic Faith Words** sacred • Read about Blessed Margaret of Castello. ☆ Highlight how Blessed Margaret showed respect for others. ◉ **Deuteronomy 30:19–20** Proclaim "The Choice." • Explain why life is sacred. • **Share Your Faith Activity** Identify how to follow the Fifth Commandment.	☐ pencils ☐ index cards ☐ highlighter markers
Protect and Respect Pages 202–203 • Identify actions that deliberately harm human life, including that of the unborn, the sick, and elderly, as grave sins • Relate the Fifth Commandment to respect and care for our bodies	• **Catholic Faith Words** murder • Identify acts that harm human life. • Explain that anger, hatred, and revenge are sinful if uncontrolled. ◉ **Matthew 5:43–45** Proclaim "Love of Enemies." • **Connect Your Faith Activity** Fill in the missing letters and choose one life-giving action to practice.	☐ pencils ☐ index cards • **Optional Activity** Respect Your Body ☐ Activity Master 14 (Page 199E)
Live, 15 minutes		
Our Catholic Life Pages 204–205	• Explain that there are many concrete ways to follow the Fifth Commandment. ☆ Match the example with the correct sentence ending. • **People of Faith** Learn about Saint Gianna Molla. • **Live Your Faith Activity** Write a note.	☐ pencils ☐ crayons or markers
Celebration of the Word Page 206	• Select three readers. ▶ Rehearse "Christ, Our Light." • Follow the order of prayer.	◉ Download "Christ, Our Light."

Family + Faith Page 207

Point out that the Catholic Families page provides chapter highlights, information on how fourth graders understand faith concepts, and family prayer.

Chapter Review Page 208

◉ **aliveinchrist.osv.com**
• Customize and Download Assessments
• Email Links to eAssessments
• Interactive Student Reviews

ONLINE RESOURCES

 Go to **aliveinchrist.osv.com**

You will find:

- Interactive lesson planning with web specific content and additional activities
- Step by step lesson instruction from printed Catechist Edition for integrated lesson planning
- Custom-built assessments to download and eAssessment links
- Interactive reviews that provide scores and the option to review answers
- Sunday readings with background and questions of the week

 Go to **osvparish.com**

You will find:

- Ask the Experts Q and A
- General Catechist Helps
- Community Connections and Blogs

Sharing the Message with Fourth Graders

Respect for Life Respect for human life is foundational to Catholic teaching. Much discussion on this principle, both within the Church and in the public square, focuses on issues such as abortion and the death penalty. Fourth graders might not yet be ready to confront these issues head on, due to their graphic nature, but respect for human life is also a broader principle that has implications in the everyday lives for children this age. Is there a child who is teased because he or she looks different? Are there times when children feel tempted to hit someone else out of anger? These questions are also relevant to respect for life.

Teaching Tip: Watch for, and set limits on, comments and actions that are not respectful of others. Talk about how respect for the life and dignity of the human person is one of the most important principles of Catholic teaching.

How Fourth Graders Understand

- Fourth graders are looking for role models. Tell them about people who show respect for life and who love justice.
- Fourth graders do not always want to compete. Use cooperative games and projects with your group.
- Help fourth graders understand that anger, hatred, and fighting are ways that people fail to show respect for life.

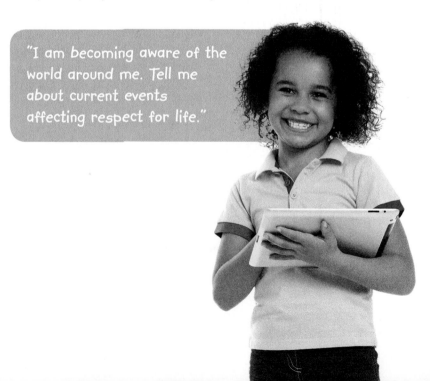

"I am becoming aware of the world around me. Tell me about current events affecting respect for life."

Chapter Connections

Chapter Story

Invite

"A Change of Heart"

Use this story to expand the chapter introduction.

- The children will relate the story to their own lives, reflecting on their respect for the lives of others.
- Connect respecting the lives of others to making a choice to respect life.

 Go to **aliveinchrist.osv.com** Lesson Planning section for this story.

NCEA IFG: ACRE Edition

Discover

Moral Formation

- Objective: To be knowledgeable about the teachings of Jesus and the Church as the basis of Christian morality and to understand Catholic Social Teaching

Communal Life

- Objectives: To know the origin, mission, structure, and communal nature of the Church; to know the rights and responsibilities of the Christian faithful

Catholic Social Teaching

Live

 Use one of these features to introduce a principle and engage the children with an activity.

- Life and Dignity of the Human Person, Pages 290–291
- Option for the Poor and Vulnerable, Pages 296–297

Music Options

 Use one or more of the following songs to enhance catechetical learning or for prayer.

- "Christ, Our Light," Live prayer, Page 206
- "My Ten Commandments," Invite, Page 199
- "God's Good Rules," Discover, Page 201
- "Loving Others," Discover, Page 203

LECTIONARY CONNECTION

 Chapter 14 highlights Lectionary-connected themes such as respect for life, the Ten Commandments, and Jesus' Passion. If your parish aligns its curriculum to the liturgical year, you could use this chapter in connection with the following Sundays.

Year A

Fifth Sunday of Lent—sanctity of life

Palm Sunday of the Passion of the Lord—Fifth Commandment

Thirtieth Sunday in Ordinary Time—respect life

Year B

Palm Sunday of the Passion of the Lord—Jesus' Passion

Sixth Sunday of Easter—love one another

Thirty-third Sunday in Ordinary Time—Resurrection

Year C

Palm Sunday of the Passion of the Lord—Jesus' Passion

Twenty-sixth Sunday in Ordinary Time—Ten Commandments

 Go to **aliveinchrist.osv.com** for a complete correlation ordered by the Sundays of the year and suggestions for how to integrate the Scripture readings into chapter lessons.

Name _____ Date _____

Respect Your Body

Think about the things that can harm your body. Draw a symbol for each of the following items, and then draw and color the barred circle "No" symbol over each drawing. Next, write a personal pledge saying what you will do to show respect for your body.

Junk food

Smoking

Not using safety equipment

Fighting

Staying up too late

Alcohol

I will respect my body by

_____

_____

_____

Signed _____

Respect Life

 Let Us Pray

Leader: God, we thank you for the precious gift of life.

"For with you is the fountain of life,
and in your light we see light." Psalm 36:10

All: Brighten our lives with a great love of life and the courage to cherish and protect it. Amen.

 Scripture

"You have heard that it was said to your ancestors, 'You shall not kill; and whoever kills will have to answer for his actions.' But I say to you, whoever is angry with his brother will have to answer for his actions, and whoever says anything mean will have to answer for his words." Based on Matthew 5:21–22

© Our Sunday Visitor

? What Do You Wonder?

- If someone makes you mad, what should you do?
- Is it okay to be mean to someone who was mean to you first?

199

Optional Activity

Chapter Story: "A Change of Heart" *Verbal/Linguistic*

Use this story after the opening prayer, before explaining that we are called to respect human life.

- Read aloud the story.
- Ask the children what the term *merchant of death* means. Nobel's invention, dynamite, killed many people.
- *Ask:* If your death notice were accidentally written today, what could it say about your respect for the lives of others?

 Go to **aliveinchrist.osv.com** for Chapter Story.

 Invite

 Let Us Pray

Invite the children to gather in the prayer space and make the Sign of the Cross. Choose one child to be the leader and one to read aloud the Psalm verse from a Bible.

Have the children move out of the prayer space and back to their seats.

Say: As Catholics, we are called to respect life—all life. Jesus taught us about the precious gift of life.

Scripture

Guide the children through the process of Scripture reflection.

- Invite them to close their eyes, be still and open their minds and hearts to what God is saying to them in this passage.
- Proclaim the Scripture.
- Maintain several moments of silence.
- *Ask:* What did you hear God say to you today?
- Invite volunteers to share.

What Do You Wonder?

Say: Words are so important that they can "kill" someone's spirit, hurt their feelings. Teasing and bullying are just some of the ways that show disrespect for life.

Invite the children to respond to the questions. Ask what else they might wonder about respecting human life or being angry.

 Music Option: Have the children sing "My Ten Commandments," downloaded from **aliveinchrist.osv.com**.

Objectives

- Deepen their awareness of human life as sacred and a gift from God from the moment of conception until the time of natural death
- Recognize that all actions that respect and protect life uphold the Fifth Commandment

All Human Life is Sacred

Ask: How do you respect life?

- Write the children's responses on the board or on chart paper.

Read aloud or summarize the introduction.

Blessed Margaret of Castello

- Tell the children that they will read about a woman who endured many hardships, but devoted her life to helping others.
- Ask the children why someone might spend their life helping people who are sick and dying.
- Invite volunteers to take turns reading the biography.
- ⭐ Have the children highlight how Blessed Margaret showed respect for others.
- Invite volunteers to share what they highlighted.
- Blessed Margaret of Castello treated people with respect and human dignity. Refer to page 318 in the Our Catholic Tradition reference section in the back of the Student Book to find out more about respecting the dignity of all people.

Discover

All Human Life is Sacred

How do you respect life?

Catholic Faith Words

sacred worthy of reverence and devotion

Sometimes we are unsure of people who look or talk differently than we do. And we may not know how to treat people who have illnesses or disabilities. But all people everywhere deserve respect. Here's the story of a woman who could not walk, but her life is an example for all of us.

Blessed Margaret of Castello

Blessed Margaret of Castello could not see or walk. She had a big lump on her back and twisted arms and legs. Her parents were ashamed of her, so they shut her up in a room and left her all alone. Finally, some kind women took Margaret in with them. She lived the rest of her life helping people who were sick and dying. After she died, another girl who could not walk came to her funeral and was miraculously cured! Even though Blessed Margaret had many things wrong with her, she knew that every life is important and that we all can do something to help others.

© Our Sunday Visitor

⭐ Highlight how Blessed Margaret showed respect for others.

ⓘ Catechist Background

Human Dignity

All human life is sacred and equal because it comes from God.

- Help the children develop an awareness of the factors that affect the respect a person receives from society.
- Help the children recognize that society often rewards external factors that should not influence the respect a person receives.

Choose Life

All human life is **sacred**, worthy of reverence and devotion, and all actions that respect and protect life uphold the Fifth Commandment. At the end of his life, Moses told the people to remember that God's law was life for them.

 **Scripture**

The Choice

I call heaven and earth today to witness against you: I have set before you life and death, the blessing and the curse. Choose life, then, that you and your descendants may live, by loving the LORD, your God, obeying his voice, and holding fast to him. For that will mean life for you . . . *Deuteronomy 30:19–20*

God's laws show the path to life and happiness. The Fifth Commandment reminds us of the fundamental respect for life that is owed to every person. Every person is made in God's image and likeness, therefore every human life is sacred from the moment of conception until the time of death.

Share Your Faith

Reflect Think about what the Fifth Commandment tells you. Unscramble the words below to fill in the sentence about what everyone deserves.

tcpesre	feil	dreasc

Every human _____ life _____

is _____ sacred _____ , and deserves

_____ respect _____ .

Share Then, talk with a partner about how you can follow the Fifth Commandment.

201

 Songs of Scripture

That You May Live

Help the children understand what it means to "heed his voice."

- Have each child draw a simple outline of an ear shape and cut it out.
- Discuss the ways they can listen for God's voice. Bible, prayer, in a trusted adult, the laws of the Church
- Direct them to write one way they can listen for God's voice on the ear.

 Use *Songs of Scripture*, Grades 4–6 CD, Track 9

Choose Life

Introduce this part of the lesson by reading aloud the paragraph.

- Invite a volunteer to read aloud the definition of *sacred*.
- Have the children make a vocabulary card for *sacred*.

 Scripture

Ask a volunteer to stand and proclaim "The Choice."

- *Ask:* What life-and-death decisions must people make daily? Possible responses: to cross a street safely, to follow safety rules at home

Have the children read silently the last paragraph to learn about why life is sacred.

 Music Option: Have the children sing, "God's Good Rules," downloaded from **aliveinchrist.osv.com**.

Activity

Read aloud the directions for the Share Your Faith activity.

- Have the children work independently to complete the activity.
- Then have the children talk with a partner about how they can follow the Fifth Commandment.

Quick Review

The Fifth Commandment says to respect and protect all human life. Human life is sacred because it comes from God.

Objectives

- Identify actions that deliberately harm human life, including that of the unborn, the sick, and elderly, as grave sins
- Relate the Fifth Commandment to respect and care for our bodies

Protect and Respect

Ask: How do you keep the Fifth Commandment?

- Write the children's responses on the board or on chart paper.

Have the children read the three paragraphs.

- Discuss the meaning of the word *murder*.
- Have the children make a vocabulary card for *murder*.

Respect for the Body

Write the word *life* on the board or on chart paper and circle it.

- Outside the circle write *smoking, drinking alcohol, not exercising,* and *eating junk food*. Explain that the words outside the circle are actions that harm life.
- Invite the children to name other actions that harm life. Add those to the chart.

Point out the photo.

- *Ask:* How are these children keeping the Fifth Commandment?

Protect and Respect

How do you keep the Fifth Commandment?

All human life is sacred, including the life of the unborn and the elderly. The life of an unborn child is fragile, and it is deserving of the greatest respect and care. The intentional ending of the life of an unborn child is a grave sin.

The taking of one's own life is suicide. It is contrary to God's gift of life and love. However, one's responsibility may be lessened by certain factors. **Murder**, the intentional killing of an innocent person, is seriously sinful. To kill in self-defense, however, is justified, if it is the only way to protect one's own life.

The Catholic Church teaches that the death penalty, or capital punishment, is almost always wrong. Alternatives, such as life in prison without parole, are preferred.

Respect for the Body

The Church teaches that your body and soul are united. You are a temple in which God's Spirit dwells. The Fifth Commandment teaches you to respect your body and those of others. Eating healthy foods and exercising are important to protect your life and health. At your age, using alcohol is an offense against the Fifth Commandment. The use of tobacco and illegal drugs is harmful to the body. Tempting or encouraging others to disrespect the gift of life is wrong, too.

> **Catholic Faith Words**
>
> **murder** the deliberate killing of another person when the killing is not in self-defense

© Our Sunday Visitor

202   Chapter 14

Optional Activity

Activity Master 14: Respect Your Body

Distribute copies of the activity found on catechist page 199E.

- This activity will remind the children not to harm their bodies.
- As an alternative, you may wish to send this activity home with the children.

Avoid Anger

Jesus said that anger can be sinful if it is not controlled. Anger can harden into hatred and lead to revenge, or getting back at someone, or to violence.

It can be difficult to show love and respect for those who bully or treat you unfairly. Jesus calls you to love in this way.

Scripture

Love of Enemies

"You have heard that it was said, 'You shall love your neighbor and hate your enemy.' But I say to you, love your enemies, and pray for those who persecute you, that you may be children of your heavenly Father, for he makes his sun rise on the bad and the good, and causes rain to fall on the just and the unjust." Matthew 5:43–45

→ What did Jesus mean when he said that God makes his sun rise on the bad and the good?

Connect Your Faith

Choose Life Fill in the missing letters in these examples of life-giving actions.

Protect unborn c [h] [i] [l] [d] r [e] n.

Set a [g] [o] [o] [d] example for others.

Forgive your e [n] e [m] ies.

Think of one life-giving action that you will practice today.

203

Scripture Background

Matthew 5:43–45

This passage from the Gospel according to Matthew is taken from the Sermon on the Mount, in which Jesus preaches to his disciples on how to live an ethical life.

- Jesus taught that laws such as "love your enemies" cannot be achieved by humans alone but through the grace of God.
- Almost every section of this sermon is repeated elsewhere in the New Testament.

Avoid Anger

Tell the children to read these two paragraphs to learn how the Fifth Commandment relates to anger, hatred and revenge.

Scripture

Invite a child to proclaim "Love of Enemies."

Discuss the question at the end of the Scripture story.

- Invite the children to share times when they have been able to avoid hatred or revenge, even when they were provoked.
- Remind the children that forgiveness is a way to show love to others, even to enemies.

Activity

Read aloud the directions for the Connect Your Faith activity.

- Have the children fill in the missing letters.
- Provide time for the children to circle one life-giving action they will practice.

▶ Music Option: Have the children sing, "Loving Others," downloaded from **aliveinchrist.osv.com**.

Quick Review

The Fifth Commandment forbids harm to life because all human life is sacred. This means that humans must treat their bodies with respect.

© Our Sunday Visitor

Live

Our Catholic Life

Ask: How can you act in the spirit of the Fifth Commandment?

- Write the children's responses on the board or on chart paper.

Write the Fifth Commandment on the board or on chart paper.

- Discuss why this Commandment might be difficult to keep.
- Invite a volunteer to read aloud the paragraph.

Ways to Respect Life

⭐ Have the children match the examples on the left with the correct sentence ending on the right.

- When everyone has finished, review the answers with the group.

⭐ Have the children draw a star next to something they have done this week to follow the Fifth Commandment.

- Invite volunteers to share what they have done this week to follow the Fifth Commandment.

Our Catholic Life

1. Match the examples with the correct sentence ending.
2. Draw a star next to something you've done this week to follow the Fifth Commandment.

How can you act in the spirit of the Fifth Commandment?

The Fifth Commandment may seem easy to follow. But as you have read, there is more to this Commandment than not killing. The Fifth Commandment also asks that you take care of and respect yourself and others.

Ways to Respect Life

Respect life	but learn to compromise.
Do not fight	by learning to relax your body or by talking to someone you trust.
Make peace	by treating younger children and babies with patience and kindness.
Don't bully	by getting to know someone who seems different.
Avoid risks	that might lead you or others to be hurt.
Control your anger	with those who have hurt you.
Appreciate uniqueness	from those whom you have hurt.
Seek forgiveness	or make fun of others.

© Our Sunday Visitor

🧍 Reaching All Learners

Kinesthetic and Interpersonal Learners

To benefit children who learn well by watching and interacting with others, consider having the children act out the situations on this page.

- Arrange the children into small groups, and assign one or two items to each group.
- Have the children act out each situation.
- Challenge the rest of the group to guess which suggestion is being demonstrated.

People of Faith

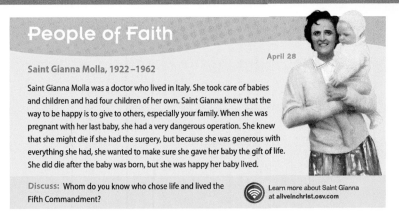

Saint Gianna Molla, 1922–1962

April 28

Saint Gianna Molla was a doctor who lived in Italy. She took care of babies and children and had four children of her own. Saint Gianna knew that the way to be happy is to give to others, especially your family. When she was pregnant with her last baby, she had a very dangerous operation. She knew that she might die if she had the surgery, but because she was generous with everything she had, she wanted to make sure she gave her baby the gift of life. She did die after the baby was born, but she was happy her baby lived.

Discuss: Whom do you know who chose life and lived the Fifth Commandment?

 Learn more about Saint Gianna at **aliveinchrist.osv.com**

Live Your Faith

Write a note to someone you have treated unfairly. In your note, explain one thing you will or would do differently because of what you've learned this week.

Catholic Social Teaching

Chapter Connections

To integrate Catholic Social Teaching into your lesson, choose one of the following features: Life and Dignity of the Human Person, pages 290–291; or Option for the Poor and Vulnerable, pages 296–297.

- Start the Live step of the process by talking about Saint Gianna Molla on page 205. Then move directly to the Catholic Social Teaching feature.
- Or, to expand the lesson, complete both pages 204 and 205, then move to the Catholic Social Teaching feature.
- Return to Chapter 14 for the prayer on page 206.

People of Faith

Tell the children about Saint Gianna Molla.

- Invite a volunteer to read aloud the People of Faith story.
- Explain that Saint Gianna Molla is a patron Saint for mothers, physicians, and unborn children.
- She is the namesake of the Gianna Center in New York City. It is the first pro-life healthcare center for women in New York.
- Saint Gianna is known for saying, "The secret of happiness is to live moment by moment and to thank God for all that he, in his goodness, sends to us day after day."
- *Ask:* Whom do you know who chose life and lives the Fifth Commandment?

 Encourage the children to go to **aliveinchrist.osv.com** at home to learn more about Saint Gianna Molla.

Activity

Discuss how a skill such as asking for forgiveness or giving forgiveness can be acquired. Point out that everyone needs practice with both skills.

- Read aloud the directions for the activity, and then ask each child to think quietly about how he or she may have wronged another person.
- Have the children write their note as directed.
- Read and comment on the children's notes privately if they wish to share them. Because of the nature of the activity, avoid sharing with the whole group.

Live

 Let Us Pray

Celebration of the Word

Tell the children that they will ask for help in obeying the Fifth Commandment.

Prepare

Choose three readers for the prayer.

- Teach the children their responses. You might want to write them on the board or on chart paper.

 Rehearse "Christ, Our Light," downloaded from **aliveinchrist.osv.com**.

Gather

Invite the children to process to the prayer space. Have the readers bring their books.

- Direct the children to ready their minds and hearts for prayer.

Pray

Follow the order of prayer on the student page.

- *Leader's concluding prayer:* Lord, we know that protecting life is within our power. Help us find the strength to do what is right.

 Conclude by singing together "Christ, Our Light."

 Live

 Let Us Pray

Celebration of the Word

Gather and begin with the Sign of the Cross.

Reader 1: A reading from the First Letter of Peter.

Read 1 Peter 3:9–12.

The word of the Lord.

All: Thanks be to God.

Reader 2: When we are given the choice to walk away or to stay and fight,

All: Help us choose your way, O Lord.

Reader 3: When we are given the chance to help people with illnesses or disabilities or an elderly person,

All: Help us choose your way, O Lord.

Leader: Let us pray.

Bow your heads as the leader prays.

All: Amen.

 Sing "Christ, Our Light"

Christ, our Light, you taught us to love.
Christ, our Light, you're always with us.
Together we learn, together we grow,
together we walk in your way.

© 2002, John Burland. All rights reserved.

206 Chapter 14

 Liturgy Link

Reflection

Ask the children to close their eyes. In a soft voice, encourage them to relax.

- Have the children reflect on questions about showing respect for life. You can use discussion questions from this chapter.

- Pause so that the children can think about how these questions apply to their lives.

Go to **aliveinchrist.osv.com** for Sunday readings, Scripture background, questions of the week, and seasonal resources.

FAMILY+FAITH
LIVING AND LEARNING TOGETHER

YOUR CHILD LEARNED >>>
This chapter is about respecting and protecting human life at all stages because life is a gift from God.

Scripture
 Read **Matthew 5:21–22** to find out what Jesus teaches us about respecting one another.

Catholics Believe
• All human life is sacred because it comes from God.
• The Fifth Commandment forbids anything that takes a human life.

To learn more, go to the *Catechism of the Catholic Church #2258, 2268–2269* at **usccb.org.**

People of Faith
This week, your child learned about Saint Gianna Molla, who was willing to sacrifice her life for that of her unborn daughter.

CHILDREN AT THIS AGE >>>
How They Understand Respect for Life Respect for human life is foundational to Catholic teaching. Much discussion on this principle, both within the Church and in the public square, focuses on issues such as abortion and the death penalty. Fourth-graders might not yet be ready to confront these issues head on, due to their graphic nature, but respect for human life is also a broader principle that has implications in the everyday lives of children this age. Is there a child who is teased because he or she looks different? Are there times when children feel tempted to hit someone else out of anger? These questions are also relevant to respect for life.

CONSIDER THIS >>>
How does your family acknowledge and celebrate that each person's life is a gift from God?

Family life is the perfect setting to celebrate each person's uniqueness. It is in the heart of family that we experience and appreciate that God creates each of us with imagination and love. As Catholics, we know that "God's creative action is present to every human life and is thus the source of its sacred value.... The Fifth Commandment calls us to foster the physical, spiritual, emotional, and social well-being of self and others" (*USCCA*, p. 389).

LET'S TALK >>>
• Ask your child to talk about how anger, teasing, and bullying relate to the Fifth Commandment.
• With your child, name ways we show respect for others and protect others and ourselves, including our bodies.

LET'S PRAY >>>
Saint Gianna Molla, pray for us that we may be faithful to God's love and always choose the path of life and hope. Amen.

For a multimedia glossary of Catholic Faith Words, Sunday readings, seasonal and Saint resources, and chapter activities go to **aliveinchrist.osv.com.**

Alive in Christ, Grade 4 Chapter 14 **207**

Family + Faith

Distribute the page to the children or parents/adult family members. Point out the chapter highlights, insights on how fourth graders understand concepts, the opportunity for the adults to reflect on their own experience and faith journey, and the family prayer.

Chapter 14 Review

(A) **Work with Words** Complete the following statements.

1. The Fifth Commandment says this: <u>You shall not kill.</u>

2. Every human life is a gift from <u>God</u>

3. One serious sin against the Fifth Commandment is <u>Possible respon</u>ses: <u>murder, suicide, taking the life of an unborn child</u>.

4. All human life is <u>sacred</u>

5. Hatred can lead to <u>revenge or violence</u>

(B) **Check Understanding** Complete each sentence with the correct word from the Word Bank.

6. One way to live the Fifth Commandment is to make <u>peace</u>.

7. Jesus said to love everyone, even your <u>enemies</u>.

8. Tempting or encouraging others to disrespect the gift of life is <u>wrong</u>.

9. Jesus explained that uncontrolled <u>anger</u> is against the Fifth Commandment.

10. Actions that <u>respect</u> and protect life uphold the Fifth Commandment.

Word Bank
peace
anger
wrong
enemies
respect

 Go to **aliveinchrist.osv.com** for an interactive review.

208 Chapter 14 Review

Chapter Review

Use Catechist Quick Reviews to highlight lesson concepts.

(A) **Work with Words**
Have the children complete the sentences.

(B) **Check Understanding**
Have the children complete each sentence with the correct word from the Word Bank.

 Go to **aliveinchrist.osv.com** to prepare customized and downloadable assessments, send eAssessments, and assign interactive reviews.

Respect Life **207–208**

KEY CONCEPT

Because God is truth, his people are called to live in the truth. The Eighth Commandment forbids lying.

DOCTRINAL CONTENT

- A martyr is a person who gives up his or her life to witness to the truth of Christ and the faith. (CCC, 2473)

- God is the source of all truth. His Word and his law call people to live in the truth. (CCC, 2465)

- The Eighth Commandment calls us to be honest in words and actions and forbids lying, gossip, and any acts against the truth. (CCC, 2464)

- Reparation is an action taken to repair the damage done from sin. (CCC, 2487)

TASKS OF CATECHESIS

Helping children grow in a faith that is "known, celebrated, lived, and expressed in prayer" (NDC, 20).

This chapter focuses on the following tasks of catechesis:

- Moral Formation
- Education for Communal Life

Catechist Background

 "Do not take a false oath, but make good to the Lord all that you vow.... Let your 'Yes' mean 'Yes,' and your 'No' mean 'No.'"
Matthew 5:33, 37

➜ **Reflect** Is it ever okay to not tell the truth?

Truth is central to your relationship with God. The Bible often refers to truth: The truth will set you free (John 8:32); Jesus calls himself "the truth" (John 14:6); Christians are called to follow the Spirit of truth (John 16:13). To become one with Jesus, you must speak the truth.

The benefits of candor and sincerity are many. Truth builds community by creating trust. It nurtures love by strengthening communication and respect. The covenant between God and humans, reflected in human relationships, depends on the constancy of truth.

Lying is more than not telling the truth. People bear false witness both by what they say and do and by what they refuse to say and do. Humans witness to falsehood whenever they are not witnessing to the truth, that is, to God.

Lying destroys reputations, relationships, and lives. Gossip and slander are all too common forms of this sin. Certainly there are levels of lies; a false compliment is clearly not the same as perjury. Still, all lying undercuts trust. False witness aimed at deliberately leading another into error or danger is especially grave. It tarnishes the honor of both the hearer and the liar and steps far away from the Gospel call to speak the truth.

➜ **Reflect** How does your life show that you respect truth?

Catechist's Prayer

Dear God, there is no greater joy than to walk in your ways. In your words and actions I find truth. Lead me to follow you and find freedom for my spirit and purpose in my life. Amen.

Lesson Plan

Objectives	Process	Materials
Invite, 10 minutes		
Live in the Truth Page 209	◯ **Psalm 86:11** Pray the opening prayer. 📖 **Based on Matthew 5:33, 37** Reflect prayerfully on the Word. • Discuss What Do You Wonder questions.	🔊 **Optional Activity** Chapter Story: "It's the Truth!"
Discover, 35 minutes		
Witness to the Truth Pages 210–211 • Define a martyr as a person who gives up his or her life to witness to the truth of Christ and the faith	• **Catholic Faith Words** martyr • Explain that Saint Thomas More had a choice to make. • Read "Saint Thomas More" and discuss the questions. • Explain that many Saints are martyrs. • **Share Your Faith Activity** Name why it is important to tell the truth.	☐ pencils ☐ index cards • **Optional Activity** Famous Martyrs ☐ Saint pictures ☐ construction paper ☐ glue
The Eighth Commandment Pages 212–213 • Recognize God as the source of all truth. His Word and his law call people to live in the truth • Identify the Eighth Commandment as calling us to be honest in words and actions and forbidding lying, gossip, and any acts against the truth • Define reparation as an action taken to repair the damage done from sin	• **Catholic Faith Words** reparation, prudence • Explain what the Eighth Commandment forbids. 📖 **John 8:31–32, 14:6** Proclaim "The Truth Will Set You Free." • **Connect Your Faith Activity** Identify scenarios that show living in the truth.	☐ pencils ☐ index cards • **Optional Activity** Gossip and Truth ☐ Activity Master 15 (Page 209E)
Live, 15 minutes		
Our Catholic Life Pages 214–215	• Explain that living the Eighth Commandment can be difficult. ☆ Use the words to complete the sentences. • **People of Faith** Learn about Saint Joan of Arc. • **Live Your Faith Activity** Design a poster.	☐ pencils ☐ crayons or markers
Prayer to the Holy Spirit Page 216	• Choose a leader. ▶ Rehearse "Spirit, Come Down." • Follow the order of prayer.	🔊 Download "Spirit, Come Down."

Family + Faith Page 217

Point out that the Catholic Families page provides chapter highlights, information on how fourth graders understand faith concepts, and family prayer.

Chapter Review Page 218

🔊 aliveinchrist.osv.com
- Customize and Download Assessments
- Email Links to eAssessments
- Interactive Student Reviews

ONLINE RESOURCES

 Go to **aliveinchrist.osv.com**

You will find:

- Interactive lesson planning with web specific content and additional activities
- Step by step lesson instruction from printed Catechist Edition for integrated lesson planning
- Custom-built assessments to download and eAssessment links
- Interactive reviews that provide scores and the option to review answers
- Sunday readings with background and questions of the week

 Go to **osvparish.com**

You will find:

- Ask the Experts Q and A
- General Catechist Helps
- Community Connections and Blogs

Sharing the Message with Fourth Graders

Telling the Truth Fourth graders are concrete thinkers who understand cause and effect. Unlike preschoolers, they know that the truth doesn't change just because we want it to. They also know that adults don't know everything, and that sometimes we can be fooled. It's important for them to see the connection between truth, trust, and relationship. We cannot really be close to people if we tell them lies, no matter how small the lies, because relationship implies trust.

Teaching Tip: Be sure to point out that we can also lie by not telling the whole truth. While it is neither prudent nor polite to always say everything we think, hiding the truth when it needs to be told is also sinful.

How Fourth Graders Understand

- Fourth graders will follow models of truthfulness. Be sure that you are always truthful with them.
- Help fourth graders feel comfortable telling the truth by creating an environment that is open, positive, and fair.
- Fourth graders need to know what you expect of them when they are working on a project. Be sure to give them clear directions.

"I know that mean words can hurt. Teach me how to affirm others."

Chapter Connections

Chapter Story

Invite

"It's the Truth!"

Use this story to expand the chapter introduction.

- The children will relate the story to their own lives, reflecting on the importance of telling the truth.
- Connect being dishonest to leading to trouble.

 Go to **aliveinchrist.osv.com** Lesson Planning section for this story.

NCEA IFG: ACRE Edition
Discover

Moral Formation

- Objective: To be knowledgeable about the teachings of Jesus and the Church as the basis of Christian morality and to understand Catholic Social Teaching

Communal Life

- Objectives: To know the origin, mission, structure, and communal nature of the Church; to know the rights and responsibilities of the Christian faithful

Catholic Social Teaching
Live

 Use one of these features to introduce a principle and engage the children with an activity.

- Rights and Responsibilities of the Human Person, Pages 294–295
- Solidarity of the Human Family, Pages 300–301

Music Options

 Use one or more of the following songs to enhance catechetical learning or for prayer.

- "Spirit, Come Down," Live Prayer, Page 216
- "C-H-O-I-C-E-S," Discover, Page 211
- "Choices," Discover, Page 211
- Jesus Is the Word," Discover, Page 213

LECTIONARY CONNECTION

 Chapter 15 highlights Lectionary-connected themes such as truth, sin, and conscience. If your parish aligns its curriculum to the liturgical year, you could use this chapter in connection with the following Sundays.

Year A

Third Sunday of Lent—Eighth Commandment

Fourth Sunday of Lent—live in the light

Thirty-first Sunday in Ordinary Time—sincerity and hypocrisy

Year B

The Most Holy Trinity—children of God

Twenty-sixth Sunday in Ordinary Time—sin

Our Lord Jesus Christ, King of the Universe—truth

Year C

First Sunday of Lent—temptation

Third Sunday of Lent—choices

Twenty-ninth Sunday in Ordinary Time—conscience

Go to **aliveinchrist.osv.com** for a complete correlation ordered by the Sundays of the year and suggestions for how to integrate the Scripture readings into chapter lessons.

Name _____   Date _____

Gossip and Truth

Gossip is one of the ways that people slip into habits that don't lead to truthful lives. Gossip can hurt people in many ways. Truth is the way to defeat gossip.

Design a comic strip that shows the terrible Gossip Monster and the harm it does. Draw a character that represents Truth fighting the monster.

The Gossip Monster attacks!

Who is hurt by the Gossip Monster?

Truth to the rescue!

The Gossip Monster is defeated!

What would you like to say to the Gossip Monster?

_____

How can you help Truth fight the Gossip Monster?

_____

 CHAPTER **15**

Live in the Truth

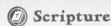 **Let Us Pray**

Leader: Your words, O Lord, are precious and true.

"Teach me, LORD, your way
that I may walk in your truth." Psalm 86:11

All: May our words echo yours, O Lord, so that your
truth may be told. Amen.

Scripture

"You have heard that it was said to those who came before
you, 'Do not tell lies to each other, but make good to the Lord all
that you promise.' Let your 'Yes' mean 'Yes,' and your 'No' mean
'No.'" Based on Matthew 5:33, 37

© Our Sunday Visitor

? What Do You Wonder?

- Is it okay not to tell the truth so you
don't hurt someone's feelings?
- Is lying really all that bad?

Live in the Truth **209**

Optional Activity

Chapter Story: "It's the Truth!" *Verbal/Linguistic*

Use this story after the opening prayer, before explaining that it is
important to tell the truth.

- Read the story aloud as the children follow along.
- Invite the children to write a saying about the importance of
telling the truth.
- *Ask:* Why do people sometimes not tell the truth?
- Transition back to the lesson instruction.

 Go to **aliveinchrist.osv.com** for Chapter Story.

Let Us Pray

Invite the children to gather in the
prayer space and make the Sign of
the Cross. Choose a child to read
aloud the Psalm verse from a Bible.
Prompt the children's response.

Have the children move out of the
prayer space and back to their seats.

Explain that it is important for us to
tell the truth.

Say: Sometimes telling the truth
feels hard to do. God's Word offers
us some guidance about speaking
the truth.

Scripture

Guide the children through the
process of Scripture reflection.

- Invite them to close their eyes, be
still and open their minds and
hearts to what God is saying to
them in this passage.
- Proclaim the Scripture.
- Maintain several moments of
silence.
- *Ask:* What did you hear God say
to you today?
- Invite volunteers to share.

What Do You Wonder?

Say: Being a witness for Jesus
requires us to speak the truth. When
you say, "Yes," to Jesus you say, "No,"
to all the things that will take you
away from him.

Invite the children to respond to
the questions. Ask what else they
might wonder about lying and
telling the truth.

Objectives

- Define a martyr as a person who gives up his or her life to witness to the truth of Christ and the faith

Witness to the Truth

Ask: How do people show they value truth?

- Write the children's responses on the board or on chart paper.

Read aloud the introduction.

- Tell the children to listen to find out what Saint Thomas More's dilemma was.

Saint Thomas More

Show the children the location of England on a map. Explain that kings and queens were very powerful during the sixteenth century.

- Read aloud the letter.
- Ask the children to identify the two choices that Thomas More faced. to support the king and live or to support the Catholic Church and die
- *Ask:* What would you do if you were in Thomas' position?
- *Ask:* Have you ever had to decide whether to speak the truth, tell a lie, or remain silent? What happened?

Witness to the Truth

How do people show that they value truth?

Saint Thomas More, an important official in England in the sixteenth century, was imprisoned for refusing to tell a lie.

Saint Thomas More

Saint Thomas had an important decision to make. In a letter to his daughter, he discussed his dilemma.

> My dearest Meg,
>
> Your father greets you with all his affection but not much hope. The dilemma I face will not soon go away.
>
> I have been imprisoned now for some months. All I have to do to be set free is to take the Oath of Supremacy. But how can I? If I take the oath, I will be saying that Henry VIII is the supreme head of the Catholic Church in England. You know that my Catholic faith is strong, and I believe that the Pope is the true head of the Catholic Church.
>
> King Henry is angry. He is afraid that if I go against him, other people will follow my example. I am being forced to make a choice: be honest and be killed, or tell a lie and live.
>
> Pray for me.
>
> Your loving father,
> Thomas More

→ What important decision did Saint Thomas More have to make?
→ What would you do if you were in Thomas' position?

210 Chapter 15

Optional Activity

Famous Martyrs *Visual/Spatial*

Perform an Internet search, and print pictures and stories of Catholic martyrs.

- Have the children cut out the pictures and mount them on construction paper.
- Then have the children glue the appropriate story to the back of each picture.
- Share the stories in a "wall of fame" gallery.

Speak and Act the Truth

Saint Thomas More chose to remain true to his beliefs and speak the truth. As a result, the king had him killed, but the Catholic Church named him a Saint. Many Saints have suffered torture and death for the sake of their faith. A person who stays faithful to Christ and suffers and dies rather than denying the truth is called a **martyr**. Martyrs live the truth by backing up their words with actions.

You will probably not be called on to be a martyr. But every follower of Jesus is called to live in the truth. By your actions, you show your faithfulness to Jesus and the truth of his message.

Catholic Faith Words

martyr a person who gives up his or her life to witness to the truth of Christ and the faith. The word *martyr* means "witness."

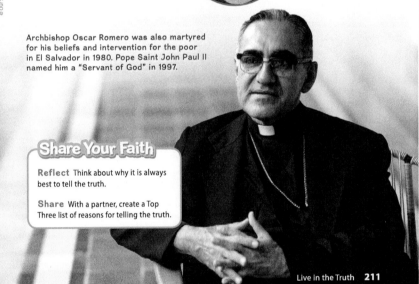

Jean Donovan was an American missionary martyr. She was killed with three other women in 1980, while working as part of a Diocesan Mission Project in El Salvador.

Archbishop Oscar Romero was also martyred for his beliefs and intervention for the poor in El Salvador in 1980. Pope Saint John Paul II named him a "Servant of God" in 1997.

Share Your Faith

Reflect Think about why it is always best to tell the truth.

Share With a partner, create a Top Three list of reasons for telling the truth.

Live in the Truth **211**

Speak and Act the Truth

Have the children read these two paragraphs to learn about people who stand up for truth.

Work with Words

Invite a volunteer to read aloud the definition of *martyr*.

- Have the children make a vocabulary card for the term *martyr*.
- Tell the children that the Church recognizes many martyrs as Saints.
- Explain that early Christians who were killed because of their beliefs are also considered martyrs. Over the centuries, many Catholics have died for their faith.
- Ask why Thomas More and others were willing to give up their lives to witness to the truth. Possible responses: They wanted to remain faithful to Christ; they knew that the truth was important.

 Music Option: Have the children sing, "C-H-O-I-C-E-S" or "Choices," downloaded from **aliveinchrist.osv.com**.

Activity

Read aloud the directions for the Share Your Faith activity.

- Have the children work with a partner to create a list of reasons for telling the truth.

Quick Review

Followers of Jesus are called to live in the truth. Martyrs are people who die for the truths of faith.

ⓘ Catechist Background

Catholic Martyrs

Many Catholic Saints have been martyrs as well.

- Maximilian Kolbe was martyred at Auschwitz, Saint Stephen was the first martyr for Christ, and Saint Charles Lwanga was the leader of the Ugandan martyrs.
- Martyrs young and old have come from all times, races, and regions of the world.

Objectives

- Recognize God as the source of all truth. His Word and his law call people to live in the truth
- Identify the Eighth Commandment as calling us to be honest in words and actions and forbidding lying, gossip, and any acts against the truth
- Define reparation as an action taken to repair the damage done from sin

The Eighth Commandment

Ask: What does the Eighth Commandment call you to do?

- Write the children's responses on the board or on chart paper.

Read aloud the text.

- Remind the children of Jesus' answer to the question: Who is my neighbor? Everyone is your neighbor.

- Point out that Jesus might say that the Eighth Commandment is "You shall not bear false witness against anyone."

Work with Words

Invite a volunteer to read aloud the definition of *reparation*.

- Have the children make a vocabulary card for the term *reparation*.

Discover

The Eighth Commandment

What does the Eighth Commandment call you to do?

God is the source of all truth. His Word and his law call people to live in the truth. The Eighth Commandment says this: You shall not bear false witness against your neighbor.

The Eighth Commandment forbids lying, or purposely not telling the truth. Lying can take many forms. If a person lies in court when under oath, he or she commits perjury, or false witness. Gossip is talking about another person behind his or her back. Gossip may or may not be a lie, but all gossip can harm the good reputation of another person.

All lies are unjust and unloving. All require **reparation**, or repair. Reparation may be as simple as an apology, or it may take more work, such as trying to help a person get back the reputation you have hurt.

➔ Why is reparation important?

Catholic Faith Words

reparation an action taken to repair the damage done from sin

prudence the Cardinal Virtue that helps us be practical and make correct decisions on what is right and good, with the help of the Holy Spirit and a well-formed conscience

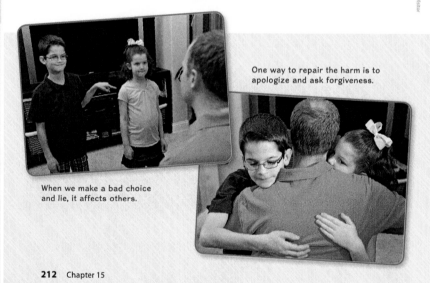

One way to repair the harm is to apologize and ask forgiveness.

When we make a bad choice and lie, it affects others.

Optional Activity

Activity Master 15: Gossip and Truth

Distribute copies of the activity found on catechist page 209E.

- Have the children design their comic strips and share them with the group.

- As an alternative, you may wish to send this activity home with the children.

Jesus Is the Truth

Living in the spirit of the Eighth Commandment is more than not lying. You must choose to act with **prudence** and make correct decisions on what is right and good. When you are truthful, you are living as a follower of Jesus, who always told the truth.

Scripture

The Truth Will Set You Free

[Jesus said] "If you remain in my word, you will truly be my disciples, and you will know the truth, and the truth will set you free. . . . I am the way and the truth and the life. No one comes to the Father except through me." John 8:31–32, 14:6

People trusted what Jesus did and said. When you are truthful, people trust you. When you promise to tell the truth, you have a special duty. Let your "yes" mean "yes" and your "no" mean "no." Telling the truth will set you free to follow Jesus and to live in love.

Connect Your Faith

Live the Truth Read the following list, and mark an X if a statement talks about living in truth and an O if it does not. For each statement marked with an O, tell one way the person could make up for his or her wrong choice.

X Juanita heard an unkind story about a classmate. She did not repeat it.

O Scott bragged falsely about how good he was at sports.

O Samantha told her parents that she was going to the library, but instead she went to the park.

X Matt discovered that his friend had shoplifted, but he did not gossip about it.

Live in the Truth **213**

© Our Sunday Visitor

Scripture Background

John 8:31–32, 14:6

John 14:6 ("I am the way and the truth and the life") is part of the Last Supper Discourses.

- As one of the last lessons Jesus gave his disciples, this message is of extreme importance.
- With his next words, Jesus specifies how he is the way and the truth and the life; "No one comes to the Father except through me."

Jesus Is the Truth

Ask the children to explain the difference between being truthful and not lying.

- Have the children read silently the paragraph to learn the difference.
- Have the children make a vocabulary card for *prudence*.

Scripture

Choose a child to proclaim "The Truth Will Set You Free."

- Discuss what Jesus meant when he said, "The truth will set you free."

Read aloud the last paragraph.

- Remind the children that having people trust you is a good consequence of being truthful.

Music Option: Have the children sing, "Jesus Is the Word," downloaded from **aliveinchrist.osv.com**.

Activity

Read aloud the directions for the Share Your Faith activity.

- After the children have marked their responses, ask them to gesture "thumbs up" if the statement describes living the truth and "thumbs down" if it does not.
- Discuss as a group ways to make the wrong choices right.

Quick Review

The Eighth Commandment forbids lying. You must make up for the harm done by any lies you tell. Jesus said, "The truth will set you free."

Live in the Truth **213**

Our Catholic Life

Ask: How can you live in the spirit of the Eighth Commandment?

- Write the children's responses on the board or on chart paper.

Summarize the first paragraph of text.

- Discuss how telling what seems to be a simple lie may lead to a complicated situation.

Invite volunteers to read the second and third paragraphs.

- *Ask:* Why is it important to tell the truth? Possible responses: People do not trust liars, lying is against God's law, lying can hurt others

Choosing Truth

Point out the activity.

⭐ Have the children use the words in the left column to complete the sentences on the right.

- Invite volunteers to read aloud each completed statement.

- *Ask:* Has anyone ever been dishonest with you? How did it make you feel?

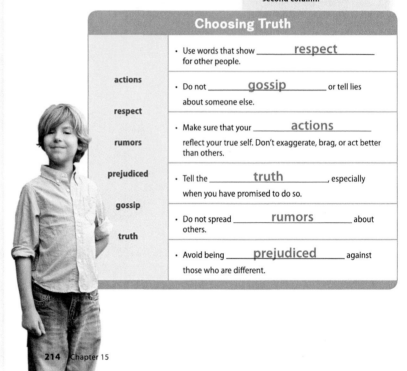

Live

Our Catholic Life

How can you live in the spirit of the Eighth Commandment?

Sometimes being honest can be difficult. It is never easy to admit to having done something wrong when you know that you may be punished. But being honest with others and yourself is what God asks of you in the Eighth Commandment.

Imagine what your life would be like if no one trusted you. No friend would tell you a secret. No one would believe anything that you said.

Sounds lonely, doesn't it? Besides, dishonesty is against God's law, and it can lead to hurting others. God's grace and practicing virtues can help us choose honesty.

 Use words from the first column to fill in the sentences in the second column.

Choosing Truth

actions
respect
rumors
prejudiced
gossip
truth

- Use words that show ___**respect**___ for other people.

- Do not ___**gossip**___ or tell lies about someone else.

- Make sure that your ___**actions**___ reflect your true self. Don't exaggerate, brag, or act better than others.

- Tell the ___**truth**___, especially when you have promised to do so.

- Do not spread ___**rumors**___ about others.

- Avoid being ___**prejudiced**___ against those who are different.

214 Chapter 15

© Our Sunday Visitor

✓ Quick Tip

Confront

It may become necessary to confront people who have spread gossip. Encourage the children to handle the situation in the following way.

- Pray for guidance.
- Take along a trusted friend as a mediator.
- Plan the meeting so that both people have a chance to speak.
- Work for a peaceful resolution.

People of Faith

Saint Joan of Arc, 1412–1431

May 30

It isn't always easy to tell the truth. Saint Joan of Arc became a martyr because she told the truth. Joan was a teenager when she had visions and heard voices. They told her to lead an army to fight for truth and save France from invaders. She bravely told the truth about her visions and voices and saved France in many battles. However, Joan was accused of being against the Church and of being a witch. She was burned at the stake. Many books and movies have been written about her.

Discuss: Talk about a time when you told the truth even though it was difficult.

Learn more about Saint Joan at **aliveinchrist.osv.com**

Live Your Faith

Design a poster that explains the importance of telling the truth. Include a slogan to make your message clear, and explain your poster to your family and friends. You may also want to write your slogan on a piece of paper to keep with you in your pocket as a reminder.

© Our Sunday Visitor

Live in the Truth **215**

Catholic Social Teaching

Chapter Connections

To integrate Catholic Social Teaching into your lesson, choose one of the following features: Rights and Responsibilities of the Human Person, pages 294–295; or Solidarity of the Human Family, pages 300–301.

- Start by talking about Saint Joan of Arc on page 215. Then move directly to the Catholic Social Teaching feature.
- Or, to expand the lesson, complete both pages 214 and 215, then move to the Catholic Social Teaching feature.
- Return to Chapter 15 for the prayer on page 216.

People of Faith

Tell the children about Saint Joan of Arc.

- Invite a volunteer to read aloud the People of Faith story.
- Explain that at a very early age, Saint Joan of Arc heard the voices of Saint Michael, Saint Catherine, and Saint Margaret. At first the messages were personal and general. It was not until she was sixteen that the voices told her to go to the King of France and help him defend France.
- Surprisingly, this young girl and her small army had a series of military successes until she was captured.
- Saint Joan of Arc is the patron Saint of the soldiers of France.
- *Say:* Talk about a time when you told the truth even though you thought it was difficult.

Encourage the children to go to **aliveinchrist.osv.com** at home to learn more about Saint Joan of Arc.

Activity

Read aloud and discuss the directions for the Live Your Faith activity as a group.

- Allow time for the children to complete their posters.
- Invite volunteers to share their drawings.

Live

 Let Us Pray
Prayer to the Holy Spirit

Tell the children that the Spirit of Truth is another name for the Holy Spirit.

Prepare

Choose a leader for the prayer service.

- Teach the children their response.

 Rehearse "Spirit, Come Down," downloaded from **aliveinchrist.osv.com**.

Gather

Invite the children to process to the prayer space.

- Direct the children to prepare their minds and hearts for prayer.

Pray

Follow the order of prayer on the student page.

- For a Scripture reading, consider Psalm 15; Proverbs 12:17, 19, 22; John 1:14–18; or John 18:37–38.

 Conclude by singing together "Spirit, Come Down."

Live

 Let Us Pray
Prayer to the Holy Spirit

Gather and begin with the Sign of the Cross.

Leader: Whenever we are afraid to tell the truth,

All: Spirit of Truth, guide us!

Leader: Whenever we are tempted to gossip,

All: Spirit of Truth, guide us!

Leader: Whenever we are faced with choices about telling the truth,

All: Spirit of Truth, guide us!

Leader: Whenever we falsely judge another,

All: Spirit of Truth, guide us!

Leader: God of all truth, whenever we face choices about telling the truth, guide us to your light. Give us strength to make good choices. We ask this in Jesus' name.

All: Amen.

 Sing "Spirit, Come Down"
Spirit, Spirit, Spirit,
come down from Heaven.
Spirit, Spirit,
and seal us with your love.
© 2001, Janet Vogt and Mark Friedman.
Published by OCP. All rights reserved.

216 Chapter 15

 Liturgy Link

Reminders of the Holy Spirit

Consider enhancing the prayer service connection to the Holy Spirit by encouraging the children to wear red clothes or accessories to the session.

- Point out that red is associated not only with the Holy Spirit, but also with enthusiasm, or zeal.

 Go to **aliveinchrist.osv.com** for Sunday readings, Scripture background, questions of the week, and seasonal resources.

FAMILY+FAITH
LIVING AND LEARNING TOGETHER

YOUR CHILD LEARNED >>>
This chapter explains the Eighth Commandment and explores Jesus' call to live in the truth and repair the damage done from sin.

Scripture
 Read **Matthew 5:33, 37** to find out about the relationship between grace and truth.

Catholics Believe
• Because God is truth, his people are called to live in the truth.
• The Eighth Commandment forbids lying.
To learn more, go to the *Catechism of the Catholic Church #1741, 2465–2470* at **usccb.org**.

People of Faith
This week, your child learned about Saint Joan of Arc. As a result of her visions, she saved France in many battles. She is the patron of women in the military.

CHILDREN AT THIS AGE >>>
How They Understand Telling the Truth Your child is probably a concrete thinker who understands cause and effect. Unlike preschoolers, children this age know that the truth doesn't change just because we want it to. They also know that adults don't know everything, and that sometimes we can be fooled. It's important for children to see the connection between truth, trust, and relationship. We cannot really be close to people if we tell them lies, no matter how small the lies, because relationship implies trust.

CONSIDER THIS >>>
How important is truth in your relationships?

Most of us expect honesty in our relationships even if we do not always welcome it. Truth is central to our relationship with God. As Catholics, we know that "God is the source of truth. Jesus not only taught the truth; he also said, 'I am the truth' (cf. John 14:6). The Hebrew word for truth, *emeth*, refers to truth in words and truthfulness in deeds. Jesus both personalized truth and spoke nothing but the truth" (*USCCA, p. 431*).

LET'S TALK >>>
• Ask your child to explain the Eighth Commandment.
• Share a time when you had to decide to lie or tell the truth, or when someone else lied to you. How did it feel? What did you do?

LET'S PRAY >>>
Saint Joan of Arc, pray for us that we may be strong in our faith and always have the courage to speak and live the truth. Amen.

For a multimedia glossary of Catholic Faith Words, Sunday readings, seasonal and Saint resources, and chapter activities go to **aliveinchrist.osv.com**.

Chapter 15 Review

A Work with Words **Fill in the circle next to the answer that best completes each statement.**

1. A _____ is someone who gives up his or her life to witness to the truth of Christ and the faith.
   ○ priest
   ○ deacon
   ● martyr

2. _____ are sins against the Eighth Commandment.
   ● Lying and gossip
   ○ Stealing and lying
   ○ Gossip and murder

3. _____ is the action taken to repair the damage done by sin.
   ○ Perjury
   ○ Sin
   ● Reparation

4. The Eighth Commandment is "You shall not _____."
   ○ kill
   ● bear false witness against your neighbor
   ○ keep holy the Lord's Day

5. _____ are called to live in the truth.
   ○ Only martyrs
   ○ Only priests and deacons
   ● All of us

B Check Understanding **Complete each sentence with the correct word from the Word Bank.**

> **Word Bank**
>
> martyr   truth
> prudence   gossip
> lying

6. Jesus calls you to live in the _____truth_____.

7. Thomas More was a _____martyr_____ and a Saint.

8. _____Lying_____ is purposely not telling the truth.

9. _____Gossip_____ is talking about another person behind his or her back.

10. _____Prudence_____ is being practical and making correct decisions with the help of the Holy Spirit and a well-formed conscience.

 Go to aliveinchrist.osv.com for an interactive review.

Family + Faith

Distribute the page to the children or parents/adult family members. Point out the chapter highlights, insights on how fourth graders understand concepts, the opportunity for the adults to reflect on their own experience and faith journey, and the family prayer.

Chapter Review

Use Catechist Quick Reviews to highlight lesson concepts.

A **Work with Words**
Have the children fill in the circle next to the answer that best completes each statement.

B **Check Understanding**
Have the children complete each sentence with the correct word from the Word Bank.

 Go to **aliveinchrist.osv.com** to prepare customized and downloadable assessments, send eAssessments, and assign interactive reviews.

Live in the Truth   **217–218**

Use Catechist Quick Reviews in each chapter to highlight lesson concepts for this unit and prepare for the Unit Review.

Have the children complete the Review pages. Then discuss the answers as a group. Review any concepts with which the children are having difficulty.

Ⓐ **Work with Words**
Have the children use the clues to solve the puzzle.

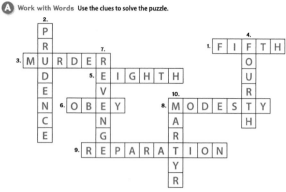

Ⓐ Work with Words Use the clues to solve the puzzle.

Across

1. This Commandment says: You shall not kill.

3. The deliberate killing of another person

5. This Commandment says: You shall not bear false witness against your neighbor.

6. To do things or act in certain ways that are requested by those in authority

8. The virtue that helps people dress, talk, and move in appropriate ways

9. Action taken to repair the damage done from sin

Down

2. The virtue that helps us be practical and make correct decisions

4. This Commandment specifically addresses sons and daughters.

7. Continuing the cycle of anger and hatred

10. Someone who gives up his or her life to witness to the truth of Christ and the faith

Morality **219**

© Our Sunday Visitor

B Check Understanding **Fill in the circle next to the best answer.**

11. Jesus said, "I am the way and the _____ and the life."

   ○ light
   ● truth
   ○ leader

12. Saint Thomas More was killed for refusing to say that the king of England was the head of the Catholic Church. More believed that the _____ was the true head of the Church.

   ● Pope
   ○ bishop
   ○ queen

13. God's plan for humans includes living _____ families.

   ○ without
   ● with
   ○ around

14. All actions that respect and protect life obey the _____ Commandment.

   ○ Ninth
   ○ Sixth
   ● Fifth

15. When you are _____, you are living as a follower of Jesus.

   ○ sinful
   ● truthful
   ○ greedy

B **Check Understanding**
Have the children fill in the circle next to the best answer.

C **Make Connections**
Have the children write a brief response to each question or statement.

Go to **aliveinchrist.osv.com** to prepare customized and downloadable assessments, send eAssessments, and assign interactive reviews.

C Make Connections **Write a brief response to each question or statement.**

16. List two ways that school helps you respect and take care of your body.
   <u>Possible responses: through health class and gym</u>
   <u>class, through sports, by providing healthful lunches</u>

17. List two ways that you respect and take care of your body at home.
   <u>Possible responses: get enough sleep, exercise,</u>
   <u>avoid drugs</u>

18. Why will breaking the Eighth Commandment eventually leave you feeling lonely?
   <u>Possible responses: No one will trust me anymore.</u>
   <u>I will not have friends.</u>

19. Explain what you have learned about family.
   <u>Possible responses: Families need to be united; the</u>
   <u>Fourth, Sixth, and Ninth Commandments teach</u>
   <u>family love.</u>

20. What have you learned about being a faithful follower of Christ?
   <u>Responses will vary.</u>

Sacraments

Our Catholic Tradition

- The Paschal Mystery is celebrated in the seasons of the liturgical year and through the Sacraments. (CCC, 1171)

- Christ instituted the Seven Sacraments as effective signs of God's life and love that give us grace. (CCC, 1131)

- The Eucharist is the heart of the Church's life. (CCC, 1407)

- The Sacraments of Healing are about conversion, forgiveness, and healing. (CCC, 1421)

How does Jesus' saving work continue through the Seven Sacraments and the celebration of the liturgical year?

Unit 6 Overview

Chapter 16

The children will:

- describe the Paschal Mystery as the mystery of Jesus' suffering, Death, Resurrection, and Ascension through which he saved all humans from the power of sin and everlasting death
- recognize the liturgical year as made up of the feasts and seasons of the Church calendar that celebrate the Paschal Mystery of Christ
- name the seasons of the Church year as Advent, Christmas, Ordinary Time, Lent, Triduum, and Easter

 Catholic Social Teaching: Live Your Faith

- Call to Family, Community, and Participation, Pages 292–293
- Solidarity of the Human Family, Pages 300–301

Chapter 17

The children will:

- recognize that God the Father sent his only Son, Jesus, as a sign of his love for all people
- recognize that each of the Seven Sacraments are effective signs of God's life, instituted by Christ and given to the Church, so that Jesus can continue his saving work in the world
- begin to develop an understanding that the visible signs and Divine actions in each celebration give grace and allow us to share in God's work
- identify that the Sacrament of the Eucharist is at the heart of Christian life

 Catholic Social Teaching: Live Your Faith

- Option for the Poor and Vulnerable, Pages 296–297
- Solidarity of the Human Family, Pages 300–301

Chapter 18

The children will:

- explore conversion, turning away from sin and responding to God's love and forgiveness, relating their own lives to the example of Zacchaeus
- understand that in the Sacrament of Penance and Reconciliation, we receive God's forgiveness of sins through the Church and are strengthened by grace to make peace and avoid temptation
- discover that the Sacrament of the Anointing of the Sick brings Jesus' healing touch to strengthen, comfort and forgive the sins of those who are seriously ill or close to death

 Songs of Scripture "The Blind Man"

 Catholic Social Teaching: Live Your Faith

- Rights and Responsibilities of the Human Person, Pages 294–295
- Option for the Poor and Vulnerable, Pages 296–297

Preview Unit Theme

Ask: What is the unit theme?

Summarize that the unit focuses on the Sacraments.

Invite volunteers to read aloud each of the bullets in Our Catholic Tradition.

Explain to the children that they will learn about these things in the next three chapters.

Have the children study the photos and images. Invite volunteers to describe what they see. What do these images say about the unit theme?

Ask: How does Jesus' saving work continue through the Seven Sacraments and the celebration of the liturgical year?

After some discussion, explain to the children that they will be exploring this question in this unit.

KEY CONCEPT

The liturgical year celebrates the Paschal Mystery. The seasons of the liturgical year include Advent, Christmas, Lent, Triduum, Easter, and Ordinary Time.

DOCTRINAL CONTENT

- The Paschal Mystery is the mystery of Jesus' suffering, Death, Resurrection, and Ascension through which he saved all humans from the power of sin and everlasting death. (CCC, 571)
- The liturgical year is made up of the feasts and seasons of the Church calendar that celebrate the Paschal Mystery of Christ. (CCC, 1171)
- The seasons of the Church year are Advent, Christmas, Ordinary Time, Lent, Triduum, and Easter. (CCC, 1168–1169)

TASKS OF CATECHESIS

Helping children grow in a faith that is "known, celebrated, lived, and expressed in prayer" (NDC, 20).

This chapter focuses on the following tasks of catechesis:

- Promoting Knowledge of the Faith
- Liturgical Education

Catechist Background

My deliverance and honor are with God, my strong rock; my refuge is with God. Trust God at all times, my people! Pour out your hearts to God our refuge! Psalm 62:8–9

➤ **Reflect** How is Jesus with you in each moment of your day?

The rhythm of the liturgical seasons matches the cycle of life. During the Church year, the faithful experience the anticipation of Advent; rejoice at the Savior's birth on Christmas; live faithfully in Ordinary Time; grow reflective in Lent; and know suffering, death, and rising to new life in Christ through the Triduum and Easter. Catholics do not simply watch this drama unfold; they are drawn into the reality of God's continuing presence in their lives. This presence is reinforced as Catholics recall Christ's life and the Paschal Mystery at every Mass.

The mystery began on Holy Thursday evening. It moved through suffering on the Cross to the miracle of an empty tomb on Easter morning. As Jesus revealed himself to the disciples on Easter evening, the mystery moved to joy in the knowledge that Jesus had saved all humans from sin and death and made his followers full participants in new life. Through the Sacrament of Baptism, all Church members share in the Paschal Mystery. United with Christ, they become true sons and daughters of the heavenly Father.

➤ **Reflect** How do you show your belief in the Paschal Mystery?

Catechist's Prayer

Jesus, you walked the journey of life while loving others generously. By learning from and teaching about you, may I know the Father's will in my life. Amen.

Lesson Plan

Objectives	Process	Materials

Invite, 10 minutes

The Liturgical Year Page 223

- Psalm 34:2 Pray the opening prayer.
- Psalm 62:8–9 Reflect prayerfully on the Word.
- Discuss What Do You Wonder questions.

- **Optional Activity** Chapter Story: "The Life Cycle"

Discover, 35 minutes

A Time for Everything Pages 224–225
- Describe the Paschal Mystery as the mystery of Jesus' suffering, Death, Resurrection, and Ascension through which he saved all humans from the power of sin and everlasting death
- Recognize the liturgical year as made up of the feasts and seasons of the Church calendar that celebrate the Paschal Mystery of Christ

- **Catholic Faith Words** Ascension, Paschal Mystery, liturgical year
- Explain that all living things have a life cycle.
- Ecclesiastes 3:1–8 Proclaim "The Right Time."
- Explain that Jesus' cycle of life did not end with his Death.
- Introduce the liturgical year as the feasts and seasons of the Church calendar.
- **Share Your Faith Activity** Reflect on best and worst times of the past week.

- ☐ pencils
- ☐ index cards

The Church's Seasons Pages 226–227
- Name the seasons of the Church year as Advent, Christmas, Ordinary Time, Lent, Triduum, and Easter

- Recall that the Paschal Mystery is celebrated in the liturgical year.
- Read about and discuss each of the seasons of the liturgical year.
- **Connect Your Faith Activity** Design symbols to illustrate the saving actions of Jesus that each season celebrates.

- ☐ pencils
- ☐ crayons or markers
- **Optional Activity** Seasons and Feast Days
- ☐ Activity Master 16 (Page 223E)

Live, 15 minutes

Our Catholic Life Pages 228–229

- Explain that each Church season is celebrated in a different way.
- ☆ Write one way to celebrate each Church season.
- **People of Faith** Learn about Saint Juan Diego.
- **Live Your Faith Activity** Draw one way to celebrate the current liturgical season.

- ☐ pencils
- ☐ crayons or markers
- ☐ banners or ribbons

Prayer of Praise Page 230

- Select a child to be the leader.
- Rehearse "We Proclaim Your Death, O Lord."
- Follow the order of prayer.

- Download "We Proclaim Your Death, O Lord."

Family + Faith Page 231
Point out that the Catholic Families page provides chapter highlights, information on how fourth graders understand faith concepts, and family prayer.

Chapter Review Page 232
- aliveinchrist.osv.com
  - Customize and Download Assessments
  - Email Links to eAssessments
  - Interactive Student Reviews

ONLINE RESOURCES

 Go to **aliveinchrist.osv.com**

You will find:

- Interactive lesson planning with web specific content and additional activities
- Step by step lesson instruction from printed Catechist Edition for integrated lesson planning
- Custom-built assessments to download and eAssessment links
- Interactive reviews that provide scores and the option to review answers
- Sunday readings with background and questions of the week

 Go to **osvparish.com**

You will find:

- Ask the Experts Q and A
- General Catechist Helps
- Community Connections and Blogs

Sharing the Message with Fourth Graders

The Church Year Fourth graders have better "internal calendars" than do younger children. They can calculate how long it will be to Christmas or Easter, for example. As they learn about the Church year, their ability to understand time can help them feel involved in the celebrations and seasons of the Church calendar. This is especially true when they have an opportunity to mark time in faith formation or the home with a sacred space that reflects the current season (e.g., altar cloths of green, purple, red or white and icons that fit the season).

Teaching Tip: Be sure to recognize the changing of Church seasons through the décor and activities you use in the room.

How Fourth Graders Understand

- Sometimes children just do not know the answers. Take time to help fourth graders discover them.
- To put information in order, fourth graders may need to see it as well as hear it. Help them learn both auditorily and visually.
- Show the children where each part of the liturgical year falls on the calendar.

"I like to learn through movement. Incorporate gestures into the session activities."

Chapter Story

"The Life Cycle"

Use this story to expand the chapter introduction.

- The children will relate the story to their own lives, reflecting on the seasons.
- Connect the seasons with their ongoing cycle of seasonal changes.

 Go to **aliveinchrist.osv.com** Lesson Planning section for this story.

NCEA IFG: ACRE Edition

Discover

Knowledge of the Faith

- Objective: To know and understand basic Catholic teaching about the Incarnate Word Jesus Christ as the way, truth, and life

Liturgical Life

- Objective: To know the Paschal Mystery of Jesus: in the Church's liturgical life—feasts, seasons, symbols, and practices—and in the Sacraments as signs and instruments of grace

Catholic Social Teaching

Live

 Use one of these features to introduce a principle and engage the children with an activity.

- Call to Family, Community, and Participation, Pages 292–293
- Solidarity of the Human Family, Pages 300–301

Music Options

 Use one or more of the following songs to enhance catechetical learning or for prayer.

- "We Proclaim Your Death, O Lord," Live Prayer, Page 230
- "A Circle of Colors," Discover, Page 227
- "Jesus, Come to Us," Discover, Page 227

LECTIONARY CONNECTION

Chapter 16 highlights Lectionary-connected themes such as Jesus' Passion, the Paschal Mystery, and the Second Coming. If your parish aligns its curriculum to the liturgical year, you could use this chapter in connection with the following Sundays.

Year A

First Sunday of Advent—Second Coming

Easter Sunday—Jesus' Death and Resurrection

Twenty-second Sunday in Ordinary Time—Death, Resurrection, Ascension

Year B

First Sunday of Advent—Second Coming

Palm Sunday of the Lord's Passion—Christ's Passion

Easter Sunday—Jesus' Death and Resurrection

Year C

The Epiphany of the Lord—birth of Jesus

Second Sunday of Easter—Resurrection

The Most Holy Trinity—promise of the Holy Spirit

 Go to **aliveinchrist.osv.com** for a complete correlation ordered by the Sundays of the year and suggestions for how to integrate the Scripture readings into chapter lessons.

Name _____ Date _____

Seasons and Feast Days

Place the feast day (special day) in its correct season by writing it beneath the name of the season. Refer to a liturgical calendar if you have difficulty placing some feasts.

Advent

Christmas

Lent

Triduum

Easter

Ordinary Time

Immaculate Conception	Assumption of Mary
Christ the King	Ash Wednesday
Ascension	Baptism of Jesus
Epiphany	Pentecost
Holy Family	Good Friday
Saint Nicholas	Holy Saturday
Holy Thursday	

The Liturgical Year

 © Our Sunday Visitor

♥ Let Us Pray

Leader: Loving Lord, we praise you and give you thanks no matter the time, no matter the season.

"I will bless the LORD at all times; his praise shall be always in my mouth." Psalm 34:2

All: Loving Lord, we praise you and give you thanks no matter the time, no matter the season.

🕮 Scripture

My deliverance and honor are with God, my strong rock; my refuge is with God. Trust God at all times, my people! Pour out your hearts to God our refuge!

Psalm 62:8–9

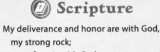

❓ What Do You Wonder?

- Why does the Church tell the story of Jesus' life over and over again?
- Is Jesus really with you in each moment of your day?

223

Optional Activity

Chapter Story: "The Life Cycle" *Verbal/Linguistic*

Use this story after the opening prayer, before explaining that year after year, we give thanks to God for the gift of his Son, Jesus.

- Ask the children to describe the life cycle of the butterfly from egg to caterpillar to cocoon to butterfly.
- Read the story aloud as the children follow along.
- Discuss one seasonal change that happens where you live. Then transition back to the lesson instruction.

🛜 Go to **aliveinchrist.osv.com** for Chapter Story.

♥ Let Us Pray

Invite the children to gather in the prayer space and make the Sign of the Cross. Choose a child to read aloud the Psalm verse from a Bible.

Have the children move out of the prayer space and back to their seats.

Explain that we give thanks to God for the gift of his Son, Jesus.

Say: Time after time, year after year, we offer God heartfelt praise and thanks for sending us Jesus.

🕮 Scripture

Guide the children through the process of Scripture reflection.

- Invite them to close their eyes, be still and open their minds and hearts to what God is saying to them in this passage.
- Proclaim the Scripture.
- Maintain several moments of silence.
- *Ask:* What did you hear God say to you today?
- Invite volunteers to share.

What Do You Wonder?

Say: We celebrate Jesus' life, Death, Resurrection, and Ascension each Mass, and especially during Holy Week and Easter. By joining our life with Jesus, we receive the gift of knowing that he is with us in each moment of our lives.

Invite the children to respond to the questions. Ask what else they might wonder about Jesus' life, Death, Resurrection, Ascension, and presence with us.

Objectives

- Describe the Paschal Mystery as the mystery of Jesus' suffering, Death, Resurrection, and Ascension through which he saved all humans from the power of sin and everlasting death

- Recognize the liturgical year as made up of the feasts and seasons of the Church calendar that celebrate the Paschal Mystery of Christ

A Time for Everything

Ask: What is the Paschal Mystery?

- List the children's responses on the board or on chart paper.

Read aloud the first paragraph.

- Tell the children that a poet observed and wrote in the Bible about different times and events in life.

 Scripture

Organize the children in two groups, facing one another. Have them proclaim aloud "The Right Time," with the first group reading the first line of the couplet and the other group reading the second line.

- *Ask:* What message was God giving us in this poem?

- Ask the children if this Scripture passage is familiar.

- Invite the children to share when they have heard this reading.
  Possible responses include: at Mass, a wedding, or a funeral

---

 Discover

A Time for Everything

What is the Paschal Mystery?

All living things follow a pattern. They come to life, they grow and develop, and finally they die. This pattern is called a life cycle. Every year, as the seasons change, you see changes in the world around you. God tells us about the importance of seasons and cycles in one of the Wisdom Books in the Bible.

 Scripture

The Right Time
There is an appointed time for everything,
and a time for every affair under the heavens.
A time to give birth, and a time to die;
a time to plant, and a time to uproot the plant . . .
A time to weep, and a time to laugh;
a time to mourn, and a time to dance . . .
A time to seek, and a time to lose;
a time to keep, and a time to cast away . . .
A time to love, and a time to hate;
a time of war, and a time of peace. Ecclesiastes 3:1–8

→ What message was God giving us in this poem?

© Our Sunday Visitor

224

 Scripture Background

Ecclesiastes 3:1–8

This passage stresses that God has a plan that humans do not fully understand and that all aspects of life are under his loving providence.

- The verses indicate that joy and sorrow are part of the human condition for individuals as well as for society as a whole.

- The verses following this excerpt urge people to "be glad and to do well during life," appreciating the gifts that God has given them.

The Paschal Mystery

Jesus experienced the natural cycle of life, but his cycle did not end with his Death on the Cross. God the Father raised Jesus from the dead and to new life. Then Jesus ascended to join his Father in Heaven. The suffering, Death, Resurrection, and **Ascension** of Jesus are called the **Paschal Mystery**. This mystery reveals that Jesus saved all humans from the power of sin and everlasting death.

The Church celebrates this mystery in every Sacrament and especially at every Eucharist. Every Sunday we gather with the parish community to celebrate the new life that Jesus' Resurrection gives us.

The Liturgical Year

From week to week at Mass, you may notice different readings, hymns, and colors. These mark the seasons of the Church's year, called the **liturgical year**. The liturgical year begins on the first Sunday of Advent, usually around December 1, and ends with the feast of Christ the King.

Catholic Faith Words

Ascension when the Risen Jesus was taken up to Heaven to be with God the Father forever

Paschal Mystery the mystery of Jesus' suffering, Death, Resurrection, and Ascension

liturgical year the feasts and seasons of the Church calendar that celebrate the Paschal Mystery of Christ

Share Your Faith

Reflect Think about what you did last week. In the boxes, sketch one of the symbols for the "times" of your life. If Monday was a happy time, draw a smiling face to show that you were happy. Use different symbols to represent your "times."

Share With a partner, share some of the best and worst times you had last week.

✓ **Quick Tip**

Seasonal Predictions

Before each liturgical season, have the children predict changes that they expect in the parish church environment.

- Prompt their predictions with questions about colors, decoration, and so on.
- At the start of a new season, walk through the parish church and see if the predictions were correct.

The Paschal Mystery

Tell the children that they will hear about Jesus' becoming human and experiencing the cycle of human life.

- Read aloud the text.
- Stress the importance of the Mass as a celebration of the Paschal Mystery.

The Liturgical Year

Invite a volunteer to read aloud the text.

- *Ask:* What signs of the present liturgical season do you see?

Work with Words

Invite three volunteers to each read a definition of the Catholic Faith Words, *Ascension*, *Paschal Mystery*, and *liturgical year*.

- Distribute index cards and have the children make vocabulary cards for each term.

Activity

Read aloud the directions for the Share Your Faith activity.

- Have the children work independently to write their ideas.
- When everyone has finished, have them discuss their ideas with a partner.

Quick Review

The Paschal Mystery is Jesus' cycle of life, Death, and new life. The Paschal Mystery is celebrated in the Mass and in the seasons of the Church year.

Discover

Objective
- Name the seasons of the Church year as Advent, Christmas, Ordinary Time, Lent, Triduum, and Easter

The Church's Seasons

Ask: What are the seasons of the liturgical year?

- Write the children's responses on the board or on chart paper.

Review the meaning of Paschal Mystery.

- Summarize the first paragraph.
- Tell the children that the meaning of the Paschal Mystery is celebrated each year within the seasons that the Church celebrates.

Advent
Read aloud the text.
- Point out the Advent season on a calendar.

Christmas
Invite a volunteer to read aloud the text.
- Point out the length of this season.
- *Ask:* How does your family and parish prepare for Christmas during Advent?

Lent
Read aloud the section on Lent.
- Discuss the mood of the Church during the Lenten Season.
- Show the children the dates of Lent on a current calendar.

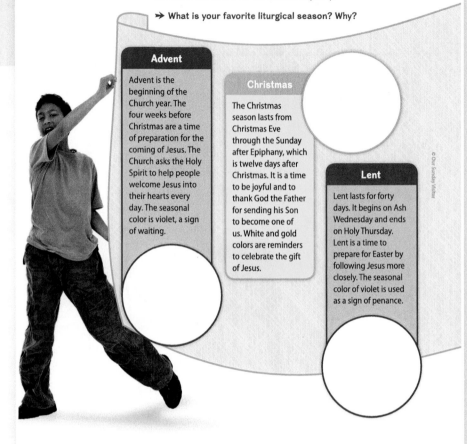

The Church's Seasons
What are the seasons of the liturgical year?

Just as the seasons of the year mark the cycles of life and death in nature, the seasons of the liturgical year mark and celebrate the events of the Paschal Mystery.

➔ **What is your favorite liturgical season? Why?**

Advent
Advent is the beginning of the Church year. The four weeks before Christmas are a time of preparation for the coming of Jesus. The Church asks the Holy Spirit to help people welcome Jesus into their hearts every day. The seasonal color is violet, a sign of waiting.

Christmas
The Christmas season lasts from Christmas Eve through the Sunday after Epiphany, which is twelve days after Christmas. It is a time to be joyful and to thank God the Father for sending his Son to become one of us. White and gold colors are reminders to celebrate the gift of Jesus.

Lent
Lent lasts for forty days. It begins on Ash Wednesday and ends on Holy Thursday. Lent is a time to prepare for Easter by following Jesus more closely. The seasonal color of violet is used as a sign of penance.

© Our Sunday Visitor

226   Chapter 16

 **Quick Tip**

Consumerism
Television commercials promote Christmas messages by mid-October. Easter candy and decorations appear shortly after Valentine's Day.

- Remind the children that the purpose of advertising is to sell things, but the purpose of holy days is to celebrate the works of God.
- Point out that Jewish and Islamic holy days are not as commercialized; discuss some possible reasons for this.

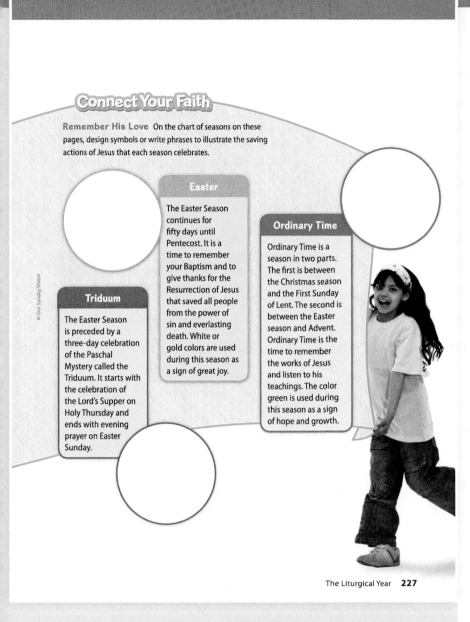

Connect Your Faith

Remember His Love On the chart of seasons on these pages, design symbols or write phrases to illustrate the saving actions of Jesus that each season celebrates.

Easter

The Easter Season continues for fifty days until Pentecost. It is a time to remember your Baptism and to give thanks for the Resurrection of Jesus that saved all people from the power of sin and everlasting death. White or gold colors are used during this season as a sign of great joy.

Ordinary Time

Ordinary Time is a season in two parts. The first is between the Christmas season and the First Sunday of Lent. The second is between the Easter season and Advent. Ordinary Time is the time to remember the works of Jesus and listen to his teachings. The color green is used during this season as a sign of hope and growth.

Triduum

The Easter Season is preceded by a three-day celebration of the Paschal Mystery called the Triduum. It starts with the celebration of the Lord's Supper on Holy Thursday and ends with evening prayer on Easter Sunday.

The Liturgical Year **227**

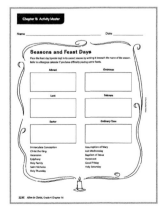

Triduum

Read aloud this section.

- Ask the children what they should remember during the Triduum. the Paschal Mystery

Easter

Read aloud this section.

- Point out that this is the second longest season of the Church's year. Only Ordinary Time is longer.

Ordinary Time

Read this section aloud.

- Point out that Ordinary Time takes place in two parts.
- *Ask:* What is the color green a sign of? hope and growth

Refer to pages 312–313 in Our Catholic Tradition to find out more about the liturgical year.

 Music Option: Have the children sing, "A Circle of Colors" or "Jesus, Come to Us," downloaded from **aliveinchrist.osv.com**.

Activity

Read aloud the directions for the Connect Your Faith activity.

- Have the children work independently to complete the activity.
- Afterward, invite volunteers to share their symbols or phrases with the group.

Quick Review

The seasons of Advent, Christmas, Lent, Triduum, Easter, and Ordinary Time make up the Church year.

Optional Activity

Activity Master 16: Seasons and Feast Days

Distribute copies of the activity found on page 223E.

- Provide a liturgical calendar or access to the Internet to assist the children in this activity.
- As an alternative, you may wish to send this activity home with the children.

Our Catholic Life

Ask: How do you celebrate the seasons of the Church year?

- Write the children's responses on the board or on chart paper.

Read aloud both paragraphs.

Celebrating the Seasons

Invite each of five volunteers to read aloud one of the blocks of text in the chart.

- After each season, pause and ask the children to share what emotions each season brings to mind.
- Point out the pictures.
- *Ask:* What season are the people in each picture celebrating?
  Ordinary Time, Advent
- Invite volunteers to share how their family or parish celebrates each of these seasons. For example, some families pray with an Advent wreath during Advent or pray the Stations of the Cross during Lent.
- ⭐ Have the children write in each box one other way they can celebrate the Church seasons. Encourage them to use ideas from the discussion.

Live

Our Catholic Life

How do you celebrate the seasons of the Church year?

The seasons in nature affect the way you think and act. For example, you would not try to go ice fishing in the middle of summer. The Church also wants you to think and act according to her seasons.

Each season of the Church year gives you a different way to look at Jesus and the people and the world around you. Here are some ways to pray and live according to the seasons.

 In each of the boxes, write one other way you can celebrate that Church season.

Celebrating the Seasons

Christmas	Celebrate Jesus' birth by looking for the love of Jesus in everyone you meet.
Ordinary Time	Learn more about Jesus by reading the Bible. Imitate his love for those who are poor, suffering, or sick.
Advent	Prepare for Jesus' coming into your heart by practicing patience.
Lent	Pray, fast, and focus your attention upon acts of penance. These actions will prepare you to celebrate Easter.
Easter	Celebrate the wonderful news that you have been saved. Share your experiences of how God has worked in your life.

 228

© Our Sunday Visitor

✓ Quick Tip

Celebrate

Celebrating liturgy is central to the Church year.

- The joy felt at the great feasts is celebrated with symbols, prayers, community observances, and family gatherings.
- Point out to the children that celebrations outside of church often reflect the occasion within the liturgical calendar. For example, Christmas gifts echo the gift of God sending his Son.

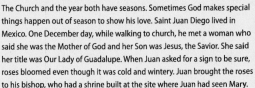
People of Faith

Saint Juan Diego, 1474–1548

December 9

The Church and the year both have seasons. Sometimes God makes special things happen out of season to show his love. Saint Juan Diego lived in Mexico. One December day, while walking to church, he met a woman who said she was the Mother of God and her Son was Jesus, the Savior. She said her title was Our Lady of Guadalupe. When Juan asked for a sign to be sure, roses bloomed even though it was cold and wintery. Juan brought the roses to his bishop, who had a shrine built at the site where Juan had seen Mary.

Discuss: When has God shown you a sign of love?

 Learn more about Saint Juan Diego at **aliveinchrist.osv.com**

Live Your Faith

Recall the liturgical season the Church is currently celebrating. Name and draw one thing you can do to celebrate this season now.

 ## Catholic Social Teaching

Chapter Connections

To integrate Catholic Social Teaching into your lesson, choose one of the following features: Call to Family, Community, and Participation, pages 292–293; or Solidarity of the Human Family, pages 300–301.

- Start the Live step of the process by talking about Saint Juan Diego on page 229. Then move directly to the Catholic Social Teaching feature.
- Or, to expand the lesson, complete both pages 228 and 229, then move to the Catholic Social Teaching feature.
- Return to Chapter 16 for the prayer on page 230.

People of Faith

Tell the children about Saint Juan Diego.

- Invite a volunteer to read aloud the People of Faith story.
- Explain that Saint Juan Diego walked fifteen miles every day to attend Mass.
- On cold mornings he wore a woven cloak, called a tilma. The Blessed Virgin Mary appeared to him the first time as he was walking to Mass.
- When Juan Diego opened his tilma to show the bishop the flowers, the bishop was shocked to see the image of the Lady imprinted on his tilma.
- News of the miracle spread quickly through Mexico.
- In the seven years that followed eight million people were converted to the Catholic faith.
- *Discuss:* When has God shown you a sign of love?

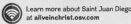 Encourage the children to go to **aliveinchrist.osv.com** at home to learn more about Saint Juan Diego.

Activity

Read aloud the directions and discuss the Live Your Faith activity as a group.

- Allow time for the children to draw their pictures.
- Invite volunteers to share their drawings.

Let Us Pray
Prayer of Praise

Tell the children that today they will express the joy of the Paschal Mystery.

Prepare

Choose a leader for the celebration.

- Show the children their responses.
- Provide banners or ribbons, if possible. Show the children how they can carry and wave the ribbons and banners during the procession.

 Rehearse "We Proclaim Your Death, O Lord," downloaded from **aliveinchrist.osv.com**.

Gather

Invite the children to process to the prayer space.

- Invite the children to be seated.
- Allow the children to get settled and prepare their minds and hearts for prayer.

Pray

Follow the order of prayer on the student page.

- Optional Bible readings are Psalm 33:1–5 and Luke 24:1–8.
- *Leader's concluding prayer:*
  Our Father, we praise and thank you for the gift of your Son.

 Conclude by singing together "We Proclaim Your Death, O Lord."

 Let Us Pray
Prayer of Praise

Gather and begin with the Sign of the Cross.

Leader: God, our good Father, you sent Jesus, your Son, to rescue us from the power of sin and everlasting death.

All: We proclaim your Death, O Lord.

Leader: Jesus, you came into this world of darkness as the light. Your words of love touched those who were sick and weak. You forgave sinners and freed them from shame.

All: Jesus lives with us.

Leader: Jesus, you died on the Cross, a sacrifice of love to set us free from our sins.

All: Jesus died for us.

Leader: Jesus, you were raised from the dead and ascended into Heaven. You sent the Holy Spirit to be with us always. We hope to share eternal life with you.

All: We wait in joyful hope!

Leader: Let us pray.

Bow your heads as the leader prays.

All: Amen.

 Sing "We Proclaim Your Death, O Lord"

 ## Liturgy Link

Procession

When worship involves stopping and starting movements, a brief rehearsal is helpful.

- Show the children where they will process and at what pace to move.
- Remind them to leave enough space so that they do not bump into one another.

Go to **aliveinchrist.osv.com** for Sunday readings, Scripture background, questions of the week, and seasonal resources.

YOUR CHILD LEARNED >>>

This chapter explains that the Paschal Mystery is the mystery of Christ's suffering, Death, Resurrection, and Ascension, and that the feasts and seasons of the liturgical year celebrate the Paschal Mystery of Christ.

Scripture
 Read **Psalm 62:8–9** to find out about the importance of giving thanks to God.

Catholics Believe
• The liturgical year celebrates the Paschal Mystery.
• The seasons of the liturgical year include Advent, Christmas, Lent, Triduum, Easter, and Ordinary Time.

To learn more, go to the *Catechism of the Catholic Church #1067–1068, 1168–1171* at **usccb.org**.

People of Faith
This week, your child learned about Saint Juan Diego. Our Lady of Guadalupe appeared to him as he walked to church one morning.

CHILDREN AT THIS AGE >>>

How They Understand the Church Year Your child has a better "internal calendar" than he or she did as a preschooler. Children this age can calculate how long it will be until Christmas or Easter, for example. As they learn about the Church year, their ability to understand time can help them feel involved in the celebrations and seasons of the Church calendar. This is especially true when they have an opportunity to mark time in the home with a sacred space that reflects the current season (for example, cloths of green, purple, red, or white and icons that fit the season).

CONSIDER THIS >>>

When have you longed for a flower to remain in bloom or for a child to not grow up too quickly?

All living things follow a cycle. They come to life, grow and develop, and finally die. The rhythm of the liturgical seasons of the Church flow through our lives just as the cycle of life. As Catholics, we know that "in the Liturgical Year, the Church celebrates the whole mystery of Christ from the Incarnation until the day of Pentecost and the expectation of Christ's second coming. The summit of the Liturgical Year is the Easter Triduum—from the evening of Holy Thursday to the evening of Easter Sunday" (*USCCA, p. 173*).

LET'S TALK >>>
• Ask your child to tell you about the liturgical year.
• Share memories of the ways your family has celebrated different Church holidays.

LET'S PRAY >>>
O God, help us grow closer to you by our worship at the Eucharist, our learning of our Catholic faith, and our devotion to prayer. Amen.

For a multimedia glossary of Catholic Faith Words, Sunday readings, seasonal and Saint resources, and chapter activities go to **aliveinchrist.osv.com**.

Family + Faith

Distribute the page to the children or parents/adult family members. Point out the chapter highlights, insights on how fourth graders understand concepts, the opportunity for the adults to reflect on their own experience and faith journey, and the family prayer.

Chapter 16 Review

A Work with Words **Match each description in Column 1 with the correct term in Column 2.**

Column 1	Column 2
1. a time of penance	Advent
2. celebrates the birth of Jesus	Christmas
3. focuses on the Resurrection of Jesus	Ordinary Time
4. prepares for the coming of Jesus	Lent
5. focuses on Jesus' work and teachings	Easter

B Check Understanding **Complete each statement with the correct term from the Word Bank.**

Word Bank

liturgical	Paschal	Thursday
works	Triduum	

6. The ____Paschal____ Mystery is the mystery of Jesus' suffering, Death, Resurrection, and Ascension.

7. The ____liturgical____ year is the cycle of feasts and seasons that celebrate the Paschal Mystery of Christ.

8. ____Triduum____ is a celebration of the Passion, Death, and Resurrection of Christ.

9. In the Church year, the Triduum begins on Holy ____Thursday____ evening and concludes on Easter Sunday night.

10. Ordinary Time is the time to remember the ____works____ of Jesus and listen to his teachings.

Go to **aliveinchrist.osv.com** for an interactive review.

Chapter Review

Use Catechist Quick Reviews to highlight lesson concepts.

A **Work with Words**
Match each description in Column 1 to the correct term in Column 2.

B **Check Understanding**
Complete each statement with the correct term from the Word Bank.

 Go to **aliveinchrist.osv.com** to prepare customized and downloadable assessments, send eAssessments, and assign interactive reviews.

The Liturgical Year   **231–232**

KEY CONCEPT

The Seven Sacraments are effective signs, instituted by Christ, that give grace and continue his saving work in the world. The Sacrament of the Eucharist is at the heart of Christian life.

DOCTRINAL CONTENT

- God the Father sent his only Son, Jesus, as a sign of his love for all people. (CCC, 458)

- The Seven Sacraments are effective signs of God's life, instituted by Christ and given to the Church, so that Jesus can continue his saving work in the world. (CCC, 1127)

- The visible signs and Divine actions in each celebration give grace and allow us to share in God's work. (CCC, 1128, 1131)

- The Sacrament of the Eucharist, in which we receive the gift of Jesus Christ's Body and Blood in Holy Communion, is at the heart of Catholic life. (CCC, 1322, 1324)

TASKS OF CATECHESIS

Helping children grow in a faith that is "known, celebrated, lived, and expressed in prayer" (NDC, 20).

This chapter focuses on the following tasks of catechesis:

- Promoting Knowledge of the Faith

- Liturgical Education

Catechist Background

 Blessed be the God and Father of our Lord Jesus Christ, who has blessed us in Christ with every spiritual blessing in the heavens. Ephesians 1:3

→ **Reflect** When do you celebrate Jesus' life and love?

Signs and symbols are staples of communication. People use signs to welcome and to warn. Symbols can be as disparate as birthday candles and wedding rings. Signs and symbols point to realities that are greater and richer than the symbols themselves. Sacraments bring about these realities.

Spiritual realities are manifested through symbols as well. The Seven Sacraments are filled with symbols of many types. These include symbols of the physical world: fire, water, light, and darkness; rituals taken from daily actions: washing, eating, and drinking; and ancient actions from God's earliest covenants: anointing and the laying on of hands. In all of these ways and more, the Church celebrates the origin of the Seven Sacraments in Jesus. Through the Sacraments, believers are enveloped in the mystery of God.

Eucharist is a word with many levels of meaning. When translated literally, it means "thanksgiving." When you celebrate the Eucharist, you receive Jesus himself, share a sacred meal, offer yourself in sacrifice in union with Christ, remember the saving actions of Jesus, and praise and thank God for acting on your behalf. At the very heart of the faith, Catholics are first, finally, and always people of the Eucharist.

→ **Reflect** How is Eucharist a participation in the Body of Christ?

Catechist's Prayer

 Loving God, the signs of your presence are all around me. Help me see them with new eyes and understand them afresh. Amen.

Lesson Plan

Objectives	Process	Materials

Invite, 10 minutes

The Seven Sacraments Page 233

- 🔵 **Psalm 100:1–2** Pray the opening prayer.
- 📖 **Ephesians 1:3, 7–8** Reflect prayerfully on the Word.
- Discuss What Do You Wonder questions.

- 🔘 **Optional Activity** Chapter Story: "I Will Remember"

Discover, 35 minutes

Present Through Time Pages 234–235
- Recognize that God the Father sent his only Son, Jesus, as a sign of his love for all people
- Recognize that each of the Seven Sacraments are effective signs of God's life, instituted by Christ and given to the Church, so that Jesus can continue his saving work in the world
- Begin to develop an understanding that the visible signs and Divine actions in each celebration give grace and allow us to share in God's work

- **Catholic Faith Words** Incarnation, Seven Sacraments
- Explain that the Incarnation is a sign of God's love for us.
- 📖 **John 14:6–7** Proclaim the Scripture story.
- Explain that Jesus is present in the Seven Sacraments.
- **Share Your Faith Activity** Explain how Jesus is present in one of the Seven Sacraments to a partner.
- ☆ Underline what Jesus promised the disciples and how he fulfills this promise today.

- ☐ pencils
- ☐ index cards
- • **Optional Activity** Seven Sacraments
- ☐ Activity Master 17 (Page 233E)

The Eucharist Pages 236–237
- Identify that the Sacrament of the Eucharist is at the heart of Christian life

- **Catholic Faith Words** Eucharist
- Explain that Jesus ate meals with friends.
- 📖 **Luke 22:17–20** Proclaim "The Last Supper."
- Explain Jesus' presence in the Eucharist.
- **Connect Your Faith Activity** Write a paragraph about the Sacraments.

- ☐ pencils
- ☐ index cards

Live, 15 minutes

Our Catholic Life Pages 238–239

- Explain participation in Mass.
- ☆ Identify when you feel close to God at Mass.
- **People of Faith** Learn about Saint Margaret Mary Alacoque.
- **Live Your Faith Activity** Make a poster.

- ☐ pencils
- ☐ crayons or markers
- ☐ Student Books

Prayer of Petition Page 240

- ▶ Rehearse "We Come to the Table."
- Follow the order of prayer.

- 🔘 Download "We Come to the Table."

Family + Faith Page 241

Point out that the Catholic Families page provides chapter highlights, information on how fourth graders understand faith concepts, and family prayer.

Chapter Review Page 242

🔘 **aliveinchrist.osv.com**
- Customize and Download Assessments
- Email Links to eAssessments
- Interactive Student Reviews

ONLINE RESOURCES

 Go to **aliveinchrist.osv.com**

You will find:

- Interactive lesson planning with web specific content and additional activities
- Step by step lesson instruction from printed Catechist Edition for integrated lesson planning
- Custom-built assessments to download and eAssessment links
- Interactive reviews that provide scores and the option to review answers
- Sunday readings with background and questions of the week

 Go to **osvparish.com**

You will find:

- Ask the Experts Q and A
- General Catechist Helps
- Community Connections and Blogs

Sharing the Message with Fourth Graders

The Seven Sacraments Fourth graders, while still bound to their five senses, are better able than younger children to see the connections between rituals and their meanings. This can help them gain a deeper appreciation of the Seven Sacraments as they know that what they are seeing and hearing in sacramental celebrations is a sign of, and participation in, something invisible as well.

Teaching Tip: When talking with the children about a Sacrament, see if they can identify the human actions we can see that help us work together with God, and the Divine actions (the things God does) that we can't see but know by faith.

How Fourth Graders Understand

- Fourth graders are becoming aware of the community around them. Tell them about services for people in need and how they can offer support.
- Fourth graders enjoy social activities. During the sessions, include activities that allow the children to talk and work with others.
- Remind the children that Jesus wants them to be a physical presence of his love in the world.

"I like to be helpful. Show me ways to serve others."

Chapter Story

Invite

"I Will Remember"

Use this story to expand the chapter introduction.

- The children will relate the story to their own lives, reflecting on the important people in their lives.
- Connect the important people to the ways we remember them.

 Go to **aliveinchrist.osv.com** Lesson Planning section for this story.

NCEA IFG: ACRE Edition

Discover

Knowledge of the Faith

- Objective: To know and understand basic Catholic teaching about the Incarnate Word Jesus Christ as the way, truth, and life

Liturgical Life

- Objective: To know the Paschal Mystery of Jesus: in the Church's liturgical life—feasts, seasons, symbols, and practices—and in the Sacraments as signs and instruments of grace

Catholic Social Teaching

Live

 Use one of these features to introduce a principle and engage the children with an activity.

- Option for the Poor and Vulnerable, Pages 296–297
- Solidarity of the Human Family, Pages 300–301

Music Options

 Use one or more of the following songs to enhance catechetical learning or for prayer.

- "We Come to the Table," Live Prayer, Page 240
- "Savior of the World," Discover, Page 234
- "The Seven Sacraments," Discover, Page 235
- "The Supper of the Lamb," Discover, Page 236
- "We Come to Worship You," Live, Page 238

LECTIONARY CONNECTION

Chapter 17 highlights Lectionary-connected themes such as Eucharist, Real Presence, and the Sacraments. If your parish aligns its curriculum to the liturgical year, you could use this chapter in connection with the following Sundays.

Year A

Third Sunday of Easter—Real Presence

Fifth Sunday of Easter—Jesus as Way, Truth, and Life

The Most Holy Body and Blood of Christ—Eucharist

Year B

Fifth Sunday of Easter—Eucharist

The Most Holy Body and Blood of Christ—Eucharist

Twenty-seventh Sunday in Ordinary Time—Marriage

Year C

Sixth Sunday of Easter—Confirmation

The Most Holy Body and Blood of Christ—Eucharist

Thirty-second Sunday in Ordinary Time—Matrimony

 Go to **aliveinchrist.osv.com** for a complete correlation ordered by the Sundays of the year and suggestions for how to integrate the Scripture readings into chapter lessons.

Name _____ Date _____

Seven Sacraments

Design a stained-glass window that represents the Seven Sacraments. Divide this outline of a stained-glass window into seven parts. In each part, create a colorful symbol for one of the Seven Sacraments.

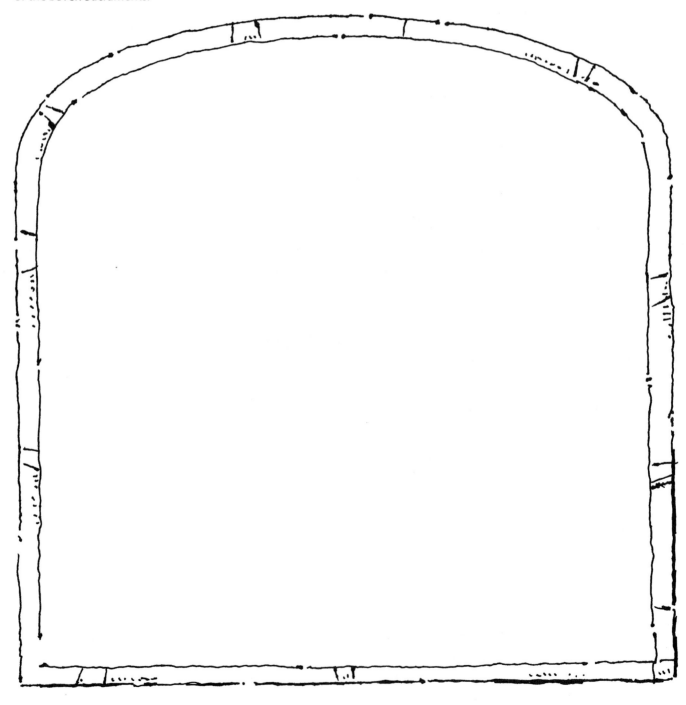

The Seven Sacraments

 Let Us Pray

Leader: With joy and gladness, Lord, we celebrate the signs of your great love.

"Shout joyfully to the LORD, all you lands;
    serve the LORD with gladness;
    come before him with joyful song." Psalm 100:1–2

All: With wonderful signs of your love, you bless us, Lord. No wonder we shout, "Praise and thanks!" Amen.

 Scripture

Blessed be the God and Father of our Lord Jesus Christ, who has blessed us in Christ with every spiritual blessing in the heavens. . . . In him we have redemption . . . the forgiveness of transgressions, in accord with the riches of his grace that he lavished upon us. Ephesians 1:3, 7–8

? What Do You Wonder?

- How do you continue to receive spiritual blessings?
- When do you celebrate Jesus' life and love?

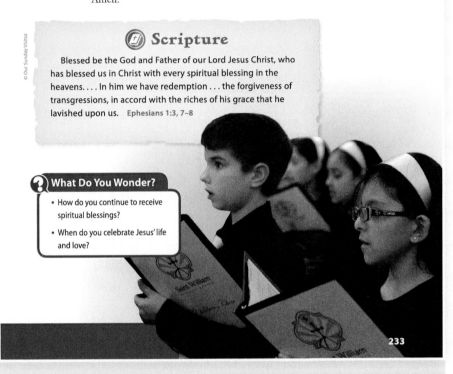

233

Optional Activity

Chapter Story: "I Will Remember" *Verbal/Linguistic*

Use this story after the opening prayer, before explaining that the Seven Sacraments are signs of God's love for us.

- Invite a child to read aloud the story.
- *Ask:* Why are the flowers in Juana's garden signs to her that her *abuelita* is living with and loved by God?
- After asking what things remind them of the special people in their lives, continue with the lesson instruction.

 Go to **aliveinchrist.osv.com** for Chapter Story.

 Let Us Pray

Invite the children to gather in the prayer space and make the Sign of the Cross. Choose a child to read aloud the Psalm verse from a Bible. Prompt the children's response.

Have the children move out of the prayer space and back to their seats.

Explain that the Seven Sacraments are signs of God's love for us.

Say: We bless God the Father for sending his Son, who gives us the Seven Sacraments as powerful signs of God's love for us.

 Scripture

Guide the children through the process of Scripture reflection.

- Invite them to close their eyes, be still and open their minds and hearts to what God is saying to them in this passage.
- Proclaim the Scripture.
- Maintain several moments of silence.
- *Ask:* What did you hear God say to you today?
- Invite volunteers to share.

What Do You Wonder?

Say: We celebrate these signs with gladness, for we know that in our celebration, Jesus is present with us. In our celebration, we are made sharers in the life and love of God.

Invite the children to respond to the questions. Ask what else they might wonder about blessings or the Sacraments.

Objectives

- Recognize that God the Father sent his only Son, Jesus, as a sign of his love for all people

- Recognize that each of the Seven Sacraments are effective signs of God's life, instituted by Christ and given to the Church, so that Jesus can continue his saving work in the world

- Begin to develop an understanding that the visible signs and Divine actions in each celebration give grace and allow us to share in God's work

Present Through Time

Ask: What is a Sacrament?

- Write the children's responses on the board or on chart paper.

Read aloud the first two paragraphs.

- Ask the children what signs of God's presence they have seen today.

- Ask the children to listen as you tell them about a special sign that God sent the whole world. Then proclaim the Scripture story.

- Encourage the children to memorize John 14:6–7.

Work with Words

Invite a volunteer to read aloud the definition of *Incarnation*.

- Have the children make vocabulary cards for the term.

 Music Option: Have the children sing, "Savior of the World," downloaded from **aliveinchrist.osv.com**.

Present Through Time

What is a Sacrament?

Your life is filled with many signs. However, some signs have a deeper meaning, like a trophy that you worked hard to win or an American flag. Christians received the most precious sign of all in the **Incarnation**, when the Son of God became man. God the Father sent his Son, Jesus, as a sign of his love for all people. He pointed the way to God for all who followed him.

Jesus welcomed people like Peter and Zacchaeus, and they changed their lives for him. Jesus showed people God the Father's forgiveness. He healed some and called others to serve. Through Jesus' words and actions, many people experienced God's saving love. Because he is both Divine and human, Jesus made God and his love present.

"No one comes to the Father except through me," Jesus said to his Apostles at the Last Supper. "If you know me, then you will also know my Father. From now on you do know him and have seen him" (John 14:6–7).

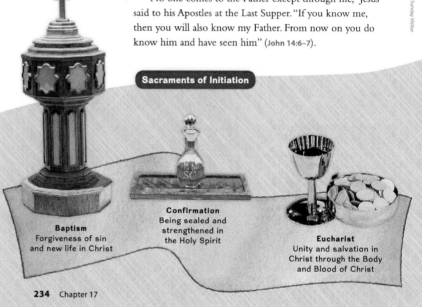

Sacraments of Initiation

Baptism Forgiveness of sin and new life in Christ

Confirmation Being sealed and strengthened in the Holy Spirit

Eucharist Unity and salvation in Christ through the Body and Blood of Christ

234 Chapter 17

Scripture Background

John 14:6–7

These verses are preceded by an appeal to believe in Jesus, not only because of his words, but also because of his deeds.

- John 14:6–7 emphasizes that Jesus is the means of salvation.

- By knowing Jesus, Christians will know God the Father, because the Father and Son, with the Holy Spirit, are one God in the Holy Trinity.

Visible Signs and Divine Actions

It was only after Jesus' Resurrection that his Apostles began to understand that Jesus was really God! Jesus had promised his followers that he would always be with them and that they would continue his saving work. A very important way that Jesus does this is through the **Seven Sacraments**. The Sacraments are effective signs of God's life, instituted by Christ and given to the Church. They are actions of the Holy Spirit at work in Christ's Body, the Church. Jesus is present in each of the Sacraments.

In each of the Sacraments, there are visible signs and Divine actions that give grace and allow us to share in God's work. Each one celebrates a way that Jesus' saving work continues in the world.

Underline what Jesus promised the disciples and one way he fulfills this promise today.

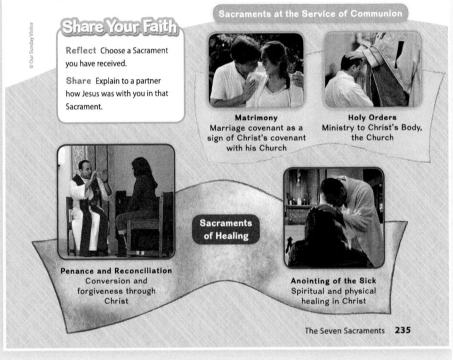

Share Your Faith

Reflect Choose a Sacrament you have received.

Share Explain to a partner how Jesus was with you in that Sacrament.

Sacraments at the Service of Communion

Matrimony
Marriage covenant as a sign of Christ's covenant with his Church

Holy Orders
Ministry to Christ's Body, the Church

Sacraments of Healing

Penance and Reconciliation
Conversion and forgiveness through Christ

Anointing of the Sick
Spiritual and physical healing in Christ

The Seven Sacraments **235**

Optional Activity

Activity Master 17: Seven Sacraments

Distribute copies of the activity found on catechist page 233E.

- This activity reviews the Seven Sacraments and the idea of symbols.
- As an alternative, you may wish to send this activity home with the children.

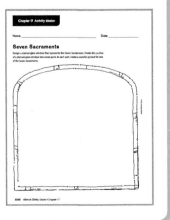

Visible Signs and Divine Actions

Read aloud the text. Have the children listen to find out how Jesus is present today.

 Have the children underline what Jesus promised the disciples and one way he fulfills this promise today.

Work with Words

Invite a volunteer to read aloud the definition of *Seven Sacraments*.

- Have the children make vocabulary cards.

Call attention to the ribbon of Sacraments along the bottom of the pages.

- As you read about each of the Seven Sacraments, have the children raise their hands if they have celebrated or seen that particular Sacrament.
- Invite volunteers to share experiences of the Sacraments.

Refer to page 314 in Our Catholic Tradition for more about the Seven Sacraments.

 Music Option: Have the children sing, "The Seven Sacraments," downloaded from **aliveinchrist.osv.com**.

Activity

Read aloud the directions and have the children complete the activity.

Quick Review

Jesus shares his life and love with us. Sacraments are special signs and celebrations that come from Jesus and allow us to share in God's life and love.

Discover

Objective

- Identify that the Sacrament of the Eucharist is at the heart of Christian life

The Eucharist

Ask: What is the heart of our Catholic life?

- Write the children's responses on the board or on chart paper.

Tell the children that they will now focus on the Sacrament of the Eucharist.

- Read aloud the introductory paragraph.

Point out the painting and read aloud the caption.

- Invite the children to tell what they see in the painting.
- Tell the children that they are going to hear the Scripture account, "The Last Supper," that tells about this painting.

 **Scripture**

Proclaim "The Last Supper."

- Ask the children where they have heard these words of Jesus before. at Mass

Read aloud the last paragraph.

- *Ask:* What did Jesus' followers do when they gathered weekly?

 Music Option: Have the children sing, "The Supper of the Lamb," downloaded from **aliveinchrist.osv.com**.

Discover

The Last Supper, by Remigio Cantagallina

The Eucharist

What is the heart of our Catholic life?

Jesus often ate meals with his friends. On the night before he died, Jesus shared a Passover meal with his Apostles.

 **Scripture**

The Last Supper

Then [Jesus] took a cup, gave thanks, and said, "Take this and share it among yourselves; for I tell you [that] from this time on I shall not drink of the fruit of the vine until the kingdom of God comes." Then he took the bread, said the blessing, broke it, and gave it to them, saying, "This is my body, which will be given for you; do this in memory of me." And likewise the cup after they had eaten, saying, "This cup is the new covenant in my blood, which will be shed for you." Luke 22:17–20

After Jesus was raised to new life and returned to the Father, his followers gathered weekly for the "breaking of the bread." They knew, as Catholics do today, that Jesus was present when they blessed and broke bread together as Jesus commanded. This celebration is called the **Eucharist**, the Sacrament in which Jesus gives himself and the bread and wine become his Body and Blood.

236   Chapter 17

 **Scripture Background**

Luke 22:17–20

The institution of the Sacrament of the Eucharist is related in this important passage, as well as in verses from the Gospels according to Matthew and Mark.

- Matthew 26:26–29 states the Christ's blood "will be shed on behalf of many for the forgiveness of sins."
- Mark 14:22–25 gives a similar account.

Act of Thanksgiving

In the Eucharist, we remember, give thanks for, and share in the life, Death, and Resurrection of Jesus. The word *Eucharist* means "thanksgiving." At the beginning of Mass, you ask God's mercy because of your sins. Your venial sins can be forgiven by your participation in the Eucharist. You listen to the Word of God. You thank God the Father for the great gift of his Son. When you receive Jesus in Holy Communion, you are united with the other members of the Body of Christ.

When Jesus told the Apostles to "do this in memory of me," he did not mean only that they should break bread together. He meant that they should live their lives as he did. Living the Eucharist means loving, welcoming, and forgiving others. You live the Eucharist when you share with those who do not have what you do.

→ When did you first receive Jesus in Holy Communion? Tell what you remember about the day.

> **Catholic Faith Words**
>
> **Eucharist** the Sacrament in which Jesus gives himself and the bread and wine become his Body and Blood

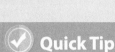

Activity

The Sacraments Use some of these terms in a paragraph about the Sacraments.

_____
_____
_____
_____
_____
_____
_____

Word List
• • • • • • • • • • •
Eucharist
God's Word
Holy Communion
Divine action
Body of Christ

237

© Our Sunday Visitor

✓ Quick Tip

Living the Eucharist

The U.S. Conference of Catholic Bishops calls Catholics to be "engaged and challenged, encouraged and empowered" to live the faith every day (*Sharing Catholic Social Teaching*, p. 9).

• Give each child a self-stick note on which to write one way that he or she might bring Christ's love to the world.

Act of Thanksgiving

Invite a volunteer to read aloud the first paragraph.

• Tell the children to listen to find out the meaning of the word *Eucharist* and what happens during the celebration of the Sacrament.

Work with Words

Have the children create vocabulary cards for *Eucharist*.

Ask: What do the words *living the Eucharist* mean?

• Explain that Jesus is really and truly with us, or present, in the Eucharist—Body, Blood, Soul, and Divinity. This is called Real Presence. Because Jesus is with us in the Eucharist, we receive strength from it to live a certain way.

Read aloud the last paragraph.

• *Ask:* When did you first receive Jesus in Holy Communion?

• Invite the children to tell what they remember about the day.

Activity

Read aloud the directions for the Connect Your Faith activity.

• Confirm that the children understand the terms.

• Provide time for the children to write their paragraphs.

Quick Review

The Eucharist unites Jesus with his followers. Living the Eucharist means continuing Jesus' work in the world.

Our Catholic Life

Ask: How can you participate actively in Mass?

- Write the children's responses on the board or on chart paper.

Read aloud the first two paragraphs.

Take Part

Invite each of six volunteers to read aloud one of the suggestions.

⭐ Have the children place a star beside the part of the Mass in which they feel especially close to God. Then have them draw a heart next to one part they will concentrate on more next week.

Point out the picture.

- Invite the children to tell what is happening in the picture.
- Remind the children that sharing a sign of peace is one way of participating in Mass.

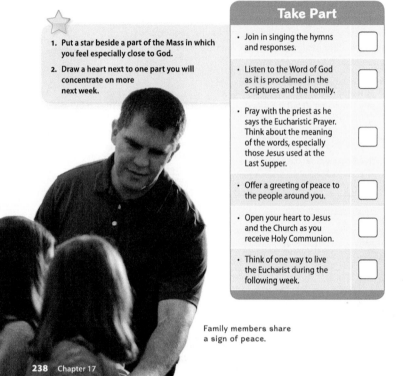

Our Catholic Life

How can you participate actively in Mass?

Do you go to Mass or do you participate in Mass? Do you know the difference? If you arrive at church on Sunday, slink into the pew, and daydream for the next hour, you are only going to Mass.

Mass is an excellent time for you to take an active role in your relationship with God. It is your chance to join with the rest of your parish in lifting your voices and souls in praise of God.

1. Put a star beside a part of the Mass in which you feel especially close to God.
2. Draw a heart next to one part you will concentrate on more next week.

Take Part

- Join in singing the hymns and responses. ☐
- Listen to the Word of God as it is proclaimed in the Scriptures and the homily. ☐
- Pray with the priest as he says the Eucharistic Prayer. Think about the meaning of the words, especially those Jesus used at the Last Supper. ☐
- Offer a greeting of peace to the people around you. ☐
- Open your heart to Jesus and the Church as you receive Holy Communion. ☐
- Think of one way to live the Eucharist during the following week. ☐

© Our Sunday Visitor

Family members share a sign of peace.

238 Chapter 17

✓ Quick Tip

Give Thanks

Attending Mass weekly affords Catholics an opportunity to show their thanks for being part of creation.

- Have the children listen to see how often the people thank God during Mass.
- Scripture lessons read during Mass show that God appreciates but does not need our expressions of thanks.

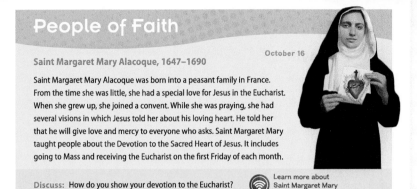

People of Faith

Saint Margaret Mary Alacoque, 1647–1690

October 16

Saint Margaret Mary Alacoque was born into a peasant family in France. From the time she was little, she had a special love for Jesus in the Eucharist. When she grew up, she joined a convent. While she was praying, she had several visions in which Jesus told her about his loving heart. He told her that he will give love and mercy to everyone who asks. Saint Margaret Mary taught people about the Devotion to the Sacred Heart of Jesus. It includes going to Mass and receiving the Eucharist on the first Friday of each month.

Discuss: How do you show your devotion to the Eucharist?

Learn more about Saint Margaret Mary at **aliveinchrist.osv.com**

Live Your Faith

Make a Eucharist Poster Create a poster for your parish hall or church entrance for people to see as they come to Mass. On your poster, draw some ways people can live the Eucharist.

© Our Sunday Visitor

The Seven Sacraments **239**

🌐 Catholic Social Teaching

Chapter Connections

To integrate Catholic Social Teaching into your lesson, choose one of the following features: Option for the Poor and Vulnerable, pages 296–297; or Solidarity of the Human Family, pages 300–301.

- Start the Live step of the process by talking about Saint Margaret Mary Alacoque on page 239. Then move directly to the Catholic Social Teaching feature.

- Or, to expand the lesson, complete both pages 238 and 239, then move to the Catholic Social Teaching feature.

- Return to Chapter 17 for the prayer on page 240.

People of Faith

Tell the children about Saint Margaret Mary Alacoque.

- Invite a volunteer to read aloud the People of Faith story.

- Explain that Saint Margaret Mary Alacoque endured many hardships in her life. When she was eight years old, her father died of pneumonia. Because of financial hardship, she was sent to a convent to attend school. A few years later she contracted rheumatic fever and was sent home.

- The family farm had been taken over by relatives. Margaret and her mother were treated like servants. When her eldest brother turned eighteen, however, the farm was legally his. Finally the family had possession of their home once again.

- *Ask:* How do you show your devotion to the Eucharist?

 Encourage the children to go to **aliveinchrist.osv.com** at home to learn more about Saint Margaret Mary Alacoque.

Activity

Read aloud the directions and discuss the Live Your Faith activity as a group.

- Allow time for the children to design their posters.

- Invite volunteers to share their drawings.

Let Us Pray

Prayer of Petition

Tell the children that this is a traditional prayer by Saint Francis de Sales. It asks God to help us prepare to receive him each time we celebrate the Eucharist.

Prepare

 Rehearse "We Come to the Table," downloaded from **aliveinchrist.osv.com**.

Gather

Invite the children to process to the prayer space. Have each child bring their book.

 Play "We Come to the Table" as the children process.

- Invite the children to be seated and place their books on their laps.
- Allow the children to get settled and prepare their minds and hearts for prayer.

Pray

Follow the order of prayer on the student page.

 Conclude by singing together "We Come to the Table."

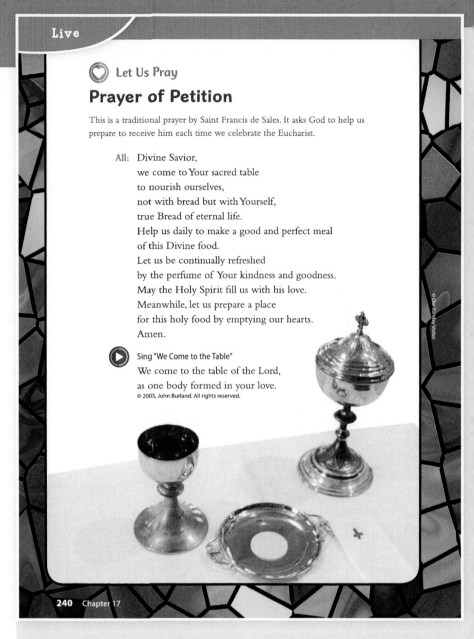

Live

 Let Us Pray

Prayer of Petition

This is a traditional prayer by Saint Francis de Sales. It asks God to help us prepare to receive him each time we celebrate the Eucharist.

All: Divine Savior,
we come to Your sacred table
to nourish ourselves,
not with bread but with Yourself,
true Bread of eternal life.
Help us daily to make a good and perfect meal
of this Divine food.
Let us be continually refreshed
by the perfume of Your kindness and goodness.
May the Holy Spirit fill us with his love.
Meanwhile, let us prepare a place
for this holy food by emptying our hearts.
Amen.

Sing "We Come to the Table"
We come to the table of the Lord,
as one body formed in your love.

 Liturgy Link

Offering

When members of the assembly bring forward the gifts during Mass, everyone is reminded of the need to offer themselves to God.

- Perhaps an offering could be part of your celebration.
- Invite the children to bring donations or nonperishable food items when they gather for prayer.

Go to **aliveinchrist.osv.com** for Sunday readings, Scripture background, questions of the week, and seasonal resources.

FAMILY+FAITH
LIVING AND LEARNING TOGETHER

YOUR CHILD LEARNED >>>
This chapter explains that in the celebration of each Sacrament, there are visible signs and Divine actions that give grace and allow us to share in God's work.

Scripture
Read **Ephesians 1:3, 7–8** to find a blessing for God for all the blessings the early Christians received.

Catholics Believe
• The Seven Sacraments are effective signs, instituted by Christ, that give grace and continue his saving work in the world.
• The Sacrament of the Eucharist is at the heart of Christian life.
To learn more, go to the *Catechism of the Catholic Church #1210, 1407* at usccb.org.

People of Faith
This week, your child learned about Saint Margaret Mary Alacoque, the promoter of the Devotion to the Sacred Heart of Jesus.

CHILDREN AT THIS AGE >>>
How They Understand the Sacraments Fourth-graders, while still bound to their five senses, are better able than younger children to see the connections between rituals and their meanings. This can help them gain a deeper appreciation of the Seven Sacraments as they know that what they are seeing and hearing in sacramental celebrations is a sign of, and participation in, something invisible as well.

CONSIDER THIS >>>
Who do you know who understands the Eucharist as a sacred gift and not an obligation?

Perhaps we might see it the same way if we became more aware that Jesus' gift of his life is given again for us each time we receive the Eucharist. We need to open our hearts to receive the gift we long for: the gift of knowing we are loved that perfectly, that completely. As Catholics, "we need to remember that the Eucharist is the summit and source of our Christian life. Why? Because in the Eucharist is found the entire treasure of the Church—Jesus Christ" (*USCCA, p.228*).

LET'S TALK >>>
• Ask your child to name the Seven Sacraments.
• Talk about the different Sacraments family members have celebrated.

LET'S PRAY >>>
Saint Margaret Mary Alacoque, pray for us that we may learn to love Jesus in the Eucharist as much as you did. Amen.

For a multimedia glossary of Catholic Faith Words, Sunday readings, seasonal and Saint resources, and chapter activities go to **aliveinchrist.osv.com**.

Family + Faith

Distribute the page to the children or parents/adult family members. Point out the chapter highlights, insights on how fourth graders understand concepts, the opportunity for the adults to reflect on their own experience and faith journey, and the family prayer.

Chapter 17 Review

(A) Work with Words Fill in the circle next to the answer that best completes each statement.

1. There are _____ Sacraments.
   - ● seven
   - ○ eight
   - ○ nine

2. _____ is present in all of the Sacraments.
   - ○ Water
   - ● Jesus
   - ○ The Bible

3. The early Christians _____ the Eucharist.
   - ● celebrated
   - ○ did not celebrate
   - ○ invented

4. Eucharist means " _____ ."
   - ○ morality
   - ○ Heaven
   - ● thanksgiving

5. When you _____ , you continue Jesus' work in the world.
   - ○ go to religion class
   - ○ sing hymns
   - ● live the Eucharist

(B) Check Understanding Complete each sentence by circling the correct answer. Then answer the last two questions.

6. After Jesus' Resurrection, the Apostles began to understand that (he was God/he was gone forever).

7. The Sacraments are actions of the (priest/Holy Spirit) at work in Christ's Body, the Church.

8. When you receive Jesus in Holy Communion, you (forgive/are united with) the other members of the Body of Christ.

9. What are some ways you can live the Eucharist?
   Possible responses: by welcoming, by forgiving, by helping others

10. What are some ways you can participate actively in the Mass?
    Possible responses: sing hymns, pray, pay attention to the homily

Go to **aliveinchrist.osv.com** for an interactive review.

Chapter Review

Use Catechist Quick Reviews to highlight lesson concepts.

(A) Work with Words
Have the children fill in the circle next to the answer that best completes each statement.

(B) Check Understanding
Complete each sentence by circling the correct answer. Write answers to the last two questions.

Go to **aliveinchrist.osv.com** to prepare customized and downloadable assessments, send eAssessments, and assign interactive reviews.

KEY CONCEPT

God's forgiveness is offered to all who are truly sorry and seek it. The Sacraments of Reconciliation and the Anointing of the Sick celebrate God's healing love.

DOCTRINAL CONTENT

- Conversion involves turning away from sin and responding to God's love and forgiveness. (CCC, 1427–1428)

- In Penance and Reconciliation, we receive God's forgiveness of sins through the Church and are strengthened by grace to make peace and avoid temptation. (CCC, 1468–1469)

- The Sacrament of the Anointing of the Sick brings Jesus' healing touch to strengthen, comfort, and forgive the sins of those who are seriously ill or close to death. (CCC, 1532)

TASKS OF CATECHESIS

Helping children grow in a faith that is "known, celebrated, lived, and expressed in prayer" (NDC, 20).

This chapter focuses on the following tasks of catechesis:

- Liturgical Education
- Moral Formation

Catechist Background

"Then I declared my sin to you; my guilt I did not hide. I said, 'I confess my transgression to the LORD,' and you took away the guilt of my sin." Psalm 32:5

→ **Reflect** Why might you feel nervous about telling your sins to a priest?

The Church's Sacraments of Healing are Anointing of the Sick and Penance and Reconciliation. Humans are fallible and fragile on many levels. On one level, their bodies grow older and deteriorate; debilitating illnesses may come gradually or suddenly. On another level, people sometimes choose to do an immoral act because they put their own interests above God or others or because they succumb to peer pressure. They sin, and their conscience grows callous.

God's plan for humans, body and soul, flesh and spirit, is to be whole and well. Your loving God knows your physical and spiritual weaknesses and responds by offering you his healing grace. Jesus was a healer. He gave his Church the mission of continuing his healing ministry by the power of the Holy Spirit. The Sacraments of Healing make you strong as you travel forward on your journey of faith.

Forgiving and reconciling are closely related, but quite distinct. Forgiveness involves letting go of sin and accepting God's forgiveness. It means getting past hurt and anger; it is the choice to change your thoughts, attitudes, and actions toward another person. Reconciliation means restoring the relationship. Reconciliation brings friends, families, and even nations together again. When you reconcile, you reconnect to others—and to God, whose arms are always open and ready to receive you.

→ **Reflect** When do you feel the need to reconnect with God?

Catechist's Prayer

Generous God, your love for me is immeasurable. Help me remember all of the forgiveness and mercy you have offered me. Amen.

Lesson Plan

Objectives	Process	Materials

Invite, 10 minutes

Healing and Reconciliation Page 243

- ○ Psalm 25:6 Pray the opening prayer.
- Psalm 32:1–3, 5 Reflect prayerfully on the Word.
- Discuss What Do You Wonder questions.

○ **Optional Activity** Chapter Story: "After School"

Discover, 35 minutes

God's Forgiveness Pages 244–245

- Explore conversion, turning away from sin and responding to God's love and forgiveness, relating their own lives to the example of Zacchaeus
- Understand that in the Sacrament of Penance and Reconciliation, we receive God's forgiveness of sins through the Church and are strengthened by grace to make peace and avoid temptation

- **Catholic Faith Words** repent, Sacrament of Penance and Reconciliation, confession, temptation
- Explain that Jesus showed God's forgiveness.
- Luke 19:1–10 Proclaim "The Story of Zacchaeus."
- God is always ready and waiting to forgive.
- The Church continues God's forgiveness in the Sacrament of Penance and Reconciliation.
- **Share Your Faith Activity** Reflect on an experience of forgiveness.

☐ pencils
☐ index cards
☐ crayons or markers

The Sacraments of Healing Pages 246–247

- Discover that the Sacrament of the Anointing of the Sick brings Jesus' healing touch to strengthen, comfort, and forgive the sins of those who are seriously ill or close to death

- **Catholic Faith Words** sacramental seal, penance, absolution, Sacrament of the Anointing of the Sick
- ☆ Underline what God will do for those who are truly sorry.
- Introduce the Sacrament of the Anointing of the Sick.
- John 9:1–18 Proclaim "The Man Born Blind."
- **Connect Your Faith Activity** Identify what God has provided us for healing.

☐ pencils
☐ index cards
☐ crayons or markers
- **Optional Activity** What Will Help?
☐ Activity Master 18 (Page 243E)

Live, 15 minutes

Our Catholic Life Pages 248–249

- Explain that celebrating the Sacrament of Reconciliation takes some preparation.
- ☆ Match the steps to the correct explanation.
- **People of Faith** Learn about Venerable Matt Talbot.
- **Live Your Faith Activity** Write a message.

☐ pencils
☐ crayons or markers
☐ construction paper and other art supplies

Our Lady, Queen of Peace Page 250

- ▶ Rehearse "Salve Regina."
- Follow the order of prayer.

○ Download "Salve Regina."

Family + Faith Page 251

Point out that the Catholic Families page provides chapter highlights, information on how fourth graders understand faith concepts, and family prayer.

Chapter Review Page 252

○ aliveinchrist.osv.com

- Customize and Download Assessments
- Email Links to eAssessments
- Interactive Student Reviews

ONLINE RESOURCES

 Go to **aliveinchrist.osv.com**

You will find:

- Interactive lesson planning with web specific content and additional activities
- Step by step lesson instruction from printed Catechist Edition for integrated lesson planning
- Custom-built assessments to download and eAssessment links
- Interactive reviews that provide scores and the option to review answers
- Sunday readings with background and questions of the week

 Go to **osvparish.com**

You will find:

- Ask the Experts Q and A
- General Catechist Helps
- Community Connections and Blogs

Sharing the Message with Fourth Graders

Healing and Reconciliation For fourth graders, right and wrong are deeper concepts than they were when they were younger. Morality is not just about what other people see us doing. It is also about who we are and what we do when no one seems to be watching. It is important that as children grow in their ability to form their consciences, they have continued opportunity to seek God's forgiveness through the Sacrament of Penance and Reconciliation.

Teaching Tip: Remind parents of the importance of providing opportunities for their children to celebrate the Sacrament of Penance and Reconciliation. Send notes home that remind families of weekly Reconciliation times as well as parish Penance services.

How Fourth Graders Understand

- Fairness is important to fourth graders. Make sure that everyone knows and follows the rules.
- Using signs like the sign of peace can help fourth graders understand the meaning of forgiveness. Include them in your lesson.
- Challenge fourth graders to imagine ways to follow Jesus' example of forgiveness in their own lives.

"Sometimes it is not easy for me to forgive. Remind me when I forget."

Chapter Connections

Chapter Story

Invite

"After School"

Use this story to expand the chapter introduction.

- The children will relate the story to their own lives, reflecting their experience of forgiveness.
- Connect forgiveness with both forgiving others and being forgiven.

 Go to **aliveinchrist.osv.com** Lesson Planning section for this story.

NCEA IFG: ACRE Edition

Discover

Liturgical Life

- Objective: To know the Paschal Mystery of Jesus: in the Church's liturgical life—feasts, seasons, symbols, and practices—and in the Sacraments as signs and instruments of grace

Moral Formation

- Objective: To be knowledgeable about the teachings of Jesus and the Church as the basis of Christian morality and to understand Catholic Social Teaching

Catholic Social Teaching

Live

 Use one of these features to introduce a principle and engage the children with an activity.

- Right and Responsibilities of the Human Person, Pages 294–295
- Option for the Poor and Vulnerable, Pages 296–297

Music Options

 Use one or more of the following songs to enhance catechetical learning or for prayer.

- "Salve Regina," Live Prayer, Page 250
- "Zacchaeus," Discover, Page 244
- "God of Mercy," Discover, Page 245
- "Heal Us Lord," Discover, Page 247
- "Hail Mary: Gentle Woman," Live Prayer, Page 250

LECTIONARY CONNECTION

 Chapter 18 highlights Lectionary-connected themes such as healing, forgiveness, and conversion. If your parish aligns its curriculum to the liturgical year, you could use this chapter in connection with the following Sundays.

Year A

First Sunday of Lent—temptation

Twenty-third Sunday in Ordinary Time—sin, forgiveness

Twenty-sixth Sunday in Ordinary Time—forgiveness

Year B

Fourth Sunday of Lent—grace

Fifth Sunday of Lent—follow Jesus

Thirtieth Sunday in Ordinary Time—Anointing of the Sick

Year C

Twenty-fourth Sunday in Ordinary Time—forgiveness

Twenty-eighth Sunday in Ordinary Time—healing

Thirty-first Sunday in Ordinary Time—conversion

Go to **aliveinchrist.osv.com** for a complete correlation ordered by the Sundays of the year and suggestions for how to integrate the Scripture readings into chapter lessons.

Name _____ Date _____

What Will Help?

For each picture in the left column, draw a kind of healing that will help the situation.
Use the empty boxes in the right column for your drawings.

Healing and Reconciliation

Let Us Pray

Leader: Merciful God, be always with us as we pray.

"Remember your compassion and your mercy,
O LORD,
for they are ages old." **Psalm 25:6**

All: Jesus, no matter how many times we sin, you call us back to you. Help us to admit our sin and ask for your forgiveness. Amen.

© Our Sunday Visitor

Scripture

"Blessed is the one whose fault is removed,
whose sin is forgiven.
Blessed is the man to whom the LORD imputes no guilt,
in whose spirit [there] is no deceit.
Because I kept silent, my bones wasted away;
I groaned all day long.
Then I declared my sin to you;
my guilt I did not hide.
I said, 'I confess my transgression to the LORD,'
and you took away the guilt of my sin."

Psalm 32:1–3, 5

? What Do You Wonder?

• Is there a limit to how much God will forgive?

• Why might you feel nervous telling your sins to the priest?

243

Optional Activity

Chapter Story: "After School" *Verbal/Linguistic*

Use this story after the opening prayer, before explaining that we feel sorrow and guilt after we have hurt someone.

• Read the story aloud as the children follow along.

• Ask: Why was Mrs. Whelan angry with Denise?

• *Ask:* What does Denise need to do?

• After discussing the answers to the questions, transition back to the lesson instruction.

 Go to **aliveinchrist.osv.com** for Chapter Story.

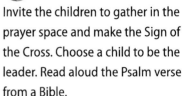

Invite

♥ Let Us Pray

Invite the children to gather in the prayer space and make the Sign of the Cross. Choose a child to be the leader. Read aloud the Psalm verse from a Bible.

Have the children move out of the prayer space and back to their seats.

Say: When we do something harmful to someone we love, we feel sorrow and guilt. Looking at the face of the person we hurt helps us realize this.

Scripture

Guide the children through the process of Scripture reflection.

• Invite them to close their eyes, be still and open their minds and hearts to what God is saying to them in this passage.

• Proclaim the Scripture.

• Maintain several moments of silence.

• *Ask:* What did you hear God say to you today?

• Invite volunteers to share.

What Do You Wonder?

Say: Even though God already knows what we have done, we still need to confess our sin. In telling God, through the priest, we experience God's forgiveness in the Sacrament of Penance and Reconciliation.

Invite the children to respond to the questions. Ask what else they might wonder about God's forgiveness or the Sacraments of Healing.

Discover

Objectives

- Explore conversion, turning away from sin and responding to God's love and forgiveness, relating their own lives to the example of Zacchaeus

- Understand that in the Sacrament of Penance and Reconciliation, we receive God's forgiveness of sins through the Church and are strengthened by grace to make peace and avoid temptation

God's Forgiveness

Ask: Who is forgiven?

- Write the children's responses on the board or on chart paper.

Invite a volunteer to read aloud the first paragraph.

Scripture

Proclaim "The Story of Zacchaeus."

- *Ask:* Why was Zacchaeus unpopular? He cheated people.

- *Ask:* How did Zacchaeus change after he met Jesus? He repaid those he had cheated and gave money to those who were poor.

- Point out that Jesus offered friendship, and that this led to the change in Zacchaeus.

- *Ask:* Who has taught you the most about forgiveness? What did the person or persons say or do?

 Music Option: Have the children sing, "Zacchaeus," downloaded from **aliveinchrist.osv.com**.

God's Forgiveness

Who is forgiven?

Jesus showed God's forgiveness to others through his words and actions. In this story, Jesus meets a wealthy tax collector who decides to **repent** and become his follower.

Catholic Faith Words

repent to turn our lives away from sin and toward God

Sacrament of Penance and Reconciliation the Sacrament in which God's forgiveness for sin is given through the Church

confession an essential element of the Sacrament of Penance and Reconciliation, when you tell your sins to the priest; another name for the Sacrament

temptation an attraction to sin; wanting to do something we should not or not do something we should

Scripture

The Story of Zacchaeus

One day, Jesus was passing through the town of Jericho. Zacchaeus, a rich tax collector, wanted to see Jesus and learn about him. Zacchaeus was short, so he climbed a tree to see over the crowd.

Jesus noticed Zacchaeus in the tree. He said, "Zacchaeus, come down quickly, for today I must stay at your house." Zacchaeus came down happily.

The crowd complained, saying that Jesus should not stay with Zacchaeus because Zacchaeus was a sinner.

Zacchaeus told Jesus that he would give money to those who were poor. He offered to give anyone he had cheated four times the amount of money that he owed to that person.

"Today salvation has come to this house," said Jesus. "For the Son of Man has come to seek and to save what was lost." Based on Luke 19:1–10

→ Who has taught you the most about forgiveness? What did the person or persons say or do?

© Our Sunday Visitor

244 Chapter 18

Scripture Background

Luke 19:1–10

The rich tax collector in this story, Zacchaeus, provides a contrast to the rich young man who would not follow Jesus because he would not give up his possessions.

- Zacchaeus got rich by cheating people.

- After encountering Jesus, he exemplifies a right attitude toward wealth.

Conversion

God is always ready and waiting to forgive. He welcomes you back, just as Jesus welcomed Zacchaeus. When you turn away from sin and respond to God's love and forgiveness, you are experiencing conversion. Conversion is about becoming the people God intends us to be.

During his life, Jesus forgave many people in his Father's name. After his Resurrection, Jesus told his disciples that he would send the Holy Spirit, who would give them the power to forgive sins. Today, the Church continues to celebrate God's forgiveness in the **Sacrament of Penance and Reconciliation**. Sometimes this Sacrament is called **confession**, for the element of the Sacrament when we tell our sins to the priest. In this Sacrament, you receive God's forgiveness of sins through the Church. The grace of this Sacrament strengthens you to make peace with those whom you may have hurt. It also strengthens you against the attraction to sin called **temptation**.

© Our Sunday Visitor

Activity

Reflect Think of someone who has forgiven you or you have forgiven. Why did you or that person need forgiveness?

Share With a classmate, discuss ways to show you are sorry and make peace with others. Then, tell one way that you can be more forgiving of others.

_____

Healing and Reconciliation   **245**

Conversion

Read aloud the first paragraph.

- Point out the word *conversion*. Tell the children that it means "a change of heart."
- *Ask:* Who experienced conversion in the Scripture story? Zacchaeus
- Have the children read silently the second paragraph to learn how the Church continues Jesus' actions.

Work with Words

Invite four volunteers to each read aloud one of the Catholic Faith Words definitions.

- Have the children make vocabulary cards.

Refer to page 315 in the Our Catholic Tradition reference section in the back of the Student Book to find out more about the Sacrament of Penance and Reconciliation.

Music Option: Have the children sing, "God of Mercy," downloaded from **aliveinchrist.osv.com**.

Activity

Read aloud the directions for the Share Your Faith activity.

- Allow the children to reflect on their experience.
- Provide time for the children to discuss with a partner.

Quick Review

Jesus shares his life and love with us. Sacraments are special signs and celebrations that come from Jesus and allow us to share in God's life and love.

Discover

Objective

- Discover that the Sacrament of Anointing of the Sick brings Jesus' healing touch to strengthen, comfort and forgive the sins of those who are seriously ill or close to death

The Sacraments of Healing

Ask: How does the Church celebrate forgiveness and healing?

- Write the children's responses on the board or on chart paper.
- Tell the children that there is more to learn about how the Church celebrates God's forgiveness.

Invite volunteers to take turns reading aloud the paragraphs.

- Pause after each paragraph and review any terms that may be unfamiliar to the children.
- Invite the children to underline what God will do for us when we confess our sins and are truly sorry during the Sacrament of Penance and Reconciliation.
- *Ask:* Why is it important to celebrate the Sacrament of Penance and Reconciliation? to help you turn away from sin and toward God

Work with Words

Distribute index cards and have the children make vocabulary cards for each of the Catholic Faith Words.

The Sacraments of Healing

How does the Church celebrate forgiveness and healing?

> **Catholic Faith Words**
>
> **sacramental seal** a rule that a priest is not to share anything he hears in confession
>
> **penance** the prayer, offering, or good work the priest gives you in the Sacrament of Reconciliation
>
> **absolution** words spoken by the priest during the Sacrament of Penance and Reconciliation to grant forgiveness of sins in God's name

Celebrating the Sacrament of Penance and Reconciliation is a public sign that you are willing to turn away from sin and toward the love of God and the community.

Begin with an examination of conscience, a prayerful reflection on how you have lived the Ten Commandments, the Beatitudes, and other Church teachings. It helps us know whether what we've done is right or wrong.

When you confess your sins to a priest, you ask for God's forgiveness through the power the Holy Spirit gives to the Church. The priest cannot tell anyone the sins confessed in the Sacrament. This is called the **sacramental seal**, or seal of confession.

Contrition is being sorry for your sins and wanting to live better. God will forgive all sins, even mortal sins, if you are truly sorry and want to change your heart.

God forgives your sins, but the effects of your sins are still in the world. You must do what you can to repair the harm your sin has caused. Part of making up for your sin is to do the prayer, offering, or good work that the priest gives you as a **penance**.

When the priest says the words of **absolution**, he grants you forgiveness of sins in God's name.

> ⭐ Underline what God will do for us when we confess our sins and are truly sorry during the Sacrament of Reconciliation.

246 Chapter 18

Optional Activity

Activity Master 18: What Will Help?

Distribute copies of the activity found on catechist page 243E.

- Provide drawing materials so that the children can complete the activity.
- As an alternative, you may wish to send this activity home with the children.

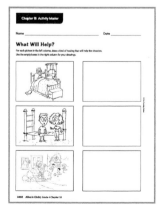

God's Healing Love

Today, the Church anoints the sick or dying through the **Sacrament of the Anointing of the Sick**. This Sacrament strengthens those who celebrate it and reminds them of God's healing love. God's love and mercy are available to all who turn to him.

In Jesus' time, people thought that sickness was God's punishment for someone's sin. But Jesus taught that this is not the case.

Catholic Faith Words

Sacrament of the Anointing of the Sick the Sacrament that brings Jesus' healing touch to strengthen, comfort, and forgive the sins of those who are seriously ill or close to death

 ### Scripture

The Man Born Blind

One day, Jesus saw a man who had been blind from birth. His disciples asked him, "Why is this man blind? Is it because of his own sin or that of his parents?"

Jesus answered, "Neither he nor his parents sinned; it is so that the works of God might be made more visible through him."

Jesus rubbed clay on the man's eyes and told him to go to a certain place and wash it off. When the man did, he could see!

Many did not believe that Jesus had done this. When the man came back, Jesus asked the man, "Do you believe in the Son of Man? . . . You have seen him and the one speaking with you is he."

The man answered, "I do believe, Lord." **Based on John 9:1–38**

Connect Your Faith

Think About Healing In the space below, name some things God has provided us for healing. Two examples are provided for you.

doctors, nurses

247

 ### Songs of Scripture

The Blind Man

Teach "The Blind Man."

- Invite the children to imagine how happy the blind man was when he washed the mud from his eyes and discovered that he could see.

- Give each child a piece of drawing paper. Ask them to draw what the blind man first saw.

> Use *Songs of Scripture*, Grades 4–6 CD, Track 10

God's Healing Love

Have the children read the first paragraph to learn about the Sacrament of the Anointing of the Sick.

- Read aloud the second paragraph to introduce the Scripture story.

- Have the children make vocabulary cards for the term *Sacrament of the Anointing of the Sick.*

Scripture

Assign parts and have the children proclaim "The Man Born Blind."

- Emphasize that God gave Jesus the power to heal people so that people could come to know God's healing love.

> Music Option: Have the children sing, "Heal Us Lord," downloaded from **aliveinchrist.osv.com**.

Activity

Read aloud the directions for the Connect Your Faith activity.

- Brainstorm answers with the whole group.

Quick Review

The Sacraments of Anointing of the Sick and Penance and Reconciliation celebrate God's forgiveness and healing.

Our Catholic Life

Ask: How can you prepare to receive God's forgiveness?

- Write the children's responses on the board or on chart paper.

Talk with the children about how they feel about preparing for the Sacrament of Penance and Reconciliation.

Read aloud or summarize the introductory paragraphs.

Before You Go

⭐ Point out the activity and have the children work independently to match the steps with the explanation.

- When everyone has finished, invite volunteers to share a step and definition until all the matches have been shared.

Ask: How do you feel after you celebrate this Sacrament?

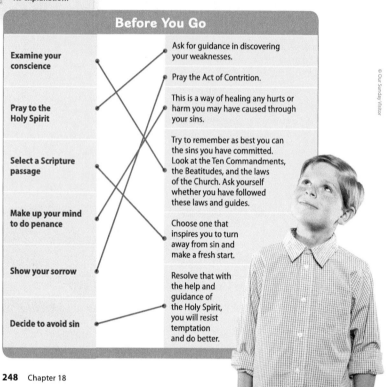

Live

Our Catholic Life

How can you prepare to receive God's forgiveness?

You may feel uncomfortable about telling your sins to a priest. Remember that the priest is not there to scare or punish you. He is acting as a servant of God. He will know your sorrow and grant you God's forgiveness.

Are you wondering how you will know what to say? Here are some suggestions to help you prepare to celebrate the Sacrament of Penance and Reconciliation.

⭐ Match the step with its explanation.

Before You Go

Examine your conscience	Ask for guidance in discovering your weaknesses.
	Pray the Act of Contrition.
Pray to the Holy Spirit	This is a way of healing any hurts or harm you may have caused through your sins.
Select a Scripture passage	Try to remember as best you can the sins you have committed. Look at the Ten Commandments, the Beatitudes, and the laws of the Church. Ask yourself whether you have followed these laws and guides.
Make up your mind to do penance	Choose one that inspires you to turn away from sin and make a fresh start.
Show your sorrow	Resolve that with the help and guidance of the Holy Spirit, you will resist temptation and do better.
Decide to avoid sin	

248   Chapter 18

© Our Sunday Visitor

✓ Quick Tip

Examine Your Conscience

This skill requires Christians to look within their souls and contemplate their characters.

- If people are truly examining their lives, they will admit to their flaws and mistakes.
- The Sacrament of Penance and Reconciliation should be considered an opportunity to ask for support in acquiring virtue and for guidance in atoning for sin.

People of Faith

Venerable Matt Talbot, 1856–1925

Matt Talbot was born in Dublin, Ireland. Many people in his family drank too much. Matt started drinking when he was young. After years of heavy drinking, he decided to stop. He realized that he had hurt many people and done many bad things. He asked for forgiveness from each person. He also received the Sacrament of Penance and asked God to forgive all his sins. For the rest of his life, he never drank again. He gave away much of his money and prayed for all those that he had hurt.

Discuss: Talk about a time when you hurt someone and had to ask forgiveness.

 Learn more about Venerable Matt at **aliveinchrist.osv.com**

Live Your Faith

Name one friend or family member who needs to hear a message of forgiveness from you. Draft your message in the space below.

_____

_____

_____

_____

_____

_____

_____

_____

_____

_____

_____

_____

Create a card with a handwritten message, and deliver it to that person.

Healing and Reconciliation **249**

 Catholic Social Teaching

Chapter Connections

To integrate Catholic Social Teaching into your lesson, choose one of the following features: Rights and Responsibilities of the Human Person, pages 294–295; or Option for the Poor and Vulnerable, pages 296–297.

- Start the Live step of the process by talking about Venerable Matt Talbot on page 249. Then move directly to the Catholic Social Teaching feature.
- Or, to expand the lesson, complete both pages 248 and 249, then move to the Catholic Social Teaching feature.
- Return to Chapter 18 for the prayer on page 250.

People of Faith

Tell the children about Venerable Matt Talbot.

- Invite a volunteer to read aloud the People of Faith story.
- Explain that Venerable Matt Talbot was able to stop drinking alcohol for life because he found strength in prayer.
- He began to attend daily Mass. In fact, he rose at 5 a.m. in order to attend Mass before work.
- He read religious books and pamphlets. He filled his days with hard work and penance.
- He slept on a wooden plank with a piece of timber for his pillow.
- Whenever he had a moment of spare time, he found a quiet place to pray.
- *Discuss:* Talk about a time when you hurt someone and had to ask forgiveness.

Encourage the children to go to **aliveinchrist.osv.com** at home to learn more about Venerable Matt Talbot.

Activity

Read aloud the directions and discuss the first part of the Live Your Faith activity as a group.

- Allow time for the children to complete their message.
- Provide materials for the children to make cards. Encourage them to deliver their cards.

Let Us Pray

Our Lady, Queen of Peace

Tell the children that today they will offer a prayer to Mary, the Queen of Peace.

Prepare

 Rehearse "Salve Regina," downloaded from **aliveinchrist.osv.com**.

Gather

Invite the children to process to the prayer space. Have each child bring their book.

- Invite the children to be seated in the prayer space.
- Allow the children to get settled and prepare their minds and hearts for prayer.

Pray

Lead the children in praying aloud together.

Conclude by singing together "Salve Regina."

Alternate Music Option: "Hail Mary: Gentle Woman"

 Let Us Pray

Our Lady, Queen of Peace

All: Most holy and immaculate Virgin,
Mother of Jesus and our loving Mother,
being his Mother, you shared in his universal kingship.
The prophets and angels proclaimed him King of peace.
With loving fervor in our hearts we salute and honor you as Queen of peace.
We pray that your intercession may protect us and all people from hatred and discord,
and direct our hearts into the ways of peace and justice which your Son taught and exemplified.
We ask your maternal care for our Holy Father who works to reconcile the nations in peace.
We seek your guidance for our President and other leaders as they strive for world peace.
Glorious Queen of peace, grant us peace in our hearts, harmony in our families, and concord throughout the world.
Immaculate Mother, as patroness of our beloved country, watch over us and protect us with your motherly love.
Amen.

Sing "Salve Regina (A Litany to Mary)"
Salve, Regína, Mater misericórdiae:
Vita dulcédo et spes nostra, salve.
Hail, Queen of Heaven, our Mother, kind and merciful:
Pray for your children. Hail, our sweetness and our hope.

 Liturgy Link

Set the Atmosphere

To establish a mood that encourages reflective prayer, use candlelight. Candles have always been used in Catholic worship.

- Use candles or battery-operated candles to quiet the atmosphere.
- In addition to or instead of the use of candles, use lower lighting to enhance the reflective nature of prayer.

Go to **aliveinchrist.osv.com** for Sunday readings, Scripture background, questions of the week, and seasonal resources.

FAMILY+FAITH
LIVING AND LEARNING TOGETHER

YOUR CHILD LEARNED >>>
This chapter explores reconciliation as it relates to the effect of sin in the world, and explains the necessity of confessing sins to a priest and trusting in Jesus' power to forgive and heal.

Scripture
Read **Psalm 32:1–3, 5** to find out about the blessing of Reconciliation.

Catholics Believe
- God's forgiveness is offered to all who are truly sorry and seek it.
- The Sacraments of Reconciliation and the Anointing of the Sick celebrate God's healing love.

To learn more, go to the *Catechism of the Catholic Church #1420–1421, 1489–1490* at **usccb.org**.

People of Faith
This week, your child learned about Venerable Matt Talbot, who is known for turning his life around with prayer and self-sacrifice.

CHILDREN AT THIS AGE >>>
How They Understand Healing and Reconciliation For fourth-graders, right and wrong are deeper concepts than they were before. Morality is not just about what other people see us doing. It is also about who we are and what we do when no one seems to be watching. It is important that as children grow in their ability to form their consciences, they have continued opportunity to seek God's forgiveness through the Sacrament of Penance and Reconciliation.

CONSIDER THIS >>>
Have you ever yearned for a relationship to be healed?

We are human, and are not perfect. Our egos or hurt feelings can get in the way of healing a relationship. Yet, God loves perfectly and offers forgiveness to all who have not loved as he asked and therefore hurt ourselves, others, and our relationship with him. As Catholics, we know that "sin should never be understood as a private or personal matter, because it harms our relationship with others and may even break our loving communion with the Church. The Sacrament of Penance repairs this break and has a renewing effect of the vitality of the Church itself" (*USCCA, p. 242*).

LET'S TALK >>>
- Ask your child to name the parts of the Sacrament of Reconciliation (contrition, confession, penance, absolution).
- Discuss how your family shares God's healing love with one another.

LET'S PRAY >>>
O God, I am heartily sorry for having offended you. Amen.

For a multimedia glossary of Catholic Faith Words, Sunday readings, seasonal and Saint resources, and chapter activities go to **aliveinchrist.osv.com**.

Family + Faith

Distribute the page to the children or parents/adult family members. Point out the chapter highlights, insights on how fourth graders understand concepts, the opportunity for the adults to reflect on their own experience and faith journey, and the family prayer.

Chapter 18 Review

A Check Understanding **Solve the crossword puzzle.**

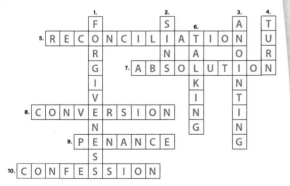

Down
1. Welcoming someone back after a wrong has been done
2. These separate you from God and others
3. This is done for those who are very sick or dying
4. God's love is available to all who _____ to him.
6. When you tell the priest your sins, you are really _____ to God.

Across
5. The Sacrament that celebrates God's forgiveness of sins is the Sacrament of Penance and _____.
7. Words spoken by the priest to forgive sin in God's name
8. Deciding to turn away from sin and turn back to God
9. The prayer, offering, or good work the priest gives you in the Sacrament of Reconciliation
10. An essential element of Reconciliation when you tell your sins to the priest

Go to **aliveinchrist.osv.com** for an interactive review.

Chapter Review

Use Catechist Quick Reviews to highlight lesson concepts.

A Check Understanding
Have the children complete the crossword puzzle.

Go to **aliveinchrist.osv.com** to prepare customized and downloadable assessments, send eAssessments, and assign interactive reviews.

Healing and Reconciliation   **251–252**

Unit Review

Use Catechist Quick Reviews in each chapter to highlight lesson concepts for this unit and prepare for the Unit Review.

Have the children complete the Review pages. Then discuss the answers as a group. Review any concepts with which the children are having difficulty.

A **Work with Words**
Have the children complete each sentence with the correct word from the Word Bank.

A Work with Words Complete each sentence with the correct word from the Word Bank.

1. The Sacrament of Penance and Reconciliation strengthens you to make __peace__ with those whom you may have hurt.

2. Absolution are the words spoken by a priest to grant God's __forgiveness__ of sins.

3. Jesus' healing touch strengthens and forgives the sins of those who are seriously ill in the Sacrament of the __Anointing__ of the Sick.

4. __Eucharist__ is the Sacrament in which Jesus gives himself and the bread and wine become his Body and Blood.

5. The cycle of the Church's feasts and seasons which celebrate the Paschal Mystery is the __liturgical__ year.

6. Through the Paschal __Mystery__, Jesus' suffering, Death, Resurrection, and Acension, we are saved from sin and death.

7. __Penance__ is the prayer, offering, or good work the priest gives you to help you make up for the effects of your sins.

8. The __Sacraments__ are effective signs of God's life, instituted by Christ and given to the Church, to give grace.

9. The __Triduum__ celebrates the Passion, Death, and Resurrection of Christ.

10. __Ordinary__ Time is a season of the Church year.

Word Bank
Triduum
Penance
Eucharist
peace
Anointing
Mystery
Ordinary
forgiveness
Sacraments
liturgical

© Our Sunday Visitor

Sacraments **253**

Unit Review

B Check Understanding Fill in the circle next to the answer that best completes the sentence.

11. Early Christians honored Jesus with "the breaking of the bread." Today this is known as _____.
    - ○ the breaking at the table
    - ○ a feast day
    - ● the Eucharist

12. Jesus showed that the most generous gift is to _____.
    - ○ spend all your money on presents
    - ○ make your own greeting cards
    - ● give your life for others

13. Two of the Seven Sacraments are _____.
    - ○ Contrition and Holy Orders
    - ○ Eucharist and Study
    - ● Baptism and Matrimony

14. The seasonal color for Advent and Lent is _____.
    - ○ green
    - ● violet
    - ○ red

15. The seasonal colors for _____ are white and gold.
    - ● Christmas and Easter
    - ○ Ordinary Time and Lent
    - ○ Pentecost and Advent

© Our Sunday Visitor

254 Unit 6 Review

C Make Connections Write responses on the lines below.

16. Name two different seasons of the Church year, and tell one way you can grow closer to God during each.
    Responses will vary.

17. Why is it important to participate actively in Mass?
    Possible responses: It helps build my relationship with God; connects me to others; brings me closer to Jesus

18. Name three things you can do to prepare for the Sacrament of Penance and Reconciliation.
    Possible responses: examine my conscience, pray, read the Bible

19. Why is it important to celebrate the Sacrament of Penance and Reconciliation?
    Possible response: I will experience healing and forgiveness when I'm truly sorry.

20. How do the Sacraments help you grow in faith?
    Possible responses: When I receive the Sacraments, I receive God's life, becoming more like Jesus; I share in Jesus' saving actions.

© Our Sunday Visitor

Sacraments **255**

B Check Understanding
Have the children fill in the circle next to the best answer.

C Make Connections
Have the children write responses to each statement or question.

Go to **aliveinchrist.osv.com** to prepare customized and downloadable assessments, send eAssessments, and assign interactive reviews.

Unit 6 Review **254–255**

Kingdom of God

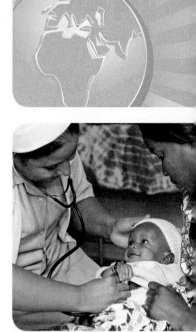

Our Catholic Tradition

- All Church members share in her mission to spread Jesus' message of God's love and promote the Kingdom of God. (CCC, 863)

- We do this by proclaiming the Gospel and being a sign of Christ to others. (CCC, 942)

- We are called to be generous stewards of our possessions and to work for the good of all people. (CCC, 2238)

- We live in God's love and do his will so that we can live forever with him in Heaven. (CCC, 1821)

How does living in God's Kingdom on Earth prepare us for God's Kingdom in Heaven?

Unit 7 Overview

Chapter 19

The children will:

- recognize that being detached from our possessions enables us to work for peace and justice in God's Kingdom
- identify that the Seventh and Tenth Commandments teach about the right attitude toward material possessions and require generosity
- name theft, greed and envy as sins against these Commandments
- appreciate that God created the world for all creatures and called humans to stewardship

 Catholic Social Teaching: Live Your Faith

- Call to Family, Community, and Participation, Pages 292–293
- Dignity of Work and Rights of Workers, Pages 298–299

Chapter 20

The children will:

- recognize that the mission of the Church is to proclaim the Gospel and work for the good of all people
- understand evangelization as sharing the Good News of Jesus through words and actions in a way that invites people to accept the Gospel
- appreciate that the Church is made up of people of many cultures and they are all united by their belief in Christ
- explore the work of missionaries as those who spread the Gospel message and Jesus' care for all people to the world

 Songs of Scripture "Come and Follow Me"

 Catholic Social Teaching: Live Your Faith

- Option for the Poor and Vulnerable, Pages 296–297
- Solidarity of the Human Family, Pages 300–301

Chapter 21

The children will:

- define Heaven as the state of eternal happiness with God
- recognize that the Holy Spirit helps us respond to God's grace and grow in friendship with him so that we may spend eternity with him
- recognize that at the time of their death they will be judged by God, called the Particular Judgment
- discuss Jesus' coming in glory at the end of time to judge all the living and the dead and the coming of God's Kingdom in its fullness, called the Last Judgment

 Catholic Social Teaching: Live Your Faith

- Life and Dignity of the Human Person, Pages 290–291
- Rights and Responsibilities of the Human Person, Pages 294–295

Preview Unit Theme

Ask: What is the unit theme?

Summarize that the unit focuses on the Kingdom of God.

Invite volunteers to read aloud each of the bullets in Our Catholic Tradition.

Explain to the children that they will learn about these things in the next three chapters.

Have the children study the photos and images. Invite volunteers to describe what they see. What do these images say about the unit theme?

Ask: How does living in God's Kingdom on Earth prepare us for God's Kingdom in Heaven?

After some discussion, explain to the children that they will be exploring this question in the next three chapters.

KEY CONCEPT

The Commandments call you to be generous and to have the right attitude toward possessions. Stewardship is the way we appreciate and use God's gifts, including our time, talent, and treasure, and the resources of creation.

DOCTRINAL CONTENT

- Being detached from our possessions enables us to work for peace and justice in God's Kingdom. (CCC, 2545–2546)
- The Seventh and Tenth Commandments teach about the right attitude toward material possessions and require generosity. (CCC, 2401, 2534)
- Theft, greed and envy are sins against these Commandments. (CCC, 2408, 2536, 2538)
- God created the world for all creatures and called humans to stewardship. (CCC, 2402)

TASKS OF CATECHESIS

Helping children grow in a faith that is "known, celebrated, lived, and expressed in prayer" (NDC, 20).

This chapter focuses on the following tasks of catechesis:

- Promoting Knowledge of the Faith
- Moral Formation

Catechist Background

"Give and gifts will be given to you; a good measure, packed together, shaken down, and overflowing, will be poured into your lap. For the measure with which you measure will in return be measured out to you." Luke 6:38

➔ **Reflect** What helps you to be generous?

Most desires, such as the desire for food, shelter, and loving relationships, are good and natural. When belongings are at the top of a person's priorities, however, desire for them often becomes extreme. Greed seeks to fulfill one's own desires without any consideration of other people's needs or wishes.

The sin of envy is a close relative of greed. Admiration for another, and even emulation, is normal. Growing unhappy at another person's success is envy. Clearly, greed and envy oppose the love and generosity to which Jesus has called his followers. Greed and envy offer nothing but dissatisfaction and an insatiable appetite for material goods and worldly pleasures. Following Jesus leads to joy and fulfillment.

What can humans give to God, who has everything? They can offer nothing and yet everything—they offer to him all that they are by opening their hearts. By not allowing the desire for material goods to control them, people are free to be centered on the real treasure— God. All humans are part of his family and must share the resources of the Earth with all, in justice and solidarity.

➔ **Reflect** How do you demonstrate generosity in daily life?

Catechist's Prayer

Gracious God, you grant me a beating heart, a thinking mind, and a giving nature. Give me one more gift—a grateful spirit to appreciate the gifts of each day. Amen.

Lesson Plan

Objectives	Process	Materials

Invite, 10 minutes

A Generous Spirit Page 257

- ♡ **Proverbs 14:21, 31** Pray the opening prayer.
- 📖 **Luke 6:38** Reflect prayerfully on the Word.
- Discuss What Do You Wonder questions.

- 🌐 **Optional Activity** Chapter Story: "The Giveaway"

Discover, 35 minutes

What Really Matters Pages 258–259

- Recognize that being detached from our possessions enables us to work for peace and justice in God's Kingdom

- Explain that Jesus helps us to understand how much is too much.
- 📖 **Luke 12:16–21** Proclaim "The Parable of the Rich Fool."
- Explain that those who do not become too attached to possessions are able to help bring about God's Kingdom.
- **Share Your Faith Activity** Identify right and wrong choices for scenarios.

- ☐ pencils

Generosity and Humility
Pages 260–261

- Identify that the Seventh and Tenth Commandments teach about the right attitude toward material possessions and require generosity
- Name theft, greed and envy as sins against these Commandments
- Appreciate that God created the world for all creatures and called humans to stewardship

- **Catholic Faith Words** envy, greed, humility, justice, stewardship
- Explain that the Seventh and Tenth Commandments teach us to have the right attitude about material possessions.
- Members of the Body of Christ are called to share their possessions with others.
- 📖 **Mark 12:41–44** Proclaim "The Poor Widow's Contribution."
- ☆ Write the name of a person who has a generous spirit.
- **Connect Your Faith Activity** Match the categories with the examples.

- ☐ pencils
- ☐ index cards
- ☐ crayons or markers
- **Optional Activity** Good Stewards
- ☐ Activity Master 19 (Page 257E)

Live, 15 minutes

Our Catholic Life Pages 262–263

- Review the Seventh and Tenth Commandments.
- ☆ Write ways to be more generous.
- **People of Faith** Learn about Saint Margaret of Scotland.
- **Live Your Faith Activity** Design an ad.

- ☐ pencils
- ☐ crayons or markers

Beatitudes for the Poor in Spirit
Page 264

- ▶ Rehearse "God's Greatest Gift."
- Designate Side 1 and Side 2.

- 🌐 Download "God's Greatest Gift."

Family + Faith Page 265

Point out that the Catholic Families page provides chapter highlights, information on how fourth graders understand faith concepts, and family prayer.

Chapter Review Page 266

🌐 aliveinchrist.osv.com

- Customize and Download Assessments
- Email Links to eAssessments
- Interactive Student Reviews

Teaching This Grade

ONLINE RESOURCES

 Go to **aliveinchrist.osv.com**

You will find:

- Interactive lesson planning with web specific content and additional activities
- Step by step lesson instruction from printed Catechist Edition for integrated lesson planning
- Custom-built assessments to download and eAssessment links
- Interactive reviews that provide scores and the option to review answers
- Sunday readings with background and questions of the week

 Go to **osvparish.com**

You will find:

- Ask the Experts Q and A
- General Catechist Helps
- Community Connections and Blogs

Sharing the Message with Fourth Graders

Being Generous Because they still think concretely, fourth graders can be very materialistic. However, they also love opportunities to give to others. Giving them practical ways to be generous helps fourth graders feel a sense of purpose and can be an important foundation for pursuing their God-given vocation as they grow.

Teaching Tip: Consider a group project that will benefit a ministry in the parish or a local charity whose goals are consistent with Catholic teaching.

How Fourth Graders Understand

- Fourth graders are beginning to be able to solve interpersonal problems. Show them some new strategies to try.
- Fourth graders enjoy working with others. Invite them to share in the responsibility for prayer.
- Envy is a huge issue for some children this age. Challenge the children to move beyond this tendency by reflecting on the gifts they have been given.

"I am learning how to be generous. Show me how to share time and attention."

Chapter Connections

Chapter Story
Invite

"The Giveaway"

Use this story to expand the chapter introduction.

- The children will relate the story to their own lives, reflecting on the gifts they have been given.
- Connect the gifts they have been given to generosity.

 Go to **aliveinchrist.osv.com** Lesson Planning section for this story.

NCEA IFG: ACRE Edition
Discover

Knowledge of the Faith

- Objective: To know and understand basic Catholic teaching about the Incarnate Word Jesus Christ as the way, truth, and life

Moral Formation

- Objective: To be knowledgeable about the teachings of Jesus and the Church as the basis of Christian morality and to understand Catholic Social Teaching

Catholic Social Teaching
Live

 Use one of these features to introduce a principle and engage the children with an activity.

- Call to Family, Community and Participation, Pages 292–293
- Dignity of Work and Rights of Workers, Pages 298–299

Music Options

 Use one or more of the following songs to enhance catechetical learning or for prayer.

- "God's Greatest Gift," Live Prayer, Page 264
- "Building God's Kingdom," Discover, Page 259
- "Seek Ye First," Discover, Page 259
- "Act Justly," Discover, Page 261
- "Raise Your Voice for Justice," Page 261
- "God's Greatest Gift," Live Prayer, Page 264

LECTIONARY CONNECTION

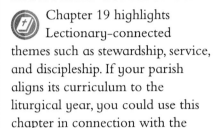 Chapter 19 highlights Lectionary-connected themes such as stewardship, service, and discipleship. If your parish aligns its curriculum to the liturgical year, you could use this chapter in connection with the following Sundays.

Year A
Twenty-fifth Sunday in Ordinary Time—grace

Twenty-ninth Sunday in Ordinary Time—stewardship

Thirty-third Sunday in Ordinary Time—stewardship

Year B
Twenty-fifth Sunday in Ordinary Time—love of others, service

Twenty-eighth Sunday in Ordinary Time—follow Jesus

Thirty-second Sunday in Ordinary Time—stewardship

Year C
First Sunday of Advent—holiness

Pentecost Sunday—Holy Spirit

Twenty-third Sunday in Ordinary Time—discipleship

Go to **aliveinchrist.osv.com** for a complete correlation ordered by the Sundays of the year and suggestions for how to integrate the Scripture readings into chapter lessons.

Name _____   Date _____

Good Stewards

Fill in the chart to show the gifts that God has given you, why each gift is important, and how you are taking care of it or using it for good. You can include material gifts, such as water, clothing, and toys, as well as spiritual gifts, such as virtues and talents.

My Gift	Why it Is Important	How I Care for It

Now draw a picture of yourself being a good steward of one of these gifts.

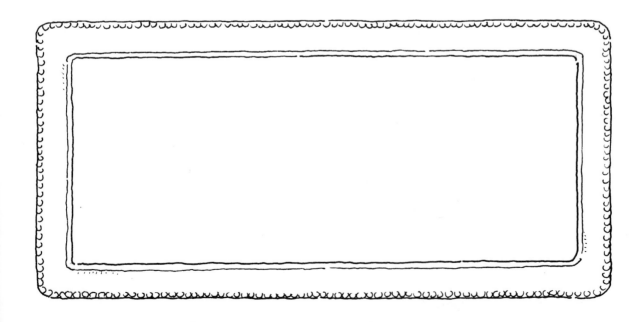

A Generous Spirit

 Let Us Pray

Leader: Create in us, O God, a generous spirit, a kind and caring heart.

"Happy is the one who is kind to the poor!
Those who are kind to the needy honor [God]."
Based on Proverbs 14:21, 31

All: Create in us, O God, a generous spirit, a kind and caring heart. Amen.

 Scripture

"Give and gifts will be given to you; a good measure, packed together, shaken down, and overflowing, will be poured into your lap. For the measure with which you measure will in return be measured out to you." Luke 6:38

? What Do You Wonder?

- How do you share your gifts with others?
- Which of the Ten Commandments helps you grow in generosity?

257

© Our Sunday Visitor

Optional Activity

Chapter Story: "The Giveaway" *Verbal/Linguistic*

Use this story after the opening prayer, before explaining that God has generously given each of us many gifts.

- Read the story aloud as the children follow along.
- *Say:* Think about something you own that someone else has admired.
- *Ask:* How difficult would it be for you to give it away? Why?
- Explain that generosity means being free in giving.

 Go to **aliveinchrist.osv.com** for Chapter Story.

Invite

 Let Us Pray

Invite the children to gather in the prayer space and make the Sign of the Cross. Choose a child to read aloud the Psalm verse from a Bible. Prompt the children's response.

Have the children move out of the prayer space and back to their seats.

Explain that God has generously given each of us many gifts.

Say: We are a gifted people. The gifts we've been given are meant to be shared.

Scripture

Guide the children through the process of Scripture reflection.

- Invite them to close their eyes, be still and open their minds and hearts to what God is saying to them in this passage.
- Proclaim the Scripture.
- Maintain several moments of silence.
- *Ask:* What did you hear God say to you today?
- Invite volunteers to share.

What Do You Wonder?

Say: We can be generous in all things. We can be generous with time, compassion, abilities, and love.

Invite the children to respond to the questions. Ask what else they might wonder about sharing their gifts and how the Ten Commandments help us to be generous.

Objective

- Recognize that being detached from our possessions enables us to work for peace and justice in God's Kingdom

What Really Matters

Ask: What does Jesus want you to know about riches?

- Write the children's responses on the board or on chart paper.

Read aloud or summarize the first paragraph.

- Tell children that they are about to hear a Scripture story about a man who obsessed about his wealth.

Scripture

Invite volunteers to read the parts of the Rich Fool, God, and the narrator. Have them proclaim "The Parable of the Rich Fool."

- *Ask:* What did the rich fool do when he ran out of space to store his harvest?
- Discuss the question that follows the Scripture story.

Call attention to the illustration.

- Invite the children to describe what they see in the illustration.

What Really Matters

What does Jesus want you to know about riches?

The difference between needs and wants is not always clear. Commercials constantly show us things that we don't really need. Sometimes it can feel like we need everything we want to make us happy. Jesus helps us to understand how much is too much through this parable.

Scripture

The Parable of the Rich Fool

There was a rich man whose land produced a bountiful harvest. He asked himself, "What shall I do? I do not have space to store my harvest." And he said, "This is what I will do. I will tear down my barns and build larger ones. There I will store all my grain and other goods. Afterward, I will say to myself, 'You have so many good things stored up for many years. It is time to rest, eat, drink, and be merry!'"

But God said to him, "You fool. Tonight your life will be taken from you. The things you have stored, to whom will they belong?"

Thus will it be for the one who stores up treasure for himself but is not rich in what matters to God.   Based on Luke 12:16–21

→ How could the Rich Fool have been richer in what matters to God?

Scripture Background

Luke 12:16–21

This parable warns against the foolishness of attaching too much importance to wealth.

- The rich farmer in this story is portrayed negatively, as an example of extreme greed. He has stored up his wealth, and has not focused on the things of God.
- The story points out that no amount of wealth can protect someone from death and or God's judgment at time of death. Instead of focusing on accumulating material possessions, we should be focused on growing in love with God and others.

Poor in Spirit

Everything that God made is good. People are good. The things that people create with love and care are good. But Jesus taught that possessions are not the most important things. Do you remember the story found in Matthew 19:16–22 about the rich young man? Jesus loved him and wanted him to be happy.

Sometimes people need to leave behind their material possessions in order to have the time and energy to do good. The Apostles left their homes, families, and jobs in order to follow Jesus and help him spread God's Word.

The first Beatitude says, "Blessed are the poor in spirit, for theirs is the kingdom of heaven" (Matthew 5:3). Those who do not become too attached to their possessions are able to work for love and peace in the world and help bring about God's Kingdom.

Share Your Faith

Reflect Describe a right and wrong choice for each of the following situations.

Share In a small group, role-play the right choice in one of these situations.

A video game that you want is on an outdoor table during a sidewalk sale.

Right _____

Wrong _____

Someone else wins an award that you wanted.

Right _____

Wrong _____

A Generous Spirit **259**

Reaching All Learners

Role-Plays

Putting themselves in another's place is enjoyable and instructive for fourth graders.

- Children who are particularly strong in social skills, word activities, and movement will have a chance to shine when performing skits.
- Praise the children for the ingenuity of their solutions, not for the quality of their acting.

Poor in Spirit

Read aloud the first paragraph.

- Have the children listen to discover what Jesus taught about possessions.

Invite volunteers to share what they remember about Jesus and the rich young man. (Matthew 19:16–22).

- *Ask:* What did Jesus tell the rich young man to do?

Have the children read silently the second and third paragraphs to learn which Beatitude talks about the right attitude toward possessions and dependence on God.

- Refer to page 317 in the Our Catholic Tradition reference section of the Student Book for more about the Beatitudes.

 Music Option: Have the children sing, "Building God's Kingdom" or "See Ye First," downloaded from **aliveinchrist.osv.com**.

Activity

Read aloud the directions for the Share Your Faith activity.

- Have the children work independently to write their ideas. After a short time, have them discuss with a partner.
- Provide time for the children to role-play the right choice in one of the situations.

Quick Review

Everything God made is good, but being too attached to possessions makes it difficult for people to love.

Objectives

- Identify that the Seventh and Tenth Commandments teach about the right attitude toward material possessions and require generosity
- Name theft, greed, and envy as sins against these Commandments
- Appreciate that God created the world for all creatures and called humans to stewardship

Generosity and Humility

Ask: What do the Seventh and Tenth Commandments teach you?

- Write the children's responses on the board or on chart paper.

Invite a volunteer to read aloud the first paragraph.

- Have the children listen to find out which two Commandments tell about the right attitude to have toward material possessions.

Work with Words

Invite a volunteer to read aloud the second paragraph.

- Have the children make vocabulary cards for *greed, envy, humility,* and *justice.*

Called to Share

Explain that almost everyone feels greed or envy at times. Point out that we can overcome these feelings.

- Tell the children to read to find out how to be happy for their own gifts and to appreciate those of other children.

- Discuss the question.

Generosity and Humility

What do the Seventh and Tenth Commandments teach you?

There are two Commandments that teach us about the right attitude to have toward our material possessions. The Seventh Commandment says this: You shall not steal. The Tenth Commandment tells us: You shall not covet your neighbor's goods.

Theft, greed, and envy are all sins against the Seventh and Tenth Commandments. Theft is taking what is not yours. When you have **envy**, you resent or are sad because someone else possesses something that you really want. Envy harms the Body of Christ because it divides God's People rather than bringing everyone together. **Greed** is the desire to gain earthly possessions without concern for what is reasonable or right.

Called to Share

Humility helps us to know that God is the source of everything good. It can help us overcome both envy and greed. Caring too much about material possessions almost always brings unhappiness and disappointment.

Justice is giving God and others what is their due. Because everything comes from God, all people have a right to what they need to live comfortably. As a member of the Body of Christ, you are called to share your possessions with others, especially those who do not have food, shelter, or decent clothing.

➜ In what ways are people your age tempted to be envious or greedy?

Catholic Faith Words

envy the sin of resenting what others have or being sad from wanting for yourself what belongs to others

greed the sin of desiring to gain earthly goods without limits or beyond what you need

humility the moral virtue that helps us to know that God is the source of everything good. Humility helps us to avoid being prideful.

justice giving God what is due him, and giving each person what he or she is due because that person is a child of God

© Our Sunday Visitor

Optional Activity

Activity Master 19: Good Stewards

Distribute copies of the activity found on catechist page 257E.

- Have the children fill in the chart with information about the gifts that God has given them.

- As an alternative, you may wish to send this activity home with the children.

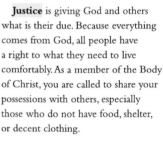

Called to Stewardship

The Seventh and Tenth Commandments require us to be generous with others. Being generous means giving more than is necessary.

God created the world for all creatures and called humans to **stewardship**. This means people are called to use natural resources well and protect the environment for everyone now and in the future; to respect all life as a gift from God; and to share time, money, and talent to help others.

> **Catholic Faith Words**
>
> **stewardship** the way we appreciate and use God's gifts, including our time, talent, and treasure, and the resources of creation

Scripture

The Poor Widow's Contribution

Jesus watched people put money into the Temple treasury. Many rich people put in large sums of money. A poor widow put in two small coins worth only a few cents. Jesus said to his disciples, "I say to you, this poor widow put in more than all the others. They contributed their extra money, but the widow has given all she had." **Based on Mark 12:41–44**

On the coin label, write the name of someone you know who has a generous spirit.

→ Why do you think the widow contributed more than the rest?

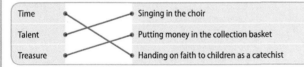

Connect Your Faith

Be a Good Steward Match the categories of stewardship on the left to the examples on the right.

Time	Singing in the choir
Talent	Putting money in the collection basket
Treasure	Handing on faith to children as a catechist

A Generous Spirit **261**

Scripture Background

Mark 12:41–44

The story of the widow's contribution comes right after Jesus' denunciation of some of the scribes.

- Jesus says of the scribes, "They devour the houses of widows and, as a pretext, recite lengthy prayers. They will receive a very severe condemnation" (Mark 12:40).

- Jesus goes on to praise the widow. He says that God prefers a sincere heart to an empty show.

Called to Stewardship

Read aloud the first paragraph.

- Invite a volunteer to read aloud the next paragraph.

Work with Words

Invite a volunteer to read aloud the definition of *stewardship*.

- Have the children make vocabulary cards.

Scripture

Invite a volunteer to proclaim "The Poor Widow's Contribution."

- *Ask:* Why do you think the widow contributed more than the rest?

- Invite the children to write the name of someone who has a generous spirit on the coin label.

> Music Option: Have the children sing, "Act Justly" or "Raise You Voice for Justice," downloaded from **aliveinchrist.osv.com**.

Activity

Point out the Connect Your Faith activity and read the directions aloud.

- Have the children complete the matching activity independently.

- Provide time for the children to check their answers with a partner.

Quick Review

The Seventh and Tenth Commandments deal with generosity and stewardship.

Our Catholic Life

Ask: How can you learn to have a more generous spirit?

- Write the children's responses on the board or on chart paper.

Review the Seventh and Tenth Commandments.

- Invite a volunteer to read aloud the first paragraph.

- Explain that when you are generous, you keep these Commandments.

- Invite a volunteer to read aloud the second paragraph.

- Ask the children to close their eyes as you read aloud the suggestions in the graph.

⭐ In the open sections, have the children write ways to follow some of these suggestions this week.

 Music Option: Have the children sing, "They'll Know We Are Christians," downloaded from **aliveinchrist.osv.com**.

Our Catholic Life

How can you learn to have a more generous spirit?

God knew that it would be easier for you to help and care for one another if you did not let possessions get in the way. He gave you the Seventh and Tenth Commandments to encourage good habits and help build a world of peace, love, and justice.

You have the ability to be as generous as God wants you to be. Here are some ideas that can help you be more generous every day.

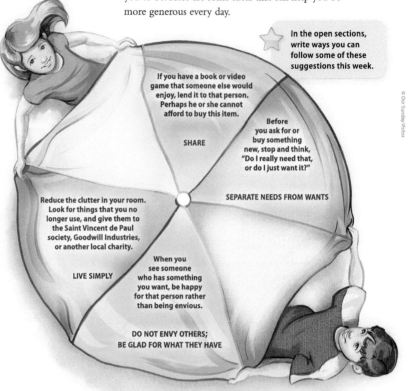

⭐ In the open sections, write ways you can follow some of these suggestions this week.

© Our Sunday Visitor

262 Chapter 19

 Quick Tip

Let Go

You and the children will present an alternative to commercialism and materialism if you try to let go of attachment to material goods. Remind the children of the following points.

- People are more important than things.
- There is serenity in simplicity.
- Jesus said that God will take care of people's needs.
- Read Luke 12:22–31 aloud, and encourage the children not to worry about material goods.

People of Faith

Saint Margaret of Scotland, 1045–1093

November 16

Saint Margaret was a princess who was shipwrecked with her family near Scotland. She married Malcolm, the Scottish king, and became a queen. Margaret was rich, but she used her money to help others. She took care of children who didn't have parents. She helped repair churches that were falling down. She even built a bridge so people didn't have to wade in a river to cross it. Saint Margaret knew that the Earth's goods were meant for the benefit of the whole human family, not just for some people.

Discuss: How does it feel when you give away something you own?

 Learn more about Saint Margaret at **aliveinchrist.osv.com**

Live Your Faith

Design and Decorate In the space below, design and decorate an ad that will remind people to be generous with one another.

A Generous Spirit **263**

 ## Catholic Social Teaching

Chapter Connections

To integrate Catholic Social Teaching into your lesson, choose one of the following features: Call to Family, Community and Participation, pages 292–293; or Dignity of Work and Rights of Workers, pages 298–299.

- Start the Live step of the process by talking about Saint Margaret of Scotland on page 263. Then move directly to the Catholic Social Teaching feature.
- Or, to expand the lesson, complete both pages 262 and 263, then move to the Catholic Social Teaching feature.
- Return to Chapter 19 for the prayer on page 264.

People of Faith

Tell the children about Saint Margaret of Scotland.

- Invite a volunteer to read aloud the People of Faith story.
- Explain that Saint Margaret of Scotland became the Queen of Scotland when she married King Malcolm.
- As Queen, she had a positive influence on her husband and his country.
- When King Malcolm realized how wise his wife was, he listened to her good advice.
- The king and queen were excellent models for everyone to follow. They prayed together. They fed crowds of poor people with their own hands. Their goal was to help make everyone happy and good.
- *Discuss:* How does it feel when you give away something you own?

 Encourage the children to go to **aliveinchrist.osv.com** at home to learn more about Saint Margaret of Scotland.

Activity

As a group, read aloud and discuss the directions for the Live Your Faith activity.

- Allow time for the children to design their ads.
- Invite volunteers to share their drawings.

Live

Let Us Pray
Beatitudes for the Poor in Spirit

Explain to the children that this prayer calls us to remember that our relationships are far more important than things. We ask God for the strength to help us to put him and his people first in our lives.

Prepare
Designate a leader, Side 1, and Side 2.

 Rehearse "God's Greatest Gift," downloaded from **aliveinchrist.osv.com**.

Gather
With music playing in the background, invite the children to process to your prayer space. Have each child bring their book.

- Have the children remain standing, with Side 1 and Side 2 each gathered together.
- Invite the children to prepare their minds and hearts for prayer.

Pray
Follow the order of prayer on the student page.

 Conclude by singing together "God's Greatest Gift."

 Live

 Let Us Pray

Beatitudes for the Poor in Spirit

This prayer calls us to remember that our relationships are far more important than things. We ask God for the strength to help us to put him and his People first in our lives.

Gather and begin with the Sign of the Cross.

Leader: Jesus calls us to be poor in spirit. We ask you, God, for the grace to allow us to see the needs of others and a heart that wants to help.

Side 1: Blessed are the poor in spirit,

Side 2: for theirs is the Kingdom of Heaven.

Side 1: Blessed are those who

Side 2: share their possessions.

All: Help us to love and care for others.

Side 2: Blessed are the poor in spirit,

Side 1: for theirs is the Kingdom of Heaven.

Side 2: Blessed are those who

Side 1: find ways to care for those who have little.

All: Help us to love and care for others.

 Sing "God's Greatest Gift"
Love, love, Jesus is love.
God's greatest gift is the gift of love.
All creation sings together,
praising God for love.

Liturgy Link

Scripture Cycles

The Gospel readings at Mass are rotated in a three-year cycle.

- The Gospel according to Matthew is read during Year A. The Beatitudes are in Matthew's Gospel.
- The Gospel according to Mark is read during Year B, and the Gospel according to Luke in Year C.
- The Gospel according to John is read every year during the seasons of Christmas, Lent, and Easter, and Ordinary Time.

Go to **aliveinchrist.osv.com** for Sunday readings, Scripture background, questions of the week, and seasonal resources.

FAMILY+FAITH
LIVING AND LEARNING TOGETHER

YOUR CHILD LEARNED >>>
This chapter examines generosity and humility and discusses theft, greed, and envy in relationship to the Seventh and Tenth Commandments, deepening the understanding that the Earth's good are meant for all.

Scripture
 Read **Luke 6:38** to find out about the importance of generosity.

Catholics Believe
- The Commandments call you to be generous and to have the right attitude toward possessions.
- Stewardship is the way we appreciate and use God's gifts, including our time, talent, and treasure, and the resources of creation.

To learn more, go to the *Catechism of the Catholic Church #299, 2402–2405* at **usccb.org**.

People of Faith
This week, your child learned about Saint Margaret of Scotland, who used her wealth to benefit the Scottish people.

CHILDREN AT THIS AGE >>>
How They Understand Being Generous Because they are still concrete thinkers, fourth-graders can be very materialistic. However, they also love opportunities to give to others. Giving them practical ways to be generous helps them feel a sense of purpose and can be an important foundation for pursuing their God-given vocation as they grow.

CONSIDER THIS >>>
Do you think your family has too much stuff?

Most desires such as for food, shelter, and loving relationships are good and natural. But when we focus too much on material things, we can become selfish and even greedy. As Catholics, we know that "the Tenth Commandment calls us to practice poverty of spirit and generosity of heart. These virtues liberate us from being slaves to money and possessions. They enable us to have a preferential love for the poor and to be witnesses of justice and peace in the world" (*USCCA pgs. 449–450*).

LET'S TALK >>>
- Ask your child to explain what envy, being poor in spirit, and humility have to do with the Seventh and Tenth Commandments.
- Talk about ways your family might change its attitude toward possessions and be even more generous with one another.

LET'S PRAY >>>
 Saint Margaret, pray for us that we may always be generous with everything we have. Amen.

For a multimedia glossary of Catholic Faith Words, Sunday readings, seasonal and Saint resources, and chapter activities go to **aliveinchrist.osv.com**.

Chapter 19 Review

A Work with Words **Fill in the circle next to the answer that best completes each statement.**

1. The _____ Commandment states that you should not steal.
   - ○ Sixth
   - ● Seventh
   - ○ Eighth

2. The way we appreciate and use God's gifts is called _____.
   - ● stewardship
   - ○ conscience
   - ○ generosity

3. The _____ Commandment states that you should not desire what others have.
   - ○ Eighth
   - ○ Ninth
   - ● Tenth

4. _____ is being sad or resentful when someone else possesses something you want.
   - ○ Stealing
   - ○ Generosity
   - ● Envy

5. _____ is the unlimited gathering of material possessions.
   - ● Greed
   - ○ Generosity
   - ○ Stewardship

B Check Understanding **Below are examples of how you can keep the Seventh and Tenth Commandments. In the space provided, write the number of the Commandment that the example refers to.**

6. [10] Donating your outgrown clothing to charity

7. [7] Finding a toy in the parking lot of a store, and turning it in to the lost and found

8. [10] Sharing your possessions with a brother or sister

9. [7] Not eating food in a grocery store until after you have paid for it

10. [10] Being thankful for what you have

 Go to **aliveinchrist.osv.com** for an interactive review.

Family + Faith

Distribute the page to the children or parents/adult family members. Point out the chapter highlights, insights on how fourth graders understand concepts, the opportunity for the adults to reflect on their own experience and faith journey, and the family prayer.

Chapter Review

Use Catechist Quick Reviews to highlight lesson concepts.

A Work with Words
Have the children fill in the circle next to the answer that best completes each statement.

B Check Understanding
Have the children write the number of the Commandment that each example illustrates.

 Go to **aliveinchrist.osv.com** to prepare customized and downloadable assessments, send eAssessments, and assign interactive reviews.

A Generous Spirit   **265–266**

KEY CONCEPT

The mission of the People of God is to proclaim the Gospel and to work for the good of all people. The Church is made up of people of many cultures, but all are united by their belief in Christ.

DOCTRINAL CONTENT

- The mission of the Church is to proclaim the Gospel and work for the good of all people. (CCC, 849)

- Evangelization is sharing the Good News of Jesus through words and actions in a way that invites people to accept the Gospel. (CCC, 853–854)

- Missionaries spread the Gospel message and Jesus' care for all people to countries all around the world. (CCC, 849–851)

- The Church is made up of people of many cultures, and they are all united by their belief in Christ. (CCC, 781)

TASKS OF CATECHESIS

Helping children grow in a faith that is "known, celebrated, lived, and expressed in prayer" (NDC, 20).

This chapter focuses on the following tasks of catechesis:

- Education for Community Life
- Missionary Initiation

Catechist Background

"You will receive power when the holy Spirit comes upon you, and you will be my witnesses in Jerusalem, throughout Judea and Samaria, and to the ends of the earth." **Acts of the Apostles 1:8**

➔ **Reflect** What would you like to tell someone about Jesus?

Differences are part of the beauty of creation. If all flowers were yellow and all birds blue, their beauty would be lost in their sameness. Catholics are called to be grateful for human diversity as well, because it is part of God's plan. The Church teaches that people with various talents and backgrounds, as well as people of different ethnicities, races, genders, and ages, share a birthright as God's children.

Catholics recognize that we must respect people who are different from us. This respect leads to treating others justly. Justice, in turn, leads to harmony among people.

Mission is one of the duties of Christianity. Spreading the Good News of salvation is an act of love that is guided by the Holy Spirit. Its hallmarks are respectful dialogue, acts of compassion, and the humble awareness that God is in charge. Rooted in prayer, the Christian mission welcomes all people.

➔ **Reflect** How do you work with God as he build his Kingdom?

Catechist's Prayer

Risen Lord, I am blessed to be embraced by your generous love. Continue to form me in your ways of compassion and concern for others. Amen.

Lesson Plan

Objectives	Process	Materials

🕙 Invite, 10 minutes

The Church in the World Page 267

- 🔵 **Isaiah 6:8** Pray the opening prayer.
- 📖 **Acts of the Apostles 1:8** Reflect prayerfully on the Word.
- Discuss What Do You Wonder questions.

🔊 **Optional Activity**
Chapter Story: "Different, Yet the Same"

🕙 Discover, 35 minutes

Make Disciples of All Nations
Pages 268–269

- Recognize that the mission of the Church is to proclaim the Gospel and work for the good of all people
- Understand evangelization as sharing the Good News of Jesus through words and actions in a way that invites people to accept the Gospel
- Appreciate that the Church is made up of people of many cultures and they are all united by their belief in Christ

- **Catholic Faith Words** Gospel, mission, evangelization
- Explain that Jesus gave his Apostles a mission.
- 📖 **Matthew 28:18–20** Proclaim "The Commissioning of the Disciples."
- Explain that Jesus wants his followers to go to all places and share the Gospel.
- Explain that Jesus reached out to all people.
- Explain that the Church celebrates worldwide diversity and is united in a common belief.
- **Share Your Faith Activity** Write a newspaper headline.

☐ pencils
☐ index cards
- **Optional Activity** Diversity Bingo
☐ Activity Master 20 (Page 267E)

The Church in Bolivia Pages 270–271

- Explore the work of missionaries as those who spread the Gospel message and Jesus' care for all people to countries around the world

- Show the children where Bolivia is on a map.
- Read about the missionaries and the Church in Bolivia.
- **Connect Your Faith Activity** Write a prayer.

☐ pencils

🕙 Live, 15 minutes

Our Catholic Life Pages 272–273

- Explain how to support missions.
- ☆ Identify ways to support missions.
- **People of Faith** Learn about Saint Junipero Serra.
- **Live Your Faith Activity** Make a list for a care package.

☐ pencils
☐ crayons or markers

Prayer of Praise Page 274

- Write prayers.
- ▶ Rehearse "Somos el Cuerpo de Christo/We Are the Body of Christ."
- Follow the order of prayer.

🔊 Download "Somos el Cuerpo de Christo/We Are the Body of Christ."

Family + Faith page 275
Point out that the Catholic Families page provides chapter highlights, information on how fourth graders understand faith concepts, and family prayer.

Chapter Review Page 276
🔊 aliveinchrist.osv.com
- Customize and Download Assessments
- Email Links to eAssessments
- Interactive Student Reviews

Teaching This Grade

ONLINE RESOURCES

 Go to **aliveinchrist.osv.com**

You will find:

- Interactive lesson planning with web specific content and additional activities
- Step by step lesson instruction from printed Catechist Edition for integrated lesson planning
- Custom-built assessments to download and eAssessment links
- Interactive reviews that provide scores and the option to review answers
- Sunday readings with background and questions of the week

 Go to **osvparish.com**

You will find:

- Ask the Experts Q and A
- General Catechist Helps
- Community Connections and Blogs

Sharing the Message with Fourth Graders

Mission Fourth graders are learning more about the world and its diverse cultures. They are growing in their ability to understand distances and the different experiences and living conditions of people around the world. For this reason, children this age are ready to learn more about the Church's missionary activity and ways in which they can participate, through praying and supporting missionaries and looking for God's call to share the Gospel in everyday life.

Teaching Tip: Have a globe or world map in the room to talk about missionaries in various places as well as to point out the various countries that were home to our Saints.

How Fourth Graders Understand

- Without assistance, fourth graders are likely to stay with one group of friends. Uses different techniques for forming groups.
- Fourth graders want to work for justice. Show them ways to work for it as a group.
- Help the children understand that acceptance of various cultures has helped Catholicism spread throughout the world.

"I like new sights and sounds. Include videos in class presentations."

Chapter Connections

Chapter Story Invite

"Different, Yet the Same"

Use this story to expand the chapter introduction.

- The children will relate the story to their own lives, reflecting on the difference they see in their group.
- Connect noticing differences to noticing similarities.

 Go to **aliveinchrist.osv.com** Lesson Planning section for this story.

NCEA IFG: ACRE Edition Discover

Communal Life

- Objectives: To know the origin, mission, structure, and communal nature of the Church; to know the rights and responsibilities of the Christian faithful

Missionary Spirit

- Objectives: To recognize the centrality of evangelization as the Church's mission and identity embodied in vocation and service; to be aware of how cultures are transformed by the Gospel

Catholic Social Teaching Live

 Use one of these features to introduce a principle and engage the children with an activity.

- Option for the Poor and Vulnerable, Pages 296–297
- Solidarity of the Human Family, Pages 300–301

Music Options

 Use one or more of the following songs to enhance catechetical learning or for prayer.

- "Somos el Cuerpo de Christo/We Are the Body of Christ," Live Prayer, Page 274
- "Take the Word of God with You," Discover, Page 271
- "The Family of God," Discover, Page 269

LECTIONARY CONNECTION

Chapter 20 highlights Lectionary-connected themes such as the Kingdom of God, call to service, and the Paschal Mystery. If your parish aligns its curriculum to the liturgical year, you could use this chapter in connection with the following Sundays.

Year A

Fifth Sunday of Lent—Paschal Mystery

Third Sunday of Easter—Paschal Mystery

The Ascension of the Lord—Paschal Mystery

Year B

Twenty-fifth Sunday in Ordinary Time—call to service

Thirty-first Sunday in Ordinary Time—love God and neighbor

Thirty-third Sunday in Ordinary Time—Kingdom of God

Year C

Thirtieth Sunday in Ordinary Time—humility

Our Lord Jesus Christ, King of the Universe—Kingdom of God

 Go to **aliveinchrist.osv.com** for a complete correlation ordered by the Sundays of the year and suggestions for how to integrate the Scripture readings into chapter lessons.

Name _____   Date _____

Diversity Bingo

How diverse is your group? Find out by having another person sign a box containing a phrase that accurately describes him or her. See how many boxes you can fill.

plays baseball	has brown eyes	likes pizza	sings well
wears glasses	was born in another country	is an only child	has a nickname
can do a handstand	has curly hair	has a pet	likes reading
has a sister	speaks another language	plays soccer	knows how to cook

The Church in the World

Let Us Pray

Leader: Lord God, you invite us to take part in the mission of your Son to share the Good News with all the world.

"I heard the voice of the Lord saying, 'Whom shall I send? Who will go for us?' 'Here I am,' I said; 'send me!'" Isaiah 6:8

All: Here we are, Lord. Send us to be your witnesses. Amen.

© Our Sunday Visitor

Scripture

[Jesus said,] "You will receive power when the holy Spirit comes upon you, and you will be my witnesses in Jerusalem, throughout Judea and Samaria, and to the ends of the earth."
Acts of the Apostles 1:8

What Do You Wonder?

• What is one thing you want to tell someone about Jesus?

• What unifies Catholics around the world?

The Church in the World **267**

Optional Activity

Chapter Story: "Different, Yet the Same" *Verbal/Linguistic*

Use this story after the opening prayer, before explaining that Jesus gives us the gift of the Holy Spirit.

• Read the story aloud as the children follow along.

• *Say:* Look at the person next to you. What things about the two of you are alike and what things are different?

• *Ask:* Which are more important: things that are the same or things that are different?

 Go to **aliveinchrist.osv.com** for Chapter Story.

Let Us Pray

Invite the children to gather in the prayer space and make the Sign of the Cross. Designate one child as leader and one to read aloud the Psalm verse from a Bible. Prompt the children's response.

Have the children move out of the prayer space and back to their seats.

Explain that Jesus gives us the gift of the Holy Spirit to give us the strength to continue his mission.

Say: Jesus does not leave us alone to continue his mission. He promises to be with us always and gives us the powerful gift that is the Holy Spirit.

Scripture

Guide the children through the process of Scripture reflection.

• Invite them to close their eyes, be still and open their minds and hearts to what God is saying to them in this passage.

• Proclaim the Scripture.

• Maintain several moments of silence.

• *Ask:* What did you hear God say to you today?

• Invite volunteers to share.

What Do You Wonder?

Say: The Holy Spirit will help us act as Jesus' witnesses no matter where we may go—even to the ends of the Earth.

Invite the children to respond to the questions. Ask what else they might wonder about telling others about Jesus or the diversity of the Church.

Objectives

- Recognize that the mission of the Church is to proclaim the Gospel and work for the good of all people
- Understand evangelization as sharing the Good News of Jesus through words and actions in a way that invites people to accept the Gospel
- Appreciate that the Church is made up of people of many cultures and they are all united by their belief in Christ

Make Disciples of All Nations

Ask: How does the Church reach out to the world?

- Write the children's responses on the board or on chart paper.

Read aloud the first paragraph to introduce the Scripture story.

Scripture

Proclaim the "The Commissioning of the Disciples."

Read aloud the last paragraph.

- *Ask:* What do Catholics and other Christians in communities around the world have in common?
  They are followers of Jesus.
- Discuss the question at the bottom of the page.

Work with Words

Invite volunteers to read aloud the Catholic Faith Words and their definitions. Then have the children make vocabulary cards for all three terms.

Make Disciples of All Nations

How does the Church reach out to the world?

At the Last Supper, Jesus told his Apostles that the Holy Spirit would come to strengthen them and guide them when he was gone. After his Resurrection, before he ascended into Heaven, Jesus gave his Apostles the following command.

Scripture

The Commissioning of the Disciples

"All power in heaven and on earth has been given to me. Go, therefore, and make disciples of all nations, baptizing them in the name of the Father, and of the Son, and of the holy Spirit, teaching them to observe all that I have commanded you. And behold, I am with you always, until the end of the age."
Matthew 28:18–20

© Our Sunday Visitor

Jesus wanted his followers to go out to all places and share the **Gospel** message of the Good News of God's Kingdom. Today, no matter where you go in the world, you will find followers of Jesus. Jesus' universal, or worldwide, **mission** on Earth was to share God's love with all people. All Catholics share in the Church's mission to announce this Good News and to share it in words and actions through her work of **evangelization**.

➜ Think about three places you will go this week. How will you live out Jesus' mission in each place?

268

Songs of Scripture

Come and Follow Me

This song emphasizes the two movements of discipleship, "Come and Go." First, we are called to learn the way of Christ and then go out into the world to bring it to others.

- On card stock, have half the children write the word *Come* and the other half write the word *Go*, in big bold letters.
- Have the children raise their signs when they sing *Come* and *Go*.

 Use *Songs of Scripture*, Grades 4–6 CD, Track 4

Jesus' Universal Mission

Jesus reached out to all people, especially people who were poor and those who were left out by others. He healed, forgave, and loved people, especially those who were considered sinners. Jesus treated everyone with dignity and respect. An important part of Jesus' mission was justice, the virtue of giving to God and people what is due to them.

Unity in the Church

There are differences in the ways the people of other countries and cultures practice their faith. Even in your parish you may notice a diversity, or variety, in the ways that people express their faith. These cultural differences strengthen the Church. She is united because of her faithfulness to the common belief handed down from the Apostles through their successors, the bishops. The Church is united in the celebration of the Mass, in the Sacraments, in prayer, and when people in every culture help bring justice to the world. You bring justice to the world by working to give others what is rightfully theirs.

> ### Catholic Faith Words
>
> **Gospel** a word that means "Good News." The Gospel message is the Good News of God's Kingdom and his saving love.
>
> **mission** a job or purpose. The Church's mission is to announce the Good News of God's Kingdom.
>
> **evangelization** sharing the Good News of Jesus through words and actions in a way that invites people to accept the Gospel

Share Your Faith

Reflect Think of all the ways that Jesus taught about and worked for justice. Write a newspaper headline that describes how Jesus brought justice to the world.

_____

_____

Share With a partner, talk about ways that you can bring justice into the world like Jesus did.

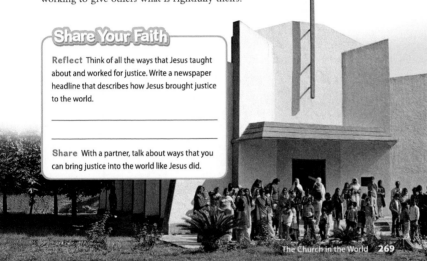

The Church in the World **269**

Jesus' Universal Mission

Have the children read silently.

- Ask the children to tell you what Jesus' mission was.

Unity in the Church

Read aloud the text.

- *Ask:* In what ways is the Catholic Church diverse worldwide? Possible responses: countries, languages, cultures

- Point out that amidst the diversity, Catholics are united through the same faith.

- Discuss what unites the Church.

- *Ask:* What cultural practices does your parish or family have?

> ▶ Music Option: Have the children sing, "The Family of God," downloaded from **aliveinchrist.osv.com**.

Activity

Read aloud the directions for the Share Your Faith activity.

- If possible, show the children some headlines from a newspaper.

- Have the children work independently to write their headlines.

- Provide time for the children to talk with a partner about ways to bring justice into the world like Jesus did.

Quick Review

The Catholic Church celebrates diversity and carries out her mission of sharing God's message.

Optional Activity

Activity Master 20: Diversity Bingo

Distribute copies of the activity found on catechist page 267E.

- This game allows the children to find out more about one another.

- As an alternative, you may wish to send this activity home with the children.

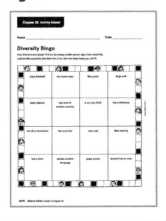

Objective

• Explore the work of missionaries as those who spread the Gospel message and Jesus' care for all people to countries all around the world

The Church in Bolivia

Ask: How does the Church include different cultures?

• Write the children's responses on the board or on chart paper.

Show the children the location of Bolivia on a world map.

• Read aloud the introductory paragraphs.

A Floating Church

Slowly read aloud the text, pausing to answer any questions.

• Have the children tell how the priest in Bolivia is like Saint Paul. The priest travels to spread the Word of God.

Point out the pictures on the page.

• Ask the children to tell what they see in each picture.

• *Ask:* How are the missionaries preaching the Gospel of Jesus in word and deed?

The People and the Mission

Have the children continue listening as you read aloud.

• *Ask:* What about the missionaries' experience in Bolivia is different from the experience in your parish?

The Church in Bolivia

How does the Church include different cultures?

Catholic missionaries bring the Catholic faith to people all over the world. They are careful to respect and include the customs of different groups in prayer and worship. Missionaries preach the Gospel of Jesus in word and deed.

In the following story told by a missionary, you will find some ways that the Church in Bolivia is like your parish and some ways that it is different from your parish.

A floating church

I work with other missionaries in the jungle region of northeast Bolivia. We travel in our parish boat to visit the people who live far apart along the Beni River. Most of the people work deep in the jungle. Some work with rubber trees, and others harvest Brazilian nuts.

On our way up the river, we tell whoever is home to gather their neighbors together for Mass, Baptisms, and marriages on the day we will return downstream. When we return, the people gather near the river. There we baptize people, celebrate Mass, and perform marriages.

✓ Quick Tip

What Do They Do?

Catholic missionaries do many types of work.

• Have the children consider the various needs that people have, such as food, shelter, and medical care.

• Point out that missionaries serve these needs.

• Challenge the children to think of ways to satisfy these needs in poor countries.

The People and the Mission

The people are happy to have us come and celebrate the Sacraments with them. Ninety-five percent of Bolivians are Catholic. Their ancestors converted to Christianity a long time ago. Many of the people we meet along the river still speak their native Indian languages. The people we meet also bring some of their native customs into their religious life.

My coworkers and I have learned the languages of the people. We spend time talking and listening to the people. We are able to help them take care of their health in a clinic, and we educate them in a school. We have helped them set up a type of company called a *cooperative*, which is owned by the people who use its services. For example, we helped the farmers set up a cooperative so that they could get fair prices for their rubber and nut crops.

Bolivia has a lot of troubles. Once, there was an uprising in a town, and I was asked to be mayor for four months. Another time, I was arrested with another priest because we had helped the people form a cooperative.

➜ What about the missionaries' experience in Bolivia is different from the experience in your parish?

➜ How does the Church include different cultures?

Connect Your Faith

Support the Missions Research what connections your parish has to mission work. Write a short prayer to support missionaries around the world.

_____

_____

_____

Reaching All Learners

See Bolivia

Children with different learning styles will understand the story better if they can see the country and conditions in which the people live.

- Work with your parish or local librarian to find a video about Bolivia. You may also be able to find a video online.

- Select a few minutes of the video with scenes similar to those described in the story.

The People and the Mission, *continued*

Distribute drawing materials. Suggest that the children draw life in Bolivia and something in your parish that is similar.

Bolivia

Continue reading aloud the text.

- Explain that a cooperative helps people share what they produce and keeps money in their community. People in power may be afraid that with the help of a cooperative, people will become educated and seek civil rights.

- Stress that missionaries build strong communities where people can have what they need to live.

▶ Music Option: Have the children sing, "Take the Word of God with You," downloaded from **aliveinchrist.osv.com**.

Activity

Read aloud the directions for the Connect Your Faith activity.

- Ask the children what they know about their parish's connection to mission work. Provide any information you may have.

- Have the children work independently to write their prayers. Encourage them to pray them silently.

Quick Review

The Church welcomes all cultures. Missionaries help others by sharing the Word of God and by providing social services.

Live

Our Catholic Life

Ask: How can you help missionaries spread God's Word?

• Write the children's responses on the board or on chart paper.

Tell the children that this page will teach them more about missionaries.

• Ask volunteers to read aloud the two paragraphs.

Ways to Help

Ask the children to read through all the ways to support missions. Then have them make suggestions for specific ways to help.

☆ Have the children put a check mark next to one thing that they could do this week to support missions. Then have them underline what they might do in the future.

• You might like to have the group discuss a project they can undertake together.

Ask: If you were a missionary, what work would you like to do and where?

Refer to pages 324–327 in the Our Catholic Tradition reference section of the Student Book for traditional prayers of the Church. These prayers can be offered for the missions. The Act of Hope and Act of Love are on page 325.

Live

Our Catholic Life

How can you help missionaries spread God's Word?

Jesus told his Apostles to go and spread his message all around the world. Today, missionaries continue this work in all corners of the world.

Missionaries give up lives of comfort to live with and help people in need. The missions provide food, medical care, and education in addition to spreading the Word of God. Many missions have very little money to buy the items needed to care for the people. Below are some ways you can help missionaries in their good work.

Ways to Help

Put a check mark next to one thing you could do this week to help support missions. Underline what you might do in the future.

Collect Medical Supplies
Collect bandages, first aid cream, or used eyeglasses.

Raise Money
Organize projects to raise money to help missionaries purchase supplies.

Send Your Support
Write a letter to a missionary, thanking him or her for doing God's work.

Gather Bibles
Collect Bibles or old hymnbooks to help missions share the Word of the Lord.

Pray for a Missionary
Say a prayer to bless a missionary and the work that he or she is doing.

© Our Sunday Visitor

272 Chapter 20

Quick Tip

Stay Hopeful

Catholics are hopeful people, mainly because they know that the end of the story will be happy: They will be with God in Heaven.

• Remind the children that hope is ever-present.

• Remind the children that all prayers will be answered, although not always in the ways that they expect.

• Teach the children to pray the Act of Hope, and include it in your group prayers. You can find the Act of Hope on page 325 in the Our Catholic Tradition reference section in the back of the Student Book.

People of Faith

Saint Junípero Serra, 1713–1784
July 1

We think missionaries go to faraway places, but two hundred years ago, the United States *was* a faraway place! Saint Junípero Serra, a Spanish priest, came to America and lived in what is now California. He built many churches and named them after Saints. Many cities still have those names, like San Diego (Saint Diego) and Santa Monica (Saint Monica). Father Serra walked from mission to mission. Once he was bitten by a snake! Although his foot hurt for the rest of his life, he still kept walking to his churches.

Discuss: How have you helped support missions?

Learn more about
Saint Junípero
at **aliveinchrist.osv.com**

Live Your Faith

Make a List Missionaries are often gone from home for a long time. What might they need? Make a list of items you would include in a care package to a missionary.

The Church in the World **273**

Catholic Social Teaching

Chapter Connections

To integrate Catholic Social Teaching into your lesson, choose one of the following features: Option for the Poor and Vulnerable, pages 296–297; or Solidarity of the Human Family, pages 300–301.

- Start the Live step of the process by talking about Blessed Junípero Serra on page 273. Then move directly to the Catholic Social Teaching feature.
- Or, to expand the lesson, complete both pages 272 and 273, then move to the Catholic Social Teaching feature.
- Return to Chapter 20 for the prayer on page 274.

People of Faith

Tell the children about Saint Junipero Serra.

- Invite a volunteer to read aloud the People of Faith story.
- Explain that Saint Junipero Serra is credited for founding the Church and helping it to grow on the West Coast of the United States.
- He came to the United States when he was thirty-seven, and he spent the rest of his life as a dedicated missionary in the New World.
- He founded twenty-one missions and converted thousands of people. He taught people about growing crops, raising cattle, and arts and crafts.
- His statue, representing the state of California, is in National Statuary Hall at the Capitol in Washington, D.C.
- *Discuss:* How have you helped support missions?

Encourage the children to go to **aliveinchrist.osv.com** at home to learn more about Saint Junipero Serra.

Activity

Read aloud the directions and discuss the first part of the Live Your Faith activity as a group.

- Allow time for the children to make a list.
- Invite volunteers to share their ideas.
- Consider putting together a care package as a group. Invite each child to choose one item to donate.

Live

 ## Let Us Pray
Prayer of Praise

Explain to the children that this prayer helps us reflect on and appreciate the diversity of God's people, a gift of God to each of us.

Prepare

Have each child choose a country that they have studied in geography or one they have heard about in the news recently. Invite them to look at the sample prayer statements in the prayer and write one for their chosen country.

> ▶ Rehearse "Somos el Cuerpo de Cristo/We Are the Body of Christ," downloaded from **aliveinchrist.osv.com**.

Gather

Invite the children to process to the prayer space. Have each child bring their book and the prayer they have written.

- Invite the children to be seated in a circle and prepare their minds and hearts for prayer.

Pray

Follow the order of prayer on the student page.

- *Prayer statements about our sisters and brothers around the world:* Invite children to take turns offering the prayers they have written.

> ▶ Conclude by singing together "Somos el Cuerpo de Cristo/ We Are the Body of Christ."

Live

 Let Us Pray
Prayer of Praise

This prayer helps us reflect on and appreciate the diversity of God's people, a gift of God to each of us.

Gather and begin with the Sign of the Cross.

Leader: Lord of the Nations, all the people of the world glorify you. We are your one family, all sisters and brothers.

Prayer statements about our sisters and brothers around the world:

- I pray for the people of _____, who _____.
- I give thanks for the people of _____, who _____.
- God created the people of _____, who _____.
- The people of God in _____ praise God by _____.

Leader: Loving God, we marvel at the diversity of the world, all people, all creation, showing your greatness. May each of us always bring your love and your Good News with us wherever we are.

All: Amen.

▶ Sing "Somos el Cuerpo de Cristo/We Are the Body of Christ"
Somos el cuerpo de Cristo.
We are the body of Christ.
Hemos oído el llamado;
we've answered "Yes" to the call of the Lord.
Somos el cuerpo de Cristo.
We are the body of Christ.
Traemos su santo mensaje.
We come to bring the Good News to the world.

 ## Liturgy Link

Movement in Prayer

As an alternative to writing a prayer statement, have the children write statements on a paper banner about the Good News of Jesus.

- During the song, have a child bring the banner to the center of the prayer area and pass it to the next child.
- Continue passing the banner while the group sings.

> Go to **aliveinchrist.osv.com** for Sunday readings, Scripture background, questions of the week, and seasonal resources.

FAMILY+FAITH
LIVING AND LEARNING TOGETHER

YOUR CHILD LEARNED >>>
This chapter discusses the mission and unity in diversity of the Catholic Church.

Scripture

Read **Acts of the Apostles 1:8** to find out what Jesus promises to send.

Catholics Believe
- The mission of the People of God is to proclaim the Gospel and to work for the good of all people.
- The Church is made up of people of many cultures, but all are united by their belief in Christ.

To learn more, go to the *Catechism of the Catholic Church #849, 858–859, 1934–1938* at **usccb.org**.

People of Faith

This week, your child learned about Saint Junípero Serra, the founder of the California mission chain.

CHILDREN AT THIS AGE >>>

How They Understand Mission Your child is probably learning more about the world and its diverse cultures. Children this age often are growing in their ability to understand distances and the different experiences and living conditions of people around the world. For this reason, your child is ready to learn more about the Church's missionary activity and ways in which they can participate, through praying and supporting missionaries and looking for God's call to share the Gospel in everyday life.

CONSIDER THIS >>>
Do you believe unity in diversity is a possibility?

Differences are part of the beauty of creation. Imagine if all the roses in the world were red. The Church is made up of many cultures, but we are all united in our belief in Christ. As Catholics, we know that "the word *catholic* means 'universal.' The Catholic Church has lived and continues to live in a diversity of cultures and languages because she is led by the Spirit of Christ to bring the Gospel to all peoples" (*USCCA, p. 129*).

LET'S TALK >>>
- Ask your child to explain how the Catholic faith is brought to the whole world.
- Talk about how your family participates in Jesus' mission to spread the Good News.

LET'S PRAY >>>
Dear God, thank you for the missionaries like Saint Junípero Serra who teach others about God and the saving grace of Jesus. Amen.

For a multimedia glossary of Catholic Faith Words, Sunday readings, seasonal and Saint resources, and chapter activities go to **aliveinchrist.osv.com**.

© Our Sunday Visitor

Chapter 20 Review

A Work with Words Complete each sentence with the correct word from the Word Bank.

Word Bank
- justice
- world
- mission
- diversity
- respect

1. Jesus' _____mission_____ was to share God's love with all people.

2. The Church is one body, made up of a great _____diversity_____ of members.

3. The mission of every person in the Church is to bring the Good News of Jesus to the _____world_____.

4. The virtue of _____justice_____ challenges followers of Jesus to work to provide for the needs and rights of others.

5. Missionaries must _____respect_____ the culture and customs of the local people.

B Check Understanding List five things that missionaries do for the people they serve.

6. Possible responses: provide food; provide medical care; spread God's message; celebrate Masses,

7. Baptisms, and weddings; help the people develop businesses

8. _____

9. _____

10. _____

© Our Sunday Visitor

Go to **aliveinchrist.osv.com** for an interactive review.

Family + Faith

Distribute the page to the children or parents/adult family members. Point out the chapter highlights, insights on how fourth graders understand concepts, the opportunity for the adults to reflect on their own experience and faith journey, and the family prayer.

Chapter Review

Use Catechist Quick Reviews to highlight lesson concepts.

A Work with Words
Have the children complete each sentence with the correct word from the Word Bank.

B Check Understanding
Have the children list five things that missionaries do for the people they serve.

Go to **aliveinchrist.osv.com** to prepare customized and downloadable assessments, send eAssessments, and assign interactive reviews.

The Church in the World   **275–276**

KEY CONCEPT

To spend eternity with God, we must first grow in friendship with him and accept his grace. The Last Judgement will mark God's final triumph over evil when Christ returns in glory and judges all the living and the dead.

DOCTRINAL CONTENT

- Heaven is a state of eternal happiness with God. (CCC, 1024)

- To spend eternity with God, we must grow in friendship with God. Through the Holy Spirit, God helps us respond to his grace and grow in friendship with him. (CCC, 1039–1041)

- At the time of our death, we will be judged by God. This is called the Particular Judgment. (CCC, 1121–1122)

- The Last Judgment refers to Jesus' coming in glory at the end of time to judge all the living and the dead and the coming of God's Kingdom in its fullness. (CCC 682, 1039)

TASKS OF CATECHESIS

Helping children grow in a faith that is "known, celebrated, lived, and expressed in prayer" (NDC, 20).

This chapter focuses on the following tasks of catechesis:

- Promoting Knowledge of the Faith
- Education for Community Life

Catechist Background

And this is the testimony: God gave us eternal life, and this life is in his Son. Whoever possesses the Son has life; whoever does not possess the Son of God does not have life. 1 John 5:11–12

➡ **Reflect** How often do you think about going to Heaven as you go through your day?

Individually, humans will stand accountable before God at the time of death. The Last Judgment refers to a different reality than this individual judgment. Scripture speaks of a time when Jesus will return. At this Second Coming, all humanity will stand before God. All humans will face the truth of their lives and their relationships with him and others.

No one knows when Jesus will return in glory. However, at that time the harmony and intimacy lost in the Garden of Eden will be reestablished and surpassed. Therefore, the Last Judgment should not be a time of fear; it is a time of completion.

Knowing that humans are accountable may produce some anxiety, but this knowledge also provides hope. Imperfections, pain, and disappointments will cease. "So faith, hope, love remain, these three; but the greatest of these is love" (1 Corinthians 13:13).

The Holy Spirit, the Third Divine Person of the Holy Trinity, motivates and guides the Church. The Spirit is generous, supplying humans with the gifts they need. These gifts are Wisdom, Understanding, Counsel, Fortitude, Knowledge, Piety, and Fear of the Lord. These are the seeds of a person's moral decisions, prayer life, love for others, and worship of God. Like seeds, these grow only with attention and nurturing.

➡ **Reflect** What Gifts of the Holy Spirit do you want to develop more fully?

Catechist's Prayer

Faithful God, thank you for sustaining me throughout the catechetical year. Thank you for the children in my group and the joy they have brought me. Amen.

Lesson Plan

Objectives	Process	Materials
Invite, 10 minutes		
Eternal Life with God Page 277	● **Psalm 34:15** Pray the opening prayer. ● **1 John 5:1–3, 11–12** Reflect prayerfully on the Word. • Discuss What Do You Wonder questions.	● **Optional Activity** Chapter Story: "With Jesus"
Discover, 35 minutes		
Being with God Pages 278–279 • Define Heaven as the state of eternal happiness with God • Recognize that the Holy Spirit helps us respond to God's grace and grow in friendship with him so that we may spend eternity with him	• **Catholic Faith Words** Heaven, Gifts of the Holy Spirit • Explain that the Holy Spirit helps us grow in friendship with God. • Explain that the Gifts of the Holy Spirit help us. • **Share Your Faith Activity** Reflect on a time of using the Gifts of the Holy Spirit.	☐ pencils ☐ index cards • **Optional Activity** Gifts of the Holy Spirit ☐ Activity Master 21 (Page 277E)
The Last Judgment Pages 280–281 • Recognize that at the time of their death they will be judged by God, called the Particular Judgment • Discuss Jesus' coming in glory at the end of time to judge all the living and the dead and the coming of God's Kingdom in its fullness, called the Last Judgment	• **Catholic Faith Words** Particular Judgment, Purgatory, Hell, Last Judgment • Explain that the Gifts of the Holy Spirit help to prepare you to be with God forever. ☆ Highlight the words *forever* and *everlasting*. ● **Matthew 25:34–40** Proclaim "The Judgment of Nations." • **Connect Your Faith Activity** Design a car magnet.	☐ pencils ☐ crayons or markers
Live, 15 minutes		
Our Catholic Life Pages 282–283	• Explain that everyone experiences times of sorrow, sadness, or loneliness. ☆ Write about times when you used a Gift. • **People of Faith** Learn about Saint Martin de Porres. • **Live Your Faith Activity** Identify how to use the Gifts of the Holy Spirit in scenarios.	☐ pencils
Prayer for the Kingdom Page 284	• Designate Side 1 and Side 2. ● Rehearse "Holy Spirit." • Follow the order of prayer.	● Download "Holy Spirit." ☐ paper ☐ pencils

---

Family + Faith Page 285

Point out that the Catholic Families page provides chapter highlights, information on how fourth graders understand faith concepts, and family prayer.

Chapter Review Page 286

● **aliveinchrist.osv.com**

• Customize and Download Assessments
• Email Links to eAssessments
• Interactive Student Reviews

ONLINE RESOURCES

 Go to **aliveinchrist.osv.com**

You will find:

- Interactive lesson planning with web specific content and additional activities
- Step by step lesson instruction from printed Catechist Edition for integrated lesson planning
- Custom-built assessments to download and eAssessment links
- Interactive reviews that provide scores and the option to review answers
- Sunday readings with background and questions of the week

 Go to **osvparish.com**

You will find:

- Ask the Experts Q and A
- General Catechist Helps
- Community Connections and Blogs

Sharing the Message with Fourth Graders

Death and Resurrection Most fourth graders have a clear sense of death as an irreversible state and know that everyone will eventually die. Fear of their parents' death is one of the most common fears of children this age, though they rarely voice it. Some children this age have experience with the deaths of grandparents and great aunts and uncles. It is helpful for them to know that death is not the end, that by faith we know that we will be reunited with those we love and can look forward to an eternity with God.

Teaching Tip: Encourage children to remember, and pray for, loved ones who have died. You might wish to do this in some visual way in the room, with photos or notes that represent deceased relatives.

How Fourth Graders Understand

- The idea of death can be puzzling and sometimes scary. Help fourth graders see that death is a part of life.
- Sometimes religious concepts are difficult to understand. Explain them simply and patiently.
- Use many examples when teaching about the Gifts of the Holy Spirit so that the children will understand that these gifts can change lives.

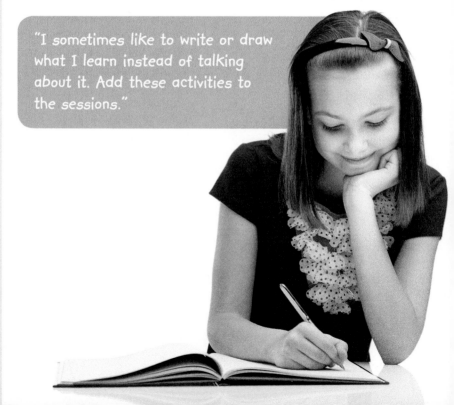

"I sometimes like to write or draw what I learn instead of talking about it. Add these activities to the sessions."

Chapter Connections

Chapter Story

Invite

"With Jesus"

- Use this story to expand the chapter introduction.
- The children will relate the story to their own lives, reflecting on their images of Heaven.

 Go to **aliveinchrist.osv.com** Lesson Planning section for this story.

NCEA IFG: ACRE Edition

Discover

Knowledge of the Faith

- Objective: To know and understand basic Catholic teaching about the Incarnate Word Jesus Christ as the way, truth, and life

Communal Life

- Objectives: To know the origin, mission, structure, and communal nature of the Church; to know the rights and responsibilities of the Christian faithful

Catholic Social Teaching

Live

Use one of these features to introduce a principle and engage the children with an activity.

- Life and Dignity of the Human Person, Pages 290–291
- Rights and Responsibilities of the Human Person, Pages 294–295

Music Options

Use one or more of the following songs to enhance catechetical learning or for prayer.

- "Holy Spirit," Live Prayer, Page 284
- "They'll Know We Are Christians," Discover, Page 281
- "Building God's Kingdom," Live, Page 282
- "Seek Ye First," Live, Page 282

LECTIONARY CONNECTION

Chapter 21 highlights Lectionary-connected themes such as justice, Second Coming, and judgment. If your parish aligns its curriculum to the liturgical year, you could use this chapter in connection with the following Sundays.

Year A

Second Sunday of Advent—justice, peace

Fifth Sunday of Easter—priesthood of all believers

Twenty-seventh Sunday in Ordinary Time—judgments, justice

Year B

First Sunday of Advent—Second Coming

Fourth Sunday of Lent—grace

Pentecost Sunday—Holy Spirit

Year C

First Sunday of Advent—Second Coming

Thirty-second Sunday in Ordinary Time—Heaven, Hell

Thirty-third Sunday in Ordinary Time—justice

 Go to **aliveinchrist.osv.com** for a complete correlation ordered by the Sundays of the year and suggestions for how to integrate the Scripture readings into chapter lessons.

Name _____   Date _____

Gifts of the Holy Spirit

Write each Gift of the Holy Spirit in the first column next to its definition in the middle column. Then, in the third column, write an example of how you use the Gift.

FORTITUDE	WISDOM	KNOWLEDGE	COUNSEL
PIETY	UNDERSTANDING		FEAR OF THE LORD

Gift	Definition	I use this gift when I...
	Helps you see yourself as God sees you and act as God wants you to act	
	Helps you give good advice	
	Helps you come to know God, yourself, and others	
	Helps you be open to God's loving communication	
	Helps you recognize that God is greater and more wonderful than any created thing	
	Helps you show love and honor to God	
	Helps you stand up for what is right	

Eternal Life with God

 Let Us Pray

Leader: God, teach us to live so that some day we might share eternal life with you.

"Turn from evil and do good;
   seek peace and pursue it." Psalm 34:15

All: Give us gifts to help us see you, love you, and follow you, Lord, until the day your Kingdom comes in fullness. Amen.

© Our Sunday Visitor

Scripture

Everyone who believes that Jesus is the Christ has been born of God, and everyone who loves the father also loves the child. We know that we love the children of God when we love God and obey his Commandments. For the love of God is this, that we obey his Commandments. And his Commandments are not burdensome. And this is the testimony: God gave us eternal life, and this life is in his Son. Whoever has the Son has life; whoever does not have the Son of God does not have life. Based on 1 John 5:1–3, 11–12

? What Do You Wonder?

- Is going to Heaven on the minds of most people as they go through their day?
- Will you have your body in Heaven?

277

Optional Activity

Chapter Story: "With Jesus" *Verbal/Linguistic*

Use this story after the opening prayer, before explaining that living as a disciple of Jesus helps prepare us for eternal life.

- Read the story as the children follow along.
- *Ask:* Why do you think the little girl thought that the funeral home was Heaven? Possible responses: It was beautiful; her grandmother was there.
- *Ask:* Whom would you like to meet in Heaven?

 Go to **aliveinchrist.osv.com** for Chapter Story.

 **Invite**

 Let Us Pray

Invite the children to gather in the prayer space and make the Sign of the Cross. Invite a child to read aloud the Psalm verse from a Bible. Prompt the children's response.

Have the children move out of the prayer space and back to their seats.

Say: Living as disciples of Jesus helps us to prepare for eternal life. As we listen to God's Word today, we will hear how living in this world is connected to eternal life.

Scripture

Guide the children through the process of Scripture reflection.

- Invite them to close their eyes, be still and open their minds and hearts to what God is saying to them in this passage.
- Proclaim the Scripture.
- Maintain several moments of silence.
- *Ask:* What did you hear God say to you today?
- Invite volunteers to share.

What Do You Wonder?

Say: All choices have consequences. Heaven is the consequence of accepting God's grace and following Jesus. When you live in this world trying to love God above all things and love others as Jesus did, God is preparing a home for you in the next world, a place in the fullness of his Kingdom.

Invite the children to respond to the questions. Ask what else they might wonder about life in Heaven.

Discover

Objectives

- Define Heaven as the state of eternal happiness with God
- Recognize that the Holy Spirit helps us respond to God's grace and grow in friendship with him so that we may spend eternity with him

Being with God

Ask: How do the Gifts of the Holy Spirit help you live in friendship with God?

- Write the children's responses on the board or on chart paper.

Compare the children's ideas of Heaven with the idea of sharing life with God and all holy people forever. Then read the text aloud.

- Point out that there is much about Heaven that people will need to wait to understand. Whatever it is like, Heaven will be an experience of love and peace.
- *Ask:* What do you think will be the best thing about Heaven?
- Point out that Baptism and Confirmation, which help people grow in friendship with God, are Sacraments of the Spirit.

Work with Words

Invite a volunteer to read aloud the definition of *Heaven*.

- Have the children make vocabulary cards for *Heaven*.

© Our Sunday Visitor

Being with God

How do the Gifts of the Holy Spirit help you live in friendship with God?

Heaven is not a place in the sky among the clouds. **Heaven** is the full joy that all holy people who have lived in God's grace will share with him forever.

To spend eternity with God, you first must grow in friendship with God. Through the Holy Spirit, God helps you grow in friendship with him and with others. You receive the **Gifts of the Holy Spirit** at Baptism, and in Confirmation these gifts are strengthened in you. The seven Gifts of the Holy Spirit are wisdom, understanding, counsel, fortitude, knowledge, piety, and fear of the Lord.

These seven powerful gifts help you show care and respect to God and holy persons and things, and to follow Jesus more closely. They open your heart so that the Holy Spirit can guide you to make good and unselfish choices and live the Christian life. When we allow the Gifts of the Holy Spirit to work in our hearts, the Fruits of the Holy Spirit (see page 306 in the Our Catholic Tradition section of your book) can be seen in us.

Catholic Faith Words

Heaven the full joy of living eternally in God's presence

Gifts of the Holy Spirit seven powerful gifts God gives us to follow the guidance of the Holy Spirit and live the Christian life

278 Chapter 21

Quick Tip

Visions of Heaven

For now, accept all of the children's ideas of Heaven.

- Some will have a traditional image with angels, clouds, and harps.
- Children who are interested in the natural world may picture Heaven as a beautiful landscape or a lovely garden.
- Have the children share their thoughts of the definition of Heaven—the state of eternal happiness with God.

The Gifts of the Holy Spirit

The Gift of	Helps You
WISDOM	• see yourself as God sees you and act as God wants you to act • live in the image and likeness of God
Understanding	• get to know God, yourself, and other people better • see why you sometimes make wrong choices • learn to make better choices and forgive more freely
COUNSEL	• give good advice to others • hear the Holy Spirit, who speaks to you through the good advice and good example of others
FORTITUDE	• stand up for what is right even when doing so is difficult • face and overcome your fear, which sometimes leads to making a bad choice or failing to love
Knowledge	• be open to God's loving communication • know God in the way that you come to know someone you love and someone who loves you
Piety	• show faithful love and honor to God • recognize the importance of spending time talking and listening to God in prayer
Fear of the Lord	• know that God is greater and more wonderful than any created thing • remember to be open to the surprising and powerful goodness of God

© Our Sunday Visitor

Share Your Faith

Reflect Think and write about a time when you used one of the Gifts of the Holy Spirit.

_____

_____

Share With a partner, discuss this time in your life.

Optional Activity

Activity Master 21: Gifts of the Holy Spirit

Distribute copies of the activity found on page 277E.

- The distinction between gifts such as knowledge and wisdom may be challenging. Remind the children to refer to their texts.
- As an alternative, you may wish to send this activity home with the children.

The Gifts of the Holy Spirit

Direct the children's attention to the chart.

- Tell the children that this chart tells how the Gifts of the Holy Spirit help you grow in friendship with God.
- Work through the chart with the children, reading each bar as a sentence: "The gift of … helps you …."
- Stop after each sentence and ask the children how that gift might be used by someone their age.
- Remind the children that using these gifts will help them prepare for the joy of being with God in Heaven.

Have the children refer to page 309 in the Our Catholic Tradition reference section of the Student Book for more about the Gifts of the Holy Spirit and the Fruits of the Holy Spirit.

Activity

Read aloud the directions for the Share Your Faith activity.

- Give the children time to complete the activity individually.
- Ask volunteers to share a time when they used a gift of the Holy Spirit.

Quick Review

Heaven is not a place; it is eternal life and happiness with God. The Gifts of the Holy Spirit help people make good choices.

Discover

Objectives

- Recognize that at the time of their death they will be judged by God, called the Particular Judgment
- Discuss Jesus' coming in glory at the end of time to judge all the living and the dead and the coming of God's Kingdom in fullness, called the Last Judgment

The Last Judgment

Ask: How does a person prepare for the Last Judgment?

- Write the children's responses on the board or on chart paper.

Tell the children that everyone has the choice to accept or reject God's grace and the Gifts of the Holy Spirit.

- Read aloud the first paragraph.
- Point out that God welcomes all who love him above all things and love their neighbor as themselves.
- Read aloud the second paragraph.
- Tell the children that those who choose to reject God are separated from him forever. Tell the children that permanent separation from God is called Hell.
- ☆ Have the children highlight the words *forever* and *everlasting* in the text and talk about their meanings today.

Work with Words

Review the definition of each Catholic Faith Word.

The Last Judgment

How does a person prepare for the Last Judgment?

The Gifts of the Holy Spirit help you turn away from selfish actions and prepare you to be with God forever. All through your life, you have the choice of accepting or rejecting the grace offered through Jesus. At the time of your death, God will judge how well you have accepted and used his gifts. This is called the **Particular Judgment**.

Jesus asks you to love God above all things and your neighbor as yourself. If you have faith in God and are open to the grace he gives you to live his plan for your life, the everlasting happiness of Heaven will eventually be yours. Sometimes people are in friendship with God but need to be purified to be with him in Heaven. This period of final cleansing is called **Purgatory**. Some people sin greatly and reject God's love. They refuse his grace and forgiveness. These sinners will be separated <u>forever</u> from God because of their own choices. That separation is called **Hell**.

> Highlight the words *forever* and *everlasting* in the text. Talk about what these words mean to us and in our life with God today.

All Souls Day celebrations remember those who have died and celebrate their lives.

Catholic Faith Words

Particular Judgment the individual judgment by God at the time of a person's death; when God decides, after a person's death, where that person will spend eternity according to his or her faith and works

Purgatory a state of final cleansing after death and before entering Heaven

Hell being separated from God forever because of a choice to turn away from him and not seek forgiveness

© Our Sunday Visitor

ⓘ Catechist Background

Judgment

Scripture and the teachings of the Church point out that we will be judged by our actions.

- Children often think about judgment in terms of what they have done wrong.
- Help the children reflect on how they live their faith in right words, actions, and examples.

At the end of time, all people who have ever lived will rise again and appear before God for judgment. This **Last Judgment** will not change each person's Particular Judgment. Rather, it will mark the coming of God's Kingdom in its fullness. This is the time when Christ will come again in glory.

Catholic Faith Words

Last Judgment God's final triumph over evil that will occur at the end of time, when Christ returns and judges all the living and the dead

Scripture

The Judgment of the Nations

"Then the king will say to those on his right, '. . . Inherit the kingdom prepared for you. . . . For I was hungry and you gave me food, I was thirsty and you gave me drink, a stranger and you welcomed me, naked and you clothed me, ill and you cared for me, in prison and you visited me.' Then the righteous will answer him and say, 'Lord, when did we see you hungry and feed you, or thirsty and give you drink? When did we see you a stranger and welcome you, or naked and clothe you? When did we see you ill or in prison, and visit you?' And the king will say to them in reply, 'Amen, I say to you, whatever you did for one of these least brothers of mine, you did for me.'"

Matthew 25:34–40

→ Who is the king in this story? Who are the righteous?

Connect Your Faith

Express Yourself Design a car magnet with a saying about living according to how you will be judged.

281

Scripture Background

Matthew 25:34–40

This passage is followed by a similar passage in which those who have not obeyed God are sent to "eternal punishment."

- If you choose to share verses 41-46, consider whether the children are mature enough for the images in the passage.
- If you share the passage with children, explain it carefully.

The Last Judgment,

continued

Read aloud the first paragraph.

- Tell the children to listen to find out what will happen to all people at the end of time.
- Review the definition of *Last Judgment* and have the children make vocabulary cards.

Scripture

Explain that Jesus described the Last Judgment for his followers.

- Proclaim "The Judgment of the Nations."
- *Ask:* Who is the king in this story?
- *Ask:* Who are the righteous?

 Music Option: Have the children sing "They'll Know We Are Christians," downloaded from **aliveinchrist.osv.com**.

Activity

Point out the Connect Your Faith activity and read aloud the directions.

- Have the children work with a partner to design a car magnet.
- Invite volunteers to share their designs.

Quick Review

People are judged on how well they have allowed God's grace to transform their lives. Particular Judgment occurs after a person dies. The Last Judgment happens at the end of time, when Jesus comes in glory.

Our Catholic Life

Ask: How can you grow in friendship with God?

- Write the children's responses on the board or on chart paper.

Invite a volunteer to read aloud the first paragraph.

- Have the children recall a time when they were sorrowful, lonely, or uncertain.
- Explain that everyone's life has times like these.

Read aloud the second paragraph.

Using the Gifts of the Spirit

Read through the suggestions for coping with troubled times.

 In the space provided, have the children write about a time when they did these things.

- *Ask:* What are other times to reach out to God?

 Music Option: Have the children sing "Building God's Kingdom" or "Seek Ye First," downloaded from **aliveinchrist.osv.com**.

Our Catholic Life

How can you grow in friendship with God?

God our Father, by the Holy Spirit, has given you seven powerful gifts to help you grow in friendship with him. He is always there to help and encourage you as you use these gifts in your life.

Sometimes you might feel lonely or unsure of what you should do. During these times, you can reach out to God and to others. Here are some examples.

 In the spaces below, write about a time when you did these things.

Using the Gifts of the Spirit

Look for Guidance
When you are faced with a difficult choice, remember the Gifts of the Holy Spirit. Pray for the Spirit's help.

Reach Out
When you meet a person who is lonely, afraid, or suffering, reach out with words and actions of love.

_____

_____

Stop and Pray
When you are rushed or stressed, stop and pray. Feel God's presence and find comfort.

_____

_____

Notice the Beauty
When you experience sadness, look around at the beauty of God's creation and the blessings you have been given.

_____

_____

Give Thanks
When you feel joy or happiness, thank God, the source of all goodness.

© Our Sunday Visitor

✓ Quick Tip

Lament

Every life includes sad times. Lamenting means expressing sad feelings and giving them validity.

- Tell the children to express their feelings when they feel hurt or sad.
- Teach the children to have empathy with those who are suffering. Tell them to listen to others and try to help ease their pain.

People of Faith

Saint Martin de Porres, 1579–1639

November 3

Saint Martin de Porres was born in Lima, Peru. His father was Spanish, and his mother was a freed black slave. Martin became a Dominican brother. He spent his life doing good works. He went throughout the city, caring for those who were sick and poor. He was a blessing to all he met, even animals. Because he was meek and pure of heart, he saw that the simplest work honored God if it served others. He would ask people for donations to help the poor, as well. Saint Martin lived the Beatitudes and worked for the Kingdom his whole life.

Discuss: How will you prepare for eternal life with God?

 Learn more about
Saint Martin de Porres
at **aliveinchrist.osv.com**

Live Your Faith

Name and Describe Look at the pictures and name the Gift of the Holy Spirit represented in each one. Then, in the space below, describe how you could use these gifts in your everyday life.

_____ helps me _____ at home.

_____ helps me _____ at school.

When I feel _____ , _____ helps

me _____ .

Eternal Life with God **283**

Catholic Social Teaching

Chapter Connections

To integrate Catholic Social Teaching into your lesson, choose one of the following features: Life and Dignity of the Human Person, pages 290–291; or Rights and Responsibilities of the Human Person, pages 294–295.

- Start the Live step of the process by talking about Saint Martin de Porres on page 283. Then move directly to the Catholic Social Teaching feature.
- Or, to expand the lesson, complete both pages 282 and 283, then move to the Catholic Social Teaching feature.
- Return to Chapter 21 for the prayer on page 284.

People of Faith

Tell the children about Saint Martin de Porres.

- Invite a volunteer to read aloud the People of Faith story.
- Explain that Saint Martin de Porres was known for his work with the poor. He established an orphanage and a children's hospital.
- There are many miracles attributed to Saint Martin. They include miraculous knowledge, instantaneous cures and being able to communicate with animals.
- He is the first black Saint of the Americas. He is the patron Saint of mixed-race people and everyone seeking racial harmony.
- *Discuss:* How can you prepare for eternal life with God?

 Encourage the children to go to **aliveinchrist.osv.com** at home to learn more about Saint Martin de Porres.

Activity

Read aloud the directions and discuss the first part of the Live Your Faith activity as a group.

- Allow time for the children to write their answers.
- Invite volunteers to share what they have written.

Let Us Pray

Prayer for the Kingdom

Explain to the children that this prayer will help us celebrate God's reign. We promise to continue to work with God as he builds his Kingdom.

Prepare

- Have paper and letter-size envelopes ready for the children.
- Designate Side 1 and Side 2.

 Rehearse "Holy Spirit," downloaded from **aliveinchrist.osv.com**.

Gather

Invite the children to process to the prayer space. Have each child bring their book and a pencil.

- Ask them to be seated in a circle.

Pray

Follow the order of prayer on the student page.

- *Remembering:* Invite the children to share stories or experiences they remember they have talked about this year of people who have worked for building the Kingdom of God, both in today's world and in the past.

- *Our Summer Promise:* Give each child a piece of paper and invite them to write *promise*, or *covenant*, naming one way they will practically and concretely work for building the Kingdom of God during the summer months. Then, give them an envelope, ask them to address it to themselves and place their promise inside.

Live

 Let Us Pray

Prayer for the Kingdom

Gather and begin with the Sign of the Cross.

Leader: Because you call us, All-Loving God, we want to live each day working for the justice, love, and peace of your Reign.

All: We will be followers of Jesus, praying and living each day: "Your Kingdom come."

Remembering
Our Summer Promise

Leader: Your Kingdom come.

Side 1: May your Kingdom come

Side 2: into our hearts and into our world.

Side 1: Open our hearts

Side 2: to those who are poor, sick, lonely, and suffering.

Side 1: Make us one Body in Christ

Side 2: through the gifts of your Spirit.

All: Help us ready ourselves for the banquet of Heaven. Amen.

 Sing "Holy Spirit"

© Our Sunday Visitor

Liturgy Link

Circle Gathering

This prayer, with its Remembering activity, is a good one for the group to share in a circle.

- Have the children bring their books.
- Invite them to think about stories or experiences they remember from this year of people who have worked for building the Kingdom of God.
- When you are ready, ask the children to turn to page 284.

 Go to **aliveinchrist.osv.com** for Sunday readings, Scripture background, questions of the week, and seasonal resources.

FAMILY+FAITH
LIVING AND LEARNING TOGETHER

YOUR CHILD LEARNED >>>
This chapter examines the Gifts of the Holy Spirit, defines Heaven as the state of eternal happiness with God, and recognizes that acting as members of God's Kingdom on Earth prepares us for the fullness of God's Kingdom in Heaven.

Scripture
 Read **1 John 5:1–3, 11–12** to find out more about the connection between the Son of God and eternal life.

Catholics Believe
- To spend eternity with God, we first must grow in friendship with him and accept his grace.
- The Last Judgment will mark God's final triumph over evil when Christ returns in glory and judges all the living and the dead.

To learn more, go to the *Catechism of the Catholic Church #681–682* at usccb.org.

People of Faith
This week, your child learned about Saint Martin de Porres, who spent his life working for the Kingdom.

CHILDREN AT THIS AGE >>>
How They Understand Death and Resurrection
Your child probably has a clear sense of death as an irreversible state and knows that everyone will eventually die. Fear of their parents' death is one of the most common fears of children this age, though they rarely voice it. Some children have had experience with the deaths of grandparents and great aunts and uncles. It is helpful for them to know that death is not the end, and that by faith we know that we will be reunited with those we love and can look forward to an eternity with God.

CONSIDER THIS >>>
How many times have you thought, "Why isn't someone holding him accountable?"

An important lesson that you will teach your children is the need for consequences. We are accountable for what we choose and the consequences that follow our words and actions. The need for accountability stretches past this lifetime into the next world. God, our perfect parent, will allow us the consequences of a lifetime of choices. As Catholics, we understand that "immediately after death, each person comes before God and is judged individually (the particular judgment) and enters into heaven, Purgatory, or hell" *(USCCA, p. 156)*.

LET'S TALK >>>
- Ask your child to tell you about the seven Gifts of the Holy Spirit.
- Share how these gifts help you to follow Jesus.

LET'S PRAY >>>
Saint Martin, help us do simple things with love, so that we may always be prepared to meet God at the end of time. Amen.

For a multimedia glossary of Catholic Faith Words, Sunday readings, seasonal and Saint resources, and chapter activities go to **aliveinchrist.osv.com**.

Family + Faith

Distribute the page to the children or parents/adult family members. Point out the chapter highlights, insights on how fourth graders understand concepts, the opportunity for the adults to reflect on their own experience and faith journey, and the family prayer.

Chapter 21 Review

A **Work with Words** Fill in the circle of the choice that best completes each sentence.

1. _____ Judgment is the individual judgment by God at the time of a person's death.
   - ○ Last
   - ● Particular
   - ○ Strong

2. The _____ Judgment will occur when Jesus returns to judge all who have ever lived.
   - ● Last
   - ○ Particular
   - ○ Lord's

3. A separation from God forever is called _____.
   - ○ sin
   - ● Hell
   - ○ Purgatory

4. The Last Judgment _____ change your Particular Judgment.
   - ○ will
   - ● will not
   - ○ should

5. Heaven is the _____ of full joy, living eternally in God's presence.
   - ● state
   - ○ place
   - ○ room

B **Check Understanding** For each statement, write the correct Gift of the Holy Spirit being used.

6. Josh gives his best friend good advice, telling him not to shoplift.
   Counsel

7. Kim didn't do her homework, but she decides to tell her teacher the truth.
   Fortitude or courage

8. Tasha was ready to steal a DVD. When she remembered what she learned in religion class, she put the DVD back.
   Understanding

9. Madison is overwhelmed with the beauty of the night sky, and she thinks of God.
   Fear of the Lord or awe and wonder

10. Amelia is struggling with a decision. She thinks about what Jesus would do.
    Wisdom

Go to **aliveinchrist.osv.com** for an interactive review.

Chapter Review

Use Catechist Quick Reviews to highlight lesson concepts.

A **Work with Words**
Have the children fill in the circle of the choice that best completes each sentence.

B **Check Understanding**
For each statement, have the children write the correct gift of the Holy Spirit being used.

 Go to **aliveinchrist.osv.com** to prepare customized and downloadable assessments, send eAssessments, and assign interactive reviews.

Eternal Life with God **285–286**

Use Catechist Quick Reviews in each chapter to highlight lesson concepts for this unit and prepare for the Unit Review.

Have the children complete the Review pages. Then discuss the answers as a group. Review any concepts with which the children are having difficulty.

(A) Work with Words
Have the children complete each sentence with the correct term.

(A) Work with Words Complete each sentence with the correct term.

1. To _____resent_____ or want for yourself what belongs to others is called envy.

2. Variety, especially among people, is known as _____diversity_____.

3. The _____Last_____ _____Judgment_____ will occur at the end of time, when Christ returns to judge the living and the dead.

4. The virtue of giving to God and people what is due them is called _____justice_____.

5. _____Greed_____ is the desire to gain earthly goods without limits or beyond what you need.

6. The _____poor_____ _____in_____ _____spirit_____ are those who do not become too attached to their possessions and are able to help bring about God's reign.

7. The job or purpose of sharing the Good News of Jesus and the Kingdom of God is known as a _____mission_____.

8. _____Stewardship_____ is the way we appreciate and use God's gifts and the resources of creation.

9. The full joy of living eternally in God's presence is _____Heaven_____.

10. _____Particular_____ _____Judgment_____ is the individual judgment by God at the time of a person's death.

UNIT 7 Unit Review

B Check Understanding Fill in the circle next to the answer that best completes each statement.

11. In the Parable of the Rich Fool, Jesus teaches that the rich man is not concerned with _____.
- ● what matters to God
- ○ being merry
- ○ riches

12. _____ left their homes, families, and jobs in order to follow Jesus and help him spread God's Word.
- ○ The Israelites
- ○ Adam and Eve
- ● The Apostles

13. Missionaries follow Jesus' example by reaching out to _____ people, especially those who are sick and those who are poor.
- ○ most
- ● all
- ○ some

14. Being separated from God forever as a result of a person's choice to sin and reject God's forgiveness is called _____.
- ● Hell
- ○ greed
- ○ Heaven

15. You receive the Gifts of the Holy Spirit in Baptism and Confirmation, including _____.
- ○ wisdom
- ○ piety
- ● both wisdom and piety

288 Unit 7 Review

C Make Connections Use the five words in the Word Bank to write a brief paragraph that answers the following question: What can you do in your life now to prepare for when you will see God?

Word Bank
- generous
- mission
- Heaven
- judgment
- Holy Spirit

16–20. <u>Responses will vary.</u>

_____

_____

_____

_____

_____

_____

_____

_____

_____

_____

_____

_____

_____

_____

_____

_____

_____

_____

_____

_____

_____

_____

Kingdom of God **289**

B Check Understanding
Have the children fill in the circle next to the answer that best completes each statement.

C Make Connections
Have the children use the five words in the Word Bank to write a brief paragraph that answers the question.

Go to **aliveinchrist.osv.com** to prepare customized and downloadable assessments, send eAssessments, and assign interactive reviews.

Unit 7 Review **288–289**

Live Your Faith
&
Our Catholic Tradition
Reference Section

Live Your Faith

" Let us keep a place for Christ in our lives, let us care for one another and let us be loving custodians of creation. "

—Pope Francis via Twitter, March 19, 2013

The Seven Themes of Catholic Social Teaching

The Catholic Church's Social Teaching helps build a just society and shows us how to live lives of holiness amidst the challenges of modern society. The wisdom of this tradition can be understood best through a direct reading of Church documents, but here is a synopsis of each of the seven key themes that are part of our Catholic Social Tradition.

Life and Dignity of the Human Person

Each person is created in God's image and all people have rights that flow from their human dignity. The equal dignity of all people means we must work to eliminate social and economic inequalities. We strive to value all people over our personal wealth or possessions.

Call to Family, Community, and Participation

In order for our society to be healthy, we must all make positive contributions to it, bringing to it the light of the Gospels. We can do this by finding practical ways to participate more fully in our own families, in our parishes, and in our communities.

Rights and Responsibilities of the Human Person

Every person has a right to life and the rights needed to live in dignity. The fundamental rights of all people are freedom, justice, and the basic necessities of everyday life. As individuals and as a society, we must work to protect these rights for all people.

Option for the Poor and Vulnerable

God loves all people, and he calls us to love one another as he loves us. In a world where many people live in great poverty while others enjoy great wealth, we must pay special attention to the needs of the poor and reach out to them in Christian charity.

The Dignity of Work and the Rights of Workers

Through labor all people participate in the work of creation and all workers have the following rights that must be protected: the right to productive work, to fair wages, and to pursue economic opportunity. Catholics believe that our work can be a valuable way to serve God and others.

Solidarity of the Human Family

All people—rich and poor, young and old, weak and strong—have equal dignity and rights that flow from that dignity. As part of one human family, we are all dependent on one another and responsible for one another, and must work to reduce social inequalities and provide for one another's needs.

Care for God's Creation

God is the Creator of all people and all that exists in nature. He has given us the bounty of the Earth and its resources and has entrusted us with its care. We are called to respond by protecting and caring for all God's creation for generations to come.

 Go to **aliveinchrist.osv.com** for a complete listing of chapters and Church year lessons correlated to the themes of Catholic Social Teaching.

About This Principle This section presents an overview of the theological foundation of the theme so that catechists have background information at point of use.

Wrap Instruction An easy to follow side column provides catechists with directions and activities for presenting the Catholic Social Teaching in developmentally appropriate ways.

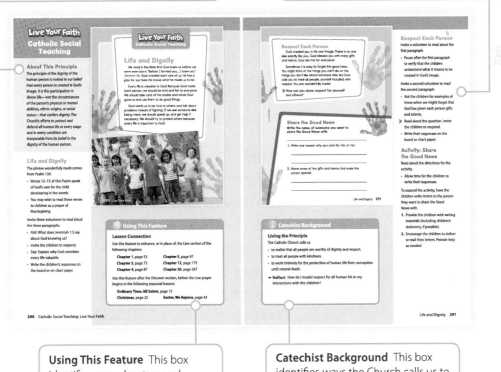

Using This Feature This box identifies core chapters and seasonal lessons to which the Live Your Faith feature is connected.

Catechist Background This box identifies ways the Church calls us to practice the principle and includes a question for catechist reflection.

Live Your Faith
Catholic Social Teaching

About This Principle

We are called by God to respect life when making decisions involving life, death, hunger, poverty, war, and peace. Many of the problems we see in the world today arise from a failure to protect and respect the human dignity of all persons. The Catholic Church teaches that everyone has human dignity, because each individual is created in the image of God.

Life and Dignity of the Human Person

Ask: Why do all people deserve respect?

- Remind the children that because God made each person, we need to treat everyone with respect.

Read aloud the first paragraph.

- Point out that although God created each of us, we are unique and special.

- Invite the children to share with a partner three things about themselves that make them unique or special.

Read aloud the second paragraph.

- Explain that because God made each person, we need to treat ourselves and others with dignity.

Encourage the children to memorize the Scripture verse from Jeremiah. Tell them that they can recite this verse when they are having a difficult day and recall God's love and care for them.

Live Your Faith
Catholic Social Teaching

Life and Dignity of the Human Person

In Scripture God tells us, "Before I formed you in the womb I knew you" (Jeremiah 1:5). God created each of us. Every person is unique and unrepeatable. God has a special plan for each of our lives. He knows what he made us to be.

Because God made each person, we should treat each person with dignity. Every life is valuable to God. We should take care of the bodies and minds God gave us and use them to do good things. God calls us to be kind toward others and to solve problems peacefully instead of fighting. If we see someone being bullied, teased, or disrespected, we need to speak up and get help from an adult if necessary. We should help protect others because every life is important to God.

290 Live Your Faith

Using This Feature

Lesson Connection

Use this feature to enhance, or in place of, the Live section of the following chapters:

Chapter 1, page 59   **Chapter 13**, page 195

Chapter 4, page 93   **Chapter 14**, page 205

Chapter 8, page 137   **Chapter 21**, page 283

Chapter 9, page 147

Use this feature after the Discover section, before the Live Prayer begins in the following seasonal lessons:

Advent, page 18   **Triduum**, page 33   **Ascension**, page 45

Life and Dignity

All humans have a special place in God's plan. As followers of Jesus, you have a duty to help one another use God's gifts to live as he has called you to live.

God wants all people to have the food, water, and shelter they need to live happy and healthy lives. He also wants you to treat all people with respect. Part of showing respect for people is asking them what they need and then helping them to help themselves.

⟩ **What are some ways you can show respect for human life and dignity?**

Needs Around the World

What types of aid are needed by people who are poor around the world? How would these types of aid improve the people's lives? Discuss these issues with a partner and then answer the following questions.

1. When we help the poor, we also learn valuable lessons. What is something we can learn from helping others?

   _____

   _____

2. How might this lesson help us be better followers of Jesus?

   _____

   _____

Catechist Background

Living the Principle

The Catholic Church calls us

- to realize that all human life is sacred and that all people are worthy of human dignity and respect.
- to recognize that the Fifth Commandment is also a mandate to promote and preserve life.
- to be aware that ignoring the call to respect human life and dignity leads to grave personal and social sin.

→ **Reflect** How is respect for human life and dignity a part of your vocation as a catechist?

Life and Dignity

Read aloud both paragraphs.

- Call attention to the photographs.
- Ask the children to tell you what they see in each picture.
- Explain that the people in the pictures are working to promote human life and dignity.
- ⟩ Have the children discuss the question on the page in small groups. Invite sharing with the large group.

See pages CE52–CE53 for more information on all seven Catholic Social Teaching principles.

Activity: Needs Around the World

Read aloud the directions for the activity.

- Have the children discuss the questions with a partner or talk together as a large group.
- After the discussion, have the children work independently to complete the activity.

To expand this lesson, have the children make banners using the words *life, health, respect*, and *dignity*.

1. Have the children cut out letters for each word and glue them to poster board or a large piece of felt.
2. Direct the children to add words that begin with each letter.
3. Provide time for the children to decorate their banners.

Live Your Faith
Catholic Social Teaching

About This Principle

The obligation of Catholics is stated simply: They are called to belong. They are not asked to belong. They are called—as to a vocation—to be responsible for family members and to participate as members of communities. Furthermore, Catholics cannot deny anyone else's call to active participation. They must allow others to serve our communities and answer the call to help.

Call to Family, Community, and Participation

Ask: Why did God give us communities?

- Write the children's responses on the board or on chart paper.

Read aloud the first paragraph.

- Point out that God gave us communities so that we could take care of one another.

Invite a volunteer to read aloud the second paragraph.

- *Ask:* Why does the Church use the term "domestic Church" to describe families? Possible responses: the family is where we learn about God, it is where we learn how to live a Christian life, it is the first place we learn what it means to live in a community, it is where we learn how to love others

Live Your Faith
Catholic Social Teaching

Call to Family, Community, and Participation

From the very beginning, God made people to be in relationship with one another. Scripture tells us, "The LORD God said: It is not good for the man to be alone. I will make a helper suited to him" (Genesis 2:18). God gave us communities so that we could take care of one another.

The family is a very special type of community. Our Church teaches that the family is the "school of holiness" and the "domestic Church." These names reflect the Catholic teaching that the family is where we learn who God is and how to live a Christian life. It is the first place where we learn what it means to live in a community. The family is where we learn how to love others.

© Our Sunday Visitor

292 Live Your Faith

 Using This Feature

Lesson Connection

Use this feature to enhance, or in place of, the Live section of the following chapters:

Chapter 3, page 79   **Chapter 12**, page 181

Chapter 5, page 103   **Chapter 13**, page 195

Chapter 10, page 161   **Chapter 16**, page 229

Chapter 11, page 171   **Chapter 19**, page 263

Use this feature after the Discover section, before the Live Prayer begins in the following seasonal lessons:

Christmas, page 23   **Lent**, page 27

Call to Community

God made people to live with and for others. Humans belong to one another because God is Father of all, and Jesus is everyone's brother and Savior.

A community is a group of people who share common beliefs and activities. The first community you belong to is your family. You belong to the Church community through Baptism. You also belong to other communities, such as neighborhoods, towns or cities, and the world. Baptized Christians have a responsibility to participate in all of these communities.

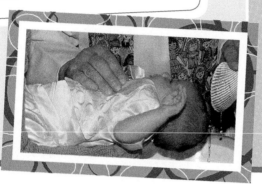

An Ideal Community

Use the diagram to design an ideal community. The diagram represents the main street and two cross streets in a neighborhood. Draw housing, schools, parks, stores and services the community might need.

1. How can you and your friends take more responsibility for your community?

2. What are you willing to do to help others in the neighborhood or world community live better lives?

_____

Call to Family, Community, and Participation **293**

Call to Community

Invite volunteers to read aloud the paragraphs.

- *Ask:* How are human beings all connected? because God is Father of all and Jesus is everyone's brother and Savior

- Explain the call to community by having the children reflect on all of the people who help them in the parish community.

- Have the children write a caption for the photograph that describes how the child is becoming part of the community. Invite volunteers to share their captions.

See pages CE52–CE53 for more information on all seven Catholic Social Teaching principles.

Activity: An Ideal Community

Ask the children to describe their ideal community. List their ideas on the board or on chart paper.

- Explain to the children that they will be community designers.
- Read aloud the directions for the activity.
- Have the children work individually or in pairs to complete the activity.

Live Your Faith
Catholic Social Teaching

About This Principle

This principle emphasizes the balance between what is due to people and what their responsibilities are. Humans are entitled to life and the means to sustain it: food, shelter, and medical care. They are also entitled to sustenance for their intellect in the form of education and employment. Because humans live in community with other people, Catholics must help ensure these rights for others. They also have a responsibility to honor God for these gifts.

Rights and Responsibilities of the Human Person

Ask: What does Jesus say about how we should treat our neighbor?

- Write the children's responses on the board or on chart paper.

Read aloud the first paragraph.

- Explain that rights are freedoms or things that every person needs or should have.
- Explain that responsibilities are our duties, or the things we must do.

Read aloud the second paragraph.

- Emphasize that Jesus tells us to "love your neighbor as yourself" (Mark 12:31).
- Ask the children to name the things that everyone has a right to.
- Ask the children to explain what we are responsible for doing.

Live Your Faith
Catholic Social Teaching

Rights and Responsibilities of the Human Person

Because God made every person, everyone has rights and responsibilities. Rights are the freedoms or things every person needs and should have. Responsibilities are our duties, or the things we must do.

Jesus tells us to "love your neighbor as yourself" (Mark 12:31). The *Catechism* teaches that "respect for the human person considers the other 'another self'" (CCC, 1944). We respect the rights that come from people's dignity as human beings. Everyone has a right to food, shelter, clothing, rest, and the right to see a doctor if they need one. We also have a responsibility to treat others well and work together for the good of everyone.

294

🌐 Using This Feature

Lesson Connection

Use this feature to enhance, or in place of, the Live section of the following chapters:

Chapter 3, page 79   **Chapter 15**, page 215

Chapter 6, page 113   **Chapter 18**, page 249

Chapter 12, page 181   **Chapter 21**, page 283

Use this feature after the Discover section, before the Live Prayer begins in the following seasonal lessons:

Lent, page 27   **Triduum**, page 33

Ascension, page 45   **Pentecost**, page 48

Rights and Responsibilities

God's plan is that every person should be treated with dignity. Every person, everywhere, has a right to life and to the things needed to live, such as food, clothing, shelter, and education.

With human rights come human responsibilities. Part of your mission to follow Jesus is to work for the human rights of all people. It is not fair that some people have things they do not need while others have nothing. All Christians have the responsibility to see that people everywhere are treated fairly and have what they need to live. The Catholic Church calls all of its members to find ways to fight hunger and homelessness. One way to work for human rights is to care for the needs of those who are homeless.

≫ **What human rights and responsibilities can you name?**

Sharing Food

Another way to work for human rights is to gather food for a local food bank. To accomplish this, you will need a plan. Check off each task as you complete it.

1. ☐ Find a food bank nearby and ask what kinds of food are needed.

2. ☐ Decide when and where you will collect the food, and how you will let people know about your food drive.

3. ☐ Get containers for the food, and encourage class members to collect and arrange to have it delivered.

4. ☐ Make cards to thank those who have donated, and think about how to collect food other times during the year.

Do Your Part Ask yourself: Which of the project jobs could I do best? Do I have my own money that I can use to buy food? Can I earn money to buy food for the poor?

Rights and Responsibilities of the Human Person **295**

ⓘ Catechist Background

Living the Principle

The Catholic Church calls us

- to find ways to reaffirm one another spiritually.
- to serve one another by practicing the Corporal Works of Mercy.
- to deepen our relationships with God by following the first three Commandments.

➔ **Reflect** How does my teaching style affirm the rights of the children?

Rights and Responsibilities

Read aloud the first paragraph.

- Ask the children how Jesus cared for people's human rights. Possible response: He fed and healed people. He spoke to people about caring for the poor.
- Invite the children to discuss the responsibilities they have.
- *Say:* All Christians have responsibilities to God's family.

Read aloud the second paragraph.

- Ask the children how we fulfill our responsibilities to other people. by making certain that they have what they need
- ≫ Have the children discuss the question together as a large group.

See pages CE52–CE53 for more information on all seven Catholic Social Teaching principles.

Activity: Sharing Food

Read aloud the directions for the activity.

- After sharing the food drive idea with the children, ask which Corporal Works of Mercy the group would be performing. feeding the hungry, giving drink to the thirsty
- Refer to page 317 in the Our Catholic Tradition reference section in the back of the Student Book for a list of the Corporal Works of Mercy.
- Work with the children to assign tasks. You will need adult assistance for many of the tasks.
- Have the children reflect on and answer the questions.

Live Your Faith

Catholic Social Teaching

About This Principle

In this expression, option means that when people have a choice, they must choose to serve the needs of the weakest first. This principle requires Catholics to set aside bureaucratic definitions and program goals and to focus on distributing resources to those who need them most. People must focus public policy on making the riches of our nations, including food, medical care, and education, available to all.

Option for the Poor and Vulnerable

Ask: Why do the needs of the poor come first?

• Record the children's responses.

Introduce the topic. See pages CE52–CE53 for more information on all seven Catholic Social Teaching principles.

Read aloud the first paragraph.

• Invite a volunteer to reread the Scripture passage.

• Invite the children to explain what the Scripture passage means.
  whatever we do for someone in need, we do for Jesus, and we should treat people in need the same as we would treat Jesus

Read aloud the second paragraph.

• Explain that Catholics put the needs of the poor first. This is called *preferential option for the poor*.

Live Your Faith
Catholic Social Teaching

Option for the Poor and Vulnerable

In Scripture, Jesus says, "whatever you did for one of these least brothers of mine, you did for me" (Matthew 25:40). Whatever we have done for people who are poor or needy, we have also done for him, and what we have not done for them, we haven't done for Jesus. This means we should treat people in need the same way we would treat Jesus himself. We should give special priority to people who are hungry, thirsty, homeless, or alone.

Saint Rose of Lima said, "When we serve the poor and the sick, we serve Jesus." Our Church teaches that we should have special love and care for those who are poor, and put their needs first. This is called the preferential option for the poor. The *Catechism* teaches that "God blesses those who come to the aid of the poor and rebukes those who turn away from them … It is by what they have done for the poor that Jesus Christ will recognize his chosen ones" (CCC, 2443).

© Our Sunday Visitor

296 Live Your Faith

 Using This Feature

Lesson Connection

Use this feature to enhance, or in place of, the Live section of the following chapters:

Chapter 6, page 113   **Chapter 17**, page 239

Chapter 7, page 127   **Chapter 18**, page 249

Chapter 11, page 171   **Chapter 20**, page 273

Chapter 14, page 205

Use this feature after the Discover section, before the Live Prayer begins in the following seasonal lessons:

Ordinary Time, page 12   **Advent**, page 18

Option for the Poor

The crowds that came to hear Jesus preach included many people who were poor or sick. Jesus wanted his Church to be a Church for the poor. Jesus told people who were poor that they were blessed in God's eyes. God's Kingdom belonged to them.

For Catholics, the needs of those who are poor come first. Every Catholic parish is called to serve people who are poor. This is a job that parishioners must do in order to live their faith.

A family that has plenty of money or belongings has a duty to share its good fortune and help meet the needs of those who have less. Every country has a duty to use its wealth to help its citizens who are poor. Rich countries have a duty to help countries that do not have as much.

≫ What are some ways that families, parishes, and countries could show that they put the needs of the poor first?

How Can You Help?

Tell about a time when you put the needs of others before your own. What good thing happened because of your action?

_____

_____

Think of ways that you, or a group to which you belong, might help in the following situations:

1. A friend hurt themselves on the way home from school.
2. A woman is poor and has a sick child.
3. A homeless person is outside on a cold night.
4. A shelter is running low on supplies such as blankets and clothes.

Option for the Poor and Vulnerable **297**

Catechist Background

Living the Principle

The Catholic Church calls us

- to share what we have with others.
- to be active advocates for those who are less fortunate.
- to know that our efforts for others will be rewarded when we are judged by God.

➜ **Reflect** How am I preparing the children for a life of service to the poor and vulnerable?

Option for the Poor

Explain that vulnerable people have few resources, such as money or food, to help them live. Therefore this teaching means that Catholics should choose to do what is most helpful for those who are poor.

Read aloud the first paragraph.

- Help the children recall Gospel accounts in which Jesus cured or fed people who were poor.

Invite volunteers to read aloud the next two paragraphs.

≫ Have the children discuss the question in small groups. Invite sharing with the large group.

Activity: How Can You Help?

Read aloud the directions for the activity.

- Have the children work independently to complete the activity.
- Afterward, invite the children to share their responses.
- From the children's responses, lead the children into a discussion about how Catholics can best serve those in need.

To expand this lesson, have the children study homelessness in the United States. They can investigate the following questions:

1. How many homeless people are there?
2. How many of these are children?
3. Do some parts of the country have more homeless people than other parts? Why?

Live Your Faith
Catholic Social Teaching

About This Principle

Work, whether done by volunteers or paid employees, elevates the workers. Through our work, we share in God's plan for creation by making resources into something new. Workers have an obligation to use their time and talents for God and their employers. However, workers also have the rights that are defended by the Catholic Church. These include safe working conditions, reasonable hours, and fair wages.

The Dignity of Work and Rights of Workers

Ask: Why is work important?

- Write the children's responses on the board or on chart paper.

Read the first paragraph aloud.

- Explain that work helps people earn money to buy necessities like food. It also gives meaning to their lives. For example, a teacher may find meaning in her work as she sees the children learn and grow throughout the school year.

Read aloud the second paragraph.

- Explain that workers have rights. They have the right to fair wages and fair treatment by their employers.
- Point out that workers and their employers should treat one another with respect and solve conflicts peacefully.

Live Your Faith
Catholic Social Teaching

The Dignity of Work and Rights of Workers

All adults have a right and responsibility to work. Work helps people earn money to buy food and other necessities. It also helps to give their lives meaning as they cooperate with God's creation. Everyone should have access to meaningful work, whether that work is within the home or outside the home.

Scripture and Catholic Tradition teach that workers deserve to be treated with justice by their employers: "you shall not exploit a poor and needy hired servant" (Deuteronomy 24:14). Workers have a right to a fair wage for their work (see Leviticus 19:13; Deuteronomy 24:15). When there is a conflict between workers and employers, workers have a right to get together and express their opinions. Workers and their employers should treat one another with respect and solve conflicts peacefully.

© Our Sunday Visitor

298   Live Your Faith

🌐 Using This Feature

Lesson Connection

Use this feature to enhance, or in place of, the Live section of the following chapters:

Chapter 5, page 103   **Chapter 19**, page 263
Chapter 10, page 161

Use this feature after the Discover section, before the Live Prayer begins in the following seasonal lesson:

Pentecost, page 48

The Dignity of Work

Work is more than just a way to make money or complete a task. God calls you to discover your unique gifts and talents and to use them in your work. When you do this, your work becomes part of God's continuing work of creation. Through work, people can see that they have dignity as gifted children of God.

≫ When have you used your gifts and talents along with those of others?

One kind of work is no more important than another. Each person's work can help his or her community and the people who live there. How much a job pays is not important. Every worker and every kind of work is important and worthy of respect.

≫ What kinds of work do you respect most? Why?

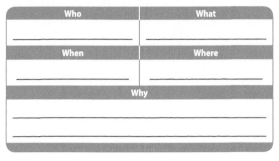

Design an Action Plan

In your group, you may have people with several different gifts and talents, all of which are important and deserve respect. These gifts can be put to good use in a parish ministry or community outreach to help others. Work together to design an action plan that will benefit your community.

Who	What
_____	_____
When	**Where**
_____	_____
Why	
_____	
_____	

Catechist Background

Living the Principle

The Catholic Church calls us

- to serve God and one another through our work.
- to work cooperatively to achieve good for ourselves and the human community.
- to respect the achievements of all workers, no matter what their jobs.

➔ **Reflect** How do I show respect for the children or my co-workers?

The Dignity of Work

Invite a volunteer to read aloud the first paragraph.

≫ Invite the children to share when they have used their gifts and talents along with those of others.

Read aloud the second paragraph.

≫ Ask the children to share what kinds of work they most respect and why.

- Discuss how all workers deserve respect because they share in God's creative work.
- Discuss how the photos show the dignity of each worker.

Help the children understand the meanings of the terms *dignity* and *rights* with regard to work. Explain the following points.

- All workers have dignity because of their efforts to make the world a better place.
- People have a right to jobs that will use their talents and pay just wages.
- The Church supports the rights of workers.

See pages CE52–CE53 for more information on all seven Catholic Social Teaching principles.

Activity: Design an Action Plan

Read aloud the directions for the activity.

- Work together as a large group to design an action plan.

About This Principle

We know that everyone belongs to the human family. However, we do not always act as though we know it. We accept political and racial divisions, refer to us and them, and are quick to distinguish ourselves from others. We seldom reflect on the needs and goals of all humans. As Catholics, if we truly believe in the solidarity of the human family, we will avoid wars, meet everyone's needs, and feel sorrow at the death of any person. We will answer the call to stand up for and take care of one another.

Solidarity of the Human Family

Ask: If God created each of us unique, how are we also one?

- Record the children's responses.

Read aloud the first paragraph.

- Emphasize that God calls everyone to be his children. The differences we see between ourselves and others are often not important to God.

Read aloud the second paragraph.

- Explain that *justice* is giving to God and each person what is due to them. We seek fairness for all people because we are all children of God.

- Emphasize that working for justice between people will help us to live in peace with one another.

Live Your Faith
Catholic Social Teaching

Solidarity of the Human Family

Our world includes people of different nations, races, cultures, beliefs, and economic levels. But God created each one of us. We are one. In fact, Scripture tells us that "there is no partiality with God" (Romans 2:11). The differences that we see between others and ourselves are not important to him. God calls everyone to be his children.

Because God created all people, we have an obligation to treat everyone with love, kindness, and justice. In the Beatitudes, Jesus says, "blessed are the peacemakers, for they will be called children of God" (Matthew 5:9). Working for justice between people will help us to live in peace with one another.

300   Live Your Faith

🌐 Using This Feature

Lesson Connection

Use this feature to enhance, or in place of, the Live section of the following chapters:

Chapter 2, page 69   **Chapter 16**, page 229

Chapter 7, page 127   **Chapter 17**, page 239

Chapter 8, page 137   **Chapter 20**, page 273

Chapter 15, page 215

Use this feature after the Discover section, before the Live Prayer begins in the following seasonal lessons:

Ordinary Time, page 12   **Christmas**, page 18   **Easter**, page 39

Solidarity

When you look at the word solidarity, you can see the word solid. To stand in solidarity with others means to stand strong, or solid, next to them, helping them with their problems and sharing their joys. United, both groups of people become brothers and sisters in the one family of God.

The Call to Unity

Sometimes it may be difficult to see God's plan for solidarity and unity. Countries fight one another in wars. Family members argue. Friends sometimes walk away angry. But Christians are called to look for ways to grow in unity and peace. Bringing people together to solve problems is one way.

> ≫ How can you help your family live in unity? How can you help the world live in solidarity?

Building It Up

Building a house is hard work. It takes lots of time, many people, and special tools. Building solidarity can be hard work, too. Many people must work together to build solidarity, and they need to have the right tools. Tell how each of these "tools" could help people build solidarity.

1. teaching and learning

_____

2. listening and talking

_____

3. praying

_____

4. helping

_____

5. receiving help

_____

ⓘ Catechist Background

Living the Principle

The Catholic Church calls us

- to show solidarity with the family of God.
- to respect the lives of all people.
- to truthfully defend the rights of others.

→ **Reflect** How can my group and I be models of solidarity?

Solidarity

Invite a volunteer to read aloud the paragraph.

- Ask the children when they have stood up for a family member or friend.
- Discuss their reasons for doing so and the results.

The Call to Unity

Invite a volunteer to read aloud the paragraph.

- Discuss what it means to stand in solidarity with other people.
- Have the children give examples of what this means for schoolmates.

≫ Discuss the questions together as a group.

See pages CE52–CE53 for more information on all seven Catholic Social Teaching principles.

Activity: Building It Up

Read aloud the directions for the activity.

- Have the children work in groups to trade ideas about how each of the "tools" helps build solidarity.
- Invite the groups to share with the large group.

To expand this session, have the children research the United Nations. Explain that the United Nations works to avoid war by promoting unity between countries. Have the children find out the following:

1. Why was it started?
2. How long has it been in existence?
3. How does it operate?
4. What does it do to promote world peace?

Live Your Faith
Catholic Social Teaching

About This Principle

Everything in God's creation should work in harmony. Our task, as Catholics, is to recognize that harmony and live within it. When we work in harmony with creation, we take and use only what is appropriate. If we consider ourselves true stewards of creation, we will not take more than we need of anything. This discipline must extend to manufactured products, because the process of making them also results in waste and pollution.

Care for God's Creation

Ask: What is the role of humans in creation?

- Write the children's responses on the board or on chart paper.

Introduce the topic. See pages CE52–CE53 for more information on all seven Catholic Social Teaching principles.

Read aloud the first paragraph.

- Ask the children what God said about what he made. it was very good
- Point out that God gave humans the responsibility to care for all of God's creation.

Read aloud the second paragraph.

- Explain that the common good is the good of everyone.
- Emphasize that God asks us to take care of the environment and all living things.

Live Your Faith
Catholic Social Teaching

Care for God's Creation

When God created the world—the animals, plants, and all natural things—he looked at what he had made and called it "very good" (Genesis 1:31). God made people the stewards of the "fish of the sea, the birds of the air, and all the living things that crawl on the earth" (Genesis 1:28). That means humans have a responsibility to care for all of God's creation.

Catholic Tradition teaches us that God created the Earth and all living things for the common good—the good of everyone. God asks us to take care of the environment and all living things, so that they can be enjoyed by everyone today and in future generations. The *Catechism* teaches us that we owe animals kindness, because they give glory to God just by being what they were made to be.

© Our Sunday Visitor

302 Live Your Faith

🌐 Using This Feature

Lesson Connection

Use this feature to enhance, or in place of, the Live section of the following chapters:

Chapter 1, page 59   **Chapter 9**, page 147
Chapter 4, page 93

Use this feature after the Discover section, before the Live Prayer begins in the following seasonal lesson:

Easter, page 39

Care for Creation

You show that you care for creation by taking care of resources such as land and plants and by using them well. This is a way to thank God for the many gifts he has given you.

Humans are part of creation, too. In fact, humans are a very special part of creation because God created people in his image.

When you take care of other people and treat them with love, you are doing your part in God's plan. Helping other people shows that you recognize his creation of human life as a special and precious gift.

Kinds of Care

In the spaces below, list some things that are necessary for God's creation to grow.

1. What does a plant need to grow healthy and strong?

_____

2. What does a person need to grow healthy and strong?

_____

3. What does a pet need to grow healthy and strong?

_____

Compare the lists. Which items are the same?

_____

(i) Catechist Background

Living the Principle

The Catholic Church calls us

- to use resources for the benefit of all creatures.
- to act as trustees, not owners, of the world's goods.
- to show our respect for God through our management of the environment.

→ **Reflect** How can you model caring for creation for your group?

Care for Creation

Invite volunteers to read aloud the text.

- *Ask:* How can you take care of resources such as land and plants? Possible responses: recycling, conserving energy use, not using harmful chemicals on lawns or plants

- Point out the photograph. Ask the children what it reveals about humans' role in creation.

- *Ask:* How can you show that you care for God's creation? Possible response: visit an elderly person; adopt a pet; tend a garden

Activity: Kinds of Care

Read aloud the directions for the activity.

- Point out that plants, animals, and humans are all part of creation, and that all need care in order to survive and grow.

- Have the children work in pairs to complete the activity.

- Discuss the children's responses with the entire group.

To expand this session, have the children make a large mural on the creation theme.

1. Provide a large sheet of paper for the mural.

2. Have the children sketch their ideas on a small sheet of paper.

3. Combine ideas, and enlarge the sketch on the large piece of paper.

Scripture

About the Old Testament

The Pentateuch is the first five books of the Old Testament—Genesis, Exodus, Leviticus, Numbers, and Deuteronomy. The word *pentateuch* means "five containers." In the beginning the Pentateuch was written on leather or papyrus and each book was kept in a separate container. Jewish people call these books the Torah. The books of the Pentateuch tell of the beginning of human relationship with God. They also tell us the story of God's loving actions for humans.

The Wisdom books of the Old Testament provide guidance in human behavior. Wisdom is a spiritual gift that allows a person to know God's purpose and plan. These books remind us that God's wisdom is always greater than human knowledge.

Many prophets were authors of Old Testament books. A prophet is a person sent by God to call people back to their covenant with God.

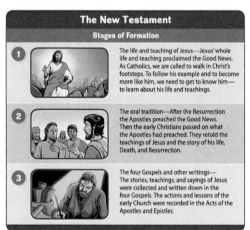

The New Testament

Stages of Formation

1. The life and teaching of Jesus—Jesus' whole life and teaching proclaimed the Good News. As Catholics, we are called to walk in Christ's footsteps. To follow his example and to become more like him, we need to get to know him—to learn about his life and teachings.

2. The oral tradition—After the Resurrection the Apostles preached the Good News. Then the early Christians passed on what the Apostles had preached. They retold the teachings of Jesus and the story of his life, Death, and Resurrection.

3. The four Gospels and other writings—The stories, teachings, and sayings of Jesus were collected and written down in the four Gospels. The actions and lessons of the early Church were recorded in the Acts of the Apostles and Epistles.

The Covenant

The covenant is the sacred agreement joining God and humans. When God made the covenant with Noah after the flood, he promised never to destroy the Earth again. God renewed the covenant with Abram (Abraham), promising him that his descendants would be "as numerous as the stars in the sky" (Genesis 26:4).

Years later, when the descendants of Abraham were slaves in Egypt, God used Moses to lead his People away in the Exodus, or "the road out." At Mount Sinai the covenant was renewed with Moses. God guided the Israelites to the Promised Land. In return, the Israelites were called to love only God and to follow his Law, the Ten Commandments.

Finally, through the Paschal Mystery—Jesus' life, Death, Resurrection, and Ascension—the covenant was fulfilled and a new covenant was created. The new covenant is open to all who remain faithful to God.

God renewed his covenant with Abraham and Moses, ultimately establishing the new covenant in Jesus.

Optional Activity

Old Testament Passages

Prepare a list of citations from the Old Testament, and have the children find these citations in their Bibles.

- Ask the children to write the main idea of each passage next to its citation.
- Then have the children compare their findings with a partner.

Optional Activity

New Testament Letters

Invite the children to familiarize themselves with a selection of New Testament Letters.

- Invite volunteers to proclaim the following Scripture texts: Romans 1:8–12; 1 Corinthians 4:18–21; 1 Corinthians 12:14–26; and 2 Thessalonians 3:1–6.
- Have the children summarize in their own words the issues that these selections address. Offer help as needed.

The Creeds

A creed is a statement of the Church's belief.

Apostles' Creed

This is one of the Church's oldest creeds. It is a summary of Christian beliefs taught since the time of the Apostles. This creed is used in the celebration of Baptism and is often used at Mass during the Season of Easter and in Masses with children. This creed is part of the Rosary.

I believe in God,
the Father almighty,
Creator of heaven and earth,
and in Jesus Christ, his only Son,
   our Lord,

At the words that follow, up to and including the Virgin Mary, all bow.

who was conceived by the Holy Spirit,
born of the Virgin Mary,
suffered under Pontius Pilate,
was crucified, died and was buried;
he descended into hell;
on the third day he rose again from the
   dead;
he ascended into heaven,
and is seated at the right hand
of God the Father almighty;
from there he will come to judge
the living and the dead.
I believe in the Holy Spirit,
the holy catholic Church,
the communion of Saints,
the forgiveness of sins,
the resurrection of the body,
and life everlasting. Amen.

Nicene Creed

This creed, which is prayed at Mass, was written over a thousand years ago by leaders of the Church who met at a city named Nicaea. It is a summary of basic beliefs about God the Father, God the Son, and God the Holy Spirit, the Church, and other teachings of our faith.

I believe in one God,
the Father almighty,
maker of heaven and earth,
of all things visible and invisible.

I believe in one Lord Jesus Christ,
the Only Begotten Son of God,
born of the Father before all ages.
God from God, Light from Light,
true God from true God,
begotten, not made, consubstantial
   with the Father;
through him all things were made.
For us men and for our salvation
he came down from heaven,

At the words that follow up to and including and became man, all bow.

and by the Holy Spirit was incarnate
   of the Virgin Mary,
and became man.

For our sake he was crucified under
   Pontius Pilate,
he suffered death and was buried,

and rose again on the third day
in accordance with the Scriptures.
He ascended into heaven
and is seated at the right hand of
   the Father.
He will come again in glory
to judge the living and the dead
and his kingdom will have no end.

I believe in the Holy Spirit, the Lord,
   the giver of life,
who proceeds from the Father and
   the Son,
who with the Father and the Son is
   adored and glorified,
who has spoken through the prophets.

I believe in one, holy, catholic and
   apostolic Church.
I confess one Baptism for the
   forgiveness of sins
and I look forward to the resurrection
   of the dead
and the life of the world to come.
   Amen.

Optional Activity

Apostles' Creed

Tell the children that the Apostles' Creed is a summary of Christian beliefs. It contains the truths taught by the Apostles, and it highlights what we believe as Catholics. At some Masses with younger children, we profess the Apostles' Creed.

- Have the children write this prayer in the middle of a piece of paper.
- Provide them with colored pencils and markers to add illustrations or drawings around the text to create an "illuminated" manuscript page.
- Encourage the children to work in pairs to memorize this prayer.

Optional Activity

Nicene Creed Puzzles

Because this is the creed we usually pray at Mass, it is important to help the children memorize this prayer.

- Make a copy of the Nicene Creed for each child.
- Cut each copy of the prayer into strips, each containing a line or phrase of the prayer.
- Place the strips into an envelope, one complete set of prayer strips for each envelope.
- Distribute envelopes to the children, one envelope for each child.
- To begin, have the children work in pairs to assemble their puzzles.
- After some time, have the children work independently.
- Encourage the children to use their puzzles at home to memorize the Nicene Creed.

The Holy Trinity

God is revealed in three Divine Persons: God the Father, our Creator and sustainer; God the Son, our Savior; and God the Holy Spirit, our guide. Each of the Persons of the Trinity is separate from the other Persons. However, the Father, Son, and Holy Spirit are one and the same God. The Holy Trinity is the central mystery of the Catholic faith.

The mission of God the Son and God the Holy Spirit is to bring people into the love of the Trinity—the perfect love that exists in the Father, Son, and Holy Spirit.

God the Father

God created all things. The beauty of creation reflects the beauty of the Creator. He cares for and loves all. In his Divine providence, God guides everything toward himself.

God the Son

Jesus is the Son of God. The Son of God became man in order to save all people from the power of sin and everlasting death. Jesus was truly man and yet was truly God, fully divine while fully human. He became human, being born of the Virgin Mary. Except for sin, Jesus was human in every way.

Through the teachings of Jesus, people come to know about the Kingdom of God and how to live for God's reign. From the Sermon on the Mount and other teachings, people learn to live in love. Jesus taught everyone how to live the Ten Commandments—by loving God and all of his creation.

The Holy Trinity is often represented by an equilateral triangle, three interwoven circles, a circle of three fish, or a shamrock.

Jesus' Resurrection showed him as the Messiah, the Savior. By his Death Jesus conquered sin. By rising to new life, Jesus conquered death and so saved all humans from the power of sin and everlasting death.

The Ascension happened forty days after the Resurrection, when Jesus ascended to Heaven to join the glory of God the Father. At the Ascension Jesus commanded the Apostles to continue his mission by teaching and guiding people toward God's Kingdom.

God the Holy Spirit

The Holy Spirit continues to guide people in the Christian life. Through the teachings of Jesus, we learn how to live in love. Through the strength and wisdom of the Holy Spirit, we are able to lead this life of love. The Holy Spirit breathes into the faithful his Gifts.

Gifts of the Holy Spirit	Fruits of the Holy Spirit
You receive the Gifts of the Holy Spirit through the Sacraments of Baptism and Confirmation. These gifts help you grow in relationship with God and others.	The qualities that can be seen in us when we allow the Holy Spirit to work in our hearts.
Wisdom Understanding Right judgment (Counsel) Courage (Fortitude) Knowledge Reverence (Piety) Wonder and awe (Fear of the Lord)	Charity Joy Peace Kindness Patience Goodness Gentleness Faithfulness Modesty Self-Control Chastity Fortitude

Optional Activity

The Holy Trinity

Have the children make three dimensional symbols of the Holy Trinity.

- Tell the children to use known symbols or to create symbols of their own.
- Provide the children with construction paper, scissors, staplers, and glue. Display the completed Holy Trinity symbols.

Optional Activity

Mary

Assign stories about Mary for the children to read. Reading such stories will help them reflect on Mary's faith in God.

- Encourage the children to retell some of the stories to the group.
- Possible stories from the Gospel according to Luke include Luke 1:26–38, 1:39–56, 2:1–14, 2:22–38, and 2:41–52.

Church

Church authority is based on the authority Jesus gave to Peter when he gave him the "keys to the kingdom" (Matthew 16:19) and the authority Jesus gives his disciples to forgive sins in his name (see John 20:23). Church authority also flows from the command from Jesus to his Apostles to make disciples of people everywhere, teaching them to live as Jesus taught and baptizing them in the name of the Father, Son, and Holy Spirit. (See Matthew 28:18–20). Speaking to his Apostles, Jesus also promised to send the Holy Spirit as the Spirit of Truth that would guide them "into all truth." The official teaching authority of the Church is the Magisterium, which is made up of the Pope and the bishops. The Magisterium teaches with the authority given by Jesus and the guidance of the Holy Spirit.

Mission

The Church has the mission to help bring justice to everyone. The principles of social justice are respect for all persons, equality for all persons, and oneness in the family of God with responsibility for one another. These principles can be accomplished with the fair distribution of goods, fair wages for work, and fair resolution in conflicts.

Pope

The Pope's title of "Servant of the Servants" began with Pope Gregory the Great. The Bible says that "[W]hoever wishes to be first among you will be the slave of all" (Mark 10:44). The many titles for the Pope include: Bishop of Rome, Vicar of Christ, Supreme Pontiff of the Universal Church, Patriarch of the West, Primate of Italy, Successor of Saint Peter, Prince of the Apostles, Servant of the Servants of God, and Sovereign of Vatican City.

Saints

Canonization is the process by which the Church recognizes faithful people as Saints. During each of the three stages of becoming a Saint, the faithful person has a different title—first Venerable, then Blessed, and finally Saint.

Mary is the greatest of Saints. We have many teachings about her. The Immaculate Conception means that Mary was preserved from Original Sin from the first moment of conception. The Feast of the Immaculate Conception is December 8. On this date, the Catholics of Paraguay celebrate the feast day of the Virgin of Caacupe. Centuries ago, the Virgin Mary appeared in the Paraguayan countryside. A church was built in the place where she had appeared, and many pilgrims to that church have experienced miracles. Today December 8 is as special a celebration to the Catholics of Paraguay as Christmas is. Many honor Mary every year by making a pilgrimage, or long walk, to the church of the Virgin of Caacupe.

Last Things

Purgatory

At death most people are not ready for Heaven and God's eternal friendship. However, they have not broken their relationship with God. These souls are given time in Purgatory. Purgatory means "purifying." Purgatory helps the soul prepare for life with God. The soul becomes more faithful and loving.

Particular Judgment

When people die, they are judged by how fully they have responded to God's call and the grace he has offered through Jesus. This judgment is called Particular Judgment. Souls will be given reward or punishment at this time.

General Judgment

General Judgment, or the Last Judgment, will occur at the Second Coming of Christ. This judgment represents God's triumph over evil. General Judgment will mark the arrival of God's Kingdom in its fullness. General Judgment will happen to all people, living and dead. However, this judgment will not change the Particular Judgment received by each soul.

Optional Activity

Mission

Supply the children with news articles on Catholic Social Teaching issues.

- Ask each child to read an article and tell the group how the article illustrates real-world applications of Catholic Social Teaching.
- Help the children identify in their articles any of the principles of Catholic Social Teaching found on page 310.

Optional Activity

Saints

Direct each child to research the life of a Saint. The research should focus on the Saint's contribution to his or her local faith community or the wider Church.

- Ask the children to illustrate their Saints' contributions.
- Put the illustrations together to make a Saint mural.

The Liturgical Year

Advent

Four Sundays of Advent

Christmas

Christmas Day
Feast of the Holy Family
Feast of Epiphany

Ordinary Time

Sundays between Epiphany and
Ash Wednesday

Before Lent begins, the palms from Palm
Sunday from the prior year are collected
and burned. The ashes are then used for
the Ash Wednesday service.

312

Lent

Lent begins on Ash Wednesday, and continues with the Five Sundays of Lent, including Passion or Palm Sunday.

Lent is a time of fasting, prayer, and almsgiving. The forty days of Lent remind Christians of the number of days Jesus spent fasting in the desert. The forty days also represent the number of years the Israelites spent wandering in the desert after the Exodus.

Lent begins with Ash Wednesday, a day of penance. The last Friday in Lent, Good Friday, is also a day of penance. All Catholics from their eighteenth to their fifty-ninth birthdays must fast on days of penance: They eat light meals and have no food between meals. On Ash Wednesday and on all Fridays during Lent, abstinence is required for Catholics fourteen years of age or older. This means that they may not eat meat. Fasting, abstinence, and personal reflection during Lent help prepare Catholics for the celebration of Easter.

Triduum

The Triduum, which means "three days," starts with the celebration of the Lord's Supper on Holy Thursday. Good Friday is observed with a Liturgy of the Word, Veneration of the Cross, and a Communion service. On Holy Saturday evening the Easter Vigil is celebrated. The Triduum ends with evening prayer on Easter Sunday. Because the Triduum celebrates the Paschal Mystery—the life, Death, and Resurrection of Jesus—it is the high point of the entire Church year.

Easter Season

The Easter season begins on Easter Sunday and continues with the Second through Seventh Sundays of Easter, culminating with Pentecost Sunday (fifty days after Easter).

The Paschal Candle is a symbol of Christ and of Easter. This candle is lit from the Easter fire during the Easter Vigil. Throughout the fifty days of the Easter Season, the candle burns during the liturgy. After the Easter Season it is used during Baptisms and funerals as a symbol of the Resurrection.

Ordinary Time

Sundays between Pentecost and
the First Sunday of Advent

313

Optional Activity

Advent or Lent

Invite the children to make either Advent calendars to count down the days until Christmas or Lenten calendars to count down the days until Easter.

- Suggest that the calendars include symbols and colors of the liturgical season.
- Refer to a liturgical calendar for assistance. You can find one online at **usccb.org**.

Optional Activity

Triduum Triptychs

A triptych is a piece of art created on three separate panels that are hinged together. Have the children draw their triptychs for the Triduum.

- The art on each panel should represent one day of the Triduum and a symbol for that day.
- Ask each child to explain his or her symbols to a partner. Display the triptychs for others to see.

The Seven Sacraments

The Catholic Church celebrates Seven Sacraments—special signs and celebrations of Jesus' presence. Jesus gave us the Sacraments to allow us to share in God's life and work. There are three groups of Sacraments.

Sacraments	
Sacraments of Initiation	
These are the three Sacraments that celebrate membership into the Catholic Church.	• Baptism • Confirmation • Eucharist
Sacraments of Healing	
In these Sacraments, God's forgiveness and healing are given to those suffering physical and spiritual sickness.	• Penance and Reconciliation • Anointing of the Sick
Sacraments at the Service of Communion	
These Sacraments celebrate people's commitment to serve God and the community and help build up the People of God.	• Holy Orders • Matrimony (Marriage)

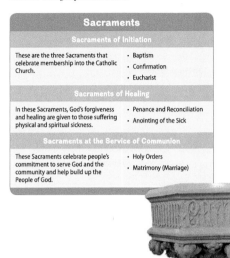

Holy water is water that has been blessed. It is used during the Sacrament of Baptism as well as for the blessing of people or objects. Fonts of holy water are placed at the entrances of churches so that people may bless themselves and recall the meaning of Baptism as they make the Sign of the Cross.

The Sacrament of Penance and Reconciliation

The Sacrament of Reconciliation is also known as the Sacrament of Penance or the Sacrament of Confession. In this Sacrament, sin is forgiven and the one who has sinned is reconciled with God, with himself or herself, and with the Church community. The essential elements for Reconciliation are contrition (sorrow for the sin), confession, absolution by the priest, and satisfaction (attempting to correct or undo the wrong done).

Rite for Reconciliation of Individual Penitents

1. Welcome
2. Reading from Scripture
3. Confession of Sins and Acceptance of a Penance
4. Act of Contrition (See page 324.)
5. Absolution
6. Closing Prayer

Rite for Reconciliation of Several Penitents

1. Greeting
2. Celebration of the Word
3. Homily
4. Examination of Conscience
5. General Confession of Sin/Litany of Contrition
6. The Lord's Prayer

7. Individual Confession of Sins, Acceptance of a Penance, and Absolution:

Prayer of Absolution

God, the Father of mercies,
through the death and resurrection
   of his Son
has reconciled the world to himself
and sent the Holy Spirit among us
for the forgiveness of sins;
through the ministry of the Church
may God give you pardon and peace,
and I absolve you from your sins
in the name of the Father, and of
   the Son,
and of the Holy Spirit.

8. Closing Prayer

Examination of Conscience

For help with examining your conscience, use the following steps:

1. Pray for the Holy Spirit's help in making a fresh start.
2. Look at your life in the light of the Beatitudes, the Ten Commandments, the Great Commandment, and the Precepts of the Church.
3. Ask yourself these questions: Where have I fallen short of what God wants for me? Whom have I hurt? What have I done that I knew was wrong? What have I not done that I should have done? Have I made the necessary changes in bad habits? What areas am I still having trouble with? Am I sincerely sorry for all my sins?

Optional Activity

Reconciliation

Ask each child to compose an Act of Contrition.

- As the children are working on their prayers, reinforce the absolute confidentiality of the Sacrament of Penance and Reconciliation.

Point out that even civil laws respect the seal of the confessional.

- Invite volunteers to read their newly composed prayers.

Optional Activity

Conscience

Have the children work in small groups to compose questions that will be used in an examination of conscience.

- Assign group members to read the Ten Commandments, the Beatitudes, or the Precepts of the Church and to use these labels as a basis for their questions.

- Remind the children that a regular examination of conscience helps ensure continued growth in faith.

God's Laws

God gives us laws to help us live by the covenant. These laws guide us in loving God and our neighbor.

Laws are rules that help people live as members of a community and behave in an acceptable manner.

Divine law is the eternal law of God. It includes physical law and moral law. The law of gravity is an example of physical law. A moral law is one that humans understand through reasoning (you may not steal) and through Divine Revelation (keep holy the Lord's Day).

Natural moral law consists of those decisions and duties that all humans accept as right. For example, people everywhere understand that no one may kill another unjustly. Everyone must obey natural moral law.

The Ten Commandments

1. I am the Lord your God: you shall not have strange gods before me.
2. You shall not take the name of the Lord your God in vain.
3. Remember to keep holy the Lord's Day.
4. Honor your father and your mother.
5. You shall not kill.
6. You shall not commit adultery.
7. You shall not steal.
8. You shall not bear false witness against your neighbor.
9. You shall not covet your neighbor's wife.
10. You shall not covet your neighbor's goods.

The Beatitudes

The Beatitudes are sayings of Jesus that show us the way to true happiness in God's Kingdom. The Beatitudes are listed in the Gospel according to Matthew (see Matthew 5:3–10). See also Chapter 7.

The New Commandment

Jesus also gave his followers a New Commandment: "love one another. As I have loved you, so you also should love one another" (John 13:34).

Corporal and Spiritual Works of Mercy

The Corporal Works of Mercy draw Catholics to the care of the physical needs of others. The Spiritual Works of Mercy guide us to care for the spiritual needs of people.

Corporal	Spiritual
• Feed the hungry	• Warn the sinner
• Give drink to the thirsty	• Teach the ignorant
• Clothe the naked	• Counsel the doubtful
• Shelter the homeless	• Comfort the sorrowful
• Visit the sick	• Bear wrongs patiently
• Visit the imprisoned	• Forgive injuries
	• Pray for the living and the dead

Precepts of the Church

The following precepts are important duties of all Catholics.

1. Take part in the Mass on Sundays and holy days. Keep these days holy and avoid unnecessary work.
2. Celebrate the Sacrament of Reconciliation at least once a year.
3. Receive Holy Communion at least once a year during the Easter Season.
4. Fast and abstain on days of penance.
5. Give your time, gifts, and money to support the Church.

Optional Activity

The Ten Commandments

Ask each child to copy the Ten Commandments on a sheet of paper.

- Invite the children to decorate their papers so that they resemble scrolls and to display them in a prominent place at home.
- During the next session, challenge the children to recite from memory the Ten Commandments.

Optional Activity

Corporal Works of Mercy

Have the children create a mural that illustrates the Corporal Works of Mercy.

- Help the children generate ideas for the mural by providing them with examples of the Corporal Works of Mercy from the parish bulletin, diocesan newspaper, or other media.

Free Will and Conscience

God's image is his likeness that is present in you because you are his creation. You are called to respect the dignity of all people because everyone is made in God's image.

- Freedom means you are able to choose and act with few limitations. We are given freedom by God that we may choose to do good things.

- Free will is the gift from God that allows humans to make their own choices. Because you are free to choose between right and wrong, you are responsible for your choices and actions.

- Conscience is a gift from God that helps us judge whether actions are right or wrong. It is important for us to know God's laws so our conscience can help us make good decisions. Conscience helps you choose what is right. It involves free will and reason working together. You must form your conscience properly. If not formed properly, your conscience can lead you to choose what is wrong.

Forming your conscience is a lifelong process. It involves practicing virtues and avoiding sin and people or situations that may lead you to sin. You can turn to good people for advice, to Church teachings for guidance, and to God for help in educating your conscience.

Grace

God gives you two types of grace. Sanctifying grace is the gift of God's life in you. It gives you the desire to live and act within God's plan.

Actual grace is the gift of God's life in you that helps you think or act in a particular situation according to God's plan. Actual grace opens you to understanding and strengthens your will.

Virtue and Sin

Virtues are good qualities or habits of goodness. The word virtue means "strength." Practicing virtue can give you the strength to make loving choices.

Types of Virtues

Theological Virtues	Cardinal Virtues
Faith Hope Charity (Love)	Prudence (careful judgment) Fortitude (courage) Justice (giving people their due) Temperance (moderation, balance)

Sin is a turning away from God and a failure to love. Sin affects both the individual and the community. A person may be sorry for his or her sin, ask forgiveness for it, accept punishment for it, and resolve to do better. In this case, the experience may actually help the person develop as a Christian and avoid sin in the future. However, a person who makes a habit of sin will harm his or her development, set a poor example, and bring sorrow to others. Society suffers when people disobey God's law and the just laws of society. There are many types of sin.

- Original Sin is the human condition of weakness and the tendency toward sin that resulted from the choice of Adam and Eve, our first parents, to disobey God. Baptism restores the relationship of loving grace in which all people were created.

- Actual sin is any thought, word, act, or failure to act that goes against God's law. Sin is always a choice, never a mistake.

- Mortal sin causes a person's relationship with God to be broken.

A mortal sin is a serious act, such as murder. In order for it to be a mortal sin, there must be a deliberate choice to commit the act; it is never an accident.

- Venial sin weakens a person's relationship with God but does not destroy it. Venial sin often comes from bad habits. It can lead to mortal sin.

- Social sin happens when one person's sins affect the larger community. Poverty and racism are examples of social sin.

Optional Activity

Grace

Have the children work together in small groups to write prayers to the Holy Spirit.

- Each group's prayer should include a request for an increase in one of the Gifts of the Holy Spirit (see page 309) and thanksgiving for the gift of God's grace.

- Pray one of these prayers during the opening prayer of each session.

Optional Activity

Virtues

Have the children create bookmarks that incorporate the symbols of the Theological Virtues (*faith:* a cross; *hope:* an anchor; *love:* a heart).

- Provide the children with appropriate art supplies.

- You may also wish to have the children brainstorm symbols for the Cardinal Virtues to use for the bookmarks.

Basic Prayers

These are essential prayers that every Catholic should know. Latin is the official, universal language of the Church. As members of the Catholic Church, we usually pray in the language that we speak, but we sometimes pray in Latin, the common language of the Church.

Sign of the Cross

In the name of the Father,
and of the Son,
and of the Holy Spirit.
Amen.

Signum Crucis

In nómine Patris
et Fílii
et Spíritus Sancti.
Amen.

The Lord's Prayer

Our Father, who art in heaven,
hallowed be thy name;
thy kingdom come,
thy will be done
on earth as it is in heaven.
Give us this day our daily bread,
and forgive us our trespasses,
as we forgive those who trespass
    against us;
and lead us not into temptation,
but deliver us from evil.
Amen.

Pater Noster

Pater noster qui es in cælis:
santificétur Nomen Tuum;
advéniat Regnum Tuum;
fiat volúntas Tua,
sicut in cælo, et in terra.
Panem nostrum
cotidiánum da nobis hódie;
et dimítte nobis débita nostra,
sicut et nos
dimíttus debitóribus nostris;
et ne nos indúcas in tentatiónem;
sed líbera nos a Malo.

The Hail Mary

Hail, Mary, full of grace,
the Lord is with thee.
Blessed art thou among women
and blessed is the fruit of thy womb,
    Jesus.
Holy Mary, Mother of God,
pray for us sinners,
now and at the hour of our death.
Amen.

Ave Maria

Ave, María, grátia plena,
Dóminus tecum.
Benedícta tu in muliéribus,
et benedíctus fructus ventris
    tui, Iesus.
Sancta María, Mater Dei,
ora pro nobis peccatóribus,
nunc et in hora mortis nostræ.
    Amen.

Glory Be

Glory be to the Father
and to the Son
and to the Holy Spirit,
as it was in the beginning
is now, and ever shall be
world without end.
Amen.

Gloria Patri

Gloria Patri
et Filio
et Spíritui Sancto.
Sicut erat in princípio
et nunc et semper
et in sæcula sæculorum.
Amen.

Angelus

V. The angel spoke God's message to Mary,
R. and she conceived of the Holy Spirit.
Hail, Mary . . .
V. "I am the lowly servant of the Lord:
R. let it be done to me according to your word."
Hail, Mary . . .
V. And the Word became flesh,
R. and lived among us.
Hail, Mary . . .
V. Pray for us, holy Mother of God,

R. that we may become worthy of the promises of Christ.
Let us pray.

Lord,
fill our hearts with your grace:
once, through the message of an angel you revealed to us the Incarnation of your Son;
now, through his suffering and death lead us to the glory of his resurrection.

We ask this through Christ our Lord.
Amen.

Optional Activity

Lord's Prayer

Have the children suggest reverent gestures to accompany the phrases of the Lord's Prayer.

- After the children have practiced using their gestures while saying the prayer, have them share with partners or another group of children.
- Use the gestures as part of the Lord's Prayer during future prayer services.

Optional Activity

Angelus

In this prayer, the angel of the Lord spoke God's message to Mary. Through quiet prayer and contemplation, we can attempt to discern God's special message to us.

- Have the children create images of angel messengers.
- Provide them with the appropriate art supplies and simple outlines of an angel to copy if they wish.
- Have them include a small banner across the bottom of the angel.
- After a few moments of silent prayer, ask them to write in the banner one word or short phrase that they feel that God may be asking them to focus on or work on. (This could include ideas such as Family, Friends, Be more forgiving, Love others.)

Memorare

Remember, most loving Virgin Mary, never was it heard that anyone who turned to you for help was left unaided. Inspired by this confidence, though burdened by my sins, I run to your protection for you are my mother. Mother of the Word of God, do not despise my words of pleading but be merciful and hear my prayer. Amen.

Hail, Holy Queen

Hail, Holy Queen, Mother of Mercy, our life, our sweetness and our hope. To you do we cry, poor banished children of Eve. To you do we send up our sighs, mourning and weeping in this valley of tears. Turn then, most gracious advocate, your eyes of mercy toward us, and after this exile show unto us the blessed fruit of thy womb, Jesus. O clement, O loving, O sweet Virgin Mary.

Prayer to the Holy Spirit

Come, Holy Spirit, fill the hearts of your faithful. And kindle in them the fire of your love. Send forth your Spirit and they will be created. And you will renew the face of the earth. Let us pray. Lord, by the light of the Holy Spirit you have taught the hearts of your faithful. In the same Spirit help us to relish what is right and always rejoice in your consolation. We ask this through Christ our Lord. Amen.

Prayers from the Sacraments

I Confess/*Confiteor*

I confess to almighty God and to you, my brothers and sisters, that I have greatly sinned, in my thoughts and in my words, in what I have done and in what I have failed to do,

Gently strike your chest with a closed fist.

through my fault, through my fault, through my most grievous fault;

Continue:

therefore I ask blessed Mary ever-Virgin, all the Angels and Saints, and you, my brothers and sisters, to pray for me to the Lord our God.

Gloria

Glory to God in the highest, and on earth peace to people of good will. We praise you, we bless you, we adore you, we glorify you, we give you thanks for your great glory, Lord God, heavenly King, O God, almighty Father. Lord Jesus Christ, Only Begotten Son, Lord God, Lamb of God, Son of the Father,

you take away the sins of the world, have mercy on us; you take away the sins of the world, receive our prayer; you are seated at the right hand of the Father, have mercy on us. For you alone are the Holy One, you alone are the Lord, you alone are the Most High, Jesus Christ, with the Holy Spirit, in the glory of God the Father. Amen.

Holy, Holy, Holy Lord

Holy, Holy, Holy Lord God of hosts. Heaven and earth are full of your glory. Hosanna in the highest. Blessed is he who comes in the name of the Lord. Hosanna in the highest.

Sanctus, Sanctus, Sanctus

Sanctus, Sanctus, Sanctus Dominus Deus Sabaoth. Pleni sunt coeli et terra gloria tua. Hosanna in excelsis. Benedictus qui venit in nomine Domini. Hosanna in excelsis

---

Optional Activity

Prayer to the Holy Spirit

Invite the children to create banners or other liturgical art that reflects the imagery of this prayer.

- Encourage the children to pray this prayer before making a decision, facing a challenge, or in other situations in which the Holy Spirit's wisdom or guidance would be especially welcome.

Optional Activity

Agnus Dei (Lamb of God)

The reference to Jesus as the Lamb of God in this litany prayer comes from John 1:29 and Revelation 5:6–13, as well as other Scripture passages.

- Have the children write the Latin version of the Lamb of God on prayer cards.
- Have them draw peace symbols around the edges of the card.
- Together, read aloud the Agnus Dei prayer.

 You may wish to play for the children "The Supper of the Lamb" downloaded from the Grade 4 music section on **aliveinchrist.osv.com** to familiarize them with the new language in the English translation of the Third Edition of the *Roman Missal*.

Lamb of God

Lamb of God, you take away the
sins of the world,
have mercy on us.
Lamb of God, you take away the
sins of the world,
have mercy on us.
Lamb of God, you take away the
sins of the world,
grant us peace.

Act of Contrition

Contrition is the sorrow that rises up in
the soul, making you repent past sins and
plan not to sin again. To repent is to turn
back from the sin and ask God's mercy.

My God, I am sorry for my sins with all
my heart.
In choosing to do wrong
and failing to do good,
I have sinned against you
whom I should love above all things.
I firmly intend, with your help,
to do penance,
to sin no more,
and to avoid whatever leads me to sin.
Our Savior Jesus Christ
suffered and died for us.
In his name, my God, have mercy.

Agnus Dei

Agnus Dei, qui tollis peccata mundi:
miserere nobis.
Agnus Dei, qui tollis peccata mundi:
miserere nobis.
Agnus Dei, qui tollis peccata mundi:
dona nobis pacem

The Jesus Prayer

Lord Jesus Christ, Son of God,
have mercy upon me, a sinner.

The Apostles' Creed

See page 306 for this prayer.

The Nicene Creed

See page 307 for this prayer.

Personal and Family Prayers

Act of Faith

O God, we firmly believe that you are
one God in three Divine Persons, Father,
Son, and Holy Spirit; we believe that
your Divine Son became man and died
for our sins, and that he will come to
judge the living and the dead. We believe
these and all the truths that the holy
Catholic Church teaches because you
have revealed them, and you can neither
deceive nor be deceived.

Act of Hope

O God, relying on your almighty power
and your endless mercy and promises,
we hope to gain pardon for our sins, the
help of your grace, and life everlasting,
through the saving actions of Jesus
Christ, our Lord and Redeemer.

Act of Love

O God, we love you above all things,
with our whole heart and soul, because
you are all good and worthy of all love.
We love our neighbor as ourselves for
the love of you. We forgive all who have
injured us and ask pardon of all whom
we have injured.

Grail Prayer

Lord Jesus,
I give you my hands to do your work.
I give you my feet to go your way.
I give you my eyes to see as you do.
I give you my tongue to speak your words.
I give you my mind that you may think
in me.

Above all, I give you my heart
that you may love in me your Father
and all mankind.
I give you my whole self that
you may grow in me,
so that it is you, Lord Jesus,
who will live and work and pray in me.
Amen.

Morning Prayer

God be in my head, and in my
understanding;
God be in my eyes, and in my looking;
God be in my mouth, and in my speaking;
God be in my heart, and in my thinking;
God be at my end, and at my departing.
Amen.

Evening Prayer

Lord, from the rising of the sun to its
setting your name is worthy of all praise.
Let our prayer come like incense before
you. May the lifting up of our hands be
as an evening sacrifice acceptable
to you,
Lord our God.
Amen.

Optional Activity

Act of Contrition

Tell the children that the Act of Contrition is a prayer of sorrow. Through it we tell God we are sorry and want to do better, and we ask him to help us avoid temptation.

- Talk about the difference between someone just saying "I am sorry," and someone showing that he or she is really sorry.
- Have the children write a prayer of sorrow in their own words.
- Encourage them to share their prayers with their families.

Optional Activity

Act of Love

Recognizing God's presence is not always easy because he usually makes his presence known to us in the quiet of our hearts.

- Explain to the children that we often have to make an effort to hear God's voice in the busy worlds we live in.
- Have them list five "noises" or things that might make it hard for them to hear his voice.
- Ask volunteers to share some of the items from their lists, and encourage the group to offer suggestions for quieting those noises.

Praying with the Saints

When we pray with the Saints, we ask them to pray to God for us and to pray with us. The Saints are with Christ. They speak for us when we need help.

One of the most popular devotions to Mary is the Rosary. It focuses on the twenty mysteries that describe events in the lives of Jesus and Mary.

How to Pray the Rosary

1. Pray the Sign of the Cross and say the Apostles' Creed.
2. Pray the Lord's Prayer.
3. Pray three Hail Marys.
4. Pray the Glory Be to the Father.
5. Say the first mystery; then pray the Lord's Prayer.
6. Pray ten Hail Marys while meditating on the mystery.
7. Pray the Glory Be to the Father.
8. Say the second mystery; then pray the Lord's Prayer.
Repeat 6 and 7 and continue with the third, fourth, and fifth mysteries in the same manner.
9. Pray the Hail, Holy Queen.

The Mysteries of the Rosary

The Joyful Mysteries
The Annunciation
The Visitation
The Nativity
The Presentation in the Temple
The Finding in the Temple

The Sorrowful Mysteries
The Agony in the Garden
The Scourging at the Pillar
The Crowning with Thorns
The Carrying of the Cross
The Crucifixion and Death

The Luminous Mysteries
The Baptism of Jesus
The Wedding at Cana
The Proclamation of the Kingdom
The Transfiguration
The Institution of the Eucharist

The Glorious Mysteries
The Resurrection
The Ascension
The Descent of the Holy Spirit
The Assumption of Mary
The Coronation of Mary in Heaven

Litany of St. Joseph

A litany is a prayer with one line that is meant to be repeated over and over again so that those praying are caught up in the prayer itself. In Litanies of the Saints we call to the Saints to intercede for us.

Lord, have mercy.	Lord, have mercy.
Christ, have mercy.	Christ, have mercy.
Lord, have mercy.	Lord, have mercy.
Good Saint Joseph,	pray for us.
Descendant of the House of David,	pray for us.
Husband of Mary,	pray for us.
Foster father of Jesus,	pray for us.
Guardian of Christ,	pray for us.
Support of the holy family,	pray for us.
Model of workers,	pray for us.
Example to parents,	pray for us.
Comfort of the dying,	pray for us.
Provider of food to the hungry,	pray for us.
Companion of the poor,	pray for us.
Protector of the Church,	pray for us.

Merciful God,
grant that we may learn from Saint Joseph to care for the members of our families and share what we have with the poor. We ask this through Christ our Lord. Amen.

Optional Activity

The Mysteries of the Rosary

Symbols that represent the Joyful Mysteries include green leaves or white rosettes. Scripture passages and reflections that apply to these mysteries include: the Annunciation (humility), Luke 1:26–38; the Visitation (charity), Luke 1:39–45; the Nativity (poverty), Luke 2:1–20; the Presentation (obedience), Luke 2:22–35; and the Finding of Jesus in the Temple (piety), Luke 2:41–52.

- Organize the children into five small groups and assign each group one of the Joyful Mysteries.
- Provide each group with the Scripture passages from Luke that apply to their mystery, as well as the concept to reflect on.
- After reading aloud the passage, encourage the groups to take some time to think about the reflections and then discuss how these ideas apply to the mysteries they read about.

Optional Activity

Litany of Saint Joseph

A litany is a form of prayer used in celebrations and processions consisting of a number of petitions. Pray this litany together.

- Explain the format of the litany to the children.
- Ask them to use their books to follow along with the prayer.
- As the leader, read all of the first column text.
- Each time you finish your line, pause so that the children can give the appropriate responses from the second column.

Catholic **Faith Words**

A

absolution words spoken by the priest during the Sacrament of Penance and Reconciliation to grant forgiveness in God's name **(246)**

ark of the covenant a wooden chest that housed the tablets of the Ten Commandments. The Israelites carried it wherever they went as a reminder that God was with them. **(76)**

Ascension when the Risen Jesus was taken up to Heaven to be with God the Father forever **(225)**

B

beatification the second step in the process of becoming a Saint, in which a Venerable person is recognized by the Church as having brought about a miracle through his or her prayers of intercession **(166)**

Beatitudes teachings of Jesus that show the way to true happiness and tell the way to live in God's Kingdom now and always **(122)**

blasphemy the sin of showing disrespect for the name of God, Jesus Christ, Mary, or the Saints in words or action **(144)**

C

canonization a declaration by the Pope naming a person a Saint. Canonized Saints have special feast days or memorials in the Church's calendar. **(166)**

Cardinal Virtues the four principal moral virtues —prudence, temperance, justice, and fortitude—that help us live as children of God and from which the other moral virtues flow. We strengthen these good habits through God's grace and our own efforts. **(191)**

charity the Theological Virtue of love. It directs us to love God above all things and our neighbor as ourselves, for the love of God **(134)**

chastity a moral virtue and one of the Fruits of the Holy Spirit that helps us to act and think in ways that are appropriate and pure **(192)**

common good the good of everyone, with particular concern for those who might be most vulnerable to harm **(100)**

confession another name for the Sacrament of Penance and Reconciliation; an essential element of the Sacrament when you tell your sins to the priest **(244)**

conscience the God-given ability that helps us judge whether actions are right or wrong. It is important for us to know God's laws so our conscience can help us make good decisions. **(110)**

Corporal Works of Mercy actions that show care for the physical needs of others **(135)**

covenant a sacred promise or agreement between God and humans **(3, 67)**

D – E

Divine Revelation the way God makes himself, and his plan for humans, known to us **(57)**

envy the sin of resenting what others have or being sad from wanting for yourself what belongs to others **(260)**

eternal life life forever with God for all who die in his friendship **(122)**

Eucharist the Sacrament in which Jesus gives himself and the bread and wine become his Body and Blood **(237)**

evangelization sharing the Good News of Jesus through words and actions in a way that invites people to accept the Gospel **(269)**

faith the Theological Virtue that makes it possible for us to believe in God and all that he helps us understand about himself. Faith leads you to obey God. **(134)**

faithful to be constant and loyal in your commitments to God and others, just as he is faithful to you **(67)**

fortitude the Cardinal Virtue that helps you show courage, have strength to get through difficult times, and not give up on doing good **(192)**

free will the God-given freedom and ability to make choices. God created us with free will so we can have the freedom to choose good. **(109)**

Gifts of the Holy Spirit seven powerful Gifts God gives us to follow the guidance of the Holy Spirit and live the Christian life **(278)**

Gospel a word that means "Good News." The Gospel message is the Good News of God's Kingdom and his saving love. **(269)**

grace God's free and loving gift to humans of his own life and help **(109)**

Great Commandment the twofold command to love God above all and your neighbor as yourself. It sums up all God's laws. **(132)**

greed the sin of desiring to gain earthly goods without limits or beyond what you need **(260)**

Heaven the joy of living eternally in God's presence **(278)**

Hell being separated from God forever because of a choice to turn away from him and not seek forgiveness **(280)**

Holy Trinity the mystery of one God in three Divine Persons: Father, Son, and Holy Spirit **(98)**

hope the Theological Virtue that helps us trust in the true happiness God wants us to have and in Jesus' promises of eternal life, and to rely on the help of the Holy Spirit **(134)**

human dignity the worth each person has because he or she is made in the image of God **(88)**

humility the moral virtue that helps us to know that God is the source of everything good. Humility helps us to avoid being prideful. **(260)**

idolatry the sin of worshipping an object or a person instead of God. It is letting anything or anyone become more important than God. **(143)**

Immaculate Conception the truth that God kept Mary free from sin from the first moment of her life **(169)**

Incarnation the mystery that the Son of God became man in order to save all people **(234)**

justice giving God what is due him. This virtue also means giving each person what he or she is due because that person is a child of God. **(260)**

Kingdom of God God's rule of peace, justice, and love that exists in Heaven, but has not yet come in its fullness on Earth **(157)**

laity all of the baptized people in the Church who share in God's mission but are not priests or consecrated sisters or brothers; sometimes called lay people **(158)**

Last Judgment God's final triumph over evil that will occur at the end of time, when Christ returns and judges all the living and the dead (281)

liturgical year the feasts and seasons of the Church calendar that celebrate the Paschal Mystery of Christ (225)

M – N

Magisterium the teaching office of the Church, which is all of the bishops in union with the Pope (178)

martyr a person who gives up his or her life to witness to the truth of Christ and the faith. The word martyr means "witness." (211)

Mary the Mother of Jesus, the Mother of God. She is also called "Our Lady" because she is our Mother and the Mother of the Church. (168)

mercy kindness and concern for those who are suffering. God has mercy on us even though we are sinners. (122)

mission a job or purpose. The Church's mission is to announce the Good News of God's Kingdom. (269)

modesty a moral virtue and one of the Fruits of the Holy Spirit that helps us dress, talk, and move in appropriate ways (192)

morality living in right relationship with God, yourself, and others. It is putting your beliefs into action. (100)

mortal sin serious sin that causes a person's relationship with God to be broken (91)

murder the deliberate killing of another person when the killing is not in self-defense (202)

O

Original Sin the sin of our first parents, Adam and Eve, which led to the sinful condition of the human race from its beginning (64)

P

Particular Judgment the individual judgment by God at the time of a person's death; when God decides, after a person's death, where that person will spend eternity according to his or her faith and works (280)

Paschal Mystery the mystery of Jesus' suffering, Death, Resurrection, and Ascension (225)

patron Saint a Saint who has a particular connection to a cause, place, type of work, or person. For example, if a person or city shares the name of a Saint, that Saint is a patron. (169)

peace a state of calm when things are in their proper order and people settle problems with kindness and justice (125)

penance the prayer, offering, or good work the priest gives you in the Sacrament of Penance (246)

Precepts of the Church some of the minimum requirements given by Church leaders for deepening our relationship with God and the Church (178)

providence God's loving care for all things; God's will and plan for creation (56)

prudence the Cardinal Virtue that helps us be practical and make correct decisions on what is right and good, with the help of the Holy Spirit and a well-formed conscience (212)

Purgatory a state of final cleansing after death and before entering Heaven (280)

R

reparation an action taken to repair the damage done from sin (212)

repent to turn our lives away from sin and toward God (244)

Resurrection the event of Jesus being raised from Death to new life by God the Father through the power of the Holy Spirit **(144)**

Sacrament of Penance and Reconciliation the Sacrament in which God's forgiveness for sin is given through the Church **(244)**

Sacrament of the Anointing of the Sick the Sacrament that brings Jesus' healing touch to strengthen, comfort, and forgive the sins of those who are seriously ill or close to death **(247)**

sacramental seal a rule that a priest is not to share anything he hears in confession **(246)**

sacred worthy of reverence and devotion **(200)**

Sacred Scripture another name for the Bible; Sacred Scripture is the inspired Word of God written by humans **(4, 57)**

Sacred Tradition God's Word to the Church, safeguarded by the Apostles and their successors, the bishops, and handed down verbally—in her creeds, Sacraments, and other teachings—to future generations **(57)**

Saint a person whom the Church declares has led a holy life and is enjoying eternal life with God in Heaven **(166)**

salvation the loving action of God's forgiveness of sins and the restoration of friendship with him brought by Jesus **(64)**

Seven Sacraments effective signs of God's life, instituted by Christ and given to the Church. In the celebration of each Sacrament, there are visible signs and Divine actions that give grace and allow us to share in God's work. **(234)**

sin a deliberate thought, word, deed, or omission contrary to the law of God. Sins hurt our relationship with God and other people. **(91)**

soul the spiritual part of a human that lives forever **(88)**

Spiritual Works of Mercy actions that address the needs of the heart, mind, and soul **(135)**

stewardship the way we appreciate and use God's gifts, including our time, talent, and treasure, and the resources of creation **(261)**

temperance the Cardinal Virtue that helps us use moderation, be disciplined, and have self-control **(192)**

temptation an attraction to sin; wanting to do something we should not or not do something we should **(244)**

Ten Commandments the summary of laws that God gave Moses on Mount Sinai. They tell what is necessary in order to love God and others. **(76)**

Theological Virtues the virtues of faith, hope, and charity, which are gifts from God that guide our relationship with him **(134)**

venial sin a sin that weakens a person's relationship with God but does not destroy it **(91)**

vocation God's plan for our lives; the purpose for which he made us **(157)**

vows solemn promises that are made to or before God **(157)**

worship to adore and praise God, especially in the liturgy and in prayer **(143)**

Index

Index

The Subcommittee on the Catechism, United States Conference of Catholic Bishops, has found this catechetical series, copyright 2014, to be in conformity with the *Catechism of the Catholic Church*.

Nihil Obstat
Rev. Fr. Jeremiah L. Payne, S.Th.L.
Censor Librorum, Diocese of Orlando

Imprimatur
✠ Most Rev. John Noonan
Bishop of Orlando
March 26, 2013

For permission to reprint copyrighted materials, grateful acknowledgment is made to the following sources:

Allelu! Growing and Celebrating with Jesus ® Music CD © Our Sunday Visitor, Inc. Music written and produced by Sweetwater Productions. All rights of the owners of these works are reserved.

English translation of the *Catechism of the Catholic Church for the United States of America* copyright © 1994, United States Catholic Conference, Inc.—Libreria Editrice Vaticana. English translation of the *Catechism of the Catholic Church: Modifications from the Editio Typica* copyright © 1997, United States Catholic Conference, Inc.—Libreria Editrice Vaticana. Used by permission. All rights reserved.

Scripture texts in this work are taken from the *New American Bible, revised edition* © 2010, 1991, 1986, 1970 Confraternity of Christian Doctrine, Washington, D.C., and are used by permission of the copyright owner. All Rights Reserved. No part of the *New American Bible* may be reproduced in any form without permission in writing from the copyright owner.

Excerpts from the *United States Catholic Catechism for Adults*, copyright © 2006, United States Catholic Conference, Inc.—Libreria Editrice Vaticana.

Excerpts from the English translation of *The Roman Missal* © 2010, International Commission on English in the Liturgy Corporation (ICEL): All rights reserved.

The English translation of the Act of Contrition from the *Rite of Penance* © 1974, ICEL: English translation. All rights reserved.

Twenty-Third Publications, A Division of Bayard: "Grail Prayer" from *500 Prayers for Catholic Schools and Parish Youth Groups* by Filomena Tassi and Peter Tassi. Text copyright © Filomena Tassi and Peter Tassi.

United States Conference of Catholic Bishops, Inc., Washington, D.C.: "Hail, Holy Queen" from *Catholic Household Blessings and Prayers*. Translation copyright © 1989 by United States Catholic Conference, Inc.

Additional acknowledgments appear on page 335.

Alive in Christ Parish Grade 4 Student Book
ISBN: 978-1-61278-049-8
Item Number: CU5251

1 2 3 4 5 6 7 8 015016 17 16 15 14 13
Webcrafters, Inc.; Madison, WI; USA; June 2013; Job# 105391

© Our Sunday Visitor

© Our Sunday Visitor

Activity Master
Answer Keys

Activity Master Answer Keys

Chapter 1 Activity Master, p. 53E

1. −
2. −
3. +
4. +
5. +
6. −
7. −
8. −
9. +
10. +

11–14. Responses will vary.

Chapter 2 Activity Master, p. 63E

Chapter 3 Activity Master, p. 73E

1. (egasrtn) = **strange**; (dsog) = **gods**
2. (etka) = **take**; (aniv) = **vain**
3. (memReerb) = **Remember**; (ylho) = **holy**
4. (fteahr) = **father**; (tomhre) = **mother**
5. (llhsa) = **shall**; (ikll) = **kill**
6. (mocmit) = **commit**; (adtrulye) = **adultery**
7. (halls) = **shall**; (lstae) = **steal**
8. (flsae) = **false**; (tiwnses) = **witness**
9. (vocet) = **covet**; (weif) = **wife**
10. (cotve) = **covet**; (gdoos) = **goods**

Chapter 4 Activity Master, p. 87E

Scripture	Whom did Jesus treat with dignity?	How did Jesus show that he respected the person?
1. Matthew 8:1–4	a man with leprosy	Jesus touched and healed him.
2. Mark 2:13–17	tax collectors and sinners	Jesus ate with them and spent time with them.
3. Luke 7:36–50	a sinful woman	Jesus allowed the woman to kiss and anoint his feet; he forgave her.
4. Luke 19:1–10	Zacchaeus	Jesus stayed at his house.
5. John 4:4–42	a Samaritan woman	Jesus spoke with her and promised her "living water."

Chapter 5 Activity Master, p. 97E

Board Game

Chapter 6 Activity Master, p. 107E

1. GOOD
2. SIN
3. STUDY
4. RULE
5. BETTER
6. RELY
7. CLOSER

Puzzle Solution: Let your conscience be your guide.

Chapter 7 Activity Master, p. 121E

Section 1
1. I could help Mom with cooking dinner.
2. I could spend time with my younger brother.

Section 2
1. I could visit Mr. Hatsumi and ask him what he needs.
2. I could volunteer to walk Mr. Hatsumi's dog or take his trash to the curb.

Section 3
1. I could invite him to come to my house to play.
2. I could create a sympathy card for him.

Section 4
1. I could invite Bryn to my lunch table.
2. I could show Bryn where the buses are after school.

Chapter 8 Activity Master, p. 131E

Answers will vary.

Chapter 9 Activity Master, p. 141E

```
A   J   Y   O   Z   U   E   P   T   M   E
J   E   S   U   S   C   H   R   I   S   T
Q   F   A   D   K   M   O   N   Q   D   S
B   W   V   N   L   I   L   G   H   C   Y
C   P   I   R   O   L   Y   D   S   Z   D
M   G   O   Q   R   H   S   O   N   B   L
T   S   R   N   D   R   P   E   D   K   J
K   R   X   G   U   V   I   Z   U   T   N
P   F   A   T   H   E   R   L   W   O   Q
W   B   N   E   D   O   I   B   X   A   B
G   Z   C   R   E   A   T   O   R   J   I
```

Chapter 10 Activity Master, p. 155E

1. C A T [E] [C] H I [S] [T]

2. M [U] [S] I C [I] [A] N

3. S E [R] [V] E [R]

4. D [E] A [C] [O] N

5. L [E] C T [O] R

6. Y [O] [U] T H

   M I [N] I S T [E] [R]

7. P [R] [I] E S [T]

8. R E [L] [I] G I [O] [U] [S]

   L I F E

1–8. Responses will vary.

Chapter 11 Activity Master, p. 165E

Saint Nicholas, sack of coins
Saint Blaise, candles
Saint Peter, keys
Saint Patrick, shamrock
Saint Kateri Tekakwitha, canoe
Saint Catherine of Siena, book—Doctor of the Church
Saint Joseph, carpentry tools
Saint Francis of Assisi, forest animals
Saint Martha, apron and dust pan

Chapter 12 Activity Master, p. 175E

Check children's coloring.

Chapter 13 Activity Master, p. 189E

Check children's artwork.

Chapter 14 Activity Master, p. 199E

Check children's artwork.

Chapter 15 Activity Master, p. 209E

Check children's artwork.

Chapter 16 Activity Master, p. 223E

Advent: **Immaculate Conception**
Christmas: **Epiphany, Holy Family, Saint Nicholas**
Lent: **Ash Wednesday**
Triduum: **Holy Thursday, Good Friday, Holy Saturday**
Easter: **Pentecost, Ascension**
Ordinary Time: **Assumption of Mary, Baptism of Jesus, Christ the King**

Chapter 17 Activity Master, p. 233E

Check children's artwork.

Chapter 18 Activity Master, p. 243E

Check children's artwork.

Chapter 19 Activity Master, p. 257E

Check children's work.

Chapter 20 Activity Master, p. 267E

Answers will vary.

Chapter 21 Activity Master, p. 277E

Gift	Definition	I use this gift when I...
wisdom	Helps you see yourself as God sees you and act as God wants you to act	Answers will vary.
counsel	Helps you give good advice	Answers will vary.
understanding	Helps you come to know God, yourself, and others	Answers will vary.
knowledge	Helps you be open to God's loving communication	Answers will vary.
fear of the Lord	Helps you recognize that God is greater and more wonderful than any created thing	Answers will vary.
piety	Helps you show love and honor to God	Answers will vary.
fortitude	Helps you stand up for what is right	Answers will vary.

CCC 1669: endnote #174–174 Cf. *Gen* 12:2; *Lk* 6:28; *Rom* 12:14; 1 *Pet* 3:9.)